Ex Post Economic Evaluation of Competition Policy

Ex Post Economic Evaluation of Competition Policy

The EU Experience

Edited by

Fabienne Ilzkovitz

Adriaan Dierx

Wolters Kluwer

Published by:
Kluwer Law International B.V.
PO Box 316
2400 AH Alphen aan den Rijn
The Netherlands
E-mail: international-sales@wolterskluwer.com
Website: lrus.wolterskluwer.com

Sold and distributed in North, Central and South America by:
Wolters Kluwer Legal & Regulatory U.S.
7201 McKinney Circle
Frederick, MD 21704
United States of America
Email: customer.service@wolterskluwer.com

Sold and distributed in all other countries by:
Air Business Subscriptions
Rockwood House
Haywards Heath
West Sussex
RH16 3DH
United Kingdom
Email: international-customerservice@wolterskluwer.com

ISBN 978-94-035-1294-5

e-Book: ISBN 978-94-035-1282-2
web-PDF: ISBN 978-94-035-1290-7

Editors

Fabienne Ilzkovitz is the Principal Advisor responsible for the economic evaluation of competition policy within the Directorate-General for Competition of the European Commission. Since 2014, she has coordinated various ex post evaluation projects, ranging from the ex post evaluation of specific competition policy interventions to the assessment of the macroeconomic impact of EU competition policy as a whole. Previously, she held the position of Director responsible for the implementation of EU competition policy in the area of transport and postal services in the Directorate-General for Competition.

Before moving to the Directorate-General for Competition, Fabienne Ilzkovitz led several teams of economists in the Directorate-General for Economic and Financial Affairs of the European Commission. In this Directorate-General, she managed and contributed to important European projects, such as the economic impact of the internal market, the analysis of the external aspects of the Economic and Monetary Union, the impact of structural reforms on productivity and growth, the reform of the European system of merger control and the organisation of product market monitoring. She has published widely in peer-reviewed journals, books and working papers on issues dealing with European integration, competition policy and industrial economics.

Fabienne Ilzkovitz is also Associate Professor of Economics in the Solvay Brussels School of Economics and Management at the Université Libre de Bruxelles (ULB). She teaches on issues related to European economic integration and European economic policies in the Bachelor programme and animates a seminar on the economic evaluation of European regulation and policies in the Business Master programme.

Adriaan Dierx is a Senior Expert on ex post economic evaluation within the Directorate-General for Competition of the European Commission. He has managed a number of studies aimed at assessing the economic impact of the European Commission's competition policy interventions. Previously, he was entrusted with the investigation of antitrust infringements and merger proposals in the transport, postal and other services sectors.

Before moving to the Directorate-General for Competition, Dr Dierx was responsible for analysing EU market integration, competitiveness and innovation policies within the Directorate-General for Economic and Financial Affairs. He has been intensively involved in discussions on how to stimulate structural reforms within the European Union with a view to improve its economic performance.

Dr Dierx holds a PhD in Economics from the University of Pittsburgh. He has published on EU competition policy, structural reform, economic integration and regional development issues in international journals, books and European Economy working papers.

Contributors

Luca Aguzzoni is an economist with a specialisation in quantitative methods and competition policy. He currently works in the Chief Economist Team of the Directorate-General for Competition (European Commission). He has extensive work experience in merger cases and State aid cases including the ex post evaluation of merger decisions and State aid interventions.

Before joining the European Commission, Luca worked as a senior consultant for private clients and public bodies on both cases and research assignments, including also litigation cases in front of national courts. His sectoral experience covers several sectors from media and telecommunications to chemical products and manufacturing. Before working on competition policy, he also worked on public finance issues (pension/social security) for the UK Department of Work and Pensions and for the International Labour Organization (ILO). Luca first graduated at Bocconi University and holds a PhD in Economics from the European University Institute (Florence). Luca has made regular publications in peer-reviewed journals in the domain of competition policy and industrial economics.

Veit Böckers is Competition Economist in the Strategy Department of METRO AG company. There, he works on antitrust cases, mergers and as an empirical market analyst. He joined METRO in 2018 from the economic consultancy CEG where he worked on several cartel damage cases. Veit holds a PhD in Economics from the Düsseldorf Institute for Competition Economics.

Paolo Buccirossi is the Director and founder of Lear, an economic consultancy specialising in competition and regulatory matters. He has advised private clients and public institutions on a wide range of competition issues before the European Commission and several national competition authorities. Paolo has prepared witness statements in private litigation cases and assisted clients during regulatory reviews.

Before founding Lear Dr Buccirossi was an economic advisor at the Italian Competition Authority where he conducted several investigations concerning antitrust infringements in several sectors, including telecommunications, media and transportation. Dr Buccirossi holds an MSc in Public Economics and a PhD in Economics awarded by the University of Rome La Sapienza. He is the editor of the Handbook of Antitrust Economics and has published several research papers in leading economic journals. Dr Buccirossi is an Adjunct Professor of Economics of Competition Law at the University of Rome Tor Vergata and a Visiting Professor at the College of Europe.

Mattia Cai is a Research Fellow within the European Commission's Joint Research Centre. In his current position, his role is to support the activities of Directorates-General for Competition, for Internal Market, Industry, Entrepreneurship and SMEs, and EUROSTAT, with data analysis and modelling.

Prior to joining the European Commission in 2016, he held academic positions at the University of Padova, Bocconi University and the Free University of Bolzano-Bozen. During that time, he worked on a number of applied research projects in the areas of agricultural, environmental and regional economics. He holds a PhD in Agricultural Economics from the University of Padova, Italy.

Roberta Cardani is a Scientific Officer at the Economic and Financial Analysis Unit of the Joint Research Centre (JRC-Ispra), where she is mainly involved in the projects regarding the ex post evaluation of competition policy enforcement in the European Union; and the model-based quantification of the main drivers of real GDP growth in the euro area. She also works on the development of the Global Multi-country model.

Dr Cardani holds a PhD in Economics from the Catholic University (Milan) and BA in Economics from Bocconi University. She has been visiting research fellow at the University of Cambridge, San Francisco Federal Reserve Bank, European Central Bank and Dutch Central Bank. Before joining the JRC, Dr Cardani was a researcher at University of Milano-Bicocca and Pavia.

Her research interests span the fields of macroeconomic modelling, business cycles analysis, fiscal and monetary economics, and firm dynamics. She has published on monetary, fiscal policies and forecasting issues in international peer-reviewed journals.

Luca Di Martile is a competition economist working in the private practice. He has extensive experience in competition policy related matters in a wide range of industries and sectors, including chemical, metallurgical, manufacturing, aviation, and mobile telecommunication. Prior to joining the private sector, Luca worked as an economist at the Chief Economist Team of the Directorate-General for Competition of the European Commission, where he applied quantitative techniques in the review of merger and antitrust cases, as well as ex post merger evaluations. Luca graduated from Bocconi University and holds an MSc in Economics from the University of Amsterdam.

Tomaso Duso is the Head of the Firms and Markets Department at the Deutsches Institut für Wirtschaftsforschung (DIW Berlin), a Professor of empirical industrial economics at the Technische Universität (TU) Berlin, and the spokesperson of the

Berlin Centre for Consumer Policies (BCCP). He is also a Research Fellow for the CEPR and CESIfo.

His research interests are in applied econometrics in the fields of industrial organisation and management. In particular, his research focuses on the ex post evaluation of competition policies and product market regulations. His papers have been published in The Review of Economics and Statistics, The Economic Journal, The Journal of Law and Economics, European Economic Review, and Journal of Management Studies, among other academic journals.

Tomaso advised several public bodies, such as various Directorates-General of the European Commission, the UK Competition Commission as well as the UK Competition and Markets Authority, the Dutch Authority for Consumers and Markets, the OECD, and the European Bank for Reconstruction and Development on competition policy issues.

Richard Havell is an Economic Adviser at the UK Competition and Markets Authority, and is the present Head of Research and Evaluation within its Office of the Chief Economic Adviser. He has led the economic analysis of several mergers while there.

Before moving to the Competition and Markets Authority, Dr Havell was an Associate Principal in Charles River Associates' European Competition Practice. While there, he worked on mergers, antitrust and litigation cases in multiple industries and jurisdictions, including the Visa interchange fee litigation in the UK High Court and the merger between Uber and Yandex Taxi in Russia. His work focussed in particular on two-sided and digital markets.

Dr Havell holds a PhD in Economics from the University of East Anglia, where he was a Research Associate at the Centre for Competition Policy. His research there focussed on empirical analysis of European cartels and on ex post evaluations of merger decisions.

Sven Heim is Assistant Professor of Economics at the Centre for Industrial Economics (CERNA) at Mines ParisTech and a Research Associate at the Department of Economics of Innovation and Industrial Dynamics at the Centre for European Economic Research Mannheim (ZEW). Before he was a doctoral and post-doctoral researcher at ZEW in the research group Competition and Regulation. His research interests cover energy and environmental economics, applied econometrics, competition and regulation, and information economics.

Kai Hüschelrath is Professor of Economics at the University of Applied Sciences in Schmalkalden (Germany). He studied economics and management at the University of Würzburg and received his PhD in Economics from WHU Otto Beisheim School of Management in Vallendar.

Before joining the faculty in Schmalkalden, he worked as an economist in the London office of Frontier Economics and as a researcher (and later head of research group) at the ZEW Centre for European Economic Research in Mannheim. His research mainly concentrates on the entire fields of industrial organisation and law and economics with a particular focus on competitive strategy and competition policy.

He has published in well-known general interest and field journals such as the Review of Economics and Statistics, the European Economic Review, the International Journal of Industrial Organization, the Journal of Economics & Management Strategy or the International Review of Law and Economics. He also has substantial experience in advising both private companies and public authorities in competitive strategy and competition policy matters.

Yannis Katsoulacos is Professor of Economics at the Department of Economic Science of the Athens University of Economics and Business) (1994-). He was the Chairman of the Department (2011-2015), the University Vice-rector (2007-2011) and the Director of the Program of Post-graduate Studies (and founder of the post-graduate programmes) in Applied Economics and Finance (2000-2018). Currently he is a Visiting Professor at the European Institute, London School of Economics (2018-2019) and ESSEC Business School (2019-2020). He holds a PhD and an MSc in Economics from the London School of Economics.

He was a Research Fellow of the London Centre of Economic Policy Research (CEPR, 1992-2001) and has published over 100 articles (over 45 in international, including leading, refereed scientific journals) and 10 books on competition policy, industrial organisation, the economics of technical change and the new economy.

He served as a Commissioner of the Hellenic Competition Commission (1995-2005) and was a member of the committees that were responsible for the three main amendments that modernised Greek Competition Law, in 1995, 2000 and 2011. He is Senior Academic Consultant for the European Competition Practice of CRA International (2011-).

In 2005, he initiated and is since then in charge for organising the CRESSE Annual International Summer School and Conference in Competition and Regulation, currently one of the leading conferences in the world in this area.

Alessia Marrazzo is a Consultant at Lear, an economic consultancy specialising in competition and regulatory matters. She helps clients providing robust and sound economic analyses in follow-on damages actions and she has been involved in several cases before the Italian Competition Authority involving abuses of dominance and cartels. She specialises in damages quantification methods and causal inference techniques. She has also worked on international arbitration cases, related to disputes between the Government and major telecom operators in the Mexican market.

Before joining Lear, Alessia worked as a trainee at the Directorate-General for Competition (European Commission). During her stay at the Commission, she took part in a project on the ex post evaluation of the effectiveness of remedies accepted by the Commission. Alessia holds an MSc in Competition and Market Regulation from Barcelona Graduate School of Economics, and an MSc in Economic and Finance from the University of Naples Federico II. She is also a PhD candidate in Economics at the University of Bologna.

Franco Mariuzzo is Associate Professor in the School of Economics and member of the Centre for Competition Policy at University of East Anglia (UEA), UK. His research interest is in industrial organisation and competition policy. He has co-investigated two studies commissioned by the European Commission. Dr Mariuzzo holds a PhD in Quantitative Economics from the University of Venice. Prior to joining UEA, he has worked at Mannheim Institute for the Economics of Ageing, Trinity College Dublin, University of Groeningen and University College Dublin.

He has published his research in the Economic and Social Review, Economic Inquiry, Energy Policy, International Journal of Industrial Organization, Journal of Economics and Management Strategies, Review of Economics and Statistics, Review of Industrial Organization, and contributed to various peer-reviewed books.

Salvatore Nava is a Consultant at Lear, an economic consultancy specialising in competition and regulatory matters. He assists private companies in proceedings before the Italian competition authority, including anticompetitive agreements, abuses of dominance and merger cases. Salvatore has also been involved in various antitrust damages cases in the media, energy and consumer goods industries and in technical assistance projects undertaken by Lear on behalf of the World Bank Group. While at Lear, Salvatore has spent four months as an external consultant for a leading UK regulator, where he was involved in the data analysis for a market study.

Prior to joining Lear, Salvatore worked for two years for a competition economics consultancy based in London, and he was involved in a number of assignments, ranging from cases of antitrust damages estimation to submissions on behalf of various clients to courts and regulators – covering a wide range of industries such as financial services, commodity trading, aviation, construction and healthcare services. Salvatore holds advanced degrees in Economics and Industrial Economics from the University of Rome Tor Vergata and the University of East Anglia respectively.

Peter Ormosi is an Associate Professor of Competition Economics and a member of the Centre for Competition Policy at the University of East Anglia. Before joining academia, he worked for the Hungarian Competition Authority (2000-2002) and the OECD (2003-2005). His research is mapped around various topics in law and economics, including the analysis of the effect of private sanctions, measuring cartel detection and deterrence, the anticompetitive effects of mergers, and the ex post evaluation of the impact of competition enforcement including the analysis of the deterrent effect of law enforcement.

Peter is currently working on measuring the distributional impact of competition policy, and on more general questions of law and economics, such as the reputational effects of crime. He has published in both economics and law journals of international excellence. He has provided advice and delivered various reports for the Competition and Markets Authority, the European Commission, the OECD, UNCTAD, and the World Bank on issues related to impact evaluation and the estimation of the consumer benefits of competition policy. He is also a member of the UK Competition and Markets Authority's Academic Board.

Penelope Papandropoulos has been working since 2007 at the European Commission. She has worked in the Directorate-General for Competition (in the team of the Chief

Economist) and as a member of the Competition Commissioner's cabinet (for Vice-President Almunia and currently for Executive Vice-President Vestager). Between 2007 and 2014, she predominantly worked on merger cases, contributing to high profile merger cases such as Google/DoubleClick, Fortis/ABN Amro, Oracle/Sun Microsystems, BHP Billiton / Rio Tinto, Western Digital/Hitachi, Lufthansa/Brussels Airlines, UPS/TNT and many others. In 2015-2019, she was coordinating the work of the Chief Economist Team in State aid matters. Prior to working at the Commission, Dr Papandropoulos was for several years an economic consultant at Charles River Associates (CRA International), and previously Lexecon. Dr Papandropoulos holds a PhD in Economics from the Université Libre de Bruxelles.

Rodrigo Peduzzi is an official of the European Commission, currently working as Case Handler in the Directorate-General for Competition dealing with State aid for Research, Development and Innovation, for Important Projects of Common European Interest and for the Environment. Previously, he worked in the Directorate-General for Competition's State aid strategy Unit and was primarily in charge of coordinating the introduction of the new ex post evaluation requirement within State aid control. He joined the European Commission in 2010, initially dealing with competitiveness policies and better regulation. Before joining the Commission, he worked for several years in an Italian employer organisation where he was in charge of EU economic and competition policies.

Filippo Pericoli is an Economist at the Joint Research Centre of the European Commission. He is involved in many research projects regarding among others: the macroeconomic impact of competitions policy; risk sharing and resilience; macroeconomic forecasting; efficiency of numerical algorithms for Bayesian econometrics.

Previously he was Senior Adviser at the Directorate-General of the Treasury of the Italian Ministry of Economy and Finance, where he worked as economist and as applied econometrician in the field of macroeconomic analysis and forecasting. In this period, he contributed to writing the official documents and reports of the Ministry.

Dr Pericoli holds a PhD in Economics from the University La Sapienza, and he has been working in the following universities: Rome Tre, Sapienza, LUISS, Tor Vergata, and Boston University. He participated to a high number of international conferences, is author of many articles in peer-reviewed journals in the field of risk sharing, applied econometrics and forecasting.

Nicole Robins heads Oxera's State aid practice and is the partner in charge of Oxera's Brussels office. She advises clients on a wide range of economic and financial issues in State aid cases relating to assessments of the market economy operator principle (MEOP), the application of State aid rules for services of general economic interest (SGEI), and the compatibility of aid, as well as ex post evaluations of aid schemes. Nicole co-directed Oxera's study for the Directorate-General for Competition on the ex post assessment of the impact of aid on competition.

She provides advice on State aid compliance, and advises beneficiaries, complainants and Member States during investigations by the European Commission and in State aid litigation cases in front of the European courts.

She has given expert economic evidence in front of the General Court on State aid matters on a number of occasions. Nicole also teaches the State aid module on the King's College Economics for Competition Law postgraduate course.

Cornelius Schmidt is an Economic Analyst within the Chief Economist Team of the Directorate-General for Competition of the European Commission. While he is covering all competition policy instruments, his focus is on State aid, including ex post evaluation of State aid. He dealt with a large number of evaluation plans for State aid schemes submitted to the European Commission. Dr Schmidt holds a PhD in Financial Economics. His scholarly work appeared recently in a top-tier academic journal.

Philipp Schmidt-Dengler is Professor of Economics at the University of Vienna. He completed his undergraduate Studies at the University of Vienna, holds an MA from Queen's University and received a PhD in Economics from Yale University in 2005. Before joining the University of Vienna in September 2014, he was a Professor at the Universität Mannheim, a Lecturer and subsequently Reader at the London School of Economics and Political Science. Philipp Schmidt-Dengler was a member of the Panel of Academic Advisors to the UK Competition Commission.

He is a Co-editor of the International Journal of Industrial Organization and Associate Editor of the Journal of Applied Econometrics, Research Fellow of the Centre for Economic Policy Research in London, and Affiliate of the CESifo Research Network in Munich. He is also a Scientific Consultant at the Austrian Institute of Economic Research. His research interests are industrial economics, competition policy, applied microeconomics and econometric policy evaluation, with a focus on firm behaviour.

Maurizio Strazzeri is a PhD student at the Graduate School of Decision Sciences at the University of Konstanz. Before moving to Konstanz, he studied economics at the University of Giessen and the University of Wisconsin-Milwaukee. His research interests are migration, labour economics and applied econometrics.

Florian Szücs obtained a PhD in Economics from the University of Vienna in 2011. Before accepting an assistant professor position at the Vienna University of Economics and Business, he was a postdoctoral researcher at DIW Berlin. His research interests include empirical industrial organisation, innovation and law and economics. He has published in top-refereed economics journals including the Economic Journal, the European Economic Review and the International Journal of Industrial Organization.

David Ulph has been Professor of Economics at the University of St Andrews since 2006. In addition he is a Member of the UK Competition Appeal Tribunal, a Commissioner of the Scottish Fiscal Commission and a Member of the NHS Pay Review Body. Prior to joining St Andrews he was Chief Economist at HM Revenue & Customs (previously Inland Revenue) from 2001-2006. Before that, he was Professor and Head of Department at the University of Bristol (1984-1992) and University College London (1992-1997). He was Executive Director of the ESRC Centre for Economic Learning and Social Evolution from 1997-2001 and of the Scottish Institute for Research in Economics from 2010-2017.

He has published extensively on the economics of: (i) enforcement of competition policy; (ii) enforcement of tax policy; (iii) industrial organisation and innovation; (iv) design of environmental policy, particularly climate change.

He is a Fellow of the Royal Society of Edinburgh and of the Royal Society of Arts. In 2016, he was made a Commander of the Order of the British Empire (CBE) in recognition of his contribution to Economics and Social Sciences.

Summary of Contents

Table of Contents

List of Tables

List of Figures

Acknowledgements

This edited volume is a collective effort of many contributors. It brings together recent work on the ex post economic evaluation of EU competition policy, both by external experts and senior Commission officials. We are much indebted to the authors of the different chapters for their wholehearted collaboration. Our thanks are also due to Karin Hunin, who provided invaluable assistance in preparing the initial layout of this publication and in carefully checking the different submissions received, and to Peer Schulze, who prepared the index of keywords. We would also like to thank Simon Bellamy of Kluwer Law International for his much-appreciated advice throughout the publication process and Mrs. Sudha Elangovan of NewGen Knowledge Works for the final production of this volume. We are particularly grateful to Johannes Laitenberger, who as Director General of DG Competition initiated this publication project and offered encouragement throughout the process, as well as to Olivier Guersent, the current Director General, who oversaw its completion. Finally, a word of thanks goes to our families for their unwavering support.

Foreword

In their book *Good Economics for Hard Times: Better Answers to Our Biggest Problems*, Abhijit Banerjee and Esther Duflo make the point that 'What is dangerous is not making mistakes, but to be so enamored of one's point of view that one does not let facts get in the way. To make progress, we have to constantly go back to the facts, acknowledge our errors, and move on.' In 2019, Banerjee and Duflo (together with Michael Kremer) were awarded the Nobel Prize for economics for their experimental approach to assessing public policy interventions. This is a recognition of the importance of having evidence-based policymaking and of using tools such as evaluations for improving the regulatory environment and policy enforcement.

The present volume fits within this framework and aims at illustrating our experience with and providing guidance on the ex post economic evaluation of competition policy. My predecessor, Johannes Laitenberger, took the very welcome initiative to launch the publication of this volume, and when taking over in his position, I was delighted to support and further pursue this project.

Nowadays, international organisations (such as the European Commission, the OECD and the World Bank) as well as national administrations increasingly use ex post evaluations to assess the value added of their policy interventions for society. The European Commission in particular has made a significant effort to strengthen the evidence base for its policy proposals. In line with the 'evaluate first' principle, each proposal for revision of an important existing regulation should be backed up by a robust ex post evaluation of the performance of the existing regulation.

In this context, the Directorate-General for Competition has developed its activities in the domain of ex post economic evaluation of EU competition policy. The main objectives of this work are to improve competition policy rules and decision-making practices, to enhance transparency and accountability to external stakeholders and citizens, to collect solid evidence in support of competition advocacy, and to defend the legitimacy of competition policy.

This volume assembles and summarises the various ex post evaluation studies that have been initiated by the Directorate-General for Competition since 2014. These studies include ex post evaluations of merger interventions, antitrust decisions and

State aids as well as an analysis of the macroeconomic impact of competition policy. Together, they constitute a body of knowledge that is of interest to competition policy analysts and practitioners as it takes stock of progress made and sets out a path for the future development of competition policy.

It is my intention to continue developing ex post evaluation activities within the Directorate-General, drawing lessons from the experience described in this volume. Although ex post evaluation is costly in terms of resources, it offers a good return on investment as it is a powerful tool for strengthening competition policy enforcement and supporting competition advocacy. Therefore, competition authorities have an interest in developing an evaluation culture within their organisation and in gaining access to the necessary expertise. A close collaboration with academics and experts is indispensable to ensure the use of state-of-the-art methodologies and have an open discussion of the evaluation results obtained.

It is essential that evaluations are designed from the outset to provide answers to issues of concern to policy makers. Globalisation and digitalisation have drastically changed the business environment and therefore, it is not surprising that questions about the future of competition enforcement have moved into the mainstream of Europe's policy debate. Ex post evaluations should contribute to feed this debate with facts, as highlighted by Banerjee and Duflo.

There are also a number of areas in which further research is necessary. They are spelled out in detail in the remainder of this volume. Let me highlight a few. While the price effects of individual merger decisions have been investigated thoroughly in the economic literature, less is known about their effects on innovation, which is the principal determinant of competition in digital markets. Ex post evaluations of antitrust and State aid decisions are relatively scarce. The State Aid Modernisation has given an impulse to the development of ex post evaluations in that domain, but antitrust still poses a challenge. Understanding the deterrent effects of our interventions and identifying the measures that could contribute to increase these deterrent effects would also improve the impact of our competition rules. Finally, more work is needed to determine the effects of competition policy on the economy as a whole. To make progress, access to quality data is fundamental and the Directorate-General for Competition will make an effort to improve the collection and organisation of its data. We remain committed to continue the dialogue on these issues with competition policy practitioners and academics in order to further stimulate research in this area.

Olivier Guersent

Preface: Contents and Main Lessons Learnt

Since 2014, the European Commission and its Directorate-General for Competition have developed an expertise on the ex post economic evaluation of EU competition policy. This is reflected in a literature review carried out in 2015 (*see* Ilzkovitz and Dierx, 2015) and in a number of papers and study reports prepared either in-house or by external evaluation and competition policy experts. The studies presented in this volume build on this work and range from the ex post evaluation of specific competition policy interventions to the assessment of the macroeconomic impact of EU competition policy as a whole. They have a common goal of increasing the understanding of the impact of competition policy decisions taken and of informing and improving future decision-making practices. They thereby contribute to raising the transparency of the EU decision-making process and defending the legitimacy of its competition policy interventions.

This preface provides a short summary of the different chapters in this volume. It draws the main lessons from our five-year experience with ex post economic evaluation in the Directorate-General for Competition and highlights areas for further research.

CONTENTS OF THE EDITED VOLUME

This volume includes an introductory chapter and four parts. The introductory chapter describes the main principles and instruments of EU competition policy, and it clarifies the role and scope of ex post economic evaluation in this field. Parts I, II and III are devoted to ex post evaluations of competition policy interventions under the three main instruments of EU competition policy: merger control, antitrust and State aid. Part IV considers the broader impact of competition policy as a whole.

Part I: The Ex Post Evaluation of Merger Interventions

Ex post evaluations of merger interventions have been carried out most frequently, both by competition authorities and academics. One reason is that the theory of harm is well defined and therefore easier to investigate. Moreover, there are many more merger decisions than abuse of dominance decisions or cartel prohibitions. In view of the relatively large number of quantitative ex post evaluations of individual merger decisions carried out in the EU, we thought it could be instructive to include in this volume chapters that summarise the principal conclusions of such evaluations. Chapter 2 is the meta-retrospective of ex post evaluation studies of mergers decisions taken in EU jurisdictions. Chapter 3 reviews quantitative ex post evaluations of merger decisions affecting mobile telecoms markets. Chapter 4, on the contrary, is devoted to the ex post evaluation of a single merger in the UK mobile telecoms market.

The meta-retrospective study by Peter Ormosi, Richard Havell and Franco Mariuzzo described in Chapter 2 is based on twenty-nine ex post evaluations, covering mergers in thirteen industries and six EU jurisdictions. Most of the decisions subject to an ex post evaluation were taken in the first decade of this century. Seventeen mergers were unconditionally approved, ten were remedied and two were blocked. For this sample of European mergers, the authors find that approved mergers are followed by a price increase of 5%, on average, while remedied mergers are not followed by a price-increase, on average. This evidence suggests that, in the EU, remedies have been effective in eliminating anticompetitive effects. This conclusion differs from that of another meta-study carried out by John Kwoka (2013) in the US. Kwoka finds that in the US sample of studies, remedied mergers are followed by a large price increase (of 16% for conduct remedies and 8% for divestitures).[1] Ormosi et al. correctly emphasise that it would be misleading to draw strong conclusions on the relative effectiveness of EU and US jurisdictions from a comparison of these two meta-studies. The diverging results could well be due to differences in the two samples of ex post evaluations. The authors also attempt to identify cases where there was a potential error in the merger decision. However, they find little evidence of genuine competition policy errors. In conclusion, the authors argue that retrospective studies can be very instructive to competition authorities and that therefore such studies should be further developed, for example, by investigating the non-price effects of mergers.

Chapter 3, by Luca Agguzoni and Luca Di Martile, provides an overview of the quantitative analyses of the impact of merger decisions in the EU mobile telecommunication sector over the past fifteen years. The mergers that were approved – some subject to conditions – led to a reduction in the number of mobile network operators active in the countries concerned. The resulting higher within-country market concentration triggered a policy debate on the effects of the increased concentration on competition in the mobile telecom markets. This was reflected in a substantial number of ex post evaluation studies carried out both by academics and competition authorities. Therefore, this chapter is able to exploit a rich set of sixteen quantitative ex post

1. For unconditionally approved mergers, Kwoka finds a price increase of the same order of magnitude (around 7%) as Ormosi et al.

evaluations of EU mobile telecom mergers. About half of the ex post evaluations of individual merger decisions use a Difference-in-Differences or structural model approach to conduct the evaluation. The other studies apply regression analyses to assess the impact of the observed changes in market structure on prices and investment. Based on this review, it appears that mergers in the EU mobile telecom industry have led to higher prices, especially in highly concentrated markets. This is true in particular for unconditionally approved mergers and for mergers with ineffective remedies. The impact of the mergers on investment is less clear: the results of the reviewed studies are quite diverse, reflecting the specificity of each merger case analysed. Moreover, there is a great heterogeneity in terms of study design, data used and modelling choices made. Therefore, the chapter concludes that the policy debate is far from settled. A more in-depth analysis of recent merger cases and an improved data collection effort should help to make further progress in this area.

Chapter 4 is devoted to the five-to-four T-Mobile/Orange UK merger case, which is one of the mergers also included in the review of ex post studies presented in Chapter 3. In March 2010, the European Commission cleared the merger proposal. However, the merger approval decision was conditional on behavioural and structural remedies, which aimed to ensure that Three, the 'maverick' in the UK mobile telecoms market, would continue to be an effective competitor. This chapter, written by Paolo Buccirossi, Alessia Marazzo and Salvatore Nava, uses a Difference-in-Differences approach to investigate the effects of the merger clearance decision, inclusive of remedies, on mobile telecommunication prices and investment in the UK. This quantitative analysis shows that the combination of the merger and the associated remedies resulted in a price decline ranging between 9% and 19% for medium-to-high intensity users of mobile services in the UK. The Difference-in-Differences approach does not allow for a separate identification of the merger with and without remedies. However, the descriptive analysis concludes that the remedies may have contributed to maintaining competitive conditions in the UK market for mobile services, with Three continuing to increase its market share. The Difference-in-Differences analysis did not find a significant effect of the merger on the level of investment. Nevertheless, based on their descriptive analysis the authors conclude that the merger has not hindered the development of 4G services in the UK, with all mobile operators making investments in the provision of such services. This chapter offers a good illustration of the benefits of combining descriptive and counterfactual-based evaluations to get more robust and rich results. It also pleads for more reliable indicators of prices and investment in the telecommunications industry, in order to strengthen the empirical foundation of the evaluation results obtained.

Part II: The Ex Post Evaluation of Antitrust Decisions

The number of studies aimed at evaluating antitrust enforcement is very limited because there are fewer decisions in this area, the theory of harm is more difficult to analyse and differs from one case to another, and the definition of the counterfactual is more complex. To close this gap, the Directorate-General for Competition asked academics and consultants to work in this area. The result of this work is presented in Part II of this volume, which includes two quantitative ex post evaluations of abuse of dominance cases, one in the Polish fixed telecommunications market and the other in the German electricity market.

Chapter 5, by Alessia Marazzo, Paolo Bucirossi and Salvatore Nava, presents an ex post evaluation of the 2011 decision by the European Commission prohibiting an abuse of dominant position by the incumbent operator, Telekomunikacja Polska (TP), in the Polish fixed telecommunications market. In this decision, the European Commission established that TP had abused its dominant position over the period August 2005-October 2009 by hindering the access of other operators to its nationwide DSL[2] network. The ex post evaluation combines a descriptive investigation of the evolution of broadband penetration and prices with a Difference-in-Differences analysis. It shows that the anticompetitive conduct of TP indeed hindered the access of other operators to the TP network, having a negative effect on DSL broadband penetration in Poland. Before the European Commission's intervention, the level of broadband penetration in Poland was 0.75 percentage points below that in other European countries with the same regulatory framework, corresponding to a difference of 30,000 Polish subscribers. However, the refusal by TP to give access to its DSL network encouraged competitors and new entrants to invest in alternative technologies. This observation triggers the interest in further work on the relative importance of promoting competition between different technological platforms (inter-platform competition) versus competition within the same network (intra-platform competition). The chapter is less conclusive on the effects of TP's abuse on prices. Nevertheless, it appears that – contrary to what is observed elsewhere in Europe – prices charged for DSL-based broadband services in Poland were higher than prices of alternative broadband services over the entire period of analysis, which might be interpreted as an effect of the abuse.

Chapter 6, by Veit Böckers, Tomaso Duso and Florian Szücs, concerns the alleged abuse by E.ON of its dominant position in the German wholesale electricity market. In 2008, the European Commission investigated claims that E.ON had abused its dominant position in the German electricity market by withdrawing available generation capacity from the wholesale market. The Commission was concerned that the withdrawal of the electricity generation plants was part of a strategy aimed at increasing wholesale electricity prices. To address such concerns, E.ON made the commitment to divest 5000 MW electricity generation plants to other market players. In 2008, the European Commission made the commitments binding. The chapter provides convincing evidence – based on a Difference-in-Differences analysis – that the implementation by E.ON of its commitment reduced wholesale electricity prices. This reduction in price was particularly strong during peak hours (when there was a relative shortage of production capacity), which led to a convergence between peak and off-peak prices. The analysis also illustrates the extent to which the reduction in wholesale prices is passed on to end customers. The degree of pass-through is less for incumbents with large market power than for smaller independent electricity suppliers, supporting the

2. Digital Subscriber Line (DSL) is the technology that allows transmitting digital data over telephone lines.

idea that the pass-through of upstream price reductions to downstream markets depends on the market power of the retailer. Finally, the authors of this chapter argue in favour of a better availability of reliable data to develop robust quantitative ex post evaluations. They stress that data availability is an important consideration when deciding whether to go ahead with an ex post economic evaluation and that constructing an appropriate dataset is an essential first step in the ex post evaluation process.

Part III: Ex Post Evaluation of State Aid

The third part of this book explores the role of ex post evaluation in the area of State aids. Chapter 7 describes the increased importance of ex post evaluation since the State Aid Modernisation. The three following chapters in Part III concern quantitative ex post evaluations of three different types of State aids: an aid provided to a regional airport in the UK over the period 2006-2011; national and regional aid schemes aimed at supporting the deployment of broadband in rural areas of Germany, which were approved by the European Commission between 2008 and 2010; and restructuring aid decisions taken by the European Commission between 2000 and 2012.

Chapter 7, by Penelope Papandropoulos, Rodrigo Peduzzi and Cornelius Schmidt, describes how the State Aid Modernisation (SAM) of 2012-2016 led to a burst of ex post evaluations in the domain of State aids. One of the main elements of the SAM was the expansion of the scope of the General Block Exemption Regulation (GBER), which under certain conditions permitted EU Member States to grant aids without having to notify them ex ante to the European Commission. The wider scope of the GBER under the SAM has gone hand-in-hand with safeguards to preserve competition in the internal market and ensure the good use of public money. In particular, from 2014 on, EU Member States were required to assess whether the large State aid schemes achieved their intended objective without leading to distortions of competition. The chapter provides an overview of the methods used in State aid evaluations and presents the lessons drawn by the European Commission from its assessment of the evaluation plans submitted by the Member States up until May 2019. In particular, the chapter spells out the conditions for a successful ex post evaluation of a State aid scheme: the schemes should be designed from the outset with an evaluation strategy in mind as this facilitates the collection of the data that are necessary for the evaluation; and evaluation experts should be involved at an early stage. Moreover, the evaluation process is smoother if based on comprehensive evaluation plans, if the interim reports already include intermediate results and if the European Commission and the Member States establish regular contact to discuss problems and difficulties encountered. Finally, the chapter discusses future challenges faced by State aid evaluations, in particular how to ensure the further development of an ex post evaluation culture in the Member States and how to use the results of these ex post evaluations as a key tool to promote an effective EU State aid policy.

Most evaluations of State aid measures and schemes are aimed at assessing the effectiveness of the aid, i.e., does it achieve its intended objectives. Chapter 8, on the contrary, focuses on the effects of State aid on competition. In this chapter, Nicole

Robins, undertakes an empirical analysis to assess the competitive impact of the aid received by the Newquay Airport over the period 2006-2011, which aimed at improving connectivity in a relatively remote area of the UK. Robins' empirical strategy is based on a combination of interviews with market participants, a descriptive analysis of the evolution in the number of passengers on different airport routes and Difference-in-Differences estimations based on a dynamic panel data model, which allow isolating the impact of the aid from other market developments. The effect of the aid is measured by the difference in passenger traffic between the routes potentially affected by the aid (the treated group) and the routes at UK airports unlikely to have been affected (the control group). The chapter shows that aid to Newquay airport was likely to have had a significant negative impact on passenger traffic at some neighbouring airports and might even have contributed to the closure of one of these airports. This raises questions about the effectiveness of the funding provided by the UK government for the conversion of the military airport at Newquay into a commercial airport, as it may have led to the closure of another commercial airport operating below capacity. It also confirms the presumption made in the 2014 revision of the aviation State aid guidelines that an aid to an airport in the catchment area of another airport that is already operating below capacity can have distortive effects under certain circumstances.

Chapter 9 investigates the impact of aid schemes approved by the European Commission during 2008-2010 to support the development of basic broadband infrastructure in rural areas of Germany. This State aid evaluation offers a comprehensive analysis of these schemes, looking not only at their effectiveness in promoting broadband coverage but also at the effects of the aid on market entry, allowing to assess whether these schemes could have led to a crowding-out effect on competitors. The empirical strategy combines different methodologies. It starts with a descriptive analysis of the evolution of broadband coverage and the number of internet service providers in German municipalities. Then, it uses matching techniques to construct a set of non-aided western German municipalities that is as similar as possible to the sample of aided municipalities. Subsequently, the Difference-in-Differences approach is used to compare broadband coverage and market entry in aided municipalities with the matched non-aided municipalities. The study finds that the aid schemes were successful in increasing broadband coverage in aided municipalities, estimating that these municipalities gained the equivalent of two to three years in broadband development, compared to similar non-aided municipalities. The study also concludes that the aid schemes did not create distortions of competition, as the number of internet service providers grew more rapidly in aided municipalities. Finally, the aid schemes seemed to be most effective when offering medium-size aids and where most needed (i.e., in municipalities with a low DSL coverage, e.g.).

The last chapter in Part III, by Sven Heim, Kai Hüschelrath, Philipp-Schmidt-Dengler and Maurizio Strazzeri, focuses on the causal impact of restructuring aids provided by the EU Member States. It assesses the impact of fifty-six approval decisions by the European Commission between 2000 and 2012 on the survival probability and financial viability of aided firms. As a background, the chapter provides an overview of the institutional framework and of the literature on rescue and restructuring aids in the European Union. The chapter's empirical strategy is based on matching techniques and survival models. Matching techniques are used to constitute a control group of non-aided firms that are comparable to the aided firms. The comparison of the observed survival probability and financial viability between aided firms and matched non-aided firms allows estimating the effect of restructuring aids provided. The authors find that restructuring aid increases a firm's average survival time by approximately eight to fifteen years, depending on the definition of survival used. They also provide evidence that, in the long-term aid, recipients have a significantly higher probability for improvement in their financial viability than matched non-aided firms. The authors therefore conclude that the European Commission's rescue and restructuring aid policy is effective. The next step in the analysis would be to analyse the overall welfare effects of rescue and restructuring aids, looking not only at their direct effects on aid beneficiaries but also at indirect effects of the granting of aid on competition, trade, employment, investment and economic growth.

Part IV: The Broader Impact of EU Competition Policy

The fourth and last part of this book aims at giving a picture of the broader impact of EU competition policy. This part includes three chapters, moving from the direct benefits of competition policy interventions for consumers in terms of avoided price increases (Chapter 11) to their deterrent effects (Chapter 12) and finally to their sectoral and macroeconomic effects (Chapter 13).

Chapter 11, by Adriaan Dierx and Fabienne Ilzkovitz, examines how to measure the direct effects of competition policy interventions. Based on the customer savings approach, adopted by an increasing number of competition authorities, the European Commission calculates the direct benefits of merger interventions and cartel decisions for customers. Customer savings are calculated as the multiple of the estimated price reduction resulting from the European Commission's intervention, the turnover in the market concerned and the estimated duration of the price effect. However, the customer savings approach ignores the deterrent and non-price effects of competition policy interventions and does not take into account the benefits resulting from other activities than merger interventions and cartel prohibitions, such as abuse of dominance cases and State aid control. Despite these limitations, this method is very informative about the broader impact of competition policy interventions. The customer savings associated with cartel prohibitions and merger interventions over the period 2012-2018 amounted up to 0.1% of EU GDP. A limited number of important decisions account for a large share of these customer savings: these decisions concern cartels in the trucks and financial derivatives markets as well as mergers in the beer market, in mobile telecommunications and in the market for basic metals.

Chapter 12, by Adriaan Dierx, Fabienne Ilzkovitz, Yannis Katsoulacos and David Ulph, reviews the alternative approaches proposed in the literature to assess the deterrent effects of cartel and merger enforcement policies. There is agreement in the literature that the deterrent effects of competition policy largely outweigh its direct effects. However, the measurement of deterrent effects – i.e., the extent to which competition policy enforcement discourages anticompetitive behaviour – is challenging. It requires information on changes in future behaviour of market players, which can be associated with competition policy interventions. The simplest measurement method relies on surveys of companies and their legal advisors. These surveys indicate that three to eight mergers are deterred per merger intervention by a competition authority and that five to twenty-eight cartels are deterred for every cartel detected. These survey results have a number of limitations. In particular, the survey results may be biased because the sample of interviewees is not randomly selected. Therefore, new statistical and theoretical modelling tools have been developed, particularly in the area of cartels, allowing refining the results of surveys. According to these models, the amount of deterred harm resulting from cartel prohibitions is six to seventeen times that of detected harm. Measures to increase the deterrent effects of cartel policy aim at increasing the probability of detection (e.g., through leniency programmes), at augmenting the expected punishment (via fines and private damages actions), and at reducing the risk of recidivism (by monitoring past cartel members and increasing fines for repeat offenders). In the area of mergers, there is less consensus on the type of competition policy intervention – prohibition or clearance with remedies – having the strongest deterrent effects and this could be investigated further. Another avenue of future research consists in testing the hypothesis that the deterrent effects of cartel prohibitions and merger interventions are primarily felt in the markets and sectors directly affected by the competition authorities' interventions. Such sectoral deterrence analysis needs to be further explored and first attempt in that direction is made in the last chapter of this volume.

Chapter 13, by Fabienne Ilzkovitz, Mattia Cai, Roberta Cardani, Adriaan Dierx and Filippo Pericoli, provides an assessment of the macroeconomic and sectoral impact of merger interventions and cartel prohibitions by the European Commission over the period 2012-2018. The macroeconomic simulations presented in this chapter consider both the direct and the deterrent effects of competition policy interventions. On the one hand, inter-temporal deterrence effects arise from companies' expectations that the European Commission will continue its competition policy interventions well into the future. On the other hand, sectoral deterrence effects come from the transmission of the direct effects of competition policy interventions in a given market to the remainder of the sector to which this market belongs. Model simulations show that the macroeconomic impact of competition policy interventions (including deterrent effects) may lead to 0.3 % increase in GDP, an effect of the same order of magnitude as the estimated impact of the implementation of the EU Service Directive. However, the effect is somewhat smaller than that of the European Fund for Strategic Investments (+ 0.9 %), which was at the core of the 2015 Juncker Plan. These positive effects are robust to variations in different assumptions concerning the level of price increase avoided by competition policy interventions and the magnitude of the deterrent effects. An input-output model is used to exploit available information on the distribution of merger and cartel interventions by industry and to explore how the avoided price increase resulting from a competition policy intervention in a given industry is transmitted to the prices in other industries. The chapter shows that the industry spillover price effects of competition policy interventions may be as important as their within-industry price effects. Taking into account these spillover price effects, the average annual price reduction associated with competition policy interventions over the period 2012-2018 is significant (-0.2%). Large price reductions occur in industries that are important for the purchasing power of consumers (motor vehicles, financial services) and the competitiveness of the European economy (telecommunications, electronics).

MAIN LESSONS LEARNT AND AREAS FOR FURTHER WORK

Ex post evaluation is a relatively recent activity of competition authorities. Nevertheless, an evaluation culture has developed gradually within the European Union. Over the last twenty years, the scope of the ex post analysis has widened, more solid methodologies have been employed and the accuracy of analysis has improved. Nowadays, there is a broad agreement that the quality of competition policy rules and interventions can be improved through the ex post evaluation of past practice. Moreover, ex post evaluation is a useful tool to defend to a wider public the legitimacy of the work carried out. However, given their complexity, ex post evaluation analyses still have to overcome several pitfalls, in particular to enhance their robustness and their informative power for future decision and policy-making.

A number of lessons can already be learnt from the experience of competition authorities and academics with ex post evaluations. Broadly speaking, there are two main conditions for getting successful ex post economic evaluations: access to good data and selection of an appropriate and robust methodology.

Good Data Are Essential

Access to good data is essential, in particular for quantitative evaluations. For example, the ex post evaluation of an individual competition policy intervention requires market data covering the period before and after the date of the intervention, as well as comparable data on other geographic or sectoral markets, which can be used as a control. The selection of an appropriate control group to be used as a counterfactual is the basis of a robust and informative evaluation. A sufficient time gap between the competition policy intervention and the ex post analysis should be observed to be able to see the effects of the intervention. Data availability and quality (including the degree of granularity and completeness of the data as well as the robustness of the indicators considered) should be a criterion for the selection of the cases to be evaluated.

Ideally, the collection of data to be used for ex post evaluation purposes could already commence at the time of the decision. This would imply that the selection of the competition policy intervention to be subjected to an ex post evaluation is made at a very early stage. In any event, a budget for data acquisition should be set aside from the beginning of the study. Useful data can be obtained from market participants. However, they may be reluctant to collect and release them, unless the competition authority has legal powers obliging them to cooperate. For qualitative studies based on surveys and interviews, the participation of stakeholders is fundamental and a refusal by market participants to cooperate may be a real obstacle. Therefore, if ex post evaluation activities have to develop further, one could consider giving more legal powers to competition authorities to collect data for that purpose.

Select an Appropriate and Robust Methodology

The choice of methodology depends on a number of factors, such as the objective of the evaluation, the nature of data available, the time available for the study and the skills of the evaluation team. It is also important to recognise the limitations of the different methodologies, which need to be properly taken into account when interpreting the results obtained. The use of a combination of methods increases the robustness of the results. A descriptive analysis of market developments can usefully complement a more sophisticated quantitative analysis, as it can help to identify ex ante the assumptions to be tested and to interpret ex post the empirical results obtained. Likewise, surveys and interviews can be used to better understand market developments. At the same time, our experience with ex post evaluations has taught us that studies with too ambitious a scope have limitations in terms of the possible depth of analysis.

Different methodologies require a different expertise, which is not always available in the same team. On the one hand, evaluators associated with competition authorities may be more familiar with the competition policy interventions under investigation and have better access to the relevant sources of information. However, to ensure that the analysis is impartial, the ex post assessment should be performed by a different team from the one involved in the competition policy decision being evaluated. On the other hand, external evaluators may have a better knowledge of more complex 'state of the art' methodologies and can provide a fresh perspective. Moreover, working with external experts may increase the credibility of results, as they would be considered as more independent than the competition authority responsible for the decision. A combination of internal and external expertise may thus be the right way to achieve a balance between independence and effectiveness of the evaluation. A close monitoring of outsourced studies by the internal staff of the competition authority and the early involvement of academic experts are examples of good practice. Similarly, a sharing of experience with other competition authorities and international organisations helps to deliver better outcomes overall.

While Diverting Resources from Enforcement, Ex Post Evaluations Are a Good Investment for Competition Authorities

To sum up, ex post evaluations require time and resources. Such analyses are expensive, relying not only on the availability of well-trained empirical economists but also on an infrastructure for the collection, safe storage and processing of data. The direct costs of performing an ex post evaluation primarily relate to human resources requirements if done in-house and the competition authority study budget if the evaluation is outsourced. While internal ex post evaluations divert resources from enforcement activities in the short term, they provide more learning opportunities thereby contributing to the efficiency and effectiveness of competition policy enforcement in the medium term.

Four Main Areas for Further Research

Despite recent progress made with the ex post evaluation of competition policy, gaps remain. For future work, we believe that an effort has to be made in four main directions. First, to extend the use of robust ex post evaluations beyond communication and advocacy purposes and encourage their usage for decision-making and policy design. Second, to expand the quantitative analysis of the effects of competition policy interventions in the areas of abuse of dominance and State aids. Third, to widen the scope of the ex post analysis by considering other effects than the direct price effects of competition policy interventions: a more in-depth analysis of the non-price effects and of the indirect (deterrent) effects of such interventions would be valuable for policy makers. Fourth, to develop the work on the sector and macroeconomic impact of competition policy.

Encourage the Usage of Ex Post Evaluations for Decision-Making and Policy Design

At present, the ex post evaluations of competition policy interventions are used more for advocacy purposes than for improving future decision-making. The reason is that it is difficult to generalise the results of ex post evaluations of individual decisions, which by their nature are quite case specific. In the area of merger control, for example, it would be worthwhile to check for a relatively large sample of merger decisions whether expectations about market developments at the time of the decision were ultimately realised. This descriptive analysis was successfully implemented by competition authorities in Canada, New Zealand and the United Kingdom, allowing them to draw general lessons on how to improve the enforcement of merger control.

Thus far, public consultations have been the main tool used to check what did work and what did not work before undertaking a reform of a competition policy regulation. While this type of qualitative analysis relying on the views of market players and industry experts is very informative, it is less precise than a full-fledged ex post evaluation of the costs and benefits of a specific competition policy regulation or instrument. For example, one could consider conducting an ex post evaluation of the costs and benefits of the EU State aid control system, which has come under some criticism over the recent period. On the one hand, this system is essential to avoid distortions of competition in the European Internal Market. On the other hand, the absence of a State aid control in other large jurisdictions may create unfair conditions of competition for EU companies vis-à-vis competitors subsidised by governments of third countries. An ex post evaluation of the effectiveness of the EU State aid control could contribute to having a well-informed debate within this context.

Expand Ex Post Evaluations in the Areas of Abuse of Dominance and State Aids

Most of the empirical work has focused on the price effects of merger interventions and cartel prohibition.[3] However, much less work has been done in other areas of competition policy, such as interventions in cases of abuse of dominance and State aid. We hope that this volume, which includes two ex post evaluations of abuse of dominance cases and three State aid evaluations, will encourage further research in these areas.

In recent years, the European Commission has taken a number of important decisions concerning abuse of dominance in the digital economy. It would be interesting to carry out ex post evaluations of these decisions, after sufficient time has passed for their effects to be observable. In the area of State aid, the impulse given by the requirement of the SAM that EU Member States conduct ex post evaluations of large State aid schemes will be felt for years to come. The challenge here is to ensure that the ex post evaluations carried out will be reflected in improvements in the new State aid schemes to be proposed by the Member States.

Consider Other Effects than the Direct Price Effects of Competition Policy Interventions

The empirical analysis is almost exclusively devoted to the price effects of competition policy interventions on the markets directly affected by these interventions. Less is known about the effects of competition policy enforcement on other measures of market performance, such as innovation, quality and diversity of products. Analysing the impact of competition policy enforcement on innovation is particularly relevant in this period of rapid digitalisation of the economy. In digital markets, innovation is the principal determinant of competitive performance. Entry barriers tend to be high and dominance is often entrenched. In such markets, competition policy should ensure that the dominant player does not diminish the incentives and possibilities for competitors to innovate. However, analysing how specific competition policy interventions have affected firms' innovation activities is quite challenging. For this reason, the European Commission's Directorate-General for Competition has commissioned a feasibility study on the microeconomic impact of competition policies on innovation. This feasibility study, which was carried out by Ormosi et al. (2017), offers some interesting insights on how to make progress in analysing the impact of competition policy enforcement on innovation. The study includes a survey of the relevant literature as well as an ex post assessment of the recent consolidation of the hard-disk drive market.

3. The motivation for the assessment of decisions concerning cartels is different from the ones related to mergers and abuse of dominant positions. As cartels are prohibited per se in most jurisdictions, the decision is by definition appropriate. Therefore, ex post evaluations of cartel decisions focus on calculating the magnitude of the overcharge (or increase in price) imposed by the cartel in order to determine whether the fines imposed have sufficiently strong deterrent effects against future cartels (*see* OECD, 2016).

We have decided not to include the study in this volume because this is an area that merits further reflection.

The direct effects of each competition policy intervention tend to be limited to the small number of markets targeted by the intervention. The indirect effects are much wider: companies that observe interventions by competition authorities pay greater attention to competition rules and may refrain from engaging in anticompetitive behaviour themselves, even if they are not directly affected by such intervention. There is agreement on the importance of such deterrent effects because they give a greater leverage to competition policy interventions. As competition authorities do not have the resources to tackle all or even most of the anticompetitive actions that could potentially be taken, it is important that their interventions discourage other misbehaviours from occurring in the first place or refrain recidivism for a long period of time. However, there is much uncertainty about the size of the deterrent effects. This volume suggests alternative methods to measure the order of magnitude of the deterrent effects of cartel enforcement and merger control. Such measurements could then be used to: (i) obtain a better assessment of the macroeconomic impact of competition policy; (ii) improve the design of competition rules; and (iii) prioritise the allocation of resources across different competition policy instruments.

Develop the Work on the Sector and Macroeconomic Impact of Competition Policy

The work presented in this volume on the sectoral and macroeconomic impact of competition policy could be further developed as well. At the sector level, a better understanding of the effects of competition policy enforcement on market functioning and sector performance could help competition authorities to better operate in important sectors of the economy. An intervention by a competition authority in a given market affects not only the parties directly concerned by the decision, but other market participants as well. Moreover, multiple decisions within a single market or sector may have larger effects than the sum of each individual decision. Similarly, the interactions between merger interventions, antitrust prohibitions and State aid decisions within a given market or sector are insufficiently explored. A better knowledge about the connections between competition policy instruments and between competition and regulatory policies in key sectors, such as energy, transport and telecommunications, would allow defining a more appropriate policy framework.

At the macroeconomic level, we have presented some work proposing a new approach to measure the impact of competition policy interventions on GDP growth and employment. This is a first step in establishing a link between microeconomic competition policy interventions and their price and mark-up impact, allowing translating the effects of these interventions at the macroeconomic level. However, there are other channels than mark-up and price reduction, through which competition policy interventions have a macroeconomic impact, such as the business dynamism and innovation channels. These channels should be further investigated. Finally, price reductions generally associated with competition policy interventions are particularly beneficial for low-income people and therefore, competition policy could also have positive distributional effects. However, the literature in this area remains in its infancy.

In conclusion, we believe that ex post evaluation activities have a clear value added for competition authorities. We hope that, by presenting a collection of interesting ex post evaluations on a wide range of topics, this volume will stimulate further work in this area.

Fabienne Ilzkovitz
Adriaan Dierx

REFERENCES

Ilzkovitz F. and Dierx A. (2015), 'Ex-post economic evaluation of competition policy enforcement: a review of the literature', DG Competition staff paper, Publications Office of the European Union, June.

Kwoka J.E. Jr. (2013), 'Does merger control work? A retrospective on EU enforcement actions and merger outcomes', *Antitrust Law Journal*, 78(3), pp. 619-650.

OECD (2016), 'Reference guide on ex-post evaluation of competition agencies' enforcement decisions', April.

Ormosi P., Bennato A.R., Davies S. and Mariuzzo F. (2017), 'Feasibility study on the microeconomic impact of the enforcement of competition polices on innovation', Report prepared for the Directorate-General for Competition, European Commission.

CHAPTER 1

EU Competition Policy and Ex Post Evaluation: Key Concepts*

Fabienne Ilzkovitz & Adriaan Dierx

This introductory chapter offers a historical perspective on the development of the regulatory framework for the three main instruments of EU competition policy: antitrust, State aid control and merger control. Traditionally, the European Commission has used public consultations to evaluate existing regulations and assess the impact of its policy proposals in these areas. More recently, such qualitative evaluations have been complemented by quantitative evaluations that provide hard evidence on the impact of competition policy interventions. In this light, the chapter defines the objectives and scope of ex post evaluations carried out in the competition policy domain. Then, it gives an overview of the quantitative and qualitative evaluation methods that have been used to assess ex post what has been the impact of competition policy in both the EU and elsewhere.

§1.01 INTRODUCTION

This introductory chapter has two main objectives: first, to summarise the main principles and instruments of EU competition policy; and second, to describe the role and scope of ex post economic evaluation in this field. Section 1.02 presents the regulatory framework in the three main areas of the EU competition policy: antitrust enforcement, State aid control and merger control. It describes how this regulatory framework has evolved during its sixty-year history, how ex post evaluation has traditionally been used and what are the main challenges for competition policy. Section 1.03 focuses on ex post economic evaluation toolbox. Based on the ex post evaluation practice of competition authorities and academic research, this section considers the objectives, scope and methodologies of current ex post economic evaluation practice in the competition policy domain. Section 1.04 concludes.

* This chapter has been written under the sole responsibility of the authors and does not represent the views of the European Commission.

§1.02 A SHORT HISTORY OF EU COMPETITION POLICY

Since the Treaty of Rome (1957), competition policy has been at the core of the process of EU economic integration. Europe's founding fathers already emphasised the importance of EU competition policy for the smooth functioning of the common market and, to avoid distortions of competition at the European level, they gave exclusive competence within this area to the European Union. In its Preamble, the Treaty of Rome refers to the objective of establishing free and fair competition. The Treaty itself contains rules prohibiting public and private practices that could undermine competition.[1] Even though the Treaty gives exclusive powers to the European Commission to ensure that these rules are correctly applied, in its enforcement practice the Commission works in close cooperation with national competition authorities. EU competition policy enforcement decisions are subject to review by the European Courts.

The approach to competition policy adopted at the EU level considers that competition is not an end in itself but a tool that contributes to improving the functioning of markets to the benefit of consumers. Competition should improve the efficiency of companies and encourage them to innovate. This has a positive impact for consumers, who benefit from lower prices and a wider range of better quality products. To improve the conditions of competition, EU competition policy builds on three main instruments: (1) antitrust rules, which seek to prevent anticompetitive practices, such as cartels and abuses of dominant position; (2) State aid control, which prevents public money from being wasted by focusing aid where it helps correct market failures without impairing competition; and (3) merger control, which aims at preserving competitive market structures by controlling mergers and acquisitions. The remainder of this section briefly reviews the rules governing these three instruments. It also describes the main reforms aimed at increasing the efficiency of the competition policy framework as a tool to create a better functioning internal market. The section concludes with a discussion of the use of ex post evaluation in the three competition policy instruments and of current and future challenges for competition policy.

[A] Antitrust

Antitrust policy covers measures aimed at preventing or controlling cartels and agreements between companies as well as abuses of dominant positions (*see* Box 1.1).

Box 1.1: Antitrust policy (Articles 101 and 102 of the Treaty on the Functioning of the European Union, TFEU)

The basic provisions of the EU antitrust rules are set out in Articles 101 and 102 of the TFEU.

1. In particular, Article 85 of the Treaty of Rome (which became Article 101 of the Treaty on the Functioning of the European Union – TFEU), Article 86 (which became Article 102 of the TFEU) and Articles 92-94 (Articles 107-109 of the TFEU).

Article 101 prohibits anticompetitive agreements, in other words all agreements that have as their object or effect the distortion of competition within the internal market. This covers horizontal agreements (between undertakings operating at the same level of the value-added chain) and vertical agreements (undertakings operating at different levels, such as producers and distributors). Under Article 101(1), an agreement is regarded as anticompetitive by nature if the participants agree to: (i) fix prices; (ii) limit production; (iii) share markets; (iv) apply dissimilar conditions to equivalent transactions; and (v) subject the conclusion of contracts to the acceptance of supplementary obligations. These practices are therefore illegal, as are cartels, which are explicit or tacit agreements between competitors to fix prices, limit supply or share the market.

But Article 101(1) does not apply to agreements which fulfil the four cumulative conditions set out in Article 101(3), namely: (1) the agreements must contribute to general welfare (improving the production or distribution of goods or technical progress); (2) consumers must receive a fair share of the resulting benefits; (3) the restrictions are indispensable to the attainment of these objectives; and (4) the agreements do not eliminate competition. For example, agreements aimed at developing common technical standards for the entire internal market and those intended to promote research and development and technology transfers are often compatible with the competition rules. Lastly, small enterprises can cooperate with each other if this allows them to compete better with larger companies.

Article 102 prohibits the abuse of a dominant position. A 'dominant position' is defined as the ability to behave independently of one's competitors and customers.[2] A dominant position is not anticompetitive in itself,[3] but once a dominant position is established an abuse may occur. There are two categories of abuses: (1) exploitative abuses, whereby a company exploits its dominant position to extract additional profits from its suppliers and customers by imposing unfair purchasing or selling prices or other unfair trading conditions; and (2) exclusionary abuses, whereby company's behaviour is designed to eliminate competitors, for instance, by means of predatory pricing (in other words, artificially low prices), of special discounts for certain customers which smaller competitors cannot match, of refusal to grant access to essential inputs or infrastructure to new entrants.

The initial role of antitrust policy was to accompany and support the gradual dismantling of barriers to trade within the common market. To facilitate the implementation of Treaty Articles 85 and 86, the Council adopted Regulation (EEC) No. 17/62, which clarified the provisions of the Treaty. This Regulation granted substantial powers to the Commission since it conferred on it a dual monopoly: information (any

2. *See*, *Continental Can*, Commission decision of 9 December 1971.
3. Judgment of the Court of 14 February 1978, *United Brands Company and United Brands Continentaal BV v. Commission of the European Communities*, Case 27/76.

company that wanted to be exempt from the prohibition of an agreement had to notify it to the Commission) and decision-making (the Commission alone decided whether an agreement was admissible), including the imposition of sanctions in the form of fines.

Over the decades, the centralised system of notifications increasingly confined the European Commission to a reactive role due to the high number of notifications received: for example, proceedings initiated by the European Commission accounted for only 13% of new cases registered over the period 1988-1998 (*see* European Commission, 1999). In addition, by the start of the twenty-first century, both companies and Member States had acquired greater knowledge and experience of European competition rules. Consequently, the European Commission undertook a major reform enabling it to adopt a more proactive policy towards agreements and abuses of dominant positions that severely restrict competition in the internal market.

Within the framework of this reform, the European Commission decided to abolish the centralised system of notifications of agreements and replace it with a decentralised system in which the Commission, national competition authorities and courts are empowered to enforce the antitrust rules. The new arrangements for applying antitrust procedures, introduced by the Regulation No. 1/2003, were intended to ensure more effective compliance with the rules and to reduce red tape for businesses. This Regulation largely relies on market players assessing ex ante the compatibility of their practices with the EU competition rules, and on targeted ex post enforcement action by the European and national competition authorities.

The advantage of these new arrangements is that the European Commission has wider scope for priority setting and for investigating cases and inquiry in key economic sectors, as well as less conventional forms of anticompetitive behaviour observed in rapidly expanding sectors. However, this also implies greater cooperation between the national competition authorities and the Commission in order to guarantee the consistent enforcement of the rules and efficient allocation of tasks. That is why a European Competition Network (ECN) was set up to foster cooperation and the exchange of best practices between national authorities.

Another innovation introduced by Regulation No. 1/2003 is the option of increased use of remedies and commitments. Article 7 of the Regulation allows the European Commission to require companies to end a particular infringement and, for this purpose, to impose any behavioural or structural remedies which are proportionate to the infringement and necessary to bring it effectively to an end. As for Article 9, it allows the companies concerned to offer commitments to meet the concerns expressed to them by the European Commission in its preliminary assessment, and allows the Commission to make those commitments binding on the companies. This procedure allows the European Commission to resolve cases more quickly while ensuring companies' compliance with competition rules.

Following the adoption of Regulation (EC) No. 1/2003, the Directorate-General for Competition changed its working methods in two ways. First, it adopted new instruments, a leniency policy and sector enquiries, which enabled it to continue identifying major infringements of the rules despite the absence of the notification system. Second, it took measures to speed up its decisions.

The leniency policy is intended to encourage companies to report cartels by granting them immunity or a reduction in fines. This approach proved effective: the European Commission's decisions on cartels tripled following its introduction in 1996 (Wils, 2016). More recently though, the effectiveness of the leniency programme seems to have diminished. This could be attributable to many factors, including that there are fewer cartels to report. Nevertheless, in March 2017 the European Commission decided to supplement the leniency programme by a new whistleblowing tool, which allows individuals to supply information anonymously to the Commission about secret cartels.

Sector inquiries are investigations that the European Commission carries out into sectors of the economy and into types of agreements across various sectors, when it believes that a competition in a specific market may be impaired. If it finds grounds for doing so, the Commission may assess – at a later stage – whether it needs to open specific investigations to ensure the respect of EU rules on restrictive agreements and abuse of dominant position. Since 1999, six sector inquiries have been conducted in sectors such as telecommunications, the media, financial services, energy, pharmaceuticals and e-commerce.

Following the entry into force of the 2003 antitrust modernisation package, the Directorate-General for Competition made an additional effort to improve internal operations. In 2005, it introduced a two-stage procedure allowing it to identify more quickly and efficiently cases that warranted an in-depth investigation and should be given priority, and to close other cases. The criteria used to determine priority include the extent of the harm to consumers, the strategic nature of the sector, the impact on the functioning of the internal market and the complexity of the investigation (*see* Lowe, 2009).

The European Commission also encouraged the use of negotiated procedures, which can contribute to increasing the speed of decisions. In the area of cartels, for example, the Commission introduced a settlement procedure in 2008, which allows the parties to take note of the evidence in the Commission's file and to admit their involvement and liability in relation to the cartel. In exchange for this admission, the Commission can reduce the amount of the fine by 10%. During the period 2010-2018, the Commission adopted twenty-eight negotiated decisions out of a total of forty-two decisions on cartels. In the area of abuse, the Commission imposed interim measures for the first time in more than fifteen years (in the 2019 Broadcom investigation). However, the purpose of such interim measures is not to speed up proceedings, but rather to prevent irreparable harm to competition in fast moving markets. Over the recent period, investigations have become more complex and based on voluminous files of information. In light of the limited resources available to competition authorities, there is an increasing need to prioritise. Ex post evaluations can make a contribution to deciding how and where to prioritise.

[B] State Aid Control

In 2018, Member States spent EUR 120.6 billion or 0.8% of EU GDP on State aid (*see* European Commission, 2019a). The main objective of EU State aid control is to ensure that this large amount of spending is used to promote objectives of common interest without distorting competition. State aid control ensures an effective use of public resources. It also helps maintain a level playing field between companies in the internal market by making sure that Member States do not engage in subsidy races.

As a first step, State aid control weighs the positive and negative effects of an aid measure. Aid may be justified to correct market failures or for reasons of equity (*see* Box 1.2). Market failures may be the result of externalities, asymmetric information, coordination problems or market power. In the event of market failure, it must be verified that the aid is both effective and proportionate. For the aid to be effective, it must cause a change in behaviour of the aid beneficiary. The amount of aid needs to be proportionate to the size of the market failure. Other considerations may play a role as well. For example, certain aids may be considered compatible with the internal market to the extent to which they help to improve fairness. This is the case, for example, of regional aid or aid for the financing of services of general interest, such as mail delivery in sparsely populated and peripheral areas.

Box 1.2: State aid control (Articles 107-109 of the TFEU)

State aid is prohibited on the basis of Article 107(1) TFEU, unless it is authorised because it fulfils the conditions under Article 107(2) or (3). Article 107(1) specifies the criteria that must be fulfilled in order for a measure to be considered as an aid (*see* Verouden and Werner (2016)): (i) use of State resources (in various forms such as grants, tax relief, interest-rate subsidies, guarantees); (ii) an advantage granted to an undertaking, i.e., an entity with an economic activity; (iii) selectivity of the measure (granted to certain sectors or certain undertakings); (iv) effect on trade between Member States; and (v) risk of distortions of competition. If these conditions are fulfilled and the measure does not fall below a certain *de minimis* threshold (EUR 200,000 over three years), it is considered as an aid, which can be authorised only if it meets the compatibility criteria under Article 107(2) or (3). For instance, the European Commission may authorise aid that contributes to an objective of general interest, such as aid for research and innovation, environmental aid, aid for broadband networks, regional development aid, aid for SME, aid for the promotion of training or to remedy a serious disturbance in the economy of a Member State.[4]

The governments of the Member States must notify to the European Commission aid that they intend to grant. The aid may be granted only once authorisation has been received from the Commission. However, the European Commission

4. It was on that basis in particular that aid was granted to European banks in difficulties following the economic and financial crisis of 2008.

has laid down block exemption regulations detailing the aid schemes and measures, which are deemed to be compatible and do not need to be notified. Over the period 2015-2019, only 8% of notified cases required the opening of a formal investigation procedure and only 4% led to a negative decision requiring recovery of the State aid. If governments of EU Member States have granted incompatible aid, the European Commission may request that the aid be paid back. This has happened for example in the case of the corporate tax rulings.

Any positive effects of the aid must be compared with its negative effects, which may be due to distortions of competition that result in inefficiencies in the allocation of resources. For example, distortions of competition may arise if the aid has the effect of preventing the exit of inefficient firms from the market, as may be the case for poorly devised rescue and restructuring aid, or if the aid increases the market power of a beneficiary that already has a dominant position.

Aid may also give rise to distortions in the international allocation of resources where certain governments subsidise their domestic firms to protect them from foreign competition or grant aid to attract foreign investors. Negative cross-border externalities that can undermine the functioning of the internal market are one of the key elements justifying State aid control at European level. Moreover, European State aid control helps to ensure a proper use of public resources in the different EU Member States.

The principle of State aid control by a supranational authority has been present since the Treaty of Rome. However, State aid control did not become reality until 1968, when the customs union was established. At that time, there was a need to prevent Member States from replacing custom duties with subsidies to protect their companies from foreign competition. It would take a further two decades for State aid control to become a full-fledged competition policy instrument and for the European Commission to request the recovery of unlawful aid that was incompatible with the Treaty (*see* European Commission, 2011). In the early 1990s, German unification, the breaking-up of monopolies in the network industries, the audio-visual sector and financial services, and the creation of the internal market brought about an increase in importance of State aid control. Subsequently, the prospect of Economic and Monetary Union underlined the importance of fiscal discipline and further increased the need for supervision and regulation of State support (*see* Mederer et al., 2008). In 2013, the European Commission started to review rulings by national tax authorities that give individual companies clarity in advance, on how corporate taxes will be calculated. Such rulings may under certain conditions provide selective advantages to a company and therefore be considered as State aid. A number of negative decisions requiring the recovery of the State aid have since been adopted as a result of the Commission review. Most recently, an effort has been made to incorporate aid into the European Commission's sustainable and inclusive growth strategy.

Since the end of the 1990s, the regulatory framework of State aid control has undergone three major reforms: the first defined what still constitutes today the architecture of State aid control, the second was the 2005-2009 State Aid Action Plan (SAAP) and the third was State Aid Modernisation (SAM) from 2012 to 2014 (European

Commission, 2012). These reforms had three important objectives: (1) to enable the Commission to focus on aid cases with potentially the most distortive effects on competition in the internal market while giving the Member States more responsibility for the implementation of State aid control; (2) to improve the analysis of the effects of aid in order to foster aid in support of sustainable growth and discourage wasteful and unproductive aid; and (3) to increase the transparency of procedures and rules and simplify them in order to speed up the adoption of decisions and reduce the administrative burden for companies.

Figure 1.1 Framework for State Aid

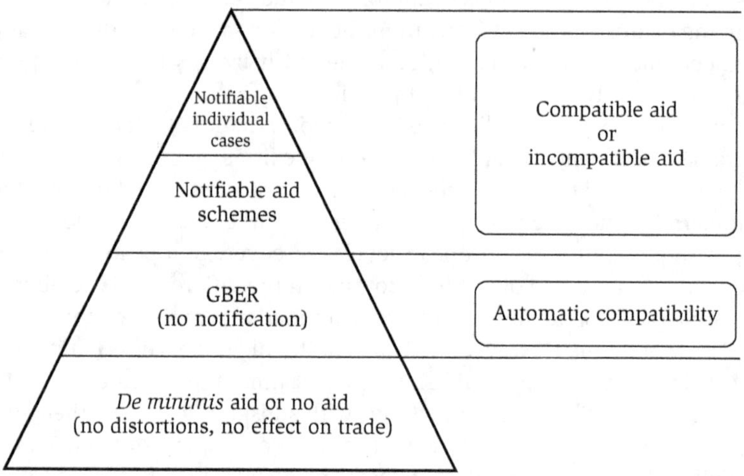

A first major reform was introduced at the end of the 1990s, with the adoption of Council Regulation No. 994/98, also known as the 'enabling regulation', which allows the Commission to adopt regulations exempting certain categories of horizontal aid from notification. This Regulation laid the foundations of the future General Block Exemption Regulation (GBER), which, together with the *de minimis* threshold, is at the basis of the current framework for aid (*see* Figure 1.1).

In 2005, a second innovative package of reforms was launched under the SAAP,[5] which was based on four principles. First, State aid should be targeted at activities that contributed to growth, competitiveness or the creation of sustainable jobs. Second, in order to identify this 'good' aid, it was essential to define a more sophisticated economic approach for making the trade-off between the positive and negative effects of aid. Third, the SAAP sought to reduce the time taken to reach decisions, in particular by extending the scope of the GBER and reducing the number of aid measures that had to be notified. Finally, the SAAP sought a greater sharing of responsibilities between the European Commission and the EU Member States.

5. *See* European Commission (2005a).

The Communication on EU SAM was issued in 2012. It served three main purposes. First, State aid control would seek to promote aid that supports sustainable growth and contributes to the improvement of the quality of public finances by discouraging wasteful and counter-productive subsidies. Second, State aid control would focus on cases with the biggest impact on the internal market. Sector inquiries were foreseen in the event of suspected distortions of competition, while the scope of the GBER was further extended to include cases of a local nature with little effect on cross-border trade. The extension of the GBER went hand in hand with the requirement that the EU Member States become more transparent about their State aids - i.e., to inform market participants about big individual aid awards - and conduct ex post evaluations of large State aid schemes. Third, procedures would be streamlined in order to speed up the decision-making process. Decision-making is also facilitated by the greater cooperation between the European Commission and national governments within the High Level Forum on SAM and the associated working groups.

The 2018 State aid scoreboard shows that the objective of broadening the scope of the GBER has been achieved: 82% of aid measures granted in 2018 and 38% of the total aid amount were exempt from notification (European Commission, 2018). Accordingly, the number of aid measures notified to the Commission has fallen significantly. Moreover, the trend away from sectoral and defensive aids has continued: while in the 1990s sectoral and rescue and restructuring aid accounted for over 50% of total aids, in 2016, around 94% of total State aid spending was allocated to horizontal objectives of common interest, such as environmental protection, R&D&I and regional development. In particular, there has been a marked increase in total expenditure on environmental and energy measures.

Another important initiative of the Commission concerns 'Important Projects of Common European Interest' (IPCEI). In its June 2014 Communication, the European Commission (2014) sets out criteria under which Member States' support of transnational projects of strategic significance for the EU may be considered to be compatible with the internal market under EU State aid rules. The objective of this initiative is to encourage Member States to channel their public spending to large projects that make a clear contribution to economic growth, jobs and the competitiveness of the EU. When private initiatives do not materialise because of the significant risks and the transnational cooperation that such projects entail, Member States may fill the funding gap to overcome such market failures and boost the realisation of projects that otherwise would not have taken off. The IPCEI rules support investments for R&D&I and first industrial deployment on condition that the projects receiving this funding are highly innovative and do not cover mass production or commercial activities. They also require extensive commitments for the dissemination and spillover of new knowledge throughout the EU as well as a detailed competition assessment to minimise any undue distortions in the internal market. The first application of the 2014 Communication outside the field of infrastructure took place in December 2018 and concerned an integrated project jointly notified by France, German, Italy and the UK for research and innovation in microelectronics. A second application from the EU Battery Alliance has been prepared with the aim of building a strategic value chain for car batteries in Europe.

[C] Merger Control

Merger control is the most recent instrument in European competition policy. A first 'merger regulation' aimed at controlling concentrations with a Community dimension (Regulation No. 4064/89) was adopted in December 1989 and entered into force on 21 September 1990. Before this Regulation was adopted, the European Commission had exercised a degree of control over mergers, first on the basis of Article 86[6] (now Article 102) and subsequently on the basis of Article 85 (now Article 101). However, the outcome was unsatisfactory, in particular because of the impossibility of exercising ex ante control on the basis of these articles. The recognition by the Court of Justice in 1987 that the European Commission could use Article 85 to control a concentration[7] paved the way for a systematic use of Article 85, which culminated in the adoption of the merger regulation in 1989.

Another key factor in the introduction of merger control was the project of creating an internal market by 31 December 1992. EU market integration increased the incentive for businesses to merge and acquire assets across national borders. Combining their activities enables businesses to develop new products more efficiently or to reduce their costs, thereby leading to benefits for consumers. However, certain merger transactions also risk harming consumers if, by reducing competition, they increase prices, reduce product choice or hamper innovation. The European Union's competition policy had to adapt to this new environment by controlling mergers with a Community dimension. This control would prevent cross-border mergers from reducing competition within the internal market.

Box 1.3: Merger control (Council Regulation (EC) No. 139/2004)

EU merger control rules give the European Commission the power to prohibit mergers and acquisitions that pose a significant threat to competition. The availability of a merger control system at European level means that companies operating in several Member States only need a single authorisation to merge, which is valid throughout the European Union (one-stop shop). The only merger operations that need to be notified to the European Commission are those involving undertakings with a turnover above a certain threshold and whose activities take place in several Member States.

A merger can be prohibited if the merging companies are the main competitors on the relevant market and if it can be established that the merger would significantly impede effective competition in the European Union. However, the European Commission only rarely prohibits a merger: since the implementation of the merger regulation, thirty mergers have been prohibited to date, which represents 0.4% of the total number of mergers notified to the Commission (*see* European Commission, 2019b). If a merger has a negative effect on competition,

6. In the *Continental Can* case of 1971, the Commission for the first time prohibited a merger on the basis of Article 86 of the Treaty.
7. Philip Morris judgment of 17 November 1987 (Joined Cases 142 and 156/84).

the European Commission can impose binding measures or conditions on the merging companies to avoid any distortions of competition once the merger takes place. If the European Commission concludes that the proposed merger does not restrict competition, it is approved without conditions. This is the case for 93% of the mergers that are notified to the Commission.

A key reform of merger control was the adoption of a new merger regulation in 2004 (*see* Box 1.3).[8] In substance, the two main modifications of the merger regulation were the introduction of a new test for assessing mergers and the recognition of efficiencies as an integral part of the analysis of the effects of mergers. Based on the new test, mergers that significantly impede effective competition are prohibited. This new test allowed the Commission to extend its review beyond the question of whether the merger would place the company in a dominant position or strengthen its ability to reinforce such a position. It was better suited to oligopolistic market structures, in which a merger could significantly reduce effective competition without creating or strengthening a dominant position, and it encouraged an economic analysis of cases that went beyond the more formalistic approach based on market shares. As regards efficiencies, the new merger regulation specified the three criteria that must be met for efficiency arguments put forward by the parties to be taken into account: they must be: (1) verifiable; (2) specific to the concentration (i.e., not achievable by means other than the merger); and (3) passed on to consumers.

At the same time, the European Commission also decided to upgrade the capability of its Directorate-General for Competition to undertake economic analyses by setting up a team of economists responsible for ensuring the economic rigour of decisions under the authority of a Chief Economist. The team provides methodological assistance and contributes to the economic analysis of individual decisions.

The period following the adoption of the new merger regulation was a generally stable period during which the Commission adopted guidelines and communications to clarify and specify the circumstances in which a merger was expected to have anticompetitive effects with a view to deterring certain mergers with a high risk of being prohibited.

This period was also characterised by an effort to streamline procedures. In 2013, the Commission adopted a series of measures aimed at simplifying the merger control procedures in order to lessen the administrative burden on companies wishing to merge, and thereby reduce the associated costs. This merger simplification package was implemented in 2014 and, in particular, it allowed broadening the scope of the simplified procedure governing the handling of unproblematic mergers. As a result, in more than 70% of cases, the European Commission decisions are taken by means of a simplified procedure.

At the same time as improving implementation, the European Commission launched an initiative focusing on a broader review of the functioning of the 2004 Merger Regulation. Based on a public consultation conducted in 2016 the Commission

8. Regulation (EC) No. 139/2004 on the control of concentrations between undertakings.

concluded that, on the whole, the 2004 Regulation was working well and that a fundamental overhaul was not necessary. Nevertheless, a reflection is underway whether EU merger control procedures should be further simplified and whether other thresholds than the currently used turnover-based thresholds should be applied in cases where the company being acquired has a high value but only a low turnover.

[D] Use of Ex Post Evaluation in the Three Policy Instruments

Traditionally, the European Commission has used public consultations to evaluate existing regulations and get feedback of new policy proposals, as illustrated by the above-mentioned review of the 2004 Merger Regulation. In competition policy, court judgments play an important role as well, primarily to validate individual decisions in antitrust, State aid control and merger control. A judgment by the Court to overturn one or more specific decisions may have wider consequences, as it will motivate the European Commission to review the relevant regulation to see if it is still fit for purpose. As an example, the decision by the Court to overturn three merger decisions around the turn of the century, added to the incentive for the European Commission to propose the 'new' Merger Regulations of 2004.

Both public consultations and court judgements are qualitative in nature. More recently, such qualitative evaluations have been complemented by quantitative evaluations that allow getting an idea about the size of the impact of competition policy interventions and – when using more sophisticated Counterfactual Impact Evaluation (CIE) techniques – identifying the causal effects of such interventions. The first example of an evaluation by the European Commission that used quantitative data analysis (in addition to structured interviews and questionnaires) was the 2005 merger remedies study. In this study the European Commission (2005b) assessed the implementation and effectiveness of the remedies imposed on merging companies. The study finds that divestment remedies are rather effective as 94% of the divested businesses are still alive three to five years after the divestiture and therefore continue to exercise some degree of competitive constraint on the merged entity. However, the effectiveness of remedies giving access to infrastructure or technology appears to be relatively low.

More recently, CIE tools, including in particular the Difference-in-Differences technique, have increasingly been used to evaluate the impact of individual merger decisions, and to a lesser extent of antitrust decisions and State aid measures and schemes, as described later on in this book. As such studies allow measuring ex post the impact of interventions in different markets and sectors based on hard evidence, they are more convincing as a tool to illustrate the benefits for consumers of competition policy interventions. In recent years, ex post evaluations have been used as well to illustrate to a wider public the broader benefits of competition and competition policy enforcement.

[E] New Challenges for Competition Policy

Looking back, one can conclude that the various reforms undertaken over the last sixty years in the competition policy domain have contributed to an improved division of responsibilities between the European Commission and the EU Member States. This has allowed the European Commission to focus on the cases with the largest risk of market distortions and fostered the development of an EU competition culture in the Member States. Moreover, the oversight by the European courts has incited the European Commission, and indirectly the national competition authorities, to improve enforcement practices and strengthened the economic and legal underpinnings of EU competition policy.

EU competition policy will continue evolving, because it is faced with new challenges. Four main challenges can be identified: (1) speed, quality and relevance; (2) collaboration with the EU Member States; (3) digitalisation; and (4) globalisation. By providing convincing evidence and analysis, ex post evaluations can help competition policy adapt to these new challenges, without compromising its basic principles. In this section, we set out these challenges and consider how to best deal with them.

[1] Reconcile Speed, Quality and Relevance

Despite the different steps taken towards modernisation of different tools of competition policy, the first challenge remains to reconcile the speed, quality and relevance of the decisions taken. The gradual shift towards an economic, effects-based approach in antitrust has increased the complexity of the competition authorities' investigations, as this approach requires an empirical investigation of the potentially anticompetitive effects of the companies' behaviour. A similar shift can be observed in merger and State aid control. Moreover, the files submitted by the parties (and by the EU Member States in the case of State aid control) for investigation by the European Commission have become much more voluminous. Consequently, the human and IT resources needed to investigate and conclude cases have increased exponentially. At the same time, there is the pressure in this digital age to take decisions ever more rapidly. Markets are undergoing rapid change and decisions need to be taken in good time for them to remain relevant, without making sacrifices in terms of quality. It is therefore essential that competition authorities make an effort to define priorities by targeting sectors, markets and practices posing the greatest risk to the proper functioning of markets.

The European Commission has employed various methods to better identify priority actions and speed up procedures, including sector enquiries, the introduction of new tools to increase its capacity to detect competition policy infractions ex officio, and a reflection on how to improve time-consuming procedures such as access to file. In addition, ex post evaluation techniques have been used to see if its interventions had the desired effects. Finally, the increased decentralisation of competition policy enforcement to the EU Member States has allowed the European Commission to devote its resources to the most urgent and important cases.

[2] Develop Further the Collaboration with the EU Member States

The process of decentralisation of competition policy in antitrust and State aid control also implies a greater collaboration between Commission and Member States to ensure the necessary coherence in the application of common rules. In the area of antitrust, for example, national competition authorities have adopted 85 % of all decisions enforcing Article 101 and 102 TFEU since 2004. The powers of the national competition authorities were further strengthened by the ECN + Directive[9] of 2018. The Directive aims to ensure that when applying the common EU antitrust rules, national competition authorities have the resources and the appropriate enforcement tools in order to bring about a genuine common competition enforcement area.

In the area of merger control, the ECN's EU Merger Working Group, established in 2010, aims fostering increased consistency, convergence and cooperation amongst EU merger jurisdictions. The group's mandate is to identify areas of possible improvements regarding issues arising in relation to mergers with cross-border impact, and to explore possible solutions, focusing on what is feasible within the existing legal frameworks, and drawing from agency practices and experience.

In the area of State aid control, the bilateral collaboration between the European Commission and national governments on specific cases is complemented by multilateral discussions in the High Level Forum on SAM and its associated working groups. Such discussions facilitate the exchange of best practices (in terms of ex post evaluation, e.g.) as well as the sharing of Member States' experience with SAM and the way forward.

[3] To Adapt to the Digitalisation of the Economy

The digitalisation of the economy poses a serious challenge for EU competition authorities. Digital markets have a number of technological and economic characteristics, such as economies of scale, network effects, switching costs, lock-in effects and the strategic role of data, which can give rise to market concentration and high mark-ups for winners in the digital economy. Once winners obtain a dominant position in the market, they are easily tempted to engage in anticompetitive behaviour.

In antitrust, the European Commission has already had to intervene a number of times to prevent firms in the digital sector from using their dominant position in one market to foreclose competition in neighbouring markets, for example, by reducing interoperability or requiring exclusivity. Over the recent period, the European Commission adopted important decisions addressing anticompetitive practices implemented by digital platforms. In the subdomain of cartels, new algorithms may help facilitate collusive behaviour that is much harder to detect. In the area of State aid, there is a need to ensure an appropriate balance between public and private financing of infrastructure investments, for example, for the roll out of 5G. Finally, in the area of

9. Directive (EU) 2019/1 of the European Parliament and of the Council of 11 December 2018 to empower the competition authorities of the Member States to be more effective enforcers and to ensure the proper functioning of the internal market.

merger control, there is great concern about the potential danger of 'killer' acquisitions, in which innovative start-ups are bought by dominant incumbents before they can develop into serious competitors. These acquisitions currently are not covered by merger control, because they do not meet the turnover thresholds commonly included in merger regulations. Currently, a debate is ongoing whether such acquisitions should be brought under the control of competition authorities, for example, by introducing a criterion related to the purchase price of the merger target.

In light of these various challenges associated with the digitalisation of the economy, the European Commission launched in 2019 a reflection on possible changes for competition policy in the digital sector (*see* Crémer et al., 2019). The main objective of this reflection is to improve the effectiveness of competition policy enforcement within the current legal framework by adapting it to the new realities of digital markets.

[4] Competition Policy in a Globalised World

Globalisation has gone hand in hand – in the US and perhaps to a lesser extent in the EU – with a rising market concentration and increasing mark-ups for the top decile firms (*see, for example*, De Loecker and Eeckhout, 2017 and Bajgar et al., 2019). These observations have fostered research on the causes and effects of increased concentration and mark-ups (*see* International Monetary Fund, 2019). In a globalised world, interaction between firms in different countries is much easier, and markets take on an increasingly international dimension. Access to these international markets allows the most efficient firms to grow larger, raise their market share and increase mark-ups. In this context, the capacity and willingness of competition authorities to tackle the increase in market power associated with globalisation has been put into question. Following this line of reasoning would imply a strengthening of competition policy enforcement.

However, there are contrary arguments seeming to favour a weakening of competition policy enforcement. EU merger rules, for example, have been criticised for not sufficiently taking into account the global dimension of the markets concerned and the pressure on EU industry from foreign competitors. As a result, they would prevent the emergence of European champions big enough to take on global competition. This criticism gained particular importance following the European Commission's prohibition in early 2019 of the proposed Siemens/Alstom merger. Similarly, European businesses often express support for a watering down of EU State aid rules. They use the argument that EU State aid rules do not protect EU firms from 'unfair' conditions of competition vis-à-vis foreign companies benefitting from subsidies granted by third-country governments.

As shown by the description of the evolution over time of the three main instruments of competition policy, the European Commission regularly re-examines its competition tools and is ready to adapt them where appropriate to ensure that they continue to play their role. However, the competitiveness of the EU economy at the global level depends on a level playing field within the internal market that provides businesses with the incentive to invest, innovate and grow. It is therefore important not to compromise the good functioning of the internal market, which is an important achievement of the process of EU integration. There are other tools, policies and actions better suited than competition policy to create fair conditions of competition at world level. A review of competition rules should therefore be carried out within a broader context taking into account the respective roles that these other tools, policies and actions could play.

§1.03 EX POST EVALUATION OF COMPETITION POLICY: DEFINITION, SCOPE, OBJECTIVES AND METHODOLOGIES

Over the past two decades, competition authorities worldwide have become increasingly interested in conducting ex post evaluations of their interventions. As reported by Kovacic (2006), the scepticism expressed at the end of the 1990s about the benefits of competition policy was a catalyst for competition authorities to start evaluating their activities. More recently, competition policy has faced different types of criticisms. Some have questioned its capacity to tackle the increase in market power of big companies in digital markets; others have considered that competition rules have not sufficiently evolved to take account of the globalisation of the economy. In the context of this debate, it has been all the more important to defend the legitimacy of competition policy on the basis of credible ex post evaluations of past practices.

The previous section has shown that ex post evaluation has played a role in all important reforms of the regulatory framework of the EU competition policy. However, this ex post evaluation was rather qualitative in nature and based for a large part on the public consultation of stakeholders. Only recently has the Directorate-General for Competition started to conduct quantitative ex post evaluations. At the same time, a culture of quantitative evaluation has emerged in a small number of national competition authorities that had the resources required for such work. In addition to the European Commission, the UK and Dutch competition authorities are leading amongst EU agencies but other EU competition authorities have also started to be active in this domain. In 2016, the OECD published a reference guide to assist competition authorities in carrying out robust ex post evaluations. With this volume, we also hope to contribute to the further development of evaluation activities both by competition authorities and academics.

In this section, we define the concept of ex post evaluation of competition policy both from a micro- and a macro-perspective. Subsequently, we describe the objectives and the scope of evaluation activities in the competition policy domain as well as the different methodologies used.

[A] Definition of Ex Post Economic Evaluation of Competition Policy

Evaluation is the systematic identification of the effects of a specific intervention or policy. The recent work by the European Commission in this domain should be seen within the context of its Better Regulation Agenda adopted in 2015. As part of this agenda, the European Commission committed to evaluate its rules and regulations before revising them (the 'evaluate first' principle) and to provide an objective and credible evidence-base for its policy proposals and decisions. This broader commitment also applies to the regulatory framework for competition policy and its implementation in the form of merger, antitrust and State aid interventions.

A distinction can be made between ex ante and ex post (or retrospective) evaluation. The former aims at using evidence to predict the impact of a specific action – legislative or non-legislative, spending programmes or other measures – and on that basis, assess whether it is justified and how it should work to achieve certain objectives. The latter is defined as a critical, evidence-based judgment of the extent to which an action has met the needs it aimed to satisfy and actually achieved its expected effects. It goes beyond an assessment of whether something happened or not, and looks at causality – whether the action taken by a given party altered behaviours and led to the expected changes and/or any other unintended or unexpected changes.

Ex post economic evaluation of competition policy looks at the economic effects of competition policy enforcement and its underlying regulatory framework. Enforcement is made visible by decisions taken in the different domains of competition policy (antitrust enforcement, State aid control and merger control). The economic effects include the impact of competition policy on prices, mark-ups, non-price effects (such as business dynamism and innovation) and ultimately productivity, employment and growth. A distinction can be made between the direct and indirect economic effects of competition policy actions. On the one hand, competition interventions have a direct impact on the conditions of competition, for example, by eliminating a cartel or by prohibiting a merger that would have reduced competition and led to an increase in prices for consumers. On the other hand, these interventions also have an indirect benefit via their deterrent effects. For example, the imposition of high fines on cartels is expected to deter other companies from entering into such illegal agreements. The deterrent effects are much more difficult to measure (*see also* Chapter 12). Both direct and indirect economic effects of competition policy improve the conditions of competition in product markets. The resulting improvement in market performance may also engender macroeconomic benefits as explained in Chapter 13.

[B] Scope of Ex Post Evaluation Activities

The scope of ex post evaluation activities is very broad. Evaluations may cover individual enforcement decisions, modifications of the regulatory framework and other activities of competition authorities including sector inquiries, advocacy actions and the collaboration with other competition authorities. The degree of aggregation of an evaluation can range from the microeconomic impact of specific decisions or regulatory modifications in a given market to the broader impact of competition policy enforcement at the sector and macroeconomic level.

The main differences between microeconomic ex post evaluations of competition policy decisions or regulations at a market level and macroeconomic evaluations of the broader impact of competition policy lies in two main factors (*see also* OECD, 2012). First, microeconomic ex post evaluations always concern specific interventions or rules, whose effects are examined in detail, while evaluations of the broader impact concern a wide group of interventions (e.g., the benefits of all merger decisions). Second, ex post evaluations of specific interventions or regulations assess their impact on the relevant markets in terms of microeconomic outcomes (such as the prices of the affected goods, mark-ups and market power of the affected companies, entries on the affected markets, etc.), while the evaluations of the broader impact focus on the aggregate, macroeconomic performance (as measured by total customer benefits or GDP growth).

Ilzkovitz and Dierx (2015) provide an overview of the evaluation activities carried out by academics and competition authorities in these different areas. Their literature review shows that most of the existing empirical work is concentrated on the impact of merger and cartel[10] decisions. Within the context of the SAM, investigations of the effectiveness of State aid schemes have started to be carried out. However, little has been done to evaluate the EU system of State aid control, antitrust decisions halting the abuse of dominance, and other activities of competition authorities, including competition advocacy. At a more macroeconomic level, some evaluations have been done to assess the customer savings resulting from cartel prohibitions and merger interventions. However, relatively little is known about the impact of competition policy on GDP or employment growth.

As part of an effort to close these gaps, the European Commission's Directorate-General for Competition has commissioned two ex post economic evaluations of abuse of dominance cases (presented in Part II of this volume). It has also developed work on the deterrent and macroeconomic impact of competition policy, with a view to complement the customer savings results, which only give a partial view of the broader impact of competition policy (*see* Part IV).

[C] Objectives of Ex Post Evaluations

Broadly speaking, one can distinguish five main reasons why competition authorities undertake evaluations: (1) to enhance decision-making and enforcement practice; (2) to improve the effectiveness of competition law; (3) to set internal priorities; (4) to defend the legitimacy of competition policy enforcement and to advocate competition; and (5) to improve the transparency of policy decisions. In 2012, the OECD carried out a survey of competition authorities to gauge their reasons for conducts ex post evaluations (*see* Box 1.4).

10. The present volume does not include an ex post economic evaluation of a cartel decision, because there is little dispute about the negative economic effects of this type of antitrust infringement.

Box 1.4: OECD survey of competition authorities on the reasons for performing ex post evaluations

In 2012, the OECD decided to explore the reasons for performing ex post evaluations, grouping them into three categories: (1) evaluations for accountability and transparency; (2) evaluations of specific interventions and their impact on the affected markets; and (3) evaluations of the broader impact of competition policy.

Based on a survey of forty-six competition authorities, the OECD (2012) finds that 96% of them are required by law or by their statutes to account for their expenditures (e.g., in their annual report). Fifty-six per cent of the competition authorities investigate the market impact of specific interventions in order to enhance decision-making and enforcement practices, to set internal priorities, or to improve the effectiveness of the regulatory framework. Finally, 40% of the competition authorities surveyed assess the broader impact of competition policy for competition (policy) advocacy purposes and to defend the legitimacy of their interventions.

First, an ex post evaluation of a specific competition policy intervention can help to determine whether the intervention has been effective, for example, by comparing the actual outcome with the likely outcomes of alternative courses of action. By doing so, ex post evaluations can contribute to improving the quality of enforcement practice. Evaluation activities may also cover the analytical tools and econometric techniques used in case investigations. Learning from past successes and detecting past errors lead to better decisions and a competition policy enforcement that is more effective. However, it is not always easy for a competition authority to make public that an error has been made if the decision is still under investigation by the Court.

Second, the quality of competition law can benefit from ex post evaluations as well. Assessing to what extent the overall architecture of competition policy has contributed to the achievement of the objectives set out in the European competition law helps to understand its effectiveness. The application of competition rules is based on notices, guidelines and regulations that need to be revised periodically. Any policy reform ideally should include an ex post assessment of existing regulations before options for reform are considered. By improving procedures that are ineffective, the competition agencies can significantly increase their productive efficiency.

Third, ex post evaluations can also help in setting priorities and identifying activities on which to concentrate. Evaluations can help spot areas of weak enforcement where the interventions are likely to have the largest impact. In this way, they can contribute to productivity gains for the competition authority concerned, for instance by streamlining procedures and improving the allocation of resources.

Fourth, it is important to be able to demonstrate the benefits of competition policy in terms of market functioning and consumer welfare. Competition authorities allocate a significant proportion of their resources to advocacy activities, notably for the purpose of better defending the legitimacy of their work to a wider public. Advocacy activities are more efficient when they are supported by a sound ex post analysis of the impact of past competition enforcement. Moreover, the robustness of the results and the independence of the evaluators are essential for competition agencies to be credible. At the macroeconomic level, an increasing number of competition authorities employ customer savings calculations to show the overall benefits of competition policy.

The fifth and final objective of ex post evaluations is the enhancement of the transparency of policy decisions by allowing external parties to be aware of the work of competition authorities. The public scrutiny of the activities of a public authority that relies on public funds contributes to sound policy-making and enforcement. However, it implies not only the publication of the final decision taken by the competition authority but also being more open about the process leading to that final decision.

[D] Methodologies

[1] Overview of Quantitative and Qualitative Evaluation Methods

Evaluating the impact of a policy or a decision can be based on three main analytical tools (*see* Martini, 2012). These three analytical tools are the descriptive analysis, the counterfactual impact evaluation (CIE) and the theory-based evaluation (TBE). Table 1.1 describes the evaluation questions that these tools aim to address and the analytical challenges that need to be overcome.

Table 1.1 Main Analytical Tools for Ex Post Evaluation of Policies

Analytical Tool	*Descriptive Analysis*	*Counterfactual Impact Evaluation*	*Theory-Based Evaluation*
Main evaluation question	Determines what has been achieved	Determines whether a given intervention produces the desired effects in terms of outcome	Determines why a given intervention produces the desired effect in terms of outcome (or the theory of change)
Main analytical challenge	To find good indicators of what did happen after the intervention	To establish a causal relationship between interventions and outcomes	To identify the cause-effects mechanisms

When the purpose of the evaluation is to show the results of an intervention, a simple descriptive analysis can be used, which depicts the situation before and after the intervention. For example, we can look at the number of cartels detected before and after the introduction of a leniency policy. However, when the objective is to support future decisions, the evaluation must go a step further and establish a causal link between the intervention and the outcomes. This may be achieved by using a so-called

CIE. With this type of quasi-experimental method, it is possible, for example, to distinguish the impact of a merger decision on the prices in the market concerned from other factors having affected this price, such as changes in demand and supply conditions. Finally, when one is interested in the channels through which the intervention produces its outcome, the evaluation needs to build a theory explaining the mechanisms at work. For example, one can use a macroeconomic model to analyse the channels through which a change in mark-up resulting from competition policy interventions will affect GDP growth.

Amongst the family of CIEs, the Difference-in-Differences approach is most widely used to analyse the impact of specific competition policy interventions. This type of approach can provide reliable and robust estimates of the impact of an intervention. However, it requires a large dataset and if the assumptions underlying this approach are not fulfilled, the results may be biased. Another problem with this approach is that the results of a single retrospective study are difficult to generalise. Therefore, this type of analysis would tell very little about the degree of over- or under-enforcement more generally. This is the reason why other methodologies, such as descriptive analyses or meta-retrospectives, are used to analyse the effects of policy actions involving a greater number of decisions.

A further distinction can be made between quantitative and qualitative methods for the ex post evaluation of competition policy. Following Bergman (2008), quantitative methods are defined as methods that result in numerical estimates of progress made towards the relevant competition policy objective. For example, one can estimate the customer savings associated with cartel decisions and merger interventions during a given period. By contrast, qualitative analyses do not result in a numerical estimate and they can only provide an indication of the sign of the effects. Nevertheless, they can be used to analyse a broader range of effects, such as non-price effects, which tend to be more difficult to quantify, or to summarise the views on guidelines and regulations of the stakeholders who have to comply with these rules. Qualitative techniques, such as interviews and surveys, are not necessarily easy to implement and can be resource intensive. Moreover, they are by nature subjective. Table 1.2 proposes a typology of the different evaluation methods.

Table 1.2 Typology of Different Evaluation Methods

Methods	*Descriptive*	*Counterfactual Based*	*Theory-Based*
Quantitative	Before-and-After and cross-sectional studies Event studies Customer savings calculations	Quasi-experimental (Difference-in-Differences, matching methods, regression discontinuity design, etc.)	Estimation and simulation of econometric models (structural or macroeconomic) Estimation of reduced form equation
		Meta-retrospectives	
Qualitative	Court judgments Surveys, interviews	Not available	Structured interviews Public consultation

As can be seen from Table 1.2, there is not a single way to perform an ex post evaluation of competition policy. This introductory section is not meant to suggest the most appropriate methodological approach as this choice depends on a wide array of factors: the objective of the analysis, the existing data as well as the human and IT resources available to carry out the study. In particular, a careful analysis of the data needs and of the feasibility of the project is required. Data are often very costly. Therefore, a thorough consideration of the cost and availability of data should be made very early in the process, as it makes some methods more suited for some cases than others. Another issue to consider before starting an ex post evaluation is that the time gap between the competition policy intervention and the execution of the ex post analysis should be sufficient. The length of the desirable time gap depends on the type of intervention being evaluated, on the effects being analysed and on the methodology used. It is important to find the right balance between the time needed for the effects to manifest themselves and the risk of new events occurring and making the identification of these effects difficult. Based on experience, the gap should range between a minimum of three years and a maximum of ten years.

The different methodological approaches are complementary and, though challenging, a combination of approaches would be optimal for drawing robust and comprehensive conclusions. For example, most of the studies dealing with individual competition policy decisions presented in this book combine a quantitative description of market developments before and after the decision and a Difference-in-Differences analysis. One rarely sees evaluations employing multiple (i.e., three or more) methods because they tend to be more costly and because different evaluation methods require different types of expertise.

The remainder of this subsection provides an overview of the main methodologies available for ex post evaluations of competition policy, making a distinction between quantitative and qualitative ones. It is important to stress that this subsection only aims at introducing these methodologies. It explains the intuition for the different methods, discusses their main strengths and weaknesses and provides examples of their use in other chapters of this volume. It is not our intention to discuss in detail all the technical aspects of the methodologies.

[2] Quantitative Methods

This subsection presents a number of quantitative methods for the ex post evaluation of competition policy. Table 1.3 summarises the strengths and weaknesses of the different methods and refers to the chapter(s) in this volume where the methods are used.

Table 1.3 Overview of Quantitative Methods

Method	*Strengths*	*Weaknesses*	*Illustration of the Method in this Volume*
Descriptive analyses			
Before-and-After and cross-sectional studies	Increase understanding of market developments Informative for future decisions Smaller data and expertise requirements	Failure to control for other factors affecting market functioning Need to be complemented by other analyses	*T-Mobile/Orange UK* merger case (Chapter 4) *Telekomunikacja Polska* antitrust case (Chapter 5) E.ON alleged abuse of dominant position (Chapter 6) Newquay Airport State aid case (Chapter 8) Broadband State aid schemes in Germany (Chapter 9)
Event studies	Prompt assessment of a competition policy decision Capability to assess impact of any type of decision, including merger prohibitions Smaller data and expertise requirements	Detect correlation, not causality Assume that financial markets are efficient Can only be used to study firms quoted on the stock market Can only be used to study firms that are not diversified and which get a large share of their revenues in the affected markets	Quoted in Chapter 12 as a method to assess the deterrent effects of merger control

Method	*Strengths*	*Weaknesses*	*Illustration of the Method in this Volume*
Customer savings calculations	Simple and easily understood method Well suited for advocacy and communication purposes	Based on a number of assumptions (even if well founded and conservative) Neglect deterrence effects, spillover effects to other markets and non-price effects	The direct effects of competition policy interventions (Chapter 11)
Counterfactual Impact Evaluation*			
Difference-in-Differences	Identify a causal relationship between the competition policy decision and market outcomes Provide statistically robust estimates of the impact of the decision	Require a proper counterfactual Need to have a good set of control variables to properly identify the impact of the intervention More data intensive and require econometric expertise Method not suited to analyse certain types of individual decisions (e.g., merger prohibitions) and results cannot be generalised	The reviews of merger decisions in the EU (Chapter 2) and in the EU mobile telecommunications sector (Chapter 3) consider ex post evaluations based on Difference-in-Differences *T-Mobile/Orange UK* merger case (Chapter 4) *Telekomunikacja Polska* antitrust case (Chapter 5) E.ON alleged abuse of dominant position (Chapter 6) Newquay Airport State aid case (Chapter 8) Broadband State aid schemes in Germany(Chapter 9)

* In addition, Chapters 3 (Review of merger decisions in the EU mobile telecommunications sector), 7 (Role of ex post evaluation in the area of State aids) and 10 (Impact of restructuring aids) make reference to CIE studies using synthetic control groups, regression discontinuity design and instrumental variables,respectively.

Method	*Strengths*	*Weaknesses*	*Illustration of the Method in this Volume*
Matching techniques	Improve match between treatment and control groups leading to better estimates of the treatment effect	Require a large dataset to conduct the matching	Broadband State aid schemes in Germany (Chapter 9) Impact of restructuring aid (Chapter 10)
Theory-Based Evaluation			
Structural models	Allow for the estimation of the full welfare effect of a competition policy decision Allow to analyse the effects of a wider range of decisions (e.g., merger prohibitions or comparison of alternative remedies)	Not adapted to analyse complex markets Requires making assumptions on both demand and supply curve and on how firms compete in the market. Results are sensitive to these underlying assumptions Require a large dataset, strong econometric skills Trade-off between richness of the model and its simplicity	The reviews of merger decisions in the EU (Chapter 2) and in the EU mobile telecommunications sector (Chapter 3) consider ex post evaluations based on structural models
Reduced form estimations (including cross-sectional and panel data analyses)	No need to define a counterfactual Can be used to analyse a wide range of effects	Need to have a good set of control variable to properly isolate the impact of the effect analysed Requires large data set and good econometric skills	The review of merger decisions in the EU mobile telecommunications sector (Chapter 3) describes multi-event panel data analyses

Method	*Strengths*	*Weaknesses*	*Illustration of the Method in this Volume*
Macroeconomic models	Integrated framework allowing taking into account the economy-wide interactions resulting from competition policy enforcement Allow to compare the benefits of competition policy to that of other structural policies and to put the work of competition authorities into a broader perspective Well suited for communication and advocacy purposes	Difficult to find macroeconomic indicators of competition policy and of competition Black box model based on a number of assumptions Defining the chain of events describing the impact of competition policy in the medium to long term on the whole economy is very complex	The macroeconomic and sectoral impact of competition policy (Chapter 13)
Meta-retrospectives	Combination of results from different studies and different methodologies allows identifying conclusions on which there is a consensus	Sample of studies in the meta-retrospectives not representative and not random, making the conclusions specific to the analysed sample	A review of merger decisions in the EU (Chapter 2)

[a] Before-and-After and Cross-Sectional Studies

Descriptive studies can be employed to compare market developments in the period before and after the decision (Before-and-After methods) or market developments after the decision in the affected market and in comparable geographic or product markets not influenced by the decision (cross-sectional methods). This type of approach can help to formulate a number of assumptions to be tested with more robust empirical analyses. For example, in the *Telekomunikacja Polska* (TP) antitrust case, a descriptive analysis is used in a first step to provide an overview of the Polish fixed telecoms markets in the period during and after the abuse. This analysis seems to indicate that the TP abuse delayed the development of DSL penetration and increased DSL prices in the Polish markets. In a second step, these assumptions are tested using a Difference-in-Differences approach.

Before-and-After studies can also be employed to assess whether key assumptions about market characteristics (such as competitive constraints or the take-up of new technologies) and ex ante expectations about market developments (such as the viability of the divested entity or the entry of new competitors) at the time of the decision turned out to be true ex post. As shown in Table 1.4, three competition authorities (the Bureau of Competition of Canada in 2007, the UK Office of Fair Trading and the Competition Commission in 2009 and 2015 and the New Zealand Competition Commission in 2014 and 2015) successfully implemented studies using this approach (often in combination with other methods) to evaluate their merger decisions.

Table 1.4 Experience of Competition Authorities with Descriptive Analyses of Merger Decisions

Competition Authority (year)	*Number and Type of Merger Decisions Selected*	*Methods Used*	*Assumptions Tested*
Canada (2007)	3 unconditional clearances	Before-and-After study Interviews Regression analysis	Market entry Buyer market power Economic reasoning
UK (2009)	4 unconditional clearances, 3 conditional clearances and 1 prohibition	Before-and-After study Questionnaires Interviews Merger simulations	Soundness of the decision Market entry
New Zealand (2014-2015)	18 cleared mergers	Before-and-After study Interviews	Entry and expansion of competitors Success divestitures Buyer market power
UK (2017)	8 unconditional and conditional clearances (5 in Phase I and 3 in Phase II)	Before-and-After study Interviews	Entry and expansion

This type of comparison between the predictions underpinning a merger intervention on the one hand and the market outcomes on the other hand can provide useful insights into the effectiveness of the analytical tools used in the merger examination. In case of discrepancies between ex ante expectations and ex post results, such an assessment can help to pinpoint pitfalls and errors in the analysis and to draw recommendations on how to improve the decision-making process. However, if the aim is to investigate the reasons why the competition authority's ex ante expectations did not materialise ex post, the Before-and-After study has to be complemented with more robust empirical analyses.

The great advantage of Before-and-After and cross-sectional studies is that they require less technical expertise and data. However, the drawback of such an approach is that it does not control for other factors that may have contributed to the changes observed in the market of interest. Such reservations notwithstanding, these descriptive analyses can be very informative for future decision-making, especially when they are complemented by robust quantitative analyses.

[b] Event Studies

Event studies track the changes in the stock prices of competitors to the parties directly affected by a competition policy intervention. Stock market reactions at the time of the intervention are used to assess the effects of the competition policy decision on competition. If a decision is procompetitive and results in a price reduction in the affected market, one may expect that the future returns of competitors will be negatively affected by the decision. On the other hand, if the decision is anticompetitive, expected returns and stock prices of competitors should go up. Chapter 12 illustrates how event studies can be employed to measure the deterrent effects of merger interventions. The chapter makes the point that merger control has strong deterrent effects on anticompetitive mergers in particular. Therefore, more stringent merger control should make newly proposed mergers more procompetitive on average and have detrimental effects on the stock prices of non-merging rival firms.

Event studies do not require data on how the market has been affected by the competition policy intervention but only data on the reactions of the stock market at the time of the intervention. Event studies can thus be used to assess any kind of market intervention affecting firms that are quoted in the stock market. In particular, they may be used to assess the impact of merger prohibition decisions. The Difference-in-Differences method, on the contrary, is not well suited to evaluate the impact of a merger prohibition decision because the difficulty of defining the counterfactual: what would have happened if the merger had been approved?

The principal advantage of event studies is that they deliver a prompt assessment of the competitive effects of the decision taken. Moreover, such studies require relatively few data (i.e., time series of stock prices of the firms directly or indirectly affected by the competition policy intervention) and less sophisticated econometric skills. On the other hand, event studies do not enable the identification of a causal relationship between the competition policy intervention and the stock price evolution, but just a correlation between the two. They offer an immediate, but imprecise, measure of the correctness of the decision. Implicitly, they assume that financial markets are efficient and that the share price movements in reaction to a competition policy intervention represent the rational expectations of investors about the likely impact of the intervention on the future profitability of the firms. If this assumption is not satisfied, the results are not robust. Finally, a large share of the revenues of the companies operating in the affected markets must originate from these markets. If this condition is not satisfied, it is unlikely that the competition policy intervention will be reflected in share price movements of these companies. As an increasing number of quoted companies are multinationals or conglomerates operating in different product and geographic markets, this condition is not necessarily satisfied.

[c] Customer Savings Calculations

Customer savings calculations by competition authorities attempt to quantify the monetary value that customers save due to competition policy decisions, such as a merger interventions or cartel prohibitions. The customer savings from a given competition policy intervention equal the product of the price increase avoided due to the intervention, the size of the affected market and the expected duration of the price effect. In calculating the customer savings associated with their decisions, competition authorities adopt conservative assumptions from the literature on the avoided price increase. The two other elements of the product reflect case-specific information that is collected by competition authorities over the course of their case investigations.

The customer savings are a macroeconomic measure of the effects of the competition policy interventions made by a competition authority over a given period. For example, Chapter 11 shows that the customer savings associated with cartel prohibitions and merger interventions by the European Commission amounted to 0.1% of EU GDP over the period 2012-2018. The advantage of customer savings calculations is that they can be easily understood and provide clear numerical outcomes. Moreover, the fact that they are based on case-specific information and cautious assumptions increases their credibility and makes them well suited for communication and advocacy purposes.

The main limitation is that customer savings calculations take into consideration only the direct benefits for customers in terms of the price increase prevented. They ignore the dynamic and non-price effects, in terms of innovation, quality and choice, of competition policy interventions as well as their deterrent effects and spillovers to other markets. These effects may be significant, but the uncertainty over their magnitude is so great that competition agencies have refrained from attempting to measure them. Consequently, the customer benefits approach underestimates the total impact of competition policy interventions.

[d] Quasi-experimental Methods, Including the Difference-in-Differences Approach

Quasi-experimental methods are based on the comparison of developments in markets that have and have not been affected by one or more competition policy interventions, before and after these interventions. An evaluation of the impact of a merger decision, for example, would be based on the comparison of price developments in affected and non-affected markets, before and after the merger decision.

The definition of the control group, which permits assessing what would have happened in the absence of the decision (the 'counterfactual'), is crucial for the identification of the impact of the competition policy decision. To get around the fact that the counterfactual is unobservable, ex post evaluations seek to compare the actual outcomes for parties affected by the competition policy enforcement decision (the 'treatment' group) with outcomes for non-affected parties which are as similar as possible to the affected parties (the 'control' group). The challenge for CIEs is therefore twofold: first, to identify suitable parties in both the treatment group and the control group; and second, to obtain the relevant data. While data on the affected parties pre-treatment may already have been gathered during the case investigation, the collection of data for the post-treatment period and for non-affected parties is likely to be far more difficult.

Box 1.5: Counterfactual Impact Evaluation methods

Within the CIE literature, a basic distinction is made between experimental and quasi-experimental evaluation designs (European Commission, 2013).

Under the experimental approach, parties would be randomly assigned to either the treatment or the control group, in order to ensure that the groups are statistically equivalent (except for the fact that one is affected by the competition policy enforcement decision while the other is not). However, it would appear to be politically unacceptable to randomly select the parties being subjected to a competition policy enforcement decision. Consequently, the experimental approach would seem to be of little use in practice in this domain.

As an alternative, a number of quasi-experimental methods have been developed which seek to mimic randomisation:

- propensity score matching, which matches treated parties affected by the enforcement decisions with non-treated parties sharing similar observable characteristics;
- the regression discontinuity approach, which focuses on the difference in performance between treated and non-treated parties close to the borderline;
- the Difference-in-Differences approach, which is based on the assumption that the changes over time in the performance of treated and non-treated parties are the same;

- the synthetic control method, which constructs a control group as a weighted combination of non-treated parties. This weighted combination closely tracks the changes over time in the performance of the treatment group during the pre-treatment period;
- instrumental variable techniques, which require the identification of an instrument that influences parties' performance only through its relation with the enforcement decision. This technique is mostly used to correct for the possible endogeneity of the enforcement decision.

Amongst the different quasi-experimental methods (*see* Box 1.5 for an overview of these methods), the Difference-in-Differences approach has been most commonly used as a tool for assessing the impact of a competition policy enforcement decision on a given outcome. The ex post evaluations of individual EU competition policy decisions analysed in Chapters 4, 5, 6, 8 and 9 employ this methodology. The Difference-in-Differences approach is based on a comparison of changes over time in outcomes between the treated group that is affected by the decision (A in Figure 1.2) and the non-affected control group (B in Figure 1.2). The difference in performance between the treatment group and the control group before the treatment (A – B) is subtracted from their difference in performance after the treatment (C – D) to arrive at the estimated impact of the competition policy intervention.

Figure 1.2 Difference-in-Differences Method

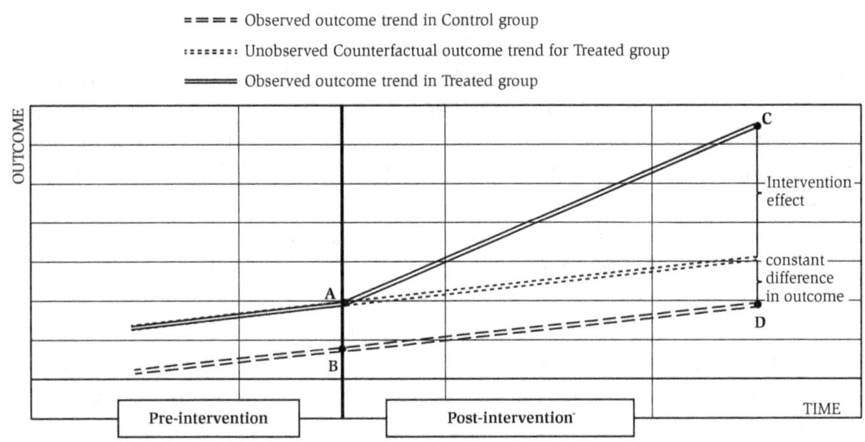

In other words, the Difference-in-Differences approach compares the changes in the treated markets before and after the decision with the changes that occurred over the same period in a comparable market not influenced by the decision. The reliability of this approach rests on the assumption that, absent the treatment, the difference between the treated group and the control group would have stayed constant over time (i.e., the 'common trend assumption'). Moreover, there should be no spillover effects of the treatment on the control group. If these conditions are not fulfilled, a selection bias may emerge and affect the outcome of the evaluation exercise.

Difference-in-Differences studies are very popular because they offer reliable and statistically robust estimates of the impact of a competition policy intervention. Their main advantage is that they allow identifying a causal relationship between a specific intervention by a competition authority and market outcomes. While the Difference-in-Differences framework is most often used to assess the price effects of mergers, the same approach can also be used to investigate the effect of a merger on other variables such as investment and innovation. Alternatively, if suitable data are available, the approach can be used to determine ex post what has been the impact of a decision in an abuse of dominance case or the granting of State aid support.

In practice, however, this approach may be quite challenging. First, one needs to ensure that the counterfactual is not affected by the intervention. Second, a set of control variables needs to be defined in order to properly isolate the impact of the intervention from other events. Third, data requirements may be substantial. Finally, this approach can only be used to assess enforcement decisions that lead to a change in market conditions. For example, while they can be used to evaluate merger clearance decisions, they cannot be employed in the case of merger prohibitions. Moreover, in the case of a merger clearance subject to remedies, the Difference-in-Differences approach does not permit making a distinction between the effects of the merger clearance and the associated remedies.

[e] Structural Models

A structural model offers a theory-based description of how competition works in a given market. It requires a detailed specification of demand, supply and equilibrium conditions, as well as the estimation of key structural parameters (such as price elasticities on the demand side and cost/technology parameters on the supply side). However, after the model has been properly specified and the structural parameters estimated, it can be used to simulate market outcomes, including equilibrium prices, market shares, profit margins and consumer welfare, under alternative scenarios.[11] In the practice of competition policy enforcement, structural models are used mainly to predict ex ante what will be the likely price effects of a merger. However, they can be adapted to perform ex post merger evaluations.

Structural models are very adaptable to the particular case under investigation. They allow simulating any counterfactual, e.g. what would be the market outcomes in the absence of the competition policy intervention? They can also be used to disentangle the impact of a merger from that of associated remedies imposed by the competition authority. Another potential advantage is that they allow estimating the full welfare effect of a policy intervention, which is not possible when applying the Difference-in-Differences approach. For example, in the ex post evaluation of State aid

11. Ilzkovitz and Dierx (2015), Ormosi et al. (2015) and OECD (2016) offer a more detailed description of the key steps in structural model simulations.

given to the UK Newquay airport, the Difference-in-Differences analysis suggests that the aid had contributed to the closure of another airport in the same region. This makes one wonder whether the aid, which aimed to improve regional connectivity, is justified from a welfare perspective.

However, structural models also have limitations. According to the OECD (2016), they are best suited to analyse consumer goods markets, but less well adapted for an investigation of intermediate product markets or markets characterised by complex strategic decision-making (e.g., by firms having to make a simultaneous decision on innovation and prices). Moreover, they are not tailored to model anticompetitive conducts such as predatory pricing, margin squeezes, etc. There is a trade-off between the richness of the model and its simplicity. Simple models are easier to estimate and the estimated model coefficients tend to be more robust. Nevertheless, the outcomes of structural model simulations remain rather sensitive to the underlying assumptions. Therefore, to achieve credible results both a large dataset and strong econometric skills are required.

[f] Reduced Form Estimations (Including Panel Regressions)

If insufficient data are available to conduct structural model estimations, the estimation of a reduced form offers an alternative tool to assess the impact of competition policy interventions. However, while structural models fully reflect some underlying economic theory, the relation between the reduced form and its economic underpinning tends to be weaker. Nevertheless, a well-specified reduced form allows testing whether (competition) policy interventions have the intended effects at the industry or macroeconomic level.

The principal challenge of reduced form estimations - as is the case for Difference-in-Differences analyses - is to properly control for other factors that may have an effect on the outcome variable of interest. A failure to do so can lead to a bias in the estimated effect. However, contrary to the Difference-in-Differences method, there is no need to define a counterfactual.

Reduced form estimations can be used to analyse a wide range of effects. In Chapter 3, for example, panel regression analyses are conducted to assess the effects of past episodes of concentration on market performance in terms of prices and investments in the EU mobile telecommunication sector.

[g] Macroeconomic Models

While structural models have been used mostly to analyse the impact of individual competition policy interventions in well-defined markets, they are not well adapted to assess the effects of competition policy enforcement on the economy as a whole. Customer savings can be used as an indicator of the size of such macroeconomic effects. However, as discussed above, customer savings underestimate the full macroeconomic impact of competition policy interventions as they only consider the direct benefits for consumers of the avoided price increases. Macroeconomic models take the next step by providing information on the impact of competition policy enforcement on macroeconomic variables, such as GDP growth, employment and productivity.

While the academic literature on the macroeconomic impact of competition is quite extensive, there has been much less empirical work on the macroeconomic impact of competition policy, certainly in comparison with other policies affecting the conditions of competition, such as trade liberalisation or deregulation policies. This lack of empirical analysis may be explained by the difficulties associated with this type of work. First, it is not straightforward to find appropriate indicators of the strength of competition policy. Second, in order to make the link with macroeconomic outcome variables, it is necessary to establish a causal relationship between competition policy and competition. Third, the definition of appropriate indicators of competition provides a further challenge, as illustrated by the recent debate on how to construct and interpret measures of mark-up (*see, for example*, De Loecker and Eeckhout, 2018). Fourth, it is harder to track the chain of events, which may follow competition policy interventions in the medium to long term, than to look at the immediate impact of a specific competition policy decision in a given market. Finally, the macro-model to be developed should have a microeconomic foundation describing the channels through which the changes in the conditions of competition affect macroeconomic performance. Chapter 13 attempts to overcome these difficulties and present a comprehensive assessment of the macroeconomic impact of competition policy interventions by the European Commission since 2012.

The main advantage of the approach used in Chapter 13 is that it is based on a fully developed econometric model that allows taking into account the economy-wide interactions resulting from competition policy enforcement. Estimating the impact of competition policy enforcement on GDP growth and employment also allows putting the work of competition authorities in a broader perspective and comparing the benefits of competition policy to that of other structural policies. Moreover, macroeconomic impact indicators summarise the benefits of competition policy in a way that is easy to understand for a wider public, making them a powerful communication tool. However, models are a simplified representation of reality, which is based on assumptions. This is why it is important to analyse the sensitivity of results to the main assumptions made and to treat the results obtained as indicators of the order of magnitude of the impact rather a precise estimate.

[h] Meta-retrospectives

Meta-retrospective studies rest on the analysis, often through simple statistical comparisons, of the outcomes of a large number of ex post evaluations with the objective of drawing more general conclusions and lessons. A meta-analysis of retrospective studies investigating a particular question may offer additional insights that individual studies are unable to offer. By contrasting and combining results from different studies, meta-retrospectives allow distinguishing issues on which there is a broad consensus in the literature from areas where there remain discrepancies between the results obtained.

The main problem with this approach is that the sample of cases studied included in the meta-retrospective is not necessarily representative of the case population. Typically, published studies are more likely to be included in the sample, because they tend to be more accessible and are considered more reliable. Consequently, the sample of studies taken into account is not a random sample and any conclusions drawn are specific to the analysed sample.

Meta-retrospectives can be based on studies applying different methodologies if these methodologies deliver quantitative results that can be combined in a summary indicator. Chapter 2 in this volume is a meta-retrospective that covers EU merger evaluation studies using different quantitative methodologies and that provides an average price impact of unconditionally approved and remedied mergers. By contrast, Chapter 3 cannot be considered as a meta-retrospective, as it does not attempt to represent by a summary indicator the results of different quantitative studies (Difference-in Differences, structural models and reduced form estimations) of mergers in the EU mobile telecommunication sector. *A priori*, one could argue that results are more robust if studies based on different quantitative methodologies come to statistically comparable results.

[3] Qualitative Methods

The focus of the studies presented in this volume is on the economic, quantitative impact of competition policy interventions. However, for the sake of completeness, this subsection gives an overview of qualitative methods that can be used in ex post evaluations of competition policy interventions (*see* Table 1.5).

Table 1.5 Qualitative Methods

Method	*Strengths*	*Weaknesses*	*Illustration of This Method*
Court judgments	Good indication of the quality of the decision or the relevance of regulations and guidelines concerned	Address mainly legal and procedural issues	Reference to court judgment in the *Telekomunikacja Polska* antitrust case (Chapter 5)
Surveys and interviews	Allow assessing effects that are not easily quantifiable (non-price or deterrent effects)	Less precise Subjective measure	Assessment of deterrent effects of competition policy (Chapter 12)
Structured interviews and public consultations	Allow to get views of stakeholders on a wide range of competition policy issues	Can be manipulated for strategic reasons	References to interviews in the case of Newquay Airport in the UK (Chapter 8)

Most of the qualitative ex post evaluation tools are better suited to address legal or procedural issues rather than economic questions (e.g., court judgments). Nevertheless, qualitative methods are valuable as complements to the quantitative ex post evaluation tools presented above. Moreover, in the event that quantitative data are not available or that the acquisition of such data is too costly, the effects of a competition policy intervention can only been determined through a more qualitative assessment.

[a] Court Judgments

Amongst the various qualitative evaluation methods, court judgments are most deep-rooted in the system. In most countries, competition policy decisions can be appealed in court by the parties concerned. While court judgments in response to such appeals mostly address legal and procedural issues, increasingly courts view it as their obligation to evaluate the economic arguments underlying the decisions of the competition authorities as well.

Whether or not a decision is upheld in court may be considered as a first indication of the quality of the decision taken. For example, in Chapter 5, the fact that the General Court upheld the decision of the European Commission that the Polish incumbent, Telekomunikacja Polska, abused its dominant position can be considered as a first indication that the decision was justified. Similarly, if the court upholds a high percentage of decisions taken by competition authorities in a given competition policy domain, the conclusion may be drawn that the underlying policy guidelines and regulations are functioning as intended.

[b] Surveys and Interviews

In making their ex ante assessment of a merger proposal or an allegation of anticompetitive behaviour, competition authorities commonly rely on surveys and interviews of competitors, suppliers and customers. An ex post evaluation whether the merger or antitrust decision taken was the appropriate one, could equally rely on such information. The range of respondents to surveys aimed at assessing the quality of competition policy enforcement decisions could be widened beyond the parties directly concerned by such decisions or competition rules. Competition lawyers and consultants as well as other competition authorities should be well placed to pass judgment on the enforcement measures taken.

There are two important steps in organising surveys: the design of the questionnaire and the selection of the sample. In designing the questionnaire, one has to balance the desire to obtain a rich set of information and the wish to get a high response rate. Close-ended questions ask the respondent to choose one or more answers from a number of options while open-ended questions ask the respondent to formulate his or her own answer. Close-ended questions may lead to a higher rate of response while open-ended questions may be useful to obtain information not originally anticipated. Open questions are more often used in structured interviews (*see* next subsection) of small groups of people particularly qualified in the domain surveyed. The other important step is to define the size, composition and characteristics of the target population. It is essential to select a representative sample if the whole target population cannot be covered by the survey.

Surveys and interviews allow getting information on a broad range of issues that cannot be easily quantified, such as the quality of products sold or the deterrent effects of competition policy enforcement. For example, surveys are the most commonly used tool to estimate the deterrent effects of cartel prohibitions and merger interventions (*see* Chapter 12): businesses and legal advisors are being asked to estimate the number of cartels and anticompetitive mergers deterred for every cartel or anticompetitive merger detected. However, by their nature, surveys are subjective measures of the effects of competition policy interventions and survey respondents may have strategic considerations when answering the questions addressed to them. Moreover, surveys and interviews are less precise than quantitative analysis and can only give an indication of the sign of the effects. This is the reason why ideally surveys and peer reviews should be complemented by quantitative assessments or the judgement of independent experts. Another challenge inherent to surveys and interviews is to obtain the cooperation of the respondents and interviewees. Finally, the information obtained via these channels is not necessarily easy to summarise.

[c] Structured Interviews, Public Consultations

A structured interview consists in an interview based on a well-defined questionnaire, which aims at testing with a focus group the validity of certain assumptions or specific preliminary findings. This is why structured interview are often used as part of a TBE. The main differences with surveys or non-structured interviews are that: (i) the focus group, in principle, should consist of informed people; and (ii) the interview is based on a precise questionnaire, with a view to test a specific theory or mechanism.

Similarly, a public consultation can be organised to get views of stakeholders on competition policy rules. In principle, public consultations are conducted with stakeholders having a certain degree of knowledge of the subject matter under investigation. They go beyond a simple survey by providing the respondents with background information, allowing them to consider a wide range of arguments on the subject matter. In some cases, respondents engage in trade-off exercises in which they are required to make graduated choices amongst competing priorities, just as policymakers must do.

The main goal of public consultations is to improve the efficiency and transparency of the decision-making process and increase the involvement of key stakeholders in important competition policy reforms. Public consultations are often organised before undertaking a substantial revision of a regulation with the aim of finding out what worked or did not work as intended. This why public consultations can be considered as qualitative ex post evaluations. For example, in January 2019, the European Commission launched a public consultation on the prolongation of the State aid regulations and guidelines, which were reformed as part of the SAM package and are scheduled to expire by the end of 2020.

Structured interviews and public consultations have some of the same limitations as simple interviews and surveys: the results are subjective and can be manipulated for strategic reasons. However, if the interview is properly structured, such sources of bias should be more easily identified.

§1.04 CONCLUSION

EU competition policy has evolved over the last sixty years, and it has continuously adapted to the changing environment. Historically, modifications in the regulatory framework for competition policy have been driven by court judgments and the outcomes of public consultations. More recently, such qualitative evaluations have been complemented by quantitative, ex post evaluations of competition policy interventions that are aimed at identifying the causal effects of such interventions. Looking forward, EU competition policy will continue evolving as it needs to maintain the speed, quality and relevance of decisions taken at the EU level under the new conditions created by the digitalisation and globalisation of the EU economy.

Within this context, the European Commission will go on examining its competition rules regularly to check if they are still fit for purpose. Evidence-based ex post evaluations are essential in this process. Significant progress has been made in the development of analytical tools for the ex post evaluation of competition policy rules and enforcement decisions. This chapter provides an overview of these tools, highlighting their strengths and weaknesses.

REFERENCES

Bajgar M., Berlingieri G., Calligaris S., Criscuolo C. and Timmis J. (2019), 'Industry concentration in Europe and North America', OECD Productivity Working Papers 18, OECD Publishing.

Bergman M.A. (2008), 'Quis custodiet ipsos custodes? or measuring and evaluating the effectiveness of competition enforcement', *De Economist*, 156(4), pp. 387-409.

Crémer J., de Montjoye Y.-A. and Schweitzer H. (2019), 'Competition policy for the digital era', Report for the European Commission, Publications Office of the European Union.

De Loecker J. and Eeckhout J. (2017), 'The rise of market power and the macroeconomic implications', NBER Working Paper No. 23687, August.

De Loecker J. and Eeckhout J. (2018), 'Some thoughts on the debate about (aggregate) markup measurement'.

European Commission (1999), 'White paper on modernisation of the rules implementing articles 85 and 86 of the EC treaty', Commission Programme No. 99/027.

European Commission (2005a), 'State Aid Action Plan. Less and better targeted State aid: a roadmap for State aid reform 2005-2009', COM(2005) 107 final.

European Commission (2005b), 'Merger remedies study', DG Competition staff paper, October.

European Commission (2011), 'Report on Competition Policy 2010', Directorate-General for Competition, Publications Office of the European Union.

European Commission (2012), 'EU State Aid Modernisation (SAM)', COM(2012) 209 final.

European Commission (2013), 'Design and commissioning of counterfactual impact evaluations - A practical guidance for ESF managing authorities', Directorate-General for Employment, Social Affairs and Inclusion, Publications Office of the European Union.

European Commission (2014), 'Criteria for the analysis of the compatibility with the internal market of State aid to promote the execution of important projects of common European interest', Communication from the Commission, 2014/C 188/02.

European Commission (2019a), 'State aid scoreboard 2018: Results, trends and observations regarding EU28 State Aid expenditure reports for 2017'.

European Commission (2019b), 'Merger Statistics, 21 September 1990 to 28 February 2019'.

International Monetary Fund (2019), 'The rise of corporate market power and its macroeconomic effects', in: *World economic outlook: Growth slowdown, precarious recovery*, Washington, DC.

Ilzkovitz F. and Dierx A. (2015), 'Ex-post economic evaluation of competition policy enforcement: a review of the literature', DG Competition staff paper, Publications Office of the European Union, June.

Judgment of the Court of 14 February 1978, '*United Brands Company and United Brands Continentaal BV v. Commission of the European Communities*, Case 27/76', European Court Reports 1978-00207, ECLI:EU:C:1978:22.

Kovacic W.E. (2006), 'Using ex post evaluations to improve the performance of competition policy authorities', *The Journal of Corporation Law*, 31(2), pp. 504-547.

Lowe, P. (2009), 'The design of competition policy institutions for the twenty-first century: The experience of the European Commission and the Directorate-General for Competition', in: X. Vives (ed.), *Competition policy in the EU: Fifty years on from the Treaty of Rome*, Oxford University Press.

Martini A. (2012), 'Opportunities and limitations of counterfactual impact evaluation of structural funds', in: K. Olejniczak, M. Kozak, S. Bienias (eds), *Evaluating the effects of regional interventions. A look beyond current structural funds' practice*, Warzaw.

Mederer W., 'Evolution of State aid control' (2008), in: W. Mederer, N. Pesaresi and M. Van Hoof (eds), *EU Competition Law*, vol. IV, State Aid Book One, Claeys & Casteels.

OECD (2012), 'Evaluation of competition enforcement and advocacy activities: the results of an OECD survey', DAF/COMP/WP2(2012)7/FINAL.

OECD (2016), 'Reference guide on ex-post evaluation of competition agencies' enforcement decisions', April.

Ormosi P., Mariuzzo F. and Havell R. (2015), 'A review of merger decisions in the EU: what can we learn from ex-post evaluations?', Report prepared for the Directorate-General for Competition, Publications Office of the European Union, July.

Verouden V. and Werner P. (2016), 'EU State aid control: Law and Economics', Kluwer Law International.

Wils W.P.J. (2016), 'The use of leniency in EU cartel enforcement: An assessment after twenty years', *World Competition*, 39(3), pp. 327-388.

PART I The Ex Post Evaluation of Merger Interventions

CHAPTER 2

A Review of Merger Decisions in the EU*

Richard Havell, Franco Mariuzzo & Peter Ormosi

In this review of retrospective European merger studies, we provide a discussion of the price effect of the analysed mergers and examine whether the competition authority made the right decisions. We find that remedied mergers, on average, were not followed by a price increase, suggesting that, in our sample, merger interventions were effective at eliminating problems. High market concentration was more likely to lead to higher post-merger prices, but only in mergers that were not subjected to a remedy by the competition authority. We make a stylised attempt to look at a number of reasons why prices may increase post-merger and find little evidence of genuine competition authority errors.

§2.01 INTRODUCTION

The last two decades have seen an increasing amount of works by academics and competition authorities, trying to improve our understanding of the political economy of competition policy in the European Union (EU). Merger control has been one of the most researched areas, which is unsurprising, given that it is an ex ante policy instrument – i.e., the competition authority has to assess the market effect of a transaction before the transaction takes place. In this respect even if a merger decision is based on the best available evidence, there is inevitable uncertainty in the appropriateness of any intervention that follows. Because of this, it is crucial that merger control

* This chapter is partially based on a report the authors prepared for the Directorate-General for Competition, European Commission, titled *A review of merger decisions in the EU: What can we learn from ex-post evaluations?*. We thank Fabienne Ilzkovitz and Adriaan Dierx for their valuable input during the preparation of the report and for commenting on this chapter. We are also grateful for comments on various versions of this chapter to Amelia Fletcher, Luke Froeb, John Kwoka and Bruce Lyons, and the participants of the 4th E.CA Competition Law and Economics Expert Forum. The opinions expressed here are those of the authors and not necessarily those of the European Commission or the Competition and Markets Authority (CMA).

decisions are subjected to rigorous ex post evaluation exercises in order to assess how well they are achieving their task of filtering out anticompetitive mergers.

If done correctly, lessons learned from these ex post studies can be channelled back into policymaking and affect how mergers are assessed in the future. As Ashenfelter, Hosken and Weinberg (2009) point out, 'Because economic models generate explicit predictions of the competitive effects of mergers, it is relatively straightforward [...] to evaluate their performance with retrospective evidence. If these tools are proven effective, they could lead to a more efficient, objective, and accurate merger review process.' This is not to say that merger retrospectives are the panacea that unconditionally guarantees an optimal merger control design, but the evidence they provide is invaluable for any competition authority.

Since the pioneering book by Neven, Nutall and Seabright (1993) in the early nineties, we have seen a steady increase in the number of papers that ex post evaluate European merger decisions (merger retrospectives).[1] A study that brings together this body of literature can be useful for numerous reasons. First, this would provide a concise document that consistently summarises the corpus of relevant studies and extract what we have learnt from European merger control. Second, it is an obvious way of providing evidence under which conditions merger control works. Third, it can identify areas where changes would be most pressing.

The intellectual motivator of this chapter is Professor John Kwoka's (2013, 2015) who meticulously compiled study of US merger retrospectives. Kwoka collates 60 studies estimating the price effects of 53 transactions (46 mergers) in the US and presents the average price effects estimated by each study. For a smaller sub-sample (23 mergers), where he had information on the competition authority's merger decision,[2] he reports price-change estimates according to the action taken by the competition authority as an attempt to identify if an error was made in its decision. He finds that a large proportion of ex post studies estimated that the merger led to a price increase, even when remedies were imposed upon the merger. Despite this, the strength of remedies appears to be correlated with the price effects of mergers, indicating that the authorities were capable of identifying those mergers that posed the largest competitive concerns, and applied stronger remedies in such cases. Kwoka argues that the key problem faced by US competition authorities is the effectiveness of remedies, especially non-structural ones, rather than the identification of problematic mergers.

Ashenfelter et al. (2009), the OECD (2011), and Ilzkovitz et al. (2015) offer a different survey of relevant works, focusing more on methodological issues. Both works comprehensively discuss the relative advantages and disadvantages of the main methods: Difference-in-Differences, merger simulations, event studies, and surveys.

1. In this chapter we use 'merger retrospectives' and 'ex post merger evaluations' interchangeably.
2. Information is limited in other cases, where an investigation by the competition authority may have been conducted but was closed without intervention by the competition authority or even without confirmation by the competition authority to the general public that an investigation had been conducted.

The main conclusion is that there is no one-size-fits-all method, and specific circumstances can justify different choice of methods.

Both Kwoka and the OECD emphasise the selection problem in reviews of merger retrospectives: available studies are biased towards studying mergers with available data and which are on the margins of being accepted or rejected. For this reason, one has to be cautious when using these studies to derive general conclusions on antitrust agencies' merger decisions. Coate (2014) attempts to control for this problem by estimating challenge probabilities for the Federal Trade Commission (FTC), i.e., the probability that the FTC would challenge a merger. These challenge probabilities were then applied to a sample of nineteen mergers challenged by the FTC in order to infer the effectiveness of the FTC's actions. Coate finds that in cases with high estimated challenge probability the ex post study was more likely to find a price increase. Because of the correlation between challenge probability and the result of the merger retrospective Coate interprets this as evidence that the current policy is efficient – although the intervention may not be.

This chapter contributes to the already existing works in various ways. The first part of this chapter replicates Kwoka's work and applies his method to a sample of EU mergers. We look at the estimated price impacts of these mergers and briefly assess how they vary with the type of the competition authority's decision. We find that on average remedied mergers were not followed by a price increase. This suggests that European merger remedies seem effective in eliminating problems.

Exploring the relative richness of data from European merger decisions, we look at heterogeneity across the estimates, and find that more concentrated markets are more likely to lead to higher post-merger price increases. We also find that a large proportion of studies look at the merger's price effect within a year from the merger, which is likely to be inadequate for picking up dynamic effects and potential market self-corrections, which typically take longer to unfold.[3]

Finally, we attempt to evaluate the merger decision in the light of the price-change estimates. In around half of the cases, the retrospective estimate and the decision together might appear to suggest – wrongly – that the competition authority's decision was potentially erroneous. However, when put under further scrutiny, we point out that only a small number of these cases are likely to represent a genuine error in the decision, and others are possibly a result of other factors (non-price effects were given priority over price effects, faulty evidence, or random error).

§2.02 SAMPLE DESCRIPTION

To conduct our review, we looked at all retrospective studies of mergers in the EU that were published prior to April 2016. Our sample consists of quantitative studies, which ex post estimate the price effects of individual mergers. An important selection criterion that we adopted was to have information both on the price-effect estimates and the

3. Market self-correction typically refers to the market mechanism, whereby the monopoly profit attracts entry, and thus more competition, consequently reducing prices.

merger decision itself. Our sample size, where both the price-change estimate and the Competition authority's decision is available, is similar to Kwoka's. Kwoka's findings are based on 23 Difference-in-Differences estimates; our study has 20 Difference-in-Differences and 9 merger simulation estimates.[4] It is important to add that these were simulations conducted after the merger decision and should not be confused with simulations during the investigation.

[A] Evaluation Methods Used in the Sample of Studies

In general, because of its simplicity and overall good performance (in terms of unbiased estimates), the Difference-in-Differences method tends to be preferred over merger simulations in merger retrospectives. It is also true that, although the simulations in our sample were conducted ex post, they relied on ex ante information and they therefore seemingly do not fit well in our sample of merger retrospectives. In addition, merger simulations come with considerable shortcomings, the most notable of which is that they rest on strong - and often untestable - assumptions. Where comparisons have been made, the predictions of merger simulations are often found to differ substantially from observed outcomes based on a Before-and-After or Difference-in-Differences study design.[5]

Nevertheless, for expositional purposes we chose to include both methods in our analysis. Throughout the discussion, we do not express a preference for either the Difference-in-Differences or the merger simulations method as a tool for ex post merger analysis,[6] in particular since there are at least three instances where simulations show their strengths against Difference-in-Differences:[7]

(1) Difference-in-Differences method always compare the observed state of the world (factual) with a counterfactual world where the merger did not happen. Because of this, it is more limited in its ability to estimate if there was an

---

4. *See* Table 2.10 in the Appendix for an overview of the twenty-seven merger decisions examined. As two merger decisions (GSK/AstraZeneca and Carlsberg/Pripps) have been evaluated using the Difference-in-Differences method and on the basis of merger simulations, they are counted twice raising the total sample size to twenty-nine. This sample is somewhat different from the one published in the report prepared for the European Commission (*see* Ormosi et al., 2015) as four more mergers were added (Jumbo/C1000, GDF/Suez, T-Mobile/Orange and T-Mobile/tele.ring). This means that the results published in the report prepared for the European Commission have also changed.
5. For example, Peters (2006) found that the predictions of merger simulations differed from observed effects, in one case predicting an increase of 3.4-9.8% where the actual increase was 29.4%. Weinberg (2011) found that price increases of 5% resulted from a merger, which simulations indicated would raise prices by 1%. Weinberg and Hosken (2013) found that simulations consistently overestimated price effects in one case and understated them in the other, with the simulations often producing results that were double or half the actual price effects, respectively.
6. There is an ongoing debate in the empirical industrial economics literature on the relative merits of Difference-in-Differences and merger simulations in the context of policy evaluation. Probably most prominently in: Angrist and Pischke (2010), Einav and Levin (2010), and Nevo and Whinston (2010).
7. We offer a short overview of these methodologies in section 2.04.

unnecessary intervention by the competition authority, which would require estimating a world with the merger, but without the intervention. For example, one might want to know whether a merger that was blocked by the authority would have led to a price increase. In this case, the factual world is the world without the merger, and the task would be to find a counterfactual, which is as if the merger had gone ahead. This may be possible in some cases,[8] but not in general. Merger simulations allow comparisons across different counterfactuals (no merger, unconditional merger, remedied merger, alternative remedy), making it a better tool for estimating whether mergers would have led to a price increase in the absence of an intervention (e.g., blocking the merger, or a remedy).

(2) Because they do not estimate demand parameters, Difference-in-Differences methods are unable to evaluate changes in welfare, something that can be done in merger simulations.

(3) Finally, Difference-in-Differences methods may suffer from the contagious/umbrella effect, in which case the counterfactual responds to the merger, making it hard to identify the causal effect of the merger on the outcome.[9] Merger simulations use hypothetical equilibria of the merger and the counterfactual groups (e.g., merger against the no-merger world, or a remedy against an alternative remedy world). Because of this, the counterfactual is never affected by the merger.

Our selection criteria for merger simulation studies was that the study was conducted after the merger, rigorous structural models were used to estimate parameters of the demand system, and these parameters were then plugged into a merger simulation to estimate the price effect of the merger.

[B] Merger Characteristics

We found twenty-two relevant studies including twenty-nine ex post evaluations. One key selection criterion was that we had to be able to link the study to an enforcement decision. This ruled out a number of aggregate studies.

Table 2.1 describes some of the main characteristics of the sample of merger retrospectives analysed in this study.[10] All of these are true mergers (e.g., no joint ventures are included in the sample). The mergers span thirteen different industries. These industries are: hospitals with six mergers studied; petrol retailing with four mergers, supermarkets, brewing (with one having been studied with both methods) with three mergers each; telecoms and iron ore mining with two mergers each; and

8. For example, in the UK mergers do not require pre-notification and thus can temporarily exist before a remedy is imposed. This temporary period can be used as a control for the merger without remedy.
9. For example, using rivals' prices as counterfactual might lead to biased results if the rivals are also affected by the price-changing effect of the merger.
10. A more detailed description of our sample is given in Table 2.10 in the Appendix.

energy supply, pharmaceuticals (studied with both methods), book retailing, video game retailing, bread making and lorries all with one merger each.

Table 2.1 Sample Description

		Total Sample		***Difference-in-Differences***		***Merger Simulations***	
		N	*Proportion (%)*	*N*	*Proportion (%)*	*N*	*Proportion (%)*
Country	European Union	8	27.59	5	25	3	33.33
	France	2	6.9	2	10		
	Netherlands	7	24.14	7	35		
	Spain	1	3.23	1	5		
	Sweden	5	17.24	2	10	3	33.33
	United Kingdom	6	20.69	3	15	3	33.33
Decision	Approve	17	58.62	14	70	3	33.33
	Remedy	10	34.48	6	30	4	44.44
	Block	2	6.9			2	22.22
Industry	Book retailing	1	3.45	1	5		
	Break making	1	3.45			1	11.11
	Brewing	4	13.79	1	5	3	33.33
	Car parking	1	3.45	1	5		
	Video game retailing	1	3.45	1	5		
	Energy supply	1	3.45	1	5		
	Hospitals	6	20.69	6	30		
	Iron ore mining	2	6.9			2	22.22
	Lorries	1	3.45			1	11.11
	Petrol retailing	4	13.79	4	20		
	Pharmaceuticals	2	6.9	1	5	1	11.11
	Supermarkets	3	10.34	2	10	1	11.11
	Telecoms	2	6.9	2	10		

There is some variation in the geographical distribution of sample cases. The three main jurisdictions in the sample account for 21 of the merger retrospectives. The European Union assessed 8 of the mergers, the Netherlands 7, and the United Kingdom 6 mergers. Sweden has 5 merger retrospectives in the sample, France has 2, and Spain has 1. Two of the mergers in the sample were decided upon by competition authorities in the 1990s, the remaining mergers were in the 2000s. The earliest merger decision studied was in 1995 and the most recent in 2012. The mean lag between a merger decision and a study of that merger decision is seven year (which explains the lack of recent mergers in the sample).

Seventeen of the mergers were unconditionally approved, ten were remedied, and two mergers in the sample of ex post evaluation studies were blocked by the competition authority. Difference-in-Differences method is used predominantly for unconditionally approved mergers; interventions (remedy or block) were more likely looked at using merger simulations.[11]

[C] Potential Sample Biases

Any attempt to reach a conclusion about the overall nature of merger enforcement through the analysis of a group of ex post studies must acknowledge that the mergers analysed by individual studies are not a representative sample of all mergers. Kwoka suggests that the mergers of most interest to academics are those that raised the most complex questions and where the competition authorities faced a hard decision. He also points out that markets with publicly available data will be most attractive to academics for study. This biases Kwoka's sample towards regulated industries with data reporting requirements, such as airlines and petrol retailing industries where data is often collected and released publicly by third parties.

The sample of EU merger retrospectives collected by this study is naturally susceptible to the same biases, although given the large proportion of unconditionally approved mergers in our sample we believe it is much less likely that case selection was motivated by the complexity of the merger investigation. In any case, we acknowledge that non-random issues, such as data availability could have driven sample selection. For this reason, the interpretation of our findings and conclusions should be limited to this sample and we caution against any generalisation.

§2.03 RESULTS: PRICE EFFECT OF THE TRANSACTIONS

In order to summarise the effect of the analysed mergers, it is useful to reduce each study to a single figure that captures the estimated price effects. Kwoka carefully details the procedure he used to solve the same problem, which we follow. Where a single figure is reported as the measured effect, this figure is taken. When the author presents multiple figures from various specifications and indicates that a particular figure is preferred, this figure is taken. Where multiple results are presented alongside each other, then a simple mean is calculated and this is taken as the effect measured by the study. In a few cases, it was necessary to convert nominal price changes into percentage figures.

Although we make continuous references to Kwoka's work, we caution against any comparison of these figures with US studies, as the characteristics of the two samples of mergers might be very different in the two studies. For example, it is possible (given the higher proportion of remedied mergers in the sample) that the US sample contains a higher proportion of mergers in more concentrated markets.

11. This is unsurprising given that, as mentioned above, merger simulations enable a wider choice of counterfactuals that may be required when assessing the effect of interventions.

Table 2.2 displays the headline price-effect estimates, broken down by whether they detected a price increase or decrease in comparison to a counterfactual. In merger retrospectives the typical counterfactual is the merger not occurring (comparing the actual realised price with the counterfactual price). However, two of the studies relate to blocked mergers. In these cases, the factual is the no-merger world against the estimated counterfactual of an unconditionally approved merger.[12] Because of this, in blocked mergers an estimated price increase implies desirable outcome (as it refers to the price increase avoided by the blocking of the merger). For this reason, we judged that it would be misleading to include blocked merger estimates in this table. For the same reason we have taken out the blocked mergers from all discussion where mean price effects are reported and the blocked cases are not separately identifiable.[13]

Table 2.2 Mean Price Effect by Direction of Price Change and Type of Study

	Difference-in-Differences			*Merger Simulations*			*Full Sample*		
	Mean (%)	*Std. Dev. (%)*	*N*	*Mean (%)*	*Std. Dev. (%)*	*N*	*Mean (%)*	*Std. Dev. (%)*	*N*
Overall	1.67	11.70	20	6.93	12.11	7	3.04	11.80	27
Increase	8.8	13.15	9	8.19	12.76	6	8.55	12.53	15
No increase	-4.16	6.19	11	-0.6		1	-3.87	5.99	12

The sample average price effect records an increase of 3%. A more nuanced look at the data reveals that around three-quarters of the price-change estimates are smaller than 5%. The overall mean price increase is larger when the merger simulations were used. This seems to be driven by price decreasing mergers, as the average price increase seemed to be the same (8%) irrespective of the method used. Difference-in-Differences methods were more likely to report a post-merger price drop.

It is important to add that, by definition, merger simulations always give a positive price-change estimate if no efficiencies are incorporated in the models. Only two of the studies mention efficiencies in detail. However, they report them by

12. The approved merger, which in fact did not happen, is simulated.
13. Two of the estimates were much higher than in other cases. The use of the term outlier would be somewhat deceptive in this case as these large price-change estimates are exactly the ones that we should be most interested in. Both in the Difference-in-Differences and the merger simulation samples the 'outlier' is the *GSK/Astra Zeneca* merger (42% and 36% price increase respectively). The large price increases were probably due to the merging parties' already dominant position and the lack of entry that the competition authority anticipated at the time of approving the merger. The price increase in this case was likely to have been made worse by a regulation that required pharmaceutical products to be sold in smaller packages. The reduction in the size was not accompanied by a proportionate reduction in the prices, which made the large increase in the unit price a lot less conspicuous. Because we are pooling average price effects together, these figures could have a disproportionately large effect on the averages, which might give a misleading picture of the average price effect. Nevertheless, even after removing the 'outliers' we would arrive to the same qualitative conclusion.

simulating the level of efficiencies that would be needed to eliminate any negative welfare effects. As all these merger simulation studies were conducted after the merger, we feel that it was a forgone opportunity to not incorporate post-merger information on cost savings.

[A] Price Effects and Competition Authority's Actions

We divided the cases into three categories: approved, remedied and blocked. Kwoka distinguished between five groups of cases: cleared, opposed,[14] divestiture, conduct/conditions, and no information. There are no mergers in our dataset where we do not know the competition authority's merger decision. Only one merger in our sample had a behavioural remedy (the weakening of vertical ties in the Scottish and Newcastle/Courage merger) so we treated all remedied mergers as a single category.

Table 2.3 Mean Price Effect by Intervention and Type of Study

	Difference-in-Differences			*Merger Simulations*			*Full Sample*		
	Mean (%)	*Std. Dev. (%)*	*N*	*Mean (%)*	*Std. Dev. (%)*	*N*	*Mean (%)*	*Std. Dev. (%)*	*N*
Unconditionally approved	3.44	13.35	13	13.10	18.10	3	5.14	14.15	16
Remedied	-2.47	5.19	7	2.31	2.90	4	-0.55	4.88	11
Blocked			0	30.65	35.85	2	30.65	35.58	2

Table 2.3 shows the price outcomes of mergers by methodology and competition authority's action. The average price increase in unconditionally approved mergers is around 5%, and around 3.5% if only looking at the Difference-in-Differences estimates. For remedied mergers prices, on average, did not increase (-0.6% for the full sample and -2.5% if we look at Difference-in-Differences estimates only).[15] Three of the eleven studies of mergers with remedies estimated a post-remedy price increase (two of them resulting from a merger simulation); three estimated no price change and the remaining five were negative price-effect estimates.

14. The prosecutorial system in the US allows for a class of mergers that we see only rarely in the EU – mergers that the competition authority opposed, but which were not blocked by the Court. These cases offer the potential to test for Type I error – i.e., if prices stay the same or go down following the merger, it would suggest a Type I error (too much intervention) by the competition authority in respect of the original merger decision. In the EU, such cases rarely exists (except in very specific circumstances – e.g., where mergers are cleared only on the basis that the turnover concerned is too small or whether authorities make procedural errors which allows the merger to go through (e.g., missing deadlines). We had neither in our sample of cases.
15. We would caution against interpreting this as evidence that the remedies were 'too tough' and 'over-fixed' the problem: both the small size of the sample (11) and the limited average price effect (-0.6%) do not warrant drawing general conclusions.

A stylised conclusion – based solely on these findings – would be that European competition authorities are good at finding the right intervention. However, there are some cases where intervention would have been justified (hence, the on average positive estimated price effect of unconditionally approved mergers).

In his meta-study of US ex post merger evaluations Kwoka (2013) finds that unconditionally approved mergers are followed by a price increase of around 7%, which is similar to the 5% reported here for mergers that have been unconditionally approved by European competition authorities. However, in contrast to our results Kwoka finds that in the US sample of studies, remedied mergers were followed by a large price increase (of 16% for conduct remedies and of 8% for divestitures).

Again, it is important to emphasise that a comparison of the effectiveness of the jurisdictions (US versus EU) based on these findings would be misleading without knowing more of the characteristics of the sample of analysed cases. First, limitations of small sample size apply to both samples. Second, it is possible that the US sample is composed predominantly of high-concentration, problematic mergers, whilst the EU sample contains more benign cases. The cases studied for ex post evaluation are highly unlikely to represent a random sample drawn from the full set of merger decisions. For this reason, the difference in the main conclusions of Kwoka's work and this study could be simply due to the differences in the way the two samples are generated. Moreover, price effect is only one of the variables upon which the competition authority draws conclusions on the merger. It is equally possible that other considerations (such as quality or efficiency improvements) dominated the merger decision.

[B] Examining Heterogeneity Across Merger Studies

Reporting on merger decisions tends to be more transparent in Europe than in the US, which allows us to take a cursory look at some of the merger characteristics. For example, it is possible that large price increases are typical to very concentrated markets, i.e., markets that raised complex issues for investigators. It is also possible that variation in the design of the studies affected the price estimates. Finally, industry-specific conditions in some markets might be more/less susceptible to a larger/smaller price increase.

[1] Market Structure

Changes in market concentration can serve as an indicator of the likely market power effect of the merger. Accordingly, market structure considerations have a prominent place in EU merger control guidelines. Where they were available, we collected information on three different measures of market concentration (number of post-merger firms, combined post-merger market share, and Herfindahl-Hirschman Index (HHI), and these are introduced in Table 2.4.

Table 2.4 Market Structure in the Sample Mergers (Difference-in-Differences and Merger Simulations)[16]

		N	*Mean*	*Std. Dev.*	*Min*	*Max*
Number of post-merger firms		23	7.17	3.43	1	15
Market shares	Combined post-merger	23	0.35	0.19	0.07	0.87
HHI	Pre-merger	15	2261	1450	656	6668
	Post-merger	15	2888	1943	693	8825
	Change	15	627	575	27	2157

Table 2.5 reports the average estimated price-effect with respect to market concentration. Our sample size was too small for conducting a regression analysis. Therefore, we are only reporting simple comparisons of means. For each measurement of market concentration, we broke down the sample into two groups, below and above the median measure of concentration. For example, the median of the combined post-merger market shares is 35%, therefore we report the average of the price-change estimates for cases where the combined post-merger market share is less than or equal to 35% and cases where it is more. In this context, a market is less concentrated if the combined market share is less than or equal to 35%, if the pre-merger HHI is less than or equal to 2050, if the post-merger HHI is less than or equal to 2600, or if the number of firms in the market is more than 5.

Table 2.5 suggests that market concentration is a strong driver of the estimated price-effect of the merger. Average estimates of post-merger price increase were less than or equal to 2% where the market was less concentrated. In more concentrated markets, the average estimated price increase was substantially larger (between 6% and 10%). It also appears that the post-merger price increase depends on whether the competition authority intervened. Large price increases were observed on average if the merger had been unconditionally approved. In the sample, remedies had been able to reduce post-merger price-increases even in concentrated markets.[17]

16. Because of missing values the frequency is lower than the total number of mergers in our sample.
17. Of course, this does not mean that these figures should be used as thresholds above which mergers should be intervened.

Table 2.5 The Estimated Price Effect of Mergers by Market Concentration (Difference-in-Differences and Merger Simulations)

		Full Sample		*Unconditionally Approved*		*Remedied*	
Measure of Concentration		*N*	*Mean Price-Change (%) (std.err)*	*N*	*Mean Price-Change (%) (std.err)*	*N*	*Mean Price-Change (%) (std.err)*
Combined post-merger market share of merged firms (%)	≤ 35%	11	0.59 (2.29)	9	0.76 (2.52)	2	-0.17 (0.61)
	> 35%	12	6.53 (16.45)	7	9.67 (21.50)	5	2.12 (3.03)
Pre-merger HHI	≤ 2050	7	0.33 (1.58)	5	-0.18 (1.29)	2	1.63 (1.93)
	> 2050	8	9.71 (19.00)	4	22.92 (18.20)	4	-3.5 (6.76)
Post-merger HHI	≤ 2600	7	0.34 (2.42)	4	-0.22 (1.49)	3	1.09 (3.57)
	> 2600	8	9.71 (18.92)	5	18.34 (18.85)	3	-4.67 (7.09)
Change in HHI	≤ 400	6	2.06 (5.49)	5	2.42 (6.05)	1	0.26
	> 400	9	7.52 (18.07)	4	19.67 (21.44)	5	-2.2 (6.53)
Number of firms	> 5	12	1.53 (2.24)	5	1.62 (1.64)	7	1.64 (2.72)
	≤ 5	9	7.88 (18.37)	7	12.57 (18.24)	2	-8.5 (3.53)

The sample size of course warrants a large amount of caution when trying to extrapolate from these results. Nevertheless, these figures confirm that for our limited sample of mergers, price increases happen – as theory would predict – in more concentrated markets. This would suggest that market structure might serve as a useful first screen of merger decisions.[18] Another interesting finding is that on average remedies appear effective in avoiding price increases in concentrated markets (as measured by the HHIs and the number of firms in the market). This does not mean that there was no error (as we will further discuss in section 2.05). This reinforces our earlier finding that merger control in the EU is good at finding the right remedy. However, some mergers with high concentration had been unconditionally approved, and were followed by a price increase.

18. Kwoka and Gu (2015) arrive at a similar conclusion.

[2] Data Window

Studies differ considerably in their research design, which could contribute to some of the variation in the magnitude of price-effect estimates. Here we picked one particular feature, the span of the data that was used for estimating the impact of a merger or an intervention.[19] We believe this is important, because it is possible that the immediate price-shock, caused by the merger, is self-corrected by the market within few years following the merger.[20] It seems unlikely that the competition authority would choose to intervene if it believed that market correction would offset the price increase within one or two years after the merger. On the other hand, longer spanning data is more likely to contain confounding effects (effects other than the merger). For this reason, a badly chosen time period may provide misleading price-effect estimates.

Our focus is only on Difference-in-Differences studies, where the choice of data span is relevant. Although all the relevant studies highlighted a single price-change as a preferred estimate, some of them estimated the post-merger price impact for each consecutive year following the merger. For example, the Dutch hospital merger study estimates how post-merger prices changed in the first to the fifth year after the merger. Although it uses the over-time average estimated price-change as its preferred one, it also reports price-change estimates for each year following the merger. For the purposes of analysing how post-merger prices evolve over time, we treat the estimates for each separately estimated years as a single observation. We recorded fifty-one such estimates.

Table 2.6 suggests a quadratic relationship between the time passed after the merger and the price-change estimate, peaking at two years after the merger. Accepting the figures in Table 2.6 at their face value would suggest that prices only increase for a few years after the merger, and eventually start dropping. This however, should not imply that market self-correction mechanisms fix unremedied mergers and therefore, there is no need for merger control. The unremedied mergers were approved, exactly because the competition authority may have anticipated these correcting forces to eliminate any price increase. On the other hand, in remedied mergers, probably the remedy eliminated the price-increasing effects of the merger.

Of course, these numbers have to be handled with caution; the sample size is very small for formal testing. Nevertheless, it appears that it does matter when the study is conducted, and it strongly matters whether the study used a model that pooled post-merger data or estimated effects for each year following the merger. A study using data from the immediate aftermath of the merger may not fully reflect all the effects of the merger. Similarly, a study that estimates a post-merger average effect (over-time) masks important information about post-merger price dynamics.[21] Mariuzzo and

19. Kwoka (2015, p. 63) also briefly discusses the data window issue in US studies.
20. *See, for example,* Focarelli and Panetta (2003), who find that post-merger prices first increased after mergers in the bank deposit market, but from the third year following the merger they reverted to (or below) pre-merger levels.
21. Mariuzzo and Ormosi (2016) show this for a large sample of cases including US merger retrospectives as well.

Ormosi (2018) show how much this is a problem.[22] In choosing the appropriate time span of the data, one should take into account what the competition authority's decision was. For example, if the competition authority predicted that the initial price increase would be neutralised by subsequent entry then the data span should be sufficiently long to pick up these effects. Most merger guidelines posit that a merger should be considered unproblematic if any potential problem can be expected to be eliminated within two years of the merger. Therefore, it seems obvious that at any merger retrospective analysis should allow for at least a two-year post-merger window.

Table 2.6 The Estimated Price Effects of the Merger (in %) by the Year of the Price Change Estimate[23]

Year		*Full Sample*		*Unconditionally Approved*		*Remedied*	
		Over-time Mean	*Dynamic*[24]	*Over-time Mean*	*Dynamic*	*Over-time Mean*	*Dynamic*
1	N	13	11	8	10	5	1
	Average price change	3.60	1.14	4.80	1.45	1.69	-1.90
	(*Std. Dev.*)	(9.31)	(4.71)	(11.91)	(4.84)	(2.10)	
2	N	3	10	2	9	1	1
	Average price change	9.00	3.51	11.00	4.12	5	-2
	(*Std. Dev.*)	(31.19)	(5.16)	(43.84)	(5.07)		
2+	N	0	14	0	14	0	0
	Average price change		2.70		2.70		
	(*Std. Dev.*)		(4.34)		(4.34)		

[3] The Relevant Industry

Table 2.7 shows that there are four industries in the sample where three or more studies were conducted. From these, some simple observations can be made. For

22. The argument in Mariuzzo and Ormosi (2018) is not that longer time spans should be applied, but that the dynamics of price changes should also be evaluated. For example, when data is only available for two post-merger years, the evaluation should look at the annual effects, rather than just a two-year mean effect.
23. Because the timing of the study only varied in the case of Difference-in-Differences estimates (and not for simulations), this table only contains these estimates.
24. Where a study estimated multiple price effects for different periods, the 'Over-time mean' refers to the mean of these estimates, and 'Dynamic' refers to the estimate of the price effect in the final period of the analysed time window. Mechanisms that may act to counteract increasing prices after a merger, such as the entry or expansion of a competitor, may take time to happen, leading to the estimated price increases being smaller in the Dynamic estimates.

hospitals and brewing, the price-change estimates show considerable variation. On the other hand, for petrol retail and supermarkets the estimates are relatively small. This raises an important point. Based on price-change estimates, one would be inclined to conclude that petrol retail mergers do not harm consumers once remedies have been imposed. Any such conclusion would ignore the possibility that even a small price change can have large welfare implications in certain circumstances. Such is the case in petrol retail, as petrol prices are likely to represent a large proportion of household expenses, demand is probably very inelastic, and at retail level, it is unlikely that mergers would lead to large cost savings. Without wanting to use the findings of a handful of merger price-effect estimates to make general policy conclusions, it appears that the characteristics of the analysed industry have to be taken into account when interpreting the price-effect estimates. A full-fledged merger simulation would allow the analysis of the welfare impact of the merger.

Table 2.7 Price Effect by Industry (Difference-in-Differences and Merger Simulations)

Industry	*N*	*Average Price Change (%)*	*Std. Dev.*	*Min*	*Max*
Hospitals	6	2.35	4.69	-2.1	10
Petrol retailing	4	0.67	0.50	0	1.2
Brewing	4	10.9	3.70	-2	5
Supermarkets	3	-0.71	1.46	-2.4	0.26
Pharmaceuticals	2	38	5.66	34	42
Iron ore mining	2	3.6	1.41	2.6	4.6
Telecommunications	2	1	16.97	-11	13
Video game retailing	1	-20			
Book retailing	1	0			
Car parking	1	3			
Energy supply	1	-6			
Bread making	1	2.7			
Lorries	1	5.3			

§2.04 METHODOLOGICAL LESSONS

In conducting our review, we have identified a number of methodological lessons. Most of these relate to Difference-in-Differences studies but we also make a short reference to ex post merger simulations.

[A] Difference-in-Differences

At the heart of these studies is the choice of the counterfactual. If there is sufficient local and/or regional variation in the data then a carefully selected set of local markets can be used as counterfactual. If, on the other hand, such data is not available and there is no local variation (e.g., if firms compete nationally rather than locally) then a different counterfactual, such as a competitor or a group of competitors, may have to be used.

Depending on the counterfactual, some of the assumptions required for unbiased estimates might be more likely violated. For example, a key assumption for Difference-in-Differences studies is that there are no spillover effects (i.e., the analysed event only affected the treatment group and not the counterfactual). This is unlikely to be the case if the counterfactual is the rivals' prices, which are likely to have been affected by the merger. The specific problem in this case is that the counterfactual price also absorbs some of the price effects; therefore, any estimate from a Difference-in-Differences analysis will be biased downwards.

When data is available for local markets and the data shows sufficient variation across these markets then choosing a better performing counterfactual is easier. Nevertheless, it is important to emphasise that this choice should not be arbitrary, but rely on formal methods. Propensity Score Matching (PSM) is a frequently used device for finding a counterfactual that is sufficiently similar to the treatment market (i.e., it converges to the ideal situation, where the counterfactual is the same as the treatment but for the analysed event).[25]

Even where formal methods for counterfactual selection are not possible, the merger study should always examine the implications of the given counterfactual choice. For example, if local markets cannot be used, and competitors are used as control, then the study should examine in detail whether any assumption of an unbiased Difference-in-Differences estimator has been violated and what this may imply for the acquired estimates.

Another key methodological point relates to the dimensions of the panel data. The data used for Difference-in-Differences analysis has two key dimensions: the number of individuals observed (e.g., markets, firms, or products) and the number of time periods. Datasets vary in their disaggregation, which determines the dimensions of the data, which in turn can be used to inform the researcher on the adequate methods (e.g., how to model the error terms). Panel data with a large number of time periods (time-series dominant) can be prone to all the issues that one would encounter in time-series analysis (e.g., non-stationarity, autocorrelation). Such time-series issues are less likely to be a problem in data with large number of individuals and a small number of time periods (cross-section dominated).[26]

25. Other, less frequently used techniques exist for choosing a counterfactual that is not affected by spillover effects. Probably the most elaborate of these was proposed by Choné and Linnemer (2012), who design an iterative technique using radii around spatial points to select a local market that was not affected by a merger.

26. For example, if there is autocorrelation in the data and the research does not deal with it, then the estimated model is likely to return spurious results. This is due to the problem that if there is positive correlation between the dependent variable (usually price) at different time periods,

Ideally, if the time-series aspect of the data is correctly handled, it is good to have large frequency data that spans sufficiently long before and after the event. However, in some circumstances the data only allows a distinction between before and after prices for a large number of individuals (cross-sections). Although this situation would eliminate concerns about non-stationarity, or serial correlation, it would of course limit the richness of the analysis. Moreover, a simple before and after breakdown of data (i.e., respectively aggregating all data before and after the analysed event) may be problematic because it does not allow testing of the parallel trend assumption between the treatment market/product and the counterfactual. The assumption of parallel trends is one of the conditions of unbiased estimates. If the treatment and the counterfactual time series of prices follow non-parallel patterns then the estimated effect of an intervention will also contain some other underlying differences between the treatment and counterfactual. With many time periods we can test if the treatment and the counterfactual groups follow a parallel pattern before the analysed event, to prove that any deviation from parallel after the event is due to the analysed event.

Another central assumption to the Difference-in-Differences method is that the analysed event is exogenous, i.e., the incidence of the merger is not correlated with the error term in the model. Endogeneity can be due to unobserved factors that were driving the decision to merge. For example, if the price effect of a merger is estimated and the researcher has no information on costs, but the merger is driven by the parties' willingness to reduce their costs, then the estimated price effect will suffer from endogeneity bias. Endogeneity could also be due to reversed causality, i.e., where a change in the price is what is driving the analysed event not the other way around.

In practise, it is not trivial how to deal with such endogeneity, and many of the previous studies simply assume that the analysed event is exogenous. This is a possibility in many cases, for example, when analysing the local (e.g., country-specific), and product-specific effects of a largely diversified global merger, the decision to merge at the local level is likely to be exogenous (based on a global decision at the headquarters of the firm). Nevertheless, when the situation is not so clear-cut, the most prudent practice is to try and find out what triggered the analysed event. Information on this can be collected through a qualitative analysis (e.g., a questionnaire administered to market participants or market experts). In merger cases there might be signs suggesting that the merger was proposed by the parties to reduce their costs. With this information in hand, it becomes even more important to try to acquire costs data and include it in the model to reduce the chances of biased results.[27]

Although the consensus is that Difference-in-Differences methods are a simple, versatile, and reliable method for estimating the impact of competition policy related events, it has limitations when it comes to merger retrospectives. First, they are well

---

then the standard errors estimated using a simple OLS regression will be biased downwards. This could lead to statistically significant findings even where they do not exist.

27. Many studies control for costs in order to (at least partially) deal with endogeneity. But often it only means the price of some raw material. It is important to bear in mind that the cost-minimising considerations (e.g., rationalising production) that may drive many mergers might be unrelated to the price of these input factors. Therefore, these controls may achieve very little in eliminating endogeneity.

designed for estimating changes in a simple outcome variable (most frequently price) in a reduced form context. However, they are inadequate for welfare analysis. Assume that in two cases the Difference-in-Differences estimates show a price increase of 1% in each case. Based simply on a Difference-in-Differences study, one would conclude that the two mergers had a similar effect. However, it is possible that the two cases have completely different welfare implications. For example, in a market where goods are homogenous, demand is inelastic and customers buy frequently (e.g., petrol) a 1% price increase may have much more serious welfare effects than in a market with differentiated products, more elastic demand, or infrequent purchases (say television sets). One would need to go beyond these estimates – potentially using a structural model – to explore the differences in the two cases.

Second, if the purpose of the ex post study is to evaluate the quality of the competition authority's merger decision then Difference-in-Differences may not be the best for analysing all possible scenarios. For example, in many jurisdictions the ability of Difference-in-Differences to identify Type I errors (too much intervention) is limited. The intuition is simple: Difference-in-Differences estimates in merger evaluations show the difference in prices between the factual world (world with the remedied or unconditionally approved merger) and the counterfactual world (no merger). If the estimates imply that prices increased post-merger, then there was possibly a Type II error (insufficient intervention) in the decision. However, if prices do not increase, and a remedy was required by the authority, then we have two possibilities: (1) the remedy was the right decision; and (2) the intervention was unnecessary, and prices would have remained the same even without the remedy (hence, there was possibly a Type I error). Because in a Difference-in-Differences model the counterfactual is always the no-merger world, it often does not allow the researcher to compare the factual price (price with a remedy) with a counterfactual world of merger with no remedy.

There are of course important exceptions, where Difference-in-Differences studies can still inform us about Type I errors. For example, in the US, it is possible that the DOJ or FTC decides to block a merger, and the Court overrules this decision, and the merger goes ahead. In this case the Difference-in-Differences study compares prices between the merger and the no-merger world. If prices do not increase then it can be concluded that blocking the merger would have meant an unnecessarily strong intervention (Type I error). Another example is the UK system, where mergers do not need pre-notification. If a merger is consummated and there is sufficient time before a remedy is imposed, a Difference-in-Differences analysis could identify if the remedy was overly strong by comparing prices without the merger, prices under the factual world of the remedied merger and prices during the period when no remedy was implemented. If the no-remedy world does not show a price increase, then it would suggest that a Type I error (unnecessary remedy) was made. Of course, any such conclusion is strongly contingent on the exact details of the case. The bottom-line is: the number and types of counterfactuals that can be created from available data determines how far our interpretations of the potential competition authority errors can go.

[B] Merger Simulations

There is no consensus about the full merits of using simulations in ex post studies. One of the main problems is that depending on the assumptions, completely different results can be derived. Whereas in Difference-in-Differences it is possible to empirically test the viability of the assumptions, the same is not always true in simulations, where, for example, one may get very different results depending on assumptions about demand, or the type of competition in the market, or the model used.

The academic community is also divided on the relative merits of Difference-in-Differences and simulations. Without wanting to provide judgement in this debate, we take a more dovish stance and argue that both methods can be useful in some cases and have weaknesses in others. Their respective usefulness depends on the research question and the available data. Simulations are frequently used in merger analysis during the investigation to help predict the outcome of the merger. Here we only focus on simulations that are done after the analysed event. Based on the type of data used, we can distinguish between three types of ex post simulations.

(1) *Simulations using ex ante information*: Whilst, strictly speaking, these do not provide ex post estimates, they still have very important value in assessing/evaluating the decision of the authority. For example in mergers, during the investigation a full-fledged simulation provides probably the best prediction of merger outcomes. Nevertheless, it is rare that the authority has time for these complex exercises. Doing an ex post simulation using ex ante data can tell us what the most-informed decision of the authority would have been, from which we can determine how far away the actual decision was from this most-informed prediction.
(2) *Simulations using ex post data*: Naturally, to derive truly ex post estimates using simulations, we have to rely on ex post data. The purpose of this exercise is the same as in ex ante simulations. The effect of an event is simulated but in this case the structural parameters are estimated using ex post data, and the pre-event situation is simulated using these parameters but accounting for any change that happened post-event (e.g., in the case of mergers, this would account for any post-merger cost savings, or how entry and exit affected the market).
(3) *Simulations using ex ante and ex post data*: Although this is the most laborious of our three categories – as it requires estimating the pre and post equilibria separately –, it has the advantage that it allows testing a key assumption used in simulations: whether the pre- and post-structural parameters remain unchanged.

In an ideal world, of course one would be able to estimate effects using both Difference-in-Differences and simulation methods. Typically, there is a large overlap in the data required, and especially where a simulation is being conducted, it should be relatively simple to use the same data to also run simple Difference-in-Differences models. Using the Difference-in-Differences estimate can help guide the research through the simulations and eliminate the results that are due to 'wrong' assumptions, for example, by showing whether the products of another firm were affected by the merger and so should be considered a part of the relevant market. However, such an exercise would be an onerous task for the authorities.

Another possibility is to combine Difference-in-Differences studies with a more qualitative approach. Difference-in-Differences could identify the cases where post-merger prices increased, and the authority could look at these cases in more detail to establish what – if anything – went wrong with the decision. For example, it can assess the precision of its predictions on post-merger entry and exit and examine whether these factors (or a lack of them) contributed to the unforeseen price increase.

§2.05 POLICY IMPLICATIONS: DO PRICE INCREASES INDICATE A POTENTIAL ERROR BY THE COMPETITION AUTHORITY?

It is important to clarify the terminology used in this section. We identify cases where the competition authority's decision did not eliminate a price increase. As a shorthand terminology, for the purposes of this work, we refer to these cases as 'potential errors'. We use the word potential to acknowledge that there are numerous situations where the competition authority made no error and yet the merger decision was followed by a price increase (*see also* Table 2.8).

[A] Is a Potential Error Really an Error by the Competition Authority?

In fifteen cases in our sample, the merger was followed by a price increase. It would be tempting to jump to the conclusion that the competition authority made an error in these decisions. However, this might not necessarily be the case. Werden (2015) identifies four types of 'error' sources: faulty facts, erroneous economics, bad breaks, and random variation. He argues – and we echo this argument – that the ex post merger study should try to investigate and establish what caused the potential error. To some extent, some of the studies in our sample did this. Where this was available, we report these findings; otherwise, we try to establish the source of the potential error by combining information from the merger study and the competition authority's merger decision report.

Below we discuss five sources that may have led to a price increase following a merger decision by the competition authority. These are: (1) erroneous analysis, (2) non-price effects outweigh price effects, (3) faulty evidence, (4) random variation, and (5) small price increase. We would argue that only the case of erroneous analysis can be classified as an error by the competition authority.

[1] Erroneous Analysis

It is possible that the competition authority had all information at hand that should have enabled it to reasonably predict the price increase, but it made an erroneous assessment leading up to a decision that did not stop the negative effects of the merger.

One example could be the inappropriate use of quantitative techniques. An upward-price-pressure type analysis may be a good indicator of the closeness of competition in heterogeneous markets but it is sensitive to the values of input (diversion ratios) and can provide a misleading indicator for whether to conduct a detailed investigation or not.[28] For example, Varma (2009) found that in broad markets where the merging firms' products are the first and second choices for a large proportion of their pre-merger buyers, upward pricing pressure indices may be high even where the market shares of the merging firms are small and the competitive constraints they face from other firms are large. Similarly, if simulations are used in the investigation and the wrong assumption is made, then the results will suffer from the resulting biases. Another source of erroneous analysis might come from the inadequate analysis of available evidence, or analysis based on no solid evidence.

A good example is the merger between *GSK and Astra Zeneca*. According to the authors of the ex post study, a post-merger price increase was likely to be due to errors in the competition authority's analysis. The authors – who were involved in the investigation as experts – estimated at the time of the investigation that the merger would significantly increase prices. Yet, the competition authority decided to unconditionally clear the merger, based on its assessment that sufficient competition from other main market segments would prevent any such price increase, and that the coming deregulation of the pharmaceutical industry would encourage new entry and competition, which did not happen.

[2] Non-price Effects Outweigh Price Effects

In most cases, the merger has a range of effects on factors other than price. For example, a merger might lead to quality improvement, or wider penetration of the relevant products. In these cases even if the competition authority had perfectly foreseen a small price increase, these could have been tolerated if the merger positively contributed to other components of consumer welfare.

In the *Agip/Esso* merger prices increased for Esso. The authors of the ex post study argue that this might have been caused by the fact that Esso stations became part of Agip with a reputation for higher quality, so the price increase can be attributed to an upwards brand repositioning of Esso stations. Although this seems like a credible explanation, the reputation effects are not identifiable from the data. Despite the potential for a small price increase, the competition authority – the European Commission – allowed the merger in light of the parties' low market shares. Any price changes that could be expected would have no economically significant effect on final consumer prices (due to the high tax on gasoline that makes up most of the price).

In the case of *Lukoil/Jet*, only Lukoil's prices increased. The ex post study claims that this might have been due to the 'considerable expansion' in Lukoil's presence and

28. Upward pricing pressure tools are used to get an idea of the likelihood of a merger with anticompetitive effects. Its simplest forms are often used in first stage screening of mergers.

recognition.[29] However, from the case report it does not seem that the competition authority used this as an argument for approving a potentially price-increasing merger.

[3] Faulty Evidence

'Errors' might have been caused by relying on faulty facts, which led to inaccurate forecasts. The ex post study in these cases should investigate any potentially faulty information gathered during the investigation. One possible source of faulty information may come from surveys of industry representatives, which could have painted a misleading picture of entry conditions based on which the competition authority unconditionally approved the merger. If there was no entry post-merger and prices did increase, then this flawed information would have led to a potential Type II error (not intervening when it should have). Whether relying on faulty information should be recognised as an 'error' by the competition authority is a difficult question. From our conversations with competition authority officials we found that opinions differ: some see the use of faulty evidence as a mistake of the competition authority, whilst others consider that the reliability of information used by competition authority may depend on the rate and quality of responses to their requests for information and therefore, there are cases where verification of the evidence becomes practically impossible.

Without detailed information on the merger investigations, we cannot identify which cases were based on faulty evidence. The competition authorities themselves would be in a better position to look at their past decisions every time a post-merger price increase is observed, and assess the validity of the evidence used for deciding on the merger. Such evidence could concern market characteristics (e.g., competitive constraints, countervailing buyer power, and take-up of new technologies) or ex ante expectations about market developments (e.g., prices, entry of new competitors, and performance of divested entity). This evaluation approach has been used by competition authorities in Canada (*see* Neumann and Sanderson, 2007), New Zealand (*see* Csorgo and Chitale, 2015), and the UK (*see* Deloitte, 2009) to gain a better understanding of the reasons for possible errors made in the decision making process.

In the *Ziekenhuis Hilversum/Gooi-Noord* merger it appears that, the competition authority expected consumers to switch, which did not happen. It is not clear from the decision and the study whether this was based on a faulty analysis or faulty evidence.

[4] Random Variation

We need to make an important caveat that applies to all ex post merger evaluations. In any individual merger study, a small post-merger price increase/drop may not imply an error of the competition authority. At the time of the decision, post-merger prices

29. There is an interesting debate in the mergers world about whether a repositioning that is due to new ownership is necessarily a significant lessening of competition/significant impediment to effective competition (SLC/SIEC), if it would have occurred even if that new owner was not a competitor (but, for example, had different branding). In this case, one could potentially observe a post-merger price rise without this implying an SLC/SIEC or a Type II error.

cannot be predicted with full certainty, and randomness can overwrite even the most studious predictions, making precise price-effect predictions impossible.[30]

To give some illustration, say that a merger is approved without intervention and an ex post evaluation finds a price increase. Does this mean that the competition authority potentially made an error? During the merger investigation, the competition authority looks at the expected price change of a merger and unconditionally approves mergers if the anticipated price change, $\Delta P \leq \widetilde{\Delta P}$, where $\widetilde{\Delta P}$ is the specific value of ΔP, above which the competition authority intervenes a merger. Let us assume that the competition authority is unbiased, namely $\widetilde{\Delta P} = 0$.

Say that F(ΔP) is the cumulative probability distribution of ΔP: if the merger is allowed even though $E(\Delta P) > 0$ then the competition authority makes a Type II error (allows bad mergers). If the competition authority intervenes in the merger even though $E(\Delta P) < 0$ the competition authority makes a Type I error, i.e., it intervenes where it should not have. If $E(\Delta P) = 0$ then the competition authority would (rightly) allow the merger to go ahead unconditionally. But even in this case, there is a $1 - F(0)$ chance that the merger leads to a price increase.

To be able to decide whether the competition authority was right or wrong, ideally one would look at the distribution of ΔP that the authority predicted during its investigation, and the value of $\widetilde{\Delta P}$, not just the actual ΔP that the ex post evaluation estimated. To give a numerical example: if $\widetilde{\Delta P}$ is the median of ΔP, then $1 - F(\widetilde{\Delta P}) = 0.5$. If there are two possible price effects: −5 and +5 then $E(\Delta P) = 0.5 \times (-5) + 0.5 \times (+5)$; therefore, the competition authority is rightly deciding to allow the merger without remedy. But even a merger like this, with a zero expected price increase, will turn out, for random reasons, to raise the price about half the time.[31]

The above simple thought experiment suggests that there is always the possibility of a random error in the merger decision. It is needless to add that the issue of random variation is a largely abstract one in most assessments. If the ex post study could observe the distribution of expected post-merger prices at the time of the decision then one would be able to assess whether the actual price effect fell within the realm of random variation. Of course, we cannot think of a scenario where this would be possible and thus, unsurprisingly, we found no considerations of random variation in any of our sample studies.

In terms of how to deal with random variation at the individual case level, probably the best advice comes from Werden (2015), who argues that this 'error' is likely to only lead to small post-merger price changes. If – pre-merger – the competition authority had accounted for all available information, and post-merger we eliminated the possibility of all other potential errors then the remaining (random) variation in the post-merger price distribution (as anticipated pre-merger) must be small.

Of course random variation can be separated from systematic biases in merger decisions if one has a sufficiently large sample of price-effect estimates – which is the main objective of reviews such as this and that of Kwoka. For example, if the mean price effect in a large body of merger retrospectives shows an average of 3% price

30. The importance of this point is also highlighted by Carlton (2009) and Werden (2015).
31. *See also* Carlton (2009) for a similar argument.

increase following un-intervened mergers, it would highlight a systematic bias of merger control being too lax. Random variation would in this case scatter the individual estimates around this mean.

[5] Small Price Increase

The overwhelming majority of studies in our sample estimated a price increase of less than 5% following the merger. Some of this may be due to random variation (*see* above). It is also possible that a small price increase is not considered a sufficiently significant impediment to competition to justify blocking/intervening a merger.

A small price increase after the merger is likely to have a negligible effect on consumers. For this reason, the competition authority might choose its intervention threshold as $\widetilde{\Delta P} > 0$. Of course, antitrust agencies will always exhibit some discretion in the selection of an appropriate threshold, particularly given the uncertainty in the market and the possibility that a merger may bring efficiency gains.

The *Carlsberg/Pripps* study provides evidence that the divestiture of a number of beer varieties to a fringe competitor was the best possible remedy and although it raised the prices in comparison to the no-merger equilibrium, it was still preferred to blocking the merger. Although no specific explanation is given, this might be due to efficiencies that in the long run would outweigh the small price increase, or due to the expectation of new entrants who will in the long run reduce the price to the pre-merger level.

Finally, another issue is important to flag up if a study finds no (or little) post-merger price-increase, especially if the market is concentrated and/or there are concerns about collusion. It is possible in these cases that the firms had been colluding before the merger and the merger was a response to changes in the dynamics of the collusive process.[32] In this case, the merger is less likely to further increase prices because they had already been at a collusive level. In the *DISA/Shell* study, the authors point out that this could have played a role in their finding that post-merger prices did not increase.

[B] Which Cases Are More Likely to Attract Potential Errors?

We now turn to examining the characteristics of the cases where there was a post-merger price-increase. Based on the above discussion we define potential error as mergers that were followed by a price increase larger than 1%.[33] For example, we could assume any price change of 1% or less to be due to random variation, or small enough to be overridden by efficiency gains. For this reason, we changed all price changes no larger than 1% to zero and redefined the 'no error' and 'potential error' groups of merger decisions accordingly (*see* Table 2.8).

32. Davies, Ormosi, and Graffenberger (2015) provide evidence that a breakdown in collusion is likely to lead to mergers between previous colluders.
33. Many competition authorities use a conservative 1% assumption on the price effect of the mergers where such effects cannot be estimated. *See, for example*, USDOJ Antitrust Division Congressional Budget Submissions.

Given our definition of a potential error (mergers where prices increased by more than 1% post-merger), the first line of Table 2.8 simply expresses the averages for the samples of price increasing and other mergers. Potential errors were more common in more concentrated industries: the HHI mean for the six mergers with potential error was significantly higher than the HHI mean for the nine mergers with no error (both pre- and post-merger).[34] This is no surprise. Unconditionally approved mergers make up most of our sample. The decision not to intervene in a merger in a concentrated market is more likely to turn out to be erroneous. When we removed small price changes from the potential error group, we redefined this sub-sample to only include cases with larger price effects (dominantly price increases). Larger price increases are connected with higher market concentration, which is very much in line with what theory would suggest.[35] These findings also reinforce that measures of market concentration give a good first approximation to the likely competitive issues a merger would raise.[36] Finally, price increases were more likely in merger simulation studies. As pointed out earlier, these studies always estimate a price increase when efficiencies are not accounted for. Moreover, it is true that merger simulations were used for mergers that were more problematic. No significant effects on estimated post-merger price increases were found from the number of firms remaining in the market following the merger, the post-merger market share of the combined firm, the decision of the competition authority to intervene in the merger, and the number of years between the merger decision and the data used in the study.

Table 2.8 Sample Means Broken Down by Potential Competition Authority Error (Difference-in-Differences and Merger Simulations)

		No Error		*Potential Error*	
		N[37]	*Mean*	*N*	*Mean*
Price effect[38]		15	-2.98***	12	10.55***
Number of post-merger firms		12	6.75	11	7.62
HHI	Pre-merger	9	1530***	6	2540***
	Post-merger	9	1874***	6	3251***
Combined post-merger market share		13	0.33	10	0.38
Decision year		15	2005	14	2004

34. We used a t-test for testing difference in means.
35. This was also concluded by Kwoka and Gu (2015).
36. Looking at EU merger decisions, both Bergman et al. (2005) and Garrod and Lyons (2016) find that a second phase investigation was more likely in more concentrated markets.
37. Data was not available for all measures of market structure at the same extent – which explains the varying number of observations.
38. We excluded the two blocked mergers from the price effect statistics as they refer to a hypothetical price effect.

		No Error		Potential Error	
		N[37]	Mean	N	Mean
Method (0 – DiD, 1 – merger simulation)		15	0.13*	14	0.35*
Competition authority decision (0 – no intervention, 1 – intervention)		15	0.4	14	0.28
Number of years between merger decision and data		15	1.6	14	1.6
*,**,*** implies t-test significance in the difference between means at 90%, 95% and 99% respectively.					

Of course, the above discussion was limited by our access to information on the individual cases. Competition authorities would be in a better position to investigate if there was a potential error in their decision. This may take the form of a two-step procedure: in the first step, a quantitative ex post study provides evidence of the price effect of the merger, and in the second step a qualitative investigation identifies if the predictions (e.g., regarding entry, or cost savings) of the competition authority were correct, or whether a decision error was made in anticipating some of the key effects of the merger. Alternatively, if the data available are insufficient to carry out a proper quantitative analysis, a well-done qualitative analysis may suffice.

§2.06 WHY ARE THERE FEWER MERGER RETROSPECTIVES IN THE EU?

Although we have seen a rise in the number of European merger retrospectives, there are still significantly more such studies carried out in the US. This of course raises the question: why is there such a gap between the two sides of the Atlantic? Of course, we cannot provide a definitive answer to this question, but we can look at some of the differences between the two sets of studies that might provide at least a partial explanation.

[A] Data Used

As shown in Table 2.9, the US studies are concentrated around a few industries: petroleum (petrol retail), academic publishing, airlines, and hospitals[39] giving most of the retrospective studies. In Europe there is also some concentration but to a seemingly lesser extent. Also, typically industries that had more than one mergers studied were

39. *See, for example,* Ashenfelter et al. (2011) for a retrospective analysis of US hospital mergers.

covered by the same study (e.g., the 6 Dutch hospital mergers, the 2 mining mergers, or 2 studies covering the 4 petrol retail mergers).

The high concentration of sampled industries in the US may be due to data availability. For example, nine studies looked at eighteen mergers in the airline industry. A large proportion of these studies rely on a quarterly dataset published by the US Department of Transportation (DOT), which contains a 10% sample of all flight itineraries used in the US. Similarly, merger retrospectives on petrol retail mergers almost invariably use data from the Oil Price Information Service (OPIS), which is high-quality, proprietary data.

Table 2.9 Number of Mergers Studied in the US and in Europe (by Industry)

Number of Merger Retrospectives in the US	*Industry*	*Number of Merger Retrospectives in Europe*
13	**Petrol retailing**	4
10	**Academic journals**	0
18	**Airlines**	0
3	**Railways**	0
6	**Hospitals**	6
0	**Brewing**	4
2	**Microfilms**	0
0	**Pharmaceuticals**	2
0	**Telecoms**	2
0	**Book retailing**	1
0	**Energy supply**	1
0	**Video game retailing**	1
0	**Car parking**	1
0	**Supermarkets**	3
1	**Banking**	0
1	**Breakfast syrup**	0
1	**Cement**	0
1	**Conventional motor oil**	0
1	**Corrugating medium**	0
1	**Feminine hygiene products**	0
0	**Bread making**	1
0	**Iron ore mining**	2
0	**Lorries**	1

Contrary to the US, we did not find two studies in the EU sample that used data from the same source. It is less likely that data similar to the DOT dataset is available in Europe. However, at Member State level industry regulators would always be a good potential data source, which was made use of in the Dutch hospital merger studies. Of course, proprietary data would be available at EU level, but the cost of such data might form an imperative obstacle to using them for merger studies. In places where the competition authority is bound by a commitment to regularly deliver ex post evaluations (e.g., CMA UK), it might have a budgetary allocation for buying such data. On the other hand, smaller authorities are understandably more constrained by their scarce resources.

[B] Who Conducted the Study?

When it comes to conducting these evaluations, agencies would be well positioned given their better access to relevant data, information about the decision, and industry sources. However, academics are more likely to be seen as representing independent opinion. Moreover, conducting a full-fledged ex post assessment of mergers is a resource-demanding exercise, which the authorities typically lack the time for.

In the US, more than 4/5 of the merger retrospectives (used in Kwoka) had officials from the FTC, DOJ, or the Government Accountability Office as authors or co-authors. In the EU, only a third of the studies were authored or co-authored by officials from competition authorities.

This difference may be explained by simple organisational anomalies between authorities on the two sides of the Atlantic. Alone in the FTC there are approximately eighty staff with PhD in applied microeconomics. This figure dwarfs the number of staff with similar qualifications in EU agencies (around thirty within DG Competition's Chief Economist Team).

[C] Judicial Review

It is also possible that the difference in the competition authority's commitment to ex post evaluations also matters. In the EU, the Court can challenge the competition authority's decision ex post. This might explain why these authorities could be more reluctant to publish the results of ex post evaluations. On the other hand, in the US, the Court procedure plays a much more central role in the decision making process; therefore, the analysed mergers are typically not subject to further judicial review. This may explain why US authorities have more incentives (or less of a disincentive) to assess the decisions.

For all the above reasons it would be important to provide more incentives to deliver ex post merger studies in Europe. A formal commitment of the competition authority to such activities could help ensure that some of the budget is allocated to these activities and that political disincentives do not obstruct the decision to conduct retrospective merger analyses.

On the plus side, there are signs of more competition authority involvement in conducting merger retrospectives in the EU. The CMA in the UK has already been regularly conducting these studies: as it 'has a public commitment to evaluate each year at least one of its previous interventions'.[40] Recently, the European Commission (both by commissioning external experts, and through the teams of its Chief Competition Economist and Principal Adviser), and the Dutch competition authority, have also been active in delivering ex post assessments of their merger decisions.

§2.07 CONCLUSION

This chapter provided a detailed review of ex post studies on the merger decisions of EU antitrust agencies. One of our objectives was to replicate Kwoka's (2013) study on US merger retrospectives with European merger cases. Although the sample size puts obvious limitations on the general validity of our conclusions, some patterns still emerge. In the sample of European studies, mergers typically only increased prices by a small amount, and such price increases happened mainly in unconditionally approved mergers. We also found that market concentration is a strong driver of the estimated price effect of the merger. The average price increase in markets that are considered un-concentrated based on conventional measures of concentration is less than 2%. In concentrated markets, on the other hand, the average price increase is substantially larger, although the remedies managed to mitigate the post-merger price hike even in concentrated markets.

We do not stop at summarising the individual price-effect estimates of the sample studies. Instead, we attempt to look at these estimates in combination with the merger decision to be able to identify cases where there was potentially an error in the merger decision. We tried to categorise these potentially erroneous decisions into five groups: (1) erroneous analysis, (2) non-price effects outweigh price effects, (3) faulty evidence, (4) random variation, and (5) small price increase, and argue that we can only talk about a genuine error in the decision in the case of (1). The overwhelming majority of our sample studies do not seem to fall in this category. Nevertheless, the purpose of this exercise was not to identify where the competition authority made an error, as this could be best done by the agencies themselves on a case-by-case basis. Instead, we wanted to draw attention to the importance of authorities assessing their own decisions, giving some framework to identify genuine errors.

We strongly argue that we would need many more retrospective studies in order to be able to identify not only errors in particular decisions but errors that are more systematic in merger control. Ex post studies of mergers are often seen as a resource intensive exercise but it needs not be the case. For example, studies on mergers in the same industry may offer considerable synergies. Where data is collected on an industry, it is relatively easy to expand the time span in order to be able to assess the impact of multiple mergers.

Finally, this chapter only looked at the price effect of mergers. It would be equally important to systematically review what we know about non-price effects.[41] Some agencies regularly conduct such evaluations, typically using qualitative tools to

40. *See* Shell/Rontec study in Office of Fair trading (2014), p. 4.
41. *See* Ormosi et al. (2015) for a first attempt in this direction.

examine the effect of mergers on factors such as entry, market structure, investments, or service quality.[42] These studies and their review could provide an invaluable source of information, especially when paired with a price estimating ex post study.

42. For example, the UK Competition Commission regularly looks at a number of past mergers and interviews market players and customers on how market conditions developed post-merger.

APPENDIX: LIST OF MERGERS INCLUDED IN THIS STUDY

Table 2.10 List of Mergers Included in this Study (Both Difference-in-Differences and Merger Simulations)

Merger	*Study*	*Jurisdiction*	*Decision Year*	*Industry*	*Competition Authority's Decision*	*Method**	*Price Effect (%)*
DISA/Shell	Perdiguero and González (2012)	ES	2004	Petrol retailing	Approved	DiD	0
Agip/Esso	Csorba, Koltay and Farkas (2011)	EU	2007	Petrol retailing	Approved	DiD	0.7
Lukoil/Jet	Csorba, Koltay and Farkas (2011)	EU	2007	Petrol retailing	Approved	DiD	0.8
Volvo/Scania	Ivaldi and Verboven (2005)	EU	2000	Lorries	Blocked	MS	5.3
Rio Tinto/North	Lundmark and Wårell (2008)	EU	2000	Iron ore mining	Approved	MS	2.6
CVRD/Caemi	Lundmark and Wårell (2008)	EU	2008	Iron ore mining	Remedied	MS	4.6
T-Mobile/Orange	European Commission (2015)	EU	2007	Telecoms	Approved	DiD	13
T-Mobile/tele.ring	European Commission (2015)	EU	2006	Telecoms	Remedied	DiD	-11
GDF/Suez	European Commission (2016)	EU	2006	Energy supply	Remedied	DiD	-6
Carrefour/Promodes	Allain, et al. (2017)	FR	2000	Supermarkets	Remedied	DiD	-2.4
Vinci/GTM	Choné and Linnemer (2012)	FR	2001	Car parking	Remedied	DiD	3

Merger	*Study*	*Jurisdiction*	*Decision Year*	*Industry*	*Competition Authority's Decision*	*Method**	*Price Effect (%)*
Ziekenhuis Hilversum/Gooi-Noord	Kemp, Kersten and Severijnen (2012)	NL	2005	Hospitals	Approved	DiD	4
Erasmus MC/Havenziekenhuis Rotterdam	Kemp, Kersten and Severijnen (2012)	NL	2005	Hospitals	Approved	DiD	-1.3
MC Alkmaar/Gemini Ziekenhuis	Kemp, Kersten and Severijnen (2012)	NL	2007	Hospitals	Approved	DiD	10
St. Lucas/Delfzicht ziekenhuis	Kemp, Kersten and Severijnen (2012)	NL	2008	Hospitals	Approved	DiD	4.5
Walcheren/ Oosterschelde-ziekenhuizen	Kemp, Kersten and Severijnen (2012)	NL	2009	Hospitals	Approved	DiD	-1
Bethesda/ Scheperziekenhuis	Kemp, Kersten and Severijnen (2012)	NL	2009	Hospitals	Approved	DiD	-2.1
Jumbo/C1000	Argentesi et al. (2016)	NL	2012	Supermarkets	Remedied	DiD	0
GSK/AstraZeneca	Björnerstedt & Verboven (2013)	SV	2009	Pharmaceuticals	Approved	DiD	42
GSK/AstraZeneca	Björnerstedt & Verboven (2013)	SV	2009	Pharmaceuticals	Approved	MS	34
Cerealia/Schulstad	Nilsson & Strand (2005)	SV	2003	Bread making	Approved	MS	2.7
Carlsberg/Pripps	Friberg & Romahn (2015)	SV	2001	Brewing	Remedied	DiD	-2
Carlsberg/Pripps	Friberg & Romahn (2015)	SV	2001	Brewing	Remedied	MS	5

Merger	Study	Jurisdiction	Decision Year	Industry	Competition Authority's Decision	Method*	Price Effect (%)
Game/Gamestation	Aguzzoni et al. (2013)	UK	2008	Video game retailing	Approved	DiD	-20
Waterstones/Ottokars	Aguzzoni et al. (2016)	UK	2006	Book retailing	Approved	DiD	0
Shell/Rontec	Office of Fair Trading (2014)	UK	2012	Petrol retailing	Remedied	DiD	1.2
Scottish&Newcastle/Courage	Pinkse and Slade (2004), Slade (2009)	UK	1995	Brewing	Remedied	MS	-0.6
Bass/Carlsberg-Tetley	Pinkse and Slade (2004), Slade (2009)	UK	1997	Brewing	Blocked	MS	56
Morrisons/Safeway	Skrainka (2012)	UK	2004	Supermarkets	Remedied	MS	0.26

* Difference-in-Differences (DiD) or merger simulations (MS).

REFERENCES

Angrist J.D. and Pischke J.-S. (2010), 'The credibility revolution in empirical economics: How better research design is taking the con out of econometrics', *The Journal of economic perspectives*, 24(2), pp. 3-30.

Ashenfelter O.C., Hosken D. and Weinberg M. (2009), 'Generating evidence to guide merger enforcement', *Competition Policy International*, 5(1), pp. 57, 72.

Ashenfelter O.C., Hosken D., Vita M. and Weinberg M. (2011), 'Retrospective analysis of hospital mergers', *International Journal of the Economics of Business*, 18(1), pp. 5-16.

Bergman M.A., Jakobsson M. and Razo C. (2005), 'An econometric analysis of the European Commission's merger decisions', *International Journal of Industrial Organization*, 23(9), pp. 717-737.

Carlton D.W. (2009), 'Why we need to measure the effect of merger policy and how to do it', National Bureau of Economic Research Working Paper No. 14719.

Choné P. and Linnemer L. (2012), 'A treatment effect method for merger analysis with an application to parking prices in Paris', *The Journal of Industrial Economics*, 60(4), pp. 631-656.

Coate M.B. (2014), 'A meta-study of merger retrospectives in the United States'.

Csorgo L. and Chitale H. (2015), 'Targeted ex post evaluations in a data poor world', OECD DAF/COMP/WP2(2015)10.

Davies S.W., Ormosi P.L. and Graffenberger M. (2015), 'Mergers after cartels: How markets react to cartel breakdown', *The Journal of Law and Economics*, 58(3), pp. 561-583.

Deloitte (2009), 'Review of merger decisions under the Enterprise Act 2002', Report prepared for the Competition Commission, Office of Fair Trading and the Department for Business, Enterprise and Regulatory Reform, 18 March.

Einav L. and Levin J. (2010), 'Empirical industrial organization: A progress report', *Journal of Economic Perspectives*, 24(2), pp. 145-162.

Focarelli D. and Panetta F. (2003), 'Are mergers beneficial to consumers? Evidence from the market for bank deposits', *The American Economic Review*, 93(4), pp. 1152-1172.

Garrod L. and Lyons B. (2016), 'Early settlement in European merger control', *The Journal of Industrial Economics*, 64(1), pp. 27-63.

Ilzkovitz F. and Dierx A. (2015), 'Ex-post economic evaluation of competition policy enforcement: A review of the literature', DG Competition staff paper, Publications Office of the European Union.

Kwoka J.E. Jr. (2013), 'Does merger control work? A retrospective on US enforcement actions and merger outcomes', *Antitrust Law Journal*, 78(3), pp. 619-650.

Kwoka J.E. (2015), 'Mergers, merger control, and remedies: A retrospective analysis of U.S. policy', *MIT Press*.

Kwoka J.E. and Gu C. (2015), 'Predicting merger outcomes: The accuracy of stock market event studies, market structure characteristics, and agency decisions', *The Journal of Law and Economics*, 58(3), pp. 519-543.

Mariuzzo F. and Ormosi P.L. (2016), 'Post-Merger Price Dynamics Matter, So Why Do Merger Retrospectives Ignore Them? ', CCP Working Paper 16-5.

Mariuzzo F. and Ormosi P.L. (2018), 'Post-merger price variation matters, so why do merger retrospectives ignore it?', *Review of Industrial Organization* (forthcoming).

Neumann M. and Sanderson M. (2007), 'Ex post merger review: An Evaluation of three Competition Bureau merger assessments', Final Report of CRA, August.

Neven D.J., Nuttall R. and Seabright P. (1993), 'Merger in daylight: The economics and politics of European merger control', Centre for Economic Policy Research, London.

Nevo A. and Whinston M.D. (2010), 'Taking the dogma out of econometrics: Structural modeling and credible inference', *Journal of Economic Perspectives*, 24(2), pp. 69-82.

OECD (2011), 'Impact evaluation of merger decisions', DAF/COMP(2011)24.

Ormosi P., Mariuzzo F., Havell R. with Fletcher A. and Lyons B. (2015), 'A review of merger decisions in the EU: What can we learn from ex-post evaluations?', Report prepared for the Directorate-General for Competition of the European Commission, Publications Office of the European Union, July.

Peters C. (2006), 'Evaluating the performance of merger simulation: Evidence from the U.S. airline industry', *Journal of Law and Economics*, 49(2), pp. 627-49.

Varma G.D. (2009). 'Will use of the upward pricing pressure test lead to an increase in the level of merger enforcement', *Antitrust*, 24(1), pp. 27-32.

Weinberg M.C. (2011), 'More evidence on the performance of merger simulations', *The American Economic Review*, 101(3), pp. 51–55.

Weinberg M.C. and Hosken D. (2013), 'Evidence on the accuracy of merger simulations', *Review of Economics and Statistics*, 95(5), pp. 1584-1600.

Werden G.J. (2015), 'Inconvenient truths on merger retrospective studies', *Journal of Antitrust Enforcement*, 3(2), pp. 287-301.

STUDIES CITED AND USED TO CREATE OUR SAMPLE

Aguzzoni L., Argentesi E., Buccirossi P., Ciari L., Duso T., Tognoni M. and Vitale C. (2013), 'They played the merger game: A retrospective analysis in the UK videogames market', Discussion Paper 1330, DIW Berlin.

Aguzzoni L., Argentesi E., Ciari L., Duso T. and Tognoni M. (2016), 'Ex post merger evaluation in the U.K. retail market for books', *The Journal of Industrial Economics*, 64(1), pp. 170-200.

Argentesi E., Buccirossi P., Cervone R., Duso T. and Marrazzo A. (2016), 'The effect of retail mergers on prices and variety: An ex-post evaluation', DICE Discussion Paper No. 225.

Allain M.L., Chambolle C., Turolla S. and Villas-Boas S.B. (2017), 'Retail mergers and food prices: Evidence from France', *The Journal of Industrial Economics*, 65(3), pp. 469-509.

Björnerstedt J. and Verboven F. (2013), 'Does merger simulation work? Evidence from the Swedish analgesics market', Working Paper, Katholieke Universiteit Leuven.

Choné P. and Linnemer L. (2012), 'A treatment effect method for merger analysis with an application to parking prices in Paris', *The Journal of Industrial Economics*, 60(4), pp. 631-656.

Csorba G., Koltay G. and Farkas D. (2011), 'Separating the ex post effects of mergers: An analysis of structural changes on the Hungarian retail gasoline market', Discussion Papers, Hungarian Academy of Sciences.

European Commission (2015), 'Ex-post evaluation analysis of two mobile telecom mergers: T-Mobile/tele.ring in Austria and T-Mobile/Orange in the Netherlands'.

European Commission (2016), 'The economic impact of the enforcement of competition policies on the functioning of EU energy markets'.

Friberg R. and Romahn A. (2015), 'Divestiture requirements as a tool for competition policy: A case from the Swedish beer market', *International Journal of Industrial Organization*, 42, pp. 1-18.

Ivaldi M. and Verboven F. (2005), 'Quantifying the effects from horizontal mergers in European competition policy', *International Journal of Industrial Organization*, 23(9), pp. 669-691.

Kemp R.G., Kersten N. and Severijnen A.M. (2012), 'Price effects of Dutch hospital mergers: an ex-post assessment of hip surgery', *De Economist*, 160(3), pp. 237-255.

Lundmark R. and Wårell L. (2008), 'Horizontal mergers in the iron ore industry – An application of PCAIDS', *Resources Policy*, 33(3), pp. 129-141.

Nilsson A. and Strand N. (2005), 'On simulation and reality: a Swedish example', in: P.A.G. van Bergeijk and E. Kloosterhuis (eds.), *Modelling European mergers: theory, competition policy and case studies*, Edward Elgar Publishing, pp. 184-189.

Office of Fair Trading (2014), 'Shell – Rontec: An evaluation of the OFT's conditional clearance of the merger'.

Perdiguero J. and Jiménez González J.L. (2012), 'Mergers and difference-in-difference estimator: Why firms do not increase prices?', IREA Working Paper 2012/05, University of Barcelona.

Pinkse J. and Slade M.E. (2004), 'Mergers, brand competition, and the price of a pint', *European Economic Review*, 48(3), pp. 617-643.

Skrainka B.S. (2012), 'The geography of grocery demand in the UK: An evaluation of the 2003 Morrisons-Safeway merger', University of Chicago.

Slade M.E. (2009), 'Merger simulations of unilateral effects: What can we learn from the UK brewing industry?' in: Bruce Lyons (ed.), *Cases in European competition policy: the economic analysis*, Cambridge University Press, New York, pp. 312-346.

CHAPTER 3

The Impact of Mobile Telecom Mergers on Prices and Quality: Evidence from Quantitative Studies*

Luca Aguzzoni & Luca Di Martile

Over the last fifteen years, a policy debate has taken place among regulators, competition authorities and industry stakeholders, centred on the impact of mergers on market outcomes in the mobile telecom industry of the European Union. A number of reports and studies contributed to this debate putting forward analyses quantifying the effects of past mergers on prices and quality of mobile telecom services, but often reaching different conclusions. This chapter offers a review of this literature, proposing a categorisation of the studies, explaining their differences and attempting to draw some conclusions on the status of the debate. The available evidence indicates that, in some of the merger episodes investigated, mergers between mobile operators may have led to price increases. At the same time, there is also weaker evidence suggesting that higher concentration may be associated with larger investments at the firm level, although it is not established to what extent this increased investment is indicative of greater consumer benefits. One clear message is that national mobile telecom markets, merger episodes and competition authorities' interventions show a high degree of heterogeneity. For these reasons, general conclusions should be drawn and interpreted carefully and the impact of each merger would in any case depend on its own characteristics. Finally, a number of recent not yet fully studied mobile merger episodes offer ample space for further research in this area.

* This chapter has been written under the sole responsibility of the authors and does not represent the views of the European Commission.

§3.01 INTRODUCTION

Over the last fifteen years, and in particular since the early 2010, the mobile telecom industry in the European Union has witnessed several mergers and acquisitions. As a result, the number of mobile operators active in the countries concerned has declined and within-country market concentration increased. These mergers triggered a policy debate on the effects of the increased concentration on the functioning of mobile telecom markets. On the one hand, supporters of more concentration argue that the mergers have allowed mobile telecom operators to combine and optimise their resources in order to fund more investments and to increase innovation and quality of service to end-customers. On the other hand, critics of rising concentration argue that the relationship between mergers and quality of service is unclear and that the decrease in the number of mobile operators has had a negative effect on competition and on end-customers through an increase in prices.

One of the first studies that attempted to investigate this relationship and set the foundation of the debate is Frontier Economics (2015). Prepared for the GSMA, the association of mobile telecom operators, Frontier Economics (2015) studies past episodes of concentrations to assess the effects of the increase in concentration[1] in mobile telecom markets on both prices and quality/innovation.[2] The study concludes that mergers in the mobile sector do not necessarily lead to higher prices, as there is no statistically significant relation between concentration levels and prices. Similarly, the study does not find any statistically significant relation between the level of concentration in the mobile telecom market and investment. However, it argues that under certain conditions mergers are likely to increase the incentives of the merging parties to invest and to innovate.

Frontier Economics (2015) bases its claim upon several elements, one of which is the seminal work of Aghion et al. (2005), which finds that the relation between concentration and innovation has the form of an inverted U-shape. This finding indicates that a high level of concentration (i.e., associated with few competing companies) and a low level of concentration (i.e., associated with many competing companies) are related to a low level of innovation. In this model, innovation is then maximised in-between high and low concentration levels. A possible explanation for this type of relation, and one often put forward to justify it, is that in markets with many companies, due to the intense competition, the expected profits that the companies would gain by innovating are not enough to cover the costs of the investments required.

The work of Aghion et al. (2005) does not relate specifically to mobile telecom investments as it rather considers R&D activity measured by patents. However, even assuming a similarity between innovation and investment decisions, the inverted U-shaped relation between concentration and innovation found in Aghion et al. (2005) may not be present in all technological-intensive industries, as shown by Igami and Uetake (2019) that find a plateau-shaped relation between the number of companies

1. Specifically, Frontier Economics (2015) focuses on 4 to 3 mergers.
2. The details of the study are presented later on in this chapter.

and innovation in the hard disk drive industry. Hence, according to this latter study, innovation does not decrease as competition increases. Furthermore, the theory whereby a low level of concentration is associated with a low level of innovation does not specify which level of concentration is low enough to generate a decrease in innovation, something that most likely depends on the industry under investigation.

Furthermore, as Federico (2017) points out, the approach of Aghion et al. (2005) does not shed light on the specific impact of mergers on innovation. As pointed out, Aghion et al. (2005) looks at concentration measures without considering what led to those concentration level (e.g., acquisitions versus organic growth). Moreover, no consideration is given to the possible effects of mergers on the incentives to innovate as it takes those incentives as fixed. In this respect, Motta and Tarantino (2017) and Federico, Langus and Valletti (2018) develop theoretical models to study how mergers change the incentives to innovate. Based on their theoretical models, those studies find that generally mergers have a negative impact on innovation. By contrast, Denicolò and Polo (2018a) argue that mergers may actually spur investment and innovation by preventing and/or eliminating duplication between the merging parties. In a subsequent paper, Denicolò and Polo (2018b) further argue that the effect of mergers on investment and innovation is not straightforward, as mergers may both increase or decrease investment and innovation.

Following Frontier Economics (2015), several other studies have been published on mergers in the mobile telecom industry. These studies often propose different and conflicting findings. This chapter presents a review of the studies that try to measure empirically the effects of mergers on market outcomes and limits its scope to the mobile telecom industry. Although the authors of this chapter have at times contributed to the policy debate, here they attempt to be as neutral as possible, and not to take sides in the debate. The objective of this chapter is to take stock of the past empirical studies, to draw some general conclusions when possible, and to suggest areas that would benefit from further research.

The chapter is organised as follows. Section 3.02 describes the main characteristics of mobile telecom markets in the European Union, focusing on aspects crucial for competition, such as the characteristics of the network infrastructure, and on important developments in terms of price and quality of services. Section 3.03 gives an overview of the mergers between mobile network operators (MNOs) assessed by the European Commission over the period 2006-2018. Section 3.04 presents the sixteen ex post evaluations of EU mobile telecom mergers analysed in this chapter, making a distinction in terms of their scope, the methodology used and the effects considered. Section 3.05 compares the results and main conclusions of these ex post evaluations. Finally, section 3.06 concludes and proposes areas for further work.

§3.02 MOBILE TELECOM MARKETS IN THE EUROPEAN UNION

From a competition policy perspective, mobile telecom markets in the European Union are defined at the national level. Although some operators are present in more than one country, they do not share the same infrastructure across countries. Moreover, until recently, international calls within the European Union made use of roaming fees, eliminating the potential gains for national consumers of using cheaper non-national telecom services and fragmenting the telecom markets in the European Union. In 2017, following the adoption of a series of regulations of the European Union,[3] retail roaming surcharges were abolished in Europe. As a result, tariffs set in one country will also apply in other countries within the Union without additional fees. However, the purpose of the regulations was not to establish a single European mobile telecom market where operators based in one country would compete against operators in other countries. Rather, the objective was to facilitate the movement of citizens within the European Union. In fact, the regulations limited the permanent or prolonged use of roaming, preventing direct competition between operators in different countries. Therefore, in the current regulatory scenario, competition still takes place at the national, rather than the European level.

A common feature across the national mobile telecom markets in the EU has been the technological development in the industry throughout its history. In its early years of development during the 1990s, mobile telecommunication could only carry voice communication, Short Message Service ('SMS') and, more rarely, Multimedia Messaging Services ('MMS'). This was the time of the so-called 2G (second-generation) cellular technology.[4,5] In the late 1990s, the 3G technology was developed, which represented an important breakthrough in the industry: mobile data transmission. This allowed users to navigate the internet and to have access to other services such as, for example, emails from their mobile devices. It was only with the development of the 4G technology in the late 2000s, however, that the performance and reliability of mobile data transmission took off. The fourth generation technology opened up countless new possibilities and applications of mobile services, from video streaming to online gaming. Finally, the next milestone in the mobile telecom industry will be the 5G technology with its increased network connectivity and the 'internet of things'[6] that is expected to hit the market in the 2020s.

Developments in mobile data (speed and data volumes) are an essential feature of modern mobile communication (*see* section 3.03[B]). Over time, mobile data speed through cellular technologies has been increasing at nearly exponential rates. Mobile speed passed from almost 10 Kilobits per second (Kbps) with 2G (GSM), to 2 Mbps with

3. Regulation 531/2012 on roaming on public mobile communications networks within the Union, Regulation 2015/2120 laying down measures concerning open internet access and amending Directive 2002/22/EC on universal service and users' rights relating to electronic communications networks and services and Regulation 2017/920 amending Regulation (EU) No. 531/2012 as regards rules for wholesale roaming markets.
4. The first generation of cellular technology, the 1G, was developed in the 1980s, but its use was not widespread among the public.
5. Cellular technology is what mobile phone networks are based on. This technology gave mobile phones the name 'cell phones'. Cellular technology refers to having many small interconnected transmitters as opposed to one big one.
6. The Internet of things is the interconnection via the internet of devices (such as vehicles or home appliances) that contain electronics, software and connectivity, which allow them to connect, interact and exchange data.

3G, to 100 Mbps with 4G (LTE). Estimates indicate that the maximum theoretical speed of 5G technology will be 10,000 Mbps, i.e., 10 Gbps.

The development of faster and more reliable mobile network technologies went hand in hand with the development of compact but powerful mobile devices. Nowadays mobile devices can have the same performance that just ten years ago only desktop computers could achieve. Another important feature of mobile devices is that they are generally tied to the latest cellular technology. Old devices are unlikely to be able to connect to the 4G network. Likewise, today's devices are unlikely to be able to connect to the 5G network of the future.

The two parallel technological developments (of mobile network connectivity, on the one hand, and of mobile devices, on the other hand) have shaped the way consumers see and use mobile services. Gradually, people have shifted their use from voice and SMS communication to data transmission. This shift in consumer preferences has had important repercussions in the industry, such as the introduction of VoIP services ('Voice over IP', i.e., making voice calls through the internet using mobile data), and the birth of 'Over The Top' (OTT) services[7] replacing the more traditional voice and SMS services.

Mobile telecom markets are characterised by some specific features that set them apart from markets in other industries, and which are pivotal for the ex post assessment of mergers in the mobile telecom sector. The following subsections provide a brief description of the main features of mobile telecom markets, underlining the most important ones for competition.

[A] Mobile Networks

The primary feature of mobile telecom markets is the presence of network infrastructures for mobile telecommunication (the 'mobile network'). A mobile network is essentially the product of two components: spectrum and cell sites.

The *spectrum* relates to the radio frequencies that allow communication and transfer of data over the airwaves. It is a 'scarce resource', in the sense that its amount and consumption are limited. In the European mobile telecom markets, the amount of spectrum available for mobile telecommunication is regulated by national authorities, which assign it to mobile telecom operators, using spectrum auctions. There is a relatively strong variation in the cost of the spectrum across the European countries.[8] As noted by London Economics (2015), this is likely due to different competitive conditions and different auction designs across countries.

The amount of spectrum is also the primary barrier to entry of new MNOs (*see* section 3.02[C]), as its cost can be very significant. For example, from the second half

7. An OTT service is any service that provides a product over the Internet and bypasses traditional distribution. Services that come as OTT are most typically related to media and communication.
8. The frequency of the spectrum is measured in MHz (or GHz). The spectrum performance is closely linked to its frequency. As a rule of thumb, the lower the spectrum frequency, the wider will be the coverage that the spectrum can achieve, and the higher will be its ability to penetrate building walls.

of 2018 on, several countries in Europe have started organising and conducting 5G spectrum auctions, with frequencies in the 3.4-3.8 GHz range. Mobile operators spent in total approximately EUR 4.3 billion in Italy, EUR 4.1 billion in Germany, GBP 1.2 billion in UK and EUR 438 million in Spain. To encourage competition, spectrum is sometimes reserved and provided at advantageous terms by national regulators to new or recently entered operators.

The *cell sites* are the physical locations where antennae and other electronic equipments for mobile telecommunication are mounted. In cities, they are generally located on the top of buildings or on other structures high enough from the ground. The spectrum is installed on the technical equipment in each cell site, which then gives an umbrella-shaped coverage for mobile telecommunication. Not having signal on the mobile phone means that the device is not able to connect to a cell site, most likely because it is too far away and outside the reach of the cell sites' coverage. National regulators generally impose limits to the amount of cell sites in a given area, in particular to limit radio wave emissions. This means that cell sites also are a scarce resource, and in several cities, it might be challenging to find cell sites that are available to new operators.

The combination of amount of spectrum and number of cell sites determine the overall coverage, quality and performance of a mobile telecom network. As mentioned, these two elements are subject to national regulations. This gives a considerable amount of power to national regulators to shape the competitive landscape of the market, in particular regarding the design of spectrum auctions. At the same time, the high barriers to entry to acquire spectrum and sites mean that incumbent network operators usually enjoy a relative high degree of market power as they benefit from the legacy spectrum assigned to them in the past and from the legacy network of sites that they have acquired over time.

[B] Coverage, Speed and Price

As in many industries, competition in mobile telecom markets is determined by two inter-related factors: quality and price. The quality of a mobile operator is directly related to the quality of its network, which is typically measured in terms of network coverage and network speed.[9]

Network coverage refers to the size of the mobile network within the national boundaries, and is measured as the percentage of the population that is covered by the mobile network. Network coverage can be subdivided into *outdoor* and *indoor* coverage, the latter measuring the ability of mobile networks to pass through solid walls, although in many cases mobile operators only report outdoor coverage.

9. The quality of a mobile telecom experience is also related to the device of the user. However, the performance of the device can be considered independent of the specific network choice and, for the purposes of this chapter, we only consider and discuss the quality of the network.

Network speed has become a key feature of mobile networks since the introduction in recent years of mobile data and 4G technology. This is because for the other mobile services (i.e., voice and SMS) mobile data speed is unimportant, whereas it is key when, for example, watching a video on a mobile device. Speed is measured both as the download and upload speed from a mobile device. It is also important to differentiate between *theoretical* speed and *actual* speed. The former is the network speed achievable in optimal conditions (e.g., no distance from the cell site, no congestion), whereas the latter is the speed actually achieved at a given time and place. The actual speed depends on a number of factors, including the number of customers connected to the cell site at a given time. Therefore, it can vary throughout a day, and is generally measured in *peak time* and *off-peak time*.

Historically, the *price* of mobile telecom services was a pay-as-you-go system, where the payment was directly related to the consumption of mobile services (voice and SMS). Nowadays the industry has drastically shifted to a bundle approach, where all services (voice, SMS and data) are bundled together for a given price, with an *out-of-bundle* unit price for each service, in case consumption goes beyond the maximum amounts allowed in the bundle. Such bundle prices make the comparison across operators more difficult, as different operators may offer bundles of varying sizes and characteristics not directly comparable. Furthermore, mobile services are increasingly sold together with other services, like fixed telephony (voice and data), pay TV services, access to streaming libraries (with video and audio content for streaming).[10] This further complicates the comparison of bundles across operators or over time.

Figure 3.1 Mobile Price Using the Basket Approach

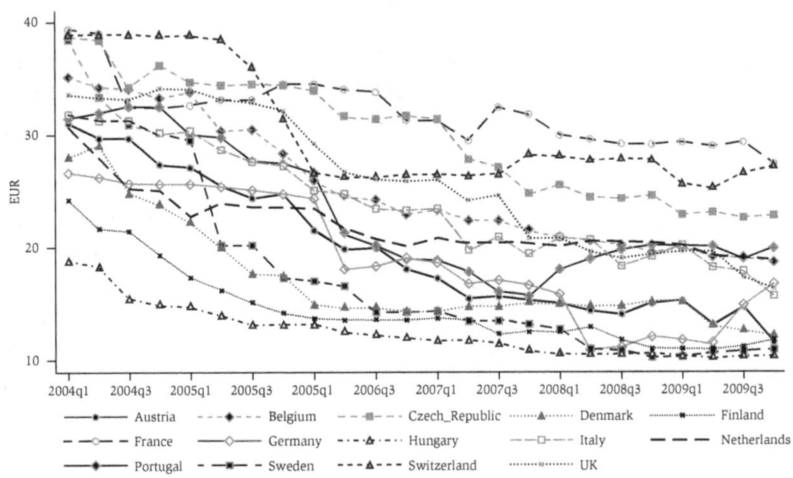

Source: Aguzzoni et al. (2018).

10. These bundles are also known as double, triple or quadruple play.

Prices in mobile telecom markets (*see* section 3.04[C] for a discussion on how to measure prices) have generally fallen since the beginning of the 2000s. Figure 3.1 shows a measure of prices in several EU countries.[11] This decrease in prices is likely driven by fast technological development in the industry as described above, which has led to a significant decrease in the service costs for the operators.

[C] Mobile Network Operators and Mobile Virtual Network Operators

In terms of operators, a broad distinction can be made between Mobile Network Operators (MNOs) and Mobile Virtual Network Operators (MVNOs). The distinguishing factor between these two categories is the ownership of the network.

MNOs, on the one hand, own their mobile network. This allows them to have full control over the quality of their services. Competition among MNOs plays out at two levels: competition on the quality of the services, which depends on the characteristics of the network, and competition on the price of the services. Moreover, MNOs are not only active in the retail (consumer) market but also in the upstream wholesale market by selling access to the retail market to MVNOs.

MVNOs, on the other hand, have a contractual agreement with an MNO through which they gain access to the MNO's network and operate mobile services at the retail level. This grants MVNOs limited to no control over the service quality, and sometimes even limit their ability to set prices independently. MVNOs are at the same time competitors and customers of the MNOs.[12] Due to their dependence on MNOs, MVNOs are often considered as having a lower impact on the competitive dynamics in the retail market than MNOs.

[D] Network Sharing and Roaming Agreement

MNOs usually own their own network, but it is often the case that some part of the mobile network (mast, radio access network equipment or even spectrum) is shared among two or more MNOs. Indeed, in several European markets MNOs have concluded agreements whereby they share, to a different extent, their mobile network. Such arrangements are referred to as *network sharing*.

There are at least three types of network sharing, which differ by the extent to which the assets of the MNOs are shared. These are passive sharing, active sharing and spectrum sharing. Passive sharing allows MNOs to use each other's cell sites to mount their own equipment. The location and possibly the towers will be shared, but the technical equipment will be held separate. Differently, an active sharing agreement also includes the sharing of the technical (active) equipment, with the traffic of the

11. Prices are measured by using the basket expenditure approach, *see* section 3.04[C] for more detail.
12. Several subcategories of MVNOs exist. However, this further subdivision is not relevant for this chapter.

different MNOs being handled separately using specialised software. Finally, spectrum sharing (often called active spectrum sharing) also allows operators to share their respective spectrum. A spectrum sharing agreement covering the whole spectrum endowments of the operators in the full national area implies that in essence the operators bound by this agreement have the same network. Table 3.1 lists the network sharing agreements within the European Union as of 2015.

Network sharing, and the possibility to enter into such agreements, is also relevant in competition policy enforcement. This is because, in some merger cases, the possibility to enter into a network sharing agreement was considered a less anticompetitive alternative to the full merger between two independent MNOs. The reason is that the network sharing agreement brings about many of the network synergies and quality improvements claimed by merging parties, without necessarily leading to the same level of anticompetitive behaviour.

Different from network sharing are *roaming agreements*. In roaming agreements, one party (an MNO or MVNO) purchases the right for its own customers' traffic to be carried by another MNO's network. Access rights to an MNO's network through a roaming agreement can be segmented or limited across several dimensions. For example, access can account only for a given cellular technology, a given geographic area or a given amount of traffic. While in network sharing, the parties involved can be considered as partners in a joint venture, having a mutual dependency on one another, roaming agreements are more similar to contracts between a provider and a customer, with one party being completely dependent on the other party. The wholesale agreements between MNOs and MVNOs are a form of roaming agreements. Likewise, the agreements for international roaming services involving operators in different countries are another form of roaming agreements.

In many cases, however, roaming agreements involve competing MNOs within the same country. In particular, new operators generally do not have a full coverage throughout the country from day one. Furthermore, they often enter with a business model that disregards legacy cellular technology (like 2G), for which they do not own the necessary spectrum. New entrants fill the gap in their networks through roaming agreements with their competing incumbent MNOs.

Table 3.1 Network Sharing Agreements in the European Union

	Year of Agreement	*Passive; Active; or Spectrum*	*Duration*	*Mobile Network Operators*
BE	2009	Passive		Orange (Mobistar) / KPN (BASE)
CY		Site sharing and national roaming arrangements		Vodafone / Areeba
CZ	2011	Active	6 years	O2 Czech Republic / T-Mobile CR
DE	2009	Passive	10 years	Vodafone Germany / Telefonica
DK	2011	Spectrum	20 years	TeliaSonera Denmark / Telenor Denmark
EL	2013	Active	15 years	Vodafone Greece / Wind Hellas
ES	2006 2009	Active Passive	10 years	Vodafone Spain / Orange Spain Vodafone Spain / Telefonica
FI	2014	Spectrum		TeliaSonera Finland / DNA
FR	2014	Active		SFR / Bouygues
HU	2015	Active		Magyar Telekom / Telenor Hungary
IE	2009 2011 2012	Passive Passive Passive	10 years 19 years	Vodafone Ireland / Hutchison (3) Hutchison (3) / Eircom Vodafone Ireland / Hutchison (3)
IT	2007 2009	Passive Passive	6 years	Vodafone Italia / TIM TIM / Hutchison (3)
NL	2013	Passive		T-Mobile / Tele2
PL	2011	Active	15 years	T-Mobile (PTC) / P4 (Play)
RO	2013	Active		Vodafone / Orange
SE	2001 2001 2009	Spectrum Spectrum Spectrum		TeliaSonera / Tele2 Telenor Sweden / Hutchison (3) Tele2 / Telenor Sweden
UK	2007 2012	Active Active		EE / Hutchison (3) Vodafone UK / Telefonica O2 UK

Source: London Economics (2015).

§3.03 AN OVERVIEW OF THE LATEST EU MOBILE MERGER DECISIONS

Table 3.2 lists the eleven merger cases between MNOs assessed by the European Commission between 2006 and 2018.[13] Two cases entailed a concentration from five to four MNOs, T-Mobile/tele.ring in Austria in 2006 and T-Mobile/Orange in the UK in 2010. Both mergers were cleared conditional on remedies (divestiture of spectrum in both cases and a national roaming agreement in the UK case). In the other nine cases, there was a concentration from four to three MNOs. Among these nine cases, three mergers were unconditionally cleared (TPG IV/APAX/Q-Telecom in Greece in 2006, T-Mobile/Orange in the Netherlands in 2007 and T-Mobile/Tele2 in the Netherlands in 2018), four mergers were cleared subject to remedies (Hutchison 3G/Orange in Austria in 2012, Hutchison 3G/Telefonica Ireland in Ireland in 2014, Telefonica/E-plus in Germany in 2014 and Hutchison 3G/WIND in Italy in 2016), one merger was prohibited (Hutchison 3G/Telefonica UK in United Kingdom in 2016) and one merger was withdrawn (Teliasonera/Telenor in Denmark in 2015).

Competition authorities often require conditions from the merging parties in order to approve the merger, the so-called remedies. The extent of such conditions can differ considerably, depending on the alleged harm brought about by the proposed transactions. Remedies from merging parties in the mobile telecom industry vary from extending the current terms of the agreements with MVNOs, to a divestment of spectrum and cell sites, paving the ground for the entry of a new MNO. Such remedies have the potential (and to some extent the intent) to change the market outcome entirely relative to a scenario in which the merger goes through without remedies. However, the presence (or absence) of remedies is often overlooked in studies examining the competitive effects of mergers. Many of the ex post evaluations examined in this chapter do not make any distinction between mergers with and without remedies and do not assess the effectiveness of the different types of remedies imposed.

From 2012 onwards the seven merger cases notified to the European Commission reduced the number of competitors in the market from four to three. In six of these cases (with the exception of the acquisition of Tele2 by T-Mobile NL in the Netherlands in 2018), the mergers raised serious competition concerns: remedies where required in four cases, the concentration was prohibited in one case and, in another case, the merger proposal was withdrawn. In all the four cases with remedies, the accepted remedies included provisions for granting network access to one or more MVNOs at competitive prices. In addition, in the Hutchison 3G/Wind merger in Italy in 2016, the remedies also included provisions for the entry of a new MNO, to which the merging

13. This table exclusively contains mobile telecom mergers assessed by the European Commission. It excludes mergers between MNOs and fixed operators, mergers between MNOs and MVNOs as well as mergers examined by national competition authorities of the European Union. In line with the applicable rules on jurisdiction, mergers that involve parties generating a large part of their revenues in a given Member State are typically dealt with by the national competition authorities. This is the case for instance in the KPN/Telfort merger in the Netherlands that is discussed later in this chapter.

parties had to divest spectrum and cell sites. For some commentators,[14] these latest developments indicate a shift of the European Commission's assessment both toward more scrutiny of mobile merger consolidation and toward structural solutions (as opposed to MVNO-based behavioural remedies) as suitable remedies to remove the competitive concerns.

*Table 3.2 Mobile Network Operator Mergers Assessed by the EC (2006-2018)**

Year	*Transaction*	*Country*	*Number of Players*	*Type of Decision*	*Type of Remedy*
2006	TPG IV / Apax / Q-Telecom	EL	4 → 3	Clearance in Phase I	
2006	T-Mobile / tele.ring*	AT	5 → 4	Clearance with remedies in Phase II	Divestiture of spectrum and sites (used e.g. for hardware and antennas)
2007	T-Mobile / Orange*	NL	4 → 3	Clearance in Phase I	
2010	T-Mobile / Orange*	UK	5 → 4	Clearance with remedies in Phase I	National roaming Divestiture of spectrum
2012	Hutchison 3G / Orange*	AT	4 → 3	Clearance with remedies in Phase II	Divestiture of spectrum MVNO-access
2014	Hutchison 3G / Telefonica Ireland*	IE	4 → 3	Clearance with remedies in Phase II	MVNO-access Network sharing agreement
2014	Telefonica / E-plus*	DE	4 → 3	Clearance with remedies in Phase II	MVNO-access Divestiture of spectrum
2015	Teliasonera / Telenor	DK	4 → 3	Transaction withdrawn	
2016	Hutchison 3G / Telefonica UK	UK	4 → 3	Prohibition	
2016	Hutchison 3G / WIND	IT	4 → 3	Clearance with remedies in Phase II	New MNO entry with divestiture of spectrum and sites
2018	T-Mobile NL / Tele2 NL	NL	4 → 3	Clearance in Phase II	

* These mergers have been the subject of ex post evaluations reviewed in this chapter.

14. Schubert (2016) and Powell and Czapracka (2017).

However, the European Commission recently cleared a four-to-three merger without conditions. In the T-Mobile NL/Tele2 NL case, the European Commission concluded that the proposed merger was unlikely to lead to significant price increases because of the limited combined market position of the merging parties (around 25% market share) and the small potential changes in the conditions of competition for MVNOs in the Dutch mobile telecom market.

Six of the mergers reported in Table 3.2 have been the subject of one or more ex post evaluation assessments (as a single case study or as part of a wider market study). These ex post evaluations aimed at studying the impact of the merger decisions on the developments of relevant market outcomes such as prices, investments and quality of services offered. These studies and their findings are discussed in the following section.

§3.04 DESCRIPTION OF THE EX POST EVALUATIONS OF EU MOBILE TELECOM MERGERS

The mobile telecom industry is likely the industry that has attracted the most attention in terms of ex post evaluation studies of merger decisions in the European Union. In the past few years, several studies have been conducted and at least fourteen different publicly available studies can be identified (*see* Table 3.3[15]).

Several of these studies have been directly commissioned by private entities such as mobile operators or industry associations. For example, the GSMA, the association representing MNOs worldwide, has been particularly active in commissioning and producing studies on this matter. On the other hand, public institutions have also been involved in this field. In particular, the Directorate-General for Competition of the European Commission, the Austrian and the UK telecom regulators (RTR and Ofcom respectively), the Body of European Regulators for Electronic Communications (BEREC) and the Austrian and the Dutch competition authorities have all contributed to the debate either by commissioning studies to third parties or by conducting in-house studies on the subject. A selection of these studies has been published as papers in peer-reviewed journals. Almost all the studies have involved, directly or indirectly, mobile operators, industry associations, competition authorities or regulators.[16]

This proliferation of studies looking at the effects of consolidation in the mobile telecom industry may be explained by both *demand* and *supply* factors. On the one hand, the last mobile merger wave of 2012-2016 likely increased the demand, from both regulators/competition authorities and firms, for a better understanding of the impact of mobile telecom mergers on relevant market outcomes (prices, innovation, quality, choice).[17] On the other hand, the mobile telecom industry is characterised by

15. Table 3.3 has sixteen entries because two studies (Frontier Economics, 2015 and WIK-Consult, 2015) appear twice as they include both case and industry studies.
16. Possibly the only exception is Csorba and Papai (2015).
17. In this respect, the ex post evaluations of the impact of past mergers have been used directly or indirectly to inform the policy debate on mobile mergers. Although these studies were considered in the decision process related to certain competition cases, there is no evidence that

a relatively good supply of relevant data both at the country level and at the single mobile operator level, with basic information on pricing, revenue and investments usually easily accessible either from publicly available sources or from data providers. This data availability, not easily found in other industries, might also have contributed to the large number of ex post evaluations conducted on this industry.

Despite being motivated by similar research questions, the studies reviewed in this chapter often obtain different results and reach different conclusions when analysing similar events or in some cases even the same event. The apparent inconsistencies in the findings of these studies may be explained by the specific choices in relation to methodologies, outcome variables, periods covered and level of aggregation (individual case study or industry study). Therefore, before discussing the results, it is useful to consider the different analytical approaches that have been taken across the different studies and provide a classification on this basis.

This substantial body of research can be classified under different dimensions. In the following, we analyse it under three broad dimensions: (1) scope of study, (2) methodology and (3) outcome variables (prices, investments, quality). Table 3.3 below presents an overview of these studies under the above classification and the following subsections provide more details on the main characteristics of the studies.

[A] Scope of the Studies

Two clearly defined sets of ex post evaluations of EU mobile telecom mergers can be distinguished: (1) case studies of a single merger decision and (2) industry wide studies pooling several consolidation (and entry) events together.

In the first type of studies, the aim is to assess a single merger decision. The outcomes post-merger are compared to the outcomes pre-merger or to the estimated counterfactual outcomes, i.e., outcomes that would have been expected to develop in the absence of the merger. The outcomes considered typically include measures of prices, investments and quality of service offered. These studies often combine a descriptive analysis of market developments and a quantitative empirical analysis aimed at identifying the impact of the merger. Results are assessed in isolation, for each single merger episode, and are not pooled across different cases. These studies usually exploit both a time dimension, as they compare outcomes over time (i.e., at least pre- and post-merger), and a cross-sectional dimension by comparing the country in which the merger takes place with a number of comparator countries that are not subject to changes in the market structure. Nine of the studies shown in Table 3.3 fall under this first category: Aguzzoni et al. (2015), WIK-Consult (2015), Frontier Economics (2015), Houngbonon (2015), RTR (2016), BWB (2016), Lear et al. (2017), GSMA (2017) and BEREC (2018).

their results shaped any particular merger decision. As an example, *see* the discussion in Annex B of the European Commission's decision of 11 May 2016 in case M.7612 – Hutchison 3G UK/Telefónica UK, in which some of the studies mentioned in this chapter are considered (Frontier Economics 2015; HSBC 2015; BWB 2016; RTR 2016; and Genakos et al., 2018;). The decision makes the point that: 'In any event, the Commission does not consider that the results from ex post studies can replace the specific assessment of the Transaction'.

Table 3.3 Scope, Methodologies and Variables Considered in the Ex Post Evaluation Studies

1. Case Studies	*Merger Case*					
Study	*Scope of the Analysis*	*Country/Period Covered*	*Method*	*Outcome Variables*[18]		*Comparators/Control Variables*
				Price	*Quality*	
Aguzzoni et al. (2015) * Prepared for DG Competition, ACM and RTR * Aguzzoni et al. (2018) is drawn from this report	T-Mobile/tele.ring (2006)	Austria 2004-2010	Difference-in-Differences Synthetic control method	Basket Price		12 European control countries MTR, GDP growth
	T-Mobile/Orange (2007)	Netherlands 2004-2010				
WIK-Consult (2015) * Prepared for Ofcom	T-Mobile/Orange (2007)	Netherlands 2005-2014	Descriptive analysis	Basket price	Capex/ subscribers	
	Hutchison 3G/ Orange (2012)	Austria 2005-2014		Basket price		
	Hutchison 3G/ Telefonica (2014)	Ireland 2005-2014		Average revenue/Gb		
	Telefonica/E-plus (2014)	Germany 2005-2015		Mobile price index of the German Federal Statistics Office		

18. Outcome variables are described in more detail in section 3.04[C].

1. Case Studies	*Merger Case*					
Study	*Scope of the Analysis*	*Country/Period Covered*	*Method*	*Outcome Variables*[18]		*Comparators/Control Variables*
				Price	*Quality*	
Frontier Economics (2015) * Prepared for GSMA	Hutchison 3G/ Orange (2012)	Austria 2005-2014	Descriptive analysis	ARPU, Price of voice, SMS and data per Mb		
Houngbonon G.V., (2015) * Benefits from financial support of Orange. Also reported by HSBC (2015)	Entry of Free (2012) Hutchison 3G/ Orange (2012)	France Austria 2013q1–2014q4 (no pre-merger or pre-entry observation)	Double differencing within a hedonic pricing model	Monthly price of tariff		Matching with 38 control countries Korea best match for France Italy best match for Austria
RTR (2016)	Hutchison 3G/ Orange (2012)	Austria 2011-2014	Difference-in-Differences Synthetic control method	Basket Price		14 EU control countries MTR, GDP growth
BWB (2016)	Hutchison 3G/ Orange (2012)	Austria 2011-2014	Merger simulation (demand estimation)	Basket price with actual usage at tariff level		Cost per subscriber
Lear et al. (2017) * Prepared for DG Competition	T-Mobile/Orange (2010)	United Kingdom 2009-2014	Difference-in-Differences Synthetic control method	Basket price	Capex	9/11 EU control countries MTR, GDP growth, VAT, exchange rate, GDP per capita

GSMA (2017)	Hutchison 3G/Orange (2012)	Austria 2011-2016	Difference-in-Differences Synthetic control method		4G coverage 4G/3G network speed	17 EU control countries GDP per capita, rural population, population density, 3G coverage/speed
BEREC (2018)	Hutchison 3G/Orange (2012)	Austria 2011H1-2016H1	Difference-in-Differences Synthetic control method	Basket price	Network test	7/10 EU control countries MTR, GDP growth
	Hutchison 3G/Telefonica (2014)	Ireland 2012H1-2016H1				
	Telefonica/E-plus (2014)	Germany 2012H2-2016H1				

2. Industry Studies							
Study	*Scope of the Analysis*	*Country/Period Covered*	*Method*	*Outcome Variables*[19]		*Measure of Intensity of Competition*[20]	*Comparators/ Control Variables*
				Price	*Quality*		
Affeldt P. and Nitsche R., (2014) * Draws on work conducted for Telefonica	Concentration and prices	23 European countries 2003-2012	Panel regression	Effective price per minute		HHI, number of competitors	Mean Capex per subscribers, GDP per capita

19. Outcome variables are described in more detail in section 3.04[C].
20. In some studies, instrumental variables are used to deal with the problem of endogeneity of the variable measuring market structure/competition (for a discussion, *see* section 3.04[B]). If used, the instruments are also listed in this column of the table.

2. Industry Studies							
Study	*Scope of the Analysis*	*Country/Period Covered*	*Method*	*Outcome Variables*[19]		*Measure of Intensity of Competition*[20]	*Comparators/ Control Variables*
				Price	*Quality*		
Csorba G. and Papai Z., (2015)	Concentration and prices	27 European countries 2003-2010	Panel regression	Basket price		Number of competitors: lagged variables used as instrument	GDP per capita, population, exchange rate, inflation, VAT, MTR, market share, MVNO presence, mobile penetration
Frontier Economics (2015) * Prepared for GSMA	Concentration, efficiencies and investment	24 European countries with 3 or 4 market players 2000-2014	Panel regression	Average revenue per minute	Capex per subscriber	HHI, lagged variables used as instrument	Dummy for: 4 players, 3G network, 4G network, auction. GDP per capita, share of prepaid connections, Capex
Houngbonon G.V. & Jeanjean F. (2016) * An author is affiliated with Orange. Also reported by HSBC (2015).	Concentration and investment	66 operators/22 national markets, EU and worldwide 2003-2012	Panel estimation		Capex/ Capex per subscriber	Lerner index with instruments: Lerner index lag and year of entry	Working age population, population density, fixed telephone penetration, MNO hosting MVNO

Houngbonon G.V. & Jeanjean F. (2017) * An author is affiliated with Orange.	Concentration and investment	17 EU countries 2006-2015	Panel estimation		Capex	Number of competitors and market share asymmetry, with instruments: political ideology and MTR	Population size, GDP per capita, competition from fixed line, number of operators
WIK-Consult(2015) * Prepared for Ofcom	Concentration and investment	12 countries (8 EU + Australia, Japan, South Korea and US) 2005-2013	Panel estimation		Capex / Capex per subscriber	Number of competitors, HHI	GDP per capita, timing of 4G auctions and launch, percentage of rural population, EBITDA
Genakos C., Valletti T. and Verboven F. (2018) * Draws on work conducted for Centre on Regulation in Europe	Concentration, prices and investment	28 OECD countries 2009-2014	Panel regression	Basket price Average revenue per user	Capex at firm and country level EBITDA margin	HHI with instruments: difference in MTR between most and least regulated MNO; number of competitors; cumulative entry/exit	Prepaid tariff dummy, GDP per capita, MTR

In the second type of studies, the aim is to assess the effects of a change in market structure in the industry. Rather than assessing the impact of a single episode, those studies group together several episodes of changes in the market structure (i.e., entry, exit and mergers), at different points in time and in different countries. The following studies fall under the second category: Affeldt and Nitsche (2014), Csorba and Papai (2015), Frontier Economics (2015), Houngbonon and Jeanjean (2016 and 2017), WIK-Consult (2015) and Genakos et al. (2018).

[B] Methodologies

A second relevant dimension to classify ex post studies is the adopted methodology.[21] The focus of this section is on quantitative methodologies as the reviewed studies are essentially quantitative studies that aim to identify a causal relationship between mergers or changes in market structure, on the one hand, and market outcomes (e.g., prices or investment), on the other hand. These studies often complement their quantitative analysis with a description of the market evolution (including a description of market players, market shares, price developments, etc.). Such a description can contribute to support the empirical strategy and findings. Two studies (Frontier Economics, 2015 and WIK-Consult, 2015) offer a relatively detailed descriptive analysis. Qualitative methodologies (e.g., surveys, interviews) might also be successfully applied to study EU mobile merger cases. However, in the available body of research, qualitative methods have not been very prominent yet.[22]

The adopted quantitative methodologies mainly include Difference-in-Differences, synthetic control group, merger simulation and panel regression analysis. The first three methodologies are mostly used in case studies and the latter in industry wide studies.

A challenge faced by the type of quantitative analyses reviewed in this chapter, whatever the methodology used, is the so-called endogeneity problem.[23] Typically, in an econometric regression framework, an assumption made is that the event under study (independent variable) is exogenous, meaning that this event (merger or change in market structure) shall not be dependent on the outcome variable (the dependent variable). Violation of this assumption leads to a bias in the estimated effect of the merger or the change in market structure on market outcomes. One main source of endogeneity is the failure of the estimated model to take into account important control variables (omitted variables). For example, some unobserved market specific changes in demand (e.g., changes in consumers taste) might affect the decision to merge of two

21. For a description of the methodologies applied to ex post evaluation, *see* Ilzkovitz and Dierx (2015) and Chapter 1 of this book.
22. For a qualitative analysis of a non-consummated mobile merger in the US, *see* Lepore (2017).
23. *See* Evans et al. (1993) for a discussion of endogeneity in price concentration studies. For a discussion of the problem of endogeneity in the context of ex post evaluations, *see* Ormosi et al. (2015) and Chapter 2.

firms. If the outcome variable is price and the unobserved changes have an impact both on the price level and the decision to merge, then the estimated effect of the merger on prices will be biased as it does not take into account the separate impact on price of the unobserved changes in demand. Another possible source of endogeneity is reverse causality between the dependent variable (price) and the independent variable (merger or change in market structure). For example, a slump in prices might trigger mergers in order for the merging parties to regain market power or to generate cost savings, while at the same time the merger will also affect the price in the market.

In some instances, it is possible to argue that changes in market structures might be exogenous and not dependent on the outcome variables of interest (price or investment). For example, a merger could also be triggered by other considerations like the decision of a smaller competitor to expand through acquisitions. In other instances, the validity of the exogeneity assumption might be more debatable. In these cases, there are different ways to deal with the endogeneity problem. The first approach is to use individual level (market or country) fixed effects in the estimated model. These fixed effects aim to capture the time invariant unobserved characteristics, thereby reducing possible omitted variable biases. This first solution is usually implemented in the reviewed econometric studies. Another approach is to use instruments, that is, finding variables that are independent from the relevant outcome variable (price or investment) but explain the endogenous variable (merger decision or the market structure). This second approach is implemented in a number of studies, especially when measures of market concentrations based on market shares (as firms' market shares are dependent on the firms' prices or investments) are used as opposed to discrete changes like merger events.

[1] Difference-in-Differences

Most of the case studies on mobile telecom mergers have adopted the so-called Difference-in-Differences methodology. This is the case for Aguzzoni et al. (2015), RTR (2016), Lear et al. (2017), GSMA (2017) and BEREC (2018). All these studies, with the exception of GSMA (2017), use the Difference-in-Differences methodology to estimate the price effects of the merger investigated. Lear et al. (2017) also estimates the impact of the merger on investments (firms' capital expenditures or Capex). GSMA (2017) estimates the impact of the merger on measures of services quality, such as 4G coverage and 4G/3G download and upload speeds of the network.

The Difference-in-Differences approach compares the outcomes of a treated group (a group that is affected by an event) to the outcomes of a control group (a group that is not affected by an event), and, at the same time, compares the outcomes of the period post-event to the outcomes of the period pre-event. Applied to merger cases, the event is the merger itself. The treated group usually consists of the merging firms or the country in which the merger takes place. The control group is a set of other foreign firms or countries not affected by the merger under investigation.

In its simplest form, the Difference-in-Differences methodology is intuitive and straightforward to apply, which also explains why it is so often used. However, Difference-in-Differences provides correct estimates only under certain conditions that may be difficult to verify. For Difference-in-Differences to represent a credible identification strategy, the control group needs to satisfy two requirements. First, it has to be subject to similar unobserved factors as the treatment group ('common trend'). Second, the studied merger should have no impact on the control group ('no spillover effects'). Under these assumptions, the variations over time in the outcome variable observed in the control group are a good approximation of the variation that would have occurred in the treated group absent the merger. If these assumptions are not satisfied then the estimates are likely to be biased. Therefore, it is important to interpret the Difference-in-Differences results with care and understand whether the specific application looks credible.

Given the importance of the common trend assumption, the selection of an appropriate control group is a key aspect of the Difference-in-Differences methodology, as not all possible comparators represent an appropriate control. In the reviewed studies the control group usually consists of a selection of similar countries (European countries, preferably of a similar size) that did not experience themselves changes in market structure (mergers, entry or exit) during the studied period. This is important, because any change in market structure included in the control group may jeopardise the estimation of the merger effect. The common trend assumption cannot be verified directly as it is not possible to test whether absent the merger the treated and control group would have evolved similarly. However, an assessment of developments pre-merger can shed light on the validity of this assumption. Such an assessment may be only descriptive based on a graphical analysis, or be more statistical when based on formal tests (Aguzzoni et al., 2015, BEREC, 2018, Lear et al., 2017).[24]

The second assumption, which requires that the control group is not affected by the merger in the treated country, poses fewer concerns. Indeed, the European mobile markets are considered national in scope. Therefore, one can assume that concentration events taking place in one country have no direct impact on other European countries.

A practical limitation of the Difference-in-Differences methodology is that it generally requires a sizeable amount of data. In principle, the ideal framework to apply Difference-in-Differences is one with many treated and control units. This is clearly not the case in studies analysing individual merger decisions, where there is generally one treated unit. However, in such cases it is still possible to make robust inference by having access to a large sample of control units. Faced with this limitation, one may be tempted to artificially increase the number of treated or control units by, for example, using less aggregated data. This should be avoided, as it may bias the statistical tests.

24. The statistical tests generally investigate the extent to which the differences between treated and control group are constant over time. A small sample size (both in terms of the length of the time series and the number of treatment and control groups) may affect the results of the common trend tests.

Therefore, estimated coefficients may be found to be statistically significant, while, in fact, they are not.[25]

[2] Synthetic Control Group

The synthetic control group method is similar in spirit to the Difference-in-Differences method. This relatively recent method was developed by Abadie and Gardeazabal (2003) and was later extended by Abadie, Diamond and Hainmueller (2010 and 2015). In the context of the evaluation of mobile telecom mergers, this approach has been applied in most of the case studies surveyed in this article: Aguzzoni et al. (2015), RTR (2016), Lear et al. (2017), GSMA (2017) and BEREC (2018).

A detailed description of this methodology is beyond the scope of this chapter.[26] In essence, the idea of the synthetic control group method is to apply a data driven routine to select an 'optimal' control group from a pool of possible control candidates. The optimal control group (the synthetic control) is the one that is the 'closest' and the 'most similar' to the treatment group before the treatment, according to a number of predictor variables that include also past realisations of the outcome variable of interest.

This method was developed in the political economy evaluation literature in which it is typical to evaluate a single treated unit versus a pool of potential controls. Therefore, it appears to be well suited for ex post evaluations of mergers that are characterised by a single treated unit as well (the market affected by the merger). Similar to Difference-in-Differences, the method works best if there is a large number of control groups. This is because a larger sample of control units allows a better estimation of the synthetic control and improves the statistical properties of the estimates. The lack of a large number of control countries (usually lower than fifteen in the reviewed studies)[27] poses a serious limitation to the use of this method applied to mobile telecom merger cases. Access to larger datasets going beyond the European Union national markets might improve the performance of this method.

[3] Merger Simulation

Only one of the reviewed studies (BWB, 2016) adopts a merger simulation approach to estimate the impact of the merger on prices. Merger simulation is a more sophisticated technique mostly used in the context of ex ante assessments of mergers rather than for

25. A detailed discussion can be found in Bertrand, Duflo and Mullainathan (2004), and Cameron, Gelbach and Miller (2008).
26. *See* Abadie et al. (2010) for a detailed discussion.
27. In the reviewed studies, the considered candidates for being control countries are less than fifteen. The reason is that many countries have to be excluded, as they themselves experience variation in the market structure, making them not suitable as a comparator (comparators need to have a stable market structure to correctly predict the impact of the merger in the treated country).

ex post evaluations. Even in sectors other than the mobile telecom industry, there are very few ex post evaluations that adopt such a methodology.[28]

The BWB study assesses the impact of the Hutchison 3G/Orange merger on prices using merger simulation techniques. This method allows estimating the counterfactual prices (prices absent the merger) based on a demand model and assuming firm profit maximisation to estimate marginal costs.[29] The impact of the merger on prices is equal to the difference between the observed prices post-merger and the predicted prices in the absence of the merger as estimated on the basis of the model. Merger simulation techniques are more data demanding than Difference-in-Differences or synthetic control applications and rely on a set of assumptions related to the structure of demand and the nature of competition. The advantage of this approach is that it does not require data from several control countries to construct the counterfactual scenario. The methodology can be applied with data on the affected country only. Moreover, the method might also be used to estimate different counterfactual scenarios, for example, separating the effect of the merger from the impact of the remedies. Hence, if very detailed data are available for a single country, merger simulations may be quite informative.

The assumptions made in the application of the merger simulation should nevertheless be closely considered before interpreting the results. Both the assumptions made at the modelling stage and the estimation of the key parameters should be scrutinised and assessed in view of the competition dynamics observed in the market. For example in the BWB (2016) study, the estimation of the price effects of the merger hinges on the forecast of the counterfactual marginal costs in the post-merger period. This forecast appears to be based on a relatively simple linear regression whose assumptions might be questioned easily.

[4] Multi-event Panel Regression Analysis

Multi-event panel regression analysis groups several merger events together rather than evaluating the impact of a single transaction on its own. The aim of this type of studies is to estimate an average relationship between some outcome variables and a measure of change in market structure, while controlling for relevant demand and cost variables. Studies of this kind are clearly related to the rich collection of papers in the industrial organisation literature, which look at the relationship between the competitive features of the markets and prices, also known as price concentration analysis.[30]

28. For other examples not related to the mobile telecom industry, *see* Miller and Weinberg (2017) and Björnerstedt and Verboven (2016).
29. First, using quantities, prices, tariff characteristics and further control variables, a demand model is estimated. Second, using prices, quantities and the coefficients of the demand function, pre-merger marginal costs are obtained from first order conditions of firms' profit maximisation. Third, counterfactual marginal costs (marginal costs post-merger in the absence of the merger) are predicted in a regression framework using usage data, time trend and other control variables. Finally, the coefficients from demand estimation and predicted counterfactual marginal costs are used to compute how prices would have evolved in the absence of the merger.
30. *See* Weiss (1989) and Newmark (2004) for a survey of this literature.

Examples of this methodology can be found in the following studies reviewed in this chapter: Affeldt and Nitsche (2014), Csorba and Papai (2015), Frontier Economics (2015), Houngbonon and Jeanjean (2016 and 2017), WIK-Consult (2015) and Genakos et al. (2018).

One often made criticism of price concentration studies is that they are not fully controlling for unobserved factors that affect both prices and market structure, the so-called endogeneity problem, mentioned at the beginning of this subsection. To address the endogeneity problem the studies discussed in this article have access to panel data thus allowing them to use country or operator fixed effects to control for unobserved time invariant country specific characteristics. All the studies reviewed in this chapter make use of fixed effects. A subset of studies, Frontier Economics (2015), Houngbonon and Jeanjean (2016 and 2017) and Genakos et al. (2018), use instrumental variables to deal with the endogeneity problem. These authors use an instrumental variable to replace the independent variable measuring the degree of competition to avoid problems of endogeneity between this measure of competition and the dependent variable. The instrumental variables most often used include mobile termination rates (MTRs), number of operators and lagged variables (*see* Table 3.3 'Industry Studies'). It is important to test the validity of the chosen instrument, as, for instance, it is done in Houngbonon and Jeanjean (2016), Houngbonon and Jeanjean (2017) and Genakos et al. (2018).

If the panel consists of two time periods and only one country experiences a change in market structure, panel regression estimates correspond to the standard Difference-in-Differences estimates. The use of multiple periods and multiple events means that the identification of the relationships of interest depends on different control groups at different points in time (*see* Genakos et al., 2018).

By grouping together many events and allowing for many treatment units, price concentration studies might have the advantage of suffering less from possible unobserved shocks that affect only the treated units at the time of the studied event. Considering many events together might average out the impact of these shocks, something that is not possible with a single case study. However, a potential disadvantage is that, by grouping together different events, there is the risk of not controlling for some case-specific heterogeneity. For example, changes in concentration levels due to mergers are treated equally as more organic changes in concentration levels, and changes in concentration due to mergers with remedies may be mixed with changes for mergers without remedies. Such sources of case-specific heterogeneity are more neatly controlled for in single case studies in which it is possible to study more in-depth the market developments around the event of interest, also from a qualitative and descriptive point of view.

[C] Outcome and Explanatory Variables

Despite their different methodological approaches, the studies under review consider two main categories of outcome variables: price and quality. Some studies use only one outcome variable while others look at both price and quality measures. Both variables are relevant competition policy outcomes directly related to consumer welfare and therefore typically assessed in merger control.[31]

At first sight, price and quality appear to be relatively intuitive outcome variables. Nevertheless, there is a significant variation in the measures of price and quality used in the different studies. As the measures of price and quality used may have an impact on the results and the conclusions that can be drawn from the analysis, a closer look at the proposed measures is necessary.

[1] Price

As noted in section 3.02[B], measuring price in the context of the mobile telecom industry poses some challenges as consumers usually purchase a bundle of services generally comprising different amounts of voice, SMS and data. Further, when consumers are purchasing mobile telecom services, they might also simultaneously conclude contracts related to other services like handset, or media content that might or might not be cross-subsidised by their mobile subscription. In addition, the offered tariffs might include some initial set-up cost, a monthly charge for a predefined bundle of consumption and pay-as-you-go rates for out-of-bundle consumption. Eventually, what consumers pay for their mobile subscription depends on their tariff plan, their consumption levels and the type of services consumed.

In this context, studying price developments in the mobile telecom industry poses the challenge of identifying a one-dimensional index to measure price. Desirable features of this index are that it should reflect the prices that actual consumers pay when making purchases and it should be consistent over time and across different countries or operators.

The studies under review propose different approaches for the estimation of this price index. Three broad approaches can be identified: revenue related measures, the basket expenditure approach and hedonic pricing models.

[a] Average Revenue Per User (ARPU)

Revenue data for mobile telecom operators are usually available and a popular metric used as a performance indicator in the mobile telecom industry is the average revenue per user (ARPU). ARPU is an aggregate revenue figure that relates total revenues to the subscriber base. ARPU depends on actual consumption (voice, data, SMS, services) and also includes revenues of side services (for example media content purchases) or revenues from call termination.[32] By definition, changes in ARPU levels might be driven by changes in consumption levels and the nature of services consumed rather

31. The European Commission Horizontal Merger Guidelines (European Commission 2004) define increased market power as 'the ability of one or more firms to profitably increase prices, reduce output, choice or quality of goods and services, diminish innovation, or otherwise influence parameters of competition'.
32. Call termination fees are paid by the calling operator to the network of the called customers. These are monetary transfers between operators that generate revenues and costs but that are not directly considered by customers in their purchasing decisions.

than by changes in prices. Moreover, there might be heterogeneity in the way ARPU is computed across mobile operators depending on the actual services offered by operators and considered in this metric. Consequently, ARPU may not be an appropriate indicator for comparisons across different countries and operators or for comparisons over time when services and usage might change. This measure is more a measure of operator's profitability than an indicator of consumer prices.[33]

Seeking to address these various issues related to the use of ARPU, two earlier studies propose to assess price effects by adjusting the ARPU measures to take into account usage. Affeldt and Nitsche (2014) consider voice revenues taking into account minutes of voice calls to define a metric called effective price per minute (EPPM). Frontier Economics (2015) uses a slightly different metric as it uses revenue (not specifically related to voice) divided by voice consumption to define the average revenue per minute (ARPM). Both metrics, as acknowledged in the respective studies, do not account for SMS and data usage. Not controlling for data usage may indeed be problematic, especially since data usage, in the period considered by these studies, was already a relevant parameter in mobile telecom packages.

[b] Basket Expenditure Approach

Most of the later studies reviewed in this chapter[34] adopt a basket expenditure approach, to estimate a price index, rather than using revenue-based metrics. The basket expenditure approach aims to represent the bills paid by consumers for their mobile telecom consumption (voice, SMS and data). By doing so, this alternative metric is directly related to the prices charged for the different services, making it more relevant for consumers as it reflects the prices they face, based on their consumption level, when deciding between different operators and tariff plans.

With access to all available tariff plans and consumption profiles, it should in principle be possible to accurately measure the evolution of consumers' expenditures on mobile telecom services while controlling for the variation in consumption levels. However, it is rarely possible to obtain access to such a detailed level of data. Among the studies reviewed, only BWB (2016) had access to a detailed dataset comprising all actual tariffs of the operators and the average consumption profiles at the single tariff level. However, this detailed dataset was available for one country (Austria) only and no comparison was possible with potential control countries. The study therefore conducts a structural estimation based only on the information of the country affected by the merger.[35]

33. For example, Genakos et al. (2018) consider that ARPU is not a meaningful measure for prices paid by consumers and use ARPU as a measure of mobile operators' performance.
34. Aguzzoni et al. (2015), WIK-Consult (2015), RTR (2016), BWB (2016), Lear et al. (2017), BEREC (2018), Csorba and Papai (2015) and Genakos et al. (2018).
35. In the case of the BWB (2016) study, access to this detailed dataset was possible because of the inspection powers of the Austrian Competition Authority, which could oblige operators to deliver the data required for the analysis. However, this power was only limited to the Austrian territory and therefore the same type of data could not be collected for possible comparator countries.

More generally, the adopted approach in several other studies is to estimate a basket based expenditure for hypothetical representative consumers. According to this approach, the first step is to estimate the consumption level of the representative consumer based on the country's national average consumption level. Then, given the consumption level, the second step consists in computing the expenditure of the representative consumer for each single tariff available at each point in time. Finally, the third step consists in the selection of the most representative tariff or tariffs to compose the basket based expenditure index. In the reviewed studies, the approach followed to make this selection is to choose the tariffs that minimise the expenditure of the representative consumer given its consumption level. In order to allow for a certain degree of uncertainty, more than one tariff is usually selected for any given point in time and for each consumption level.[36]

The expenditure index computed under this approach is representative of the level of expenditure for starting a new contract and does not necessarily reflect the conditions faced by legacy customers. At the same time, this also means that this measure provides a timely representation of price changes. Indeed price changes in the mobile industry are usually introduced in the form of new tariffs rather than by changing the price conditions of the legacy tariffs.[37]

Another important modelling choice of the basked based expenditure index is the estimation of consumption levels. In the reviewed studies, consumption levels usually vary by country (although they are assumed to be constant across operators within the same country).[38]

For what concerns the possible variation of consumption levels over time, there are two approaches with different pros and cons. The first approach is to keep the consumption level fixed for the whole period under study. This has the advantage of clearly isolating expenditure variation related to price effects only. However, the drawback could be that over time a certain consumption level becomes obsolete and not anymore representative of prevailing consumption levels. This poses the risk of selecting irrelevant tariffs in the computation of the expenditure index. Such risk is particularly important for studies that cover a longer period or for the more recent studies that cover a period in which data consumption increased significantly over a relatively short period. To account for this problem, some studies allow for changes in the consumption levels. This is usually done by using different consumption levels for different periods, while adding control variables to capture the impact of the changes

36. This selection of tariffs is needed because a consumer will likely take up the tariff that will minimise its expenditure given its consumption level. For example, a customer with a limited average consumption would not take up an unlimited plan but would rather opt for a more moderate plan or a pay-as-you-go contract.
37. Further, as the legacy customers will renew or start a new contract over time, they will also face the new conditions although with a time lag.
38. It is fair to assume that the tariffs offered in each country reflect the country specific consumption profiles and adopting the same consumption level across different countries increases the risk of picking irrelevant tariffs for some countries.

in consumption levels on expenditures.[39] However, under this approach, the impact of price changes might be confounded with consumption shifts if the price changes take place at the same time as the changes in the consumption level and if the changes in consumption levels are not properly controlled for. Among the reviewed studies, Lear et al. (2017) and Genakos et al. (2018) use both a fixed and a changing consumption level and find similar results under both approaches. BEREC (2018) also accounts for fixed and varying consumption levels reaching similar conclusions.

[c] Hedonic Pricing Model

A completely different approach to study price developments is the hedonic pricing model. Under this approach, the costs of a bundle of telecom services (that might not necessarily coincide with the customer bills)[40] is regressed on the characteristics of the bundle (minutes of voice call, GB of data) in order to isolate the impact of each tariff component. This method is proposed by Houngbonon (2015), although in a peculiar Difference-in-Differences setting that makes use of only post-merger information.[41] Another paper that uses the hedonic pricing model is Nicolle et al. (2018).[42]

With the hedonic approach, it might be possible to isolate the effect of the merger on specific components of the total tariff, such as the implicit costs of data and the implicit costs of voice. However, this method is also prone to bias, as the cost of the different components is not estimated on the basis of the actual consumption patterns but on the basis of the maximum available allowances.[43] This bias is not present in the basket expenditure approach where the expenditure is based on the average consumption and not on the maximum available allowances. Furthermore, hedonic pricing models are estimated based only on tariffs in which a user pays a monthly fee for a

---

39. If the model allows for a change in consumption level, it is important to introduce control variables in the model that are able to capture the shift in consumption levels and its consequent impact on expenditure.
40. This is because by definition the cost of a bundle does not consider possible out-of-bundle costs. By contrast, when using the basket expenditure approach, out-of-bundle costs can be taken into account.
41. The paper has access to post-merger information only for its study of the effects of the Hutchison 3G/Orange merger in Austria in 2012 and the entry of Free in France in 2013. It is not clear that the estimated effect could be ascribed to the merger or entry episodes as the appropriate pre-event comparison is lacking. Therefore, the study seems to identify the presence of different trajectories post events. However, it is not possible to relate these different trajectories to the studied events.
42. This paper is not reviewed in detail in this chapter as it mainly assesses the entry of Free in the French mobile market whereas the focus of this chapter is on the assessment of case studies concerning merger episodes.
43. This might be problematic because the cost per unit should be computed based on the actual consumption. As an example, if an operator offers a maximum allowance of 10 GB of data but the average consumption is only 5 GB, there is a risk of significantly underestimating the unit cost. At the same time, if an operator doubles the data allowance, then the model would record a reduction in price by half, when in reality the actual increase in consumption and the resulting decrease in price might be significantly lower.

predefined bundle of allowances and they do not take into account possible out-of-bundle consumption.[44] This might be problematic when studying periods or markets in which pay-as-you-go tariffs represented a significant share of the market.

[2] Quality

Beyond price, the other outcome variable considered in the literature is quality. The studies presented here propose different approaches to measure quality.

The earlier papers measure quality with indirect proxies such as investments. As the mobile telecom industry is a capital-intensive industry, it has been argued that there is a direct link between network investment and quality delivered for the benefit of the customers (Frontier Economics, 2015). However, investment is only an indirect proxy of quality. The link between investment and quality would be stronger for those investments directly related to the improvement of network quality but might be weaker for other network investments or for non-network related investments.

Several studies look at network investments (as measured by network firms' capital expenditures or network Capex) as a way to establish a closer link between investment and quality of service. Capex is a commonly available financial indicator, which might explain why it is often used. However, doubts might be raised on the effective comparability of these Capex measures across operators (as also acknowledged in Frontier Economics, 2015), especially when operators have heterogeneous networks (including their fixed network), or take part in network sharing agreements. For example, in the study by Lear et al. (2017), the authors have access to network Capex at the operator level but are unable to differentiate between mobile or fixed Capex, thereby weakening the link with mobile network quality. To account for differences in the size of the network, Capex is usually divided by the number of subscribers (e.g., in Frontier Economics 2015).

Another possible drawback of looking at Capex is that it is likely to display irregular patterns over time due to the timing of the investment decisions. Moreover, network quality might not be explained by the network investment within a single year only. Historical investments need to be taken into account as well. Whether or not to include spectrum auction fees in the Capex figures is another open question, as it further increases the fluctuations of the variable and the differences across operators or countries. Houngbonon and Jeanjean (2016 and 2017) include spectrum fees in their Capex measures whereas most of the other studies do not take such fees into account.[45]

GSMA (2017) and BEREC (2018) assess the impact of recent mergers on more direct measures of quality. The first study considers 4G Coverage and 4G/3G Network speed as a proxy for quality. This study benefits from having access to a large dataset covering multiple countries for several years, allowing the use of an econometric

44. This means that pay-as-you-go tariffs, that do not have a fixed monthly fee, would not be included unless an assumption is made on a consumption level for each component (similarly to what is done under the basket approach).
45. However, it should be noted that not all the studies clearly report how they constructed their Capex measure and what it contains.

framework to study the relationship between mergers and coverage and speed. Differently from GSMA (2017), BEREC (2018) considers a more holistic measure of quality that includes several voice and data connectivity tests and metrics.[46] This measure is therefore more comprehensive as it goes beyond considering only network coverage and speed test components, as was done in GSMA (2018). However, a limitation of BEREC (2018) is that the data and connection tests are run for Germany and Austria only, due to data availability. Therefore, BEREC (2018) can only perform a descriptive comparison of the quality developments before and after the mergers in these two countries.

[3] Explanatory Variables

The reviewed studies aim to estimate a relationship between changes in market structure/competition and some relevant measures of market outcomes. The measures considered relate to price and quality outcomes, as described in the two above subsections. However, price and quality are driven not only by the level and by the type of competition between operators, but also by other factors affecting market conditions. Therefore, it is necessary to also account for these other factors when estimating the impact of competition on price and quality. In the econometric regression framework adopted in the reviewed studies, this is often done by including (explanatory or control) variables that aim to capture these other factors affecting market outcomes.

Typically, the variables considered relate to demand or supply factors. Demand factors include the size of the population or the take up of mobile services (penetration). Another demand variable typically used is the level of or the variation in GDP, used as a proxy for income and therefore for demand for mobile services, under the assumption that higher income or an increase in income would command a higher demand for mobile services.

Supply factors aim to capture cost or technology drivers that might affect pricing or quality decisions taken by firms. Supply variables include measures of population density (or population living in rural areas), as serving a more dispersed population is likely to be more costly. Other variables are related to the timing of spectrum auctions or the timing of the launch of 3G or 4G services, as this would affect the evolution of investment costs of firms. A variable found in several studies is the MTRs. These are costs set by regulators, that MNOs pay to each other, depending on the proportion of calls terminating to each other's networks, and they should reflect elements of network costs. Beyond serving as a proxy for network cost, MTRs, or more precisely in-country differences in MTRs, can also be indicative of the degree of market asymmetry. Indeed, MTRs have been employed by regulators as a means to secure new entrants or smaller operators a stronger position in the market by allowing them to get higher termination rates

46. For more information on the methodology, *see* BEREC (2018).

than the one of established players. Therefore, it has been argued (e.g., in Genakos et al. 2018) that in-country differences in MTRs can be used as an instrument for HHI.[47]

Another way to control for other factors affecting price and quality outcomes is to introduce fixed effects allowing taking into account all time invariant characteristics, observable and non-observable, that have an influence on the relevant outcomes. For instance, the inclusion of these fixed effects implies that it is not necessary to control for population size, characteristics of the population or of the country if these variables do not change significantly over the period considered.

§3.05 EVIDENCE ON THE IMPACT OF MOBILE TELECOM MERGERS

As discussed above, two main types of studies can be identified depending on the scope of the analysis: specific case studies and industry wide studies. The discussion of the results on the impact of mobile telecom mergers necessarily needs to distinguish between these two different types of studies as they are based on different identification assumptions and have different aims.

Further, it should be noted that, in the reviewed industry wide studies, the main events leading to changes in market structure are the merger episodes. Other changes in market structure occur in case of entry or of changes in market shares of the existing players in the market (as the reviewed studies often use HHI to measure changes in market structure). However, the cases of entry are very rare and the size of the HHI variation induced by organic fluctuations in market shares is of a different and smaller order of magnitude as compared to the sharp changes implied by the merger episodes. Therefore, merger episodes are likely to be the events that contribute the most to the identification of the relationship between market structure and outcomes in the industry wide studies. However, these industry studies might not appropriately reflect the heterogeneity that is present in each merger case. In particular, one source of heterogeneity is related to the presence and extent of remedies attached to the merger. This heterogeneity is taken into consideration in single case studies but might not be controlled for in industry wide studies, which therefore might be prone to bias.

[A] Evidence Related to Single Case Studies

Table 3.4 below presents a summary of the results of the studies concerning the six mobile mergers subject to an ex post evaluation. These mergers took place during the period 2006-2014. The results of these ex post evaluations are grouped per merger case, which are presented in chronological order in the next subsections.

47. The Herfindahl-Hirschman Index (HHI) is a measure of concentration typically considered in industrial organisation. It is defined as the sum of the squares of the market shares of the firms within the industry and ranges between 0 and 10,000 (if whole percentages are used). The higher the HHI, the higher is the concentration.

Table 3.4 Summary of Evidence Related to Single Case Studies

Case Studies	*Merger Case*	*Main Findings*
Aguzzoni et al. (2015)	T-Mobile/tele.ring, AU (2006)	In Austria, it is unlikely that the merger T-Mobile/tele.ring (including the remedies) resulted in a significant price increase compared to the counterfactual of no merger.
Aguzzoni et al. (2015)	T-Mobile/Orange, NL (2007)	In the Netherlands, the earlier KPN/Telfort merger and the later T-Mobile/Orange merger are associated with a relative price increase compared to the counterfactual of no merger.
WIK-Consult (2015)	T-Mobile/Orange, NL (2007)	It cannot be excluded that the merger contributed to high mobile charges in the Netherlands.
WIK-Consult (2015)	Hutchison 3G/Orange, AT (2012)	The study reports a price increase at the time of the merger.
WIK-Consult (2015)	Hutchison 3G/Telefonica, IE (2014)	The merger led to more symmetric market positions of the leading MNOs.
WIK-Consult (2015)	Telefonica/E-plus, DE (2014)	The four players market might have preserved a competitive environment.
Frontier Economics (2015)	Hutchison 3G/Orange, AT (2012)	A descriptive before and after analysis does not find any increase in prices in Austria following the merger.
Houngbonon (2015)	Impact of the entry of a 4th operator (Free) in France (2013)	Entry of Free in France is associated with an increase in the prices for data and a decrease in the prices for voice calls[48] while the opposite is found in Austria.
Houngbonon (2015)	Hutchison 3G/Orange, AT (2012)	The H3G/Orange merger can be associated with a fall in the unit cost of mobile data when sold as part of a bundle.
RTR (2016)	Hutchison 3G/Orange, AT (2012)	The H3G/Orange and TA/Yesss! mergers in Austria led to considerable price effects in the two-year period after the merger.
BWB (2016)	Hutchison 3G/Orange, AT (2012)	The H3G/Orange and TA/Yesss! mergers in Austria led to considerable price effects within a two-year period.

48. Another study adopting a similar hedonic pricing approach, Nicolle et al. (2018), finds that in France, the computed quality-adjusted price index (encompassing both voice and data) decreased by about 42.8% and the weighted average prices without quality-adjustment decreased by 8.7% between May 2011 and December 2014. A large part of this price reduction is related to the launch of 4G services, about 60% of the impact, while increased competition associated with the entry of Free accounted for about 20%.

Case Studies	*Merger Case*	*Main Findings*
Lear et al. (2017)	T-Mobile/Orange, UK (2010)	The merger as modified by the remedies did not have negative effects on prices nor on investments as MNOs in the UK lowered their prices and possibly raised their Capex as compared to the counterfactual of no merger.
GSMA (2017)	Hutchison 3G/Orange, AT (2012)	The merger had a significant positive impact in terms of increased 4G coverage and quality (download and upload speed) relative to the counterfactual of no merger.
BEREC (2018)	Hutchison 3G/Orange, AT (2012) Hutchison 3G/Telefonica, IE (2014) Telefonica/E-plus, DE (2014)	In all three cases, there is evidence of retail price increases relative to the counterfactual of no merger. These price increases are not persistent and the effects vary across countries, user profile and time after the merger. For the German case, evidence on network connectivity indicates a worsening of quality in the short and medium terms with uncertain results for the long term.

[1] T-Mobile/tele.ring (Austria, 2006), T-Mobile/Orange (Netherlands, 2007) and T-Mobile/Orange (UK, 2010)

Among the six merger cases, two saw a change in the market structure from five to four players: the T-Mobile/tele.ring merger in Austria and the T-Mobile/Orange merger in the UK. The European Commission approved these two mergers conditional on structural remedies including the divestment of spectrum. The UK case also entailed a remedy for a national roaming agreement. The two merger cases seem to share other features as well: in both instances, the remedies strengthened the competitive position of the last entrant in the market, which happened to be Hutchison in both countries. The first merger is studied in Aguzzoni et al. (2015) and the second in Lear et al. (2017). Both studies apply a similar ex post evaluation method to study the price impact of the two merger episodes using a basket expenditures measure as a proxy for prices (as described in subsections 3.04[B] and [C]).

In both cases, the findings indicate that the mergers did not lead to an increase in prices as compared to the counterfactual of no merger. Aguzzoni et al. (2015) find that the Austrian merger as modified by the remedies leads to a relative[49] price reduction

49. In the discussion of the results, unless otherwise specified, the estimated price reduction is computed relative to the expected developments without the merger as estimated through the applied methodology (e.g., Difference-in-differences, structural model).

between 2% and 20% depending on the consumption profile considered. Lear et al. (2017) reports that the UK merger as modified by the remedies resulted in a relative price reduction between 9% and 19% depending on the consumption profiles. Therefore, in both cases, the post-merger developments indicate that the market became more competitive relative to the counterfactual of no merger at least for what concerns prices, ruling out anticompetitive effects related to the mergers. It is to be noted that both mergers entailed remedies. In the econometric analysis using a Difference-in-Differences approach, it is not possible to separate the impact of the concentration from the impact of the remedies. Therefore, it is not possible to infer what would have happened if the two mergers had been allowed without remedies or with a different configuration of the remedies.

Another merger that took place around the same period is the T-Mobile/Orange merger that occurred in 2007 in the Netherlands. In the sample of the six merger cases reviewed, this was the first merger leading to a change in market structure from four to three mobile operators. Another distinctive feature of this case relates to the absence of any remedy, as the transaction was cleared without conditions. The results (Aguzzoni et al., 2015) indicate that following the merger, prices (estimated with the basket expenditure approach) increased between 10% and 15% relative to the estimated prices absent the merger. Notably this merger took place shortly after another merger (between KPN and Telfort), which was also cleared without conditions. Therefore, it is not possible to ascribe the found price increase to the T-Mobile/Orange merger only. Rather, the available evidence indicates that the two successive episodes of market concentration together are associated with a relative price increase.

Descriptive evidence collected in WIK-Consult (2015) seems to support these findings related to the Netherlands. According to this study, it cannot be excluded that a reduction in competition following the mergers may have contributed to higher mobile charges in the Netherlands: mobile charges were among the lowest in 2006, compared to a set of 12 countries, but became relatively more expensive after the mergers (ranking of 4-6 out of 12 countries). WIK-Consult (2015) also shows that the EBITDA/revenue margin of T-Mobile increased significantly after the merger while the investments, as measured by Capex/Revenue, remained fairly constant, or even started to decline.

Due to data limitations, the above-described quantitative case studies estimate mobile prices by means of an expenditure basket approach that only considers the consumption and prices of voice and message services (notably excluding data consumption[50]). This limitation might not be problematic for the assessment of the mergers in Austria and the Netherlands, which date from 2006 and 2007 respectively. However, this might be more problematic (as acknowledged by the study itself) for the assessment of the UK merger, which was implemented in 2010 when data consumption was already a relevant competitive parameter.[51]

50. The Lear study analysing the T-Mobile/Orange merger in the UK considers two baskets: the OECD 2006 basket and the OECD 2010 basket. The 2010 OECD basket includes information on data consumption only starting from the first quarter of 2012.
51. *See* discussion in Lear et al. (2017), section 6.5, p. 100.

Because of the method used to compute basket prices (as described in subsection 3.04[C]) the above results are indicative of the price developments of the new tariffs.[52] At the same time, it cannot be excluded that the overall bills paid by actual consumers moved together with the estimated expenditure basket for new tariffs only. For example, Lear et al. (2017) show that the developments of ARPU (that include actual expenditures of the whole customer base) closely matched the developments of their expenditure basket index.

For the UK merger, Lear et al. (2017) also conducted a quantitative analysis of the effect of the merger on investments. The study concludes that the merger as modified by the remedies did not have a negative impact on investments as Capex per operator increased[53] both for the merging parties and for the other operators for which Capex data were available. The study is nevertheless cautious in interpreting this finding, as the measure of Capex is deemed imprecise (it also includes fixed-line Capex for some operators and the spectrum outlays that vary significantly across countries in terms of timing and monetary amounts).

[2] Hutchison 3G/Orange (Austria, 2012)

The next case in chronological order is the Austrian merger between Hutchison 3G and Orange in 2012. This transaction took place at the same time of the sale of Orange sub-brand Yesss![54] to the incumbent A1 Telekom Austria. The first transaction was assessed by the European Commission while the second was assessed by the Austrian Cartel Court and cleared without conditions shortly before the European Commission approved the Hutchison 3G/Orange merger subject to commitments. Hence, any study that assesses the Austrian market over that period necessarily estimates the joint effect of the two transactions, as due to their simultaneity it is not possible to separate their individual effects.[55]

The commitments offered by the merging parties in the Hutchison 3G/Orange merger consisted in: (1) the offer of spectrum to facilitate the entry of a new MNO; and (2) the offer to facilitate the market entry of MVNOs, including an upfront commitment with one MVNO. However, the first commitment never materialised and the entry of the MVNO resulting from the upfront commitment only took place in December 2014. During the course of 2015, the market entry of further MVNOs contributed to the development of the MVNO sector (RTR 2016).

The 2012 Austrian merger, as of today, is the mobile telecom concentration episode that has attracted the highest interest in terms of ex post evaluation studies as several studies assessed the impact of this transaction on prices and quality.

52. As explained in subsection 3.04[C] the basket approach is computed on the basis of the tariffs currently advertised by mobile operators ('new tariffs'). However, legacy customers could be on a different tariff plan that is not marketed anymore to new customers.
53. Although Capex per subscriber showed a decline.
54. At the time of the sale Yesss! had a market share of around 5%.
55. We therefore refer to both transactions as the '2012 Austrian merger'.

Among the studies reviewed in this article, Frontier Economics (2015) is the first to look at the price developments in Austria following the transaction, although only in descriptive terms. This study first notes that the ARPU metric had remained relatively constant until the first quarter of 2014. Based on this observation, the study argues that prices did not increase following the merger. The study also considers a corrected ARPU metric by looking at the price per average megabyte of voice, SMS and data.[56] Also considering this metric, the study finds that prices in Austria between 2013 and the first quarter of 2014 did not increase compared to the pre-merger trend of the Austrian prices.

The evidence presented by Frontier Economics (2015), however, appears to be rather weak. The developed price metric is extremely sensitive to the variation in data consumption. Moreover, the analysis is based on a simple in-country before and after approach. Under this approach, the post-merger developments absent the merger are estimated only looking at the pre-merger trend in Austrian prices. This approach therefore disregards the impact of possible developments, not captured by the pre-merger information, that would have taken place in any case in the post-merger period even absent the concentration (e.g., a steeper reduction in cost or changes in the demand that are not related to the transaction but simply to the evolution of mobile telecom markets). Not controlling for these aspects is likely to bias the analysis, especially in a rapidly changing industry such as mobile telecoms.

WIK-Consult (2015) also presents some descriptive evidence on the development of the Austrian market at the time of this merger. This study reports the evolution of a price index computed by the Austrian telecom regulator (based on a basket expenditure approach) that shows a price increase following the merger. In addition, WIK-Consult (2015) finds that the EBITDA/revenue ratio increased for all the operators in the Austrian market with the merged entity enjoying the highest EBITDA margin post-merger. WIK-Consult (2015) also reports that Hutchison 3G had the highest Capex/revenue ratio following the merger indicating a higher level of investments compared to the other operators.

Following these descriptive analyses, the Austrian Telecom Regulator (RTR, 2016) and the Austrian Competition Authority (BWB, 2016) also examined the development of the Austrian telecom market following the 2012 merger. Subsequently, BEREC (2018) did an update of the RTR (2016) study. The RTR and BWB studies conduct a quantitative estimation of the effects of the merger, with the former applying the Difference-in-Differences technique to basket prices and the latter applying a merger simulation methodology. Both studies reach similar conclusions. They conclude that prices were falling before the concentration, started increasing soon after the two mergers and started falling again later in 2015 when a number of MVNOs entered the Austrian market. In terms of estimated effects, both studies estimate a range of effects that vary with the model specification assumptions. Nevertheless, the evidence points to price increases in the order of 20% during the two years following the concentration. BEREC (2018) makes use of a longer post-merger period. It confirms the

56. This metric converts SMS and voice consumption in megabytes and then divides the price of the tariff by the average consumption.

price increase during the first years after the merger, but finds (in line with the results of RTR and BWB) that the negative effect of the merger becomes insignificant after three years when a number of MVNOs entered the Austrian market.

Another study looking at this merger is Houngbonon (2015). This study reaches a different conclusion and finds that the 2012 Hutchison 3G/Orange merger can be associated with a fall in the unit cost of mobile data when sold as part of a bundle. However, the findings of this study appear to be questionable. As already indicated in section 3.04[C][1][c], Houngbonon (2015) estimates the unit cost on the basis of maximum allowances included in the bundle (rather than actual consumption) and adopts a non-standard double differencing approach. A further peculiarity of this study is that it does not use any pre-merger observations as its starting point is the first quarter after the merger, thereby putting into doubt the identification of the impact of the merger.

Overall, the different studies reviewed in this section reach diverging conclusions with respect to the price effects of the 2012 Austrian merger, which can be due to the reasons mentioned in section 3.04 (e.g., differences in methodology, indicators used). Nevertheless, on balance and based on the joint evidence presented in the different studies, it looks plausible that following the 2012 concentration the prices paid by the average consumer of mobile telecom services increased in Austria.

For the Austrian case, it could also be argued that prices increased not because of the market concentration but rather because of the spectrum auction that took place soon after the merger. RTR (2016) considers this option in one of its robustness tests and finds that the price increases would exceed the higher costs implied by the spectrum auction. For what concerns the persistence of the effects, the evidence indicates that these relative price increases were transitory and only related to the first three years. However, a period of three years of relatively higher prices is nevertheless a source of consumer harm meriting the attention of competition authorities.

The 2012 Austrian merger also attracted considerable attention in terms of its effects on the quality of mobile telecom services. GSMA (2017) is the first structured attempt to perform a quantitative estimation of the impact of the concentration on quality in a single case study. This study documents that following the merger Hutchison had a faster 4G coverage and a faster download and upload speed than what could be predicted without the merger. In addition, the study identifies positive spillover effects on the quality of mobile telecom services in the Austrian market as a whole. BEREC (2018), on the contrary, finds that following the merger, there was an absolute deterioration in network quality metrics.[57] However, in terms of methodology, this latter study performs only a within-country analysis comparing the development of its quality metric before and after the merger whereas GSMA (2017) employs a more robust Difference-in-Differences approach.

57. BEREC (2018) uses the network test results of the magazine connect. Connect is a German print magazine which reviews telecommunications products and services. The network tests are performed in larger cities and towns and on roads connecting cities or towns. The method makes use of drive tests, walk tests as well as tests on public transport.

There is one further aspect to consider when studying the impact of mobile mergers on quality. From a merger control point of view, there are often alternatives – such as network sharing agreements – which might be less anticompetitive than a merger between two MNOs, as these agreements preserve retail competition between the two players while creating network related synergies. In the Austrian case of 2012, the European Commission decision concluded that 'there are other alternatives that would allow for LTE rollout' and that '[...] although these alternatives may be less advantageous for Hutchison 3G, they pertain to industry standard practice and must therefore be taken into account in this analysis [...] [t]he Commission therefore holds that faster LTE rollout is not merger specific'[58]. Therefore, if any improvement on quality is expected from a merger, it should be assessed against the counterfactual of what would have happened absent the merger. This assessment should not only consider the counterfactual of the two standalone companies but should also study, if appropriate given the facts of the case, the likelihood of observing a network sharing agreement or other types of alternative agreements that would lead to quality metrics similar to those of a 'full' merger.

Finally, one needs to consider whether the mechanical application of the Difference-in-Differences methodology is suitable to study the impact of a merger on quality. The price comparison across operators or countries already poses several challenges. The comparison of quality outcomes calls for even more caution. The country specificities in terms of network development might be more persistent and limit the possibility to obtain meaningful comparisons across countries absent the appropriate data and methods to account for this heterogeneity.

[3] Hutchison 3G/Telefonica (Ireland, 2014) and Telefonica/E-plus (Germany, 2014)

The two last mobile merger cases subject to an ex post evaluation study are the concentrations that took place around 2013/2014 in Ireland and Germany. Both mergers entailed a reduction from four to three independent MNOs, involved the smallest operator and latest entrant in the market and were cleared by the European Commission, conditional on remedies. Notably, in both cases, the remedy consisted in providing access to one or more MVNOs under competitive conditions and with the commitment of a fixed capacity of the network.[59] BEREC (2018) provides a quantitative study of the impact of these two mergers whereas WIK-Consult (2015) provides a descriptive analysis.

The WIK-Consult study analysed market developments in Ireland and Germany over the period 2005-2014. The study noted that, in these two countries, the market

58. Case COMP/M6497 Hutchison 3G Austria/orange Austria, paragraphs 431-432.
59. This type of remedy is different from a simple pay-as-you-go type of remedies in which MVNOs obtain access conditions based on unit tariffs. Under a fixed capacity based mechanism, the MVNO obtains a given capacity allocation for a fixed price on top of a pay per unit tariff for the traffic that goes beyond the allocated capacity. This mechanism aims to replicate the lost competitive constraint that was previously exerted by an MNO, by changing the cost structure of the MVNO, from a variable structure to a fixed structure.

consolidation led to more symmetric market positions of the leading MNOs, a structure that might provide fewer incentives for the disruptive competition of the smaller competitors. However, WIK-Consult (2015) lacks post-merger information. Therefore, it cannot provide an analysis of post-merger developments. Only for Germany, the study has access to some post-merger aggregate price information from which it concludes that the four-player market might have preserved a competitive environment.[60]

The BEREC study estimates the impact of the two mergers on retail prices using a basket expenditure approach in a Difference-in-Differences setting.[61] For both Ireland and Germany, BEREC (2018) had access to only one and a half year of price data post-merger. Therefore, only short-term effects could be estimated.

For Ireland, the study finds evidence of episodes of relative price increases. However, the price increases are not sustained over the whole period under analysis (with the exception of the prices paid by high consumption users). Therefore, it seems that the merger is associated with temporary price increases that were later reversed. It is not clear though whether this price reversal was the result of the MVNO remedy as the two MVNOs that entered the Irish market after the merger did not gain a sizeable market share and one exited the market shortly after. However, it cannot be excluded that they contributed to keep competition in the market, although they were not able to win market share.

The results for the German case are not very conclusive either. As for the Irish case, there is evidence of price increases during the considered period but the size and the persistence of these price increases is not firmly established. Moreover, the study seems to lack price information on a sizeable part of the market including the MVNO segment and the pricing of the sub-brands of MNOs. As these segments of the German market are sizeable, it is not possible to get a robust assessment of the overall price impact of the merger.

For the German case, BEREC (2018) also provides a descriptive analysis of the effects of the merger on quality.[62] The evidence shows a deterioration in quality after the merger. The study relates this evidence to possible network integration issues. As the network integration was still ongoing in 2017, it is not possible to reach firm conclusions on the overall and long-term impact of the merger on quality, both because of a lack of data and, as explained in the previous subsection, because of a lack of an appropriate methodological framework for the analysis of network quality effects.

60. This conclusion is reached by looking at the period around 2010 in which the study did not spot any price increase, despite the spectrum auction. However, this conclusion does not appear very robust as it is based on a simple observation of an aggregate price series from which it is not possible to draw firm conclusions.
61. As a robustness test, the synthetic control method is applied as well.
62. BEREC (2018) uses the network test results of the magazine connect.

[B] Evidence Related to Industry Wide Studies

Several studies attempt to uncover a more general relationship between concentration and market outcomes. The two outcomes mostly studied relate to prices and quality/investments.[63] Table 3.5 below reports the list of the seven studies considered and their main findings.

Table 3.5 Summary of Evidence Related to Industry Studies

Industry Studies	*Main Findings*
Affeldt P. and Nitsche R, (2014)	No positive relationship between concentration and prices, signs of a possible negative relationship. No conclusive results.
Csorba G. and Papai Z. (2015)	Heterogeneous effect of entry (higher effect of a 4th operator entry versus a 3rd operator entry). No price increasing effects related to mergers (both 5 to 4 and 4 to 3).
Frontier Economics (2015)	No systematic difference in prices and investments in 3 MNOs market versus 4 MNOs markets. Overall, no clear relationship between the level of competition and prices and no evidence that more intense competition increases investments.
Houngbonon G.V. & Jeanjean F. (2016)	Inverse U-shaped relationship between competition intensity and investments. Investment increases with competition as long as operators' profits are above the thresholds of 37% or 40% of their revenues.
Houngbonon G.V. & Jeanjean F. (2017)	Investment per operator increases with concentration. Industry investment rises with the number of operators in the short run, but falls in the long run.
WIK-Consult (2015)	The econometric analysis shows no linkage between higher concentration in mobile markets and an increase in profitability and investment. Investment level and improvements in consumer outcomes are likely to be driven by other factors (both related to supply and demand).
Genakos C., Valletti T. and Verboven F. (2018)	Concentration is associated with both relative price increases and higher capital investments at firm level but not at country level.

These industry studies complement the quantitative and case-specific ex post evaluations of individual mergers with descriptive or quantitative evidence of market developments in the mobile telecom industry. These studies do not directly model the impact of specific competition policy decisions and rather aim to estimate a more general relationship between competition (as measured by concentration indicators such as HHI) and market outcomes. The motivation of these studies is that, by pooling

63. For a definition of these outcome variables, *see* sections 3.04[C] and [D].

several episodes of changes in market structure (entry, exit, mergers, organic growth), it is possible to provide a more general understanding of the sector and the impact of concentration on mobile industry outcomes.

Nevertheless, for the reasons discussed in section 3.04[B][4], one needs to interpret with caution the results of sector wide studies of the mobile telecom industry. In particular, these studies mix together different events that lead to changes in market structure: episodes of entry, episodes of organic exit, episodes of exit by merger and significant variation of market shares without entry or exit, which are due to normal competitive dynamics.[64] Merger episodes are likely to drive most of the variation in the variable selected to capture the intensity of competition. However, to interpret correctly the findings it would be important to analyse if there are other events driving the variation in the measure of competition used.[65] Moreover, specifically for mergers, it is often the case that conditional and unconditional clearance decisions are pooled without distinction or any discussion of differentiation based on the extent of the accepted remedies. This possible source of heterogeneity should be appropriately considered.

At the same time, unobserved or non-controlled for country specific factors might also bias the results. For example, a number of these studies look at the impact of market concentration on network investments. However, none of the reviewed studies seems to consider that cost synergies on network developments might also be achieved through network sharing agreements. These studies do not consider that investment decisions may follow different dynamics in markets in which network sharing agreements are present. Failing to control for this important feature may have an impact on the estimates and on the interpretation of the relation between market concentration and investments. The above discussion suggests that industry wide studies should try to control for all these features, something perhaps not sufficiently done in the reviewed studies.[66]

Finally, industry studies are often not limited to EU countries and enlarge their sample to countries outside the EU. While this approach could improve the precision of the estimates, by expanding the sample, adding countries that might be significantly different from EU countries might result in decreasing the confidence on the estimated variables.

64. Studies that measure competition levels by looking at HHI would also consider changes in market share distribution as having an impact on market outcome even in the absence of entry or exit episodes.
65. In none of the reviewed industry studies, there is a clear documentation of what drives the variation in the variable(s) capturing the level of intensity of competition.
66. This feature has less of an impact when trying to estimate the price effect of mergers. Network sharing agreements have a first order impact on network decisions and hence on quality and a second order effect on prices as the operators participating in the network sharing agreements would still compete at the retail level. Therefore, a comparison across countries of network quality is likely to suffer more from not controlling for network sharing agreements than a comparison of prices.

[1] Impact of Competition on Prices

The evidence on the impact of increased concentration on prices is mixed. There are three studies that do not find any relationship in their econometric estimates: Affeldt and Nitsche (2014), Frontier Economics (2015) and Csorba and Papai (2015).

The first two studies estimate prices by a revenue-based metric scaled by the number of called minutes and measure the level of competition by the number of firms and/or the HHI index. Both measures are likely to be endogenous. However, Affeldt and Nitsche (2014) do not address this issue. Frontier Economics (2015) proposes to use as an instrument the lagged value of HHI, although no information is provided on the validity of this instrument.

Affeldt and Nitsche (2014) find that there is no robust indication of a positive relationship between concentration and prices and that there are some indications that this relation might be negative. Beyond these results, the study also documents a large heterogeneity in terms of prices across countries, due to factors other than market concentration. The study claims that differences in service quality, demand and costs are more likely to explain these price differences. For example, they point out that it is important to appropriately account for quality, as higher quality is usually associated with higher concentration and higher prices. The authors also indicate that the direction of causality between these three factors is not clear and they cannot reach a more definitive conclusion on the direction of causality.

Frontier Economics (2015) provides a descriptive analysis showing that, over the period 2000-2014, there was no systematic difference in the evolution of prices (measured as ARPM) in three-player markets as compared to four-player markets. This result is confirmed by their econometric analysis, both when they estimate the impact on prices of having a fourth operator (as compared to the baseline of only three operators) and when they more generally consider the impact on prices of market concentration, as measured by HHI. As does Affeldt and Nitsche (2014), this study concludes that other factors related to demand (GDP) and supply (availability of 4G services) are more likely to drive the differences in prices, both across countries and over time.

Overall, both studies do not provide robust conclusive evidence on the relationship between prices and concentration. This is partly due to the lack of control for the possible endogeneity of the measure of concentration, which undermines the validity of estimates and related interpretation of the results.

Differently from the two above studies, Csorba and Papai (2015) consider a basket expenditure index as price indicator and measure variation in competition by the variation in the number of operators. To account for possible endogeneity problems, the study makes use of lagged variables as instruments. The study looks at both entry and merger episodes (i.e., reductions in the number of operators). While it finds some statistically significant effects of entry (with heterogeneous effects depending on the number of original MNOs) on prices, it does not find any statistically significant effect of mergers (both for five-to-four and four-to-three mergers). One possible reason for these results is the indicator of competition. As the number of operators is a discrete variable that seldom changes, the identification of the effects is more challenging.

The study of Genakos et al. (2018) also estimates an econometric relationship between mobile prices and concentration measures. Differently from the above three studies, this latter work finds that an increase in market concentration can be associated with higher prices. More precisely, the study finds that a hypothetical asymmetric four-to-three merger involving a small operator and a larger one would increase the consumers' mobile telecom services bill by about 4-7%.

This latter study also adopts a more credible estimation approach for the following reasons. First, it uses an expenditure basket with fixed or variable consumption (appropriately controlled for) to proxy mobile prices, an indicator that appears to be more appropriate than the revenue-based metric (as discussed in section 3.04[B]). Second, it proposes a more credible strategy to address the endogeneity between the concentration measure (HHI) and the price variable, an issue that is not properly addressed in the other studies (beyond simply using lagged variables). The main instrument chosen is the asymmetry in MTRs within a country, a variable controlled by telecom regulators and correlated with market shares and hence HHI, but not directly related to prices. Other instruments used for HHI are binary indicators for the number of operators and cumulative measures of entry and exit. Genakos et al. (2018) argue that all these instruments have a direct impact on the measure of market structure (HHI) and an indirect impact on prices and investments only through their impact on HHI.[67] Nevertheless, this study still suffers from some of the other problems highlighted in the introduction of this section, like the pooling together of several merger episodes without properly controlling for the heterogeneity of the merger remedies.

[2] Impact of Competition on Investments

Five of the industry studies reviewed in this chapter estimate the impact of changes in market structure on investments. In these studies, investment is measured by capital expenditures (Capex) of mobile operators. Among the studies estimating industry wide effects, none of the reviewed studies considers a measure more directly related to the quality of mobile services, like connection speed, coverage or other more comprehensive measures. As already discussed in section 3.04[C][2], investments are not a good proxy for network quality parameters and for the benefits that consumers derive from it. Therefore, all these studies leave unanswered the more relevant question of what is the relationship between mobile telecom mergers and quality metrics relevant for consumers. Even assuming that it is possible to establish a relationship between changes in market structure and investments, it would then be necessary to relate it to quality.

67. Concerning the use of MTRs, Genakos et al. (2018), argue that the difference in MTRs between the most regulated (large incumbent) and the least regulated operator (small entrant) should boost the market share of the smallest operator and have a direct impact on HHI while the impact on prices would only be indirect through HHI. The study also provides statistical support for the choice of this and the other instruments.

Two studies, Frontier Economics (2015) and WIK-Consult (2015), conclude that there is no statistical significant relation between competition and investment. Frontier Economics (2015) finds no statistically significant relationship between the competition indicator (measured by the HHI index) and investments (measured by Capex per subscriber). It therefore concludes that a reduction of competition would not necessarily imply lower investments. This study also finds that investments as measured by Capex is driven by several other factors than competition, like the timing of the auctions, the timing of the rolling out of the network and demand features like the share of prepaid customers. Moreover, current Capex is strongly related to past Capex, suggesting some persistence of investment decisions, as can be expected in a capital-intensive industry like mobile telecom. Frontier Economics (2015) also provides a detailed overview of theoretical arguments according to which mergers would lead to higher investments. These are related to economies of scale, access to complementary assets and access to commercial partnerships allowing the deployment of innovative services. However, no quantitative evidence is provided to support the developed arguments.

Likewise, WIK-Consult (2015) finds no statistically significant relationship between measures of competition (HHI and number of operators) and the level of investments (as measured by Capex and Capex per subscriber). It also concludes that investments are driven by other factors, like the profitability and the size of operators, the country GDP or previous investments decisions. WIK-Consult (2015) does not appear to take into account the possible endogeneity between the measures of competition and investment decisions. However, it shows that the relationship between competition measures and Capex fades away after having controlled for supply and demand variables. WIK-Consult (2015) also presents some qualitative evidence to study the relationship between competition and investments. It proposes a comparison across countries (some EU countries, the United States, Japan, Australia and Korea) of several indicators related to operator profitability, market structure and demand. This analysis documents a relative high degree of heterogeneity across countries regarding factors affecting investments.

Contrary to these two studies, three studies, Houngbonon and Jeanjean (2016 and 2017) and Genakos et al. (2018), indicate that an increase in concentration has a positive impact on investment. In these studies, investment is measured by Capex and Capex per subscriber. Houngbonon and Jeanjean (2016) find support for the theory that the relationship between competition and investments is inverse U-shaped. This means that starting from low levels of competition, an increase in competition would have a positive effect on investment but beyond a certain threshold, a further increase in competition would harm investment decisions. The study also relates investment to an indicator of profitability. It shows that, if competition lowers the profitability of operators below a certain threshold, then investments are expected to fall. Houngbonon and Jeanjean (2016) further indicate that the level of competition intensity that maximises the investments is reached when operator's gross profits represent 37-40% of their revenue. When profits are above this threshold, investments increase with competition. Below this threshold, there is a trade-off between competition and investment.

A novelty of this study concerns the indicator of competition selected, which is the Lerner index.[68] The measure of mark-up used to calculate the Lerner index is EBITDA (Earnings before Interest, Taxes, Depreciation, and Amortization). The use of EBITDA raises some concerns, as it is debatable to what extent it offers an appropriate representation of concentration levels (as is the case for the standard Lerner index). Indeed, the EBITDA margin might be affected by several factors (in terms of both revenue and costs) that are not necessarily related to the intensity of competition,[69] especially in oligopolistic markets with four or three players. This modelling choice is also criticised in WIK-Consult (2015) where it is argued that the use of EBITDA to estimate mark-ups is not appropriate, as EBITDA is not computed on the basis of prices and marginal costs, as it should be according to the definition of the Lerner index. In the econometric model, the chosen competition variable is then instrumented, in a standard fashion, by its own lags and the year of entry.

In a second paper, Houngbonon and Jeanjean (2017) adopt a different methodology and use the number of firms and the asymmetry in market shares as an indicator of the level of competition. This study finds that investment per operator increases with concentration whereas industry wide investment rises with the number of operators in the short run, but falls in the long run. However, these results depend on the level of market symmetry and the relationship holds only in the case of symmetric markets. On this basis, it is not clear whether these results would apply to a typical merger case in asymmetric markets. Another result of this study is that Capex increases with market size, after having controlled for the competition measures. This is another indication that market characteristics are important drivers of investment decisions. In this study, the authors use political ideology[70] and MTRs as instruments for the number of mobile operators and for market share asymmetry, respectively.

Genakos et al. (2018) also find evidence that investment per operator increases with higher concentration.[71] They estimate that a four-to-three asymmetric merger would increase the average operator's Capex by between 7-14%. In case of a symmetric four-to-three merger, the investment per operator would increase by 19.3%. However, when looking at the same relationship and aggregating the data at country level, they do not find a statistically significant effect of concentration on investment. This latter result indicates that, while the remaining three operators may on average increase their investment, compared to the average investment in a four operators market, this increase in investments is not enough to compensate for the investments lost from the merged operator.

68. The Lerner index is a measure of market power that is defined as the mark-up (price less marginal cost) relative to price.
69. For example, EBITDA can be affected by the cost of personnel or it can include ancillary revenues or revenues from the sale of other services, which are not related to the intensity of competition.
70. In this case, the political ideology towards the welfare state is considered to have an impact on the number of operators and only an indirect impact on investments.
71. The instruments chosen for the intensity of competition variable are the same than those used for the price specification discussed in the previous subsection and include asymmetry in MTRs, binary indicators for the number of operators and cumulative entry and exit.

Thus, based on the three above-mentioned studies, it would seem that higher concentration leads to a higher average investment per operator. However, none of the studies shows that this higher average investment per operator (but lower nationwide investment as in Genakos et al., 2018) would benefit consumers in forms of higher quality. Higher investments per operator following the merger could also be related to integration costs and be even associated to a worsening in the quality of the network shortly after a merger, as some, albeit very anecdotal, evidence in BEREC (2018) indicates in the case of Austria (2012) and Germany (2013).

Finally, as highlighted in WIK-Consult (2015), it is challenging to identify a relationship between market concentration and investments. The reason is that competition related aspects have a second order effect on network investments decisions, as these are primarily influenced by supply and demand considerations not related to mergers. Therefore, absent a solid and credible identification strategy, it appears unlikely that these effects might be reliably estimated.

§3.06 CONCLUSIONS

This chapter takes stock of the lively policy debate on the impact of mergers, and more in general concentration, on market outcomes such as price, quality and innovation in the mobile telecom industry of the European Union. Over the last fifteen years, EU national mobile telecom markets shared a period of fast technological progress (in particular, the growth of mobile data) and generally falling prices. This process has been accompanied by a trend of increasing concentration that saw the exit, mostly through mergers, of several MNOs with only a few episodes of successful entry. As this increased concentration could have negative effects on market outcomes, each time that a new merger was proposed, it attracted the interest and the scrutiny of regulators, competition authorities and industry stakeholders as to its impact.

A number of reports and studies, usually commissioned or carried out by competition authorities, regulators, telecom operators or their associations, aimed to contribute to this debate and to inform policy makers. These studies looked at past mergers and changes in market structure with the aim to estimate the relationship between market concentration and market outcomes. This led to a growing literature of heterogeneous studies, often with contradicting conclusions. This chapter reviews this literature, focusing in particular on the quantitative studies, and puts them into context.

The chapter starts by introducing the mobile telecom industry in the European Union, describing the characteristics that sets it apart from other industries and highlighting the features relevant for competition among the mobile operators. It shows that the main attribute of this industry is the presence of a network infrastructure (including spectrum and cell sites) for mobile telecommunications, whose coverage and speed determine the quality of mobile services offered to consumers. This network infrastructure constitutes a high barrier to entry, giving a relatively large degree of market power to incumbent network operators. As a result, national regulators may intervene to provide access to network infrastructure to new entrants.

Two categories of operators are present in this industry, MNOs owing their network and operating at the wholesale and retail levels and MVNOs having contractual agreements with an MNO through which they have access to its network. Due to their dependence on MNOs, MVNOs may often have a lower impact on the competitive dynamics in the retail market than the MNOs. Finally, there are cases where some parts of the mobile network are shared among MNOs through network sharing or roaming agreements.

The chapter covers sixteen ex post evaluations analysing the impact of market consolidation on market outcomes in the EU mobile telecom industry. These studies can be divided into two broad categories. Single case studies investigate the impact of specific merger cases in isolation and industry wide studies aim at establishing a relation between concentration measures in the industry and market outcomes. These studies use different methodologies to identify a causal relationship between a merger or a change in market structure, on the one hand, and market outcomes, on the other hand. In the reviewed studies, the Difference-in-Differences approach and the multi-event panel regression are the most used methodologies respectively for the ex post evaluation of individual merger decision and for the industry wide studies. A common challenge faced by the quantitative analyses, whatever the methodology used, is the endogeneity between the event under study (the merger or the change in market structure) and the market outcomes. This problem is not sufficiently well addressed in most of the studies. Possible biases should then be considered when interpreting the results.

The market outcomes contemplated in the reviewed studies are price and quality. Three broad families of price measures are used in the quantitative work: (1) revenue related indicators such as ARPU; (2) basket expenditure measures estimating the bills paid by hypothetical representative consumers; and (3) hedonic pricing models regressing the costs of a bundle of telecom services on the characteristics of the bundle. Mobile network quality is often measured by the investments made by MNOs, although it is acknowledged that the link between investments and quality relevant to customers can be debatable. In this respect, only a few very recent studies considered measures of quality more directly related to customer experience, like network coverage, network speed and composite indexes covering several aspects of mobile network quality.

The results of the reviewed body of research are quite varied and often contradicting. This relates in part to the heterogeneity of the study design, the different data used and modelling choices made. One finding that emerged clearly from this review is that national mobile telecom markets and merger episodes are characterised by a high degree of heterogeneity. Therefore, understanding each case's specificities is important for the correct assessment of the possible impact of increased concentration.

Concerning prices, on balance, there is evidence that some mergers led to higher prices, in particular in already relatively concentrated markets and when no remedies had been implemented or when the accepted remedies turned out to be ineffective. Looking at single merger cases, this evidence is stronger for some cases (the 2007 T-Mobile/Orange merger in the Netherlands and the 2012 Hutchison 3G/Orange merger in Austria) and weaker in other cases. However, in the studies reviewed in this chapter, it should be noted that several of the mergers considered were approved conditional on remedies, especially when considering mergers involving a reduction from four to three operators only. Most of the time, it is not possible to disentangle the impact of the merger (absent the remedies) from that of the remedies. The two effects are typically estimated jointly. Most of the studies reviewed in the chapter do not assess the effectiveness of the remedies imposed. However, if the merger control intervention was appropriate, it should not be surprising to observe the absence of price increases following mergers as modified by the remedies.

Concerning the relationship between concentration and quality/investments, the evidence is less conclusive. On balance, there is evidence, albeit weak, that higher concentration may be associated with higher quality and investments. However, it is recognised that the factors influencing mobile operators' investment decisions are very heterogeneous and often unrelated to market concentration or mergers. Another element explaining why it is difficult to reach firm conclusions is that the available data do not allow providing a good indicator of quality relevant for consumers. Furthermore, the choice of the counterfactual scenario is more difficult when analysing the impact of market concentration on quality and investments rather than on price. It is therefore more challenging to estimate the impact of concentration on quality and investments.

Further research on the topic is needed, and several paths are available for its advancement. First, it will soon be possible to look more thoroughly at some recent merger cases. Ideal candidates are the 2016 Hutchison 3G/WIND merger in Italy and the 2018 T-Mobile NL/Tele2 NL merger in the Netherlands. Useful insights could also be gained by studying the market developments in the UK and in Denmark where, respectively, a merger was recently prohibited (Hutchison 3G/Telefonica UK in 2016) and another was withdrawn (Teliasonera/Telenor in 2015). Second, better data over a longer time period may improve the study of the relationship between concentration and quality. As mentioned above, investment has so far been the predominant metric to measure quality. Only two studies attempted to use more direct measures of quality that benefit customers. As this type of data becomes richer, more available and reliable, further research can be developed. Third, further advancements can come from the modelling choices. An aspect often not accounted for relates to the impact of network sharing agreements. These are agreements by which independent operators join their networks while competing on the retail part. Not controlling for these instances may have an impact on the estimated results, especially when considering the impact on investments and quality. Finally, the quantitative analysis might not be able in itself to overcome all the limitations discussed in this chapter. It should then be explored how to complement it with a more rigorous and systematic recourse to qualitative and descriptive analyses regarding the impact of consolidation on the mobile telecom industry.

REFERENCES

Abadie A. and Gardeazabal J. (2003), 'The economic costs of conflict: A case study of the Basque Country', *American Economic Review*, 93(1), pp. 113-132.

Abadie A., Diamond A. and Hainmueller J. (2010), 'Synthetic control methods for comparative case studies: Estimating the effect of California's tobacco control program', *Journal of the American Statistical Association*, 105(490), pp. 493-505.

Abadie A., Diamond A. and Hainmueller J. (2015), 'Comparative politics and the synthetic control method', *American Journal of Political Science*, 59(2), pp. 495-510.

Affeldt P. and Nitsche R. (2014), 'A price concentration study on European mobile telecom markets: Limitations and insights', ESMT Working Paper 14-07, November.

Aghion P., Bloom N., Blundell R., Griffith R. and Howitt P. (2005), 'Competition and innovation: An inverted-U relationship', *The Quarterly Journal of Economics*, 120(2), pp. 701-728.

Aguzzoni L., Buehler B., Di Martile L., Ecker G., Kemp R., Schwarz A. and Stil R. (2015), 'Ex-post analysis of two mobile telecom mergers: T-Mobile/tele.ring in Austria and T-Mobile/Orange in the Netherlands', study prepared for the European Commission, the Netherlands Authority for Consumers and Markets (ACM) and the Austrian Regulatory Authority for Broadcasting and Telecommunications (RTR), Publications Office of the European Union.

Aguzzoni L., Buehler B., Di Martile L., Kemp R. and Schwarz A. (2018), 'Ex-post analysis of mobile telecom mergers: The case of Austria and The Netherlands', *De Economist* 166(1), pp. 63-87.

BEREC (2018), 'BEREC Report on post-merger market developments - Price effects of mobile mergers in Austria, Ireland and Germany', BoR(18)119.

Bertrand M., Duflo E. and Mullainathan S. (2004), 'How much should we trust differences-in-differences estimates?', *The Quarterly Journal of Economics*, 119(1), pp. 249-275.

Björnerstedt J. and Verboven F. (2016), 'Does merger simulation work? Evidence from the Swedish analgesics market', *American Economic Journal: Applied Economics*, American Economic Association 8(3), pp. 125-164.

BWB (2016), 'The Austrian market for mobile telecommunication services to private customers. An ex-post evaluation of the mergers H3G/Orange and TA/Yesss!', Sectoral Inquiry BWB/AW-393, Final report, Vienna.

Cameron A.C., Gelbach J.B. and Miller D.L. (2008), 'Bootstrap-based improvements for inference with clustered errors', *The Review of Economics and Statistics*, 90(3), pp. 414-427.

Csorba G. and Papai Z. (2015), 'Does one more or one less mobile operator affect prices? A comprehensive ex-post evaluation of entries and mergers in European mobile telecommunication markets', IEHAS Discussion papers 1541, Institute of Economics, Centre for Economic and Regional Studies, Hungarian Academy of Sciences.

Denicolò, V. and Polo M. (2018a), 'Duplicative research, mergers and innovation', *Economics Letters*, 166(C), pp. 56-59, February.

Denicolò V. and Polo M. (2018b), Working paper N. 103, IEFE (Center for Research on Energy and Environmental Economics and Policy), Bocconi University, Milan, March.

European Commission (2004), Guidelines on the assessment of horizontal mergers under the Council Regulation on the control of concentrations between undertakings. Official Journal C 031, 05/02/2004, pp. 5-18.

Evans W., Froeb L. and Werden G. (1993), 'Endogeneity in the concentration-price relationship: Causes, consequences, and cures', *Journal of Industrial Economics*, 41(4), pp. 431-438.

Federico, G. (2017), 'Horizontal mergers, innovation and the competitive process', *Journal of European Competition Law & Practice*, 8(10), pp. 668-677.

Federico G., Langus G. and Valletti T. (2018), 'Horizontal mergers and product innovation', *International Journal of Industrial Organization*, 59, pp. 1-23.

Frontier Economics (2015), 'Assessing the case for in-country mobile consolidation', A report prepared for the GSMA.

Genakos C., Valletti T. and Verboven F. (2018), 'Evaluating market consolidation in mobile communications', *Economic Policy*, 33(3), pp. 45-100.

GSMA (2017), 'Assessing the impact of mobile consolidation on innovation and quality: An evaluation of the Hutchison/Orange merger in Austria'.

Houngbonon G.V. (2015), 'The impact of entry and merger on the price of mobile telecommunications services', 26th European regional conference of the international telecommunications society (ITS), Madrid, Spain, 24-27 June.

Houngbonon G.V. and Jeanjean F. (2016), 'What level of competition intensity maximises investment in the wireless industry?', *Telecommunications Policy*, 40(8), pp. 774-790.

Houngbonon G.V. and Jeanjean F. (2017), 'Optimal market structure in the mobile industry', *Information Economics and Policy*, 38, pp. 12-22.

HSBC (2015), 'Supersonic: European telecoms mergers will boost Capex, driving prices lower and speeds higher', HSBC Global Research.

Igami M. and Uetake K. (2019), 'Mergers, innovation, and entry-exit dynamics: Consolidation of the hard disk drive industry, 1996-2016', forthcoming in *the Review of Economic Studies*.

Ilzkovitz F. and Dierx A. (2015), 'Ex-post economic evaluation of competition policy enforcement: A review of the literature', Publications Office of the European Union.

Lear, DIW Berlin and Analysys Mason (2017), 'Economic impact of competition policy enforcement on the functioning of telecoms markets in the EU', Final report prepared for the Directorate-General for Competition of the European Commission, Publications Office of the European Union.

Lepore R. (2017), 'The failed AT&T/T-Mobile merger 6 years later: the but-for world that never was', *Competition Law & Policy Debate*, 3(4), pp. 76-86.

London Economics (2015), 'Competition and market outcomes in the telecom sector', Report prepared for the European Commission. Unpublished manuscript.

Miller N.H. and Weinberg M.C. (2017), 'Understanding the price effects of the MillerCoors joint venture', *Econometrica*, 85(6), pp. 1763-1791.

Motta M. and Tarantino E. (2017), 'The effect of horizontal mergers, when firms compete in prices and investments', Working Paper 987, Barcelona Graduate School of Economics.

Newmark C. (2004), 'Price concentration studies: There you go again', Manuscript prepared for the DOJ/FTC merger workshop, 'Concentration and market shares' panel'.

Nicolle A., Grzybowski L. and Zulehner C. (2018), 'Impact of competition, investment, and regulation on prices of mobile services: Evidence from France', *Economic Inquiry*, 56(2), pp. 1322-1345.

Nitsche R. and Wiethaus L. (2016), 'Efficiency defence in telecom mergers and other investment intensive industries', *European Competition Law Review*, 37(1), pp. 7-13.

Ormosi P., Mariuzzo F. and Havell R. (2015), 'A review of merger decisions in the EU: What can we learn from ex-post evaluations?', Report prepared for DG Competition, Publications Office of the European Union.

Powell M. and Czapracka K. (2017), 'The shifting sands of EU merger control - un, deux, trois piano!', *Competition Law and Policy Debate*, 3(4).

RTR (2016), 'Ex-post analysis of the merger between H3G Austria and Orange Austria', RTR-GmbH (Rundfunk & Telekom Regulierungs-GmbH), March.

Schubert S. (2016), 'Mobile fixation? A review of recent EC decisions in the telecoms sector', Competition Policy International.

Weiss L. (1989), 'Concentration and price', *The MIT Press*, Cambridge (MA).

WIK-Consult (2015), 'Competition & investment: An analysis of the drivers of investment and consumer welfare in mobile telecommunications', study prepared for Ofcom, authored by Elixmann D., Godlovitch I., Henseler-Unger I., Schwab R. and Stumpf U.

CHAPTER 4

The T-Mobile/Orange UK Merger Case*

Paolo Buccirossi, Alessia Marrazzo & Salvatore Nava

This chapter provides an ex post evaluation of the impact of the T-Mobile/Orange merger decision taken by the European Commission in March 2010. The European Commission cleared the merger, conditional on structural and behavioural remedies, in particular ensuring that Three could continue to compete in the market. This ex post evaluation is based on a Difference-in-Differences analysis of the effect of the merger, including remedies, on prices and investment in the UK market. The quantitative analysis is complemented with a descriptive analysis of market developments post-merger. The quantitative and descriptive analyses show that the merger together with the associated remedies resulted in a price decline. The quantitative analysis is less conclusive regarding the impact of the merger on investments but the descriptive analysis seems to indicate that the merger did not hinder the development of 4G services in the UK.

§4.01 INTRODUCTION

This chapter provides an ex post evaluation of the impact of the decision taken by the European Commission in March 2010 to clear the T-Mobile/Orange merger. This merger reduced the number of mobile operators in the UK market for mobile telecommunication services from five to four. As the current literature on the ex post evaluation of a five-to-four merger in telecoms is rather limited, the analysis presented here is breaking new ground.

The clearance decision taken by the European Commission was conditional upon certain behavioural and structural remedies. The quantitative and descriptive analyses

* This chapter is based on an ex post evaluation of the European Commission's decision in the *T-Mobile/Orange UK* merger case, as presented in the 2017 study *Economic impact of competition policy enforcement on the functioning of telecoms markets in the EU*, commissioned by the Directorate-General for Competition of the European Commission. *See* Lear, DIW Berlin and Analysys Mason (2017).

presented here investigate the market-wide effect of this clearance decision, inclusive of remedies, on mobile telecommunication prices and investment in the UK. It is worth pointing out that the quantitative analysis does not allow for a separate identification of the effects of the merger with and without the remedies. However, the descriptive analysis allows drawing some conclusions on the contribution of the remedies to the overall impact of the decision.

Mobile telecommunication markets are very concentrated: usually, there are no more than four mobile network operators (MNOs) in each European Union country. This concentrated market structure is mainly due to high entry barriers for new players seeking to roll out mobile network infrastructure. One of the most significant barriers is the cost of securing mobile spectrum, a scarce resource that Member States auction periodically.

Saturating mobile telecommunication markets and increasing price sensitivity of customers have led MNOs to seek cost savings, in particular through mergers and acquisitions. Since the beginning of the 2000s (*see, for example,* Mariniello and Salemi (2015) and Chapter 3), a wave of in-country consolidation in the mobile telecommunication sector has taken place in Europe. These mergers have been subject to review at national level or by the European Commission. Over the period 2006-2018 (*see also* Table 3.2, in Chapter 3), the European Commission assessed twelve mergers between MNOs: in Greece (2006), Austria (2006 and 2012), the Netherlands (2007, and 2018), the UK (2010 and 2015), Ireland (2013), Germany (2013), Denmark (2015), Italy (2016) and Sweden (2016). Most of these mergers implied a reduction in the number of MNOs, or infrastructure competitors, from four to three (Buettner, Federico and Lorincz, 2016).

These merger reviews gave rise to a lively debate on the relationship between concentration and market performance. On the one hand, competition and regulatory authorities have generally concluded that these mergers would reduce competition and lead to higher price for consumers. On the other hand, mobile telecommunication operators have advocated a more lenient merger control as they argued that mobile consolidation was necessary to enable more investment in telecommunication infrastructure and to bring better quality of service. This study can contribute to shed some light on this debate.

This chapter is structured as follows. Section 4.02 provides a short description of the decision adopted by the European Commission and of the implementation of the EU merger control in the mobile telecommunication services. Section 4.03 provides some references to studies that have been particularly useful for the empirical analysis. Section 4.04 describes the methodology used and the model estimated. Section 4.05 presents the results of the quantitative and descriptive analyses, and section 4.06 concludes.

§4.02 FACTUAL BACKGROUND

[A] Presentation of the Case Decision Being Evaluated

Prior to the merger, the UK market for retail mobile services had five MNOs (O2, Vodafone, Orange, T-Mobile and Three) as well as several Mobile Virtual Network Operators (MVNOs[1]), among which the most notable was Virgin, with many others catering for niche markets (e.g., Lebara for low-cost international calls).

In its decision, the European Commission reported that retail prices for telecommunication mobile services decreased significantly in the UK in the years prior to the merger, with this trend being accompanied by intense innovations in service and changes in pricing structure. Three emerged as the leading force in this innovation process since its entry at the end of 2004 and was considered by the Commission as the 'maverick' of the market. Three did not hold a 2G network. Thus, in order to provide voice and SMS services nationally, it entered into a 2G national roaming agreement with Orange, in addition to a 3G RAN[2] sharing agreement with T-Mobile. Under the Radio Access Network (RAN) sharing agreement, Three and T-Mobile merged their existing 3G networks, which were managed by the two companies through a joint venture.

T-Mobile and Orange were, respectively, the third and fourth operator in terms of market share: their combined share was equal to 30-40% at the time of the merger. The Commission held that market shares at the retail level, the number of remaining independent MNOs (four) and the significant presence of MVNOs would have ensured that the market remained competitive following the merger.

However, the European Commission's investigation also focused on how the merger would have affected the upstream markets and the impact that these changes could have had on the retail market. In particular, the Commission was concerned with the wholesale agreements in place between Three and each of the merging parties, and the ability and incentives of the merged entity to terminate or severely compromise them, thereby affecting Three's ability to remain a significant competitor after the merger.

Another reason for concern was the amount of contiguous spectrum at the 1800 MHz frequency band that the merged entity would have held.[3] While the prospect of further spectrum bands being made available in the years following the transaction reduced this concern, the contiguity of spectrum held by the parties would still provide them with a significant technical advantage compared to other MNOs.

1. MVNOs have a contractual agreement with an MNO through which they gain access to the MNOs network and operate mobile services at the retail level.
2. RAN sharing is a form of network sharing in which operators share passive and active elements of a network. Passive elements include space or physical infrastructure and active elements antennas and radio network controllers (RNCs). National roaming is a form of active sharing.
3. Spectrum is a significant determinant of network capacity (i.e., the number of calls that can be served simultaneously or the total bandwidth available). Contiguous spectrum is generally preferable as it enables the provision of higher speed services to end users and more consistency in the geographic coverage of moderate speed services. Contiguous spectrum also allows easier and less expensive spectrum coordination.

In light of these concerns, the merging parties submitted a set of remedies approved by the Commission. The merging parties committed to an agreement that they had reached with Three (RAN sharing agreement), entailing *inter alia* the following conditions:

- the cancellation of certain early termination rights;
- the extension in the duration of the 2G agreement, with reduced charges;
- a commitment to negotiate and conclude a network integration plan between the merged entity and Three;
- the set-up of a fast track dispute resolution mechanism.

On the spectrum issue, the remedy proposed by the parties entailed:

- the divestiture of 2x10 MHz and 2x5 MHz of spectrum in the 1800 MHz band;
- the spectrum would be divested by private sale within an undisclosed time frame. Failing that, the spectrum would be surrendered to Ofcom, which would auction it off;
- in case of a private sale, the Commission and Ofcom had to approve the purchaser.

Following the clearance of the transaction in March 2010, Orange and T-Mobile stores were rebranded as 'Everything Everywhere', subsequently shortened to 'EE', and it took two years for this new brand to emerge. The three brands have co-existed in the market for some time, with the Orange and T-Mobile brands having been phased out gradually.

[B] Institutional Background

The EU Merger Regulation (No. 139/2004 of 20 January 2004) is one of the pillars of the EU competition law. Its introduction in 1989 allowed the control of mergers having a Community dimension, a key element for a good functioning of the Single Market. The review of this regulation in 2004 strengthened the functioning of merger control at the EU level, in particular by introducing a new test, the 'significant impediment of effective competition' (SIEC) test, as the relevant criterion for examining mergers. The objective of the legislator was to introduce a test better adapted to oligopolistic market structures where a concentration can significantly reduce effective competition without creating or reinforcing a dominant position.

In its assessment of recent mobile mergers, the European Commission found that the transactions were likely to give rise to anti-competitive horizontal non-coordinated effects, despite the fact that they did not lead to the creation or strengthening of a dominant position (*see* Buehler et al., 2017). The European Commission carried out detailed qualitative and quantitative analyses of a diverse and extensive body of evidence when applying the SIEC test in mobile telecommunication mergers. The main objective of these analyses was to assess whether the merger would eliminate an important competitive force and to what extent the merging firms were close competitors. The qualitative evidence collected by the European Commission included information from the market investigation, such as past market behaviour (e.g., regarding the introduction of new tariffs and services), network performance, customer services level, brand position and degree of substitutability between firms' products. The quantitative analysis aimed at assessing the likely change in pricing incentives resulting from the merger and used different methods to assess the expected impact of the merger on prices (such as 'upward pricing pressure' based diversion ratios and calibrated merger simulations).

Mobile telecommunication markets are generally subject to ex ante regulation, particularly at the wholesale level. For instance, sector regulators are responsible for setting the auction rules, i.e., the process used to allocate spectrum among operators, for setting the interconnection rates between the networks of competing MNOs and for devising rules to facilitate market access of MVNOs. More generally, spectrum rules may alter investment in and take-up of high capacity networks affecting citizens' access to affordable telecommunication services. Describing the evolution of the regulatory framework is beyond the scope of this chapter. However, it is clear that this framework can have an important impact in creating a level playing field for firms to operate in, which in turn has an impact on market performance. The interaction between regulation and competition policy makes it more difficult to disentangle the impact of the latter on market outcomes.

§4.03 LITERATURE REVIEW

Chapter 3 of this book provides a comprehensive analysis of the main ex post evaluations of merger decisions in the mobile telecommunication sector. Therefore, in this section, we will only highlight a limited number of recent studies that are particularly relevant for our empirical analysis. Some of these studies have focused on the possible trade-off between the upward pricing pressure due to the reduction in the number of mobile telecommunication operators and the benefits (especially, related to increased investment) which might arise post-merger. Analysing this trade-off is also an objective of the ex post evaluation of the T-Mobile/Orange UK merger presented here.

To assess the price effects of the T-Mobile Orange UK merger, we employ an indicator similar to the basket expenditure used by Aguzzoni et al. in 2015 and RTR, the Austrian Regulatory Authority for Broadcasting and Telecommunications, in 2016. The study by Aguzzoni et al. (2015) evaluates the price effects of two mergers: (i) the T-Mobile/tele.ring merger in Austria (April 2006, five-to-four merger); and (ii) the T-Mobile/Orange merger in the Netherlands (August 2007, four-to-three merger). This study finds no significant price change due to the merger in Austria and a price increase in the Netherlands. The study by the RTR (2016) examines the price effects of the Orange-H3G merger in Austria (2012, four-to-three merger) and the related transaction whereby H3G spun off the Orange sub-brand Yesss! to A1 Telekom Austria. This study concludes that the merger had positive and significant effects on prices in the two years following the merger.

The analysis developed by Genakos et al. (2018) has also been particularly relevant when defining our empirical strategy. In particular, as they do, we use capital expenditure[4] per operator as an indicator of investment. Genakos et al. investigate the effects of an 'average' four-to-three symmetric merger and of a more realistic asymmetric four-to-three merger in the mobile market by using a sample of thirty-three OECD countries between 2002 and 2014. They find that the average four-to-three merger would increase the bill of end users by 16.3%[5] and the investment per operator by 19.3% in the post-merger period and that the more realistic asymmetric four-to-three merger would increase this bill by about 4-7% and the capital expenditure per operator by between 7.5% and 14%.[6] However, they do not find a statistically significant effect of concentration on investment per country.

Other recent studies present different results regarding the relationship between mergers, prices and investment. In a report prepared for GSMA, which represents the interests of mobile operators worldwide, Frontier Economics (2015) argues that the approach used by Competition Authorities may overstate post-merger price increases as they do not consider the dynamic efficiencies arising from mergers. The results of its econometric analysis[7] suggest that the relationship between mobile telecommunication prices and competition is not straightforward: Frontier Economics finds that unit prices in three-player mobile markets are not systematically higher than those in four-player markets. Moreover, there is no evidence that more intense competition increases investment in the mobile markets: the intensity of competition[8] does not have a statistically significant impact in any of their regression models. The authors also conclude that network sharing can deliver benefits over no sharing at all, but it cannot create the investment incentives resulting from mergers. Moreover, they consider that it is less certain that the benefits attributed to network sharing will be realised than those attributed to mergers.

Elixmann et al. (2015) investigate the main drivers of investment and consumer outcomes to assess whether there is a link between mobile market structure and investment: they find that there is no statistically significant linkage between consolidation or higher concentration in mobile markets and an increase in investment. Their results suggest that investment depends instead on a range of national specific factors such as mobile video usage, the timing of spectrum auctions and coverage obligations, and that there is no empirical evidence that a more 'benign' merger control approach would foster investment.

As explained in Chapter 3, one cannot yet draw clear-cut conclusions regarding the impact of mobile telecom mergers on prices and investment, as the empirical

4. Capex measures the money invested by an operator to acquire or upgrade fixed, physical, non-consumable assets, such as cell sites or equipment.
5. End-user expenditure is calculated according to a basket approach based on Teligen data, which varies over time in the main specification.
6. This paper tackles the endogeneity issues that arise when identifying the effects of market structure on prices and investments by using an Instrumental Variable (IV) approach.
7. Frontier Economics (2015) uses a panel of EU mobile network operators over the period 2000 and 2014. The source of the data used is GSMA.
8. As measured by the Herfindahl-Hirschmann Index (HHI) or the number of players in the market.

results differ from one case to another, depending not only on the specificity of the case but also on the indicators and analytical methodologies used. Therefore, expanding the number of ex post evaluations in this area, as has been done in this chapter, can contribute to improving our understanding of this complex relationship.

§4.04 EMPIRICAL STRATEGY

The goal of the empirical analysis is to evaluate the impact of the T-Mobile/Orange merger on mobile telecommunication prices and investment in the UK. This section describes the methodology used for the quantitative analysis and defines the indicators used to measure price and investment in the mobile telecommunication markets.

[A] The Identification Strategy

In order to investigate the causal relationship between the merger, as modified by its remedies, and the performance of UK mobile markets, we adopt a Difference-in-Differences approach, which is a well established and widely used methodology for ex post evaluation studies.

The Difference-in-Differences approach considers one or more specific outcomes for a group of units affected by a policy intervention (the UK mobile market) and compares them to the outcomes of a control group that was not affected by this intervention (other European markets). The variation over time in the outcome variable(s) of this control group is then used to establish what would have occurred in the absence of the intervention in the 'treated' group. Hence, the average effect of the approval merger decision (including its remedies) can be obtained by comparing the outcome(s) for the treated and control groups before and after the implementation of the merger.

The selected control group consists of MNOs from a subset of European countries. We limit the analysis to EU Member States because they have a common regulatory environment. Moreover, we exclude from the analysis any country where a major change in market structure – which we define as entry or merger of MNOs – has occurred in the four years before and after the merger (2007-2014).[9] This will ensure that major changes in market structure elsewhere in the EU do not act as confounding factors for the effect of the merger in the UK. In the empirical model, we also account for other relatively minor changes in market structure, such as entry/exit or expansion of MVNOs by controlling for the combined market shares of the MVNOs.

Based on the available data on the outcome variables, we considered two different control groups for the price and investment analyses, as shown in Table 4.1 below.

9. In Germany and Ireland, there were mergers during the 2007-2014 period, but these mergers occurred at the end and at the beginning of that period. Therefore, these two countries are included in the control group.

Table 4.1 Set of Countries and Mobile Network Operators Included in the Price and Investment Analyses

Country	*Price Analysis*	*Investment Analysis*
Belgium	Mobistar (Orange), Proximus	BASE (Telenet)
Bulgaria	None	Mtel (Telekom Austria), Telenor
Croatia	None	Hrvatski Telekom (Deutsche Telekom), Tele2, Vipnet (Telekom Austria)
Czech Republic	O2 (PPF), T-Mobile (Deutsche Telekom)	T-Mobile (Deutsche Telekom)
Denmark	TDC, Telenor	Telenor
Finland	Elisa, Sonera (TeliaSonera)	None
Germany	Deutsche Telekom (Telekom), Vodafone	E-Plus (KPN), O2 (Telefonica), Vodafone
Hungary	T-Mobile (Magyar Telekom), Telenor	T-Mobile (Magyar Telekom), Telenor
Ireland	O2 (Telefonica), Vodafone	O2 (Telefonica), eircom (Meteor)
Italy	TIM (Telecom Italia), Vodafone	VimpelCom (Wind), Vodafone
Lithuania	None	Bite, Tele2
Spain	Movistar (Telefonica), Vodafone	Orange, Vodafone
UK	O2 (Telefonica), T-Mobile	EE (BT), O2 (Telefonica), Vodafone

Source: Authors' own elaboration based on Analysys Mason Research data.

[B] Model Estimated

The basic formulation of the estimated econometric model is as follows:

$$y_{cot} = \alpha + \beta_1 \text{ merger}_t + \beta_2 \text{ treat}_c \text{ x merger}_t + X_{cot} + Z_{ct} + \mu_{co} + \tau_t + \varepsilon_{cot}$$

where the outcome for operator o in country c at time t is a function of market demand and supply factors (Z_{ct}) and other controls at the operator level (X_{cot}). We also include country-MNO specific fixed effects (μ_{co}) to account for time-invariant unobserved heterogeneity across operators in each country and in some specifications time fixed effects as well (τ_t).[10] Standard errors have been clustered at country level.[11]

10. We use time fixed effect in the Capex analysis and country-specific time trends in the price analysis. Further details are provided in section 4.05.
11. This allows the error terms to be correlated within a country and over time. The small number of available countries might introduce a downward bias in the standard error and increase the significance of the estimated effects. An alternative would be to use the wild bootstrap method but this might also introduce a bias in the standard error in case of a strong imbalance in the number of treated units relative to the number of control units (as in this case). We hence

The dummy $treat_c$ is equal to one for the treated country (the UK). The dummy $merger_t$ is equal to one in the post-merger period (i.e., second quarter of 2010 to end 2014). The coefficient of the Difference-in-Differences variable, that is the interaction variable $treat_c$ x $merger_t$, measures the additional variation experienced by the UK market, compared to the control countries, in the post-merger period. This coefficient measures the effects of the merger (as modified by the remedies) on the outcome variables.

[C] Outcome Variables

The current analysis investigates the impact of the merger (as modified by remedies) on both mobile prices and investment. Table 4.2 shows the metrics used to measure the outcome variables and their main characteristics.

Table 4.2 Outcome Variables and Metrics

Outcome Variable	*Metrics*	*Frequency*	*Source*
Price	Basket expenditure approach	Quarterly Country/operator level[12]	Teligen
Investment	Capex	Quarterly Country/operator level	GSMA

[1] Price Measure

Measuring the price of mobile services presents significant challenges. There is no one price for mobile services, but rather various sets of tariffs. Different measures have been used in the existing literature.[13]

A popular indicator is the Average Revenue Per User (ARPU). However, this measure does not allow distinguishing between price and usage level. For example, an increase in ARPU may be ascribable to either an increase in prices or an increase in usage per user, or both. To deal with this, some studies (e.g., Affeldt and Nitsche, 2014) have used ARPU while taking usage into account. However, there is no systematic information on data usage across countries and over time.

In more recent studies, Aguzzoni et al. (2015) and Genakos et al. (2018) use a basket expenditure approach. Aguzzoni et al. define representative usage profiles based on the consumption of voice and SMS, while Genakos et al. include data usage

preferred to the cluster-robust corrections and being cautious in the interpretation of the statistical significance of our results.

12. Data cover the two largest operators per country. The tariffs of one of the merging parties (Orange) are not included in the dataset.
13. *See* Chapter 3 for a brief description of the pros and cons of the alternative price measures of mobile telecommunication services.

in the basket of expenditures. Both studies identify in each period the cheapest tariff(s) available for each user profile and compute the minimum expenditure necessary to have that level of consumption. We adopted this latter approach since it has potential benefits over the aggregated measure of ARPU, most notably the fact that it enables to disentangle changes in price from changes in the level of consumption. However, the basket expenditure approach also has drawbacks. First, it requires making assumptions on the 'representative' usage profiles and, in our case, it assumes the same consumption pattern across countries. If there is significant variation in consumer behaviour across countries, the constructed prices may not reflect consumers' actual bills. Second, as it is impossible to have data for all operators at the country level, only the tariffs of the largest providers are generally used. Therefore, the constructed price index may not reflect actual price developments.

The price variables included in our quantitative analysis are constructed using OECD baskets allowing generating expenditures for different profiles of consumers. They are calculated based on Teligen data including tariffs from the two main operators in each country considered. In the following, we explain in more detail the assumptions made regarding the consumer profiles and the tariffs, due to data constrains.

First, to calculate basket expenditure, we use the consumer profiles defined by the OECD for the following reasons:

- OECD baskets and the underlying assumptions on call durations, share of off-net/on-net calls,[14] distribution of calls over day/week are based on thorough discussions with national regulators and operators as well as on consumption data submitted by operators.
- OECD baskets effectively represent a widely accepted standard for the measurement of mobile prices and as such make our results comparable to part of the existing literature in the mobile sector (e.g., Genakos et al., 2018).

Table 4.3[15] defines the OECD baskets' characteristics in terms of monthly consumption levels. The 2010 OECD basket includes information on data consumption only starting from the first quarter of 2012. Therefore, the mobile basket expenditure index will include data charges only starting from that date. To isolate price effects from usage effects we consider a constant usage pattern, which remains fixed over the period of analysis, for each profile.

14. The terms 'On-Net' and 'Off-Net' are used to describe call types. 'Off-Net' applies when the call is made on a different network, e.g., whilst you are roaming, or if you are using your home network and make a call to a number that resides with a different network provider.
15. Other assumptions, not reported in Table 4.3, concern the distribution of calls over the day and over the week and the share of on- and off-net traffic.

Table 4.3 OECD Baskets (Monthly Consumption)

Basket	*Profile*	*Calls*	*Minutes*	*SMS*	*MMS*	*Data (MB)*
OECD 2006	Low	30	60	33	1	0
	Medium	65	130	50	1	0
	High	140	280	55	1	0
OECD 2010	Low	30	60	100	0	100
	Medium	100	200	140	0	500
	High	300	600	225	0	1.000

Source: Authors' own elaboration on Analysys Mason Research data.

Second, we need to consider tariffs for these mobile services. We compute mobile expenditure based on the six cheapest tariffs for each profile, operator and period. This is tantamount to assuming that consumers behave rationally, although imperfectly so. A consumer with certain preferences, as given by his/her profile, will choose the tariff that allows him/her to spend the least. Taking the six cheapest tariffs rather than only the cheapest allows for some imperfection in this self-selection mechanism, which may be due to consumers being locked in in a tariff due to long-term plans or other switching costs.

However, no dataset covers all tariffs for all operators in the countries and period covered by our analysis. Data from Teligen represented the best option, although Teligen data cover only the two largest operators per country. Hence, the mobile basket expenditure is computed on the basis of the tariffs of two operators for each country (*see* Table 4.1 above). These data cover both pre-paid and post-paid tariffs and do not provide any separate indication of handset subsidies (if present).

Using only tariffs of the two largest operators presents limitations, especially for the UK. In the UK, the two largest carriers were O2 and T-Mobile, so prices of only one of the merging firms are in the data. This means that if the merger changed pricing for Orange products differently than T-Mobile products, this would not be reflected in our estimates. Second, an interesting question is whether the remedies were sufficient to maintain Three's competitive abilities. But without data on Three, the quantitative analysis cannot address this question. However, it will be discussed in the descriptive analysis.

[2] Investment Measure

The indicator of investment used in the quantitative analysis is capital expenditure, Capex by operator and Capex per subscriber. Capex per operator is defined as the money invested by an operator to acquire or upgrade fixed, physical, non-consumable assets, such as cell sites or equipment. Capex represents a direct measure of investment made by MNOs, and it is commonly used in studies analysing the evolution of investment in mobile markets (see for instance Genakos et al., 2018 and Frontier Economics, 2015). Dividing Capex by the number of subscribers gives a unitary measure of investment, i.e., how much the operator spends on average for each of its users.

Nonetheless, there is an intense debate on the appropriateness of Capex as investment measure in the mobile market (*see also* Chapter 3):

- Capex may not be able to capture improvements in efficiency and network quality. After the merger, larger operators can invest more efficiently in network quality achieving a higher level of quality with the same level of investment per user. This would not be captured by the Capex indicator.
- The Capex indicator does not distinguish between investment in fixed and mobile networks. This introduces heterogeneity between convergent operators (those providing both fixed and mobile services) and mobile-only operators and therefore reduces the comparability of countries with different types of operators.

While we recognise that a larger scale would allow greater efficiency, the Capex analysis would still enable us to assess whether consolidation increases Capex. Moreover, we are able to identify when the Capex may include fixed investment, in addition to the mobile investment (although we cannot identify the amount of fixed investment). This helps us deal with the second limitation.

Data on Capex have been provided by GSMA and cover only a limited number of operators per country. For the UK, we do not have enough information for H3G; rather than using partial data, we dropped all operators for which we have less than four observations in the pre- or post-merger period. This results in the exclusion of Three UK (which was the beneficiary of the remedies imposed by the Commission) from the dataset.

§4.05 RESULTS

This section discusses the results and limitations of the quantitative and descriptive analyses. The quantitative analysis seeks to estimate the effects of the merger, inclusive of the remedies, on prices and investment. The descriptive analysis looks at market trends following the merger to help interpret results from the quantitative analysis and provide insights on the role exerted by the remedies on the overall effect of the merger.

[A] Quantitative Results

[1] Effects on Prices

In this subsection, we first describe the evolution of mobile prices in the UK and in the control countries and investigate the 'common trend' requirement of the Difference-in-Differences methodology. Thereafter, we present the results of our empirical analysis.

Figure 4.1 presents the evolution of mobile basket expenditures for the medium profile user and the 2006 OECD basket, for the UK and the control countries.

Figure 4.1 Mobile Basket Expenditures in UK and Control Countries. OECD Basket 2006, Medium Profile

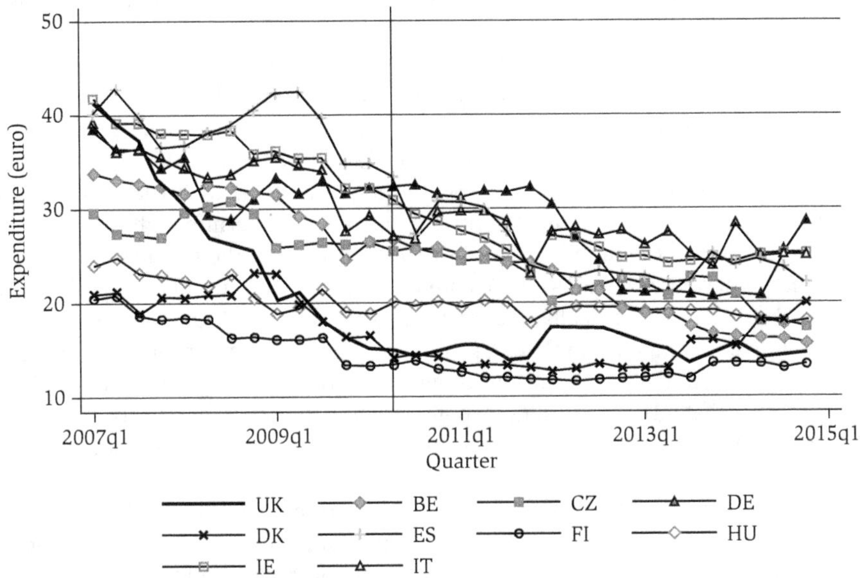

Source: Authors' own elaboration on Teligen data.

Note: The vertical line indicates the merger date (2010q2). Expenditures have been converted to euro for those countries outside the Euro area based on the exchange rate provided by Eurostat.

Mobile prices have been falling over the period 2007-2014 in all the countries considered. The increasing use of most communications services, and their widening availability, has put downward pressure on prices across Europe. However, compared to the control countries, data on mobile basket expenditure seem to suggest that the UK witnessed a steeper decline in mobile prices at least until the first quarter of 2009.

The pricing innovations introduced in the UK from 2007 on may have contributed to the steeper decline in mobile prices in the UK. These pricing innovations include the introduction of pay-as-you go (pre-paid) and SIM-only tariffs with shorter duration contracts (typically thirty days).[16] According to the 2010 Ofcom report,[17] at that date, these contracts accounted for more than one in five new pay-monthly connections and all UK operators offered GBP 15-a-month SIM-only tariffs which included unlimited text messages and at least 200 minutes a month. Interestingly, the allowances within these SIM-only tariffs are broadly comparable to those available in a twenty-four-month contract that includes a basic handset. Since the basket price index in Figure 4.1 is based on the six cheapest tariffs in each country for the two largest operators, it is strongly affected by the introduction of SIM-only plans in the UK market in 2007 and

16. *See* recital 48 of the Commission's decision COMP/M.5650 - T-Mobile/Orange.
17. *See* Ofcom (2010).

2008. The aggressive pricing strategy pursued by Three (*see* descriptive analysis in subsection 4.05[B] below) may also explain why UK mobile prices fell more than in the control countries.

The sharp price decline in the UK has implications for the empirical analysis as one of the main assumptions of the Difference-in-Differences method is that the outcome variable shows a common trend between the treated group and the control group during the benchmark period (i.e., in the period before the merger). Therefore, in the quantitative analysis, we will limit the sample period to the years 2009-2014, to prevent the pre-2009 decline affecting the calculation of the counterfactual case. In this way, we would still have five quarters pre-merger (2009q1 to 2010q1), for the two largest operators in each of the nine control countries, to determine what would have been the evolution of the mobile prices in UK, in absence of the merger.[18]

Over the period 2009-2014, the existence of a common trend can be evaluated graphically and tested empirically. Figure 4.2 describes the evolution of price outcome (i.e., mobile basket expenditure) for each of the selected usage profile and baskets, both in the UK and in the control group (unweighted average mobile expenditure in the nine countries selected). The mobile expenditure computed on the basis of the 2010 OECD baskets has a peak in 2012, due to the addition of the data component to the basket.

A simple graphical comparison between the prices in UK and in the control countries suggests that the two series share a common (and decreasing) trend in the period before the merger – at least for the medium and high profile baskets.

Further to the graphical comparison, we also performed a formal test of the common trend hypothesis. Similar to Ashenfelter et al. (2013), we first estimate the deviation of the treated country's prices from the average price of the control countries in each quarter; then we compute the slope of a linear trend of these deviations in the pre-merger period and test whether the estimated slope is statistically different from zero. Results of the test (presented at the bottom of Table 4.4) suggest that there is a difference in pre-merger trends in the UK and in the control countries, which mightaffect the precision of our estimates.

18. This is very similar to what has been done in Aguzzoni et al. (2016), for the ex post evaluation of the T-Mobile/Orange merger in the Netherlands. Their analysis uses four quarters for the pre-merger period.

Figure 4.2 Mobile Basket Expenditure, UK Against Control Group

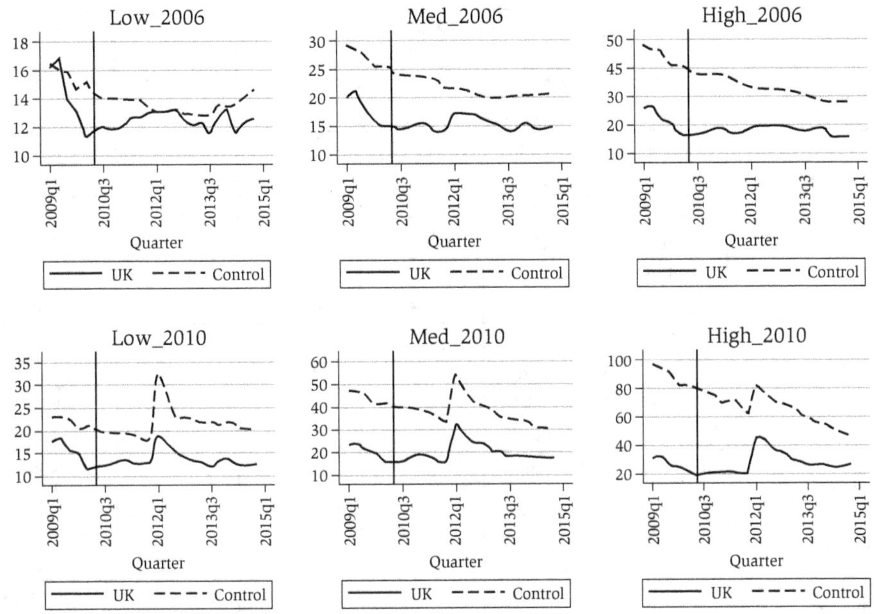

Source: Authors' own elaboration on Teligen data.

Note: The vertical line indicates the merger date (2010q2).

Table 4.4 presents the results of the empirical analysis carried on over the period 2009-2014 for six specifications. These specifications differ according to the definition of the mobile prices considered. The price variable is the natural log of expenditure for the 2006 and 2010 OECD baskets and for three consumption profiles - low, medium and high - that differ regarding to the intensity of usage. We use fixed effects at the operator and country level, and cluster standard errors at the country level. In an effort to correct for possible diverging trends in the pre-merger period, we also included country-specific time trends over the entire period of analysis.

Table 4.4 Merger Effects on Prices – Period 2009-2014

	(1)	*(2)*	*(3)*	*(4)*	*(5)*	*(6)*
Variables	*OECD2006 Low*	*OECD2006 medium*	*OECD2006 high*	*OECD2010 low*	*OECD2010 medium*	*OECD2010 high*
Post-merger[19]	-0.125** (0.050)	-0.0871* (0.047)	-0.0839* (0.045)	0.0868 (0.056)	0.112** (0.041)	0.0500 (0.058)
Treated* Post-meger	-0.0247 (0.052)	-0.0954* (0.050)	-0.112** (0.043)	-0.101 (0.066)	-0.0854* (0.042)	-0.186*** (0.047)
GDP growth	-0.0101 (0.007)	-0.00547 (0.006)	-0.00111 (0.005)	-0.0112 (0.007)	-0.00142 (0.003)	0.00927* (0.005)
MTR	-2.172* (1.014)	-2.106 (1.233)	-2.657** (0.951)	0.832 (0.979)	-0.500 (1.514)	-1.731 (1.490)
Roaming regulation	0.0797** (0.035)	0.0563* (0.029)	0.0113 (0.021)	0.0509** (0.021)	0.0221 (0.024)	-0.0158 (0.022)
VAT rate	0.0252** (0.010)	0.0210* (0.010)	0.0109 (0.010)	0.0197* (0.009)	0.00330 (0.006)	0.000746 (0.016)
Exchange rate	-0.00416** (0.002)	-0.00239** (0.001)	-0.00333*** (0.001)	-0.00375* (0.002)	-0.00250* (0.001)	-0.00496** (0.002)
Data component				0.524*** (0.079)	0.447*** (0.050)	0.325*** (0.088)
Constant	8.135*** (1.205)	11.01*** (1.153)	11.50*** (0.799)	14.60*** (1.062)	8.739*** (1.797)	16.89*** (1.880)
Observations	480	480	480	480	478	476
R-Squared	0.824	0.873	0.890	0.761	0.841	0.864
cluster	Country	Country	Country	Country	Country	Country
FE	Country* operator	Country* operator	Country* operator	Country* operator	Country* operator	Country* operator
Country-specific time trends	YES	YES	YES	YES	YES	YES
Deviation from the common trend	0.118	0.0970	0.121	0.108	0.101	0.124
Common trend test	Failed	Failed	Failed	Failed	Failed	Failed

Common trend test: 'Failed' we reject the null hypothesis of common trend at 5% level
Robust standard errors in parentheses
*** $p < 0.01$, ** $p < 0.05$, * $p < 0.1$
Source: Authors' own elaboration on Analysys Mason Research data, Eurostat and Teligen data.

19. The results in Table 4.4 indicate that UK prices declined post-merger when using the 2006 OECD basket as a price indicator, which is not reflected in Figure 4.2. However, Figure 4.2 only describes the trend of UK prices while the results in the table also take into account the impact of the control variables on prices.

Prices of mobile services seem to have fallen as a result of the merger and its remedies: this holds across all baskets and consumer profiles, but is statistically significant only for medium and high-consumption profiles. In terms of magnitude, the merger (as modified by the remedies) would seem to have caused a decrease in prices for mobile services of between 9% and 19%, for medium to high-intensity users of mobile services. The stronger effects are registered for the high-consumption profiles, for both the OECD 2006 and 2010 baskets.

Most control variables are significant and have the expected sign. For instance, lower mobile termination rates result in lower retail prices; the introduction of the roaming regulation may have caused retail prices to rise, as MNOs may have compensated the revenue lost due to the regulation with an increase in retail prices (this is usually referred to as the 'waterbed' effect); and, the inclusion of a data component translates into an increase in prices, as the underlying basket includes a wider range of services offered.

The formal common trend test suggests that there is a difference in pre-merger trends, in the UK and in the control countries, which is not explained by the control variables. The difference in price trends between the UK and the selected control countries in the pre-merger period implies that the development of mobile expenditure in the control countries may not perfectly estimate the development of mobile expenditure in UK, absent the merger. Hence, the estimate of the effects on prices might be biased.

In order to address this problem, we limited the size of the control group to the five countries with the pre-merger time trends that were most aligned with the time trend in the UK. According to this latter specification, the merger and its associated remedies resulted in price declines ranging between 20% and 42%, depending on the consumer profile. In all six specifications, the coefficients of the Treated*Post-merger dummy are negative and significant at the 5% level.

A number of additional specifications were used as robustness check. First, the pre-merger period was extended to 2008-2010q1 (using four quarters of additional observations compared to the specification presented in Table 4.4). Second, a single mobile basket combining the OECD's low, medium and high baskets in a single basket was used. Third, a variable controlling for the potential competitive pressure exercised by MVNOs was introduced in the model. These three robustness checks generally confirmed the negative price effect of the merger on prices, most notably for medium to high-intensity users.

In conclusion, although we acknowledge that the lack of a common trend might affect the precision of our estimates, we believe that the results still provide an indication of the direction of the effects of the merger (as modified by the remedies) on prices. The results presented above show that the Commission's decision to clear the merger, subject to remedies, contributed to a decline in mobile prices in the UK, at least in comparison with price developments in the EU Member States that were part of the control group.

However, there are reasons to be cautious when interpreting these results, in particular because the indicator used to measure prices – a basket expenditure approach based on OECD consumer profiles and tariffs of the two largest operators in each of the countries considered – has a number of drawbacks. First, the definition of typical consumer profiles is somewhat arbitrary and it assumes the same consumption pattern across countries. Second, while tariff data allow to track tariffs available to customers at given points in time, these do not represent prices actually paid by consumers: many of them may be locked into (or unwilling to switch from) existing price plans. Moreover, as it is impossible to have data for all operators at the country level, only the tariffs of the two largest providers are used.

For the UK, only O2 and T-Mobile are included in the sample. The quantitative analysis shows that these two operators have lowered their prices but is inconclusive on the rest of the market. Indeed, the merged entity may have used its two brands, Orange and T-Mobile, strategically – using the latter to focus on the lower end of the market. Nevertheless, evidence of a market-wide decrease in prices is backed up by the downward trend observed in retail ARPU (*see* next section). Another potential bias stemming from the data used for the price analysis is the exclusion of data services until 2012, while in fact data services appear to have been available to UK consumers from the beginning of the period of analysis. This represents a problem to the extent that data services presented value to consumers well before 2012.

[2] Effects on Capex

We are interested in understanding how – if at all – the merger (as modified by the remedies) has affected investments by MNOs. We use two indicators: average Capex per operator[20] and average Capex per operator divided by the number of subscribers. The latter is plotted in Figure 4.3.

20. For the purpose of this analysis, the merged entity is considered as a single entity over the entire period of the analysis, i.e., summing up the Capex of T-Mobile and Orange. The reason is that, in the absence of this adjustment, Capex per operator would automatically increase as a result of the reduction in the number of operators due to the merger, all else equal. Besides the merger between T-Mobile and Orange, there is no other major change in market structure in the countries covered by the analysis.

Figure 4.3 Average Capex by Operator over Number of Subscribers in the UK and the Control Group

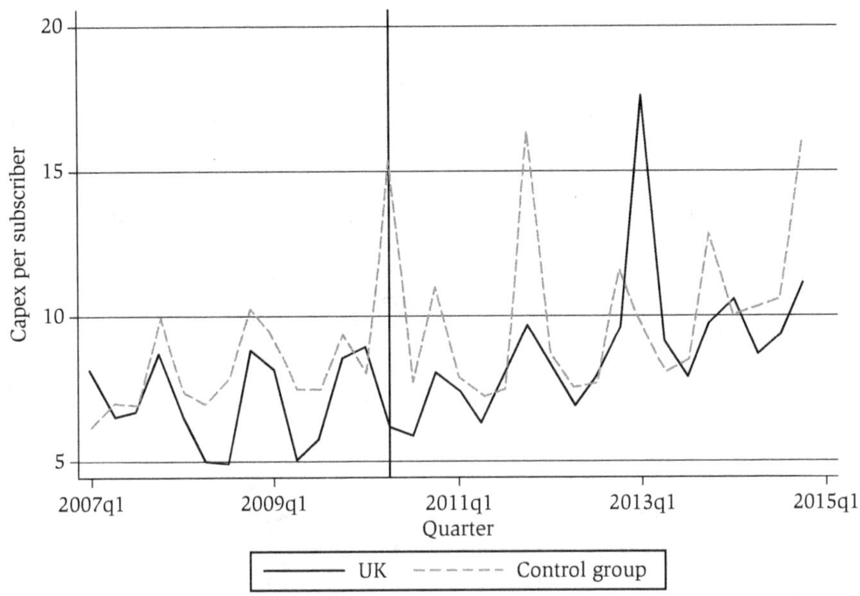

Source: Authors' own elaboration on Analysys Research data and GSMA data.

Note: The vertical line indicates the merger date (2010q2).

The time series for Capex per subscriber appear to show rather erratic trends, with some seasonal variation and other unexplained irregularities, which are even more obvious at the country or operator level. Most of the spikes are related to spectrum acquisitions. For example, in 2013q1, O2 invested EUR 671 million in spectrum, and this is reflected in the spike in the UK Capex series at that time. Similarly, in 2010q2, Telenor (Denmark) invested EUR 333 million in spectrum and SFR (France) invested EUR 1,065 million in 4G spectrum, which might explain the spikes we observe in the average Capex per subscriber for the control countries. As to the seasonality, it appears that operators will often tend to leave large expenditures to the final quarter when they have a clearer view of cash flow for the year as a whole. In the analysis, we have tried to control for such seasonality by considering additional specifications with biannual and annual data to remove some of the noise of the series and improve the precision of our estimates.

Table 4.5 below shows the main results of our analysis. The period of analysis goes from 2007-2014. We use two different dependent variables: the natural logarithm of Capex per operator (lncapex) and the natural logarithm of Capex per operator over the number of subscribers (lncapex-unit). Capex measures the total investment made by the operator, regardless of its size (although this is controlled for on the right hand side with the operator fixed effect). Dividing Capex by the number of subscribers gives a unitary measure of investment, i.e., how much the operator spends on average for each of its users.

We use the following control variables:

- A dummy variable 'fixed component' indicating whether the Capex figure for a certain operator in a given quarter includes investment in its fixed network in addition to investment in its mobile network. We expect this coefficient to be positive because investment expenditures are higher when they also include investments in the fixed network.
- A set of dummies for time of entry in the market, to control for operator fixed characteristics such as being an incumbent, a second entrant, etc.

We include country-operators fixed effect and time fixed effects. The time effects would also help us controlling for the seasonality in the Capex series. Finally, we cluster standard errors at the country level.

Table 4.5 Merger Effect on Capex – Period 2007-2014

	(1) Quarterly Data	*(2) Quarterly Data*	*(3) Biannual Data*	*(4) Biannual Data*	*(5) Annual Data*	*(6) Annual Data*
Variables	*lncapex*	*lncapex-unit*	*lncapex*	*lncapex-unit*	*lncapex*	*lncapex-unit*
Post Merger* Treated	0.240**	0.119	-0.962	0.0848	-0.923	0.0452
	(0.102)	(0.112)	(1.157)	(0.237)	(1.241)	(0.291)
Fixed component	0.212	0.223	-1.768	-0.313	-1.721	-0.336
	(0.144)	(0.166)	(1.803)	(0.405)	(1.901)	(0.518)
Ln(GDP per capita)	-0.269	-0.0350	3.628	-0.365	5.471	0.189
	(0.512)	(0.519)	(8.997)	(1.654)	(9.973)	(2.115)
Second entrant	-2.015***	0.209	-9.337	1.286	-4.648***	-0.675***
	(0.174)	(0.165)	(17.939)	(3.341)	(0.000)	(0.000)
Third entrant	-1.903***	0.889***	-5.338	-0.844	-6.637	-1.257
	(0.187)	(0.181)	(6.257)	(1.198)	(6.999)	(1.538)
Fourth entrant	-2.162***	0.719***	-5.141	-0.847	-6.518	-1.366
	(0.171)	(0.161)	(6.496)	(1.246)	(7.916)	(1.747)
Constant	18.40***	1.570	-9.556	4.483	-21.30	1.512
	(3.536)	(3.537)	(64.262)	(11.743)	(70.974)	(14.984)
Observations	726	726	384	384	192	192
R-Squared	0.919	0.621	0.411	0.429	0.418	0.457
Cluster	Country	Country	Country	Country	Country	Country
Time FE	YES	YES	YES	YES	YES	YES
FE	Country* Operator	Country* operator	Country* operator	Country* operator	Country* operator	Country* operator

Robust standard errors in parentheses

*** $p < 0.01$, ** $p < 0.05$, * $p < 0.1$

Source: Authors' own elaboration on Analysys Mason Research data and GSMA data.

Model (1) suggests that the merger (as modified by the remedies) might have caused a positive effect on Capex per operator. However, when we look at the ratio of Capex per operator over the number of subscribers (Model (2)), the effect is no longer significant, as it fades when we explicitly take into account operators' size. This may be because any positive effect on absolute Capex may have been partially offset by a growth in the number of subscribers.

Results, at both aggregate and subscribers levels, are no longer significant when we aggregate data at biannual or annual level (Models (3)-(6)) to smoothen seasonal spikes. This non-significance might be due to the reduced sample size. However, this puts into question the reliability of our results at the quarterly level. As extensively discussed above, the Capex time series is significantly affected by factors other than the merger, most notably spectrum auctions. These heterogeneous events across countries severely limit the ability of the analysis to disentangle the effect of the merger on Capex. A further limiting factor is that in some cases the available Capex figures include the investment expenditures for both fixed and mobile services. The available information (captured by the dummy *Fixed component*) imperfectly controls for such limitation.

Despite our efforts to empirically control such limitations, the shortcomings of the Capex data severely limit the identification of the causal effect of the merger on investment. Although the existing academic contributions have all used Capex to approximate investment, it is important to summarise the limitations of this indicator. Even when measured correctly, capital expenditure represents money spent on the network and is not necessarily a good proxy for the quality of the network, which is the metric of interest to consumers and policy-makers. Network quality has only a tenuous relationship with expenditure: for instance, if a larger scale allowed to spend money more efficiently, we would observe a decrease in capital expenditure but a superior network quality.

Moreover, capital expenditure is often measured unreliably. It is extracted from operators' quarterly reports and as such, it is biased by inconsistencies in reporting across operators, seasonality and noise from capital expenditure in fixed operations. In our case, such drawbacks were so severe that they limited the reliability of our results. Our Capex data exhibits seasonal spikes, which were smoothed by aggregating these data to the biannual and yearly level. However, the estimates based on the aggregated data were no longer significant, probably due to the small size of the sample.

To sum up, while the UK MNOs represented in the dataset (all but Three, the beneficiary of the remedies) would seem to have increased their investment expenditure, the data used present some features that severely limit the ability of the analysis to identify the causal relation between the merger and Capex. First, the spectrum auctions spread across the period of the analysis in different countries have created spikes in the data. Second, the measurement of Capex that combines the expenditures for both fixed and mobile services introduces heterogeneity reduces the comparability of countries with different types of operators. And third, given the incomplete operator coverage of the data, it is not possible to draw a definitive conclusion on whether the merger has raised total investment at the national level. The results, therefore, should be interpreted with caution.

[B] Descriptive Analysis

This section provides a descriptive analysis of the evolution of the UK market after the merger. This evidence might help to interpret the results obtained in the empirical analysis.

Figure 4.4 shows the market shares of both MNOs and MVNOs for the fourth quarter of 2009 – before the merger decision – and for the fourth quarter of 2014 – nearly four years after the merger and immediately before the takeover of EE by BT.

Figure 4.4 Mobile Network Operators' and Virtual Mobile Network Operators' Market Shares (Subscribers), 2009q4 and 2014q4

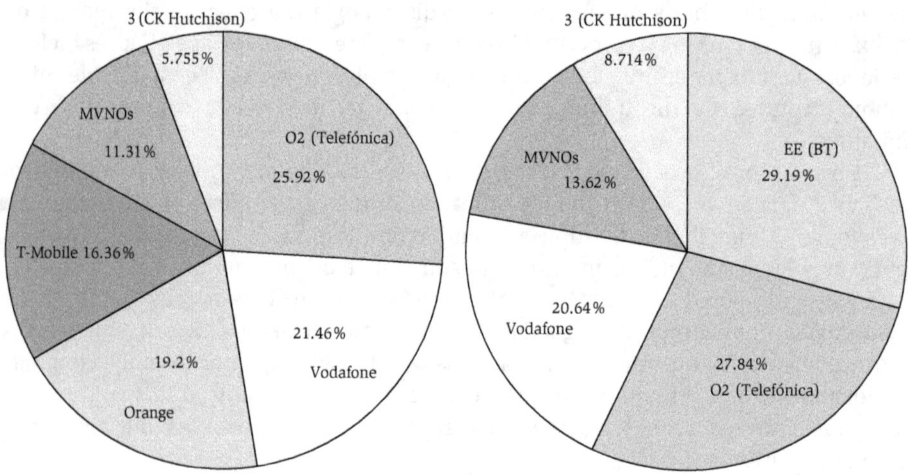

Source: Authors' own elaboration on Analysys Mason Research data.

Over that period, both O2 and Vodafone have roughly maintained their market shares, around 26-28% and 21% respectively. T-Mobile and Orange, whose aggregate share was 35.6% in late 2009, dropped (rebranded as EE) to 29.2% in 2014. On the other hand, Three has strengthened its market share from 5.7% to 8.7% market share. Similarly, the aggregate market shares of MVNOs increased to 13.6% in 2014, up from 11.3% in 2009.

The increase in the share of Three may have been caused, among other things, by its aggressive pricing strategy. Unfortunately, we do not have tariff data to analyse Three's pricing strategy. However, data on Three's ARPU (Figure 4.5) show a strong decline over the period 2010-2013, and this could corroborate an aggressive pricing strategy. The structural remedies required by the Commission (and in particular the RAN sharing agreement between the merging parties and Three) might have helped

Three to maintain the role of 'maverick'[21] in the UK market. This line of reasoning might also help explain the observed post-merger decline in mobile prices in the UK relative to that in the control group.

Figure 4.5 Mobile Network Operators' Average Revenue Per User (Euro/Subscriber)

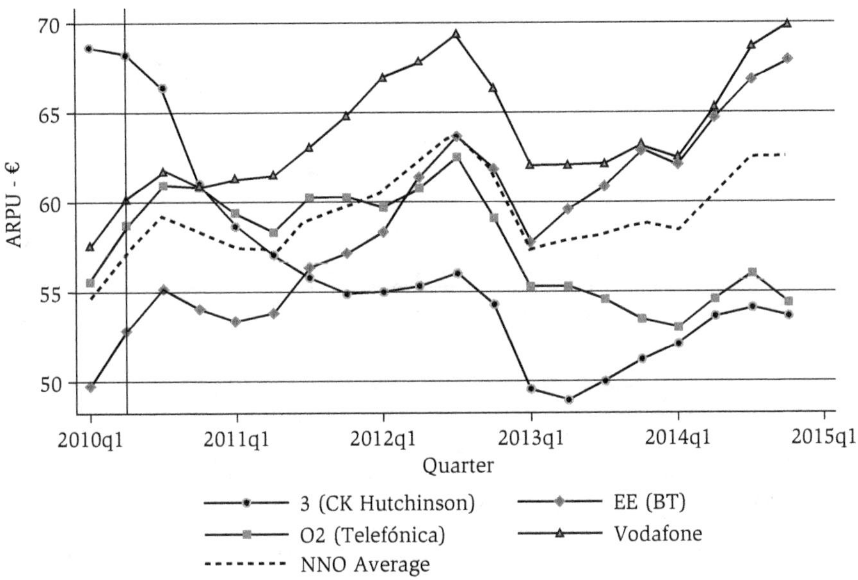

Source: Authors' own elaboration on Analysys Mason DataHub.

The level of investment by MNOs, assessed above through the analysis on Capex, may affect the speed with which innovations are deployed. For this reason, it may be interesting to look at the roll-out of 4G networks by UK MNOs around the time of the merger. Figure 4.6 describes the evolution of Long Term Evolution (LTE or 4G) coverage for UK MNOs,[22] with the dashed segments indicating coverage before 4G retail services were introduced. The vertical line - 2013q1 - indicates the time of the latest spectrum auction.

21. Elixmann et al. (2015) define the maverick as the operator most likely to introduce new services or new technologies and to implement aggressive pricing strategies.
22. This is defined as the percentage of households reached by 4G mobile broadband (LTE) networks.

Figure 4.6 4G Coverage in UK

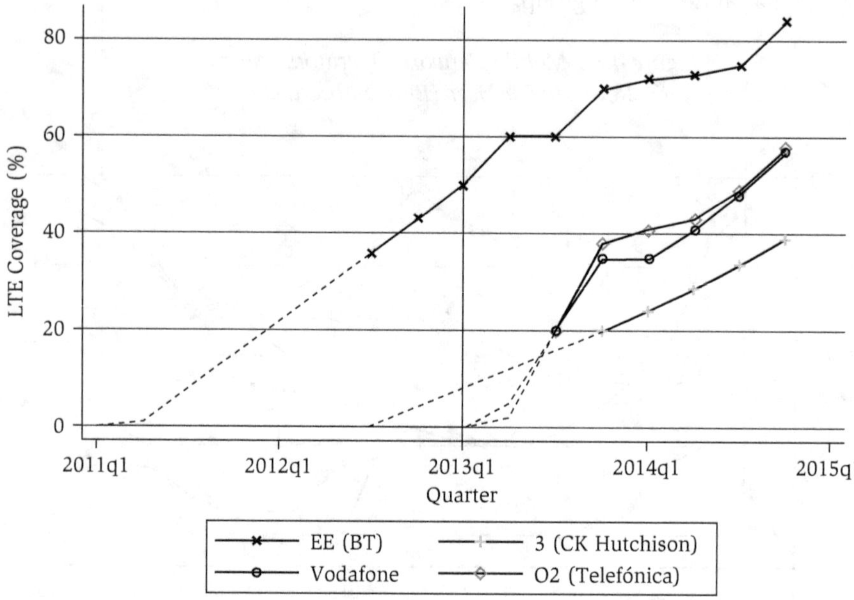

Source: Authors' own elaboration on GSMA data.

EE was the first MNO to deploy and market 4G services in October 2012. Since then, it has retained a first-mover advantage, achieving in late 2014 more than 80% population coverage. O2 and Vodafone started providing 4G services in August 2013, and had close to 60% coverage in 2014q4. Three started providing 4G services in December 2013, as the company acquired 4G spectrum (in the 2013 auction) in the 800MHz band, previously allocated to television transmission and subsequently cleared.

The remedies imposed by the European Commission (in particular the second remedy, related to the spectrum divestment) were designed to level the playing field in terms of 4G services and spectrum distribution. The above evidence confirms that, at least from 2013, all the mobile operators have invested in 4G services and that the merger has not hindered the development of these services in the UK. Figure 4.7 compares the coverage of 4G services in the UK and Italy, Germany and Spain from 2010q1 to 2014q4. The graph shows that the UK's coverage has developed in line with the other EU countries. Furthermore, the rate of 4G coverage at the national level is well within Ofcom's expectations as reported in the merger decision, i.e., full national coverage by 2017.

Figure 4.7 4G Coverage: UK Versus Italy, Germany and Spain

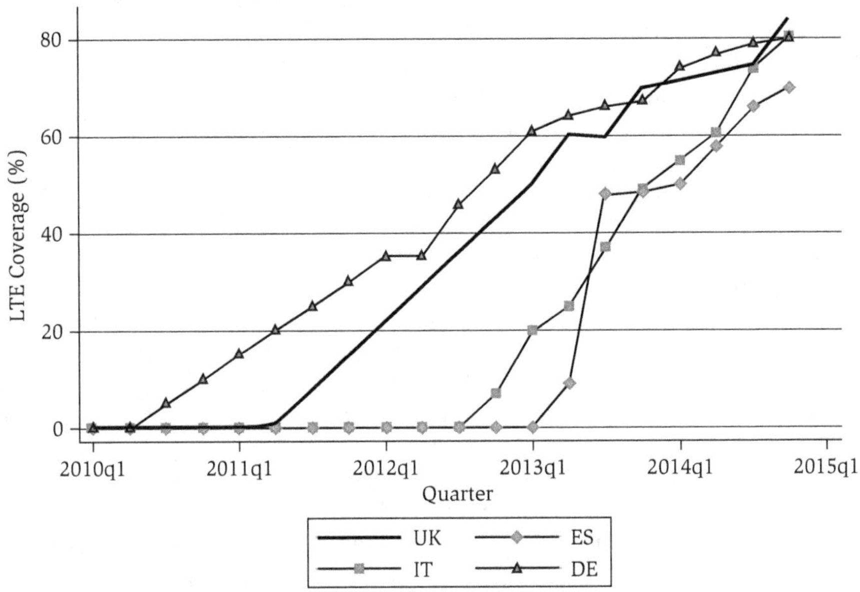

Source: Authors' own elaboration on GSMA data.

It is more difficult to draw any conclusion on the impact of the remedies on the spectrum distribution amongst competitors in the UK mobile market. Such spectrum distribution was affected not only by the remedies but also by the fact that additional spectrum bands were assigned in the 2013 auction to all four operators.

§4.06 CONCLUSION

Mobile telecommunications markets are an important element of the strategy aiming at creating a Digital Single Market in the European Union. The use of mobile telecommunication services - in particular, mobile data access - is significantly growing and is an important input for the economy. At the same time, a wave of within-country consolidation between mobile operators has taken place in the European Union. It is important that this consolidation does not lead to higher prices and lower quality of services for consumers. The EU merger control aims at avoiding these adverse consequences of mergers by imposing remedies (or more rarely) prohibiting mergers which could significantly reduce effective competition at the detriment of consumers. Ex post evaluations of past merger decisions can contribute to improve the effectiveness of this merger control by helping to understand whether the merger decisions have had their expected impact.

This case study evaluates the causal effects of the UK T-Mobile/Orange merger (together with remedies) on prices and investment per operator by using the

Difference-in-Differences methodology. It also provides a descriptive analysis of the market trends in the UK mobile telecommunication services after the merger. These quantitative and descriptive analyses seem to indicate that the merger (as modified by the remedies) has contributed to a reduction in prices of mobile services in the UK. The application of the Difference-in-Differences method shows that the merger together with the associated remedies resulted in a price decline ranging between 9% and 19% for medium to high-intensity users of mobile services in the UK. The descriptive analysis confirms that the remedies may have contributed to maintaining competitive conditions in the UK market for mobile services. Three kept on pursuing its aggressive pricing strategy in the post-merger period, which resulted in an increase of its market share. The MVNOs increased their market share as well. Overall, the market has remained competitive.

While the quantitative analysis did not find a significant effect on investment levels, the merger remedies may have contributed to maintaining a level playing field for the provision of 4G services: all mobile operators have invested in 4G services and the merger did not seem to have hindered the development of such services in the UK.

There are, however, some reasons for caution in the interpretation of these results due to the limitations of the analyses. These limitations are related to: (i) the complexity of defining and measuring prices and investments in mobile telecommunication services; (ii) the data constraints and the associated complications for the empirical analysis; and (iii) the difficulty to find a fully convincing control group due to the peculiarities of the UK market. Therefore, given the debate regarding the relationship between consolidation, prices, investment and innovation for policy makers, further research is needed to construct more reliable measures of prices and investment that can help provide more conclusive empirical evidence on these issues.

A further element that threatens the robustness of our results is endogeneity. Market structure may affect investments and innovation, but the reverse is also possible. For instance, firms may decide to merge precisely because they want to be able to spend more on their networks, or to spend more efficiently. The same holds for the price analysis: a merger may be the result, for instance, of a declining trend in prices. In such a scenario, the merger becomes a tool to respond to the declining prices, and this would make the merger endogenous and bias the estimation. In our case, the consolidation between T-Mobile and Orange might be a response to the UK price drop in the pre-merger period.

Finally, two main lessons can be drawn from this case study. First, good data are essential for robust ex post evaluations. This case study clearly illustrates the limitations created by data problems. Second, when data constraints and difficulty to find a fully convincing control groups reduces the reliability of the quantitative analysis, it is important to complement it with a descriptive analysis of market trends post-merger. The descriptive analysis presented here provides interesting information showing that the UK market had remained competitive after the merger, which supports the results of the quantitative analysis.

REFERENCES

Affeldt P. and Nitsche R. (2014), 'A price concentration study on European mobile telecom markets: Limitations and insights', ESMT Research Working Paper 14-07, ESMT European School of Management and Technology.

Aguzzoni L., Buehler B., Di Martile L., Ecker G., Kemp R., Schwarz A. and Stil R. (2015), 'Ex-post analysis of two mobile telecom mergers: T-Mobile/tele.ring in Austria and T-Mobile/Orange in the Netherlands', European Commission, Directorate-General for Competition.

Ashenfelter O.C., Hosken D.S. and Weinberg M.C. (2013), 'The price effects of a large merger of manufacturers: A case study of Maytag-Whirlpool', *American Economic Journal: Economic Policy*, 5(1), pp. 239-261.

Buehler B., Buettner T., Ocello E. and Piergiovanni M. (2017), 'Europe - The final countdown: five, four, three... no, wait!', *Competition Law & Policy Debate*, 3(4), November.

Buettner T., Federico G. and Lorincz S. (2016): 'The use of quantitative economic techniques in EU merger control', *Antitrust Magazine*, 31(1), pp. 68-75.

Elixmann D., Godlovitch I., Henseler-Unger I., Schwab R. and Stumpf U. (2015), 'Competition & investment: An analysis of the drivers of investment and consumer welfare in mobile telecommunications', WIK-Consult Report, Study for Ofcom.

Frontier Economics (2015), 'Assessing the case for in-country mobile consolidation', Report prepared for the GSMA.

Genakos C., Valletti T. and Verboven F. (2018), 'Evaluating Market Consolidation in Mobile Communications', *Economic Policy*, 33(93), pp. 45-100.

Lear, DIW Berlin and Analysys Mason (2017), 'Economic impact of competition policy enforcement on the functioning of telecoms markets in the EU', Final report prepared for the Directorate-General for Competition of the European Commission, Publications Office of the EU.

Mariniello M. and Salemi F. (2015), 'Addressing fragmentation in EU mobile telecoms markets', Research report, Bruegel Policy contribution, No. 2015/13.

Ofcom (2010), 'International Communications Market Report 2010', Research Document.

RTR (2016), 'Ex-post analysis of the merger between H3G Austria and Orange Austria'.

Part II The Ex Post Evaluation of Antitrust Decisions

CHAPTER 5

The Telekomunikacja Polska Antitrust Case*

Alessia Marrazzo, Paolo Buccirossi & Salvatore Nava

In 2009, the European Commission opened an investigation on the behaviour of Telekomunikacja Polska (TP), the incumbent operator in the Polish fixed telecoms market. In 2011, the European Commission established that TP had abused its dominant position over the period August 2005-October 2009 by hindering the access of other operators to its nation-wide legacy network. This chapter provides an ex post evaluation of this infringement decision. The evaluation combines a descriptive analysis with a quantitative assessment using the Difference-in-Differences approach, which allows identifying the causal relationships between the decision and outcomes in terms of broadband penetration and prices. It shows that the anticompetitive conduct of TP indeed hindered the access of other operators to the TP network, having a negative effect on DSL broadband penetration in Poland. However, such conduct also encouraged TP's competitors and new entrants in the wholesale telecoms market to invest in alternative technologies. The effects of the abuse on prices were less evident. Nevertheless, there is some evidence showing that the abuse might have led to higher prices of DSL-based services charged by TP.

§5.01 INTRODUCTION

This chapter provides an ex post assessment of the economic impact of a 2011 decision by the European Commission prohibiting an abuse of dominant position by the incumbent operator in the Polish fixed telecoms market. The European Commission established that Telekomunikacja Polska (TP) had abused its dominant position by hindering alternative operators from accessing its nationwide legacy network. The

* This chapter is based on an ex post evaluation of the European Commission's decision in the *TP* antitrust case, as presented in the 2017 study *Economic impact of competition policy enforcement on the functioning of telecoms markets in the EU*, commissioned by the Directorate-General for Competition of the European Commission. *See* Lear, DIW Berlin and Analysys Mason (2017).

investigation revealed that TP's conduct had resulted in harm to consumers, as reflected in lower broadband penetration, higher broadband prices and lower average broadband connection speeds.

The ex post evaluation analysis described in this chapter investigates the impact of the infringement decision adopted by the European Commission on the performance of the Polish fixed telecoms market. Using both descriptive and quantitative tools, the analysis aims at determining whether: (1) the abuse effectively distorted competition; and (2) the European Commission's decision was able to remove, partially or completely, the potentially anticompetitive effects of the abuse.

This analysis is rather novel in the field of ex post evaluation, as there are very few studies that examine the effects of abuse of dominance decisions.[1] The reason is that the ex post evaluation analysis in abuse cases is more complex than in merger cases. First, many cases are settled and consequently there are not so many prohibition decisions. It is more difficult to make a sound ex post analysis of settlement decisions, as the theory of harm is not clearly described in such decisions. Second, the definition of the counterfactual is complex. The established approach in evaluation studies is to use the period before the treatment to define the control group that will allow the evaluator to identify the evolution of the market in absence of the treatment. For example, in a merger case, information covering the period before the merger is used to identify a control group, i.e., companies not affected by the merger, whose behaviour and characteristics are similar to the merging companies. By contrast, in an abuse case, the decision brings to an end a conduct resulting in potentially anticompetitive effects on the market. The period before the intervention is thus affected by the abuse and cannot be used to estimate the counterfactual market evolution. Finally, in this particular case, it was also difficult to distinguish the impact of the European Commission's decision from that of the preceding intervention by national telecoms regulator, Urząd Komunikacji Elektronicznej (UKE). The Commission and UKE cooperated closely in bringing the abuse to an end.

This study combines a descriptive and a quantitative analysis. The use of the descriptive analysis allows to grasp a better understanding of the evolution of the European telecoms market in the analysed period, and to put into a context what have occurred in the Polish market. Moreover, it has proved very useful to complement and interpret the results of the quantitative evaluation in such a complex case.

This chapter is structured as follows. Section 5.02 provides a brief summary of the decision adopted by the European Commission and of the main events having taken place during the period covered by the analysis. Section 5.03 provides useful references to the literature analysing the economic impact of refusing access to the network and supporting the empirical strategy chosen. Section 5.04 describes the

1. *See* literature review on ex post evaluation by Ilzkovitz and Dierx (2015). Another ex post analysis of an antitrust decision using the Difference-in-Differences approach can be found in a recent study commissioned by DG Competition on the energy sector (*see* ICF and DIW Berlin, 2015). However, in that case, the identification strategy is rather specific to the energy markets under investigation and exploits the different price response to the Commission's decision between peak (8am-8pm) and off-peak prices (8pm-8am) (*see* Chapter 6).

methodology used in the quantitative analysis and defines the outcome and explanatory variables considered. Section 5.05 presents the results of the descriptive and quantitative analyses and section 5.06 concludes.

§5.02 FACTUAL BACKGROUND

[A] Presentation of the Case Decision Being Evaluated

Telekomunikacja Polska (TP), now Orange Polska S.A., is the incumbent operator in the Polish fixed telecoms market, and it has a nation-wide fixed telephone and Digital Subscriber Line (DSL) network. Since 2003, when TP was recognised as a 'significant market power' operator, TP has had an obligation to grant wholesale access to its local network via Local Loop Unbundling (LLU) and by providing bitstream access (BSA).[2] When Poland entered the EU in 2004, the national telecoms regulator, UKE, invited TP to draft a Reference Offer (RO) setting out the minimum standards to be guaranteed to alternative operators when negotiating wholesale access. However, TP's RO was considered to be insufficient to promote effective competition and UKE invited TP to present a new draft of the RO.

In April 2009, The European Commission opened an investigation against TP and, in February 2010, it issued a Statement of Objections. The European Commission decision published on 22 June 2011 found that TP consciously planned and engaged in practices aimed at hindering alternative operators from efficiently accessing its network.

More precisely, according to the European Commission, TP's conduct consisted in: (1) proposing unreasonable conditions that delayed access negotiations with alternative operators; (2) limiting access to its network; (3) limiting access to subscriber lines; and (4) refusing to provide reliable and complete information, necessary for alternative operators to make a sound decision regarding access to TP's wholesale broadband products at specific locations.[3] The European Commission concluded that TP's refusal to supply wholesale DSL services to new entrants resulted in harm to consumers as reflected in lower broadband penetration, higher broadband prices and lower average broadband connection speeds.[4] This anticompetitive conduct lasted from 3 August 2005 to 22 October 2009, when TP signed a voluntary agreement with the national telecoms regulator in which it committed to respect the existing regulatory obligations.

2. Physical unbundling or local loop unbundling is a form of wholesale access enabling alternative operators to use the physical wire connection of the incumbent to reach customer premises from a local exchange. In line with the European regulatory framework, this type of access is typically managed by the national telecom regulator. Bitstream service access refers to the situation where a wireline incumbent installs a high-speed access link to the customer's premises (e.g., by installing ADSL equipment in the local access network) and then makes this access link available to third parties, to enable them to provide high-speed services to customers. This type of access does not entail any third-party access to the copper pair in the local loop.
3. *See* recital (511), Case COMP 39.525, European Commission, (2011).
4. *See* recital (838), Case COMP 39.525, European Commission, (2011).

[B] Institutional Background

TP is one of the most recent abuse cases in telecoms markets, which have been investigated by the European Commission. Over the period 2002-2015, the Commission adopted six antitrust decisions in telecoms markets. Five of these six decisions are related to abuse of dominant position and one (Telefonica and Portugal Telecom) to an anticompetitive agreement. Figure 5.1 below shows the timeline of the antitrust decisions adopted by the European Commission.

Nearly all of the antitrust decisions taken by the European Commission investigated foreclosure conduct by incumbent operators, such as margin squeeze or refusal to supply. These decisions set both a legal and policy framework, which has been instrumental in providing direction to National Competition Authorities' activities, which were very active in this area as well: no less than 330 antitrust decisions in the telecoms markets have been taken by national competition authorities of the EU over the period 2002 and 2015.[5]

Figure 5.1 Timeline of Antitrust Decisions by the European Commission[6]

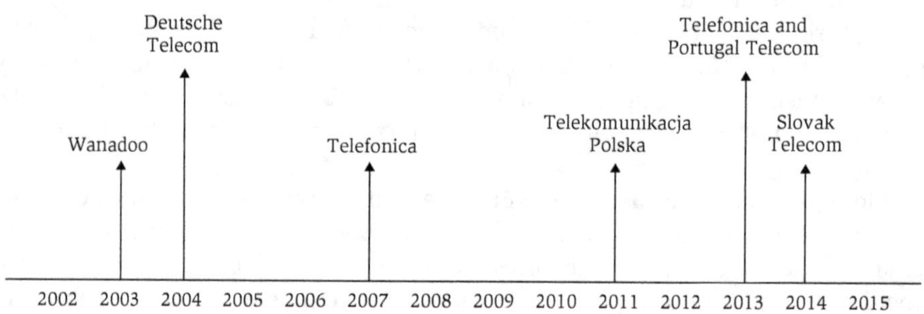

Source: Authors' own elaborations of European Commission data.

The TP case, together with *Deutsche Telekom* in Germany and *Telefonica* in Spain (both margin squeeze abuses), is an example of the interplay between competition law and regulatory policy. In the analysed case, the national regulator and the European Commission worked hand in hand to stop the anticompetitive conduct of TP and improve the conditions of competition in the Polish fixed telecoms market. Since 2004, UKE has intervened several times in this market and even sanctioned TP. The European Commission notes in its decision that only when confronted with the

5. Data on the competition policy decisions adopted by both the European Commission and the National Competition Authorities) have been collected from public websites and with the help of the National Competition Authorities. In particular, data on the European Commission decisions have been gathered from the European Commission website, while National Competition Authorities have replied to detailed questionnaires on the main characteristics of all the decisions adopted in their national telecoms markets over the period 2002-2015 (*see* Lear, DIW and Analysys Mason, 2017).
6. Case COMP 38233; Case COMP/C-1/37451, 37578, 37579; Case COMP 38784; Case COMP 39525; Case COMP 39839; Case AT 39523.

possibility of functional separation in 2009, TP signed a voluntary agreement with UKE and committed to respect the regulatory obligations signed with UKE on 22 October 2009.[7]

In spite of the above-described collaboration between the European Commission and the national sector regulator, there are a few recent examples in the literature, which instead points out that there exists a tension between regulation and competition. de Streel (2012) reviews the main abuse cases investigated by the European Commission, including the Polish case, and concludes that the interaction between regulation and competition policy might lead to a duplication of procedures. According to the author, 'the Commission uses its antitrust powers not only to ensure that competition is not distorted on the market but also to support the liberalisation programme and to control, and if necessary correct, the decisions of NRA'. The author suggests that the European Commission should inform the national regulator if a draft decision infringes EU law. If the decision is nevertheless adopted, the European Commission should open an infringement procedure under Article 258 TFEU.

TP appealed the decision before the General Court on 2 September 2011 asking for the full annulment of the European Commission's decision or, alternatively, for a reduction of the fine imposed by the European Commission. In one of the three submitted claims, TP was asking for an annulment of the fine on the basis of actions taken following the agreement with UKE. In particular, TP was advocating: (1) the considerable investments undertaken since the date of the agreement with UKE in order to modernise Polish fixed-line infrastructure for alternative operators and end-users; and (2) the voluntary cessation of the infringement, right after the agreement. On December 2015, the Court confirmed the European Commission's decision and dismissed the entire appeal of TP.

§5.03 LITERATURE REVIEW

This section presents a short review of the literature, which provides the analytical framework of the case study. A distinction is made between papers analysing the impact of the mode of competition on market performances and papers used to support the empirical strategy (such as the definition of outcome and control variables).

[A] Impact of Access on Market Performance

The papers reviewed here illustrate the impact of access regulation on telecoms market performance. Access regulation defines the mode of competition prevailing in the market, and to this extent, may have an impact on market performance. TP, by refusing to supply access to its copper network, has altered the mode of competition prevailing in the market and, in the end, affected market performance. Box 5.1 presents an overview of modes of competition in broadband services.

7. *See* recital (154), Case COMP 39.525, European Commission, (2011).

Box 5.1: Modes of competition in broadband services

Competition in the fixed telecoms markets may occur at different levels. Either, it may concern the interaction between different technological platforms or networks, or it may occur within the same network when the owner of the infrastructure is obliged to lease network elements to other firms, that will hence provide retail services relying on the same platform. In the literature, the former is often referred to as inter-platform competition and the latter as intra-platform competition (*see* Figure 5.2).

Figure 5.2 Inter- and Intra-platform Competition: State of Play in the Second Half of the Year 2010

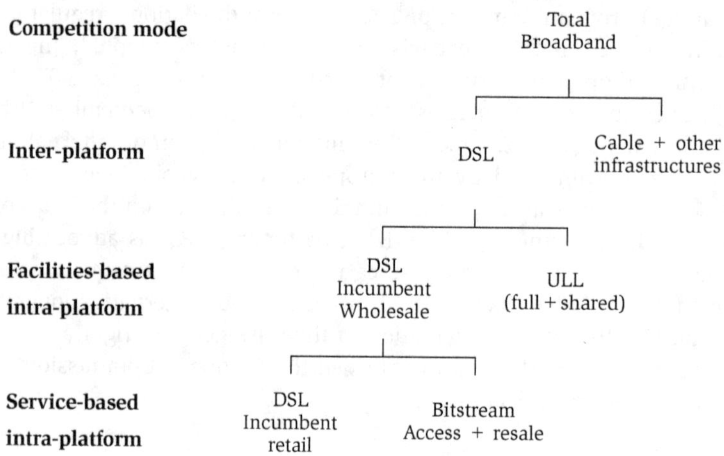

Source: Bouckaert et al. (2010).

Within inter-platform competition, each operator provides broadband services by using its own infrastructure and the associated technologies. The following technologies are generally distinguished: DSL, cable, fibre or WIMAX-wireless access. With separate platforms, the investor is not forced to share any benefits it creates as it would be with firms using its network. This could encourage investment in infrastructure but may also lead to inefficient duplication of network infrastructure.

Within intra-platform competition, alternative operators (i.e., entrants or competitors) use the existing incumbent's network. Further distinction can be made between facilities-based intra-platform competition and service-based intra-platform competition according to the type of access to the incumbent's platform gained by the competitor. Under facilities-based intra-platform, entrants lease unbundled local loop elements but have to invest their own equipment and facilities (physical unbundling or LLU). This gives alternative operators the highest degree of control of the services offered. Under service-based competition, entrants are merely reselling the incumbent's services (through bitstream access or resale services) and therefore incur little investment costs.

By refusing to give access to its copper network, TP has adversely affected the degree of intra-platform competition in the Polish market (*see* Box 5.1 for a definition). The ultimate impact on market performance is not straightforward since the provision of access to the legacy copper network is generally expected to stimulate the entry of alternative operators and promote market competition, but it may also diminish their incentives to invest in broadband infrastructure. The empirical analysis developed in this chapter will try to shed some light on this possible trade-off building upon the results available in the literature.

Since the start of the liberalisation process in the EU's the telecoms markets, regulators have typically promoted competition in retail markets by mandating access to the existing infrastructure at a regulated price. In this context, there is a wide strand of literature that investigates the impact of access regulation on broadband market performance.

Some papers argue that regulated prices for Unbundled Local Loop (ULL) access are associated with a better availability of broadband services and an increased number of retail providers (*see* Ford and Spiwak, 2004). A recent study conducted by Analysys Mason (2015) for the European Competitive Telecommunications Association (ECTA) evaluates the development and performance of European broadband markets. It observes that the coverage of Next Generation Access (NGA)[8] networks has increased significantly under the current regulatory framework and that alternative operators have played a key role in the deployment of these new networks. They also point out that access to the incumbent network (e.g., the sub-loop unbundling in Italy or Germany) or the existence of effective wholesale inputs (e.g., the existence of high quality and capillary duct network in Portugal and France) facilitates investments by alternative operators. They finally argue, 'Care should be taken when drawing conclusions about the benefits of deregulation and/or forbearance for regulation of NGA wholesale access'. Although some non-EU jurisdictions have higher NGA coverage and take-up than the EU, the absence or reduction of ex ante regulation is not a main driver of these differences. They indeed believe that the current regulatory framework has served the European broadband markets well and that effective NGA network deployment requires the support of such a regulatory policy.

Klein et al. (2014) use panel data for sixteen EU and non-EU countries covering the years 1997 to 2013 and find that the effect of LLU on penetration is positive when an intermediate level of broadband penetration has been achieved in a country.

8. NGA network are access technologies, which consist wholly or in part of optical elements that allow broadband access services with enhanced characteristics (such as higher throughput) as compared to those provided over already existing copper networks. In most cases, NGAs result in an upgrade of an already existing copper or co-axial access network.

However, they also find that the effect on penetration turns negative if the initial level of broadband penetration is relatively low or high.

Nardotto et al. (2015) show that the effect of LLU on broadband penetration is limited in early years and vanishes as the market approaches maturity. However, in their model LLU entrants offer a better quality of service than the incumbent does. Entrants use LLU to put in place quality-based differentiation strategies. Open-access policies may hence not affect broadband penetration but rather increase the quality of the service provided to the final users.

Based on the results of this strand of the literature, we might infer that, by hindering access to the incumbent's network, an abuse of dominant position impedes the development of intra-platform competition facilitated by access regulation. However, there is also a branch of the literature that shows that mandatory access to the incumbent's network may distort investment incentives in next generation networks.

For example, Bourreau et al. (2012) observe that NGA-related investment incentives are affected by the regulated access prices to the old copper networks via three effects:

(1) Replacement effect: low access prices to old-generation networks discourage infrastructure investment in NGA networks by alternative operators, as they increase the opportunity cost of this investment.
(2) Wholesale revenue effect: when the entrant does not invest in an NGA network, the incumbent enjoys wholesale revenues from its old infrastructure network and its profits are increasing with access prices.
(3) Business migration effect: if access prices to old-generation network are low, retail prices based on that network are also low. Therefore, in order to compete with the old technology, NGA network services should be offered at low prices. This effect reduces the profitability of the NGA networks, and hence the incentive to invest in them.

A recent paper from Briglauer et al. (2016) attempts to empirically test these three effects using a EU27 panel data set for the period 2004-2014. Their results show that a 1% increase in access prices (in the LLU price) raises NGA adoption and NGA network investment by almost 0.45% and 0.47% respectively.[9] Therefore, a policy measure that increased the cost of access to the incumbent's DSL network could exert a positive effect on NGA network investment and adoption (this latter effect would also reduce the gap between the retail prices of broadband services based on old and new technologies).[10]

9. The authors find that the effect of an increase in LLU price is greater for NGA network coverage than adoption. They suggest to introduce additional policies (such as tax deductions) to enhance ultra-fast broadband demand.
10. The authors also show that the effects on NGA adoption and network investment are greatly reduced in Central and Eastern European Countries (CEECs) that are characterised by a lack of a well-developed legacy infrastructure.

[B] Papers Supporting the Empirical Strategy

A number of papers have been used to inform the empirical strategy used in the quantitative analysis. Most of these papers have focused on the impact of inter/intra-platform competition on the performance of broadband markets. The underlying hypothesis is that the level of access regulation determines the extent of inter- and intra-platform competition prevailing in the markets. The presence of regulated access to the incumbent's network enhances the degree of intra-platform competition, but the ultimate impact on the performance of broadband markets is not straightforward. While some of these papers find that inter-platform competition contributes to an improved performance of telecoms markets (in terms of broadband penetration, broadband adoption and retail prices), others do not find a significant effect of inter-platform competition.[11] Below we present the main papers we build on to define the empirical strategy and the estimation model.

Bouckaert et al. (2010) estimate a model of broadband penetration to explain the differences in penetration observed between the OECD countries. Their model relies on three categories of explanatory variables: (1) competition variables, to measure the degree of inter- and intra-platform competition; (2) broadband service variables, such as speed or prices; and (3) market demographics, such as population density and dispersion, and average disposable income. Calzada and Martínez-Santos (2014) estimate a model for the prices of broadband residential plans, where the explanatory variables referred to the technical characteristics of the services, the operators' commercial strategies and measures of competition and regulation in the prices. We have used some of these variables in our empirical analysis.

Distaso et al. (2006) emphasise the role of stronger competition across technologies as the main driver to stimulate broadband adoption. Their analysis relies on an innovative measure of inter-platform competition based on a different version of the Herfindahl-Hirschmann Index (HHI). Indeed, the HHI is not computed on the basis of the share of the operators in the market, but of the technologies in use.

To conclude, there are two main policy tools to enhance competition in telecoms markets: by encouraging access to existing infrastructures (intra-platform competition) or by stimulating the development of alternative network infrastructures (inter-platform competition). This short survey of the literature does not allow drawing strong conclusions as to which of these two forms of competition is most beneficial for market outcomes, with some papers arguing that intra-platform competition is more effective and others, inter-platform.

11. The empirical analysis developed in this chapter will focus on the impact of TP's conduct on market performance and will not be able to disentangle the effect of the abuse from the effect of a change in intra/inter platform competition. Since we believe that TP, by refusing to supply access to the legacy networks, has altered the degree of intra-platform competition and ultimately affected the market's performance, we will not be able to separately estimate the effect of the abuse and the effect of a change in intra/inter platform competition on the market performance.

§5.04 EMPIRICAL STRATEGY

The goal of the empirical analysis is to evaluate the economic impact of the infringement decision adopted by the European Commission on the performance of the fixed telecoms market in Poland. More precisely, the analysis aims at assessing whether the abuse distorted competition in the fixed telecoms market, and henceforth, whether the European Commission's infringement decision was appropriate and helped to protect consumer welfare.

[A] The Identification Strategy

In order to estimate the impact of the decision, the empirical analysis relies on the Difference-in-Differences approach. The Difference-in-Differences is an established and widely used method in the ex post evaluation studies: it exploits both time and cross-section variation to identify the effect of the policy intervention (i.e., infringement decision) on the outcome variables (measuring market performance). However, in the case at hand, the identification of the 'pre-treatment' and 'post-treatment' periods is not straightforward and requires careful reflection.

As explained in the introductory section, the established approach in evaluation studies is to use the period before the treatment to define a control group that will allow estimating what would have been the evolution of the market in the absence of the treatment. In the current case, the period before the European Commission's intervention has been affected by the abuse. As we want to evaluate both the effect of the abuse and of the European Commission's decision, the ideal counterfactual should represent what would have occurred in the absence of the abuse and the decision. But the period before the abuse and the decision (before 2005) cannot be representative of a situation without abuse, given that TP has been infringing its regulatory obligations since 2003, when it was recognised as an operator with 'significant market power'.[12]

Therefore, we need to adapt the method used for the identification of the counterfactual. We will select the control group by using data for the post-intervention period. The implicit assumption is that during the post-intervention period, the functioning of the Polish market converged to that of other markets not affected by the abuse (the control group).

However, the post-intervention situation in the Polish market cannot be considered as fully independent from the treatment as it might have been influenced by the abuse, the decision and their effects. On the one hand, by hindering access to the copper network, TP's anticompetitive conduct has permanently reshaped the structure of the fixed telecoms markets in Poland. Therefore, the post-treatment period cannot truly represent what would have occurred in the absence of the abuse. On the other hand, the degree of access of alternative operators to TP's copper network clearly depends on the effectiveness of the European Commission's intervention.

12. In addition: (1) the period before 2003 would not be comparable to the period after the decision, since broadband deployment was in its early stages and the DSL network was almost inexistent; (2) data before 2004 are not available.

Having this in mind, the results of the analysis should be carefully interpreted. By relying on the post-treatment period to estimate the counterfactual, the implemented identification strategy does not allow to disentangle the effects of the abuse from the effects of the competition policy intervention. The results will estimate the impact of the abuse, as removed by the decision, on the performance of the fixed telecoms markets in Poland. It will not be possible to ascertain whether the European Commission decision has entirely restored the competitive conditions that would have prevailed in the absence of the abuse.

[B] Choice of the Control Group

The identification of the counterfactual is a crucial step in any ex post evaluation study. The counterfactual scenario should correspond to what would have occurred in the absence of the treatment. However, it is not observable and needs to be estimated by selecting an appropriate control group.

The analysis described in this chapter exploits cross-country variation and selects a set of countries that maximise the similarity between the treated fixed telecoms market (i.e., Poland) and the potential control markets in the post-intervention period. The selected control countries are European countries that are subject to the same regulatory framework as Poland. Moreover, the control group excludes all the countries that have been affected by an anticompetitive conduct over the period of analysis (2006-2014), in order to ensure that the performance of the countries in the control group is not biased by any specific event.[13] Similarly, we checked that the control group countries have not been affected by a structural change (entry or exit) over the period of analysis.[14]

On the basis of these criteria, the countries used as control group are Austria, Belgium, Bulgaria, Croatia, Cyprus, Czech Republic, Denmark, Estonia, Finland, France, Germany, Greece, Hungary, Ireland, Latvia, Lithuania, Luxembourg, Malta, and Netherlands.

The selection of the control group and the control variables is essential to correctly estimate the effect of the treatment. In this case, the presence of a common regulatory framework does not exclude the possibility that the markets in treated and control countries operate under different regulatory conditions. Therefore, in our model, we include as control variables a number of country specific factors other than

13. For this reason, we have excluded Spain, Portugal, Italy, Slovakia and Slovenia, whose fixed telecoms markets have all been investigated by the European Commission or the National Competition Authority for abuse of dominant position.
14. We used quarterly data provided by Analysys Mason to check the change in the number of operators in each country over the period 2006-2014. The number of operators in each of the selected control countries is constant over that period, which is a good (but not perfect) indication that there has been no entry or exit during that period. Please note, however, that the dataset groups the smallest operators in a country into a single entity named 'other operators' and hence we have no information to detect if their number has changed over the analysed period. We expect that the exit or entry of smaller operators, if it occurred, had a minimal impact on the competitive conditions prevailing in the country.

the anticompetitive conduct, which may contribute to explaining the difference in performance between the Polish and the control market.

To test the robustness of our results, we also considered a smaller control group, limited to CEECs. These countries implemented the EU regulatory framework later than the Western European countries and around the same time as Poland. Therefore, the situation in their fixed telecoms market might be more similar to that of the Polish market in the absence of the abuse. However, the number of CEECs which can be included in the control group after having excluded those affected by an anticompetitive conduct might be too small and not sufficiently representative for a robust econometric analysis. Therefore we consider this control group as the second best.[15]

[C] Estimation Method

The quantitative analysis evaluates the causal effects of the TP abuse on broadband penetration and retail prices by applying the Difference-in-Differences approach.[16] It compares treated and non-treated countries during and after the incumbent's abuse of its dominant position. More precisely, the period analysed covers the years 2006 to 2014: 14 quarters before the start of the European Commission's investigation in 2009 and 22 quarters thereafter.[17] The abuse period considered in this analysis starts in 2006 and ends with the opening of the European Commission's proceedings in April 2009. The benchmark period is the post-intervention period. The empirical analysis provides a measure of the average treatment effect, i.e., additional variation experienced by the Polish market compared to the control group and prior to the European Commission's intervention.

In its simplest form, the Difference-in-Differences (DiD) will be calculated as the following difference:

$$DiD = (y_t^{ABUSE} - y_t^{POST\text{-}INTERVENTION}) - (y_c^{ABUSE} - y_c^{POST\text{-}INTERVENTION}) \quad (1)$$

where y is the outcome variable in treated (t) and control (c) group.

15. The CEECs included in this smaller control group are Bulgaria, Croatia, Czech Republic, Estonia, Hungary, Latvia, Lithuania and Romania.

16. We have also tried to use the synthetic control group approach developed by Abadie and Gardeazabal (2003) and later refined by Abadie, Diamond and Hainmueller (2010 and 2015). This approach offers a data-driven procedure to construct a control group to be used as counterfactual. The control group is a weighted average of control units and the relative importance of each control unit is the outcome of an algorithm that, given some 'predictor' variables, minimises the distance between the realisations of the predictors in the treated countries and the (weighted) average of the predictors in the control countries in period before the treatment. In this case study, due to a lack of data, we did not succeed in building a synthetic control group that was sufficiently similar to the treated country (i.e., Poland) in order to arrive at significant and robust estimates.

17. Due to non-availability of data for the year 2005, the analysis will not cover this year, which corresponds to the first year of the abuse period as established by the Commission's decision. Moreover, since the Commission's investigation started in April 2009, we have decided to consider that the second quarter of 2009 is still affected by the abuse.

The post-intervention period is not a fully competitive benchmark period as it depends on the effectiveness of the European Commission's intervention (which is unknown). It follows that the coefficient of the Difference-in-Differences variable measures the effects of the abuse as removed by the intervention.

The basic formulation of the econometric model is as follows:

$$y_{ict} = \alpha + \delta abuse + \gamma_i treat_{ic} \times abuse + X_{ct} + \mu_{ic} + \tau_{ct} + \varepsilon_{ict} \quad (2)$$

where the outcome y for operator i, in country c, at time t, is a function of market demand drivers and technological conditions (X_{ct}), firm-country-specific fixed effects to account for time-invariant unobserved heterogeneity across countries (μ_{ic}), as well as country specific time trends (τ_{ct}).

The dummy $treat_{ic}$ is equal to one when the outcome is measured in the treated country/operators (Poland/Polish operators). The dummy abuse is equal to one in the abuse period, from the first quarter[18] of 2006 to the second quarter of 2009.[19] The coefficient of the Difference-in-Differences variable, the interacted variable $treat_{ic} \times abuse$, is our coefficient of interest and it measures the additional variation in the outcome variable experienced by the Polish market, compared to the control countries, prior to the European Commission's intervention.

[D] Outcome Variables

This analysis investigates the effects of TP's anticompetitive conduct on the fixed telecoms market performance, which is measured by the fixed broadband penetration, the retail prices for broadband services and the quality of these services. We first give a descriptive analysis of these variables over the period 2006-2014, comparing the situation in the Polish market with that in the European Union. Thereafter, a quantitative analysis is carried out to analyse the anticompetitive effect of the TP abuse on broadband penetration and prices in Poland.

Box 5.2: Telecoms market outcomes

Three indicators of market outcomes are used in the descriptive and quantitative analyses: broadband penetration, prices and quality.

A higher broadband penetration is an indicator of positive market outcomes since users positively value the possibility of accessing a variety of telecoms services. Fixed broadband services can be provided through many technologies (DSL, cable, fibre and wireless access) and accordingly a distinction can be made between different indicators of broadband penetration. Broadband penetration

18. Please note that data are available at quarter level.
19. We do not expect that the anticompetitive effects of the abuse terminated immediately after the Commission's intervention. Hence, we try different specifications by changing the dummy *abuse* and assuming that the effects lingered for two years after April 2009 (when the Commission initiated its proceedings). This helps us controlling for any transitory factors that might bias the estimate of the counterfactual.

may be lower in less dense and more remote areas of a country. Indeed, in certain remote areas, the investment in broadband infrastructure may not be commercially viable. In addition, these areas are also characterised by a smaller number of economic activities and the demand for broadband service might also be lower. Market demographics play a relevant role when studying the determinants of broadband penetration and should be duly taken into account when attempting to identify the effect of competition on penetration. This is the reason why we have added as a control variable in our models the percentage of rural population in each country, in addition to the number of inhabitants in each country. There has also been some impact from fixed-mobile substitution (FMS), and this is the reason why we have considered mobile data penetration at the country level as another control variable.

The level of prices is clearly one of the most relevant outcomes from the point of view of both consumers and businesses. However, the measurement of price poses several challenges in the fixed telecoms markets given the variety of the products and services on offer, the wide variation in usage profiles and the rapid technological change. This makes it difficult to identify a price measure that is comparable across consumer groups, across markets and over time. Three different approaches can be found in the literature to measure telecoms prices: (1) consumption baskets representing the average purchases of representative usage profiles; (2) averages of revenues over different measures of output (such as average revenues per MB of data) and average revenues per user; and (3) hedonic pricing models. Each of these indicators has limitations: for example, determining what the representative basket is in the first approach and how to separate price effects from output effects in the second approach.

In this chapter, we have used the average revenue per subscriber. This includes fixed retail revenues for broadband services, namely DSL, FTTH/B, cable modem, other fixed broadband services and bundled broadband services. This indicator has the advantage of being relatively easy to measure. However, it mixes different sources of revenues, which can make the comparison between countries and operators difficult if their mix of revenues is not the same. Moreover, this metric may limit the reliability of our analysis when broadband service quality differs across the selected countries and services' characteristics are not properly controlled for. This is the reason why we control for the type and the quality of the services provided by including a few control variables in our econometric model, namely the average connection speed and the percentage of voice over broadband (VoBB) or internet protocol televisions (IPTV) service subscribers.[20]

We also considered using alternative measures of prices, such as the basket expenditure approach used in Chapter 4. However, the OECD database did not include quarterly basket expenditure data for fixed telecommunication services.

20. VoIP or VoBB corresponds to voice services using Internet Protocol and IPTV corresponds to TV services including TV content delivered using Internet Protocol.

Moreover, other available data were either too aggregated or did not cover the period of interest.

Finally, this chapter presents a descriptive analysis on the evolution of broadband speed during and after the abuse. Broadband speed can be considered as a quality indicator. Most ex post evaluation analysis place their attention on prices. However, quality can also influence consumers' welfare and, whenever possible, the analysis should also be extended to the effect of the decision on the quality of the relevant products. Two measures of speed can be considered: advertised speed or actually measured speed. Advertised speed often falls short of actual connection speed and may be a biased indicator. In this report, we therefore use the average actually measured connection speed for retail broadband services.

Table 5.1 presents the indicators used to measure the outcome variables, their frequency and level of aggregation.

Table 5.1 Estimated Data on Outcome Variables

Outcome Variable	*Period*	*Metrics*	*Frequency*	*Source*
Penetration	2006-2014	Percentage of fixed subscribers over the total number of households	Quarterly data, at country/technology level	Analysys Mason
Prices	2006-2014	Revenues per subscriber	Quarterly data, at country, operator and technology level	Analysys Mason
Quality	2007-2014	Average connection speed and average peak connection speed	Quarterly data, at country level	Akamai

Source: Authors' own elaboration of Analysys Mason Research data.

Data on broadband penetration are extremely granular: for each country, it is possible to monitor the number of broadband subscribers for each technological platform (DSL, fibre, cable, fixed wireless access (FWA)) and operator. Data on revenues per subscriber measure the average end-user (business and residential) expenditure on broadband access, including bundled services such VOIP and IPTV. This metric does not only reflect the price of the broadband service, but also the quality (single broadband offer or bundle of data, voice and IPTV) and the type of service provided (*see* Box 5.2). Data on speed are aggregated at country level (rather than at operator or technology level). The limited number of observations and the level of aggregation are problematic for an econometric analysis of the effects of the abuse on broadband speed. However, we use these data for a descriptive analysis of the economic impact of the abuse.

Finally, a number of control variables have been included in the econometric model. These variables which describe supply and demand characteristics of the fixed telecoms markets are essential to allow disentangling the impact of the treatment from any other confounding factors that might have affected the trend of the outcome variables over the period of analysis. The control variables considered include:

- the percentage of rural population in each country;
- the national regulated access price at both LLU and BSA levels;
- the average population at country level;
- the average income at country level;
- the mobile data penetration at country level;
- the number of years since the launch of DSL services in each country;
- the average connection speed at country level;
- the percentage of VoBB and IPTV subscribers.

Further details on the definition of the control variables can be found in Appendix 1.

§5.05 RESULTS

[A] Descriptive Analysis

The descriptive analysis provides a preliminary overview of the evolution of the Polish fixed telecoms markets in the period during and after the abuse. It allows formulating a number of assumptions regarding the impact of the TP abuse which will be tested in the quantitative analysis. In a nutshell, the descriptive analysis seems to indicate that the TP abuse delayed the development of DSL penetration, increased DSL prices and reduced the connection speed on the fixed broadband market in Poland. At the same time, the TP abuse may also have contributed to promote the development of alternative technologies which may have reduced its negative impact overall.

[1] The Evolution of Broadband Penetration

Figure 5.3 describes the evolution in the number of DSL lines for the alternative operators in Poland. The grey bar corresponds to the number of DSL lines owned by the alternative operators, while the black bar corresponds to the number of incumbents' DSL lines over which alternative operators get access through the LLU wholesale service.

Figure 5.3 Evolution of Local Loop Unbundling Access in Poland

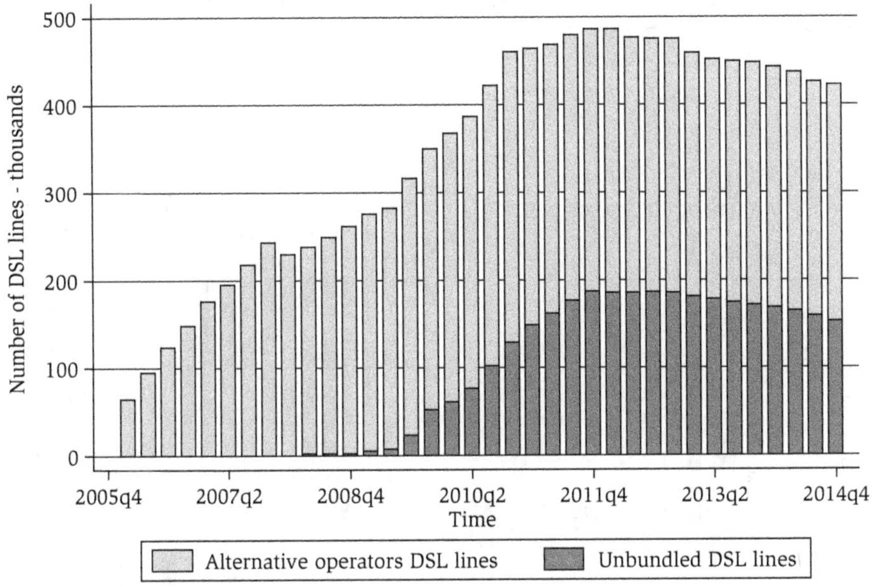

Source: Authors' own elaboration on Analysys Mason data.

Figure 5.3 clearly shows that before the European Commission's intervention, in particular before the beginning of 2009, the alternative operators were not getting access to the incumbent's network. Alternative operators active on the Polish telecoms market were providing DSL-based services mainly through their own facilities. Netia, for example, invested in its wholly owned last mile copper network from early 2007 on. This is completely different from what was occurring at the time in the rest of Europe, where alternative operators were mainly providing DSL-based services through the incumbent's network.

Figure 5.4 describes the evolution in the percentage of subscribers by technology over the period 2006-2014[21] for Poland and for the European Union as a whole. DSL was the most widespread broadband technology both in Poland and in the European Union, although its percentage (over total broadband subscribers) was decreasing over time. However, in Poland, one can observe a greater presence of alternative technologies, mainly cable and fibre connections.[22] The sizable presence of alternative technologies on the Polish telecoms market may be interpreted as a consequence of the TP

21. We considered the number of subscribers during the fourth quarter of each year.
22. The relevant fibre technologies are referred to as fibre to the home (FFTH). Fixed wireless access (FWA) is hardly present on the Polish market.

abuse. Without having access to the incumbent's network, other operators may have had the incentive to invest in alternative technologies in order to gain market share. The development of these alternative technologies may have mitigated to some extentthe negative impact of TP's abuse in the DSL market.

Figure 5.4 Share of Subscribers by Technology – EU Versus Poland

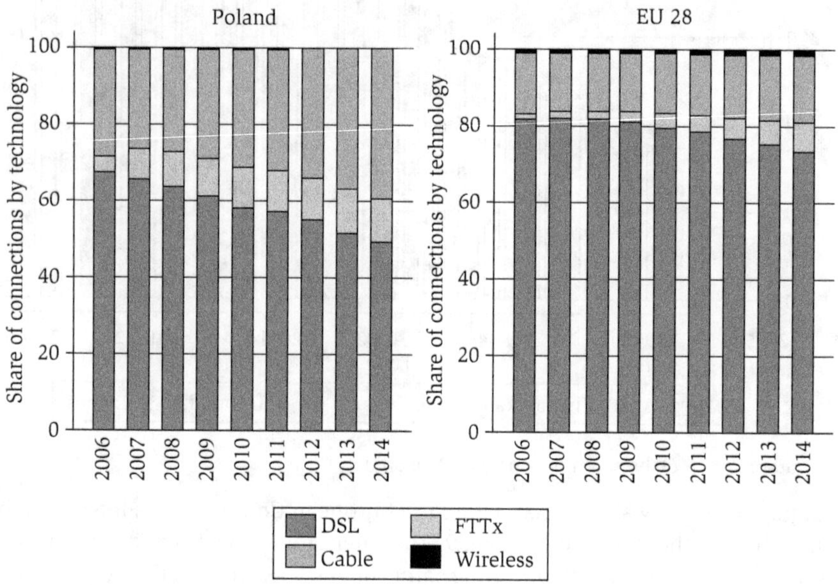

Source: Authors' own elaboration on Analysys Mason Research data. FTTx indicates either 'Fiber to the Home' or 'Fiber to the Building' technologies.

[2] The Evolution of Broadband Prices

Figure 5.5 illustrates the evolution of broadband prices (measured as broadband revenues per subscriber) in Poland. It shows that the DSL-based services are much more expensive than fibre and cable services throughout the entire period of analysis. This might be interpreted as an effect of the abuse: by refusing to provide access to its DSL network, TP foreclosed its competitors from the DSL market and thus contributed to increased DSL prices. The alternative operators invested in alternative technologies instead and thereby promoted competition in such markets. It is worth noting that prices for DSL-based services decreased after the end of the abuse (2009q3). Nevertheless, DSL-based services remain one of the most expensive services in the Polish broadband market. Conversely, in other European countries, and in particular in

Western Europe, DSL-based services were usually much cheaper than fibre services during the entire period of analysis. Indeed, fibre has been introduced more gradually in Western European countries, and it now represents a higher-quality, and hence more expensive alternative to the basic DSL services.

Figure 5.5 Evolution of Broadband Retail Prices – Poland

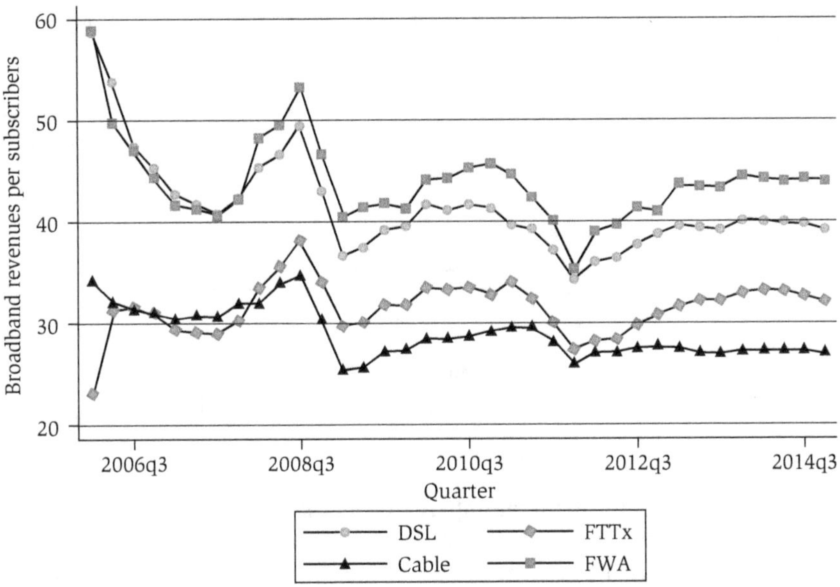

Source: Authors' own elaborations based on Analysys Mason data.

[3] The Evolution of the Average Connection Speed

Figure 5.6 describes the evolution of broadband connection speed over the period 2007-2014 in Poland, the European Union and the subset of CEECs included in the smaller control group.

Figure 5.6 Average Connection Speed in Poland, EU 28 and CEECs

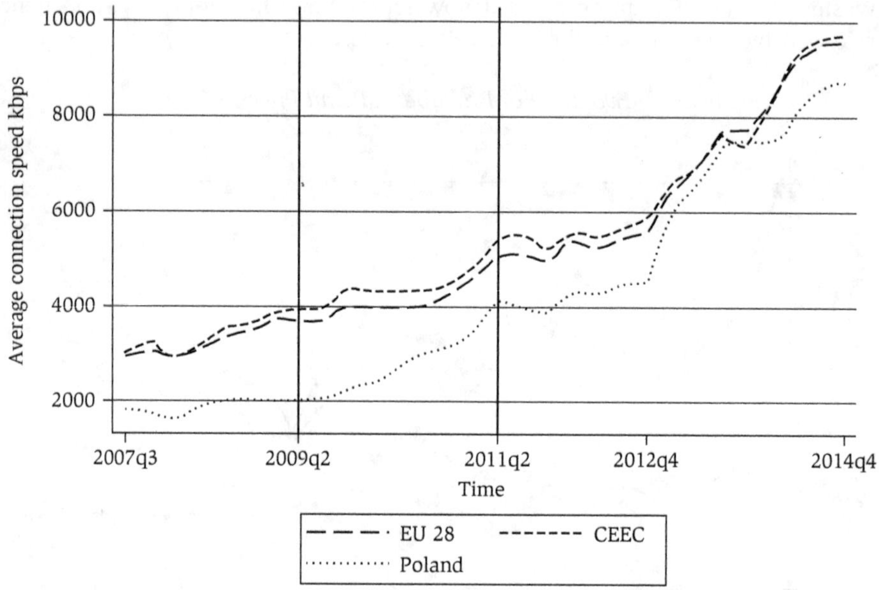

Source: Akamai's State of the Internet Report.

The three series show an increasing trend over the period of analysis: the average connection speed, which in 2007 was roughly around 3,000 kilo bites per second (kbps) on average in the EU, reached almost 10,000 kbps at the end of 2014, with a huge increase during the last quarter of 2012. The average speed in CEECs is slightly higher than the European Union average, since Estonia, Latvia and Czech Republic are characterised by broadband speed values far above the European average. Polish average connection speed, instead, is particularly low in comparison with its European peers, especially before 2011. However, from the beginning of the European Commission's investigation and especially after the European Commission's decision, the difference between the European and Polish connection speed started to narrow, which could be an indication of the positive impact of the decision on the quality of broadband services in Poland.

[B] Quantitative Results

In this subsection, we analyse the impact of the anticompetitive conduct of TP on the performance of the fixed broadband market in Poland (to the extent that such conduct was discontinued as a result of the European Commission's prohibition decision).

[1] Estimated Effects on Broadband Penetration

Figure 5.7 describes the evolution of the average broadband penetration (across all technological platforms) in Poland and its control group over the analysed period. The vertical line corresponds to the date of the European Commission's intervention (i.e., April 2009). This figure shows that the level of penetration in Poland is much lower than in the control group, both during and after the abuse. The Polish series does not show any discontinuity around the date of the European Commission's intervention. However there seems to be a slight increase in broadband penetration in Poland at the beginning of 2010.

The evidence provided by Figure 5.7 is also useful to investigate the 'common trend' requirement of the Difference-in-Differences methodology. Since the counterfactual has been estimated in the period after the European Commission's intervention, the similarity of the trend between Poland and the control group has to be evaluated on the right hand side of the graph. Indeed, the two series show a common trend in the period after the abuse at least up to 2012q3. In addition to the graphical evaluation, we also performed a formal test of the common trend hypothesis. The common trend assumption requires that there is no difference between the trends in the treated and control countries, after having considered the time-varying control variables. We hence first estimated the linear trends of the outcome variable in Poland and the control countries in the period after the European Commission's intervention, after having controlled for any demand and supply-side time-varying factor. Then we tested whether their difference was zero. The formal test confirms that there is a common trend in the development of broadband penetration in the treated and control countries: although there is a statistically significant difference at 10% level between the two trends, this is very close to zero (equal to 0.001), and this leads us to conclude that the common trend assumption is satisfied.[23]

23. This applies both to the main control group (with both Western European countries and CEECs) and the control group made up of CEECs only.

Figure 5.7 Broadband Penetration over Time – Poland Against Control Group

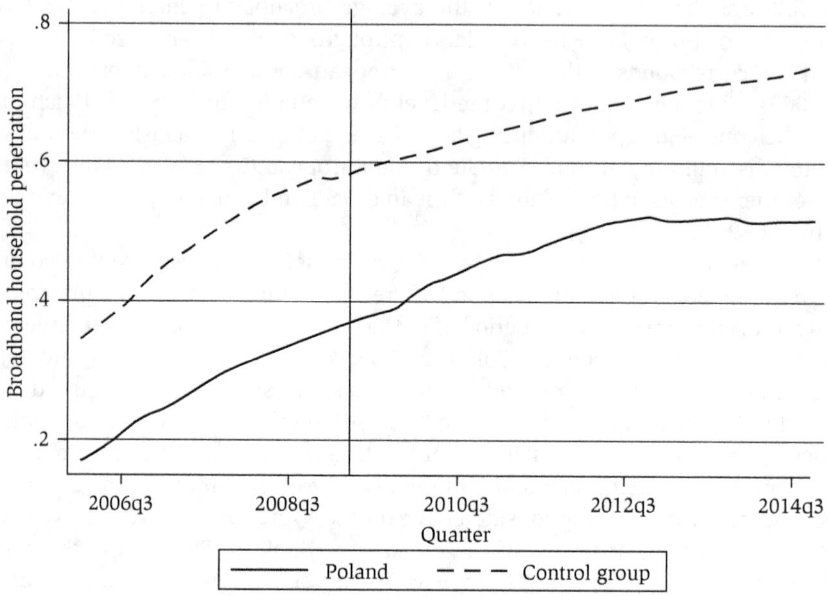

Source: Authors' own elaboration on Analysys Mason Research data.

Note: The vertical line corresponds to the European Commission intervention date (2009q2).

Table 5.2 presents the results of the empirical analysis. The dependent variable is the ratio of the number of fixed subscribers in each country to the number of households. We used country-level fixed effects and cluster standard errors[24] at the country level.[25] The variable of interest is Treated*Abuse and its coefficient measures the average impact of the abuse across all broadband technologies (*see also* subsection 5.04[D] for the definition of the other variables). Overall, the analysis indicates that the abuse had a negative impact on broadband penetration in the Polish market: the level of broadband penetration in the Polish market in the abuse period was lower than the level of broadband penetration in the selected control markets.

24. The need of clustering standard errors is related to the assumption that an unobserved random shock could be common to the observations within a group (as defined by the cluster), thereby leading to correlation between errors within the group.
25. This allows the error terms to be correlated within a country and over time. The small number of available countries might introduce a downward bias in the standard error and increase the significance of the estimated effects. An alternative would be to use the wild bootstrap method but this might also introduce a bias in the standard error in case of a strong imbalance in the number of treated units relative to the number of control units (as in this case). We hence preferred using the cluster-robust corrections and being cautious in the interpretation of the statistical significance of our results.

Table 5.2 Estimated Effects on Broadband Penetration

	(1)	*(2)*
Abuse	-0.00413** (0.0019)	0.00489 (0.0038)
Treated*Abuse	-0.00126 (0.0032)	-0.00752** (0.0030)
Income	4.39e-06*** (0.0000)	4.70e-06** (0.0000)
Mobile broadband penetration	0.0348 (0.0664)	0.0449 (0.0728)
Percentage of rural population	0.333** (0.1313)	0.350** (0.1626)
LLU pricing	-0.00156 (0.0011)	-0.00131 (0.0011)
Shared access pricing	0.000691 (0.0010)	0.000588 (0.0011)
Years from DSL launch	-0.00354*** (0.0010)	-0.00421*** (0.0014)
Constant	0.231 (0.2187)	-0.194 (0.2346)
Observations	2,880	2,320
R-Squared	0.936	0.924
Cluster	Country	Country
FE	Country	Country
Country specific trends	YES	YES

Robust standard errors in parentheses
*** $p < 0.01$, ** $p < 0.05$, * $p < 0.1$
Source: Authors' own elaboration based on Analysys Mason's data.

Model (1) shows the results of our base specification. Broadband household penetration is regressed on a number of demand and cost shifters, plus the treatment dummy variables. In this specification, we assumed that the treated (i.e., abuse) period ends at the end of the second quarter of 2009, as the European Commission opened its investigation against TP in April 2009. Model (1) suggests that, because of the anticompetitive conduct of TP, the Polish market experienced a lower level of broadband penetration. However, the estimated effect is not statistically significant.[26]

26. When the analysis is based on the restricted control group including only CEECs, we also get a negative sign for the abuse variable but the coefficient is not statistically different from zero. As already discussed, the limited number of control countries may reduce the reliability and precision of the estimate. *See* Appendix 2 for these additional results.

In Model (2), we dropped from the sample all the observations immediately following the opening of the European Commission proceedings, i.e., data from the third quarter of 2009 to the second quarter of 2011. This allows excluding from the sample the data covering the entire period of the European Commission's investigation up to the publication of the European Commission's decision. The underlying idea is that the European Commission's intervention only gradually stopped TP's anticompetitive conduct. This was confirmed by a market investigation carried out by the Polish national regulator (UKE) in 2010, which demonstrated that, at that time, there were still problems hampering fair and effective competition in the Polish broadband market. By dropping the observations immediately following the beginning of the European Commission's proceedings, we excluded from the sample all those transitory factors that could have affected market outcomes in the benchmark period. The results obtained on the basis of Model (2) suggest that, prior to the European Commission's intervention the level of broadband penetration in Poland was 0.75 percentage points lower as a result of TP's anticompetitive conduct.[27,28] This corresponds to a reduction of 30,000 Polish subscribers.

Table 5.3 investigates potential heterogeneous effects of the TP's conduct across different broadband technologies.[29] The coefficient of variable Treated*Abuse estimates the average effect of the abuse on broadband penetration, while the coefficient of variable Treated*Abuse*Technology captures the potential additional impact of the abuse on the penetration of a given broadband technology, compared to the average effect. The sum of the coefficients of Treated*Abuse and Treated*Abuse*Technology provides the overall effect of the abuse on the penetration of a particular technology.

Based on the descriptive analysis, we would expect that the abuse has negatively affected the penetration of DSL technologies, while positively impacted the penetration of cable and fibre technologies. The quantitative analysis will help us understanding whether the indication provided by the descriptive analysis can be interpreted as a causal effect of the abuse.

---

27. The outcome variable, broadband penetration may vary from 0 to 1.
28. Most of the control variables have the expected signs. The level of income has a positive and significant impact on penetration, thereby indicating that broadband penetration is higher in richer countries. The regulated wholesale access fee for the LLU has a negative impact on broadband penetration (although not significant). Surprisingly, the percentage of rural population seems to have a positive and significant impact on broadband penetration. Similarly, the period since DSL launch seems to have a negative and significant impact on penetration: we would have expected that countries with larger experience of DSL will have a higher level of broadband penetration. However, the increase in penetration might follow a non-linear trend and might flatten when the market matures. The coefficient of this variable might hence be biased by such an effect.
29. In these specifications, we dropped two years after the treatment to exclude potential transitory factors that might bias the estimates of the counterfactual.

Table 5.3 Heterogeneous Effects of the Abuse

	(3)	*(4)*	*(5)*	*(6)*
Technology	*DSL*	*FTTx*	*FWA*	*Cable*
Abuse	0.00489 (0.0038)	0.00489 (0.0038)	0.00489 (0.0038)	0.00489 (0.0038)
Treated*Abuse	-0.00296 (0.0030)	-0.0119*** (0.0030)	-0.0207*** (0.0030)	0.00556* (0.0030)
Treated*Abuse Technology	-0.0182*** (0.0000)	0.0176*** (0.0000)	0.0529*** (0.0000)	-0.0523*** (0.0000)
Technology	1.082*** (0.0903)	-0.0141 (0.1201)	-0.0750 (0.1201)	0.0272 (0.1201)
Income	4.70e-06** (0.0000)	4.70e-06** (0.0000)	4.70e-06** (0.0000)	4.70e-06** (0.0000)
Mobile broadband penetration	0.0449 (0.0728)	0.0449 (0.0728)	0.0449 (0.0728)	0.0449 (0.0728)
Percentage of rural population	0.350** (0.1626)	0.350** (0.1626)	0.350** (0.1626)	0.350** (0.1626)
LLU pricing	-0.00131 (0.0011)	-0.00131 (0.0011)	-0.00131 (0.0011)	-0.00131 (0.0011)
Shared access pricing	0.000588 (0.0011)	0.000588 (0.0011)	0.000588 (0.0011)	0.000588 (0.0011)
Years from DSL launch	-0.00421*** (0.0014)	-0.00421*** (0.0014)	-0.00421*** (0.0014)	-0.00421*** (0.0014)
Constant	-1.304*** (0.1413)	-0.221 (0.1479)	-0.221 (0.1479)	-0.221 (0.1479)
Observations	2,320	2,320	2,320	2,320
R-Squared	0.924	0.924	0.925	0.925
cluster	Country	Country	Country	Country
FE	Country	Country_ technology	Country_ technology	Country_ technology
Country specific trends	YES	YES	YES	YES

Robust standard errors in parentheses
*** $p < 0.01$, ** $p < 0.05$, * $p < 0.1$
Source: Authors' own elaboration based on Analysys Mason's data.

Model (3) estimates the potential additional effect of the abuse on the penetration of DSL services. The results of this model suggest that the abuse had an additional impact (compared to the average effect) on the penetration of DSL services, contributing to a further reduction in DSL services penetration by 1.8 percentage points. The sum of the coefficients of the two treatment variables indicates that the abuse reduced the penetration of DSL services by 2.1 percentage points in Poland. The lack of significance of the coefficient of the variable Treated*Abuse is an indication that the negative impact of the abuse on the total broadband penetration is mainly driven by its impact on the penetration of DSL services.

This assumption seems to be confirmed by the results of Models (4) and (5) which analyse the impact of the abuse on the penetration of fibre and FWA-based services. These results show that, in comparison with the control countries, Poland experienced a greater penetration of fibre and FWA-based services prior to the European Commission's intervention. This supports the idea that TP's anticompetitive conduct encouraged alternative operators to invest in alternative infrastructure, such as fibre and FWA.

All the above-mentioned results confirm the evidence provided by the descriptive analysis. The regression analysis on the penetration of cable services indicates instead that TP abuse had a negative effect on the diffusion of such services. Model (6) indeed shows that, because of the abuse, the level of penetration of cable services was lower in Poland than in its control countries.

The empirical analysis is broadly consistent with the interpretation that the TP abuse hindered the growth of broadband penetration in Poland. This indicates that the European Commission's decision was appropriate from a protection of consumer welfare perspective. However, the analysis of the heterogeneous effects of the abuse on the penetration of different technologies also shows that the abuse stimulated the penetration of alternative technologies for the provision of broadband services (fibre and FWA-based services), as anticipated in the literature and shown by the descriptive analysis.

[2] Estimated Effects on Broadband Retail Prices

In order to get a comprehensive overview of the impact of the European Commission's decision, we also look at the effect of the TP abuse on broadband retail prices.

Figure 5.8 shows the evolution in broadband prices for Poland and the selected control countries. The vertical line corresponds to the date of the start of the European Commission's investigation (i.e., April 2009).

It can be observed that the average price for broadband retail services in Poland gradually declined around the date of the European Commission's decision. The price series for the control countries was on the contrary quite flat over the analysed period.

Figure 5.8 can also be used to evaluate the existence of a common trend: the two series show quite a similar pattern in the post-abuse period. As in the broadband penetration analysis, we carried out a formal test to investigate the validity of the common trend assumption and the test confirms such assumption. The difference between the two trends is very small (it ranges from 0.006 to 0.008) and statistically-significant only at the 10% level.

Figure 5.8 Evolution of Broadband Prices – Poland Against Its Control Group

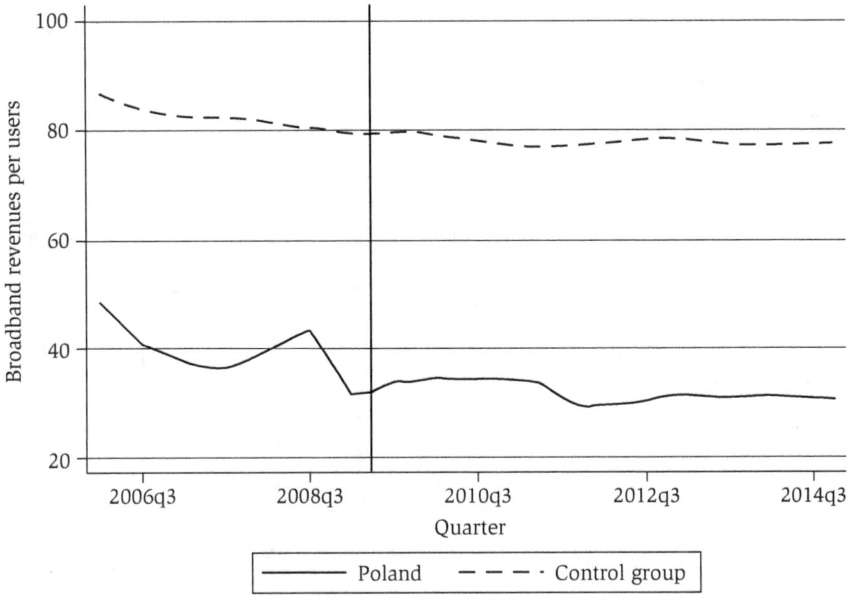

Source: Authors' own elaboration on Analysys Mason Research data.

Note: The vertical line corresponds to the European Commission intervention date (2009q2).

Table 5.4 presents the estimated effects on prices. The dependent variable in Models (1) and (2) is the natural logarithm of the average broadband revenues per user (ARPU). In Model (3) the natural logarithm of the average price charged by the incumbent for DSL-based services is used as dependent variable. We use fixed effects at the operator-technology-country level and clustered standard errors at the operator-country level. Model (1) shows the results of our base specification while in Models (2) and (3), we drop two years of observations from our sample to avoid those transitory factors that could have distorted the estimates of the market outcomes in the benchmark period.

Table 5.4 Estimated Effects on Prices

	(1)	(2)	(3)
Abuse	-0.0120 (0.0140)	-0.0263 (0.0276)	-0.0557 (0.0512)
Treated*Abuse	0.00534 (0.0441)	0.0327 (0.0857)	0.0977* (0.0482)
Income (ln)	0.00337 (0.0824)	0.00802 (0.0843)	-0.0216 (0.1319)
Mobile broadband penetration	-1.780*** (0.5341)	-1.532*** (0.5591)	-1.072** (0.4540)
Population (ln)	2.927** (1.1968)	2.489** (1.1224)	-0.202 (2.8115)
Percentage of residential subscribers	1.309*** (0.3378)	1.223*** (0.3199)	0.890** (0.4113)
LLU pricing (ln)	0.0560 (0.1504)	0.00677 (0.1701)	0.129 (0.1130)
Shared access pricing (ln)	-0.0479 (0.0596)	-0.0274 (0.0671)	0.0149 (0.0610)
Years from DSL launch	-0.000482 (0.0084)	-0.00182 (0.0096)	0.0104 (0.0102)
Constant	-51.21** (21.6456)	-34.80** (17.2366)	8.275 (51.5725)
Observations	5,909	4,758	638
R-Squared	0.871	0.855	0.973
cluster	Operator-Country	Operator-Country	Country
Country specific time trends	YES	YES	YES
FE	Operator_Tech_ Country	Operator_Tech_ Country	Operator_ Country

Robust standard errors in parentheses
*** p < 0.01, ** p < 0.05, * p < 0.1
Source: Authors' own elaboration based on Analysys Mason's data.

In Models (1) and (2), the analysis of the impact of the abuse on broadband retail prices does not provide statistically significant results. However, the direction of the effect seems to indicate that, prior to the European Commission's intervention broadband retail prices in Poland were higher because of TP's abuse.[30]

30. Most of the explanatory variables have the expected sign, although not significant. Compared to the previous analysis, the coefficient of the variable measuring mobile broadband penetration is now significant and negative. This is consistent with the fact that mobile and fixed broadband

The descriptive analysis shows that, during and after the abuse, DSL services were very expensive in Poland, compared to the alternative technologies. This is very different from what occurs in the Western countries, where fibre services are considered as the most innovative and are hence the most expensive services. The quantitative analysis did not find any significant effect of the abuse on average DSL prices. However, in Model (3) which estimates the effects of the abuse on the DSL price charged by the Polish incumbent, by comparing it to the DSL price charged by the incumbents in the selected control countries, the estimated coefficient of the variable Treated*Abuse is positive and significant. This indicates that, prior to the European Commission's intervention, TP was charging higher prices for its DSL services, compared to the incumbents in the European control countries. In particular, DSL prices charged by the Polish incumbent were 9.8 percentage points higher than what they would have been without the abuse. However, we urge caution with the interpretation of this result, in particular, because we do not get significant results if we analyse the effect of the abuse on average DSL prices.

§5.06 CONCLUSION

The objective of this chapter is to investigate the economic impact of a prohibition decision taken in 2011 by the European Commission against TP on broadband penetration and retail prices. This European Commission decision concerned the anticompetitive conduct of TP during the period August 2005-October 2009. In October 2009, TP signed a voluntary agreement with the national telecom operator UKE to comply with EU regulatory obligations and allow competitors provide broadband services via its DSL network. The qualitative and quantitative analyses presented above provide strong evidence that the TP prohibition was appropriate.

To investigate this case and the effectiveness of the prohibition decision taken by the European Commission, this chapter uses both descriptive and quantitative analyses. The quantitative analysis applies a Difference-in-Differences approach. A counterfactual scenario is defined to compare treated (Poland) and non-treated countries in order to identify the effect of the abuse on broadband penetration and prices in the Polish fixed telecoms market. A novelty of the approach used is related to the definition of this counterfactual.

The standard practice in evaluation studies is to use the period before the treatment to define a control group allowing the evaluator to identify the evolution of the market in absence of the treatment. In the present case, in the period before the abuse (pre-2005) TP was already infringing its regulatory obligations. This makes the period before the abuse not adequate to estimate the evolution of the outcome variable in the absence of TP's anticompetitive conduct. Therefore, it was decided to use the post-intervention period to select the control group. The assumption is that after the

services are substitutes, and hence the higher the diffusion of mobile telecom services, the lower the demand of fixed telecom service and the lower the fixed broadband prices.

intervention, the Polish fixed telecoms market converged to the behaviour of other markets not affected by the abuse.

This approach allowed investigating whether the abuse had distorted competition (and hence whether the infringement decisions had been appropriate) and establishing whether the decisions taken by the Polish regulator and the European Commission were able to restore competition conditions comparable to other markets where there was presumably no abuse. However, this analytical set-up made it impossible to determine whether the authorities' decisions had eliminated all abuse and to distinguish the effects of the abuse from that of the decision. The post-intervention situation in the Polish market is indeed biased by both TP's anticompetitive conduct (that has permanently affected the structure of the market) and the European Commission's intervention. Moreover, it was not possible to separate the impact of the interventions of the Polish regulator from that of the European Commission.

The qualitative and quantitative analyses presented above illustrate how the anticompetitive conduct pursued by TP hindered the access of alternative operators to its network. First, a descriptive analysis of LLU access in Poland shows that before the European Commission's intervention, the Polish alternative operators were not getting access to the TP network. Second, the quantitative analysis allows concluding that TP conduct had a negative effect on DSL broadband penetration.

Interestingly, the refusal by TP to allow access to its legacy network encouraged entrants and competitors in the wholesale market to invest in alternative technologies, thus stimulating inter-platform competition. This inter-platform competition could have contributed to reduce the negative effect on broadband penetration of the lack of intra-platform competition. This is confirmed by the descriptive analysis, which shows that one can observe a greater and earlier presence of alternative technologies on the Polish market than in the rest of the European Union. Moreover, the quantitative analysis seems to indicate that Poland has experienced a greater penetration of other technologies prior to the European Commission's intervention in comparison with the control countries.

The price analysis, however, is less straightforward. Under most model specifications, there is a positive but non-statistically significant difference between the evolution of prices in Poland and in the control countries, which can be associated with the abuse. The difficulty to find a statistically significant effect of the abuse on prices might be due to several reasons. First, the measurement of telecoms prices raises many difficulties. Second, as alternative operators were incentivised to invest in alternative technologies, this may have limited the negative effect of the abuse on broadband prices. However, in the model analysing the impact of the abuse on the DSL-based service prices charged by TP, the estimated price effect of the abuse is positive and significant. Moreover, qualitative evidence on the evolution of Polish broadband prices indicate that DSL-based service prices were higher than prices of alternative broadband services over the entire period of analysis. This differs from what is seen elsewhere in Europe, especially in Western Europe, and might be interpreted as an effect of the abuse.

Finally, while this work did not allow distinguishing the impact of the European Commission decision from that of the regulatory intervention, the analysis of facts reveals that collaboration between competition and regulatory authorities is important to ensure fair conditions of competition.

As usual with this type of frontier research, there are areas for further work. In this chapter, the empirical analysis suggests that the estimated effects on broadband penetration are mainly driven by the DSL market. TP was refusing to supply wholesale access products to its DSL network and the anticompetitive conduct mostly concerned the DSL market. This anticompetitive conduct seems to have stimulated inter-platform competition. However, the quantitative analysis did not provide sufficiently robust results to draw conclusions about the differential impact of inter- and intra-platform competition. Further work in this area would be interesting to shed some light on the debate regarding the relative importance of promoting inter- versus intra-platform competition.

It is also possible that the TP abuse had differential effects in urban and rural areas. Rural areas are typically served by the legacy network – the morphology of the territory and the low business and population density makes investment in alternative and new infrastructure less profitable. Alternative operators prefer entering urban areas since the larger, denser subscriber base allows them to recoup their investment faster. The negative effects of the abuse in the urban areas might have been counter-balanced by the deployment of alternative broadband technologies (mainly WIMAX and fibre). In rural areas, by contrast, the less favourable business case for alternative technologies is likely to make the impact of TP's anticompetitive conduct more intense. The collection of data on broadband penetration at local level might help to empirically test this argument. More generally, this study shows that the quality of data is crucial to get good ex post evaluation analysis.

APPENDIX 1: DEFINITION OF THE CONTROL VARIABLES

Table 5.5 sets out the characteristics and sources of the data that are used for the empirical analysis. We collected data for the period 2006-2014 for all the European countries.[31] Most of our data are drawn from Analysys Mason DataHub.

Table 5.5 Definition of Control Variables

Metric	*Period*	*Frequency*	*Notes/ Description*	*Source*	*Reason for Inclusion*
Control variables (supply-side)					
Territory morphology	2006-2014	Annual data	Urban, rural or mountainous areas in square kilometre	Eurostat	Measure of the cost of infrastructure deployment. In rural and mountainous areas, the cost of deploying the broadband infrastructure is higher.
Regulated access price	October 2007-October 2014	Annual data	LLU and WBA tariffs	EC Reports – Digital Scoreboard	Measure of the cost of providing retail services. The regulated price to get access to the copper network may impact the price ultimately charged in the retail market.
Population density	2006-2014	Annual data	Data at market level	Eurostat	Measure of the cost of infrastructure deployment. Due to economies of scale and scope, the cost of deploying the infrastructure is lower in more dense areas.

31. We do not have homogeneous information on Malta, Cyprus and Luxembourg.

Metric	*Period*	*Frequency*	*Notes/ Description*	*Source*	*Reason for Inclusion*
Control variables (demand-side)					
Population	2006-2014	Annual data	Data at market level. Average annual population.	Eurostat	Measure of demand.
Share of urban population	2006-2014	Annual data	Data at market level	Eurostat	Measure of demand. In urban areas, the number of economic activities is higher than in rural areas, and this may positively impact the demand for broadband services.
Income	2006-2014	Annual data	Data at market level. Average income per capita	Eurostat	Measure of demand.
GDP per capita	2006-2014	Annual data	Data at market level. Nominal GDP, seasonally and calendar adjusted data	Eurostat	Alternative measure of income and proxy to capture macroeconomic trends.
DSL launch date			Year in which DSL has been launched in each country	Analysys Mason DataHub	Countries with longer experience of broadband will have a higher level of broadband penetration.
Mobile data penetration	2006-2014	Quarterly data	Take up of mobile broadband at market level	Analysys Mason DataHub	Mobile services may be considered as substitute of fixed broadband services.
Number of households	2006-2014	Annual data	Data at market level	Eurostat	Measure of demand.

Metric	*Period*	*Frequency*	*Notes/ Description*	*Source*	*Reason for Inclusion*
IPTV and VoIP subscribers	2006-2014	Quarterly data	Data at market level	Analysys Mason DataHub	Measure of demand for highly innovative services. Also proxy for the broadband services quality.

APPENDIX 2: RESULTS OBTAINED ON THE BASIS OF THE CONTROL GROUP INCLUDING ONLY CEECs

We present here the results obtained on the basis of the smaller control group including only CEECs whose regulatory framework and morphological characteristics are similar to Poland. This might strengthen the similarity between the control and treated group in the post-abuse period.

Table 5.6 Estimated Effect of the Abuse – CEEC Control Group

	(1) *Penetration*	*(2)* *Prices*
Abuse	-0.00483 (0.0045)	-0.0383 (0.0362)
Treated*Abuse	-0.000594 (0.0037)	0.0257 (0.0871)
Income	7.35e-06** (0.0000)	0.0149 (0.0703)
Mobile broadband penetration	0.0644 (0.1250)	0.223 (0.5877)
Population		4.783*** (1.7267)
Percentage of rural population	0.173* (0.0790)	
Percentage of residential subscribers		0.819*** (0.2938)
LLU pricing	-0.000954 (0.0013)	-0.174** (0.0797)
Shared access pricing	0.000783 (0.0012)	0.152*** (0.0551)
Years from DSL launch	-0.00389 (0.0022)	
Constant	-1.148*** (0.1105)	-63.99** (24.3601)
Observations	1,044	2,018
R-Squared	0.818	0.911
cluster	Country	Operator_Country
FE	Country	Operator_Tech_Country
Country-specific trends	YES	YES

Robust standard errors in parentheses
*** $p < 0.01$, ** $p < 0.05$, * $p < 0.1$
Source: Authors' own elaboration on Analysys Mason Research data.

As for the larger control group, the formal test confirms the existence of a common trend between the treated and control series in post-abuse period. However, the use of this alternative control group to the CEECs does not improve the results of the test.

Table 5.6 shows that the results are no longer significant. However, the direction of the effect confirms the previous analysis: the abuse which was stopped by the European Commission's intervention has led to a decrease in the penetration of broadband services and an increase of broadband prices in Poland compared to its control countries. The limited number of control countries may reduce the reliability and precision of our estimate and we consider this control group as a second best.

REFERENCES

Abadie A. and Gardeazabal J. (2003), 'The economic costs of conflict: A case study of the Basque Country', *American Economic Review*, 93(1), March, pp. 113-132.

Abadie A., Diamond A. and Hainmueller J. (2010), 'Synthetic control methods for comparative case studies: Estimating the effect of California's tobacco control program', *Journal of the American Statistical Association*, 105(490), Application and Case Studies.

Abadie A., Diamond A. and Hainmueller J. (2015), 'Comparative politics and the synthetic control method', *American Journal of Political Science*, 59(2), pp. 495-510.

Analysys Mason (2015), 'The digital single market and telecoms regulation going forward', Report for ECTA (European Competitive Telecommunications Association).

Bouckaert J., van Dijk T. and Verboven F. (2010), 'Access regulation, competition, and broadband penetration: An international study', *Telecommunications Policy*, 34(11), pp. 661-671.

Bourreau M., Cambini C. and Doğan P. (2012), 'Access pricing, competition, and incentives to migrate from "old" to "new" technology', *International Journal of Industrial Organization*, 30(6), pp. 713-723.

Briglauer W., Cambini C. and Melani S. (2016), 'How to fill the digital gap? The (limited) role of regulation', ZEW – Centre for European Economic Research Discussion Paper No. 16-002.

Calzada J. and Martínez-Santos F. (2014), 'Broadband prices in the European Union: Competition and commercial strategies', *Information Economics and Policy*, 27, pp. 24-38.

de Streel A. (2012), 'The antitrust activism of the European Commission in the telecommunications sector', P. Lowe and M. Marquis (eds), *European Competition Law Annual 2012: Competition, Regulation and Public Policies*, pp. 189-208.

Distaso W., Lupi P. and Manenti F.M. (2006), 'Platform competition and broadband uptake: theory and empirical evidence from the European Union'. *Information Economics and Policy*, 18(1), pp. 87-106.

Ford G.S. and Spiwak L.J. (2004), 'The positive effects of unbundling on broadband deployment', Phoenis Center Policy Paper No. 19.

ICF and DIW Berlin (2015), 'The economic impact of enforcement of competition policies on the functioning of EU energy markets', Final report prepared for the Directorate-General for Competition of the European Commission, Publications Office of the EU.

Ilzkovitz F. and Dierx A. (2015), 'Ex-post economic evaluation of competition policy enforcement: A review of the literature', DG Competition staff paper, Publications Office of the European Union, June.

Klein G.J., Wendel J. (2014), 'The impact of local loop and retail unbundling revisited', DICE (University of Düsseldorf, Düsseldorf Institute for Competition Economics) Discussion Paper 163.

Lear, DIW Berlin and Analysys Mason (2017), 'Economic impact of competition policy enforcement on the functioning of telecoms markets in the EU', Final report prepared for the Directorate-General for Competition of the European Commission, Publications Office of the EU.

Nardotto M., Valletti T. and Verboven F. (2015), 'Unbundling the incumbent: Evidence from UK broadband', *Journal of the European Economic Association,* 13(2), pp. 330-362.

CHAPTER 6

Alleged Abuse by E.ON of Its Dominant Position in the German Wholesale Electricity Market*

Veit Böckers, Tomaso Duso & Florian Szücs

In 2008, the European Commission investigated claims that E.ON had abused its dominant position in the German electricity market by withdrawing available generation capacity from the wholesale market. The Commission was concerned that the withdrawal of the electricity generation plants was part of a strategy aimed at increasing wholesale prices. To address such concerns E.ON made the commitment to divest several power plants to other market players. On 26 November 2008 the Commission adopted a decision making this commitment binding. This chapter provides an analysis of this decision's effects on the German electricity market. It shows that wholesale electricity prices in Germany – especially during peak hours – are significantly and negatively related to the divestitures by E.ON. This reduction in wholesale prices might have contributed in turn to price reductions in the downstream retail market for electricity.

§6.01 INTRODUCTION

This chapter provides an ex post analysis of the European Commission's commitment decision of 26 November 2008 issued in response to the alleged abuse by E.ON AG of its dominant position in the German wholesale electricity market. The commitment decision imposed the divestment by E.ON of 5000 MW electricity generation plants and the sale of its high-voltage transmission grid. The ex post analysis in this chapter

* This chapter is based on an ex post evaluation of the European Commission's decision in the E.ON abuse of dominance case, as presented in the 2015 study *'The economic impact of enforcement of competition policies on the functioning of EU energy markets'* commissioned by the Directorate-General for Competition of the European Commission. For an extended analysis, *see also* Duso et al. (2018).

focuses more explicitly on the divestment of the electricity generation plants. Using quantitative tools, the analysis allows determining: (i) whether the divestment had an impact on German wholesale electricity prices; and (ii) to which extent this price shift was beneficial to the end consumer of electricity. Strictly speaking, however, the second part of the analysis cannot be considered an ex post evaluation of the commitment decision per se, as the decision solely concerned the wholesale electricity market. Rather, it allows drawing conclusions on the extent of the pass-through of the reduction in wholesale electricity prices to retail prices, which is mostly affected by the conditions of competition in the retail electricity market.

The present ex post evaluation is of particular importance because it is one of the first ex post economic assessments of a competition enforcement decision involving an abuse of dominance. It allows demonstrating the positive effects of competition policy enforcement on the level of competition in wholesale electricity markets, potentially benefitting retail customers.

This chapter is organised as follows. Section 6.02 offers some background on the functioning and institutional set-up of electricity markets in Germany. Section 6.03 gives a short description of the E.ON case. Section 6.04 contains a literature review that may help to understand better the European Commission's competition concerns in this abuse of dominance case. Section 6.05 presents the ex post evaluation methodology applied in the wholesale market analysis as well as the results obtained from this analysis. Section 6.06 covers the analysis of the potential implications of the European Commission's intervention in the wholesale market for retail electricity markets. Section 6.07 concludes and identifies areas for further work.

§6.02 THE ELECTRICITY MARKET IN GERMANY

The German electricity market is characterised by a vertical structure comprising a generation segment, a wholesale market, and retail markets (*see* Figure 6.1). A transmission system delivers the generated or imported electricity via extra high and high-voltage networks to regional supply companies, which then distribute it via medium- and low-voltage networks to electricity retailers and final consumers. A parallel balancing market ensures that actual production is equal to actual consumption in real time. In order to ensure supply on this balancing market, generators have to reserve a part of their available generation capacity for possible use during times of market shortage. This is the reserved capacity. Generators receive compensation – the capacity payments – for being available to produce electricity in case of suddenly increased demand.

Figure 6.1 The Structure of the German Electricity Market

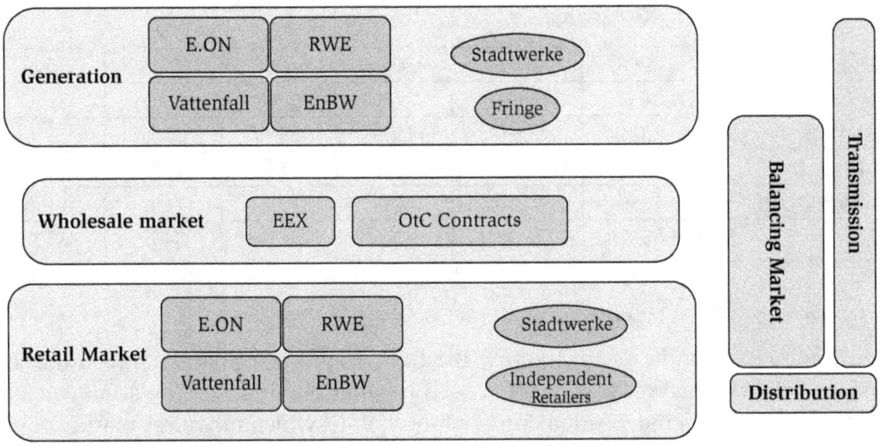

Source: ICF and DIW (2015).

For many years now, four vertically integrated, although legally unbundled, big players dominate the generation segment of the German electricity market: RWE, E.ON, EnBW and Vattenfall - also called the 'big four'. The rest of the German electricity needs is covered by the local production of a large number of municipal operators (*Stadtwerke*) and other smaller producers, or it is imported from abroad. At the retail level, the market is less concentrated since each regional market, defined as the coverage area of the low-voltage network (*see below*), includes over 100 retailers on average.

[A] Electricity Generation and the Wholesale Market

At the time of the European Commission's decision in the E.ON case (November 2008), the big four's generation capacity amounted to more than 80% of total generation capacity within Germany, with municipal operators, other small producers and imports covering the remaining 15-20%. The share of the big four in total electricity supply (as measured by electricity feed-in) during the period 2007-2009 was well over 80% as well (*see* Table 6.1). These years are of particular interest: the European Commission's energy sector inquiry was conducted in 2007 (European Commission, 2007a), the decision in the E.ON case was adopted in 2008 and E.ON's first divestments were made in 2009.

Table 6.1 Market Shares of the Big Four Electricity Companies

Generator	*Generation Capacity (MW)*			*Total Electricity Feed-in (TW/hour)*		
	2007	*2008*	*2009*	*2007*	*2008*	*2009*
RWE	34%	33%	31%	35%	36%	31%
E.ON	23%	23%	19%	23%	22%	21%
Vattenfall	17%	16%	16%	17%	15%	16%
EnBW	12%	12%	14%	12%	11%	14%
Big four	85%	84%	80%	86%	84%	82%

Source: Bundeskartellamt (2011).

In the report on its sector inquiry, the Bundeskartellamt (2011) argued that the German electricity market was characterised by joint dominance. The argument was based on estimates of the Residual Supply Index (RSI), which measures market power by the size of a supplier's available generation capacity in relation to the overall demand. The Bundeskartellamt concluded that all the big four players were possibly 'in a position to behave to an appreciable extent independently of their competitors, customers and ultimately of their consumers and to restrict competition on the first-time sales market. [...] Each of these undertakings was essential for meeting Germany's electricity demand in a considerable number of hours' (Bundeskartellamt, 2011, p. 6).

The four main generators were all vertically integrated firms and most of electricity generated was sold through their own retail outlets. The remainder was sold to other retailers via bilateral, Over-The-Counter (OTC) contracts[1] and through a centralised energy exchange market, i.e., the European Energy Exchange (EEX) market located in Leipzig. While most electricity trade between wholesalers and retailers in Germany was subject to long-term bilateral contracts between generators and retailers, a minor albeit increasing percentage of trade was conducted at the EEX.[2]

[B] Transmission and Distribution

The transmission of electricity is achieved through legally unbundled Transmission System Operators (TSOs). Nevertheless, the European Commission (Case No. COMP/M.4110 – E.ON / ENDESA, p. 10) reported that in 2004 – i.e., well before its intervention in the E.ON case – 'The operation and management of the high voltage grid (transmission) is for more than [75-85 per cent] controlled by the same four majors'. Table 6.2 indicates the big four's shares of electricity transmission and distribution for the year 2004.

1. OTC trading is done directly between two parties, without the supervision of an exchange.
2. In 2013, EEX reached a market share in German power trading of 20%, compared with 15% in 2012 (Reuters, 2014).

Table 6.2 Market Shares of the Big Four Electricity Companies in Transmission and Distribution

	Transmission *2004*	*Distribution* *2004*
RWE	[30-40%]	[15-25%]
E.ON	[25-35%]	[20-30%]
Vattenfall	[25-35%]	[< 5%]
EnBW	[5-15%]	[< 10%]

Source: European Commission, Case No. COMP/M.4110 – E.ON/ENDESA p. 10, 2004.

[C] The Retail Market

In spite of the large number of retailers present in the market, the German retail electricity market is also quite concentrated. In 2004, the big four covered more than half of the market (*see* Table 6.3). In the decade since, the overall picture did not change very much, even if the national market share of the big four showed a gradual decline and there were some movements in the market shares of individual players. In 2009 and 2010, the consolidated market shares of the big four amounted to 48% and 44% respectively.[3]

Table 6.3 Market Shares of the Big Four Electricity Companies in Retail Markets

Retail	*Large Industrial Customers* *2004*	*Small Customers* *2004*
RWE	[20-30%]	[5-15%]
E.ON	[15-25%]	[5-15%]
Vattenfall	[10-20%]	[< 10%]
EnBW	[10-20%]	[< 10%]

Source: European Commission, Case No. COMP/M.4110 – E.ON/ENDESA, p. 10, 2004.

This rather aggregated picture may be somewhat misleading as retail electricity markets are regional in scope, at least concerning households and small commercial customers. In its 2010 monitoring report, the federal network regulator (*Bundesnetzagentur*) stated that the relevant market for the electricity supply of households must be defined 'at the level of the coverage area *(Versorgungsgebiet)* –

3. Source: Bundeskartellamt (2011).

i.e., the low voltage network[4] necessary to supply [electricity]' (Bundesnetzagentur, Monitoring Report, 2010, pp. 77-79). The coverage areas differ substantially in terms of market structure, level of competition and, accordingly, retail prices. In some regions, the four big players upstream are also incumbent downstream while in others, municipal operators are incumbents, generally in the municipalities where they are based.

While in each of these coverage areas retailers offer different tariffs, incumbents are legally obliged to sell electricity at a baseline tariff (*Grundversorgungstarif*) to all households who do not explicitly choose another provider. Accordingly, this baseline tariff constitutes an upper bound for electricity retail prices in a given coverage area, because it is automatically chosen by customers unwilling or lacking the information to switch to a cheaper supplier. Strong customer inertia substantially increases the market power of the incumbent retailers. Consequently, baseline tariffs tend to be less responsive to changes in wholesale prices in comparison with the cheaper prices offered in the competitive fringe of the market.

Retail prices entail several components. On the one hand, they are affected by electricity wholesale prices that constitute the main essential input for retailers. On the other hand, they are also strongly influenced by other factors such as the (regulated) cost of transmission and distribution as well as taxes and other fees. The heterogeneity in electricity purchase costs, consumer switching behaviour, and network costs results in a significant price dispersion even within coverage areas. Typically, the most expensive tariff is the baseline tariff offered by the local incumbent, while the cheapest prices tend to be offered by smaller competitors.

Although German electricity retail markets were liberalised in 1998, initially there was very little switching among household customers and, in 2009, incumbent operators were still serving more than 70% of the German households. However, over the period 2007-2011, the number of households that switched operator grew rapidly (*see* Figure 6.2) and, by 2011, the share of final customers (also including commercial and industrial customers) that switched providers reached 11.5%. In spite of this, incumbent operators maintained a very strong customer base.

4. While the high-voltage network is used to transfer the energy from the generation plants to electricity suppliers, the low-voltage network is used to distribute the electricity to end-consumers.

Figure 6.2 Number of Final Customers Switching Providers[5]

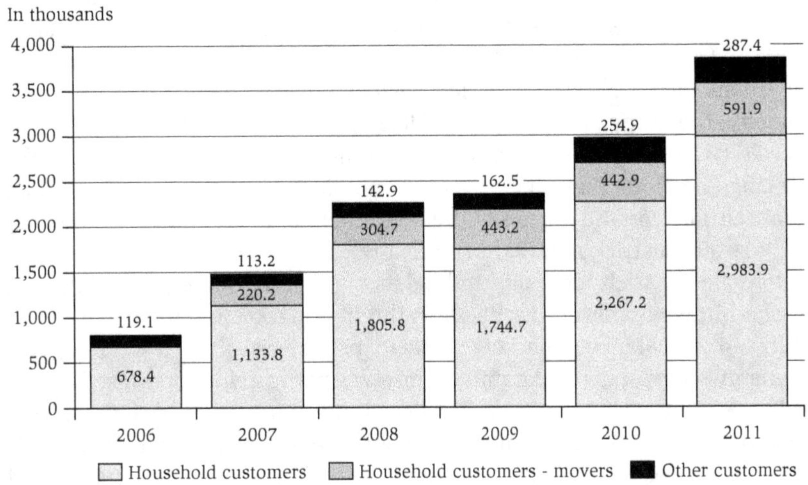

Source: Bundesnetzagentur, Monitoring Report 2012.

§6.03 DESCRIPTION OF THE E.ON ABUSE OF DOMINANCE CASE

In 2006, as a follow up to its energy sector inquiry, the European Commission initiated investigations into the German electricity market. In the course of its investigation, the Commission came to the preliminary view that E.ON might have infringed EC Treaty rules on the abuse of a dominant market position (Article 82) in two ways:

(1) As a wholesaler on the electricity market, by deliberately not offering for sale the production of certain power plants that was available and that it would have been economically rational to sell, with a view to raising prices. Moreover, the Commission had concerns that E.ON devised and implemented a strategy to deter third parties from investing in electricity generation.
(2) As a TSO, by favouring its own production affiliates and by preventing other power producers from selling balancing energy into the E.ON markets.

To address the European Commission's primary concerns, E.ON proposed to divest about 5000 MW of generation capacity in Germany. Such divestments would not only make it less likely for E.ON to withdraw capacity from the market in order to raise prices, but would also transfer generation capacity to competitors. To remedy the Commission's secondary concerns, E.ON proposed to divest its transmission system

5. Final customers switching providers include both household customers that did not change address and household customers that switched operators because of a move to a new location, as well as other, commercial and industrial customers.

business thereby removing the incentive of the TSO to favour one supplier over another.

In November 2008, the European Commission adopted a decision rendering E.ON's commitments legally binding. The various electricity generation plants were sold between January 2009 and May 2010, mostly to medium-sized market players. The divestment of E.ON's transmission system business took place in early 2010. Consequently, the European Commission decision(s) in the E.ON abuse of dominance case affected two main product markets: the German wholesale electricity market and the balancing energy market. The ex post economic evaluation in the present chapter largely concentrates on the impact of the divestment of 5000 MW generation capacity on the wholesale electricity market in Germany.

Wholesale electricity markets and balancing markets should be related because there exist arbitrage opportunities between the spot market and the balancing mechanism. Prices in the balancing markets (capacity prices) constitute a sort of opportunity cost for energy suppliers who commit themselves not to sell the reserved capacity on wholesale spot markets. Therefore, the alleged abuse in the balancing market might have had an effect on competition at the wholesale level. However, Just and Weber (2015) suggest, based on empirical evidence for the German market, that this effect is of second-order importance, particularly in the short run. The present chapter therefore focuses more explicitly on the evaluation of the impact of the generation capacity divestments on the wholesale electricity market. Nevertheless, one cannot cleanly separate the impact of E.ON's capacity divestments from that of the divestment of its transmission system business as both were completed at around the same time in early 2010.

§6.04 LITERATURE REVIEW

This section provides a short review of the literature that is relevant for a better understanding of the European Commission's concern about E.ON's behaviour. Subsection 6.04[A] describes papers analysing the costs and benefits of vertical integration in the network industries, an issue heavily debated in the literature. The combination of vertical integration with joint control of the different stages of the supply chain has been identified in the literature as both a source of efficiencies and a barrier to effective competition. Subsection 6.04[B] gives an economic perspective on the practice of withholding of electricity generation capacity, which triggered the Commission intervention in the E.ON case. Subsection 6.04[C] covers research on the pass-through of price fluctuations from wholesale to retail markets in the electricity sector.

[A] Vertical Integration

Most of the network industries historically had a vertically integrated structure in which the firms producing the initial input also owned the transmission and distribution networks. Network access was essential to be able to supply customers in the downstream, retail markets. The objective of the market liberalisation in the 1990s was to open the historical monopolies up to competition by allowing downstream competitors to have equal access to the transmission and distribution networks. E.ON used to be a typical example of a vertically integrated company, being an electricity generator, a TSO and a retailer. Its 2008 commitment to divest its high-voltage transmission grid broke up the vertical supply chain internal to the company, thereby furthering the European Commission's objective of electricity market liberalisation.

There is a large economic literature on the pros and cons of this process of vertical unbundling. The papers referred to in the next paragraphs highlight the main issues under debate. The first group of papers tends to focus on the costs of unbundling while the second group puts a greater emphasis on its benefits.

Buehler (2005) discusses the liberalisation of network industries and its potential pitfalls. He compares a monopolist's pricing strategy and incentives to invest in network reliability under different forms of market structure. He finds that both in the case of 'vertical separation' (where the network monopolist is fully separated from the imperfectly competitive downstream market) and the case of 'liberalisation' (where the network monopolist is allowed to operate in the imperfectly competitive downstream market), the incentives to invest in network costs reduction are less in comparison with a purely monopolistic market structure. Furthermore, he shows that breaking up vertically integrated supply chains in network industries may result in higher retail prices due to increased transmission costs. In the electricity sector, for example, vertical integration sector is source of substantial economies of coordination, which would be lost with the break-up of the supply chain.

Kwoka (2002) and Meyer (2012) also conclude that the benefits of vertical integration could be significant in terms of coordination and market risk economies. Coordination economies result from the technological interdependency of electricity supply: an integrated structure can internalise network externalities and lead to a more efficient exchange of information. Market risk economies include the better management of risks associated with long-term irreversible investment. In his review of the literature, Meyer (2012) finds that the losses in vertical synergies resulting from unbundling lead to an increase in costs ranging between 2% and 20% depending on the type of unbundling considered. However, he also indicates that a separation of supply stages may lead to efficiency gains due to a better management focused on specific tasks compared to a multi-product company. Finally, he notes that his study only covers the negative aspects of vertical separation while it does not take into account the positive effects in terms of increased competition.

Bolle and Breitmoser (2006) highlight the complexity of dissolving the vertically integrated supply chains. They compare the consequences of legal unbundling and ownership unbundling[6] on network access prices and the quantity of final output supplied. They conclude that legal unbundling may be the better option (as compared to ownership unbundling) since it preserves certain advantages of vertical integration

6. Under legal unbundling, the upstream generator and the network operator are two separate firms, but still connected via a holding structure while under ownership unbundling, one of these two firms has to be divested.

(e.g., it partially avoids double marginalisation[7]) while stimulating efficiency through the introduction of competitive forces downstream.

Gugler et al. (2013) provides an empirical analysis of the effects of ownership unbundling in the electricity industry electricity in sixteen European countries over the period 1998-2008. They find that ownership unbundling significantly reduces aggregate investment in the electricity industry. They also observe an investment reducing effect of third party access to the electricity transmission grid.

A second group of papers is more positive on the effects of unbundling. Pollitt (2008) provides a nuanced view of the net benefits of ownership unbundling. In principle, they should be positive, even though in the short term such benefits may be offset by the costs of reorganisation resulting from the process of ownership unbundling. Case study evidence seems to indicate that the ownership unbundling of transmission networks is a key part of successful electricity market reforms as it increased the degree of competition in generation and kept down the costs of transmission.

A number of empirical papers that investigate the effects of vertical disintegration on investments and prices support the argument that ownership unbundling may bring important benefits. Copenhagen Economics (2005) examines the impact of ownership unbundling in several EU network industries over the period 1993-2003 and concludes that higher levels of unbundling leads to price reductions and efficiency gains. Alesina et al. (2005) analyses the impact of regulatory reform in seven network industries in twenty-one OECD countries between 1975 and 1998. They conclude that investments increase with higher levels of unbundling in the gas and electricity sector. However, there is no differentiation between ownership and legal unbundling.

Nardi (2012) confirms that ownership unbundling leads to increased investments in the network, but also to a reduction in quality due to a lack of coordination across the different stages of the supply chain. This result is in line with Haucap (2007), who finds that the break-up of the supply chain is likely to reduce the operators' incentives to invest in network reliability. However, on the positive side, network operators' incentives to invest in cross-border transmission should increase, while their incentives to discriminate between independent and affiliated retailers should diminish. Unlike legal unbundling, ownership unbundling reduces the ability of integrated firms to distort downstream competition using cross-subsidies between the non-competitive part and the competitive part of the business.

In conclusion, there appears to be no consensus on whether the unbundling of the vertical supply chain in network industries (and in electricity supply more in particular) achieves net costs or benefits. However, there appears to be agreement that there is a trade-off between the vertical economies (mostly coordination economies) and incentive effects of integration on investments (mostly due to reduced market risk)

7. Double marginalisation is a phenomenon in which two firms along the supply chain in a given industry can each exert market power when setting their mark-ups. As a result, the sum of the mark-ups of the two firms is higher than what would be the mark-up of a monopolist controlling the whole supply chain.

on the one hand, and a more competitive market structure leading to price reductions and the market exit of inefficient firms, on the other hand.

[B] Withdrawal of Electricity Generation Capacity

The electric power industry faces two big constraints that determine the intrinsic mechanisms driving the electricity market. First, as power cannot be economically stored, it has to be consumed instantaneously. Consequently, the electricity prices are set every hour depending on the level of demand and the immediately available generation capacity in the market to satisfy this demand. Second, the electricity market must offer generators sufficient incentives to produce the required quantity of energy while ensuring fair prices for consumers. If the market design does not succeed in meeting the requirements of both consumers and generators of electricity, major market failures can occur.

The events in California in the early 2000s serve as an illustration. A poorly designed deregulation of California's electricity market led to a very rapid increase in wholesale prices between April 2000 and December 2000. At some point, electricity prices were nine times their average before the crisis. At the same time, the electricity supply could not meet the demand leading to several rolling blackouts. Cabral (2002) considers the different causes of the Californian energy crisis, including an increased demand for energy coupled with a low level of investment in new generation plants, which could be associated with the low electricity prices at the retail level. Moreover, generators owning both low-cost and high-cost plants had an incentive to withdraw generation capacity from the market, allowing them to charge higher prices on electricity produced with their low-cost plants, in particular during the crisis period. Cabral concludes that such strategic behaviour may indeed have contributed to the severity of the Californian energy crisis. He maintains nevertheless that the basic idea of creating competition at the level of power generations is a valid one.

Similarly, Green (2004) describes how strategic behaviour by electricity generators could have affected price developments in the England and Wales Electricity Pool during the 1990s. First, they might have engaged in strategic capacity withholding: by withdrawing low-cost plants from the market, the likelihood that high-cost plants set the spot price in wholesale markets increases. As a result, prices would be higher than they would have been if the low-cost plants had still been in operation. Second, electricity generators might have adopted a strategy of withdrawing high-cost generation plants from the market. By keeping high-cost plants unavailable for power generation, generators would be able to diminish the overall level of generation capacity in the market and hence raise the capacity payments that were 'designed to reward capacity when it is scarce'.

Capacity payments that remunerate electricity generators for being available in case needed do not infringe antitrust rules as such. However, the European Commission has had concerns that capacity payments may unduly favour particular producers and create obstacles to electricity trade across borders, in breach of EU State aid rules. Therefore, in 2015, it launched a sector inquiry on 'capacity mechanisms', which are measures taken by the EU Member States to ensure that electricity supply can match demand in the medium and long term. The conclusions of this sector inquiry are that the need for such a mechanism must be better demonstrated and that the design of most capacity mechanisms could be significantly improved. In particular, prices paid for capacity must be determined in a competitive process, and the capacity mechanisms should be open to electricity generators based in other Member States (*see* European Commission, 2016).

Tsangaris (2017) analyses the features of generation capacity withholding which allow generators to push up wholesale prices. He points out that the profitability of a generation capacity withholding strategy relies on the generator's market share in the overall generation capacity available in the spot market. Generally, small generators do not have an incentive to engage in such a practice, since they do not hold a sufficient share of the overall generation capacity for the capacity withholding substantially to affect market prices. Only a generator that accounts for an important share of total generation capacity will have the incentive to withhold such capacity from the market, because the increased profit on its remaining electricity production plants will more than compensate the profit loss due to the withholding. Tsangaris also shows that generators are more likely to enter in strategic capacity withholding in periods of high demand.

[C] Price Pass-Through from the Wholesale to the Retail Electricity Market

Since this chapter aims to assess the effects of competition policy enforcement on electricity prices, one needs to consider the interaction between wholesale and retail markets. In many wholesale markets, electricity prices are set based on bids made by generators. Such bids can vary substantially from one hour to another, and across days and seasons. In a competitive retail market, one would expect retail prices to follow the price fluctuations in the wholesale market. If electricity retailers do not have market power, then a wholesale price decrease (increase) should be reflected in a retail price decrease (increase) of the same order of magnitude. At the same time, consumers are looking for protection against price spikes, and a retailer that adjusts its prices too frequently is likely to lose customers' confidence and hence potentially part of its customer base. This phenomenon should have a dampening effect of price movements at the retail level.

Empirical studies of the pass-through of price movements in the energy sector are rather scarce. Zachmann and Von Hirschhausen (2008) and Fabra and Reguant (2014) focus on the pass-through of emission costs to electricity prices at the wholesale and retail levels. Due to the very limited elasticity of demand for electricity, there is an almost complete pass-through of positive cost shocks. However, this is not necessarily the case for negative cost shocks. Mirza and Bergland (2012) observe a similar asymmetry in their analysis of the pass-through of wholesale to retail prices in Norwegian electricity markets: retailers tend to adjust their price quicker following a price increase in wholesale markets than after a price decrease.

A recent paper by Duso and Szücs (2017) uses a panel regression model to investigate the pass-through of changes in the costs of producing electricity to changes to retail electricity prices in German. Using a linear regression of retail prices on aggregate costs while controlling for several types of fixed effects (time, type of contract, etc.) they find that the pass-through rate is on average around 60%. The rate of pass-through appears to vary significantly with demand factors, mainly customer switching behaviour and, to a lesser extent, with the market power of firms. It approaches one for the most competitive segment of the market: pass-through rates observed for independent retailers having relatively less market power appear to be significantly higher than those for other electricity retailers. Duso and Szücs also show that the rate of pass-through was increasing over time.

§6.05 IMPACT OF THE E.ON DECISION ON THE WHOLESALE ELECTRICITY MARKET IN GERMANY

Given that the E.ON decision directly affected the generation stage of the German electricity sector, the starting point for the assessment of the decision's effects should be the analysis of changes in wholesale market prices resulting from the European Commission's intervention. As the ultimate goal of competition policy enforcement is the enhancement of consumer welfare, this chapter also examines the changes observed to retail prices around the time of the Commission's decision. However, strictly speaking the retail market analysis cannot be considered as part of the ex post evaluation of the European Commission's decision. Whether or not a reduction in wholesale electricity prices is passed on to the end consumer does not depend on the European Commission's decision itself but rather more on the competitive structure of the downstream retail electricity market. Sections 6.05 and 6.06 focus on price developments in the wholesale and retail market respectively.

In theory, the effect of the E.ON decision on wholesale prices is straightforward. The divestment of power plants should lead to an increase in competition since most of the electricity production facilities were bought by medium-sized market players. Such medium-sized players would have no, or at least less, incentive to withhold electricity supply from the market unnecessarily. Therefore, the divestments should lead to an increase in the amount of electricity available in the market and hence to a decrease in wholesale prices. The objective of the Difference-in-Differences analysis presented here is to provide empirical evidence concerning this hypothesis.

[A] The Empirical Strategy

[1] The Identification Strategy

The effect of the E.ON commitment decision is identified within a Difference-in-Differences framework: the behaviour of a treatment group, which is mostly affected by the decision to divest of the power plants, is compared with the behaviour of a control group, which is not, or less, affected. By looking at the different evolution of outcomes for the two groups before and after the implementation of the divestments, we expect to be able to better control for possible spurious correlation and thus identify the effect of the E.ON decision. This suitability of the analytical framework relies on the identification of appropriate treated and control groups and on the correct choice of the before and after periods.

[a] Identification of the Treatment and Control Groups

A number of alternative options for defining the control group were considered. The first option would be to compose the control group of countries structurally similar to Germany but not affected by any abuse, merger or other relevant competition policy decisions during the sample period. However, it was impossible to find a national electricity market that was truly comparable to the German market, because Germany had pursued a unique green strategy (the so-called *Energiewende*). Direct neighbours are also a poor counterfactual because electricity markets are becoming more connected and cannot be seen as fully independent.

The second option would be the creation of a synthetic control group, which consists in defining a synthetic, hypothetical market, whose outcome pre-treatment is an almost perfect match for the outcome of the treated group. In this particular case, this 'synthetic group' group would be constructed as a weighted average of a selection of other countries, resembling Germany but not affected by the E.ON commitment decision. The difficulty of this approach lays in the selection of countries to be included in the control group. The approach is also data intensive, requiring a potentially large set of key control variables that may affect electricity prices, not only for Germany but also for all other countries used to construct the control group. This approach was abandoned because we could not satisfactorily match German electricity prices in the period before the decision with price developments in a synthetic control group.

A third identification strategy was used, which relies on the pricing dynamics of the wholesale electricity market within Germany itself. This identification strategy is based on the different price response to the European Commission's decision between peak (8am-8pm) and off-peak periods (9pm-7am). During the peak periods, more plants are in operation in order to meet the increased demand. The additional plants in operation tend to be those with low set-up and shutdown costs but with relatively high operating costs, which explains the steep slope of the supply curve during periods of peak demand. The resulting convexity of the electricity supply curve implies that prices react more strongly to changes in demand during peak periods. The logic of this identification strategy is thus that the restoration of electricity generation capacity associated with the E.ON decision moves the electricity supply curve to the right, causing a substantial decline in wholesale prices during peak periods, but only a minor decline during off-peak periods (*see* section 6.4.2 of ICF and DIW (2015)). The ex post evaluation approach used to assess the impact of the E.ON decision exploits this difference in price response between peak and off-peak periods.

As the E.ON commitment decision should cause a larger reduction in peak prices than in off-peak prices, one would expect to observe a convergence of peak and off-peak prices following the implementation of the commitment decision. Figure 6.3 represents the evolution of the monthly average day-ahead prices during peak and off-peak periods. The figure shows monthly averages to wash out the extreme daily price volatility and make the comparison clearer. While there is some seasonal variability, both peak and off-peak prices have been dropping since 2009, and there is a slight and slow convergence between the two series from 2009 on. As this descriptive evidence only suggests a possible convergence, an econometric model has been developed to control for other factors affecting these price developments.

Figure 6.3 German Monthly Peak Versus Off-Peak Prices

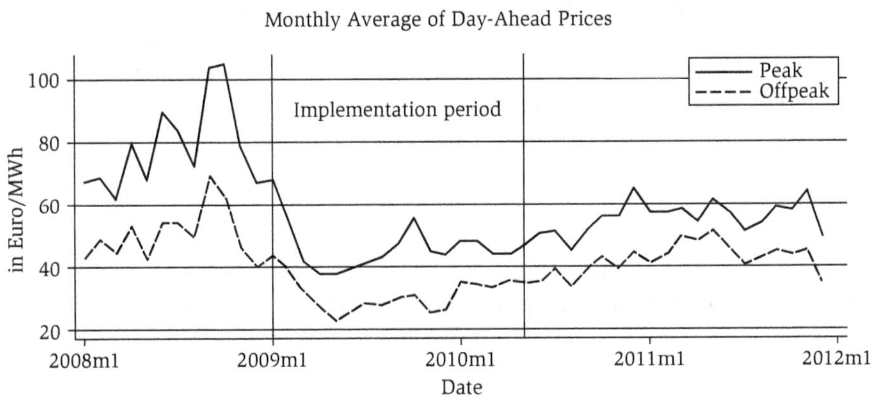

Source: *EPEX*.

[b] Identification of the Treatment Period

The treatment period corresponds to the time during which the effects of the E.ON decision (taken in November 2008) may be observed. Three sub-periods are defined: the before period (up to December 2008), the implementation period during which the remedies were implemented (from January 2009 to April 2010) and the after period (starting in May 2010). Given the high frequency of the data and because wholesale electricity markets are very dynamic and could respond swiftly to changes in supply conditions, three different impact scenarios are considered allowing identification of both the short-run and long-term effects of E.ON's divestments.

The advantage of the short-run scenario is that it may allow identifying the immediate effects of the divestments. Hence, the risk of contaminating the effect of the decision with other, unobserved factors is much lower. However, the effects of an important decision could be much more pervasive. Therefore, it is reasonable to look at the long-term impact of the decision over several years. The disadvantage of this is that the identification of the market intervention might be weakened by the existence of confounding factors, particularly in such a liquid and dynamic market.

Under the short-run scenario, the impact of each of the eight divestments implemented is assumed to be immediate and short-lived. Thus, the dummy variable Post takes on the value of 1 during the week after each of these divestments. One week after each divestment j (out of a total of eight divestments), the dummy variable Post turns to zero again and it then turns to 1 again when the next divestment is implemented. The estimated coefficient for this dummy variable measures the average cumulative short-term effect of the eight divestments.

Under the first long-term scenario, the effects of the market intervention are assumed to become apparent with the implementation of the first divestment. In this setting, the dummy variable takes on a value of 1 from the year 2009 onward.

Alternatively, one may consider that the overall effect of the decision can only be observed following the implementation of the last divestment. According to this second long-term scenario, the dummy variable takes on a value of 1 from May 2010 onward and the year 2009 is excluded from the analysis.

[2] Empirical Model

The basis empirical model used to analyse the German wholesale electricity market consists of a price equation where the wholesale price is a function of demand and supply drivers. The model is based on Böckers and Heimeshoff (2014) and takes the following form:

$$\begin{aligned}
p_{it} = {} & \beta Peak_i + \gamma Post_t + \delta Peak_i \times Post_t + \alpha_1 wind_{it} + \alpha_2 sun_{it} + \alpha_3 crossborder\ flows_t \\
& + \omega_1 uranium_t + \omega_2 coal_t + \omega_3 gas_t + \omega_4 oil_t + \omega_t emission_t \\
& + \sum_{y=2008}^{2012} \theta_y Y_{y,t} + \sum_{m=1}^{11} \vartheta_m M_{m,t} + \sum_{d=1}^{6} \mu_d D_{d,t} + \rho_1 temp_{it} + \tau_1 holiday_t + \epsilon_{it}
\end{aligned}$$

The daily power price p_{it} at day t for the group i – peak versus off-peak – is regressed on:

(1) $Peak_i$, a dummy variable equal to 1 during periods of peak demand and equal to 0 during periods of off-peak demand: the estimated coefficient β is a measure of the difference between peak and off-peak prices.
(2) $Post_t$, a dummy variable equal to 1 during the period that the effect of the decision can be felt: the estimated coefficient γ is a measure of the average price difference before and after the E.ON commitment decision. The definition of $Post_t$ varies with the short-run or long-term scenario under consideration.
(3) The variable $Peak_i \times Post_t$: the estimated coefficient δ is a measure of the treatment effect, i.e., the impact of the E.ON commitment decision as

measured by the difference in the evolution of peak versus off-peak prices before and after the E.ON decision.

(4) Demand-side variables including seasonal and business cycle dummies (day D, month M, year Y, peak and off-peak temperature, and holiday).

(5) Supply-side controls include the daily prices of input factors, represented by price indices that cover the daily international prices for commodities such as coal, gas, oil and emission certificates. Production volumes from renewable energy sources including wind and solar power are used as a control as well, as renewables brought about a significant shift in the supply curve during the period under investigation.[8]

(6) A variable measuring cross-border electricity flows, which reflects pricing constraints imposed by competition from neighbouring countries.

The double differencing implied by this Difference-in-Differences framework and the inclusion of a large set of common demand-side and supply-side drivers will help mitigate endogeneity problems due to omitted variables and create more confidence in the causal nature of the estimated treatment effect. Finally, the error terms are assumed to be auto-correlated and heteroskedastic.[9]

The price data for the wholesale analysis come from the Platts database, which provides information on prices set at the EEX power exchange. Even though most electricity is traded via OTC contracts, the electricity price determined at the EEX spot market can serve as a reference price for all of the wholesale electricity market as a whole, as there are multiple arbitrage opportunities between the spot and OTC markets. Therefore, EEX spot prices can be considered as a good proxy for wholesale electricity prices. Moreover, the EEX market is very liquid and swiftly responds to changes in electricity supplied and the intensity of competition, which makes it particularly well suited for an empirical analysis looking at the effects of commitments affecting wholesale electricity market supply. The definition and the source of the data used for the control variables are provided in Appendix.

8. Potentially, it might be important to control for additional newly installed capacity from conventional – rather than renewable – sources as it might also influence the supply curve. Data from the German regulator for the period 2007-2014 suggest that the large increase in generation capacity over the sample period comes from renewable sources. Only during the second half of 2011, some substantial changes in the generation of capacity can be observed due to the shutdown of nuclear plants following the Fukushima's accident. The reduced nuclear capacity was however compensated by an increase of gas power plants' capacity. The net change was lower than 2,000 MW and much smaller than the change in generation capacity due to renewables. Hence, these changes do not appear to affect substantially the results presented here.

9. Since the assumptions on the error term play a crucial role in making accurate inferences, several robustness checks have made to deal with the possible issue of autocorrelation in the error terms. The use of Newey-West standard error estimators having a shorter autocorrelation lag does not seem to affect the results obtained, even though some significance is lost in the short-term scenario. Similarly, bootstrapped standard errors based on 1,000 replacements tend to be somewhat larger than the Newey-West standard errors used in the main specification, making the calculated regression coefficients slightly less significant. Finally, a reduction in data frequency does not appear to affect the qualitative and quantitative results obtained.

[B] Results

[1] The Main Results

Table 6.4 reports the main results of the estimation. First, the model seems to fit the data well because it can capture between 76% and 79% of the variation in wholesale electricity prices. Second, the average difference between peak and off-peak prices varies between circa EUR 20/MWh in the short-run model and EUR 31/MWh in the long-term models. Third, an overall decrease in prices can be observed during the post period ('cumulative post effect'), mostly defined from 2009 to 2011.[10] This overall price decline may be associated with the deterioration in the economic conditions due to the economic and financial crisis of 2008. The estimated coefficients for the cumulative post effect show that on average, electricity prices have decreased by EUR 7/MWh to EUR 20/MWh depending on the model adopted.

The key question in our identification strategy is whether the divestments made by E.ON reduced the difference between peak and off-peak prices, because this convergence is what we would expect if the E.ON decision effectively reduced wholesalers' market power. The estimations for the long-term scenarios indeed show a significant convergence of peak and off-peak prices. This effect is not only statistically significant but also economically very large. Independently of the scenario (Post 2009 or Post 2010), there is a significant reduction in the price differential between peak prices and off-peak prices of around EUR 15/MWh, other things equal. The difference between peak and off-peak prices is reduced by almost 50%. Looking at short-run effects, the estimation also shows a negative, significant coefficient estimate for the dummy measuring the interaction between 'peak' and 'post', which hints at a short-run price convergence in the weeks following the implementation of the different divestments. However, the short-run convergence is relatively small (around EUR 3/MWh between peak and off-peak prices) when compared with the long-term effects.

10. The 'post' dummy cannot be identified, as it is collinear with the year dummies. Therefore, the 'post' effect is calculated as the sum of the estimated coefficients for the year dummies, the so-called cumulative post effect. In the specification represented in Column (3), where the year 2009 is dropped, the sum of the estimated coefficients of the 2010 and 2011 dummies is reported, while in Columns (1) and (2) the sums of the estimated coefficients of the 2009, 2010 and 2011 dummies are reported in the table.

Table 6.4 The Effect of the Divestments on Wholesale Electricity Prices in Germany[11]

	Short Run (1)	*Post 2009* (2)	*Post 2010* (3)
Peak	19.68*** (1.00)	31.03*** (1.79)	30.84*** (1.89)
Peak × Post	-3.22** (1.54)	-14.58*** (1.66)	-15.37*** (1.65)
Constant	46.66*** (7.92)	38.38*** (6.33)	40.32*** (7.46)
Cumulative post effect	-20.06*** (4.97)	-11.85*** (4.30)	-7.09*** (2.74)
Observations	2890	2916	2190
Adjusted R-Squared	0.76	0.79	0.78

The dependent variable is the daily average peak or off-peak price at the EEX power exchange. We control for input prices (gas, oil, coal, uranium, and emission), day, month, and year dummies, solar and wind energy production, temperature, cross-border capacities, market coupling, as well as holidays. Newey-West standard errors with a maximum lag order of autocorrelation equal to seven days are reported in parentheses.

The symbols ***, **, * represent significance at the 1%, 5% and 10% levels respectively.

Overall, the results suggest that the divestments had a significant impact on electricity prices in the German wholesale market: both the short-run and long-run differences between peak and off-peak prices was significantly reduced, *ceteris paribus*. This finding is consistent with the Commission's decision effectively stopping or at least reducing E.ON's alleged abuse of market power. The estimates of the extent of this price convergence differ, depending on the assumptions made on the relevant timing framework. The magnitude of prices convergence (with estimates of EUR 3/MWh in the short-run and EUR 15/MWh in the long-term, ceteris paribus) is significant when considering that the difference between peak and off-peak prices was EUR 30/MWh on average during the observation period. The estimations presented here each have their own advantages and disadvantages. The short-run scenario is possibly more intuitive because the short time window minimises the possibility that other unobserved factors or events create a bias. However, it might not cover long-term changes in the market structure or fail to reflect any slow adjustment in firms' bidding behaviour. The long-term effects, which can be better interpreted within a Difference-in-Differences framework, are more likely to capture permanent strategic adjustments

11. The estimated coefficients for the control variables are reported in Appendix 2. They are all significant and conform expectations. Specifically, input prices and temperature are significantly and positively related to wholesale prices. The estimated coefficients for the day and month dummies are also highly significant. Finally, the production capacity of wind and solar as well as the cross-border flows significantly decrease wholesale prices as expected.

in the bidding behaviour of both incumbents and their smaller competitors. However, they could be contaminated by other policy interventions or market changes occurring during that same period. In fact, during the years 2009-2011 several other national and EU-wide policy interventions might have affected the German electricity wholesale market. Nevertheless, the comparison of the different effects provides a quite coherent picture that consistently points to an increase in competition in the market that can be related to the European Commission's intervention in the E.ON alleged abuse of dominance case.

[2] Analysis Using Spain as a Placebo

To test the robustness of these findings, a 'placebo' tests was conducted using Spain as a placebo. Spain is a good choice because its wholesale electricity market is rather similar to that of Germany, but its electricity grid is not directly connected to that of Germany. Moreover, the Spanish authorities provide relatively good information on the main control variables, such as the production of renewable energy, cross-border electricity flows, holidays and temperature. The identification strategy is the same as the one used for Germany, comparing peak and off-peak prices and using the same definition of the before and after periods. The logic of the 'placebo' test is that: if the model indeed measures the effect of the E.ON decision and the different geographic markets are not strongly integrated, then the estimation should not give the same effects in the other countries as those observed for Germany.

During the sample period, the Spanish wholesale electricity market was not closely integrated with the German market. As Spain does not share borders with Germany, there was practically no trade of electricity between the two countries. It is therefore unlikely that the E.ON decision significantly affected Spanish prices.

Figure 6.4 shows the evolution of the monthly average peak and off-peak Spanish wholesale electricity prices. The differences between the two price series and their convergence appear much smaller than in Germany.

Figure 6.4 Spanish Monthly Peak Versus Off-Peak Prices

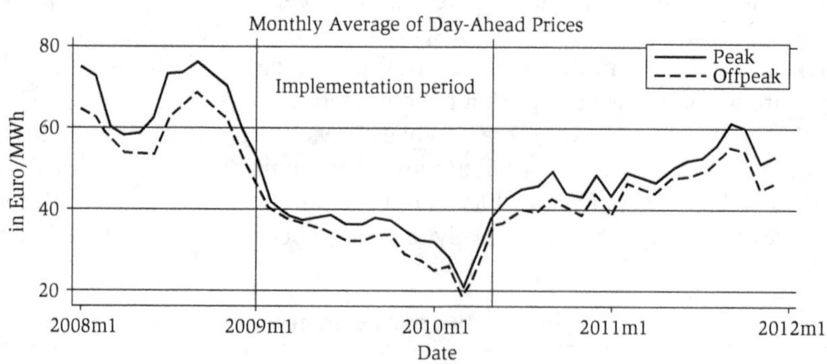

Source: *OMIE*.

The convergence pattern is further analysed within the regression framework developed above. Table 6.5 reports the regression results. Again, the model seems successful because it can explain 84% of the variation in the Spanish wholesale electricity prices. The difference between peak and off-peak prices in Spain seems to be around one-third of that in Germany and ranges between EUR 6 and EUR 10/MWh. After 2009, prices decreased on average by EUR 8 to EUR 19/MWh (the cumulative post-effect) over the regression period, a decline similar to that in Germany.

Table 6.5 The Effect of the Divestments on Wholesale Electricity Prices in Spain

	Short Run (1)	*Post 2009* (2)	*Post 2010* (3)
Peak	6.42*** (2.46)	9.52*** (2.68)	10.00*** (3.24)
Peak × Post	-1.57 (2.01)	-3.70*** (0.97)	-3.43*** (0.99)
Constant	32.79*** (4.24)	31.28*** (4.20)	32.03*** (4.63)
Cumulative post effect	-8.1* (4.64)	-19.61*** (4.58)	-13.16* (6.95)
Observations	2,878	2,878	2,148
Adjusted R-Squared	0.84	0.84	0.84

As explained above, it is unlikely that wholesale electricity prices in Spain would have been significantly affected during the one week following each individual divestment, as is done in the short-run scenario, and indeed the estimation results show no significant convergence effect in the short-run specification. So that while German prices significantly react to the implementation of the remedies, Spanish prices remain mostly unaffected.

Nevertheless, looking at the long-term specifications, a price convergence can be observed even if the convergence between peak and off-peak prices is much smaller than in Germany: between EUR 3 and 4/MWh as compared to the EUR 15/MWh price convergence for Germany. This small but significant long-term convergence is consistent with the Spanish market becoming more competitive between 2009 and 2011. Possibly, such price convergence was triggered by a strengthening of competition policy enforcement in the Spanish market, as the Spanish competition authority opened several abuse cases in the electricity sector after 2009.

In summary, it appears that peak and off-peak prices have converged in Spain as well. However, the extent of this convergence is smaller than in Germany and not necessarily linked to the E.ON commitment decision. In subsequent work, Duso et al. (2018) carried out another Placebo test by shifting the evaluation period to a time when no actual treatment occurred. In this other test, no significant long-run convergence effect was observed. The price convergence observed in Germany following the implementation of the electricity generation capacity divestments therefore supports the claim that the German model is indeed identifying, even if only imperfectly, the effects of the European Commission's decision.

§6.06 THE EVOLUTION OF RETAIL ELECTRICITY MARKETS IN GERMANY AROUND THE TIME OF THE EUROPEAN COMMISSION'S DECISION

As the objective of competition policy enforcement is to raise consumer welfare, this chapter also examines to what extent the reduction in wholesale electricity prices might have affected the functioning of retail markets. The extent of this is related to the pass-through rate: if the pass-through were low, wholesale price reductions due to antitrust interventions would have limited benefits for final consumers. Given that the European Commission's decision in the E.ON case only relates to wholesale markets, the direct impact of E.ON's commitments can only be assessed at the wholesale level. Nevertheless, the analysis of the evolution of retail markets provides quantitative evidence on the potential implications of an antitrust decision on final customers.

[A] The Empirical Strategy

The methodological approach that we adopt here is also based on a Difference-in-Differences approach.[12] The identification strategy exploits the variation in retail tariffs across local markets within Germany, across different firms, and over time. As was the case for the wholesale market analysis, the two key elements of the identification strategy used for the examination of development in the retail market are: (1) the definition of the treatment and control groups: and (2) and the definition of the before and after periods. However, the definition of these two elements differs substantially from what was discussed in the analysis of the wholesale market.

[1] The Identification Strategy

[a] Identification of the Treatment Group

As described in section 6.02, one can distinguish between three types of retailers in the German electricity market. The first group of retailers is represented by the four big vertically integrated operators: E.ON, RWE, EnBW and Vattenfall. These are very large multi-product energy firms, mostly active at all levels of the vertical production chain. The big four are incumbents both in wholesale and in retail markets and own a substantial part of the transmission and distribution networks. Yet, their operations at these different levels have been legally separated since 2002. Amongst the big four, only Vattenfall is not a long-term incumbent in the German market. Vattenfall is a Swedish utility that entered the German (and other European) market(s) on a massive scale in the late 1990s.

These big four companies are the incumbent operators in more than half of the local retail markets. They all have a strong regional focus: E.ON is particularly strong in the south (Bavaria) and east of Germany; RWE is the main incumbent in the west (particularly North-Rhine Westphalia); EnBW is the main operator in the south-west (Baden-Württemberg): and Vattenfall is particularly strong in two major city-states (Berlin and Hamburg). While there were some dynamics in their local market shares, the big four operators maintained a strong position in their core markets over the entire sample period. The big four generally offer nation-wide tariffs even though there is some cross-regional variation, particularly for their cheapest tariffs.

The second group of retailers consists of municipal operators (*Stadtwerke*) and firms with a mixed ownership structure (i.e., being partially owned by one of the big four or by municipal operators). *Stadtwerke* are often vertically integrated and, in most cases, they are multi-utilities, active not only in electricity markets but also in other markets such as gas, water, sewage and municipal waste. They mostly produce electricity for their own needs and not for sale in the wholesale markets. Municipal operators tend to be publicly owned, which may affect their objectives and pricing strategies. They are therefore likely to behave differently from both the established big four incumbents and the smaller, independent operators that mostly focus on electricity retailing.

The third category of firms active in retail electricity markets is made up of the smaller, independent operators, which are generally not vertically integrated. Their market strategy is to exploit the structural differences with the other operators in the market. They are small and have limited access to capital. They target their sales efforts to specific groups of well-informed and mobile customers, often located within a given region.

Besides different levels of vertical integration, size and possibly objectives, the three groups of firms appear to have a very heterogeneous purchasing strategy in wholesale markets. In its monitoring report in 2011, the German regulator mentions that: 'For instance, new entrants order on average only 20% of their sales volumes more than one year before its delivery to the end customers and ca. 35% during the year of the delivery. On the contrary, incumbents order more than 40% of their sales volumes more than one year in advance and only ca. 5% in the year of the delivery. Since a short-term purchasing strategy is currently on average cheaper than a long-term one, new entrant can offer at present more convenient conditions to their customers without losing money in supply and distribution' (Bundesnetzagentur, 2011, p. 41).

Finally, the very low levels of switching among households customers (*see* Figure 6.2 above) imply that incumbent firms, and especially E.ON, RWE and EnBW, have substantial market power over their captive customers.

These considerations underpin the logic of the identification strategy. Specifically, the big four are expected to react less strongly to changes in wholesale prices than small, independent retailers, the reason being that they have a larger degree of market power over their customers and use a less aggressive and more conservative purchasing strategy in wholesale markets. Given that the behaviour of municipal firms and firms with a mixed ownership structure is more difficult to predict, they are included in the treatment group as well. However, we will estimate firm-specific heterogeneous effects that may be different for each of the big four firms as well as for the *Stadtwerke* and the firms with a mixed ownership structure.

Thus, the treatment group ($treat_{im} = 1$) is composed of the local markets where one of the big four (E.ON, RWE, EnBW and Vattenfall), a municipal operator or a firm with a mixed ownership structure is incumbent because they are expected to react differently to changes in wholesale prices than independent retailers. For the big four in particular, prices are expected to increase relative to the control group of independent retailers in the post-treatment period.

[b] Additional Treatment

To increase the power of the identification strategy, the German retail electricity market is further segmented between a group of captive customers who stick to the incumbent baseline tariff – or perhaps another cheaper tariff of the incumbent – and a more mobile group of customers willing to switch and attracted by the conditions offered by independent retailers. The latter market segment is probably more competitive, which would imply that tariffs in this segment should be more responsive to changes in wholesale prices. Therefore, one would expect that the price dispersion between the highest baseline tariff and the cheapest tariff in each regional market increases post treatment in markets with one of the big four as an incumbent, in comparison with markets with an independent incumbent.

[c] Identification of the Treatment Period

As discussed in section 6.02[A], the purchase of electricity by retailers mostly works via long-term contracts. As prices are adjusted only when a new contract is negotiated, any change in wholesale prices should materialise in retail market only with a substantial delay. The German network regulator observes that: '[...] wholesale prices, which have been decreasing since the second half of 2008, started to have a positive effect on household retail prices in 2010. However, [these price reductions] are considerably delayed if compared to the wholesale market. The main reason for these delayed reductions of the suppliers' acquisition costs lies on the long-term purchasing strategy' (Bundesnetzagentur, 2011, p. 41).

While the effects of the E.ON decision on wholesale price should become visible soon after the divestments of the electricity generation plants, a corresponding decrease in retail prices should not be expected until several months later. Moreover, the decrease in retail tariffs should be more gradual in light of the fact that different retailers use different purchasing strategies. Therefore, in the Difference-in-Differences analysis presented below, the dummy variable Post takes on the value of 1 after May 2010, the date of the last divestment by E.ON.

[d] Time-Varying Treatment Effects

The price reductions in the wholesale market will only slowly affect retail tariffs because part of the electricity sold on retail markets has been purchased at the wholesale market via long-term contracts. As the existing long-term contracts expire the share of electricity purchased at a lower price increases over time. Therefore, one would expect that the impact of the European Commission's decision to be felt even more slowly on retail markets, particularly when looking at the tariffs offered by the four large vertically integrated incumbents, which tend make more use of long-term contracts (in comparison with independent retailers). Therefore, looking at time-varying treatment effects should help to improve further the identification strategy for evaluating the effects of the E.ON decision on retail tariffs.

[2] Estimation Method

The basic empirical model for the retail market analysis consists in estimating a price equation of the following form:

$$p_{imt} = \alpha + \beta_i treat_{im} + \delta Post_t + \gamma_i treat_{im} \times Post_t + X_{mt} + \mu_{im} + \tau_t + \varepsilon_{imt}$$

where the tariff set by retailer i in local market m at time t is a function of market demand and supply drivers (X_{mt}), firm-market-specific fixed effects to account for time-invariant unobserved heterogeneity across regions (μ_{im}), as well as time fixed effects to account for firm, market or firm-region invariant unobserved heterogeneity (τ_t). The error term ε_{imt} is assumed to be heteroskedastic and correlated with error terms for other observations in the same local market.[13]

The key variable of interest is treat × Post. The corresponding coefficient (γ_i) measures the difference in price changes of treated markets, where the big four, the municipal operators or retailers with a mixed ownership structure ('others') are incumbent, and non-treated markets incumbents, where independent retailers are incumbent, before and after May 2010. This coefficient is firm specific to account for the possibility of firm-specific heterogeneous effects for different firms. In particular, a different effect is expected for the big four, the municipal operators and the firms with a mixed ownership structure. The post coefficient (δ) measures any price change after the implementation of the E.ON commitments common to all firms and regions, while the coefficient β_i accounts for any idiosyncrasies between treated firms/markets and non-treated ones unrelated to the E.ON decision.

[3] The Data

The main data source for the analysis of retail prices is the German price comparison site Verivox, which provided detailed and highly disaggregated data on electricity retail prices, specifically, monthly price data between January 2007 and August 2014 for

8,241 different postal codes (located in 6,249 cities across all 16 German states) from 841 different electricity providers.

For each postal code and month, Verivox provides the price for three types of household consumption (differentiated by yearly electricity consumption: 1,500 kWh, 2,800 kWh, 4,000 kWh) and one typical commercial customer (10,000 kWh). Moreover, information is available on the incumbent operator's baseline tariff, and the overall cheapest offer for that particular local market (as defined by the postal code). Altogether, there are eight different prices for each local market and month.

Average prices vary substantially both within and across consumer groups. The baseline tariff constitutes the highest price in a given market. Therefore, one can infer the lower and upper bound of the distribution of retail prices. These bounds are used to define the variable 'price dispersion', which represents the difference between the cheapest and the most expensive price for each local market and month. Table 6.6 presents summary statistics for the baseline and cheapest tariff in the different categories of consumption. For example, a representative household with two children consuming 2,800 kWh per year could have saved EUR 139.2 per year (or more than 20%) by shifting from the baseline tariff to the cheapest tariff.

Table 6.6 The German Electricity Retail Market – Average Prices and Price Dispersion for Different Consumption Categories – January 2007 to December 2012 (in Euros with Standard Deviation in Parentheses)

	1,500 kWh	*2,800 kWh*	*4,000 kWh*	*10,000 kWh*
Baseline tariff	402.8 (36.73)	675.8 (63.15)	927.8 (88.75)	2274.9 (252.7)
Cheapest tariff	294.1 (25.14)	536.6 (29.05)	754.3 (41.85)	1917.7 (131.9)
Price dispersion	108.7 (49.62)	139.2 (60.34)	173.5 (74.16)	357.2 (186.5)

Retail prices exhibited an increasing trend over the period 2007-August 2014. This might be a little surprising given that wholesale electricity prices substantially decreased during the sample period. However, the increase in retail electricity prices over the sample period is mostly due to a substantial increase in taxes, fees, and network charges. Moreover, changes in wholesale prices only slowly pass through to retail prices because retailers tend to use long-term contracts when buying electricity. Finally, retail prices are affected by the extent of the incumbent's market power: the increase in retail electricity prices is stronger for the incumbent's baseline tariff and weaker for the overall cheapest offer. This is consistent with the expectation that market segments that are less competitive due to the presence of large vertically integrated incumbents experience stronger price increases over time.

[B] Results

This section reports on the estimation results using the basic empirical model of the local retail markets. The dependent variables is defined as: (i) the incumbent's baseline tariff; (ii) the overall cheapest offer; and (iii) the price dispersion, defined as the difference between the highest and the lowest price observed within a local market.

[1] The Main Results

Table 6.7 reports the result for the regression on the incumbent's baseline tariffs for different types of customers, i.e., households with a yearly electricity consumption of 1,500 kWh, 2,800 kWh and 4,000 kWh, respectively, and a commercial customer with a consumption of 10,000 kWh.

Table 6.7 Incumbent's Baseline Tariffs

	1,500 kWh		*2,800 kWh*		*4,000 kWh*		*10,000 kWh*	
	Coeff.	*St. Err.*	*Coeff.*	*St. Err.*	*Coeff.*	*St. Err.*	*Coeff.*	*St. Err.*
E.ON × Post	5.512***	(1.118)	9.352***	(1.904)	2.192	(2.025)	39.84***	(7.955)
RWE × Post	7.760***	(1.113)	17.34***	(1.905)	15.96***	(2.023)	64.35***	(8.034)
EnBW × Post	0.143	(1.101)	3.560*	(1.884)	-3.667*	(2.005)	27.32***	(7.888)
Vattenfall × Post	-0.287	(1.235)	1.490	(2.123)	-27.02***	(2.010)	92.45***	(8.135)
Stadtwerke × Post	-5.849***	(1.141)	-9.910***	(1.948)	-21.52***	(2.095)	-32.68***	(8.213)
Other × Post	-0.111	(1.129)	-2.020	(1.922)	-17.93***	(2.126)	-12.60	(8.005)
Constant	346.7***	(3.424)	573.8***	(5.510)	774.5***	(8.980)	1937.3***	(28.29)
Observations	480,496		480,496		482,231		479,906	
Adjusted R-Squared	0.915		0.922		0.919		0.928	

The dependent variable is the price a customer using the different consumption plans (1,500 kWh, 2,800 kWh, 4,000 kWh, and 10,000 kWh per year) would pay if he chose the incumbent's baseline tariff. The year 2009 is excluded from the regressions. Standard errors are clustered at the postal code level. t statistics in parentheses.

The symbols ***, **, * represent 1%, 5% and 10% significance levels respectively.

The Adjusted R-Squared of more than 90% in all specifications shows that the model (including control variables reflecting demand factors related to the local population structure and the number of energy-intensive plants in the local market as well as supply factors such as the number of energy firms headquartered in the local market) explains the data well. This implies that the model controls for most of the relevant drivers of retail electricity prices and accounts for most of the cross-sectional variation across different local markets. The main control variables are more precisely defined in Appendix 1 and the results of the full model estimation are presented in Appendix 3.

More interesting for the assessment whether the reduction in wholesale electricity prices was passed on to consumers are the coefficient estimates of the interaction terms between the firm dummies and the dummy for the post-intervention period which has the value of 1 from May 2010 on. These estimates measure the differential post-treatment trend for the tariffs of the incumbents that form the treatment group compared to independent incumbents. As mentioned above, the incumbents in the treatment group (notably including the big four) are expected to react less swiftly to changes in wholesale prices than independent retailers.

Consistent with this expectation, E.ON, RWE and, to a lesser extent, EnBW and Vattenfall have significantly increased their tariffs post intervention when comparing with the tariffs charged by independent incumbents, which are more likely to pass on to their customers the benefits of the reduction in wholesale electricity prices. In other words, independent incumbents reduced their baseline tariffs relative to the big four following the implementation by E.ON of its commitments to the European Commission. It is important to note however that the baseline tariffs charged by independent incumbents increased significantly over time during the period under investigation. This suggests that the baseline tariffs of the independent incumbents would have increased even more if wholesale prices had not decreased following the implementation of the E.ON decision.

The size of the coefficients' estimates is heterogeneous across firms and across consumption plans. For instance, the price increase for E.ON with respect to the independent incumbents in the 1,500 kWh consumption plan EUR 5.52 per year, which represents 1.5% of the average annual expenses for that consumption plan, represented by the constant (EUR 346.70). The baseline tariffs of municipal operators, however, decreased by EUR 5.85 per year relative to the tariffs charged by independent retailers, corresponding to around 1.7% of the annual bill. In comparison with E.ON and RWE, the relative decline in annual expenses charged by municipal operators amounted to more than EUR 10, accounting for more than 3% of the customers' annual bill.

Focusing on the baseline tariffs is clearly important because more than 70% of German households were still served by incumbent operators during the sample period. Nevertheless, it is important as well to understand the price dynamics of the most competitive segment of the market, as represented by the overall cheapest offer. Focusing on these offers also has the advantage that the control group - the independent retailers - are much more prominent because they represent 49% of the local markets considered. However, the big four companies, and particularly E.ON and RWE, are much less present as they offer the cheapest prices in less than 3% of the observations. Therefore, in some specifications the effect of the E.ON decision on the retail prices set by these companies cannot be identified. Table 6.8 shows the results.

Table 6.8 Overall Cheapest Offer

	1,500 kWh		*2,800 kWh*		*4,000 kWh*		*10,000 kWh*	
	Coeff.	*St. Err.*	*Coeff.*	*St. Err.*	*Coeff.*	*St. Err.*	*Coeff.*	*St. Err.*
E.ON × Post	2.322*	(1.189)						
RWE × Post	9.333***	(3.599)	3.384	(3.037)				
EnBW × Post	12.43**	(5.502)	-25.49***	(4.477)	6.407***	(0.916)		
Vattenfall × Post	-5.768***	(0.407)	-7.528***	(0.412)	2.487	(3.617)	-15.47***	(1.841)
Stadtwerke × Post	-13.04***	(0.430)	-9.145***	(0.527)	-3.702***	(1.233)	-68.01***	(1.393)
Other × Post	-4.474***	(0.200)	-1.406***	(0.283)	-5.489***	(0.482)	-27.11***	(1.028)
Constant	330.6***	(1.004)	545.8***	(1.284)	746.4***	(1.604)	1756.5***	(3.903)
Observations	431,105		471,453		493,538		444,261	
Adjusted R-Squared	0.830		0.736		0.788		0.871	

The dependent variable is the price a customer using the different consumption plans (1,500 kWh, 2,800 kWh, 4,000 kWh, 10,000 kWh per year) would pay if he chose the overall cheapest offer in his local market. The control category for the firm-type dummies is the group of independent firms. We control for 8,208 zip code fixed effects as well as 60-month fixed effects. Standard errors are clustered at the zip code level. t statistics in parentheses.

The symbols ***, **, * represent 1%, 5% and 10% significance level respectively.

These findings are consistent with the picture presented thus far. When it is identified, the effect on E.ON, RWE and EnBW is generally positive and significant, implying that after 1 May 2010 the retail electricity prices charged by these large integrated operators significantly increased in comparison with the independent retailers. Vattenfall and the municipal operators appear to have adopted an even more aggressive pricing policy than the independent retailers by offering some of the lowest prices in this competitive segment of the electricity market.

[2] Additional Treatment

The final piece of evidence relates to price dispersion (*see* Table 6.9). The difference between the overall most expensive offer and the cheapest offer in each local market significantly increased in markets where E.ON, RWE or EnBW was the incumbent operators, if compared to markets where the incumbent was an independent retailer. As in the previous regression, the Difference-in-Differences coefficients for Vattenfall and the municipal operators are negative and significant. In the aftermath of the E.ON decisions, these operators priced even more competitively than small independent firms.

Table 6.9 Price Dispersion (Incumbent's Baseline Tariff – Overall Cheapest Offer)

	1,500 kWh		*2,800 kWh*		*4,000 kWh*		*10,000 kWh*	
	Coeff.	*St. Err.*	*Coeff.*	*St. Err.*	*Coeff.*	*St. Err.*	*Coeff.*	*St. Err.*
E.ON × Post	3.052**	(1.421)	4.591*	(2.390)	-0.749	(2.058)	51.79***	(8.421)
RWE × Post	9.533***	(1.436)	21.46***	(2.425)	23.59***	(2.100)	118.6***	(8.512)
EnBW × Post	5.108***	(1.419)	15.12***	(2.384)	13.83***	(2.059)	97.60***	(8.482)
Vattenfall × Post	-8.530***	(1.616)	-6.184**	(2.429)	-30.27***	(2.038)	98.05***	(8.559)
Stadtwerke × Post	-3.170**	(1.447)	0.0338	(2.431)	-9.491***	(2.130)	7.183	(8.690)
Other × Post	1.197	(1.428)	6.775***	(2.394)	-2.977	(2.125)	36.76***	(8.494)
Observations	480496		480496		482226		479906	
Adjusted R-Squared	0.926		0.897		0.872		0.858	

The dependent variable is the price dispersion within a given zip code defined as the difference between the yearly prices a customer using the different consumption plans (1,500 kWh, 2,800 kWh, 4,000 kWh, 10,000 kWh per year) would pay if he chose the incumbent's baseline tariff or the cheapest tariff in his local network area. The control category for the firm-type dummies is the group of independent incumbents. We control for 8,208 zip code fixed effects as well as 60-month fixed effects. Standard errors are clustered at the zip code level. t statistics in parentheses.

The symbols ***, **, * represent 1%, 5% and 10% significance level respectively.

It appears that the pass-through to final customers of any reduction in wholesale prices greatly differs from one firm to another. In summary, the three vertically integrated incumbents (E.ON, RWE and EnBW)[14] pass on less of the wholesale price reduction than Vattenfall, the municipal operators and the independent retailers. This finding is consistent across different consumption plans. Nevertheless, caution is required in interpreting the results obtained as evidence of a causal relationship between the E.ON decision and prices charged in the retail market for electricity. However, the empirical evidence is surely consistent with the claim that the E.ON decision, by reducing market power and prices upstream, might also have contributed to lowering prices downstream.

[3] Time-Varying Treatment Effects

The results so far focus on the heterogeneous response by electricity retailers to the European Commission's E.ON decision. For each (type of) retailer, we estimated an average treatment effect over time that measures the long-term impact after 2010. However as mentioned above, we expect changes in wholesale conditions to only slowly affect retail tariffs because electricity is purchased from wholesale markets via long-term contracts. Moreover, this trend should be even slower for the tariffs offered by large, vertically integrated incumbents because they order a larger share of their sales volumes via longer-term contracts. Therefore, looking at the heterogeneity of the treatment effects over time should help us to refine our identification strategy.

To facilitate the interpretation of our analysis and because we observed that the effects for the big three German firms (E.ON, RWE and EnBW) are similar, we group these three firms into one category. We then disaggregate the implementation and the post periods into quarters and estimate time-varying effects for each quarter, i.e., instead of estimating one coefficient for the post-intervention period, we estimate thirteen different coefficients over time.

An investigation of these time-varying effects show that during the implementation period (up to March 2010), there appears to be a positive trend that leads tariffs of the big three incumbents to exceed those of the independent firms. This is what one would anticipate: E.ON, RWE and EnBW are expected to increase their prices relative to those of independent retailers as E.ON's commitments take effect. This effect gets stronger during 2010 and 2011, showing that the difference in pass-through between the three incumbents and the more competitive independent retailers increases over time, a result that is consistent as well with our expectations.

§6.07 CONCLUSION

This chapter analyses the effect of a specific competition policy intervention: the European Commission's decision concerning E.ON's alleged abuse of dominant position in the German wholesale electricity market. The decision confirmed E.ON's commitment to divest 5,000 MW of generation capacity. As the E.ON decision concerned the upstream electricity market, this chapter focuses on the effect of the decision on wholesale prices. However, to get a richer picture of the effects of the E.ON's conduct (and implicitly the decision by the European Commission in the E.ON case) on households and commercial customers, the downstream effect of the decision on retail prices is also examined. A Difference-in-Differences methodology has been applied to identify the effect of the E.ON decision in both upstream and downstream markets. The identification strategies are tailored to the specificities of the German electricity market.

The identification in the upstream market is based on the observation that electricity suppliers have more market power during peak periods when demand is higher. Since the supply schedule is highly convex and much steeper during the peak period (8am–8pm), shifts to a lower or higher capacity schedule have much larger effects during peak times. Therefore, a convergence between peak and off-peak prices is expected if market power is reduced.

The Difference-in-Differences model performs very well in explaining the variation in wholesale prices. Strong and statistically significant convergence effects are found in the short run as well as in the long term. The estimated price convergence associated with the E.ON decision equals EUR 3/MWh in the short run and EUR 15/MWh in the long term. This convergence is economically relevant, considering that the estimated difference between peak and off-peak prices is EUR 20/MWh in the short run and EUR 30/MWh over the long term. These findings are consistent with the view that the European Commission's decision, by increasing the level of competition in the German electricity market, reduced wholesale prices.

The next question is whether this significant reduction in wholesale prices had an impact on retail prices. A distinction is made between three main types of electricity retailers active in the German markets: (1) large, vertically integrated incumbents; (2) municipal operators and retailers with a mixed ownership structure; and (3) independent retailers. Structural differences affect the energy purchasing strategies of the three types of retailers, influencing in particular the share and length of their long-term contracts with wholesalers. As most contracts between electricity generators and retailers are long term, one would expect changes in the upstream market to only gradually affect retail prices as existing supply contracts are successively replaced by new ones.

The German retail market experienced a general price rise over the period 2007-2014. Nonetheless, the regression results provide evidence that the retail electricity prices increased more in the local markets where E.ON, RWE and EnBW were incumbent than in the local markets where independent retailers were incumbent. Moreover, the price dispersion between the baseline tariff charged by the incumbent and the overall cheapest offer increased more in local markets where E.ON, RWE and EnBW were incumbent than in the local markets where independent retailers were incumbent.

These findings support the idea that the pass-through of upstream price reductions to downstream markets depends on the market power by the incumbent retailer. Significant switching costs, particularly as perceived by private households, seem to create a stable customer base to be exploited by the incumbent retailer. Nonetheless, the reduction in wholesale prices allowed softening the common price rise, in particular in local markets where municipal operators or independent retailers were incumbent. These results are in line with the view that the E.ON decision, by reducing wholesale prices, might also have contributed in limiting the general rise in electricity retail prices.

One would expect the changes in wholesale conditions to affect retail tariffs only slowly because electricity is mostly purchased at wholesale markets via long-term contracts. This trend should be even slower for the tariffs offered by the large vertically integrated incumbents because they purchase a larger part of their electricity needs on the wholesale market by way of long-term contracts than independent retailers do. An analysis of the evolution of the average treatment effect over time confirms this intuition: E.ON, RWE and EnBW increased their prices relative to the prices charged by independent retailers following the implementation of E.ON's commitments and this effect became stronger over time.

This study shows that a quantitative analysis requires rich datasets. Data availability is a necessary but not a sufficient condition to obtain robust quantitative results. Quality, granularity and reliability of data are equally important. The E.ON case study benefitted from rich datasets for Germany and Spain entailing information on wholesale electricity prices and their drivers. Nevertheless, even in this case the identification strategy had to be adapted and tailored to the specific data available. Data availability is an important consideration when deciding whether or not to go ahead with an ex post economic evaluation and constructing an appropriate dataset is an essential first step in the ex post evaluation process.

A final word of caution is required. Even though the specificities of German electricity markets were used to design the empirical approach and set up the identification strategy, one cannot completely exclude alternative explanations for the results, particularly at the retail market level. Nevertheless, the empirical regularities identified in this chapter provide consistent and convincing evidence that the European Commission's decision in the E.ON abuse of dominance case had a positive influence on the functioning of German electricity markets after 2009 and benefitted consumers.

APPENDIX 1: DEFINITION OF THE MAIN CONTROL VARIABLES

Table 6.10 Main Control Variables for the Wholesale Market Analysis

Metric	*Period*	*Frequency*	*Source*	*Remarks*
Control variables (supply side)				
Coal price	2009-2011	Daily data	Platts – Argus McCloskey	
Oil price	2009-2011	Daily data	ICE Brent Europe	
Gas price	2009-2011	Daily data	ENDEX/TTF	
Emission price	2009-2011	Daily data	EEX	
Wind	2009-2011	Daily data	Network operators website	
Solar production	2009-2011	Daily data	BDEW – Solarwirtscfat.de (for installed capacity) / Deutscher Wetterdienst (for the daily sunshine duration)	As data on photovoltaic generation is not available before 2010, proxy variables are used for the whole regression period.
Control variables (demand side)				
Temperature	2009-2011	Daily data	Deutscher Wetterdienst	

Table 6.11 Main Control Variables for the Retail Market Analysis

Metric	*Period*	*Frequency*	*Source*	*Remarks*
Control variables (demand side)				
Local population structure	2009-2011	Monthly data	Regionalatlas Deutschland	Population density; birth rate minus death rate; share of non-German population
Number of energy-intensive plants	2009-2011	Monthly data	European Union Transaction Log database	145 energy-intensive plants are active in Germany
Control variables (supply side)				
Number of energy firms headquartered	2009-2011	Monthly data	Amadeus database	

APPENDIX 2: REGRESSION TABLE FOR THE WHOLESALE MARKET: FULL SPECIFICATION

Table 6.12 Wholesale Prices

	Post 2010 *(1)*	*Post 2009* *(2)*	*Short Run* *(3)*
Peak	30.84*** (1.89)	31.03*** (1.79)	19.68*** (1.00)
Peak × Post	-15.37*** (1.65)	-14.58*** (1.66)	-3.22** (1.54)
Wind capacity	-0.00*** (0.0001)	-0.00*** (0.0001)	-0.001*** (0.0001)
Sun per day	-0.004*** (0.002)	-0.004*** (0.002)	-0.004*** (0.002)
Installed solar capacity	-0.001*** (0.0002)	-0.001*** (0.0003)	-0.001*** (0.0003)
Temp off-peak	-1.05*** (0.24)	-1.04*** (0.22)	-1.23*** (0.23)
Temp sq. off-peak	0.09*** (0.03)	0.08*** (0.02)	0.10*** (0.02)
Crossboarder off-peak	0.0005** (0.0002)	0.0005** (0.0002)	0.0005** (0.0003)
Crossboarder peak	-0.001*** (0.0004)	-0.001*** (0.0003)	-0.001*** (0.0003)
Market Coupling	2.48 (2.34)	3.09 (2.13)	3.09 (2.42)
Brent	-0.02 (0.06)	0.02 (0.05)	0.03 (0.51)
TTF price	1.32*** (0.2)	1.35*** (0.13)	1.34*** (0.14)
Uranium price	-0.31*** (0.07)	-0.24*** (0.06)	-0.24*** (0.08)
EUA price	0.80*** (0.27)	0.54*** (0.18)	0.53*** (0.19)
Coal price	0.10** (0.04)	0.04 (0.04)	0.04 (0.04)
Holiday	-11.54*** (1.7)	-11.11*** (1.69)	-11.07*** (1.65)

	Post 2010 (1)	*Post 2009 (2)*	*Short Run (3)*
Temp peak	-1.48*** (0.34)	-1.54*** (0.28)	-1.35*** (0.30)
Temp sq. peak	0.07*** (0.02)	0.08*** (0.02)	0.06*** (0.02)
Tuesday	1.85 (1.15)	0.54 (0.98)	1.51** (0.43)
Wednesday	1.22 (1.68)	0.3 (1.37)	1.58** (0.46)
Thursday	2.85 (2.14)	0.37 (1.78)	2.14*** (0.48)
Friday	-2.01 (2.3)	-2.17 (1.75)	-0.13 (0.49)
Saturday	-1.39 (2.52)	-0.78 (1.87)	-6.96*** (0.73)
Sunday	-2.64 (2.44)	-1.17 (1.95)	-13.77*** (0.86)
February	-3.7 (2.32)	-1.74 (1.97)	0.45 (0.99)
March	4.58* (2.38)	4.74** (1.92)	0.11 (1.45)
April	8.66*** (1.86)	8.37*** (1.52)	0.20 (2.08)
May	1.57 (2.09)	1.12 (1.62)	-2.25 (1.98)
June	-3.36 (2.54)	-4.91*** (1.78)	-0.84 (2.07)
July	-7.09*** (2.74)	-5.09*** (1.76)	-1.23 (2.21)
August			-1.82 (2.21)
September	1.43*** (0.49)	1.51*** (0.42)	4.69** (2.23)
October	1.53*** (0.53)	1.58*** (0.45)	8.27*** (1.62)
November	2.14*** (0.54)	2.13*** (0.47)	1.07 (1.86)
December	-0.06 (0.57)	-0.12 (0.48)	-5.00*** (1.95)

	Post 2010 (1)	*Post 2009* (2)	*Short Run* (3)
2009	-7.12*** (0.81)	-6.96*** (0.72)	-12.42*** (3.16)
2010	-14.41*** (0.96)	-13.74*** (0.85)	-7.64*** (1.97)
Constant	40.32*** (7.46)	38.38*** (6.33)	46.66*** (7.92)
Cumulative post effect	-7.09*** (2.74)	-11.85*** (4.30)	-20.06*** (4.97)
Observations	2190	2916	2916
Adjusted R-Squared	0.7800	0.7900	0.7657

The dependent variable is the daily average peak or off-peak price at the EEX power exchange. Newey-West standard errors with maximum lag order of autocorrelation equal to seven days are reported in parentheses.

The symbols ***, **, * represent significance at the 1%, 5% and 10% levels respectively.

APPENDIX 3: REGRESSION TABLES FOR THE RETAIL MARKET: FULL SPECIFICATION

Table 6.13 Incumbent's Baseline Tariffs

	1,500 kWh		*2,800 kWh*		*4,000 kWh*		*10,000 kWh*	
	Coeff.	*St. Err.*	*Coeff.*	*St. Err.*	*Coeff.*	*St. Err.*	*Coeff.*	*St. Err.*
E.ON	-1.533	(3.941)	-1.991	(6.699)	1.606	(10.84)	-75.39*	(42.74)
RWE	-1.580	(3.436)	-0.539	(5.501)	21.38**	(9.612)	-14.66	(27.06)
EnBW	0.740	(9.060)	10.34	(9.469)	39.74***	(12.00)	312.7***	(48.37)
Vattenfall	-18.52***	(3.331)	-36.74***	(5.391)			-144.3***	(26.86)
Stadtwerke	0.179	(3.032)	-2.710	(5.108)	-0.105	(8.894)	-13.11	(26.19)
Other	5.821*	(3.321)	8.565	(5.365)	16.24*	(9.581)	0.507	(26.80)
E.ON × Post	5.512***	(1.118)	9.352***	(1.904)	2.192	(2.025)	39.84***	(7.955)
RWE × Post	7.760***	(1.113)	17.34***	(1.905)	15.96***	(2.023)	64.35***	(8.034)
EnBW × Post	0.143	(1.101)	3.560*	(1.884)	-3.667*	(2.005)	27.32***	(7.888)
Vattenfall × Post	-0.287	(1.235)	1.490	(2.123)	-27.02***	(2.010)	92.45***	(8.135)
Stadtwerke × Post	-5.849***	(1.141)	-9.910***	(1.948)	-21.52***	(2.095)	-32.68***	(8.213)
Other × Post	-0.111	(1.129)	-2.020	(1.922)	-17.93***	(2.126)	-12.60	(8.005)
# of EIPs	-4.180*	(2.447)	-6.468*	(3.823)	-7.317	(4.997)	-54.18*	(31.41)
Pop. Density	0.008***	(0.002)	0.016***	(0.002)	0.019***	(0.003)	0.046***	(0.008)
Share foreign	0.203	(0.159)	0.730**	(0.288)	1.556***	(0.410)	3.436***	(1.050)
Births-deaths	-0.095***	(0.009)	-0.130***	(0.014)	-0.213***	(0.019)	-0.330***	(0.052)
# energy firms	0.094*	(0.051)	0.089	(0.085)	0.069	(0.131)	0.086	(0.321)
Constant	346.7***	(3.424)	573.8***	(5.510)	774.5***	(8.980)	1937.3***	(28.29)
Observations	480,496		480,496		482,231		479,906	
Adjusted R-Squared	0.915		0.922		0.919		0.928	

The dependent variable is the price a customer using the different consumption plans (1,500 kWh, 2,800 kWh, 4,000 kWh, and 10,000 kWh per year) would pay if he chose the incumbent's baseline tariff. The year 2009 is excluded from the regressions. Standard errors are clustered at the zip code level. t statistics in parentheses.

The symbols ***, **, * represent 1%, 5% and 10% significance levels respectively.

Table 6.14 Overall Cheapest Offer

	1,500 kWh		*2,800 kWh*		*4,000 kWh*		*10,000 kWh*	
	Coeff.	*St. Err.*	*Coeff.*	*St. Err.*	*Coeff.*	*St. Err.*	*Coeff.*	*St. Err.*
E.ON	-1.046**	(0.463)	27.19***	(0.571)	0.712	(1.698)	24.20***	(1.919)
RWE	16.39***	(0.516)	16.66***	(2.217)	-0.190	(0.492)		
EnBW	6.323***	(0.286)	32.70***	(0.384)	17.57***	(0.884)		
Vattenfall	-0.889***	(0.274)	6.042***	(0.188)	5.831***	(0.208)	18.78***	(1.308)
Stadtwerke	-0.402*	(0.212)	10.29***	(0.219)	15.84***	(0.269)	63.19***	(0.963)
Other	-1.616***	(0.125)	6.187***	(0.160)	5.425***	(0.204)	17.81***	(0.799)
E.ON × Post	2.322*	(1.189)						
RWE × Post	9.333***	(3.599)	3.384	(3.037)				
EnBW × Post	12.43**	(5.502)	-25.49***	(4.477)	6.407***	(0.916)		
Vattenfall × Post	-5.768***	(0.407)	-7.528***	(0.412)	2.487	(3.617)	-15.47***	(1.841)
Stadtwerke × Post	-13.04***	(0.430)	-9.145***	(0.527)	-3.702***	(1.233)	-68.01***	(1.393)
Other × Post	-4.474***	(0.200)	-1.406***	(0.283)	-5.489***	(0.482)	-27.11***	(1.028)
# of EIPs	-1.383	(2.247)	-1.997	(3.171)	-1.303	(3.804)	-13.78**	(6.481)
pop1: density	-0.003***	(0.001)	-0.015***	(0.001)	-0.020***	(0.001)	-0.007***	(0.002)
pop2: share foreign	-0.118	(0.164)	1.140***	(0.212)	1.166***	(0.270)	-2.201***	(0.630)
pop3: births-deaths	0.156***	(0.006)	0.351***	(0.009)	0.371***	(0.012)	0.00291	(0.028)
# energy firms	0.0326	(0.030)	0.0469	(0.043)	0.101*	(0.055)	0.0463	(0.137)
Constant	330.6***	(1.004)	545.8***	(1.284)	746.4***	(1.604)	1756.5***	(3.903)
Observations	431,105		471,453		493,538		444,261	
Adjusted R-Squared	0.830		0.736		0.788		0.871	

The dependent variable is the price a customer using the different consumption plans (1,500 kWh, 2,800 kWh, 4,000 kWh, 10,000 kWh per year) would pay if he chose the overall cheapest offer in his local market. The control category for the firm-type dummies is the group of independent firms. We control for 8,208 zip code fixed effects as well as 60-month fixed effects. Standard errors are clustered at the zip code level. t statistics in parentheses.

The symbols ***, **, * represent 1%, 5% and 10% significance level respectively.

Table 6.15 Price Dispersion (Incumbent's Baseline Tariff – Overall Cheapest Offer)

	1,500 kWh		*2,800 kWh*		*4,000 kWh*		*10,000 kWh*	
	Coeff.	*St. Err.*	*Coeff.*	*St. Err.*	*Coeff.*	*St. Err.*	*Coeff.*	*St. Err.*
E.ON	-0.266	(4.266)	-7.918	(6.668)	-2.171	(9.571)	-71.61	(45.41)
RWE	0.948	(4.116)	-8.678	(5.553)	12.05	(8.655)	-59.96**	(27.65)
EnBW	3.712	(7.460)	8.717	(8.717)	41.33***	(11.20)	251.3***	(39.62)
Vattenfall	-27.83***	(4.054)	-23.03***	(5.433)			-133.8***	(27.49)
Stadtwerke	3.416	(3.648)	-3.593	(4.979)	0.502	(7.674)	-34.77	(26.92)
Other	6.382	(4.037)	3.976	(5.426)	13.15	(8.572)	-30.17	(27.47)
E.ON × Post	3.052**	(1.421)	4.591*	(2.390)	-0.749	(2.058)	51.79***	(8.421)
RWE × Post	9.533***	(1.436)	21.46***	(2.425)	23.59***	(2.100)	118.6***	(8.512)
EnBW × Post	5.108***	(1.419)	15.12***	(2.384)	13.83***	(2.059)	97.60***	(8.482)
Vattenfall × Post	-8.530***	(1.616)	-6.184**	(2.429)	-30.27***	(2.038)	98.05***	(8.559)
Stadtwerke × Post	-3.170**	(1.447)	0.0338	(2.431)	-9.491***	(2.130)	7.183	(8.690)
Other × Post	1.197	(1.428)	6.775***	(2.394)	-2.977	(2.125)	36.76***	(8.494)
# of EIPs	-3.622	(2.533)	-5.646	(4.300)	-6.550	(5.631)	-40.15	(33.40)
pop1: density	0.0123***	(0.00165)	0.0318***	(0.00247)	0.0400***	(0.00306)	0.0378***	(0.00854)
pop2: share foreign	-0.0138	(0.190)	-0.552*	(0.318)	0.00609	(0.430)	5.496***	(1.074)
pop3: births-deaths	-0.227***	(0.00901)	-0.474***	(0.0130)	-0.569***	(0.0171)	-0.204***	(0.0439)
# Amadeus firms	0.0619	(0.0571)	0.0483	(0.0940)	-0.0236	(0.140)	0.0636	(0.336)
Constant	16.97***	(3.985)	24.92***	(5.480)	23.10***	(7.956)	162.5***	(28.94)
Observations	480496		480496		482226		479906	
Adjusted R-Squared	0.926		0.897		0.872		0.858	

The dependent variable is the price dispersion within a given zip code defined as the difference between the yearly prices a customer using the different consumption plans (1,500 kWh, 2,800 kWh, 4,000 kWh, 10,000 kWh per year) would pay if he chose the incumbent's baseline tariff or the cheapest tariff in his local network area. The control category for the firm-type dummies is the group of independent incumbents. We control for 8,208 zip code fixed effects as well as sixty-month fixed effects. Standard errors are clustered at the zip code level. t statistics in parentheses.

The symbols ***, **, * represent 1%, 5%, and 10% significance level respectively.

REFERENCES

Alesina, A., Ardagna S., Nicoletti G. and Schiantarelli F. (2005), 'Regulation and investment', *Journal of the European Economic Association*, 3(4), pp. 791-825.

Bolle F. and Breitmoser Y. (2006), 'On the allocative efficiency of ownership unbundling', Discussion Paper No. 255, European University Viadrina Frankfurt (Oder), Department of Business Administration and Economics.

Böckers V. and Heimeshoff U. (2014), 'The extent of European power markets', *Energy Economics*, 46 (November), pp. 102-111.

Buehler S. (2005), 'The promise and pitfalls of restructuring network industries', *German Economic Review*, 6(2), pp. 205-228.

Bundeskartellamt (2011), 'Sector inquiry into electricity generation and wholesale markets' (B10-9/09) Report.

Bundesnetzagentur (2011), 'Monitoring Report 2011'.

Cabral L. (2002), 'The California energy crisis', *Japan and the World Economy*, 14(3), pp. 335-339.

Copenhagen Economics (2005), 'Market opening in network industries - Part II: Sectoral analyses', Report for DG Internal Market of the European Commission, September.

Duso T., Szücs F. and Böckers V. (2018), 'Abuse of dominance and antitrust enforcement in the German electricity market', DIW Berlin Discussion Paper 1685.

Duso T. and Szücs F. (2017), 'Market power and heterogeneous pass-through in German electricity retail', *European Economic Review*, (September), pp. 354-372.

European Commission (2007), 'DG Competition report on energy sector inquiry', SEC(2006) 1724, 10 January.

European Commission (2016), 'Final report of the sector inquiry on capacity mechanisms', COM(2016) 752 final, November.

Fabra N. and Reguant M. (2014), 'Pass-through of emissions costs in electricity markets', *American Economic Review*, 104(9), pp. 2872-2899.

Green R.J. (2004), 'Did English generators play Cournot? Capacity withholding in the electricity pool', Cambridge Working Papers in Economics, No. 425, Faculty of Economics, University of Cambridge.

Gugler K., Rammerstorfer M. and Schmitt S. (2013), 'Ownership unbundling and investment in electricity markets - A cross country study', *Energy Economics*, 40(C), pp. 702-713.

Haucap J. (2007), 'The costs and benefits of ownership unbundling', *Intereconomics*, 42(6), pp. 301-304.

ICF and DIW Berlin (2015), 'The economic impact of enforcement of competition policies on the functioning of EU energy markets', Final report prepared for the Directorate-General for Competition of the European Commission, Publications Office of the EU.

Just S. and Weber C. (2015), 'Strategic behavior in the German balancing energy mechanism: incentives, evidence, costs and solutions', *Journal of Regulatory Economics*, 48(2), pp. 218-243.

Kwoka J.E. (2002), 'Vertical economies in electric power: evidence on integration and its alternatives', *International Journal of Industrial Organization*, 20(5), pp. 653-671.

Meyer R. (2012), 'Vertical economies and the costs of separating electricity supply – A review of theoretical and empirical literature', *The Energy Journal*, 33(4), pp. 161-185.

Mirza F.M. and Bergland O. (2012), 'Pass-through of wholesale price to the end user retail price in the Norwegian electricity market', *Energy Economics*, 34(6), pp. 2003-2012.

Nardi P. (2012), 'Transmission network unbundling and grid investments: Evidence from the UCTE countries', *Utilities Policy*, 23(C), pp. 50-58.

Pollitt M. (2008), 'The arguments for and against ownership unbundling of energy transmission networks', *Energy Policy*, 36(2), pp. 704-713.

Reuters (2014), 'Germany's EEX saw trading growth in 2013', Financials, January 14.

Tsangaris P. (2017), '*Capacity withdrawals in the electricity wholesale market – Between Competition Law and Regulation*', Springer.

Zachmann G. and Von Hirschhausen C. (2008), 'First evidence of asymmetric cost pass-through of EU emissions allowances: Examining wholesale electricity prices in Germany', *Economic Letters*, 99(3), pp. 465-469.

PART III Ex Post Evaluation of State Aid

CHAPTER 7

The Role of Evaluation in the EU State Aid Control*

Penelope Papandropoulos, Rodrigo Peduzzi & Cornelius Schmidt

The ex post evaluation of State aid schemes is a new requirement following the State aid modernisation, which took place during the period 2012-2016. This requirement was introduced in order to assess whether these schemes achieved their intended objective without leading to distortions of competition. Up until now, forty-two evaluation plans corresponding to EUR 50 billion of aid have been approved. These plans cover the main objectives of State aid policy, including R&D&I, broadband, energy and regional aid. This chapter discusses the lessons learnt from the implementation of the new evaluation requirements. First, successful evaluation becomes easier if the aid schemes are designed from the outset with an evaluation strategy in mind and if evaluation experts are involved at an early stage, as this facilitates the collection of the necessary data. Second, the evaluation process is smoother if based on comprehensive evaluation plans, if the interim reports include already intermediate results and if Member States stay in contact with the European Commission to discuss problems and difficulties encountered. The chapter concludes with a description of future challenges for State aid evaluations, including an expansion of the use of experimental methods, the further development of an evaluation culture and the use of the results of ex post evaluations for a more effective policy implementation.

§7.01 INTRODUCTION

State aid control is an instrument of EU competition policy, which was established from the outset of the European integration process in order to ensure that State aids did not unduly distort competition in the 'common market' and did not lead to damaging subsidy races between Member States (*see also* Chapter 1 of this book). The European

* This chapter has been written under the sole responsibility of the authors and does not represent the views of the European Commission.

Commission has an exclusive competence in this field and has, in particular, the crucial task to determine whether an aid is compatible, or not, with the EU's State aid rules.[1]

State aid rules have evolved over the decades, and the European Commission has developed a detailed regulatory framework, covering procedures and substantive assessment. The evolution of the State aid rules reflects both the case law set by the EU courts and the policy priorities at the EU and national level. The latest major State aid reform is the 'State Aid Modernisation' (SAM), a thorough reform of the rulebook for State aid control, which was carried out by the European Commission during the period 2012-2016 (European Commission, 2012). The objectives of SAM were: (i) to improve the analysis of the effects of aids in order to foster aids that support sustainable growth; (ii) to focus the European Commission's enforcement on cases with the biggest impact on the internal market; and (iii) to simplify rules in order to speed up the adoption of the European Commission's State aid decisions.

One of the main building blocks of the SAM is the revised General Block Exemption Regulation (GBER),[2] with a substantially expanded scope, that increases Member States' possibilities to grant aids without the need to notify them ex ante to the European Commission. As a result, more than 96% of new measures since 2015 have been exempted from the notification requirement, compared to about 60% previously (European Commission, 2018a).

The wider scope of exemptions from the requirement to notify the European Commission of State aid cases has gone hand in hand with safeguards to preserve competition within the internal market and ensure the efficient use of public money. In particular, in 2014, the requirement to undertake ex post evaluations of large State aid schemes was introduced. This evaluation requirement was entirely new to the EU State aid architecture. The objective of this chapter is to present an overview of the work

1. In this chapter, we make a distinction between subsidies and State aid. Subsidies may involve any form of State support, while State aid is the type of support that fulfils all the criteria specified in the Treaty on the Functioning of the European Union (Article 107(1) TFEU). The European Commission has the sole prerogative to approve State aid covered by Article 107(1) of the TFEU, which in principle prohibits subsidies from State resources that are selective in favouring firms or activities and may distort competition and affect trade between Member States. Most public spending actually remains outside the realm of EU State aid control as it does not fulfil all the cumulative conditions of Article 107(1) and is thus considered as 'no aid'. For example, general measures that are available to all firms in a Member State, measures that are in line with what a private investor would do, or measures that do not distort competition or affect trade are not legally considered State aid. According to the 2019 State aid scoreboard (European Commission, 2019), EU Member States spent EUR 120.6 billion (or 0.8% of GDP) in EU State aid in 2018. This amount excludes State aid to the railway sector, State aid to compensate for the costs of delivering services of general economic interest (SGEI) and State aid to the banking sector (related to the financial crisis). It also excludes de minimis aid (i.e., individual aid below EUR 200.000 over a three-year period), measures that are considered market conform (i.e., granted on market terms) or concern non-economic activities (e.g., social security, education) or non-selective tax measures.
2. European Commission Regulation (EU) No. 651/2014 of 17 June 2014 declaring certain categories of aid compatible with the internal market in application of Articles 107 and 108 of the Treaty, OJ L 187/1. The GBER, adopted in 2014 and further extended in 2017, notably to some types of interventions for ports and for regional airports, covers a wide range of aid categories, such as regional aid, Research and Development and Innovation (R&D&I) support or aid for Small and Medium Enterprises (SMEs)

done by the EU Member States to respond to this ex post evaluation requirement and to draw first lessons from the European Commission's assessment of the evaluation plans provided so far.

At this stage, we can already say that one of the major achievements of the SAM has been to develop an evaluation culture within the realm of State aid control. While evaluation has been a common feature in many public policy domains (e.g., labour markets, education, development or health economics), this has not been the case in the area of State aids. However, partly because of the impulse given by the ex post evaluation requirement included in the SAM, a new body of empirical evidence showing the impact of State aid schemes is currently being developed within the European Union.

This chapter is structured as follows. Section 7.02 describes the origins and rationale for the introduction of the ex post evaluation requirement in State aid control. Section 7.03 presents the methods available for State aid evaluations. In section 7.04, a short literature review describes a selection of recent studies evaluating subsidy programmes. Section 7.05 discusses the experience of the European Commission in assessing evaluation plans submitted by Member States. In particular, it identifies the main lessons learnt from this experience. Section 7.06 considers future challenges, and section 7.07 concludes.

§7.02 THE ROLE OF EX POST EVALUATION IN EU STATE AID CONTROL

The ex post evaluation requirement for State aid was introduced, in particular, because the European Commission aimed at focusing its enforcement effort on the cases creating the greatest distortions to competition in the internal market. Consequently, the SAM increased the scope for EU Member States to provide non-distortive State aids without its prior authorisation. In order to give more leeway to the Member States in the design and implementation of State aid measures, one of the main modifications of the State aid regulations under the SAM reform was the broadening of the scope of the GBER. Measures implemented by Member States' authorities under the GBER are by definition not notified ex ante to the European Commission, which therefore has to rely on ex post controls.

The SAM foresees three types of ex post controls: monitoring, transparency and ex post evaluation. The first type of ex post controls is the monitoring of aid measures. Typically, each year, the European Commission selects a sample of large and significant aid measures, requests detailed information on these aid measures and assesses their actual implementation. This form of ex post control aims at verifying compliance with the legal requirements of exemption (under the GBER, e.g.) or approval (e.g., in terms of aid intensities). Second, the transparency provision requires the publication by Member States of detailed information on the beneficiaries of large aid awards (above EUR 500,000) to allow for peer review, public control and greater accountability.[3] Third, ex post evaluations investigate the effectiveness and the competition effects of State aid. The present chapter focuses on this third type of ex post control.

More precisely, the main objective of such ex post evaluations is to measure the direct and indirect impact of State aid on beneficiaries, including whether the positive effects of the aid on the behaviour of beneficiaries outweigh the possible negative effects in terms of distortions of competition. Even though Member States spend significant amounts on State aid measures, there is limited quantitative evidence on their effectiveness and on their effects on competition. In particular, there are few empirical studies assessing the causal link between State aid measures and expected outcomes in terms of investment, employment, innovation, etc. There are even fewer studies looking into the competition impact of such State aid measures.[4] Hence, the development of robust empirical evidence should constitute an important legacy of the SAM reform (*see* Verouden, 2015), bringing State aid control fully in line with the increased evaluation requirements for public policy in general.

The European Commission requests that Member States carry out ex post evaluations for both block-exempted and notified schemes. The block-exempted schemes requiring an evaluation are those schemes[5] with an average annual State aid budget above EUR 150 million in the fields of regional aid, aid for SMEs and access to finance, aid for R&D&I, energy and environmental aid and aid for broadband infrastructures. Notified aid schemes requiring an evaluation are those schemes proposed under certain guidelines adopted in the context of the SAM and where the Commission considers the evaluation exercise to be proportionate and necessary. In particular, notified aid schemes under the sectoral guidelines for broadband, regional aid, risk finance, aviation, R&D&I, environment and energy, rescue and restructuring may be subjected to an ex post evaluation if such schemes have large budgets (exceeding EUR 150 million), contain novel characteristics or when significant market, technology or regulatory changes are foreseen.

For both block-exempted and notified schemes with an evaluation requirement, Member States have to present an evaluation plan to the European Commission. Large schemes are only eligible under the GBER if the European Commission has approved the relevant evaluation plan. However, there is an initial period of six months during which the large schemes may be put into effect without having an approved evaluation plan. If the European Commission does not decide within the six-month deadline, or rejects the plan, the application of the scheme has to be suspended, meaning that no aid can be granted. Notified large schemes, on the contrary, can only be put into effect

3. The European Commission maintains a database 'State aid transparency public search', which provides information on State aid individual award data provided by Member States. Citizens and companies can easily access information about awarded aid: name of the beneficiary, amount of aid, location, sector and objective.
4. The next chapter of this book is an exception in this respect.
5. An 'aid scheme' is a programme that typically runs for a few years and can have dozen or even thousand beneficiaries selected through calls for proposals or similar mechanisms. In contrast, for an 'individual aid', the beneficiaries are selected and known in advance.

after they have been approved by the European Commission together with their evaluation plans.

Member States must propose evaluations in line with the methodological guidance provided by the European Commission services (*see* European Commission, 2014). Box 7.1 provides an overview of the key elements of the evaluation plans as presented in the methodological guidance paper.

Box 7.1: Key elements of the evaluation plans

The methodological guidance, in particular, describes the key elements of the required evaluation plans, in order to assist Member States in preparing and conducting evaluations of their aid schemes. The evaluation plans should include information on:

(1) the objective of the aid scheme to be evaluated;
(2) the evaluation questions;
(3) the result indicators;
(4) the envisaged methods to conduct the evaluation;
(5) the data collection requirements;
(6) the timeline of the evaluation, including the date of submission of the final evaluation report;
(7) the description of the independent body conducting the evaluation or the criteria that will be used for its selection; and
(8) the modalities for ensuring the publicity of the evaluation.

Member States must use the dedicated 'Supplementary Information Sheet' annexed to European Commission Regulation (EU) 2015/2282 to prepare their evaluation plans. The evaluation questions in this information sheet tackle separately the direct and indirect effects of the scheme, both positive and negative. The focus of the evaluation is on the direct effect, i.e., whether the aid indeed has the desired effect on the beneficiary. The indirect effects comprise, for example, the possible distortions of competition created by the aid. Besides the direct and indirect effects, the evaluation considers the proportionality of the aid as well as the appropriateness of the aid instrument. Proportionality of the aid means that the aid is kept to the minimum necessary and appropriateness of the aid instrument indicates whether the support measure as such was optimally chosen (e.g., a loan might lead to a better outcome than a lump-sum transfer, holding the aid amount constant).

A major contribution of the SAM has been to establish rigorous ex post evaluation requirements, relying on quasi-experimental methods.[6] Moreover, some Member

6. In March 2017, the 'Agence Nouvelle des Solidarités' (2017) published a report discussing the learnings from the UK experience of the 'What Works Centres'. This report finds that ex post evaluations using quasi-experimental methods in France are rare and, when they exist, their results are neither sufficiently disseminated nor used for policy purposes. The report suggests that

States took the initiative to improve their own policy evaluation standards along the same line.[7] This recent emphasis on quantitative, quasi-experimental evaluation methods is important as other factors could affect the behaviour of the beneficiary of the aid and make it difficult to distinguish the effect of the aid from that of these other factors, leading to biased results. For example, if an investment aid was granted to firms having already planned an investment, one could spuriously conclude from the observation of the aid being granted and the concurrent rise in investment that the aid caused the investment increase.

§7.03 COUNTERFACTUAL METHODS FOR STATE AID EVALUATION[8]

The key question in every ex post evaluation of State aid is whether there is a direct, causal impact of giving aid on the behaviour of the beneficiary. For example, does the investment aid really lead to new investments? Alternatively, would these investments have been carried out anyway and does the aid therefore constitute a windfall profit for the aid recipient?

To tackle this question, it is important to use a methodology that allows establishing a causal link between the aid and the behaviour of the aided company. For that inference, one should ideally compare the outcome for the beneficiaries of the aid (treatment group) with the outcome for non-beneficiaries (control group/counterfactual). The treatment group is usually very easy to identify. Building a good control group, on the contrary, is more challenging since it should consist of companies that did not receive aid but are otherwise, except for the aid, identical to the aid beneficiaries. The obvious question to answer why, if these control group companies are very similar to the companies that received aid, they still did not receive it.

Suppose, for example, that one wants to evaluate the direct impact of a regional aid scheme. That scheme authorised investment aid for companies in a certain region. The direct impact of the aid is the difference in investment between companies in the aided region and otherwise identical companies in non-aided regions. Such inference could only be made if the aided and non-aided companies are identical and therefore shared the very same characteristics (such as industry, size, financial strength and the like). Otherwise, one would attribute the difference in investment to the aid even though it is in fact attributable to other firm characteristics.

Ruling out that there is no systematic bias, also called selection bias, between aided and non-aided firms is often tricky. However, several empirical tools are

France could get inspiration from the UK experience of 'What Works Centres'. A call for more evaluation of innovation policies in France was also made by Pisani-Ferry (2016).

7. In a special issue on ex post evaluation of the European State Aid Law Quarterly Review, the UK practice of evaluation is discussed. The UK Treasury (HMT) has a Green Book for evaluation of public policies deemed 'substantially aligned' with the SAM requirements. *See* Wright (2018).

8. This section draws heavily on the staff working document on a 'Common methodology for State aid evaluation' (European Commission, 2014) and the references cited therein. For an academic review of recent developments in econometric methods for evaluating public policies, *see* Athey and Imbens (2017).

available to overcome this difficulty and many State aid evaluation plans rely on them. The following subsections discuss these various empirical tools.

[A] Randomised Experiments

The cleanest way to tackle the systematic difference between aid beneficiaries and control firms is to construct a randomised controlled trial (RCT). Here, intuitively, aid is awarded via a lottery. Every firm participates, but it is randomised which firm receives aid. Therefore, there are no systematic differences and the difference in behaviour between aided and non-aided firms is solely attributable to the aid.

In practice and until now, pure RCT has only played a minor role in the attribution of State aids and thus in State aid evaluation. The reason is that potential aid beneficiaries perceive it as 'unfair' as the decision to grant aid is purely determined by luck. Of course, this criticism applies to any RCT. Yet RCT is heavily relied on in medical research, where the drawbacks of having a treatment by 'lottery' seem to be counterbalanced by the fact that the RCT clearly determines whether some medicine or medical procedure has a causal impact. While it seems unrealistic to introduce a RCT within an established, large State aid scheme, we believe that newly introduced, small pilot aid schemes could rely on RCT. An evaluation of such small pilot aid schemes could deliver useful insights contributing to the efficiency of larger scale aid schemes.

The European Commission also promotes the use of RCTs in other policy fields than competition policy. For example, it encourages the use of RCT in the areas of labour market and innovation[9] policies. In the area of labour markets, RCTs have been used to show that intensifying face-to-face support services of employment agencies to unemployed people significantly facilitates their reintegration on the labour market.[10] Moreover, to incentivise innovation agencies to use RCTs, the European Commission (2017b) offers grants that are conditional on the use of RCTs.

[B] Quasi-experimental Methods

Given the resistance to the use of RCT in State aid schemes, it is important to note that other quasi-experimental methods are available, which enable evaluations in the spirit of RCTs. While there are many different methods, which all have their own merits, this section focuses on the methods most commonly used in State aid evaluations.

[1] Difference-in-Differences

In the absence of a RCT, a simple comparison between aided and non-aided beneficiaries is unlikely to show the 'true' impact of aid. The reason is that unobserved

9. For an overview of ongoing trials in innovation policy, the Innovation Growth Lab (IGL) is collating a database accessible on their website.
10. *See* European Commission (2017a, 2018b) reports on public employment services (PES) in the Netherlands and for Denmark, respectively.

differences between the two groups can explain partially the difference in their outcomes. Similarly, comparing the outcomes before and after the aid for the beneficiaries is also likely to lead to a spurious correlation because other factors than the aid could have affected the outcome. In both cases, it is impossible to disentangle the effects of the aid from other factors.

One way to mitigate the impact of these confounding factors is to look at the difference between beneficiaries and non-beneficiaries (first difference) before and after the aid (second difference). The difference between aided (treatment group) and non-aided companies (control group) before the aid is subtracted from their difference after the aid. While this very intuitive approach allows removing any (unobservable) factors that do not change over time, it assumes that both groups of companies are subject to the same economic forces. This means that, in the absence of the aid, the aided companies would have evolved just like the companies in the control group. While it is impossible to test this condition empirically, researchers gain confidence in the evaluation results if the outcomes for aided and non-aided companies exhibited a 'parallel trend' before the aid was given.

[2] Instrumental Variables

The instrumental variables technique is often used to deal with endogeneity of explanatory variables in econometric modelling. However, it has been used only to a small extent in State aid evaluations. As the aid amount is often an explanatory variable of the outcome, the question arises whether the 'State aid' variable is correlated with the outcome variable. The decision to apply for or to receive an aid might depend on many factors that are unobservable to the evaluator ('the decision is endogenous'). Without including these variables in the analysis, a simple comparison of the behaviour of aided and non-aided firms does not identify the impact of the aid. Instead, the difference could be solely explained by unobservable factors. One possibility for addressing this issue is to employ a so-called instrumental variable approach. For that approach, one searches for an 'instrumental variable' that affects the decision of the company applying for the aid but is otherwise independent of the outcome variable. Accordingly, the instrumental variable has an impact on the outcome variable solely via the aid. Employing this instrumental variable technique identifies a variation in the probability to be aided that is independent of unobservable factors. Using this 'instrumented' variation determines the impact of aid on the beneficiaries without having the concern that unobservable factors pollute the inference.

For example, imagine a national investment aid scheme where the implementation is the responsibility of regional authorities. Each region decided to spend a certain advertisement budget. Depending on the budget, firms became more or less aware of the aid scheme. If we assume that the size of the advertisement budget had nothing to do with the investment decisions other than making firms more aware of the aid scheme, we could use the advertisement budget as an instrument for the participation in the aid scheme.

[3] Regression Discontinuity Design (RDD)

Another method to address the causal inference is the RDD. For that method, the evaluator exploits the fact that in many State aid schemes the decision to award aid depends on a certain parameter, e.g., a quality score, above which beneficiaries receive the support. Below that threshold, companies do not receive any support. Intuitively, if we compare firms very close to the threshold the difference in the 'quality score' becomes negligible. Hence, we can analyse extremely similar companies on the left and on the right of the cut-off. The only difference is that companies just above the cut-off obtained aid while those below the cut-off were not aided.

These types of evaluation designs have become more common since aid is very often awarded as part of a tender. Take, for example, an environmental aid scheme under which all interested and eligible companies can make bids, and the contract is awarded to those companies that require the lowest subsidy amount for a given supply of renewable energy production. The companies bidding subsidies below the auction clearing level will actually receive the aid, while those bidding subsidies that are above this level will not receive the aid. The RDD allows comparing the investments in renewable energy for companies that 'just' won the aid with companies that lost it by a small margin.

Technically one can make a distinction between a fuzzy and a sharp RDD. For a sharp RDD, the assignment (treatment) probability increases from zero to one at the threshold. For the fuzzy RDD, instead, the increase in treatment probability is less abrupt. Nevertheless, there needs to be a significant increase in the probability around the threshold. For example, if the assignment rule is not strictly implemented, one could employ the fuzzy RDD instead of a sharp RDD.

[4] Auction Econometrics

If the aid is awarded via a tender, there is another possibility to construct the counterfactual of what the beneficiary would have done without the aid.[11] That approach relies on auction econometrics. Suppose that companies can bid for the aid needed to carry out a certain type of investment. The State wants to incentivise that investment but would like to minimise the aid. Therefore, it collects all bids but decides to finance only these companies that offer to invest with aid levels below a certain threshold. To find out how much of the investment was 'caused' by the aid, the evaluator can construct a supply curve from all bids available in that tender. The supply curve shows how much investment would be carried out depending on the aid amount given. For example, if the State wants to grant only very little aid, it will finance only the most efficient (investment/aid) projects. If the State wants to induce more investment (moving up on the supply curve), it will also need to finance less efficient

11. This approach is not part of the current version of the European Commission Staff Working Document 'Common methodology for State aid evaluation' but has been proposed in several recent evaluation plans (e.g., for the German, Spanish and Polish renewable energy schemes, SA.45461, SA.40348 and SA.43697, respectively).

projects and pay more aid. That supply curve therefore provides a counterfactual for how much investment would have been carried out without any aid (if the aid was zero) and, in turn, allows identifying how much investment was 'caused' by the aid. In addition, it allows determining how much investment was caused by changes in the aid. Figure 7.1 illustrates this analysis.

Figure 7.1 Investment Supply Curve

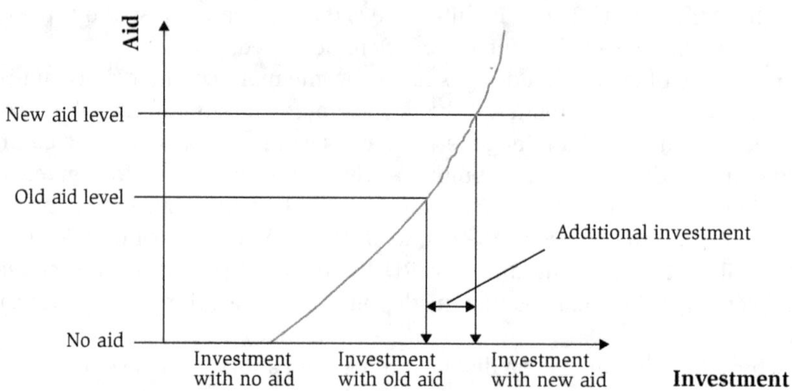

Source: Authors' own graph.

§7.04 LITERATURE REVIEW

While the literature on the evaluation of public subsidy programmes is large and diverse,[12] there are far fewer evaluations of State aid schemes or programmes.[13] This literature review therefore focuses on a small number of academic studies that evaluate

12. The What Works Centre for Local Economic Growth (2016) routinely undertakes excellent reviews of studies ('evidence reviews') that assess the impact of public policies (including public subsidies) on policy objectives. The Centre focuses on evidence regarding policy interventions in support of local economic growth, which often overlaps with the objectives of State aid evaluations, but is much wider in scope. The studies reviewed by the Centre comprise policy evaluations in the areas of, e.g., access to finance, apprenticeships, broadband, business advice, employment training, estate renewal, innovation, sports and culture as well as transport. Each study obtains a score based on their econometric execution. Whilst there are thousands of studies, only very few rely on proper quasi-experimental methods. Consequently, only a limited number of studies meet the Centre's minimum standards required to draw causal inferences for sound policy recommendations. For example, only sixteen out of thousand evaluations of the impact of subsidies on the rollout of broadband met the minimum standards. This does not mean that the studies with a low score as regards their ability to infer causality cannot be useful or insightful. Evaluation studies – even descriptive or qualitative ones – can provide interesting insights. In fact, qualitative studies are often an excellent complement to understand findings provided by quantitative models. However, establishing causality – which is often a central argument to implement policies – cannot be achieved without using appropriate methods and relevant data.
13. *See* Footnote 1 for the distinction between subsidies and State aid.

the impact of subsidy programmes in Europe applying quasi-experimental methods. Given the increasing importance of quasi-experimental methods for State aid evaluation, these studies can serve as blueprints. They clearly show which questions can be answered, which methods should be used and which data is needed to have convincing and robust empirical evidence. Even though some of these subsidy programmes may not technically qualify as 'State aid', the economic analysis would be comparable to an evaluation of a State aid scheme.

Table 7.1 Evaluations of Subsidy Programmes Relying on Quasi-experimental Methods

Study	*Type of Programme*	*Objective of the Analysis*	*Main Methodology Used*	*Data*	*Main Results*
Becker et al. (2010)	EU Structural funds	Impact on regional performance	Fuzzy RDD	Aggregate data for European regions from 1989 to 2006	Funds increase regional GDP growth but not employment.
Aguiar and Gagnepain (2017)	Fifth European Framework Programme for Research and Technological Development	Impact on EU labour productivity and profitability	Instrumental variable	Firm level data, 2000-2004 projects	Funds increase labour productivity but not profitability.
Criscuolo et al. (2019)	UK Regional Selective Assistance (RSA)	Impact on regional employment and productivity	Instrumental variable	Firm level data, 1997-2004	Funds increase employment for small firms only but have no effect on productivity.
Cerqua and Pellegrini (2014)	Italian regional aid scheme	Impact on regional activity	Sharp RDD	Firm level data, 1995-2004	Funds increase employment, investment and turnover, but not productivity.
de Blasio et al. (2018)	Italian credit guarantee scheme for SMEs	Impact on access to finance and SMEs activity	Fuzzy RDD	Loan level data, 2005-2010	Guarantee improved access to loans but no effect on interest rate paid, investment and sales.

The five notable examples of evaluations of subsidy programmes relying on quasi-experimental methods we identified are Becker et al. (2010), Aguiar and Gagnepain (2017), Criscuolo et al. (2019), Cerqua and Pellegrini (2014) and de Blasio et al. (2018). These studies assess subsidies supporting regional, R&D and SME objectives. All these studies clearly demonstrate the feasibility of applying quasi-experimental methods for the ex post evaluation of State aid schemes. Moreover, they indicate what type of data is needed for a proper ex post evaluation and offer guidance on what sources of variation to exploit for a clean empirical setting. The Table 7.1 above provides an overview of these studies.

Becker et al. (2010) analyse the causal effect of EU Structural Funds on regional performance. The EU provides grants to regions with a per capita GDP level below 75% of the EU average ('Objective 1 scheme'). Regions with a per capita GDP level above 75% are not eligible for that type of support. Examining the impact of EU funding on economic growth is challenging as richer regions may exhibit better growth prospects. The authors decide to exploit the 75% GDP per capita threshold, which creates a discontinuity in the availability of EU Structural Funds and permits the application of an RDD. While the eligibility of the scheme mostly depends on the GDP per capita ratio, it is not the sole criterion. Certain exceptions from the assignment rule lead to an imperfect assignment. This imperfect assignment does not induce a jump in the treatment probability from 0 to 1 at the threshold. Nevertheless, the treatment probability increases sharply at the threshold. Consequently, the authors do not rely on a sharp RDD, but employ a fuzzy RDD instead. Using this empirical setup and aggregate data for European regions from 1989 to 2006, the authors are able to demonstrate an impact of EU funding on GDP growth, but not on employment. Moreover, they also determine that the benefits of the EU Structural Funds in terms of GDP growth outweigh its costs by a factor of 1.2. That means that every euro (EUR) spent on an Objective 1 region returns EUR 1.2 in terms of GDP growth. This study illustrates how simple rules, like the GDP per capita rule, allow for the application of a quasi-experimental method.

Aguiar and Gagnepain (2017) analyse the effects of grants to R&D joint ventures provided by the Fifth European Framework Programme for Research and Technological Development between 1998 and 2002. As output indicators, the study focuses on labour productivity and profitability. To overcome obvious endogeneity concerns between the funding made available and technological opportunities, the authors exploit the fact that the available budget is based on social and economic criteria, in addition to the R&D prospects of the projects submitted to the programme. Therefore, part of the available budget is unrelated to the technological prospects. By exploiting the variation in social and economic criteria of the projects submitted, the authors can predict programme participation in the first stage of a two-stage regression. Subsequently, the predicted participation obtained from the first stage is used as an instrument in the second stage regression in which labour productivity and firm profitability are the dependent variables. Aguiar and Gagnepain (2017) demonstrate a substantial positive impact of the grants provided on labour productivity while there is no effect on firm profitability.

Criscuolo et al. (2019) exploit the 2000 change in eligibility criteria for the RSA programme in the UK to study the impact of regional aid on economic activity. More specifically, the weighting of observable factors (such as unemployment and GDP per capita) to determine whether a region qualified for investment subsidies was changed. By exploiting this exogenous variation via an instrumental variable approach, the authors were able to demonstrate that an increase in subsidies significantly increased manufacturing employment and reduced aggregate unemployment. These effects were not driven by the transfer of jobs from non-assisted to assisted regions, and therefore constituted 'net' job creations. The positive treatment effects were predominantly driven by smaller firms (below fifty workers). There is no effect on productivity. Overall, the study suggests that regional support schemes should target smaller companies. Moreover, they seem to be unsuitable to foster productivity, at least if the schemes mimic the setting of the RSA.

Cerqua and Pellegrini (2014) examine the effectiveness of an Italian regional aid scheme, which provided subsidies to companies located in disadvantaged regions. The scheme applied a strict ranking system based on which the aid was allocated until the funds earmarked for each region were exhausted. This budget restriction created regional cut-off points, with investment projects having a score above the cut-off point being supported and investment projects with scores below the cut-off point not being supported. This assignment system enabled the application of an RDD. Using data from 1995 to 2004, the study demonstrates that the subsidies caused increases in employment, investment and turnover, while the output per worker, used as a measure for productivity, did not change. Moreover, the subsidies did not complement owner-sourced investment and, importantly, the effects were not driven by delayed investments, which were postponed anticipating the subsidies.

de Blasio et al. (2018) analyse the impact of public guarantees on loans to SMEs. Exploiting data from 2005 to 2012 on the Italian 'Fondo di Garanzia' ('Guarantee Fund'), the study exploits the fact that the eligibility for these guarantees depended on numerous balance-sheet observables and constructs a fuzzy RDD. The authors found that guarantees increase the access to financing of SMEs, but left interest rates unchanged. Loans with a guarantee had a significantly higher probability of default in comparison to other, similar loans. The study did not detect any impact on investments or sales. Overall, it appears that this guarantee scheme did not have an actual impact on the benefitting SMEs. While these firms had more funding available, there was no impact on investment, sales or even the rate they were paying.

In addition, the three next chapters in this book use quasi-experimental methods to conduct ex post evaluations of three different types of State aid: an aid measure benefitting a regional airport in the UK over the period 2006-2011, national and regional aid schemes to support the deployment of broadband to rural areas in Germany over the period 2011-2014 and restructuring aid decisions taken by the European Commission between 2000 and 2012.

§7.05 THE IMPLEMENTATION OF EX POST EVALUATION REQUIREMENTS IN PRACTICE

In this section, we look at the implementation of the ex post evaluation requirements following the SAM reform. We first describe the State aid schemes that have been submitted for evaluation by the Member States, focusing on the types of aid schemes to be evaluated and the methodological approaches proposed in the evaluation plans sent to the European Commission. Second, we summarise the European Commission's assessments of the different evaluation plans received and the main lessons learnt.

[A] State Aid Schemes to be Evaluated by the Member States

[1] Geographical Distribution

In light of the requirement to conduct ex post evaluations of large and innovative State aid schemes, Member States have prepared evaluation plans for around fifty State aid schemes. By 30 May 2019, the European Commission had approved forty-two evaluation plans (*see* Table 7.4 in the Appendix for a complete list) covering more than half of the EU Member States, with four Member States (Germany, France, Poland and the UK) accounting for the majority of these evaluation plans.

These numbers may appear small taking into account that more than 3,000 aid measures were active in 2017 in the European Union (European Commission, 2018a). However, the forty-two schemes for which evaluation plans have been approved account for a total annual budget of EUR 50 billion. Given the fact that the total amount of aid disbursed over the period 2014-2018 amounted to approximately EUR 400 billion, it would seem that on the whole the implementation of the evaluation requirement is not too burdensome since it focuses on the 'big ticket items' only. It is also worth noting that the German renewable support scheme[14] represents almost half of the total annual budget (EUR 20 billion).

Figure 7.2 shows the number of evaluation plans approved by the European Commission for the different Member States over the period 2014-2019. For several smaller countries, there were no State aid schemes with annual budgets above the EUR 150 million threshold, and therefore no evaluation plans had to be submitted. Greece, however, decided to submit two evaluation plans: one for its entrepreneurship scheme[15] which exceeded the EUR 150 million threshold; and a second one for a notified scheme with a relatively modest annual budget of EUR 50 million, the reason being that this scheme[16] had a novel feature (i.e., the use of vouchers to support broadband take-up). Similarly, Lithuania submitted an evaluation plan for an EUR 44

14. SA.45461 EEG 2017 – Reform of the Renewable Energy Law.
15. SA.47412 – General Entrepreneurship.
16. SA.49935 – Superfast Broadband SFBB Project.

million innovative scheme providing exemptions from electricity fee payments to firms investing in technology infrastructure projects.[17]

Figure 7.2 Map of the EU Showing Evaluation Plans Adopted by Member States, by end May 2019

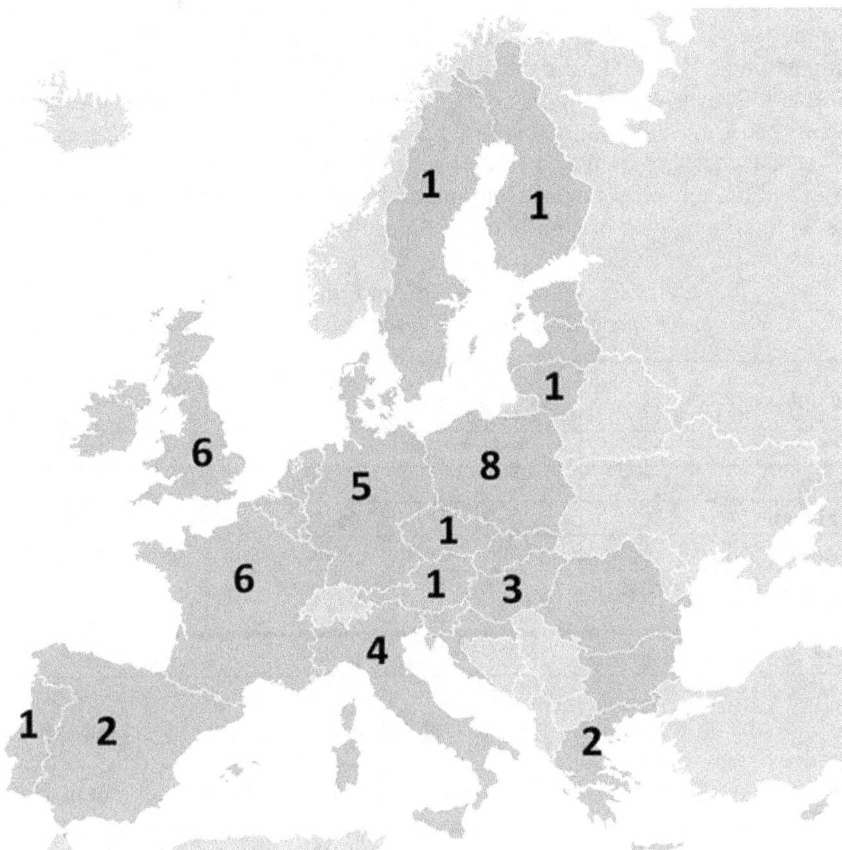

Source: Authors' own calculation; map provided by Pixabay.

[2] Type of Scheme and Aid Category

Both notified and block-exempted schemes may be subject to ex post evaluations. Almost three-quarters (in value) of the aid from schemes for which evaluation plans have been approved covers notified schemes. One reason for this large share is the

17. SA.42225 – Regional aid scheme for the promotion of the development of strategic information and communication technology (ICT) projects on strategic ICT sites.

inclusion of the German renewable support scheme, which was an EUR 20 billion notified scheme accounting for 40% of the total value of all schemes with approved evaluation plans. However, even if we exclude this scheme, the value share in approved evaluation plans of notified schemes (59%) exceeds that of block-exempted schemes (41%).

In terms of aid categories, the main areas covered by the approved evaluation plans are those reflecting major EU economic priorities: broadband, energy, regional aid and R&D&I (*see* Table 7.2). Amongst the evaluated schemes that are block-exempted under the GBER, the majority of the aid (in value) concerns regional aid or R&D&I aid. Conversely, amongst notified aid schemes, the main objectives of the aid schemes being evaluated (in value) are broadband and energy. This outcome reflects the fact that most regional and R&D&I schemes fall under the GBER, whilst (large) energy and broadband schemes continue to be subject to a full compatibility assessment within the context of a notification procedure.

Table 7.2 Value Shares of Aid Categories Covered by Approved Evaluation Plans (up to June 2019)

Aid Category	*All Aid Schemes*	*Block-Exempted Aid Schemes*	*Notified Aid Schemes*
Broadband	7%	-	10%
Energy	64%	-	87%
Regional	9%	46%	0.1%
R&D&I	9%	33%	-
Other (including mixed objectives)	11%	21%	3%
Total	*100%*	*100%*	*100%*

In terms of geographic coverage (*see* Table 7.3), regional aid schemes have the widest coverage with ten countries developing ex post evaluation studies in this area. Thereafter, one finds broadband schemes and energy schemes (six countries), followed by R&D&I schemes (four countries). Three countries are assessing schemes combining R&D&I and regional development objectives. The United Kingdom is the only country with an evaluation plan looking into risk finance and Poland is the only country looking into a scheme to promote intermodal transport.

Table 7.3 Geographic Coverage by Aid Category

Aid Category	*Geographic Coverage (Countries with an Approved Evaluation Plan)*
Broadband	Austria, France, Germany, Greece, Italy, United Kingdom
Energy	France, Germany, Poland, Spain, Sweden, United Kingdom
Regional aid (only)	Czech Republic, France, Germany, Greece, Hungary, Italy, Lithuania, Poland, Portugal, United Kingdom
R&D&I (only)	Finland, France, Germany, United Kingdom
Mix (regional, R&D&I, etc.)	Hungary, Italy, Poland
Risk finance	United Kingdom
Intermodal transport	Poland

[3] Key Elements of the Evaluation Plans Including Methods Envisaged

As described in Box 7.1, the evaluation plans must include eight key elements. The name of the scheme usually clarifies its objective. The evaluation questions spell out how the progress made towards the objective will be measured and which result indicators will be used. For example, to assess the direct impact of a renewable energy scheme, the evaluation will investigate *inter alia* whether the aid has contributed to increasing the production of energy from renewable sources. The indirect effects of such a scheme could be its effects on market concentration and on the geographical dispersion of production capacity. The appropriateness of a scheme could be measured by comparing the outcome of the scheme with the outcomes achieved in other EU Member States (with a different type of aid measure) or to the situation before amending a scheme (if the original scheme used a different aid instrument). The proportionality of the scheme could be appraised, for example, by comparing the economic impact of the supported project with the amount of aid received.

The data collection requirement is a necessary ingredient in every evaluation plan. To fulfil this requirement, it is important to have a legal basis for the collection of the data required, including the possibility to store and to link data from various data sources. Moreover, the evaluation plans should include a precise timeline for the evaluation as well as where the final evaluation report will be published (usually on the website of administration responsible for the scheme). The evaluation plan also specifies who will act as the evaluator(s), or, alternatively, spells out the criteria for their selection.

With respect to the evaluation methods used, we observe that despite the emerging evaluations relying on auction econometrics and RDDs, the Difference-in-Differences approach remains the workhorse for evaluations of State aid schemes. A great number of evaluations across all different categories of aid will rely on this method.[18] The Difference-in-Differences approaches estimate the causal effect of the aid by comparing aided firms to non-aided firms before and after the aid was granted. However, some evaluation plans intend to go further than that. For example, the German regional aid scheme (SA.39460) will include a triple difference estimator comparing the Difference-in-Differences estimator across different regions and sectors.

While instrumental variable techniques are widely used in the academic literature, only very few State aid evaluations rely on this method. For example, the regional aid scheme in Portugal (SA.42136) and the R&D&I scheme in France (SA.40266) consider instrumental variables as a possible method, without further specifying the envisaged instruments.

By contrast, the 'RDD' method is used more widely. Since tenders are increasingly employed as a tool to select the beneficiaries of the aid, more aid schemes exhibit a sharp discontinuity in the disbursement of aid, making the use of the 'RDD' method possible. Examples of aid schemes with tenders that rely, amongst other methods, on the RDD are the large renewable energy schemes in Germany (SA.45461), Spain (SA.40348) and Poland (SA.43697). However, other types of aid schemes will be evaluated using the RDD as well. These schemes comprise investment aid (Italy SA.48248), regional aid (Poland SA.43142, Portugal SA.42136), R&D&I aid (UK SA.40761, France SA.40391) and SME aid (Italy SA.47180).

Furthermore, the RDD is not restricted to the 'quality' cut-off, which divides successful and unsuccessful applicants. Other possible discontinuities relate to a shortage of budget (Greek regional investment aid scheme, SA.47412), geographical eligibility (Italian regional investment aid scheme, SA.45184), different aid intensities based on firm size (Italy investment aid SA.48248, Italy SME aid SA.47180) and the time of introduction of a revised aid scheme (UK SA.44622).

Finally, the application of auction econometrics is foreseen in three evaluation plans. For the evaluation of the 2017 German renewable energy support scheme (SA.45461), auction bids will be used to construct a supply curve for the installation of renewable energy infrastructure. The Spanish support scheme for electricity generation from renewable energy sources (SA.40348) and the Polish support scheme for renewable energy (SA.43697) will use similar approaches to establish a counterfactual. Since more aid schemes will switch to the use of a tendering process to identify aid beneficiaries, we expect that this methodology will become more important in the future, mostly as a complement to the 'RDD' method.

[B] Lessons Learnt

Since the first ex post evaluation plans were approved at the end of 2014, there has been a steep learning curve, both on the side of the European Commission and on the

18. They include broadband (e.g., Greece SA.49935, UK SA.40720), R&D&I (e.g., Germany SA.41884, France SA.40266, Poland SA.41471), regional aid (Czech Republic SA.38751, Germany SA.39460, Greece SA.47412, Hungary SA.39669, Hungary SA.48680, Italy SA.48248, Lithuania SA.46285, Poland SA.43142, Poland SA.38830, Portugal SA.42136, UK SA.39273), risk finance (France SA.44400, UK SA.40991) and aid to SMEs (Italy SA.47180).

side of the EU Member States. A number of lessons can be drawn from this first experience with evaluation plans, which could help identifying the circumstances under which ex post evaluations can be effective.

The conditions for a successful evaluation comprise the following: (i) involving evaluation experts when designing the scheme and setting up the evaluation plan; (ii) identifying all data needs and sources when designing the evaluation plan; (iii) informing the European Commission early on if obstacles are encountered and providing well-advanced interim reports; (iv) avoiding duplication of evaluations; and (v) carefully re-designing schemes in an evaluation-friendly way.

[1] Involving Evaluation Experts When Designing the Scheme and Setting Up the Evaluation Plan

In a handful of cases, Member States have asked experts to produce a 'scoping study' at the start of the evaluation process, in order to define a realistic and effective evaluation strategy. For example, the UK government asked an expert to recommend the most appropriate methodology for the evaluation of its scheme to promote broadband investment (SA.40720). Similarly, a scoping study for the Regional Growth Fund in the UK reviewed the scheme, the available data and made recommendations on data collection and the most promising methodological choices given the scheme design and the available data.

Experience suggests that involving evaluation experts[19] at an early stage of the evaluation plan can facilitate the identification of meaningful evaluation strategies and the gathering of the necessary data. Evaluation experts should work with the granting authorities to identify upfront the most promising evaluation strategies based on the design of the scheme or even help introduce features to the scheme that would enable better future evaluation.

Moreover, for administrations lacking practical ex post evaluation expertise, involving experts might save costs and reduce the administrative burden associated with this work. Indeed, experts may facilitate better-targeted evaluation plans, identify most relevant and cost-efficient data sources and, generally, ensure a smooth implementation of the plan, reducing time spent to review unsatisfactory evaluation plans and interim reports. Finally, it should be mentioned that the use of external experts is cost efficient, especially in light of the EUR 50 billion spent on schemes being evaluated.

[2] Identifying All Data Needs and Sources When Designing the Evaluation Plan

Good data are essential for robust ex post evaluations. In this respect, the examination of the initial evaluation plans received has shown that data limitations have often hampered the identification of good control groups, which is essential for a proper ex

19. These experts need not necessarily to be the ones that will carry out the actual evaluation.

post evaluation of State aid schemes. The data issues encountered with the first schemes should ideally subside over time as authorities acquire experience and gain an understanding of the data needs. For example, the proposed plans do not foresee the collection of data from rejected applicants, which makes an RDD comparing marginally accepted and marginally rejected applicants impossible. Similarly, data on certain output criteria are not available or cannot be used to compare the impact on aid beneficiaries with non-aid beneficiaries.

A lesson learnt is therefore that the identification of appropriate data needs and data sources should occur before the scheme is up and running. Otherwise, data might not be collected or could potentially not be matched with other data. Often, it is necessary to establish a sound framework for the data collection, as for example done by France for the evaluation of a risk finance scheme where a vast amount of data from several sources (including tax declarations) are made available for the evaluation.

[3] Informing the European Commission Early About Difficulties Encountered and Providing Well-Advanced Interim Reports

The first final report received in 2018 did not implement the methods foreseen in the evaluation plan and could therefore not provide evidence in line with the expectations of the initial plan.[20] This illustrates the problems that may occur if the European Commission is not informed early on (e.g., via interim reports) of any bottlenecks that may arise. In this particular case, the European Commission and the Member State have since worked together closely in order to establish a viable strategy leading to the production of an evaluation study in line with the required standards. In another problematic case, there was no interim report foreseen and the final report was sent to the European Commission with minimal interactions during its preparation. This lack of interactions meant that the Commission was not warned in advance of the difficulties faced by that Member State in following the methodology agreed in the evaluation plan. This shows again the importance of informing the European Commission of any issues with the implementation of the evaluation.

While the European Commission strongly encourages interim reports, not all reports allowed identifying future obstacles to the implementation of the evaluation plan. Indeed, the reviews of the first interim reports have indicated that the quality and depth of the analysis varies significantly. In a number of interim reports, the focus is mostly on descriptive statistics while, in others, there is a detailed description of the data and quantitative methods to be used for the evaluation. In other words, some interim reports appear to constitute advanced evaluation plans with many open questions, rather than true interim reports providing preliminary results. In these cases, it would have been preferable for the Member State to engage proactively with the European Commission, even before the interim report was due.

20. As explained in Brandtner and Vidoni (2018, p. 480), the first evaluation report submitted to the Directorate-General for Competition did not fulfil the requirements of the evaluation plan, that had previously been approved by the European Commission.

This experience illustrates the importance for Member States to stay in regular contact with the European Commission and to produce well-advanced interim reports. Hence, since 2018, regular contacts between the European Commission and the Member States are planned even before the production of an interim report. Subsequently, the Directorate-General for Competition (i.e., the strategy unit in charge of evaluation as well as the Chief Economist Team) and an external reviewer (i.e., the Competence Centre on Microeconomic Evaluation, CC-ME, at the European Commission's Joint Research Centre, JRC) review the interim report and give feedback.

[4] Avoiding Duplication of Evaluations Already Conducted Elsewhere

The argument is sometimes made that the evaluation requirement under State aid rules duplicates work already performed for EU funding agencies (e.g., structural funds) or other institutions (e.g., courts of auditors). Any duplication of work should indeed be avoided to the extent that other evaluations aim at producing systematic and robust evidence on the effectiveness of the schemes. However, in many cases, other evaluations have different purposes (e.g., compliance checks) or rely on methods that are not sufficiently robust for causal inference (e.g., surveys or case studies). The conclusions and insights from complementary studies are useful and should consequently be read in conjunction with ex post evaluation studies undertaken for State aid control.

[5] Carefully Redesigning Schemes in an Evaluation-Friendly Way

A large number of ex post evaluation plans have been prepared for aid schemes that had been running for years and tend to be renewed at expiry with limited changes. These schemes were not designed in a way that is 'evaluation-friendly'. For example, very often all eligible applicants receiving aid or budgets are unlikely to be exhausted. In other words, most schemes have no element of randomness, nor features that are conducive to robust quasi-experimental methods. Building a control group can therefore prove extremely challenging.

We believe that evaluation is of the utmost importance, especially for large schemes that are already running for a long time without any major changes. For such schemes, there is a risk that tax payers' money is not used in the most efficient and least distortive way. Therefore, the European Commission works with the Member States concerned to prepare proper evaluations contributing to an improved effectiveness of the schemes.

§7.06 FUTURE CHALLENGES

This last section discusses specific challenges for the future. We currently see three main challenges ahead. First, the European Commission intends to encourage Member States to use not only quasi-experimental evaluation methods but also consider the use of experimental designs. Second, it aims at extending the coverage of the ex post evaluations to all Member States and all categories of aid. Third, Member States and the

European Commission need to think about the policy implications of the evaluations once they have been completed.

Experimental methods are widely applied to evaluate the impact of public policies, and the European Commission considers that it would be desirable to expand its use in the area of State aids. However, many stakeholders have doubts about employing experimental methods for the evaluation of State aid schemes. The ethical arguments put forward against experimentation rely on misconceptions (*see* Bravo-Biosca, 2019). Spending millions of taxpayers' money into subsidy programmes without any evidence that they actually work would seem to be unethical as well. In particular, there is a misconception that experimentation leads to binary choices, randomly selecting the 'lucky ones' whereas the random 'unlucky ones' are unfairly denied the same benefits. Experimentation can take many other forms: pilot projects, randomisation in the type of measure (e.g., grant, tax credit, repayable advance and financial instrument), randomisation in the amounts, randomisation in the timing or randomisation across selected participants.[21]

Extending the geographical and sector coverage of the ex post evaluations would be the second challenge. In terms of geographical coverage, it is regrettable that several Member States were not required to submit an evaluation plan for State aid schemes over the period 2014-2019. This does not necessarily mean that these Member States are not evaluating their State aid schemes,[22] but rather that the annual budgets of their schemes fall below the EUR 150 million GBER threshold or does not fulfil all conditions for evaluation in the sectoral guidelines. As regards the different aid categories, most evaluation plans cover R&D&I, regional, broadband and energy schemes. There is only one evaluation for risk finance and one evaluation concerning transport. The objective would be for the ex post evaluations to cover all EU Member States and most aid categories. In this respect, the development of an evaluation culture amongst the Member States and a demonstration of the usefulness of ex post evaluations of large and innovative aid schemes in different areas would encourage Member States to undertake ex post evaluations of schemes for which such evaluations are not a legal requirement.

Based on our contacts with Member States, we perceive that an evaluation culture has been fostered by the SAM. Discussions have moved on from whether the evaluation is required to how the State aid evaluation exercise can effectively be implemented. As regards data and methodologies (and as illustrated by the first final report received and the several interim reports received thus far), encouraging developments have taken place. However, the problems identified – lack of data, difficulties in constructing a control group due to failures in the design of the State aid scheme – could imply that the first evaluation studies may not be as conclusive or

21. For example, an IGL trial by the World Bank in Latin America will randomise the granting of innovation funds only across applicants for which reviewers scoring the applications have disagreements on whether the application is high or low quality.
22. For example, the Netherlands did not submit an evaluation plan for a State aid scheme, even though the Dutch authorities are strong proponents of ex post evaluation (*see* the presentation by Theo Roelandt, Chief Analyst at DG Enterprise and Innovation of the Dutch Ministry of Economic Affairs at the Bruegel Event on ex post evaluation on 30 May 2016).

robust as one would hope for. This is indeed a question that has been raised by State aid commentators (*see, e.g.*, Nicolaides, 2015).

If final ex post evaluations do not produce clear, robust, unambiguous results, it raises several questions on what to do with these results. What should the European Commission do if the Member State claims the scheme should be changed in a certain way or kept intact in light of results that may not be robust? In which circumstances should an aid scheme be considered a success or a failure? What if the Member State does not alter the scheme in ways that are consistent with the results from the evaluation? What if similar schemes are found to have different effects in different countries? All these questions (and certainly many more) will occupy the State aid community in the years to come as both the European Commission and the Member States grapple with the evidence produced (robust or weak, positive or negative).

Whilst it is difficult to pre-judge upcoming debates, several principles will form the basis of the future discussions. First, quality matters. Studies that rely on good data and use the most robust methods should receive more weight. Second, reliable results matter. If a study indicates that a scheme has a strong incentive effect in some circumstances but not in others, these results should be taken into account in newly designed schemes. Third, cooperation and openness matter. Ex post evaluation is a mutually beneficial learning process. As final reports become public, the European Commission and Member States should ensure that these reports are widely disseminated and discussed within the State aid community but also beyond (with the academic community and the ex post evaluation community).

§7.07 CONCLUSION

In the area of State aid, ex post evaluation is a relatively new requirement. And while significant obstacles remain, our experience from dealing with State aid evaluations shows that Member States gained significant knowledge about the prerequisites of evaluations and, more commonly, agree to producing high-quality evaluations. Up until now, forty-two evaluation plans corresponding to EUR 50 billion of aid have been approved by the European Commission. These plans cover more than half of the EU Member States and reflect major EU State aid objectives: broadband, energy, regional aid and R&D&I.

In line with increasing obligations for high-quality evaluations of public policies in general, we believe the ex post evaluation requirement introduced under State aid control in 2014 will lead to three main desirable evolutions. First, ex post evaluation will contribute to an improved understanding of the actual impact of State aid on firm behaviour and competition. Second, ex post evaluation will enable Member States to design schemes that are more effective and less distortive. Third, ex post evaluation should provide reliable evidence for the European Commission to improve future rules for State aid control.

High-quality evaluations require to frontload as much as possible the work of evaluation experts at the start of the process and ideally, at the design stage of the scheme. It also requires frequent interactions between the European Commission, the

Member States and the evaluation experts to identify data issues, the use of alternative methods as soon as possible and especially in case obstacles are encountered. Similarly, Member States will learn from the experiences of others as evaluation reports are published over time.

Over the coming years, the main challenge would be to make good use of the evaluation results for policy purposes, while taking into account that the European Commission and the EU Member States are still in a learning phase and that some ex post evaluations may not produce clear and robust results. However, in the future, State aid evaluation will produce a rich body of evidence on the effectiveness of State aid in achieving policy objectives without distorting competition. This will enable a better understanding of how State aid affects behaviour and thus the development of better policies to the benefit of firms, consumers and taxpayers.

APPENDIX: LIST OF STATE AID SCHEMES TO BE EVALUATED

Table 7.4 List of State Aid Schemes to be Evaluated by the EU Member States

MS	*Type of Aid*	*Title*	*Budget [Million EUR]*	*Decision Adopted*
AT	Broadband	Broadband Austria 2020	250	17-12-2015
CZ	Regional aid	Investment incentives	437	10-12-2014
DE	Regional aid	Federal regional aid scheme (GRW)	1,126	24-02-2015
DE	R&D&I	Central Innovation Programme for SMEs (ZIM)	543	30-10-2015
DE	Energy	Support for cogeneration	1,500	24-10-2016
DE	Energy	EEG 2016	20,000	20-12-2016
DE	Broadband	NGA Germany	429	11-08-2017
EL	Regional aid	General Entrepreneurship	383	06-07-2018
EL	Broadband	Superfast Broadband (SFBB) Project - Greece	50	07-01-2019
ES	R&D&I	CDTI R&D aid scheme	800	22-06-2015
ES	Energy	RES support	6,398	10-11-2017
FI	R&D&I	TEKES aid for R&D	400	01-07-2015
FR	R&D&I	Régime cadre aides RDI 2014-2020	850	01-07-2015
FR	R&D&I	Régime ADEME Investissements d'Avenir	300	04-08-2015
FR	Regional aid	Aide fiscale à l'investissement productif outre-mer	805	04-08-2015
FR	Risk finance	Dispositif ISF PME	450	24-05-2016
FR	Broadband	Plan Très Haut Débit	1,900	07-11-2016
FR	Energy	RES schemes	753	29-09-2017
HU	Regional aid	Development Tax Benefit	246	16-01-2015
HU	Regional aid	Investment incentive scheme based on Government decree 210/2014 (VIII.27.)	175	01-06-2018
HU	Regional aid/R&D&I	Aid for regional investment from the Economic Development and Innovation Operational Program (EDIOP)	373	24-01-2019
IT	Broadband	Strategia Banda Ultra Larga	667	30-06-2016
IT	Regional aid	Credito d'imposta Sud	617	23-09-2016
IT	SMEs	Capital goods aid for SMEs	300	15-06-2017
IT	Regional aid	Contratti di sviluppo	450	12-10-2017
LT	Regional aid	ICT projects	44	08-11-2016

MS	*Type of Aid*	*Title*	*Budget [Million EUR]*	*Decision Adopted*
PL	Regional aid	Special Economic Zones	500	16-06-2015
PL	R&D&I/Risk finance	National Research and Development Centre	907	24-08-2015
PL	R&D&I/Regional aid	PARP	310	08-02-2016
PL	Regional aid	Regional aid 2014-2020	217	10-03-2016
PL	Broadband	Broadband support 2014-2020	170	15-04-2016
PL	Transport	Intermodal transport	238	31-10-2017
PL	Regional aid/R&D&I	Regional aid programme granted to some entrepreneurs for the implementation of a new investment	373	28-02-2019
PL	Energy	Renewable energy scheme	1,908	13-12-2017
PT	Regional aid	Inovação Empresarial	350	19-08-2015
SE	Energy	Biofuels tax reductions	353	14-09-2017
UK	Regional aid	Regional Growth Fund	699	11-12-2014
UK	R&D&I	Innovate UK (Technology Strategy Board)	796	10-07-2015
UK	R&D&I	SME R&D Tax Credits	648	30-09-2015
UK	Risk finance	Enterprise Investment Scheme and Venture Capital Trusts	670	09-10-2015
UK	Broadband	Extension of the National Broadband Scheme for the UK	141	26-05-2016
UK	Energy	Renewable Heat Incentive	831	27-02-2017

REFERENCES

Aguiar L. and Gagnepain Ph. (2017), 'European cooperative R&D and firm performance: Evidence based on funding differences in key actions', *International Journal of Industrial Organisation*, 53(C), pp. 1-31.

Athey S. and Imbens G. (2017), 'The state of applied econometrics: Causality and policy valuation', *Journal of Economic Perspectives*, 31(2), pp. 3-32.

Brandtner B. and Vidoni D. (2018), 'State aid evaluation – State of play and ways forward', *European State Aid Law Quarterly*, 17(4), pp. 475-482.

Becker S., Egger P. and von Ehrlich M. (2010), 'Going NUTS: The effect of EU structural funds on regional performance', *Journal of Public Economics*, 94(9-10), pp. 578-590.

Bravo-Biosca A. (2019), 'Experimental innovation policy', Innovation Policy and the Economy No 20, NBER book series, Josh Lerner and Scott Stern, editors.

Cerqua A. and Pellegrini G. (2014), 'Do subsidies to private capital boost firms' growth? A multiple regression discontinuity design approach', *Journal of Public Economics*, 109, pp. 114-126.

Criscuolo C., Martin R., Overman H.G. and Van Reenen J. (2019), 'Some causal effects of an industrial policy', *American Economic Review*, 109(1), pp. 48-85.

de Blasio G., De Mitri S., D'Ignazio A., Finaldi Russo P. and Stoppani L. (2018), 'Public guarantees to SME borrowing. A RDD evaluation', *Journal of Banking and Finance*, 96(C), pp. 73-86.

European Commission (2012), 'State aid modernisation', COM/2012/209.

European Commission (2014), 'Common methodology for State aid evaluation', European Commission Staff Working Document No. 179, 28 May.

European Commission (2017a), 'Evidence-based design of services using randomised control trials (RCTs)', report.

European Commission (2017b), 'Supporting experimentation in innovation agencies', ID: INNOSUP-06-2018, 27 October.

European Commission (2018a), 'State aid scoreboard'.

European Commission (2018b), 'Promising PES practice: Evidence based PES services: RCT for the scientific evaluation of the impact of intensified face-to-face services', report.

European Commission (2019), 'State aid scoreboard'.

Agence Nouvelles des Solidarités (2017), 'What Works Centres britanniques: quels enseignements pour des politiques fondées sur la preuve en France?', report.

Nicolaides P. (2015) 'Ex post evaluation of State aid measures', blog.

Pisani-Ferry J. (2016), 'State support for innovation: Time for questions', *Concurrences, Competition Law Review*, 2-2016, Art. No. 78529, pp. 5-7.

Verouden V. (2015), 'EU State Aid Control: The Quest for Effectiveness', *European State Aid Law Quarterly*, 14(4), pp. 459-464.

What Works Centre for Local Economic Growth (2016), 'Evidence Review 4: Access to Finance'.

Wright N. (2018), 'The UK experience of State aid evaluation', *European State Aid Law Quarterly*, 17(4), pp. 525-533.

CHAPTER 8

Ex Post Assessment of the Impact of State Aid on Competition: The Case of Newquay Airport in the UK*

Nicole Robins

The European Commission's State Aid Modernisation reforms created a new role for ex post evaluations of aid schemes. State aid evaluations effectively serve as a balancing test to assess ex post whether the realised positive effects of an aid scheme outweighed any negative effects in terms of distortions to competition and trade. Traditionally, the role for an extensive analysis of the impact of aid on competition had been relatively limited in comparison with other areas of competition policy. As such, this chapter first provides an overview of an analytical approach that can be used to assess the impact of aid on competition, before applying this framework to determine how an aid provided by the UK to Newquay Airport affected competition. The first step is to filter State aid cases to determine for which cases a more detailed analysis of the impact of the aid on competition should be undertaken. The amount of aid given to Newquay Airport and the frequency with which the aid was given, together with the number of airports in the surrounding region, suggest that the aid had the potential to create distortions of competition. The analytical results confirm that the aid led to greater competitive distortions on neighbouring airports than anticipated at the time that the aid was approved.

* This chapter is based on a study by Oxera for the European Commission. The European Commission asked Oxera to develop an analytical framework that could be used to assess the impact of aid on competition. Oxera was then requested to apply the framework to four aid measures previously approved by the European Commission across a range of sectors (including energy, manufacturing, post and transport) in order to provide further insights into the actual impact of aid on competition (*see* Oxera, 2017).

§8.01 INTRODUCTION

The main objective of the 2012 State Aid Modernisation reforms was to focus the European Commission's scrutiny on cases that pose the most significant threat to the functioning of the single market, whilst giving Member States greater responsibilities in ensuring the correct enforcement of State aid rules (*see* European Commission, 2012, p. 3). To accompany this decentralisation, the Commission gave increased prominence to the ex post evaluations of certain State aid schemes. The aim of such evaluations was to assess the actual impact of the aid and draw lessons, with a view to improving the design and effectiveness of future aid schemes (*see* European Commission, 2014c). This new role of ex post evaluations in EU State aid control will likely be further developed over the coming years.

The aim of an ex post evaluation is to assess whether the aid scheme has achieved its intended objectives and whether it has led to any significant distortions of competition and trade. State aid evaluations effectively serve as a balancing test to assess ex post whether the realised positive effects of an aid scheme outweigh the negative effects. As highlighted by the European Commission (2014c, p. 6), ex post evaluations should be conducted, as far as possible, on a quantitative basis, building on the supporting evidence identified in the evaluation plan prepared by the Member State at the time when the aid was granted.

From an ex ante perspective, the role for an extensive analysis of the likely impact of aid on competition has been more limited compared with other areas of competition policy, such as merger control, where competitive assessments are at the heart of enforcement practice. Therefore, the introduction of ex post evaluations is likely to enhance the role for sophisticated competition analysis in ex ante State aid assessments. This will complement the analysis of the effectiveness of State aid, which is currently the focus of ex ante assessments in this area.

This chapter develops an analytical framework for evaluating the competitive effects of State aid, before setting out the results from applying this framework to assess the impact on competition of a specific State aid case. In particular, the focus here is on evaluating the impact of GBP 46.8 million of aid provided by the UK government, and approved by the European Commission (2007, 2009), to convert Newquay Airport from a part military to a fully commercial airport. Using the analytical framework described in this chapter, the impact of aid received by Newquay Airport on airports in the neighbouring region is assessed through a combination of qualitative and quantitative analysis. This case study has been selected to provide insights into the potential impact of aid to airports, against the backdrop of the additional guidance introduced in the 2014 aviation State aid guidelines.

This chapter is structured as follows. Section 8.02 describes the analytical framework developed to assess the impact of State aid on competition. Section 8.03 discusses the background behind the aid granted by the UK government to develop Newquay Airport into a fully commercial airport and presents the European Commission's decisions that approved the aid. Section 8.04 sets out the methodology that has been followed to assess the competitive effects of the aid received by Newquay Airport. Section 8.05 presents the results from the analysis of the competitive effects of the aid received by Newquay Airport. Finally, section 8.06 provides an overall conclusion and discusses possible areas for future research.

§8.02 ANALYTICAL FRAMEWORK TO ASSESS THE IMPACT OF STATE AID ON COMPETITION

This section provides a short review of empirical literature analysing the effects of State aid on competition. It also proposes an analytical framework for investigating such effects.

[A] Literature Review

Empirical evidence suggests that under some circumstances State aid could have an adverse impact on market outcomes and competition. However, in practice, limited research has been undertaken to date on the impact of aid on competition, as acknowledged in recent papers by Buts and Jegers (2013, p. 92) and Coppens et al. (2015, p. 272).

Garcia and Neven (2005) follow a theoretical framework to assess the competitive effects of aid in relation to marginal costs, entry, and vertical differentiation. The authors found that the significance of any competitive distortions depends on the characteristics of the market, with more severe price distortions expected the more concentrated the market is.

Other studies aim at analysing whether State aids contribute to change the market structure. Buts and Jegers (2013) investigate the impact of fixed asset subsidies on firms' market shares in Belgium. Based on a sample of over 13,000 firms, the authors find that the aid led to an increase in market shares but only two years after the granting of the aid. Research from Coppens et al. (2015) concurs with this finding. However, the authors find that subsidies affect market shares up until six years after the aid was granted, although the impact of the aid on market shares might be expected to decline over time.

Even though aid may lead to firms increasing their market share, this does not necessarily translate into distortive effects on competition, particularly if only relatively small firms gain market share in the industry. However, Buts and Jegers (2012) find that large firms in Belgium receiving aid were more likely to gain market share, which might lead to more concentration in the industry, thus weakening competition. Using a sample of over 15,000 Belgian firms across 541 industries, they find that the greater the amount of subsidies received by an industry, the greater the impact on concentration.

Other studies consider the impact on competition of specific categories of aids. Møllgaard (2005) finds that State aid for research and development alters the relative competitive position of firms by affecting the entry and exit decisions of (potential) competitors as well as their level of investment and subsequent performance. In markets that are dependent on innovation, the author finds that State aid might create a deterrent effect on new entrants.

Rescue and restructuring aid could contribute towards improving the survival and financial viability of aided firms, as shown in Chapter 10 of this book. However, it is commonly accepted that this form of aid could create distortions to competition, as it could potentially prevent inefficient companies from exiting the market.[1] In light of this, compensatory measures may therefore be required in favour of competitors. For instance, Schweiger (2011) concludes that rescue and restructuring aid in the Slovenian manufacturing sector between 1998 and 2003 had allowed less efficient firms, which were more likely to exit the market, to survive and increase market share faster than other, potentially more efficient, firms.

Overall, the empirical evidence analysing the effects of State aid on competition is not well developed, and there is no commonly agreed analytical framework to analyse these effects. The next subsection is a first attempt in that direction.

[B] Main Elements of the Analytical Framework

To assess the competitive effects of the aid, it is important to evaluate first whether the aid was effective in changing the firm's behaviour (i.e., to assess the incentive effects of the aid). In practice, if the aid has not had a significant impact on the beneficiary's behaviour, competition is unlikely to have been unduly distorted.

The questions to be addressed through the ex post evaluation are outlined in Box 8.1 below.

Box 8.1: Questions to be addressed in the ex post evaluation

In the ex post evaluation exercise, three types of question need to be addressed:

(1) **Direct effects**. What direct incentives does the aid confer on the beneficiary? For example, what were the incentive effects? What impact did the aid have on the beneficiary; and were these effects as expected?

(2) **Indirect effects**. What were the positive and negative effects of the aid on desired policy objectives and on competition and trade? For example, what was the impact on other firms or regions? What was the impact on competition and trade? Has the aid contributed to the relevant policy objective?

(3) **Proportionality and appropriateness**. Was the aid proportionate? Was the most effective aid instrument used?

Source: European Commission (2014c).

1. For an analysis of the likely outcomes of financial distress for competing firms not receiving aid, *see* Oxera (2009).

Beyond the questions regarding the effectiveness of the aid in achieving its objectives, this chapter proposes an analytical framework to evaluate the effects of the aid on competition (*see* Figure 8.1). This framework was developed from established approaches used in other areas of competition law and economics, with adjustments to reflect the specifics of State aid control. The framework was designed to be applicable to a range of aid measures and schemes.

Although designed for ex post evaluations, the framework can in principle be applied to ex ante evaluations of State aid as well. The main difference is that the ex ante assessment of the compatibility of the aid, which is undertaken before the aid is approved by the European Commission, relies on projections of the likely impact of the aid on the company receiving it (i.e., ex ante data). This contrasts with ex post assessments, which uses actual data to assess the impact of the aid.

As shown in Figure 8.1, the framework distinguishes three main steps. The first step includes a description of the characteristics of the aid (size, breadth, frequency) as well as of the market in which the aid is granted. The second step consists of defining the counterfactual of what would have happened in the absence of the aid. The final step in this framework is to compare the counterfactual with actual data to evaluate the impact of the aid on competition. The next subsections describe each of these three steps in more detail.

Figure 8.1 Analytical Framework to Assess the Impact of Aid on Competition

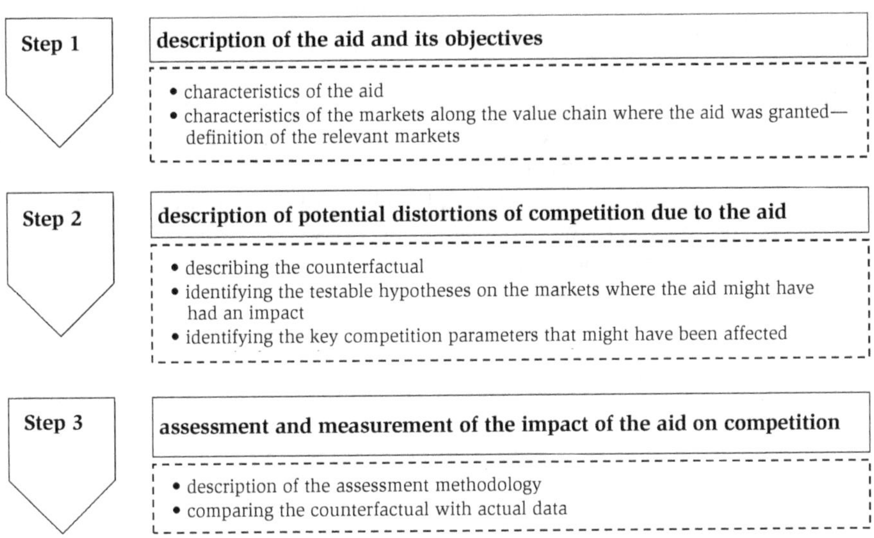

Source: Oxera (2017), p. 5.

[1] Step 1: What Are the Main Characteristics of the Aid and the Affected Markets?

State aid is intended to change market outcomes in order to correct market failures identified by a public authority. The aid is likely to affect the outcomes of normal competition; otherwise, the aid would not have its intended effect. As the impact on competition is likely to vary depending on the nature of the aid, the first step is to identify its characteristics, including its objectives and the aid instrument, as well as the characteristics of the market in which the aid is granted.

The granting of aid can commonly be viewed as an event that creates a shock in the market. The size of the shock depends largely on the nature of the event, i.e., the characteristics of the aid. To characterise the possible shock, the form, type and amount of aid granted, including the aid instrument, the number of firms receiving the aid (i.e., the degree of selectivity), the amount (in absolute value and relative to the market size) and the objectives of the aid all need to be defined.

The form of the aid matters – aid that reduces the marginal costs of production is more likely to distort competition than aid that affects fixed costs. In theory, lump-sum government funding (e.g., an airport receiving a one-off grant of EUR 1 million in a particular year) is not expected to significantly distort the recipient's incentives to operate in a commercial manner, as the grant is unlikely to have a significant impact on its marginal costs and therefore on prices.[2] By contrast, variable subsidies, such as the direct covering of any losses made by a company or subsidies that depend on the volume of output produced by the recipient, can have a greater effect on market outcomes, and are therefore more likely to distort competition.

The type and amount of aid are also important, as certain aid characteristics may have greater potential to distort certain aspects of competition. For example, a direct grant is typically considered to be more likely to be distortive than other aid instruments, such as a repayable advance.[3]

The impact of the aid also depends on the characteristics of the market in which the aid is granted. To identify the markets that may have been affected by the aid, the tools developed in antitrust and merger control can be used. The characteristics of the aid beneficiary will also influence the markets that need to be considered for the competitive assessment. For example, if the aid beneficiary is a multi-product firm that can cross-subsidise its activities, it may be necessary to take into account a number of different markets in which the firm operates, irrespective of whether the aid is targeted at a specific activity.

To identify the boundaries of the markets where the impact of the aid is likely to be greater, the geographic and product markets may need to be defined, as explained in Box 8.2.

2. In theory, companies set prices with reference to their marginal or variable costs, not fixed costs.
3. A direct grant is an unconditional and unrepayable grant. In contrast, a repayable advance (including interest) would need to be paid back to the national authority if the project is successful.

Box 8.2: Overview of the approach to defining the relevant geographic and product markets

Geographic market: The area where conditions of competition between firms are sufficiently homogeneous and can be distinguished from neighbouring areas.

It is important that the impact of the aid is not considered within too narrow a geographic market. In particular, supply-side geographic market factors, such as the extent of imports/exports from/to other regions, should be taken into account when assessing whether a geographic market is sufficiently large to reflect the potential adverse effects of the aid on competition.

Product market: The product market comprises those products and/or services that are interchangeable or substitutable by the consumer, on the basis of the products' or services' characteristics, price and intended use.

The product market can be identified by looking at how consumers respond to an increase in the price of one product (i.e., demand-side substitutability). This assessment may draw on information about the product's characteristics, prices and sales over time, as well as the customers' response to price changes.

In State aid cases, it is also often important that the product market definition reflects the response of suppliers to changes in price (i.e., supply-side substitution). For example, it may need to be considered whether, as a result of the aid, suppliers in otherwise unrelated markets might switch their means of production to serve the market in question.

Source: Oxera (2017), p. 7.

Market definition provides a reference framework for assessing the impact of the aid. It can involve the use of standard economic tools, drawing on merger control and the assessment of anticompetitive practices.[4] However, the emphasis of the market definition exercise in State aid assessments may differ slightly from the standard exercise, in the following two main areas.

First, market definition may need to focus more on the supply side. In merger control and antitrust, the theories of harm may relate to both the supply side and the demand side. On the demand side, a certain conduct may affect prices directly – for example, if competition is reduced between two producers of the same good or service (i.e., in the same part of the value chain). On the supply side, interaction between buyers and sellers might affect competition – for example, if a seller forecloses access to inputs or a buyer forecloses access to customers. By contrast, in State aid cases, demand-side effects are often the reason for the government intervention, to ensure that a certain product or service is offered at a desired price or quality that differs from the level that would exist in an environment without the aid. Therefore, the State aid assessment may need to focus more on identifying possible competitive distortions on the supply side.

4. For further details, *see* European Commission (1997).

Second, market definition may need to focus more on the medium/long run. It is possible that an aid could marginally benefit consumers in the short term, but have a more significant effect in the longer term (e.g., aid to research projects). Therefore, the market definition exercise in State aid assessments may need to focus more on the long-run effects of the aid.

It should be noted that this first step of the analysis can be used to filter the State aid cases for which an analysis of the impact of the aid is necessary. For example, it may not always be useful to undertake a detailed assessment of the relevant geographic and product markets, if the aid granted is small relative to the size of the affected market(s). In this case, the aid is unlikely to have an appreciable effect on competition.

[2] Step 2: What Are the Potential Distortions of Competition?

The second step is to identify the potential distortions of competition resulting from the aid. This involves: (i) defining the counterfactual scenario; (ii) identifying the hypotheses to be tested to determine the potential effects of the aid; and (iii) choosing the indicators to be used to measure the impact of the aid on competition.

[a] The Counterfactual Scenario

The counterfactual scenario describes what would have happened in the absence of the aid. The impact of the aid corresponds to the difference between the situation that occurred following the aid and the counterfactual scenario. To construct this counterfactual scenario, it is necessary to identify appropriate comparators or a 'control group' against which to assess the current situation. This control group consists of a group of the most comparable firms that have not received aid.[5]

The European Commission (2014c) guidelines specify the factors to be considered in order to define an appropriate control group:

- The potential for firms that receive aid to be in a different situation from those that do not receive aid, including potential selection biases between firms applying and not applying for aid.
- The common factors that explain companies' performance, such as general trends in the industry.
- The potential for firms to receive aid from multiple sources.[6]

Once the counterfactual is defined, the current situation can be compared with what would have happened in the absence of the aid. This enables the competitive distortions that the aid might create to be identified, and, consequently, the hypotheses to be tested in order to assess the impact of the aid on competition.

5. *See* European Commission (2014c), section 3.4.
6. For further details, *see* European Commission (2014c), pp. 8-10.

[b] Testable Hypotheses

To evaluate State aid schemes, the European Commission (2014c, p. 6) requests an evaluation plan at the notification stage. Among other aspects, the plan is required to specify the hypotheses to be tested to examine the impact of the aid on competition. The evaluation plan can thus be a useful starting point for the ex post assessment. However, the ex post evaluation should consider market developments since then, as the hypotheses to be tested and the appropriate counterfactual might have changed due to these subsequent market developments. For example, in the airport case study presented in section 8.03, the closure of Plymouth airport could not have been predicted at the time of the notification of the aid in 2007. However, it is interesting in the ex post evaluation to consider this development and to investigate whether this closure was due to the aid or to other factors, such as the financial crisis.

The testable hypotheses that are developed should be closely linked to the other common assessment principles required for the ex post evaluation, as outlined below:

- **The incentive effects of the aid**: the testable hypotheses developed to assess the competitive effects of the aid should be informed by the assessment of the incentive effects of the aid.
- **The assessments of market failures**: if aid is granted in the absence of a clearly established market failure, it will be more likely to distort competition since the subsidised output is more likely to displace the output of firms not receiving the aid.
- **The proportionality of aid**: if the amount of aid received by the recipient has exceeded the net costs of providing the aided service (plus a 'reasonable' profit), competition is more likely to be distorted because the aid beneficiary could use the additional funds to support its other activities.

[c] Key Competition Indicators

To measure the impact of aid on competition, a number of indicators can be used, including 'structural' indicators of competition, such as the number of firms in the industry, their market shares and the degree of concentration. For instance, the market share of the aid recipient(s) matters since it affects whether the recipient is likely to influence market outcomes. A small, capacity-constrained company that expands output because it has benefitted from aid may well remain below the threshold at which it has the power to behave independently of competitive pressures. On the other hand, if the affected market is concentrated and the aid recipient is a major player, competitors are more likely to alter their strategies in response to the aid. This may reduce the efficiency of the market. It could also result in the exit of competitors, further increasing the market share of the recipient and enhancing the scope for anticompetitive behaviour.

However, there are drawbacks in using solely market structure indicators to assess the impact of aid on competition, as market structure on its own does not always provide the full picture for analysing competition. Therefore, it is also important to consider a number of indicators that capture market outcomes (e.g., prices, volumes and quality) and market dynamics (e.g., innovation, market entry and exit, and barriers to switching). These indicators capture the interaction between competitors, firms' profitability and the evolution of market dynamics.

[3] Step 3: What Is the Actual Impact of the Aid on Competition?

The final step in the assessment is to compare the counterfactual with actual data in order to evaluate the impact of State aid on competition. This subsection discusses data collection and reviews the main analytical techniques used.

[a] Data Collection

The European Commission (2014c, p. 31) guidelines highlight the importance of the data collection process, emphasising that data must be consistent between beneficiaries and non-beneficiaries, and that it should be obtained at the most detailed level possible. Building on these guidelines, the data required for ex post evaluation should ideally be quantitative, and obtained from a combination of publicly available sources and data requests to market participants. The most useful public domain data sources are likely to include databases from national statistics offices and regulators, market studies, analysts' reports, as well as financial database packages such as Bloomberg, Datastream and Orbis. Insights may also be obtained from qualitative sources, such as interviews with key market participants.

Information should be collected over a sufficiently long time period, both before and after the aid was granted, in order to enable identification of the medium- to long-term impacts of the aid. A longer time period may be necessary in some cases, e.g., for the ex post evaluation of aid measures in industries characterised by a high level of research and development.

However, data may sometimes be difficult to obtain, particularly if the ex post assessment is conducted by independent third parties with no official powers to request data. If there are difficulties in obtaining sufficient quantitative data, depending on the hypotheses to be tested, a significant part of the assessment could be based on qualitative insights and descriptive analysis. The assessment may not necessarily require sophisticated techniques such as econometric analysis, but if the data is available, econometric analysis can add further insight.

[b] Comparing the Counterfactual with Actual Data

The simplest approach to assessing the competitive impact is to assess the evolution of key variables of interest (such as the evolution of the number of passengers across different airports). This involves plotting time series on a graph and identifying any abrupt changes in trends when the aid is introduced. Identifying breaks that are contemporaneous to the granting of the aid may sometimes be sufficient to identify the impact on competition. This approach is appropriate if there is only one effect that can account for any breaks in the trend, or if any alternative effects are likely to be negligible. If several effects that can influence competition occur at the same time, such a descriptive analysis will not be conclusive.

Therefore, if sufficient data is available, it is preferable to use the techniques outlined in Box 8.3 to determine the competitive impact of the aid and to disentangle the impact of alternative explanations.

Box 8.3: Techniques to assess the competitive impact of the aid

Comparator-based approaches

Three broad approaches, i.e., cross-sectional or time-series comparisons, Difference-in-Differences models and market structure models, can be applied to estimate the impact of the aid on competition.

Cross-sectional comparisons: Comparing different geographic or product markets. A cross-sectional analysis uses data on a comparator market that was not affected by the aid, and compares the outcomes between the market affected by the aid and the market not affected. A market is an appropriate comparator if it is subject to the same dynamics as the market affected by the aid.

Time-series comparisons: Analysing prices before, during and after the granting of aid. The assumption here is that the competitive condition in the market before the aid was granted can be used to approximate the counterfactual. This assumption is common in ex ante merger assessments, where pre-merger conditions are typically taken as the baseline. However, in ex post evaluations of aid, such an assumption may not always be appropriate since other factors, such as the stage of the economic cycle and policy changes, could lead to a difference between the before and the after comparison. If such factors are likely to be present, they should be taken into account in the estimation approach. This can be done by formulating a model that includes all relevant factors leading to changes in competition, and using econometric techniques to estimate the relationship between the aid and competition. For example, econometric analysis could be undertaken to explain the evolution of firms' market shares, with independent variables including the sector, form and type of aid, and control variables such as the firm's profitability and the stage of the economic cycle. This type of before-and-after econometric analysis is common in cartel damages cases where the amount of overcharge is estimated by comparing the pre- or post-cartel price with the price during the cartel, controlling for other factors (*see, e.g.*, Oxera, Komninos et al., 2009).

Combining the above techniques in Difference-in-Differences models: Analysing the change in price or volumes over the period of the aid, and comparing this analysis against the change in price or volumes over the same time period, but in the absence of the aid, i.e., against a market not affected by the aid. The Difference-in-Differences technique aims to overcome some of the shortcomings of cross-sectional and time-series techniques (i.e., the assumption that any unexplained difference is due solely to the impact of the aid). Difference-in-Differences estimators control for what would have happened in the absence of the aid. They do so by examining what changed over time in the aided and non-aided markets, followed by a comparison of those differences.

Market structure approaches

Models developed from the industrial organisation strand of economics are used to simulate what the market would have been like without the aid, based on actual data. The estimated impact of the aid on competition will be influenced largely by the choice of the counterfactual model. Therefore, it is important to undertake sensitivity checks on the assumptions underlying the counterfactual model.

§8.03 CONTEXT BEHIND THE AID TO NEWQUAY AIRPORT

The analytical framework described above has been applied to assess the impact on competition of the State aid received by Newquay Airport in the UK. In this section, we first describe the State aid rules in the aviation sector as applied by the European Commission in its assessment of the aid and the changes made to these rules later on. This description is followed by a short overview of the aid given to Newquay Airport and the relevant decisions by the European Commission.

[A] State Aid Rules in the Aviation Sector

The aid provided by the UK government to Newquay Airport was approved by the European Commission in 2007. At this time, the European Commission's (2005) aviation State aid guidelines were applicable. The 2005 guidelines specified that the impact of aid on competition should be evaluated case by case, depending on the markets in question. However, they presumed that small regional airports (i.e., those of a similar size to Newquay) did not generally compete with other airports, and therefore funding provided by the State to such airports was unlikely to significantly distort competition or trade (*see* paragraph 39). The one exception to this presumption was the possibility that the funding of such airports affect neighbouring airports of a similar size and with overlapping markets.[7]

In 2014, a number of changes were made to the aviation guidelines (as summarised in Box 8.4 below). These new rules aimed to ensure that airports located in regions with genuine transport needs get access to the public funding required while also maintaining a level playing field for airports and airlines irrespective of their

7. The 2005 guidelines refer to research that shows that small airports do not generally compete with other airports except, in some cases, with neighbouring airports of a similar size whose markets overlap. *See* para. 11.

business models. These changes led to a more formal requirement to evaluate the impact of aid on competition. In particular, the 2014 guidelines introduced a definition of the catchment area as 100 km or 1 hour's drive time by car, bus, train or high-speed rail (*see* European Commission, 2014b, paragraph 12). The guidelines acknowledged that the definition of the catchment area varies from airport to airport, and depends on the airport's characteristics, including its business model, location and destinations served.

Box 8.4: The European Commission's 2014 aviation State aid guidelines

The 2014 guidelines were introduced at a time of significant changes to market conditions with the emergence of the low-cost airline business model and increasing congestion at hub airports. The guidelines introduced four main changes.

Greater guidance for ensuring the compatibility of investment aid. The 2005 guidelines did not make any distinction for financing needs according to airport size. In contrast, the 2014 guidelines defined the maximum amount of aid allowed based on airport size, and required potential aid beneficiaries to identify the likely impact of the aid on traffic at other airports and other means of transport within the catchment area. As noted above, the 2014 aviation guidelines also defined the catchment area.

Transition period for operating aid. In contrast to the 2005 guidelines, the 2014 guidelines allowed airports with fewer than 3 million passengers per annum to receive operating aid during a ten-year transitional period, after which the airport was no longer allowed to receive operating aid.

Simplified rules for start-up aid. The 2014 guidelines simplified the conditions for start-up aid to airlines, with all airlines eligible to receive aid covering 50% of airport charges for new destinations over a three-year period.

Guidance for the 'Market Economy Operator Principle' (MEOP) assessment of airport-airline agreements. The 2014 guidelines emphasised that arrangements between airports and airlines are free of State aid when a private investor, operating under normal market conditions, would have accepted such terms (under the so-called MEOP). In the aviation sector, this is normally assessed through an ex ante analysis that considers whether the airport/airline arrangement is expected to lead to a positive incremental profit contribution for the airport.

Source: Oxera, based on European Commission (2014a, 2014b).

[B] Overview of the Aid Received by Newquay Airport

Newquay Airport received GBP 46.8 million of aid for infrastructure investments from the UK government. The aid funded expenditures on runway and taxiway maintenance, airfield security and safety, Civil Aviation Authority (CAA) licence compliance requirements (including a new control tower, fire station, taxiway upgrades and upgrades of utility services), as well as the purchase of land from the RAF and extensions to the airport's capacity.

The aid was provided in annual instalments over the 2006-2011 period. The primary aim of the aid was to ensure the commercial viability of Newquay Airport and enable the continuation of airfield services after the departure of the Royal Air Force (RAF) in 2008. From the perspective of the UK authorities, the objective was to improve connectivity and regional development in a relatively remote area of the UK.

In 2006, Newquay Airport handled 360,000 passengers and was therefore classified as a 'small regional airport' (European Commission, 2007, paragraph 5). The aid aimed to achieve the airport's transition from a partly military to a fully civilian airport, and to increase the passenger capacity at the airport such that it could progress towards long-term commercial sustainability (paragraph 3). In particular, the aim of the aid provided by the UK government was to increase the number of passengers at Newquay Airport to 800,000 by 2011 and to above 1.2 million passengers per annum after the expected opening of a new airport terminal in 2011, to break even by 2013-2014, and thereafter to ensure long-term commercial viability (paragraph 10).

[C] The European Commission's Decisions

In 2007, the European Commission concluded that the aid was compatible based on the 2005 aviation State aid guidelines (European Commission, 2007, paragraph 5). Following changes to the original investment plan, including an increase in the investment amount and in the level of contribution from public sources, the aid was notified again and approved once more by the European Commission in 2009. Based on the evidence submitted by the UK government, the European Commission (2009) concluded that the aid was unlikely to distort competition.

As outlined further below, the UK government argued that Newquay Airport did not compete with the three commercial airports located closest to it (Plymouth, Exeter and Bristol), as its catchment area would be almost exclusively within the county of Cornwall:

- The airport closest to Newquay Airport was Plymouth Airport.[8] According to the UK government, Plymouth Airport's main route at the time of the granting of the aid was to London Gatwick, which was operated as a joint service with Newquay. The airline serving the route, Air Southwest, flew from London Gatwick to Plymouth and then to Newquay before returning to London

8. Plymouth Airport closed in 2011. For details, *see* BBC (2011).

Gatwick. As a result, the UK government concluded that Newquay did not compete with Plymouth.

- Exeter International Airport, which is the second-closest airport to Newquay Airport, is approximately 1.5 hours by road from Newquay. According to the UK government, the traffic at Exeter International is predominantly outbound originating from Devon and Somerset, and only a small proportion of the airport's total traffic originates from, or has a destination in, Cornwall. Therefore, the UK authorities argued that there was limited overlap between the catchment areas of Exeter and Newquay airports.
- The UK government argued that Bristol Airport could not be considered as competing with Newquay since it was more than three hours away by road.

According to the UK government, Newquay would be used predominantly for inbound flights. In this respect it was different from Plymouth, Exeter and Bristol airports, which had strong outbound traffic. Only 40% of Newquay's passengers lived in Cornwall and departed on their outbound journey from Cornwall. However, the UK government did acknowledge that there was some scope for competition between Newquay Airport and the neighbouring airports in relation to outbound traffic (European Commission, 2007, paragraph 68).

Although First Great Western operates a train service from London Paddington station to Newquay station, the European Commission concluded that rail would be unlikely to constitute a competitive alternative to air transport since the journey takes approximately five hours. Based on this evidence, the Commission concluded in its Decision that 'there are no comparable competing transport systems to the region which Newquay services' (European Commission, 2007, paragraph 67).

Given the absence of geographically close competing airports and the absence of alternative high-speed means of travel, the aid was considered unlikely to significantly distort competition, based on the evidence submitted by the UK government (European Commission, 2007, paragraph 69). However, the UK government's arguments were not confirmed on an ex post basis. Moreover, some of the airports in the catchment area at the time, such as Plymouth Airport, were operating below capacity at the time that the aid to Newquay was approved.[9]

§8.04 EMPIRICAL ANALYSIS OF THE IMPACT OF AID TO NEWQUAY AIRPORT ON COMPETITION

This section presents the objectives of the empirical analysis, defines the characteristics of the aid to Newquay Airport and the markets affected by the aid, and describes the methodology adopted for the ex post assessment of the impact of the aid to Newquay Airport on competition.

9. Based on data from the UK CAA, passenger traffic at Plymouth Airport was 30% lower in 2006 than in 2005. For further details, *see also* Western Morning News (2007) and Evening Herald (2007).

[A] Objectives of the Empirical Analysis

An empirical analysis was undertaken to assess whether the aid received by Newquay Airport did indeed not have a significant impact on competition, as expected by the UK government and the European Commission.[10] A number of hypotheses were tested, including that aid to Newquay Airport:

- led to a decline in traffic on those routes that were also served by neighbouring airports (i.e., 'overlapping routes');
- had a significant impact on overall passenger traffic at neighbouring airports;
- led to changes in airlines based, capacity, and the number of routes, at neighbouring airports;
- led competing airports to charge lower net fees to airlines due to greater competition.

For this assessment, the analytical framework outlined above in section 8.02 was followed. Specifically, to test the above hypotheses, it is important: (i) to analyse the main characteristics of the aid and to identify the market(s) in which Newquay operates; (ii) to isolate the impact of the aid by defining what would have happened in the absence of the aid (i.e., in the counterfactual scenario); and (iii) to assess the actual effects of the aid on competition. These different elements are presented in the next subsections.

[B] Characteristics of the Aid and Markets Affected

This subsection applies the first step of the analytical framework defined in section 8.02.

[1] Main Characteristics of the Aid

The first step in the analytical framework consists of analysing the main characteristics of the aid in order to check whether the aid is likely to create distortions of competition. First, the aid to Newquay Airport represented a significant proportion of the revenues/assets of the airports in the neighbouring region in South West England, which is a first indication that the aid could have created a distortion of competition. Second, the aid was granted on a yearly basis affecting markets where entry represented a key driving force of competition. In fact, the aid that enabled Newquay Airport to continue its commercial operations led to the opening of new routes that competed with existing routes. Granting aid on a rolling basis in markets characterised by a degree of entry and exit is more likely to confer a competitive advantage to incumbent companies over potential entrants. In such cases, it is expected that the aid will have a

10. For details, *see* Oxera (2017), section 3.

greater impact on competition than in cases where the aid is provided only at one point in time.

In conclusion, the characteristics of the aid to Newquay Airport, in terms of the amount and frequency, are such that it has the potential to have a negative impact on competition. Therefore, a more detailed analysis of this impact is warranted.

[2] Definition of the Market Affected by the Aid

In economics terms, an airport acts as a platform, serving two separate customer groups on two sides of the market: passengers and airlines. To define the relevant markets, both types of customers need to be considered. On this basis, in order to define the market(s) in which Newquay operates, both the product and the geographic dimensions are taken into account.

[a] Product Market Dimension

The relevant market is likely to differ for various segments within the two customer groups, as they may respond differently to changes in price. Passenger segments are usually defined according to: (i) the purpose of the journey (i.e., leisure or business); (ii) long-haul or short-haul flights; (iii) charter or scheduled flights; and (iv) whether passengers are in transit or flying point to point. Newquay Airport mostly serves domestic, leisure and short-haul passengers, who typically fly point to point in the summer season. Based on discussions with various airports and airlines in the catchment area, the majority of the passengers are domestic leisure passengers visiting the local area.

The airlines operating at Newquay Airport – Flybe, Aer Lingus, Ryanair, Eurowings and Isles of Scilly Skybus – are all considered low-cost carriers, and mainly operate short-haul and point-to-point flights within Europe. Ryanair was unable to operate from either Plymouth or Exeter airports, as the runway was too short to accommodate its Boeing 737-800 aircraft. Thus, for large commercial carriers, Plymouth and Exeter airports may not be within the same product market as Newquay (Oxera, 2017, p. 21). However, for low-cost carriers and regional airlines that operate smaller aircraft, a number of regional airports may be substitutable from a product market perspective.

Aid to Newquay is unlikely to have affected other modes of transport. In particular, only a limited number of routes to/from Newquay face competition from other modes of transport, namely the routes to Plymouth and Land's End. The majority of journeys using alternative modes of transport to/from Newquay take significantly longer than by air. Therefore, these alternative forms of transport are unlikely to be affected by aid to Newquay.

[b] Geographic Market Dimension

To assess the geographic market, the ability and willingness of passengers and airlines to substitute Newquay Airport for other airports were considered. A significant proportion of Newquay's passengers are tourists visiting Cornwall. These visitors are unlikely to consider other destinations either within or outside the UK to be substitutable. Similarly, passengers flying from Newquay are unlikely to consider more than a few close airports to represent viable alternatives. For these passengers, Newquay might be in competition with other small regional airports in the same catchment area.

The analysis of the potential effects of aid to Newquay on competition therefore focuses on airports within Newquay's surrounding area. This approach is consistent with the European Commission's approach to merger assessments, where the relevant market for scheduled flights is typically defined according to origin/point of destination city-pairs. According to the European Commission (2013, paragraph 50), passengers do not consider different city-pairs to be substitutable.

To analyse which airports fall within the same geographic market, catchment area and isochrone analyses are typically used, taking into account the size, density and wealth of the local population, as well as the type and size of business in the area (European Commission, 2009, paragraph 12). The size of the airport's catchment area is likely to depend on the type of passengers at the airport. For example, in comparison to holidaymakers, business passengers are likely to be less price-sensitive and more time-sensitive, implying that the catchment area for such passengers would be smaller. Similarly, passengers flying long-haul may be willing to travel further to reach their origin airport than those flying to a nearby destination, as travelling up to an hour further to the airport is a relatively smaller increase in overall travel time for long-haul passengers than for short-haul passengers.

Table 8.1 outlines the distance from Newquay Airport to the airports in the neighbouring region. Plymouth Airport, which closed in 2011, was approximately one-hour's drive time and 75 km from Newquay Airport, while Exeter Airport was within a 1.5-hour drive time and located at 130 km.

Table 8.1 Distance from Newquay Airport to Airports in the Neighbouring Regions

Airport	*Distance (km)*	*Drive Time (hours)*
Plymouth	75	1.1
Exeter	130	1.5
Bristol	230	2.5
Bournemouth	258	3.3
Southampton	307	4.0

Source: Oxera, based on Google Maps.

As highlighted above, the catchment areas of Newquay and Exeter airports, as well as Newquay and Plymouth airports, overlap to an extent. Figures 8.2 and 8.3 illustrate a one-hour drive time around Newquay and Plymouth, as well as Newquay and Exeter, which highlights the overlap in the catchment areas.

Figure 8.2 *One-Hour Drive Time Around Newquay and Plymouth Airports*

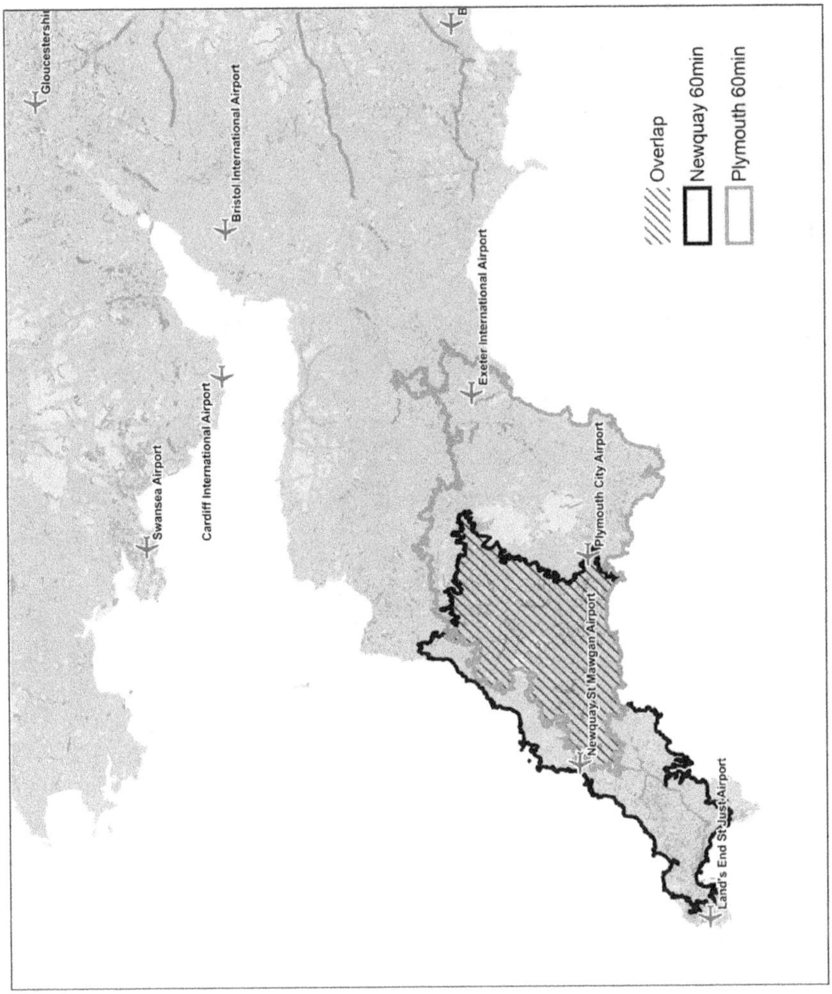

Source: Oxera analysis, based on MapInfo.

Figure 8.3 One-Hour Drive Time Around Newquay and Exeter Airports

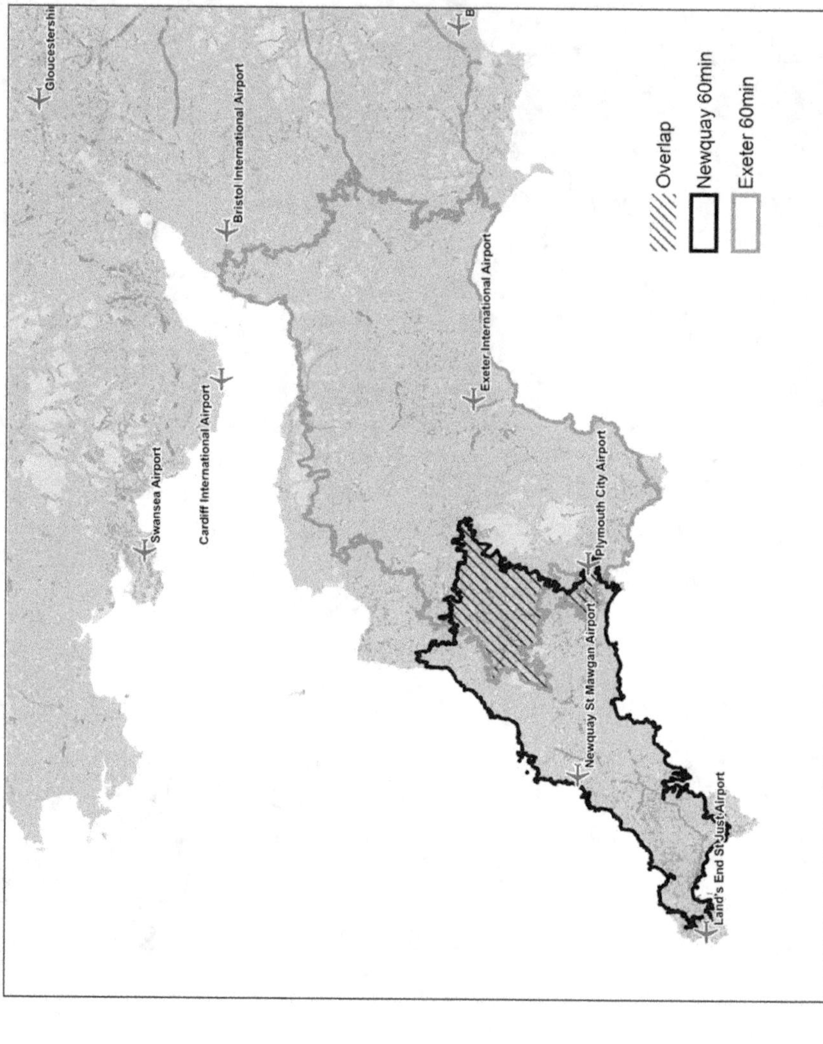

Source: Oxera analysis, based on MapInfo.

In terms of geographic scope, Newquay, Exeter and Plymouth airports (before its closure) are considered to represent the relevant market, for the reasons outlined above. Although the market could potentially be wider from the airlines' perspective, any impact of aid to Newquay on other airports is unlikely to be significant. However, to ensure the comprehensiveness of the analysis, it was also examined whether aid to Newquay Airport adversely affected Bristol Airport.

[C] Empirical Strategy

This subsection gives an overview of the three different methodologies used to assess the impact of the State aid to Newquay Airport on competition, i.e., interviews, descriptive analysis and econometric analysis (namely, Difference-in-Differences estimations based on a dynamic panel data model). Thereafter, it presents in more detail the identification strategy and the control group used in the econometric analysis.

[1] Broad Overview of the Methodologies Used

The empirical analysis is based on a combination of interviews with market participants, a descriptive analysis, as well as a quantitative analysis aimed at isolating the impact of aid to Newquay Airport from other factors that occurred at the same time, such as the global financial crisis.

Interviews were undertaken with airports in the region neighbouring Newquay Airport, as well as with the airlines operating at Newquay Airport and the surrounding airports. The interviews explored the definition of the catchment area, the awareness of Newquay Airport being granted aid, and any changes in strategy following the aid being received by Newquay Airport. The interviewees were also asked for data to complement the qualitative insights obtained from the interviews. Specifically, airports were asked to provide data on aeronautical charges, capacity investments and marketing expenditure, while airlines were asked to provide data on yields and profits per route.

To assess the impact of the aid, a descriptive analysis was undertaken, alongside a more sophisticated econometric analysis. The descriptive analysis examined the trends before the aid was granted to Newquay Airport in 2006 and after the aid was granted. Any noticeable changes in the data patterns that cannot be explained by other factors may indicate the impact of the aid. The econometric analysis was based on a dynamic panel data model to enable the impact of the aid to be isolated from other factors that occurred at the same time.

Dynamic panel data models have three main advantages over descriptive analyses. The models enable:

- the level of traffic that would have been likely in the absence of the aid to Newquay to be estimated (i.e., the counterfactual level of traffic);

- a robust quantification of the impact of the aid to Newquay, making a clear distinction from the impact of wider market developments, such as the global financial crisis;
- the joint estimation of the impact of the aid to Newquay across a number of routes, with controls for route-specific factors, as well as wider market developments that might have affected passenger traffic on those routes.

[2] Identification Strategy

To understand the potential impact of the State aid to Newquay Airport, the competitive landscape at the time when the aid was provided needs to be compared with what would have happened if the aid had not been granted (i.e., the counterfactual).

Before the aid to expand Newquay Airport's commercial passenger services was granted, the RAF provided airfield services at Newquay. Following the departure of the RAF, the airport needed to secure a licence from the CAA in the UK to continue to operate airfield services, which was a considerable investment.

As the airport was loss-making at the time and not expected to be able to generate sufficient cash flows in the near future, it was unlikely that the airport would have been able to afford its operating licence without government support (Oxera, 2017, p. 19). Furthermore, discussions with Newquay Airport during the course of the evaluation indicated that commercial operations at the airport would have ceased without the aid, and therefore Newquay Airport would have closed if it had not received the aid. In the absence of the aid to Newquay, it is assumed that Plymouth Airport would have continued its operations, whereas, in reality, the airport closed in 2011.[11]

A dynamic panel data model enabled the impact of the aid to be isolated from other market developments. The effect of the aid was measured as the difference in passenger traffic between routes that had the potential to be affected by the aid to Newquay Airport (the treatment group) and routes at those airports that were unlikely to have been affected by the aid (the control group). As illustrated in Box 8.5, passenger traffic is modelled over time for each route, assuming that past passenger numbers represent a good predictor of future levels. Seasonal fluctuations and wider industry trends, such as the impact of the global financial crisis, are captured by fixed time effects that are calibrated based on the routes in the control group.

The counterfactual scenario that implicitly underlies the dynamic panel data model is that, in the absence of the aid, Newquay Airport would have operated at a low level of traffic similar to the period before the aid, and that passenger traffic on routes to/from Newquay Airport would have developed in line with wider industry trends. The more appropriate assumption that Newquay Airport would have ceased its

11. Detailed data on Plymouth Airport's cost structure was not available to allow a robust assessment of whether the aid to Newquay contributed towards the closure of Plymouth Airport. If the necessary data had been available, it would have been important to assess whether the counterfactual level of traffic would have enabled Plymouth Airport to achieve a financially sustainable position in order to continue operations.

commercial operations in the absence of aid cannot be modelled directly in the panel data econometric analysis. Therefore, the results from the panel data models may underestimate the competitive distortions due to the aid, as the impact of the aid compared to the counterfactual where Newquay Airport would have closed would have been expected to be larger.

Box 8.5: Specification of the dynamic panel data model

The following panel data model has been estimated over the 2001-2016 period to capture trends both before and after the aid to Newquay Airport:

$$Y_{it} = \alpha_i + \delta_t + \beta Y_{it-1} + \gamma Aid_{it} + \varepsilon_{it}$$

where

Y_{it} is the number of passengers in month t for each route (i.e., route i);

α_i is a fixed route effect that captures systematic differences in passenger traffic for route i from traffic on other routes;

δ_t is a fixed time effect for month t that captures seasonality and general trends in the aviation industry across time;

Y_{it-1} is the actual number of passengers on the route in the previous month, such that β represents the lagged effect of passenger traffic in the previous month on traffic in month t;

Aid_{it} is a dummy variable that takes the value 1 if route i was potentially affected by the aid in time t. The dummy variable takes on the value 0 for all routes in the control group and all observations before January 2007, i.e., before the aid to Newquay Airport;

γ represents the short-run impact of the aid in the first month after the aid, i.e., January 2007;

$\gamma / 1 - \beta$ represents the long-run monthly impact of the aid;

ε_{it} is a route- and time-specific residual term.

This model is a Difference-in-Differences model, similar to the one developed by Stock and Watson (2007, Appendix 13.2, p. 517). The route fixed effects control for intrinsic differences between routes that are unobserved and affect the number of passengers. The fixed time effects control for differences from one period to the next, irrespective of whether aid was received. The Aid_{it} dummy variable measures the 'treatment effect', i.e., the effect of receiving the aid.

Notes: The dynamic panel data model has been estimated based on monthly route-level passenger data over 2001-2016. On average, the dataset contains fifty-five observations per route.

Source: Oxera.

[3] The Control Group

The control group should reflect the same trends and shocks over time as those faced by the treatment group, while being not affected by the aid to Newquay Airport. The treatment group is made up of routes being affected by the aid and includes specific routes from Plymouth, Exeter and Bristol airports.[12] As explained in section 8.05, the specific routes included in the treatment group may vary depending on the effects to be estimated.

The control group consists of 194 routes from Bournemouth and Southampton airports. These routes serve as a benchmark for the evolution of passenger traffic at airports that are unlikely to have been affected by the aid, given that both Bournemouth and Southampton are located more than three hours away from Newquay. However, as regional airports in the south of England, it is likely that Southampton and Bournemouth airports are affected by trends and seasonal fluctuations in passenger traffic similar to those experienced by Newquay Airport and the airports in the treatment group (namely, Plymouth, Exeter and Bristol airports). For example, it is plausible that Southampton and Bournemouth airports would have been affected by the financial crisis to the same extent as Newquay and the airports in the treatment group. Therefore, the comparison with the development of traffic at the control group of airports enables the effects of the aid to be robustly estimated separately from the impact of market-wide factors, such as the global financial crisis.

Figure 8.4 compares the evolution of passenger traffic between Plymouth, Exeter and Bristol airports (i.e., the treatment group) and the control group prior to the aid being received by Newquay Airport. It shows that fluctuations in passenger traffic for the treatment and control groups were broadly similar before the aid. This highlights the appropriateness of the control group, as it suggests that, in the absence of the aid, trends in traffic across the airports in the control and treatment groups are likely to have been similar. Bristol Airport has been included in the treatment group in order to check that aid to Newquay Airport has indeed not affected Bristol Airport, given the distance between Bristol and Newquay airports.

For the above reasons, it is appropriate to define the control group as Bournemouth and Southampton airports. The advantage of defining the control group narrowly is that the airports in this group are most likely to be affected by factors similar to those influencing Newquay, Plymouth, Exeter and Bristol airports.

That said, in principle a larger control group could have been identified, such as all regional airports in the UK, excluding Newquay, Bristol, Exeter and Plymouth airports. However, the disadvantage of such an approach is that, as the control group expands, the control group and treatment group of airports would be likely to differ in terms of how they react to shocks in the market, such as the granting of aid, or local factors. If the characteristics of the treatment group differ significantly from those of the control group (such as differences in journey purpose), the estimate of the impact of the aid may be biased.

12. The treatment group is defined as Plymouth, Exeter and Bristol airports.

Figure 8.4 Development of Monthly Average Passenger Numbers per Route Across the Treatment and Control Groups Before the Aid

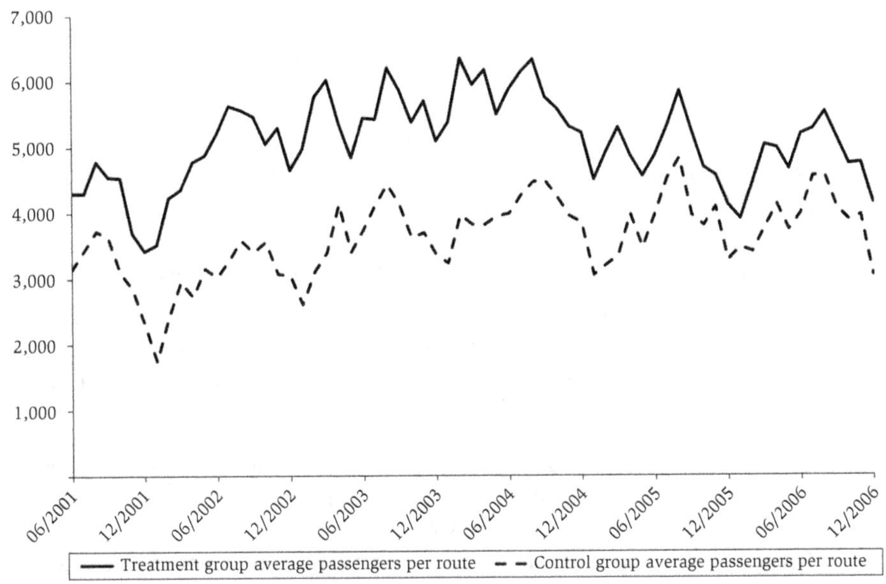

Note: Parallel trends in passenger numbers in the 2001-2006 period before the aid indicate that routes from Bournemouth and Southampton airports represent an appropriate control group.

Source: Oxera analysis, based on CAA data.

There are, however, alternative techniques that could have been used to identify the control group, such as matching techniques, which aim at pairing each beneficiary with another airport that is similar, but did not receive the aid (European Commission, 2014c, p. 20). Such matching techniques were applied to evaluate the impact of State aid schemes aimed at bringing basic broadband to rural areas in Germany (*see* Chapter 9). However, they were not used here because there were only few airports with characteristics similar to those of Newquay Airport.

§8.05 WHAT WAS THE ACTUAL IMPACT OF AID TO NEWQUAY AIRPORT ON COMPETITION?

This section presents the results of the empirical analysis using the dynamic panel data model. In those instances where the necessary detailed data is not available to allow us to conduct a quantitative analysis, information from interviews conducted with market participants are used instead to provide insights. The results are interpreted in the light of the conclusions drawn from the descriptive analysis.

[A] Did Aid to Newquay Airport Lead to a Decline in Traffic on the Overlapping Routes That Were Also Served by Neighbouring Airports?

The dynamic panel data models described above were estimated to assess the impact of the aid on specific routes from Plymouth, Exeter and Bristol airports that were also operated by Newquay Airport, including:

- Plymouth Airport's route to/from London Gatwick Airport, which represented the only route served by both Newquay and Plymouth airports prior to the aid;
- Exeter Airport's route to/from Edinburgh Airport; and
- all overlapping routes at Plymouth, Exeter and Bristol airports (i.e., all destinations from these airports that were also served by Newquay Airport).

To analyse the impact of aid to Newquay Airport on the above routes, the following dynamic panel data models were estimated, with the results reported below in Table 8.2. In all these models, the control group is the one defined in section 8.04[C][3]:

- **Model 1: Assessment of the impact of the aid on routes between Plymouth and London Gatwick**. Here, the treatment group comprised only the Plymouth route to/from London Gatwick.
- **Model 2: Assessment of the impact of the aid on routes between Exeter and Edinburgh**. The treatment group comprised the Exeter route to/from Edinburgh. Apart from the definition of the treatment group, the same model specification was adopted.
- **Model 3: Assessment of the impact of the aid on all overlapping routes at Plymouth, Exeter and Bristol airports**. This model expanded the treatment group to include all overlapping routes at Plymouth and Exeter, as well as Bristol airports.[13] The model estimated the effect of the aid on overlapping routes for each of these airports separately. As Bristol Airport is 230 km and 2.5 hours' drive time from Newquay Airport, overlapping routes at Bristol Airport were less likely to have been significantly affected by the aid to Newquay. Nevertheless, Bristol Airport was included within the analysis in order to ensure the comprehensiveness of the analysis. The treatment group therefore included all routes from Plymouth, Exeter and Bristol airports that were also served by Newquay Airport for at least one month from 2007 onwards.

As discussed below, the results show that the aid to Newquay Airport led to a significant long-term decline in traffic on overlapping routes from Plymouth to/from Gatwick and from Exeter to/from Edinburgh, as well as on all overlapping routes from both Plymouth and Exeter airports, but not Bristol Airport. The results for each of these routes are presented below, with the descriptive analysis complementing the econometric analysis.

13. Overlapping routes refer to routes to destination airports that were served by Newquay as well as Plymouth, Exeter and Bristol airports.

Table 8.2 Results of the Dynamic Panel Data Models for Overlapping Routes

	Model 1	*Model 2*	*Model 3*		
Treatment group	**Gatwick-Plymouth and Plymouth-Gatwick**	**Edinburgh-Exeter and Exeter-Edinburgh**	**All overlapping routes at Plymouth, Exeter and Bristol**		
Control group	All routes at Southampton and Bournemouth				
Treatment period	Jan 2007-Oct 2011	Jan 2007-June 2016	Jan 2007-June 2016		
Lagged effect of passenger traffic on the route in the previous month (β) (robust standard errors clustered by route in parentheses)	0.849*** (0.0207)	0.849*** (0.0206)	0.853*** (0.0149)		
			Plymouth	**Exeter**	**Bristol**
Short-run impact of the aid on passenger traffic per route each month (γ) (robust standard errors clustered by route in parentheses)	**-216.0***** (61.71)	**-356.4***** (63.37)	**-156.9***** (58.91)	**-216.3***** (74.32)	**-131.8** (191.1)
Implied long-run impact of the aid on passenger traffic per route each month $\frac{\gamma}{(1-\beta)}$	**-1,430**	**-2,360**	**-1,067**	**-1,471**	**-897**
Number of routes in the treatment group	1	1	8	24	35
Number of routes in the control group	194	194	194		
Number of observations	8,575	8,615	12,290		
Within-R-Squared	0.794	0.795	0.788		

Notes: Asterisks indicate the p-value, a measure of statistical significance, where ***, ** and * represent statistical significance at the 1%, 5% and 10% levels respectively. The short-run impact measures the marginal effect of the aid in each month. The long-run impact describes the monthly difference between the average factual and counterfactual passenger traffic after a few years. The long-run impact is calculated as the sum of short-run effects expressed as an infinite geometric series. The Appendix provides more detail on the calculation of the short-run and long-run effects.

Source: Oxera analysis, based on CAA data.

[1] Plymouth's Route to/from Gatwick

The descriptive analysis shows that passenger traffic on the Newquay route to/from Gatwick steadily increased following the capacity expansion at Newquay Airport in 2007, while that on the Plymouth route to/from Gatwick moderately declined over the same period. In particular, passenger traffic on the Newquay route doubled over the period 2006-2010, whilst passenger traffic on the Plymouth route declined by around 20% over the same period. Such a trend is consistent with Newquay potentially capturing some of the traffic that would have otherwise operated from Plymouth. However, passenger traffic at Newquay Airport did not increase in 2011 when Plymouth Airport ceased its operations. This could be due to passengers already switching from Plymouth to Newquay following the increase in the capacity of Newquay's terminal. It may also be due to the Newquay route to/from Gatwick being partly affected by the financial difficulties suffered by Air Southwest around 2010. The airline served Newquay Airport via its Gatwick-Plymouth-Newquay-Gatwick route (Department for Transport 2016, paragraph 2.116). In September 2011 the airline ceased operations.

Figure 8.5 Annual Passenger Traffic on the Newquay and Plymouth Routes to/from London Gatwick

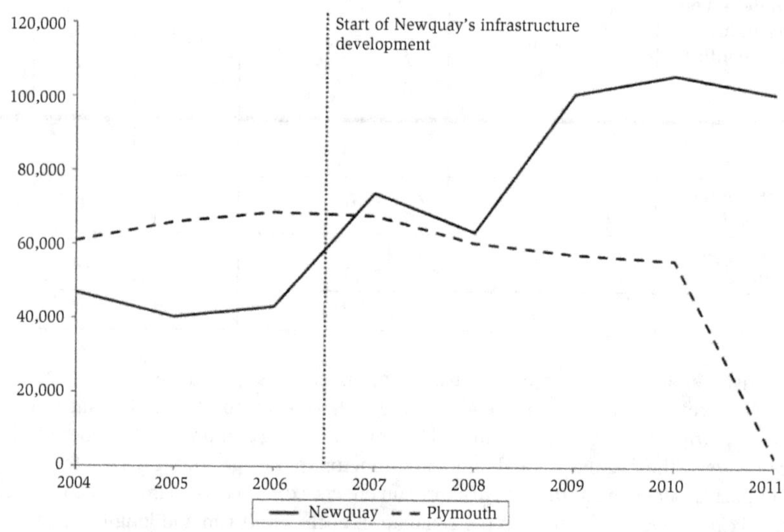

Note: Total passenger numbers include departing and arriving passengers. The figure covers the period until 2011, in light of Plymouth Airport stopping commercial operations at that time.

Source: Oxera analysis, based on CAA data.

The above trends are consistent with the hypothesis that Newquay Airport may have captured some of the traffic from Plymouth Airport following the increase in the

Newquay's terminal capacity. However, the decline in passenger traffic at Plymouth Airport could also have been due, at least partly, to the onset of the financial crisis. Therefore, econometric analysis needs to be undertaken to enable clear conclusions to be drawn about whether aid to Newquay Airport adversely affected Plymouth Airport.

The results from the dynamic panel data models presented in Table 8.2 show that the aid to Newquay Airport led to a long-term decline in passenger traffic on the Plymouth to/from London Gatwick route of around 1,430 passengers per month. This represents approximately 26% of passenger traffic on the route compared to the period prior to the aid.

[2] Exeter's Route to/from Edinburgh

The start of the Newquay-Edinburgh route appears to be associated with a decline in passenger traffic on the Exeter-Edinburgh route (*see* Figure 8.6). The evolution of traffic on the Edinburgh route is consistent with aid to Newquay Airport adversely affecting passenger traffic on that route. However, the decline might also have been partly due to the onset of the financial crisis.

Figure 8.6 Annual Passenger Traffic on the Newquay and Exeter Routes to/from Edinburgh

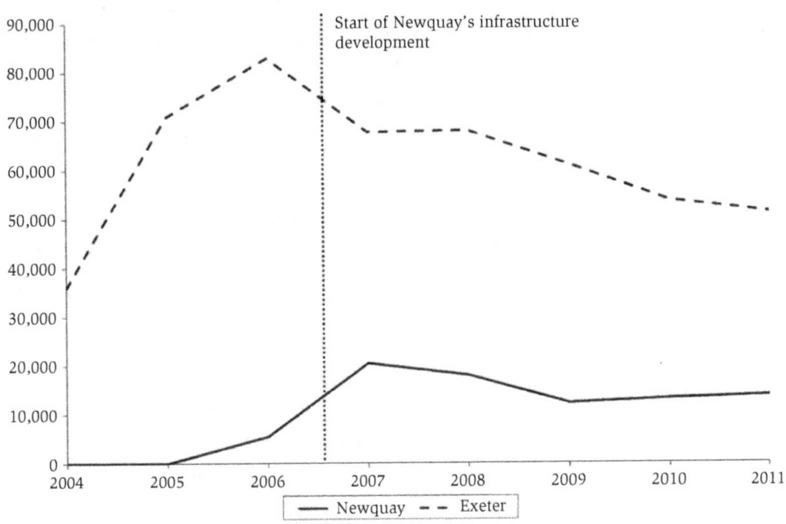

Note: Total annual passengers (including departing and arriving passengers) to Edinburgh from Newquay and Exeter airports.

Source: Oxera analysis, based on CAA data.

The results from the dynamic panel data models presented in Table 8.2 show that the aid to Newquay Airport led to approximately 2,360 fewer passengers per month on the Exeter-Edinburgh route in the long term. This represents a decline in passenger traffic of approximately 42% in the long run, all else equal.

[3] All Overlapping Routes at Plymouth, Exeter and Bristol Airports

The results from the dynamic panel data models show that the aid led to a reduction in passenger traffic across all overlapping routes at Plymouth and Exeter airports, but not at Bristol Airport, which is likely to be due to Bristol Airport being located over 230 km, around 2.5 hours' drive time, from Newquay Airport.

The overall effect on all the overlapping routes at Plymouth and Exeter airports was smaller than that observed on the individual routes between Plymouth and London Gatwick and between Exeter and Edinburgh, respectively. This result reflects the fact that the other overlapping routes at Plymouth and Exeter airports may have been less affected by the aid to Newquay than the Plymouth/Gatwick and the Exeter/Edinburgh routes.

[B] Did Aid to Newquay Airport Have a Significant Impact on Overall Levels of Passenger Traffic at Neighbouring Airports?

To assess whether the aid affected passenger traffic at neighbouring airports more generally, rather than only on overlapping routes, dynamic panel data models were estimated to quantify the impact of the aid to Newquay Airport on passenger traffic at Plymouth, Exeter and Bristol airports (*see* Table 8.3).

The results show that aid to Newquay Airport is likely to have had a significant impact on passenger traffic at Exeter and Plymouth airports, but not at Bristol Airport, as outlined below:

- **Impact of aid on Plymouth Airport**. The results suggest that aid to Newquay Airport led to an average short-term reduction of 130 passengers per route each month, amounting to 705 fewer passengers at Plymouth Airport per route each month over the long term. This represents approximately 6% of total passenger traffic per route in the period before the aid (i.e., 2004-2006).
- **Impact of aid on Exeter Airport**. The results suggest that the impact of the aid was more pronounced on Exeter Airport than Plymouth Airport. The results indicate that because of the aid to Newquay Airport monthly traffic at Exeter Airport declined by 187 passengers per route in the short-run, amounting to a long-run effect of 1,008 passengers per route. This represents approximately 9% of passenger traffic per route at Exeter Airport prior to the aid in 2004-2006.
- **Impact of aid on Bristol Airport.** The results indicate, as expected, that the aid did not have a statistically significant impact on Bristol Airport. This is likely to have been due to Bristol Airport being located 230 km, approximately 2.5 hours' drive time, from Newquay Airport, and is evidence that Newquay and Bristol airports indeed operated in different markets.

Table 8.3 Results of the Dynamic Panel Data Models for Individual Airports

Treatment group	All routes at Plymouth, Exeter and Bristol		
Control group	All routes at Southampton and Bournemouth		
Treatment period	Jan 2007-June 2016		
Lagged effect of passenger traffic on the route in the previous month (β) (robust standard errors clustered by route in parentheses)	0.815*** (0.0110)		
	Plymouth	**Exeter**	**Bristol**
Short-run impact of the aid on passenger traffic per route each month (γ) (robust standard errors clustered by route in parentheses)	-130.4** (61.28)	-186.5*** (63.32)	23.95 (80.12)
Implied long-run impact of the aid on passenger traffic per route each month $\frac{\gamma}{(1-\beta)}$	**-705**	**-1,008**	**129**
Number of routes in the treatment group	11	82	186
Number of routes in the control group	194		
Number of observations	26,229		
Within-R-Squared	0.718		

Notes: Asterisks indicate the p-value, a measure of statistical significance, where ***, ** and * represents statistical significance at the 1%, 5% and 10% levels respectively. The short-run impact measures the marginal effect of the aid in each month. The long-run impact describes the monthly difference between the average factual and counterfactual passenger traffic after a few years. The long-run impact is calculated as the sum of short-run effects expressed as an infinite geometric series. The Appendix provides more detail on the calculation of the short-run and long-run effects.

Source: Oxera analysis, based on CAA data.

Figure 8.7 shows the evolution of actual passenger traffic (i.e., the factual level of traffic) at Plymouth Airport compared with estimated traffic at Plymouth Airport in the absence of any aid to Newquay Airport (i.e., the counterfactual traffic).

Figure 8.7 Actual and Counterfactual Total Passenger Traffic at Plymouth Airport

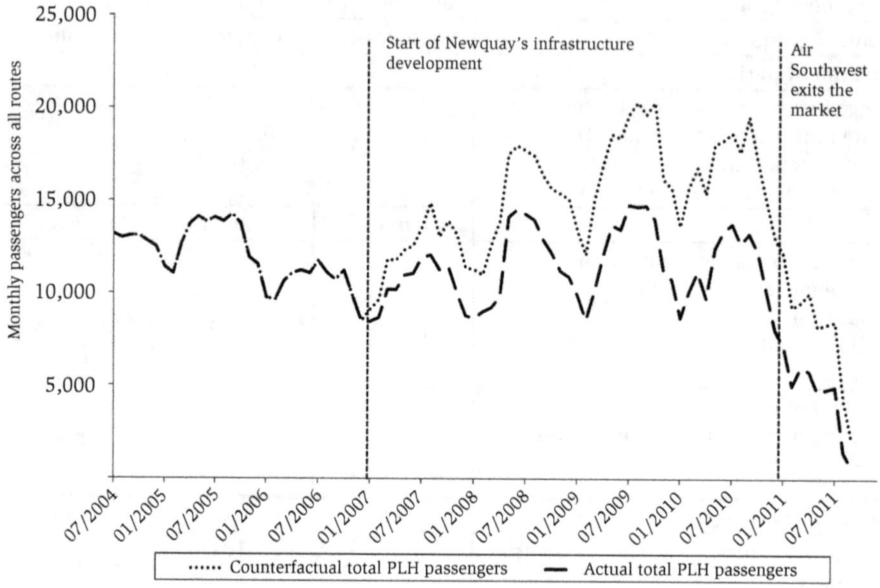

Note: Total monthly number of passengers at Plymouth Airport.

Source: Oxera analysis, based on CAA data.

In Figure 8.7, a distinction should be made between the period January 2007-January 2011 and the period following the exit of Air Southwest from the market. Over the January 2007-January 2011 period, the results from the dynamic panel model indicate that, even after controlling for market-wide factors such as the global financial crisis, Plymouth Airport is likely to have had approximately 40,000 more passengers per year in the absence of aid to Newquay Airport.[14] The data relating to Plymouth Airport's cost structure, which would be required to firmly assess whether the aid to Newquay Airport contributed towards the closure of Plymouth Airport, was not available.

Figure 8.7 also shows that traffic at Plymouth Airport declined significantly from summer 2010 onwards, which is likely to be due to the financial problems experienced by Air Southwest. In particular, Air Southwest, whose main base had been Plymouth Airport, exited the market because the level of demand for its routes was not sufficient to enable the airline to achieve financial viability. Moreover, Plymouth Airport's short runway is likely to have reduced the ability of the airport to attract other commercial airlines as it imposed restrictions on the size and type of aircraft that could operate from the airport. These factors may explain why Exeter Airport remained in operation,

14. The 40,000 additional passengers at Plymouth Airport is calculated as the average annual difference between the counterfactual level of passenger traffic at Plymouth Airport, as derived from the dynamic panel data models, and the actual level of traffic at the airport, over the period from January 2007 to January 2011.

despite the fact that the results from the dynamic panel data models show that the aid had a more pronounced effect on Exeter Airport than on Plymouth Airport.

It remains unclear whether the higher levels of passenger traffic in the absence of the aid to Newquay Airport would have enabled Plymouth Airport to continue operations after Air Southwest exited the market. Despite the factors that limited the commercial attractiveness of Plymouth Airport, the possibility that aid to Newquay contributed towards the closure of Plymouth Airport cannot be excluded.

[C] Did Aid to Newquay Airport Lead to Changes to the Airline Base, Capacity and the Number of Routes at Neighbouring Airports?

The detailed data necessary to undertake econometric analysis assessing whether aid to Newquay Airport led to changes to the airline base and airline capacity at neighbouring airports was not available. Therefore, this hypothesis was examined based on insights from the interviews with market participants.

The interviews indicated that there was no clear evidence of airlines switching entire routes to Newquay Airport following the aid, nor of airlines starting new routes from Newquay Airport instead of at the neighbouring airports. However, it cannot be ruled out that the aid led some airlines to reallocate capacity from airports neighbouring Newquay Airport.

[D] Did Aid to Newquay Airport Lead to Competing Airports Charging Lower Net Fees to Airlines due to Greater Competition?

As airlines typically negotiate the charges paid at airports, it was not possible to obtain data on charges paid by all airlines operating at Newquay Airport and the neighbouring airports.

However, one airline provided data on net charges paid by the airline at Newquay and Bristol airports. The net charges it paid remained relatively constant at Newquay Airport over the 2004-2010 period, while they increased at Bristol Airport over the 2008-2010 period. Limited insight can be drawn from this observation due to the small sample size. However, it does suggest that aid to Newquay Airport did not lead to a decrease in airline charges at the immediate neighbouring airports. This finding is consistent with insights from the interviews, as Newquay Airport considered that the aid did not have a significant impact on the airport's charges.

[E] Implications of the Results

The results show that airports are, to some extent, substitutable for at least some of the passenger traffic, and that the aid to Newquay Airport did have a significant impact on competition. These findings are consistent with the presumption in the European Commission's (2014a) aviation State aid guidelines that aid to an airport located in the catchment area of another airport that is operating below capacity (i.e., Plymouth Airport) can, under certain circumstances, have distortive effects on competition.

In addition to the factors outlined in the aviation State aid guidelines, the results indicate that the assessment of the competitive effects of the aid needs to take into account the specific circumstances of each of the airports within the neighbouring region, including the characteristics of both the airlines and the routes operated at each airport. In line with this, the results show that it is particularly important that the catchment area is defined such that it captures the specifics of the area in question.

The analysis of the impact of aid to Newquay Airport raises doubts about the effectiveness of the funding provided by the UK government, as two airports existed in the region prior to the aid (i.e., Exeter and Plymouth), and two airports existed after the aid (i.e., Exeter and Newquay). This raises questions about whether the customer benefits associated with the fact that Newquay Airport had a longer runway, and therefore could accommodate larger commercial aircraft, outweighed the costs of the aid. This question is not covered by the present analysis, which focused on the assessment of the impact of the aid on competition and did not examine whether the positive effects of the aid to Newquay Airport outweighed any potential negative effects of the aid in terms of its impact on other airports operating in the region.

§8.06 CONCLUSIONS

This chapter has proposed an analytical framework to assess the impact of State aid on competition. This framework distinguishes three main steps. The first step includes a description of the characteristics of the aid, as well as of the market in which the aid is granted. This step enables identifying those State aid cases for which a detailed analysis of the impact of the aid on competition is justified. The second step consists of defining the counterfactual: what would have happened without the aid? Finally, the third step compares the counterfactual with actual data to evaluate the impact of the aid on competition.

This framework has been applied here to assess the impact of the State aid given to Newquay Airport on competition. The analysis of the characteristics of this aid indicates that the amount of the aid given was significant in proportion of the revenues/assets of the neighbouring airports in South West England. Moreover, the aid was provided on a yearly basis over the period 2006-2011 in a market where entry represents a key driving force of competition. Based on this analysis, the chapter concluded that the aid to Newquay Airport had the potential to create distortions of competition. The product market was defined from the perspective of both airlines and passengers, including short-haul, point-to-point flights by low-cost carriers and regional airlines serving domestic leisure passengers visiting the local area. In terms of geographic scope, Newquay, Exeter and Plymouth airports (before the latter's closure) were considered to represent the relevant market because they were part of the same catchment area and thus may have been affected by the aid.

The empirical strategy was based on a combination of interviews with market participants, a descriptive analysis of market developments before and after the aid and a counterfactual impact evaluation (Difference-in-Differences) based on a dynamic panel data model. The results of this analysis show that the aid led to greater competitive distortions on neighbouring airports than anticipated at the time the aid was approved. This may be at least partly due to some airports in the neighbouring region, such as Plymouth Airport, operating below capacity at the time.

A number of lessons can be learnt from the analysis of the impact on competition resulting from the aid to Newquay Airport. First, the application of the analytical framework has shown that tools commonly used in antitrust and merger analysis can be applied to assess the impact of aid on competition. The general framework is largely similar, although it is important that the application is tailored to reflect the differences between State aid assessments and merger control and antitrust. This implies, *inter alia*, that the definition of product and geographic markets needs to focus more on the supply side and that the analysis should look more at medium- to long-term effects. Second, it is important to determine whether the aid was effective in causing behavioural change, before commencing with the assessment whether the aid had any distortive effects. Assessing the effects of aid on competition requires a prior assessment of the incentive effects of the aid. In the case of Newquay Airport, the aid created the incentive to develop it into a commercial airport.

The analysis presented in this chapter has been based on information volunteered by market participants and/or that was publicly available. This study illustrates what can be done with publicly available data. However, as highlighted in this chapter (and in more detail in the Appendix), if further data had been available, additional hypotheses could have been examined and a more in-depth assessment of the impact of the aid to Newquay Airport could have been made. As it is essential to have 'good' data to undertake a robust ex post evaluation, it is important at an early stage to identify which aid measures and schemes should be subjected to an ex post evaluation.

The analytical framework described in this chapter was applied to an individual aid measure provided to Newquay Airport. The work presented in the next chapter of this book, which analyses the effects of broadband aid schemes, shows that a framework similar to the one proposed here can also be used to assess the impact of aid schemes on competition. However, certain aspects of the assessment may be more challenging in the case of aid schemes. In particular, as a greater number of companies would have received aid, it may be more challenging to identify an appropriate counterfactual scenario in the case of an aid scheme. Matching techniques may be helpful in this respect.

In light of the growing importance of ex post evaluations in State aid control, there could be an increased role going forward for sophisticated assessments of the competitive effects of aid in State aid assessments more generally, in line with the analytical framework described in this chapter.

APPENDIX: PANEL DATA ANALYSIS

This appendix provides further details on the panel data econometric analysis described in section 8.04.

As highlighted in Box 8.6, the panel data models were defined as follows:

- The dependent variable was defined as the number of airline passengers each month, by route (by domestic and international), for all airports in the UK over the 2004-2016 period. The data was obtained from the UK CAA, and covered both scheduled and chartered traffic.
- The explanatory variables included fixed effect route effects and fixed effect time effects, the actual number of passengers on the route in the previous month and a dummy variable that took the value 1 if the route was potentially affected by the aid. In order to further improve the panel data models, additional explanatory variables could have been included on local factors/developments. This would have required the catchment area of each airport to be defined, as well as that of the destination airports, in order to identify statistics that best represent the respective areas.

The analysis was based on data that could be obtained from the public domain as well as data provided by market participants during the interviews. While efforts were made to obtain as much data as possible from market participants, there were limits on what data was available, as highlighted in Box 8.6.

Box 8.6: Data availability

The available data enabled a number of hypotheses to be tested and insights to be provided, as outlined in this chapter. However, a number of avenues were explored to obtain the following additional data so that further hypotheses could be tested.

Seat capacity and passenger numbers by airline. If data on route-level seat capacity and passenger numbers by airline had been available, this would have enabled the impact of aid to Newquay Airport on the number of available seats and load factors by route for each airline to have been examined. This analysis would have provided further insights into how airlines responded to the aid at Newquay and the extent to which airlines reallocated capacity as a result of the aid to Newquay.

Route-level profitability of airlines at Newquay and the neighbouring airports. Although this information was requested, airlines considered it too commercially sensitive to be shared outside their organisations. Data on airlines' route-level profits would have enabled an assessment to be undertaken of whether the aid to Newquay intensified competition between neighbouring airports.

Characteristics of passengers at Newquay and the neighbouring airports. Publicly available Passenger Survey reports from the CAA provide some information about passenger groups at different UK airports. However, this information was not available for Newquay or Plymouth airports, while only limited information in non-successive years was available for Exeter Airport. This information was therefore insufficient to analyse how the passenger mix might have changed at the neighbouring airports due to the aid to Newquay.

Net charges paid by airlines at Newquay and the neighbouring airports. In the course of interviews with market participants, information was requested on net charges paid by airlines at the relevant airports (i.e., charges paid by airlines less any marketing or incentive payments received by airlines). Although one airline provided information on net charges, it was not possible to obtain information on charges paid by other airlines at any of the relevant airports. While information was available about airports' published charges, as airlines typically negotiate charges with airports, the use of published charges was unlikely to yield informative results.

Plymouth Airport's cost structure. If data had been available for Plymouth Airport's cost structure, analysis could have been undertaken to assess more robustly whether, in the absence of the aid to Newquay, the counterfactual level of traffic at Plymouth would have enabled the airport to achieve a financially sustainable position in order to continue operations.

Source: Oxera.

Tables 8.2 and 8.3 show the impact of the aid to Newquay on passenger traffic on the overlapping routes, as well as on total passenger traffic, at Plymouth, Exeter and Bristol airports. The short-run impact measures the marginal effect of the aid over the subsequent month, while the long-run impact refers to the maximum monthly effect of the aid. Intuitively, the effect of the aid may accumulate over time as passengers become more aware of the additional route options to/from Newquay, and more airlines might start operating new routes to/from Newquay Airport. Box 8.7 below describes how the long-run effect has been implied from the results of the dynamic panel data models.

Box 8.7: Explanation of the short-run and long-run effects of the aid to Newquay Airport

Due to the dynamic structure of the models, the coefficient of the aid dummy γ represents the effect of the aid in the first month after the aid (the short-run effect), i.e., January 2007. The effect where $t \geq 1$, where $t = 1$ is the first month after the start of the aid, can be represented by the following equation:

$$\text{aid effect}_t = \sum_{t=1}^{T} \gamma\beta^{t-1}$$

The coefficient β represents the lagged effect of passenger traffic in the previous month on passenger traffic in month t. After a sufficient period of time following the start of the aid to Newquay, mathematically, when t reaches infinity, the long-run effect becomes: $\gamma / (1 - \beta)$

The results from the models suggest that the long-run effect of the aid to Newquay is reached after three to five years. This can be interpreted as the duration of the transitional period until Newquay is able to make maximum use of its new capacity resulting from the aid, given the level of competition.

Source: Oxera (2017).

REFERENCES

BBC (2011), 'Final day protest against Plymouth Airport's closure', news report, 23 December.

Business Cornwall (2011), 'Air Southwest calls time', 15 July.

Buts C. and Jegers M. (2012), 'A note on State aid and concentration: the case of Belgium', *European Competition Journal*, 8(1), pp. 153-162.

Buts C. and Jegers M. (2013), 'The effect of 'State aid' on market shares: An empirical investigation in an EU Member State', *Journal of Industry, Competition and Trade*, 13(1), pp. 89-100.

Coppens P., Hilken K. and Buts C. (2015), 'On the longer-term effects of State aid on market shares', *European State Aid Law Quarterly Journal*, 14(2), pp. 271-279.

Department for Transport (2016), 'A study of consultancy reports' conclusions on reopening Plymouth City Airport for commercial passenger services', December.

European Commission (1997), 'Commission notice on the definition of the relevant market for the purposes of Community competition law', *Official Journal of the European Communities*, 97/C 372/03, 9 December.

European Commission (2005), 'Community guidelines on financing of airports and start-up aid to airlines departing from regional airports', *Official Journal of the European Union*, 2005/C 312/01, 9 December.

European Commission (2007), 'State aid No N 303/2007 - United Kingdom, Newquay Cornwall Airport Development', C(2007) 4316 final, 23 October.

European Commission (2009), 'State aid N 269/2009 - United Kingdom, Newquay Cornwall Airport Development', C(2009) 4984 final, 2 July.

European Commission (2012), 'Communication from the Commission to the European Parliament, the Council, the European Economic and Social Committee and the Committee of the Regions. EU State aid modernisation (SAM)', COM(2012) 209 final, 8 May.

European Commission (2013), 'Case No COMP/M.6663 - Ryanair / Aer Lingus III', 27 February.

European Commission (2014a), 'New State aid rules for a competitive aviation industry', Competition Policy Brief, Issue 2, February.

European Commission (2014b), 'Guidelines on State aid to airports and airlines', *Official Journal of the European Union*, 2014/C 99/3, 4 April.

European Commission (2014c), 'Common methodology for State aid evaluation', Commission Staff Working Document, SWD(2014) 179 final, 28 May.

Evening Herald (2007), 'Passenger numbers plummet at airport', 16 March.

Garcia J.-A. and Neven D. (2005), 'State aid and the distortion of competition, a benchmark model', HEI Working Paper No. 06/2005.

Møllgaard P. (2005), 'Competitive effects of State aid in oligopoly', Centre of Industrial Economics, Department of Economics, Copenhagen Business School.

Oxera (2009), 'Should aid be granted to firms in difficulty? A study on counterfactual scenarios to restructuring State aid', study prepared for the European Commission, December.

Oxera and a multi-jurisdictional team of lawyers led by Dr Assimakis Komninos (2009), 'Quantifying antitrust damages: Towards non-binding guidance for courts', study prepared for the European Commission, December.

Oxera (2017), 'Ex post assessment of the impact of State aid on competition', Final report prepared for the European Commission, November.

Schweiger H. (2011), 'The impact of State aid for restructuring on the allocation of resources', European Bank for Reconstruction and Development, Working Paper No. 127, May.

Stock J.H. and Watson M.W. (2007), *Introduction to Econometrics*, Pearson Education.

Western Morning News (2007), 'Airport defends passenger slump', 17 March.

CHAPTER 9

The Impact of State Aid Schemes to Bring Basic Broadband to Rural Areas in Germany*

EU Member States have allocated significant funding towards the development of broadband infrastructure especially in rural areas. The case study summarised in this chapter investigates the impact of a 2008 national aid scheme to support broadband in Germany as well as complementary regional schemes in Bavaria and Lower Saxony. The novelty of the analysis is that it considers both the effectiveness of the aid schemes and their impact on the number of competitors. A Difference-in-Differences approach is applied to a matched sample of aided and non-aided municipalities to measure the cumulative causal effect of these State aid schemes on broadband coverage and intensity of competition at the municipal level. The results suggest that the schemes were successful in increasing broadband coverage by 12% to 21%, depending on the speed of connection. Moreover, the schemes did not impair competition. On the contrary, the number of Internet Service Providers (ISPs) in the treated municipalities grew when compared to the control group of non-treated municipalities.

§9.01 INTRODUCTION

The main objective of this State aid case evaluation is to study the effects of several State aid schemes that aimed to support the development of basic broadband infrastructure in rural areas in Germany. This is an important area for policy research, as there is limited empirical evidence on the effects of State aid in such an important domain as broadband, especially at the local level. A novelty of this analysis is that it does not only assess whether the aid schemes contributed to an increase in broadband

* This chapter is a summary reproducing the main elements of the broadband State aid evaluation conducted as part of the European Commission financed study by Lear, DIW Berlin and Analysys Mason (2017) on the *Economic impact of competition policy enforcement on the functioning of telecoms markets in the EU.*

coverage in German rural areas but it also examines whether these aid schemes created distortions to competition. So far, the literature offers little or no empirical evidence on the effects of broadband State aid schemes on competition in the market for broadband services.

Like most other European countries, Germany has allocated significant funding towards the development of broadband infrastructure as it is seen as a crucial driver for economic and social development. Between 2007 and 2015, Germany allocated almost EUR 7.9 billion to a wide range of national and regional aid schemes for basic and NGA (Next Generation Access) broadband coverage, corresponding to 4-5 % of total German State aids (excluding railway subsidies) during that period. Besides schemes aimed at pushing forward the frontier of internet access, a set of schemes has been approved to sustain basic internet access in rural areas, which lack both up-to-date infrastructure and private investments. These schemes are the focus of this ex post evaluation.

The ex post evaluation presented here investigates the impact of a national aid scheme as well as complementary regional schemes in Bavaria and Lower Saxony.[1] All three schemes (and their successors) were approved by the European Commission. The European Commission's conditions for the approval of State aid proposals are twofold. First, the aid should address the alleged market failure, i.e., the aid needs to be appropriate, proportionate, and effective. Second, it has to do so without distorting effective competition. Hence, when evaluating the European Commission's decision to give the go ahead to the broadband State aid schemes in Germany, it is necessary to look at these different dimensions.

The analysis only focusses on those schemes that subsidised basic broadband services in regions with limited coverage and not on those subsidising investments in NGA networks. These schemes are of particularly interest for several reasons. First, the regional nature of the schemes allows addressing the often complex issue of identification (i.e., the definition of a suitable untreated control group) as the affected regions can be compared to non-affected regions within a common national market. Second, the schemes are limited in scope and, therefore, their effect is easier to identify. Third, the data availability for Germany is particularly good, as detailed information on broadband coverage as well as the number and type of ISPs is available at the municipal level.

The remainder of this chapter is organised as follows. Section 9.02 provides a short description of the evaluated broadband schemes. Section 9.03 reviews the literature on the effects of State aid schemes in support of broadband network deployment. Section 9.04 outlines the empirical strategy used to evaluate ex post the impact of the national and regional State aid schemes. Section 9.05 provides a descriptive analysis of broadband coverage and the conditions of competition in German municipalities. Section 9.06 explains how the aided municipalities are matched with the non-aided municipalities as a basis for the counterfactual impact

1. The schemes referred to are N 115/2008 ('Broadband in rural areas of Germany') at the national level, as well as N 237/2008 ('Broadband support in Niedersachsen') and N 266/2008 ('Broadband in rural areas of Bayern, Germany') at the regional level.

evaluation that follows in section 9.07. Section 9.08 provides robustness checks and section 9.09 concludes.

§9.02 BROADBAND AID SCHEMES TO BE EVALUATED

This case study evaluates the impact of three broadband aid schemes, including one national scheme and two regional schemes (*see* Box 9.1). The national aid scheme was launched in July 2008 with the objective of increasing broadband coverage in rural areas in Germany that lacked such infrastructure. It was a EUR 141 million aid scheme providing incentives to private operators to offer affordable basic broadband services. While the aid scheme covered the entire country, regional authorities could only implement it if at least some areas in the region were identified as 'white areas'.[2] Eligibility for the aid scheme was determined at the municipal level and the operators directly benefitting from the aid were designated following a public tendering procedure. The local (mostly municipal) authorities were responsible for the implementation of the scheme.

Box 9.1: Objectives of aid schemes: increase in broadband coverage in rural municipalities while maintaining effective competition

The objectives of the German broadband aid schemes can be defined as follows:

- An improvement in basic broadband coverage implying an increase in the number of connections with a download transmission speed of 2 Megabits per second (2 Mbps). This case study also investigates the impact of the aid schemes on broadband coverage at higher speeds (6 Mbps, ≥ 16 Mbps). Note that broadband coverage is somewhat different from broadband take-up or penetration, which refers to the share of end-customers making use of the broadband connections available.
- The improvement in basic broadband coverage should not negatively affect effective competition as measured by the number of ISPs active within a given municipality. The aid provided was in the form of financing for infrastructure investments coupled with open-access provisions.

The aid intensity for each single infrastructure project was related to the so-called profitability gap, i.e., the 'difference in investment costs and profitability thresholds for providing similar broadband services in rural areas compared to urban areas'.[3]

2. The European Commission defines different types of areas that can apply for broadband aid: (i) white areas, where no provider is active; (ii) grey areas, where only one provider is active; and (iii) black areas, where two or more providers are active. The aid schemes discussed here were aimed at improving broadband availability in white areas only.
3. *See* Commission case decision concerning scheme N 115/2008, p. 4.

Initially, the aid was limited to a maximum amount of EUR 200,000 in public funding for each project.

The national scheme was a trigger for regional schemes in the states of Lower Saxony (Niedersachsen) and Bavaria (Bayern), which decided to mobilise additional public funding of around EUR 45 million to help reduce the digital gap in their regions. While the national scheme mostly concerned private households, the regional schemes focused primarily on broadband availability for businesses. However, municipal projects could not receive aid under a regional scheme if they were already benefitting from support under the national scheme.[4]

In its case decisions, the Commission qualified each municipal aid project as *de minimis*, i.e., it considered that due to the small amount of funding involved (less than EUR 200,000 over a period of three years in the original schemes) the aid did not have substantive anticompetitive effects or affect trade between Member States.[5] Therefore, the support provided for each individual project was not classified as State aid. Nevertheless, there was the concern that some ISPs could receive cumulative aid in excess of EUR 200,000 over three years if they were awarded State support for several local projects in different municipalities. In spite of such concerns, the Commission ruled that the distortions of competition and the effects on trade were relatively limited, while the overall impact of the measures was considered to be positive. Moreover, the Commission stated that the measures were in line with the objectives of Article 87(3)(c) of the EC Treaty because they facilitated the development of economic activities such as retail and wholesale broadband services.

In sum, between the summer of 2008 and the end of 2010, the European Commission approved several aid schemes in support of the expansion of basic broadband networks in Germany. Following the Commission's approval, the investments supported by the schemes were carried out over the period 2011-2014. The analysis presented here investigates the cumulative effect of both national and regional schemes, as it was impossible to gather specific and separate information on the amount of aid awarded under each of the schemes.

§9.03 REVIEW OF THE LITERATURE ON THE IMPACT OF BROADBAND STATE AID SCHEMES

Fast and widely available broadband connectivity is a key ingredient for growth and prosperity (*see* Elixmann and Neumann, 2013 and Nascimbene and Di Pascale, 2018). However, not all citizens or companies in a country necessarily have access to high speed or even basic broadband as the market by itself may fail to deliver it. Broadband aid schemes seek to correct this market failure. The European Commission's 2013 Broadband Guidelines regulate and incentivise the recourse to such aid schemes.

---

4. The N115/2008 scheme prohibited cumulation with any other State aid broadband measures including any separate broadband measures designed by the German states (Länder).
5. Even though prolongations and amendments increased the aid amount above *de minimis* level, the European Commission nevertheless decided to approve the schemes.

This section provides an overview of the literature analysing the impact of broadband State aid schemes on broadband coverage and penetration. Yet, there exist only few empirical evaluations of the impact of broadband State aids on broadband coverage, including in particular studies by Regeneris Consulting (2015) and Hüschelrath et al. (2019). Wallsten (2005) and Belloc et al. (2012) consider the impact of public policies on broadband penetration, while Canzian et al. (2015) focuses on the effect of broadband aid on firms' performance indicators such as sales, value added and employment.

Regeneris Consulting (2015) evaluates the effectiveness of Superfast North Yorkshire (SFNY) project. The aim of the project was to improve access to and utilisation of high-speed broadband infrastructure by SMEs in North Yorkshire.[6] The project consisted of infrastructure rollout and a business support scheme.[7] The analysis was carried out mainly through surveys, and the results suggest that SFNY met its key infrastructure target: high-speed broadband coverage has increased across the whole of North Yorkshire and York from 46% to 86%. Moreover, the number of businesses assisted and the gross number of jobs created within the business support service have exceeded the project's target.

Hüschelrath et al. (2019) assess the effects of the broadband State aid scheme of the Bavarian government, which benefitted 1129 rural municipalities over the period 2010 and 2011. The main eligibility criterion for this aid was that the municipality concerned should be underprovided in terms of broadband access (defined as having access to a download transmission speed of less than 1 Mbps). The authors apply the Difference-in-Differences method to a matched sample of aided and non-aided municipalities. The post-treatment period ran up to the year 2014. The study suggests that while the Bavarian aid scheme was effective in raising broadband coverage in rural municipalities, its economic benefits in terms of job creation were rather limited.

Wallsten (2005) studies the impact of several state-level broadband industrial and regulatory policies in the US. He shows that most state-level policies for underserved areas, tax incentives and municipal network policies seem to be ineffective. Open access policies such as telecom unbundling regulations, on the contrary, are positively correlated with broadband penetration. The results in particular suggest that the US Department of Agriculture (USDA) broader telecommunication programme is promoting rural broadband adoption.

Belloc et al. (2012) use panel data on thirty OECD countries over the period 1995-2010 to assess whether the enforcement of several public policies, such as fiscal incentives programs, subsidies or long-term loans for internet providers, have been effective in stimulating broadband penetration. Using a simple econometric model, they demonstrate that these policies positively affect the number of broadband

6. More in particular, the aim of SFNY was to deliver 77% coverage for high-speed broadband and 100 % coverage for basic broadband (2 Mbps) among premises in the North Yorkshire Intervention Area.
7. The rationale for the business support element of the project is based on an information failure whereby many businesses are unaware of the potential benefits of adoption and exploitation of broadband.

subscribers per 100 inhabitants, while their relative impact depends on the actual stage of broadband diffusion.

Canzian et al. (2015) estimate the impact of a local subsidy in the autonomous Province of Trento (Italy) to finance the installation of broadband access points in rural and remote areas that were not privately supplied. The local policy aimed at the provision of high-speed broadband technology, i.e., connections delivering download speeds of up to 20 Mbps via ADSL2+ technology. The authors conducted a quasi-experimental analysis and estimated the effect of the local policy through a Difference-in-Differences strategy. They showed that broadband availability had a significant positive effect on firms' annual sales turnover and value added. However, there seems to be no significant impact on employment.

To conclude, the existing literature on the effects of broadband State aid schemes on broadband coverage is rather scant. Some studies use qualitative techniques (e.g., surveys), while others apply the Difference-in-Differences technique to matched samples of aided and non-aided firms. Most existing studies look beyond the impact of the aid schemes on broadband coverage and investigate their impact on broadband penetration or the economic performance of firms in the affected region, as measured by changes in employment or annual turnover.

§9.04 EMPIRICAL STRATEGY

The case study adopts a Difference-in-Differences methodology to identify the joint causal effects of the broadband aid scheme of the German Federal government as well as the complementary aid schemes financed by the states of Bavaria and Lower Saxony. This section develops the empirical strategy used to determine the impact of these broadband aid schemes on basic broadband coverage and the average number of ISPs in rural municipalities of Germany.

The analysis is conducted at the level of individual municipalities because: (1) the municipalities were in charge of applying for the aid (even though the aid beneficiaries were the ISPs that developed the infrastructure); and (2) the broadband network structure is related to the old telephone prefixes, which closely correspond to the borders of the municipalities. However, potential effects coming from geographic proximity and/or spillovers across municipalities are not taken into account. This neglect of spillover effects would most likely cause an underestimation of the true average effect. Therefore, this approach provides a conservative estimate of the aid schemes' effects.

Following the description of the empirical model to be estimated, the section focused on the definition of the control group of non-aided municipalities, which should be as similar as possible to the treated group of the aided municipalities. The section concludes with the definition of the outcome and control variables used in the empirical model.

The best possible scenario for a Difference-in-Differences approach is when regional variation is available. Comparing different regions of the same country has the advantage that unobservable national institutional and regulatory trends, which are key drivers of the policy decision and the outcomes, are common across regions. Of course, to successfully use regional variation, it is necessary that the policy under investigation be applied differently across different local areas within each region. This is indeed the case in the present study, as some municipalities within the states of Bavaria and Lower Saxony requested and implemented the aid while others did not. This regional variation was exploited with the help of a panel dataset for the years 2008-2015 covering 8,000 municipalities, which represent virtually all municipalities in Western Germany (*see* Appendix 1).

[A] Estimated Model

The Difference-in-Differences model is described by the following equation:

$$y_{mt} = \alpha + \delta post_t + \gamma treat_m \times post_t + X_{mt} + \mu_m + \varepsilon_{mt}$$

where the outcome y in municipality m at year t is a function of market demand and supply conditions including geographical and technical determinants of competition and investment (X_{mt}) as well as municipality fixed-effects (μ_m), which account for the time-invariant unobserved heterogeneity across municipalities. The outcome variable y_{mt} is defined as either the basic broadband coverage or the average number of ISPs in municipality m at year t. The dummy $post_t$ is equal to one for the post-intervention year (2015), whereas the year of comparison (the base year) is the year 2010.[8] The dummy $treat_m$ is equal to one for the municipalities that were affected by the policy intervention, i.e., implemented the aid, and zero otherwise. The error term ε_{mt} is assumed to be heteroskedastic and correlated among observations in the same municipality.

The key coefficient of interest is γ, which measures the outcome change in the treated municipalities relative to the outcome change in non-treated municipalities before and after the aid: the average treatment effect. This coefficient measures the additional change in outcome for municipalities that were affected by the scheme in comparison with the change in outcome for municipalities that were not (or less) affected, as specified in more detail below. The coefficient δ measures the change in outcome that is common to all municipalities.

As the allocation of the aid was not a random treatment, a matching procedure is applied to identify appropriate treated and control groups thereby removing the possible selection bias in the sample of aided municipalities.

8. The year 2010 is used as baseline year given that the aid was awarded in 2009-2010 and the money was transferred in 2011 at the earliest. The case study analyses the impact in 2015 following the expiration of both the national and regional schemes. As a robustness check, however, the effects of the aid schemes in 2013 and 2014 are also considered. These are, as expected, qualitatively similar but smaller in size.

[B] Identification Strategy

The key element for the Difference-in-Differences approach to be successful is the clear identification of the treatment and control groups, as the treatment – i.e., the distribution of the aid – was not assigned at random. Actually, it might be expected that municipalities with certain characteristics (such as municipalities with high investment costs or low demand), which most needed the investment aid, were more likely to participate in one of the broadband aid schemes. Consequently, whether or not a municipality benefits from the aid and is part of the treatment group becomes endogenous, i.e., influenced by the municipality's characteristics. Hence, to reduce the concerns of a potential bias in the estimate of the treatment effect due non-random assignment of the treatment, the 'control' municipalities are defined as a subset of municipalities pre-selected via a matching procedure based on their observable characteristics (socio-demographic and technological). This approach tries to mimic randomness in the treatment in the sense that it generates a control group that is as similar as possible to the treated group along several and relevant observable dimensions but at the same time did not receive the treatment.

[1] Treatment Group

The treatment group consists of the aided municipalities in Bavaria and Lower Saxony. These two states are the two most important German states in terms of broadband aid. They implemented both the nationwide scheme and their own regional scheme. For both states, it is possible to get information on how much total aid each municipality had at its disposal from both the national and regional aid schemes up to 2013.

This municipality-specific information was complemented with aggregate data on the amount of public resources available to each state within the analysed schemes by the end of 2013. Bavaria alone accounted for over EUR 20 million of the around EUR 49 million of public money made available in support of broadband infrastructure in Western Germany. Public spending on broadband in Lower Saxony up until the end of 2013 amounted to EUR 6.3 million.

[2] Control Group

The control group is made up of non-aided municipalities from all states in Western German states that are as similar as possible to aided municipalities from Bavaria and Lower Saxony. The selection of these municipalities is made via a matching procedure.

[a] Objective of the Matching

The choice of the control group is crucial in any counterfactual impact analysis. The challenge is to identify those municipalities that did not obtain any State aid, but that had ex ante the same attractiveness for broadband investments as those municipalities from Bavaria and Lower Saxony that obtained the aid. A propensity score matching procedure (*see* Box 9.2) is used to select control municipalities that are similar to the treated ones in terms of observable characteristics. The objective of this matching procedure is to eliminate as much as possible any endogeneity associated with the selection of treated municipalities.

Box 9.2: Propensity score and other matching techniques

To avoid problems of selection bias in counterfactual impact evaluations, each beneficiary of the treatment has to be matched with one or more non-beneficiaries (the control group). The outcomes for the non-beneficiaries serve as a best guess of what the outcome for the beneficiary would have been had the treatment not occurred. Different matching methods have been developed to ensure that the ex ante characteristics of the beneficiary closely match those of the corresponding non-beneficiaries.

A distinction can be made between exact matching, propensity score matching and regression discontinuity design:

- Exact matching methods match beneficiaries to non-beneficiaries with the same observed characteristics. In practice though, it is almost impossible to find exact matches. Therefore, alternative matching techniques have been proposed.
- Propensity score matching methods match beneficiaries to non-beneficiaries with the same propensity score (i.e., single score summarising relevant observed characteristics). The treatment effect is then defined as the average of the differences between the outcomes for beneficiaries and matched non-beneficiaries.
- Regression discontinuity design: this matching method is based on the idea of discontinuity around a threshold, often related to the conditions for eligibility for a State aid scheme. This method assumes that the beneficiaries and non-beneficiaries of the scheme close to the threshold are similar in all other respects.

The method used here is a propensity score matching.

The first step of the matching procedure is the estimation of a logit regression to determine the probability (or 'propensity') that a municipality receives State aid in light of the observable characteristics discussed in more detail below. The matching is performed on the basis of 2008 variables (or the closest in time). As a second step, each aided municipality is matched with a non-aided municipality based on the propensity scores calculated. Note that the logit regression does not aim at explaining why a municipality implemented the aid. The only objective is to identify municipalities among the non-treated set that are as similar as possible to the treated municipalities. The third step is to check if the matched municipalities are sufficiently similar. If so, the Difference-in-Differences regression can be applied to the matched municipalities.

[b] Variables Used for the Propensity Score Matching

In the matching procedure, the following elements are considered: demographic characteristics, technological and market conditions in the municipalities, as these are among the most important determinants of the costs of investments in broadband infrastructure and the incentives to enter for ISPs (*see, for example,* Nardotto et al., 2015).[9]

A number of different specifications were tried. The trade-off is between a model that is rich enough to capture the main drivers of investment and entry, but also allows to achieve a sufficient number of control municipalities to cover most if not all treated municipalities. On that basis, the logit regression entailing the following characteristics was selected: demographic variables (total population, population density, share of population aged between 24 and 65); variables affecting the demand for broadband services (average income, share of population with tertiary education); variables that influence the technology (distance to the main distribution frame (MDF) and terrain ruggedness); and variables related to the industry in the municipality (percentage of land set aside for firms and industry).[10] Furthermore, following the matching literature (*see, for instance,* Heckman et al., 1998), a single measure of the outcome pre-treatment DSL[11] coverage (at 1 Mbps in 2008) is used.

The matching is performed based on 2008 variables (or the closest in time). By choosing a period well before the treatment, one can be more confident of including only variables that are unaffected by the treatment and, thus, avoid spurious correlation.

[C] Definition of the Outcome and Control Variables

[1] Outcome Variables

The objective of the present analysis is to analyse the effectiveness of the German broadband aid schemes as well as the possible distortions of competition resulting from such schemes.

---

9. The approach followed carefully controls for selection issues based on observable characteristics. This is a standard approach in the policy evaluation literature. Nevertheless, municipalities with certain characteristics might be more likely to participate in one of the broadband aid schemes due to unobservable characteristics, creating a selection bias. For instance, treated municipalities might have a more efficient administration that is also helpful to firms (that demand broadband) or to ISPs by making their entry easier or less cumbersome from a bureaucratic viewpoint. If this is the case, a different approach based on instrumental variables might be more appropriate. However, it is quite difficult to find appropriate instruments to tackle the potential endogeneity due to selection on unobservables. Moreover, it is well known that invalid (i.e., not exogenous) or weak instruments, might lead to larger estimation bias than simple OLS. Therefore, the authors of the study consider that the approach selected here is the best possible in order to study the causal impact of the broadband aid, also in light of the richness of the data available, which allows to control for many observable dimensions and perform several robustness checks.
10. More refined measures of industrial structure are not used, as they significantly reduced the number of matched municipalities.
11. Digital Subscriber Line (DSL) is a technology for bringing high-bandwidth information to homes and small businesses over ordinary copper telephone lines.

Basic broadband coverage is the outcome variable used to assess the effectiveness of the aid schemes. The aim is to determine whether the aid adequately addressed the targeted market failure, by comparing the development of broadband infrastructure in municipalities that benefitted from the aid schemes with the development in similar municipalities that did not receive aid.

The second dimension that needs to be evaluated is whether the scheme(s) had negative effects on competition. As a proxy for the intensity of competition, the number of ISPs active in each municipality is used. To assess whether and how the aid affected competition, the number of ISPs in municipalities that received broadband funding is compared to that in control municipalities, which did not benefit from State support.

Since the aid is supposed to be technologically neutral, the analysis looks at the impact of the aid on the number of ISPs providing broadband services through fixed line (DSL) networks, but also at its impact on the number of ISPs using other technologies – such as mobile (LTE)[12] broadband – that were also supported by the aid schemes.[13] This is possible because precise information is available on both the number and the technology of the ISPs operating in each municipality. Therefore, it is possible to distinguish between the effect of the aid on the number of both fixed line (DSL) and mobile operators – either of which are likely beneficiaries of the aid – and the effect of the aid on the number of ISPs using a different technology such as fibre, which are rather unlikely beneficiaries of the aid.

[2] Control Variables

In deciding which control variables to use in the Difference-in-Differences analysis, it is necessary to consider which external factors might affect the incentive of an ISP to invest in broadband infrastructure. In the spirit of Falck et al. (2014),[14] a distinction is made between the demographic characteristics of the local area and supply-related factors.[15]

The following demographic variables are used as controls: (i) the number of lines (households) in an area or in neighbouring areas; and (ii) the income distribution and level of education of the population. The supply-related controls are: (i) the distance to the MDF, affecting the infrastructure investments required and the quality of

12. Long Term Evolution (LTE) is a standard for 4G wireless broadband technology that offers increased network capacity and speed to mobile device users.
13. Technically, fixed line (DSL), mobile (LTE) and cable technologies can deliver basic broadband. ISPs offering DSL and LTE would probably be within the scope of the aid schemes – either as direct beneficiaries or as access seekers to the subsidised infrastructure. Cable operators, however, would likely be unwilling to provide open access to their network, which is a prerequisite for receiving State aid funding. Similarly, fibre is a technology designed for NGA and therefore, it seems unlikely that ISPs offering fibre would have been a beneficiary of the basic broadband schemes.
14. Falck et al. (2014) studies the effect of internet penetration on electoral outcomes.
15. Some of these variables have been used as well for the calculation of propensity scores used to match aided municipalities with 'similar' non-aided municipalities. However, this does not imply that they no longer have an impact on broadband coverage and the number of ISPs in the aided and non-aided municipalities.

connections; (ii) the contours of the land, characteristics of the soil and weather conditions; and (iii) other institutional settings that might have had an impact on past and future investment.

§9.05 DESCRIPTIVE ANALYSIS

Before engaging in the more sophisticated quantitative analysis of the effects of the German broadband schemes, it is useful to provide a short description of the sample of municipalities used in the empirical work and considers broad developments in terms of broadband coverage and the conditions of competition.

[A] Description of the Sample

Table 9.1 describes the principal characteristics of the sample including virtually all Western German municipalities. The average municipality is rather small, with a total population of 7,580 and an average annual income of EUR 32,000. More than a quarter of the citizens have a college degree and more than half are of working age. The average distance of the municipality to the MDF is less than 3 km, which is rather small because most municipalities contain an MDF. Finally, basic broadband coverage is 76%, on average. However, for all variables there appear to be very large differences from one municipality to another, which illustrates the importance of the matching of treated municipalities with non-treated municipalities having similar characteristics.

Table 9.1 Descriptive Statistics – Demographics[16]

	Mean	*Std. Dev.*	*Min.*	*Max.*
Total population	7,580	31,767	65	1,429,584
Average income in 2007 (1,000 EUR)	32.0	6.5	11.8	212.3
College degree	25.9	8.3	0	70.3
Population between 24 and 65 years old (%)	54.4	2.7	31.7	74.7
Population density (people per km^2)	210.9	293.9	2.4	4601.2
Unemployment rate	5.6	2.0	1.4	18.2
Ruggedness index	38.3	32.8	0.5	289.5
Land use for firms and industry (%)	0.7	1.2	0	16.4
Distance to the MDF from population centroid (meters)	2,798	1,807	11.5	14,833
Number of MDFs within municipality	0.7	1.8	0	56
DSL coverage at 1 Mbps in 2005	76.3	20.6	0	100

Source: Lear, DIW Berlin and Analysys Mason (2017).

16. For all West German municipalities in Baden-Wuerttemberg, Bavaria, Hesse, Lower Saxony, North Rhine-Westphalia, Rhineland-Palatinate, and Schleswig-Holstein.

[B] Broadband Coverage

Figure 9.1 shows the evolution of average broadband coverage in German municipalities between 2010, the year when the projects within the broadband schemes started to be designed and the funding allocated (pre-treatment period) and 2015, when the effects of the aid schemes were no longer being felt (post-treatment period). As expected, broadband coverage is both increasing over time, at every speed, and it is greater for lower speeds.

Figure 9.1 Broadband Coverage at Different Speeds (Population Coverage)

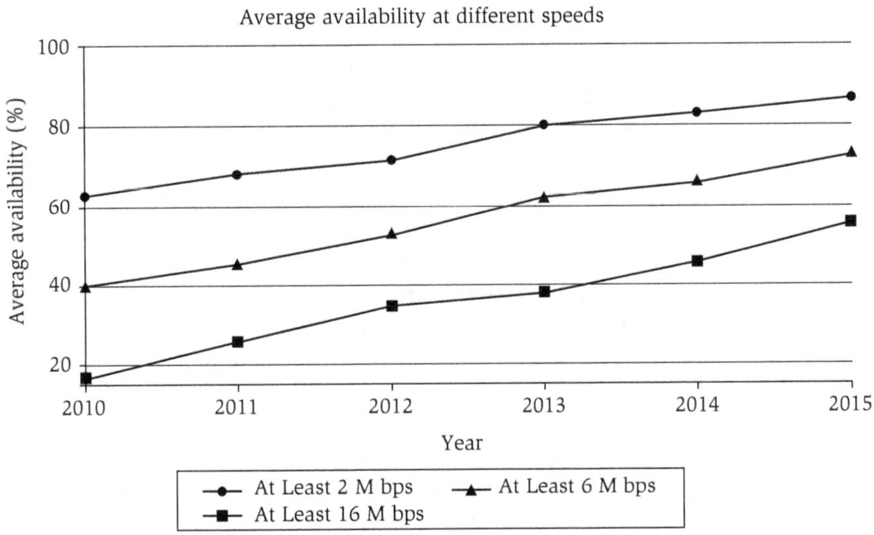

Source: Lear, DIW Berlin and Analysys Mason (2017).

[C] Number of Internet Service Providers

The other main dependent variable is the number of ISPs, which can be split up by technology used. Over the years 2010-2015, there are 248 different ISPs that appear in the database used, with a (gross) entry of 144 ISPs between 2010 and 2015. Table 9.2 shows the number of municipalities where the largest ISPs were active in 2010 and 2015.[17]

17. Note that Telefonica is considered as a single ISP, which offers both DSL and mobile technologies, in the empirical analysis. Further, Kabel Deutschland is also included among the largest ISPs, even though it is not as big as the other main ISPs. The reason is that Kabel Deutschland is the largest cable operator and it operates nation-wide. The company was acquired by Vodafone in 2014.

Table 9.2 Descriptive Statistics – Main Internet Service Providers

ISP	*Number of Municipalities 2010*	*Number of Municipalities 2015*
Deutsche Telekom AG	9,246	9,286
Vodafone GmbH	5,533	9,285
Telefonica Germany DSL	1,726	2,360
Telefonica Germany 02	3,382	7,711
Kabel Deutschland	1,514	2,741
E-Plus	-	9,270

Source: Lear, DIW Berlin and Analysys Mason (2017).

The distribution of the municipalities where ISPs are active is skewed: only 14 operators are active in more than 200 municipalities, while the 'tail' of the distribution is very long. The large majority of ISPs are local players active in less than 200 municipalities.[18] The largest players in the market are the incumbent and ex-monopolist Deutsche Telekom together with the two major pan-European operators Vodafone and Telefonica. Before it was acquired by Vodafone in 2014, Kabel Deutschland used to play a relevant role as well.

Over the years spanned by the data, a strong increase in the number of ISPs can be observed. Table 9.3 reports the frequencies of market structures in 2010 and 2015, i.e., the number (and the percentage) of municipalities with a monopoly, a duopoly, etc. More than 50% of the markets in 2010 were either a monopoly or a duopoly; whereas Xiao and Orazem (2011) consider that the presence of at least three ISPs is required to ensure that there is sufficient competition (as reflected by lower prices) in the local market. However, the picture changes dramatically over time. In 2015, more than half of the municipalities have either five or six ISPs.[19]

18. An in-depth analysis of the ownership structure of these operators confirmed that the large majority (over 95%) of them are truly independent small firms and not subsidiaries of the major ISPs.
19. While it would have been interesting to look at how entry rates have been affected by the aid schemes, this is not possible because information on the number of ISPs per municipality is only available from 2010 onwards. Hence, the number of ISPs pre- versus post-treatment can only be compared and not entry rates of ISPs.

Table 9.3 Frequencies of the Number of Internet Service Providers in 2010 and 2015, All Technologies

Number of ISPs	*2010*		*2015*	
	Count	*Share*	*Count*	*Share*
1	2,302	24.79%	0	0.00%
2	2,392	25.76%	14	0.15%
3	1,721	18.53%	710	7.65%
4	1,533	16.51%	1,838	19.79%
5	1,019	10.97%	3,075	33.11%
6	262	2.82%	2,300	24.77%
7 or more	57	0.62%	1,349	14.81%

Source: Lear, DIW Berlin and Analysys Mason (2017).

A split by technology also helps to better understand what are the driving forces behind the increase in the number of ISPs (*see* Table 9.4). It appears that mobile ISPs greatly contributed to the overall dynamism of the market. While only 22% of the municipalities had any LTE coverage in 2010, the full country was covered by 2015. By that time, almost all municipalities had at least two LTE operators and most of municipalities had three or more.

Table 9.4 Frequencies of the Number of Internet Service Providers in 2010 and 2015, by Technology

Number of ISPs	*DSL*		*Cable*		*LTE*		*FTTH*	
	2010	*2015*	*2010*	*2015*	*2010*	*2015*	*2010*	*2015*
0	4.5	0.2	68.7	54.6	77.1	0.2	98.7	90
1	54.5	0.1	30.5	17.0	21.5	1.2	1.3	9.3
2	17.8	35.3	0.8	25.6	1.4	24	0	0.6
3	11.8	37.5	0	2.6	0	52.9	0	0.1
4	10.3	18.2	0	0.2	0	20	0	0
5	1.0	7.2	0	0	0	1.7	0	0
6	0.1	1.3	0	0	0	0	0	0
7	0	0.2	0	0	0	0	0	0

Source: Lear, DIW Berlin and Analysys Mason (2017).

A significant increase in the number of operators present in the market is also observed in the DSL segment for which the median number of ISPs went from one in 2010 to three in 2015. The increase in the number of DSL operators is smaller than that in the number of LTE operation, because DSL is a more mature technology than the LTE. Moreover, the entry costs associated with the installation of fixed broadband infrastructure tends to exceed that of mobile networks. Cable is a mature technology as well even if, in 2015, the majority of German markets (55%) were still not served through this technology. Finally, fibre technologies, such as fibre to the home (FTTH), are still in their infancy, as can be seen from the last two columns.

§9.06 RESULTS OF THE MATCHING PROCEDURE

In this section, the characteristics of the aided municipalities are compared with all other municipalities in Western Germany. Subsequently, the matching procedure is applied to identify the control group and compare the characteristics of the aided municipalities with the matched municipalities in the control group.

[A] Comparison of the Characteristics of Aided Municipalities and Other Municipalities Before the Matching

In this section, the around 1,800 treated municipalities in Bavaria and Lower Saxony are compared to a sample of the other around 6,200 municipalities from Western Germany that match the treated areas in terms of observable characteristics. The main advantage of this strategy is that it is likely to find very good matches for these treated municipalities, as a large pool of 'non-treated' municipalities is available. The main disadvantage is that it cannot be certain that none of the 'control' municipalities received aid. It is therefore possible that the measurement of the treatment effect is contaminated and the estimated treatment effects exhibit a downward bias. As some municipalities in the control group may have been treated as well, the results obtained with this strategy therefore represent a lower bound on the effects of the aid schemes.

Table 9.5 reports the results of a simple comparison of the means for the main variables used. In 2010, treated municipalities in Bavaria and Lower Saxony had a smaller, less educated population, a lower population density, a lower unemployment rate and a lower ruggedness index and they were more distant from the MDF. As expected, 2005 DSL coverage at 1 Mbps in treated municipalities was below the average for Western German municipalities. As the treated municipalities appear to be different from the other municipalities in the sample in terms of observable characteristics, a matching procedure is used to eliminate these differences.

Table 9.5 Descriptive Statistics: Splitting the Sample Between Treated and Control Areas – Treated Municipalities in Bavaria and Lower Saxony Versus All Other Municipalities in West Germany

	Pre-treatment (2010)			
	With Aid		*All Other municipalities*	
	Mean	*Std. Dev.*	*Mean*	*Std. Dev.*
Total population	6,072	15,042	8,048	35,087
Average income in 2007 (1,000 EUR)	32.3	5.7	32.4	6.2
College degree (%)	22.1	7.4	26.5	7.0
Population between 24 and 65 years old (%)	54.3	2.3	54.1	2.8
Population density (people per km^2)	149.5	171.1	229.7	319.9
Unemployment rate (%)	5.3	2.0	6.0	1.7
Ruggedness index	29.9	27.6	40.7	33.8
Land use by firms and industry (%)	0.6	0.9	0.8	1.3
Distance to the MDF from population centroid (meters)	3,039	1,886	2,730	1,776
Number of MDFs within municipality	0.7	1.0	0.7	2.0
DSL coverage at 1 Mbps in 2005 (%)	74.0	19.1	77.0	20.9

Source: Lear, DIW Berlin and Analysys Mason (2017).

[B] Comparison of the Characteristics of Aided Municipalities and Other Municipalities After the Matching

The objective of the matching procedure is to select control municipalities that are as similar as possible to the treated ones in terms of observable characteristics. A logit regression is used to construct a 'propensity score' variable on which each treated municipality is matched with a control municipality. As explained in section 9.04[B], the variable used for this matching include demographic characteristics, technological and market conditions in the municipalities.

Figure 9.2 provides a visual impression of the quality of the match. The bold dots denote the difference in the value of the variables between matched and control municipalities before the matching. For instance, the unemployed rate in treated municipalities is much lower than in the other municipalities in Germany, while the average income is very similar in treated and non-treated municipalities. The crosses represent the differences among treated and non-treated municipalities after the matching. The figure clearly shows that the sample obtained with the matching procedure is such that treated and non-treated areas are much more similar than the full sample before matching.

Figure 9.2 Similarity Among Treated and Control Areas Before and After the Matching

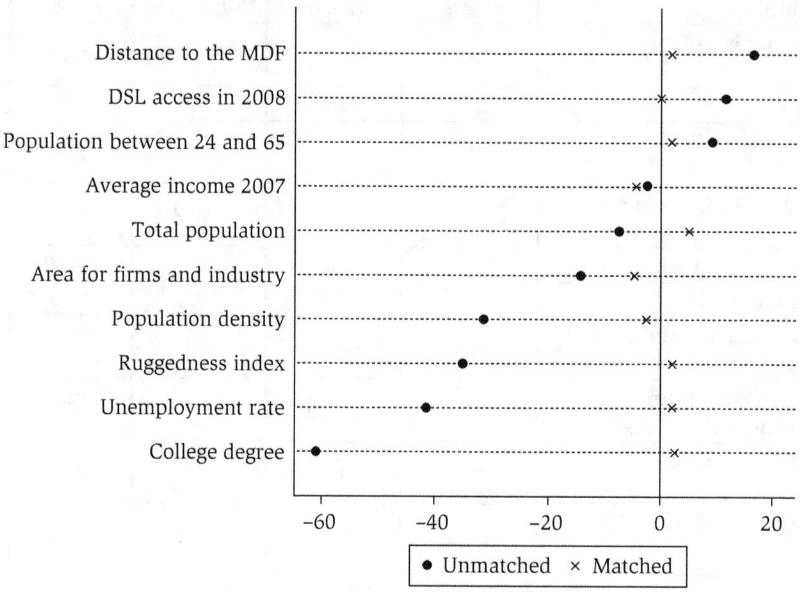

Source: Lear, DIW Berlin and Analysys Mason (2017).

Furthermore, although the common trend assumption cannot be assessed for all the outcome variables, Figure 9.3 provides a clear indication that for the 1 Mbps coverage the common trend hypothesis is satisfied.[20] Therefore, the authors of the study are confident that the matching produced a reasonable counterfactual case to perform a clean Difference-in-Differences analysis.

20. Since data on other speeds for the years before 2010 are not available, the data for 1 Mbps from Falck et al. (2014) are used to check for the common trend hypothesis.

Figure 9.3 Common Trend Hypothesis for 1 Mbps Coverage

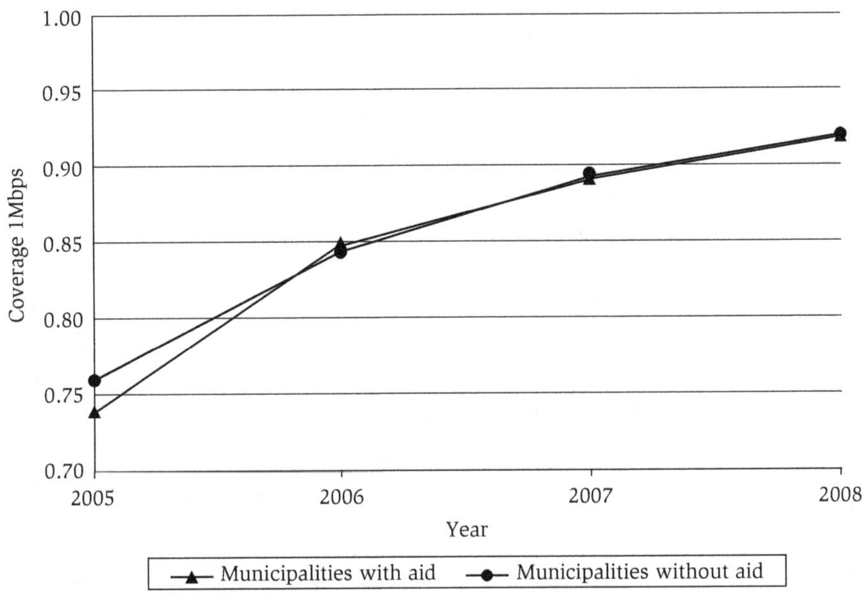

Source: Lear, DIW Berlin and Analysys Mason (2017).

§9.07 EFFECTS OF BROADBAND STATE AID SCHEMES ON COVERAGE AND NUMBER OF BROADBAND PROVIDERS

[A] Comparison Between Aided and Non-aided Municipalities After the Matching

To get a preliminary idea of the effects of the treatment, Table 9.6, reports the main variables of interest for the years 2010 and 2015. The summary statistics for the different outcome variables - broadband coverage at different speeds as well as the number of ISPs by technology - are rather similar between the aided and non-aided municipalities in 2010, as confirmed by a set of formal t-tests run for each variable. With regard to availability, municipalities that did not receive State aid have slightly more broadband coverage (for instance, 1.6% for DSL at 2 Mbps). With regard to the number of ISPs, differences in the baseline year look small and do not seem to follow a systematic pattern.

Table 9.6 Descriptive Statistics: Effect of the Aid – Treated Municipalities in Bavaria and Lower Saxony Versus Other West German Municipalities

	Pre-treatment (2010)					*Post-treatment (2015)*				
	Aided		*Non-aided*			*Aided*		*Non-aided*		
	Mean	*Std. Dev.*	*Mean*	*Std. Dev.*	*P-val*	*Mean*	*Std. Dev.*	*Mean*	*Std. Dev.*	*P-val*
Coverage DSL 2 Mbps	59.27	32.32	60.87	37.53	0.20	91.37	15.30	82.37	27.05	0.00
Coverage DSL 6 Mbps	37.05	32.43	38.70	37.65	0.19	82.88	21.81	66.51	35.56	0.00
Coverage DSL 16 Mbps	15.25	20.84	16.30	23.60	0.19	66.46	28.45	48.62	36.02	0.00
No. of ISPs (all tech)	2.81	1.37	2.79	1.42	0.63	5.52	1.21	5.25	1.18	0.00
No. of DSL operators	1.75	1.04	1.69	1.09	0.09	3.39	1.04	3.00	0.93	0.00
No. of cable operators	0.26	0.44	0.36	0.50	0.00	0.49	0.52	0.53	0.60	0.04
No. of HSDPA operators	1.82	0.78	1.72	0.82	0.00	3.84	0.90	3.63	0.83	0.00
No. of LTE operators	0.31	0.51	0.28	0.49	0.1	3.17	0.74	2.98	0.74	0.00

Source: Lear, DIW Berlin and Analysys Mason (2017). This table reports the p-value for the test of equality of the means between the sample of aided and non-aided municipalities.

Things are very different five years later, when DSL coverage is 9-18% higher in treated municipalities compared with municipalities that did not receive the State aid. The difference is larger for higher speeds: 6 Mbps and 16 Mbps. The number of ISPs also seems to have been affected by the aid, with a sharper increase in the number of ISPs in treated municipalities for all technologies. Excluding the number of cable operators (which is a 'sticky' market), all the differences of the means between treated and control areas are positive and significantly different from zero. These descriptive statistics indicate a strong treatment effect on both coverage and number of ISPs.

[B] Difference-in-Differences Analysis

Table 9.7 reports the results of the Difference-in-Differences regressions, where the authors control for all municipality-specific and time-variant fixed-effects as well as the other major drivers of broadband coverage and the number of ISPs discussed above.[21] The first three columns report the effect of the aid on broadband coverage. One can

21. For the sake of space, the coefficient estimates for all these additional variables are not reported here.

observe a large and positive post-treatment effect for all download transmission speeds as measured by the 'post-treatment' dummy. It reflects the increase in coverage over the five years that is common to all municipalities. It ranges from 24.8% for 2 Mbps to 43.5% for higher speeds (over 16 Mbps).

Further, municipalities that benefitted from the aid schemes experienced an additional large and significant increase in coverage if compared to those that did not. The average treatment effect – as measured by the coefficient's estimate for the variable 'Treated x Post-treatment' – is large and ranges between an additional increase of 11.7% for connections at 2 Mbps to almost 20% and 21% increases for connections at 6 Mbps and at speeds larger than 16 Mbps, respectively. Therefore, the analysis supports the view that the aid schemes were indeed effective in increasing broadband coverage beyond what would have happened under the counterfactual scenario represented by the control municipalities.

Table 9.7 Average Treatment Effect – Treated Municipalities in Bavaria and Lower Saxony Versus Other Municipalities in Western Germany

	Coverage			*Number of ISPs in Different Technologies*				
	2 Mbps	*6 Mbps*	*≥ 16 Mbps*	*Total ISPs*	*DSL ISPs*	*Cable ISPs*	*Mobile ISPs*	*FTTH ISPs*
Treated x Post-treatment	11.66*** (1.08)	19.79*** (1.24)	20.83*** (1.21)	0.21*** (0.05)	0.29*** (0.04)	0.06*** (0.02)	0.19*** (0.03)	0.02* (0.01)
Post-treatment	24.77*** (2.69)	35.10*** (3.04)	43.49*** (3.04)	1.77*** (0.10)	1.10*** (0.08)	0.09** (0.04)	2.78*** (0.08)	-0.09*** (0.03)
R-Squared	0.479	0.580	0.644	0.845	0.746	0.222	0.917	0.114
Observations	6,261	6,261	6,261	6,256	6,256	6,256	6,256	6,256

Source: Lear, DIW Berlin and Analysys Mason (2017).
Notes: There is a control for total population, population density, college degree, population between 24 and 65 years old, unemployment rate, industry shares at the 1-digit level, as well as municipality fixed-effects. Robust standard errors clustered at the municipality level are reported in parentheses. The symbols ***, **, * represent significance at the 1%, 5% and 10% levels, respectively.

The next four columns look at the effect of the aid on the number of ISPs. Again, the coefficient estimates for the 'post-treatment' dummy identify the trends towards an increase in the number of ISPs in municipalities that did not implement the aid. These markets have become more competitive as they have on average 1.8 additional ISPs in 2015 as compared to 2010. The growth was particularly strong in the mobile (including both LTE and HSPDA[22]) sector with an average increase of 2.8 ISPs, but was also significant in fixed-line DSL markets with an increase of 1.1 ISPs. For cable technology, one can observe a small and significant increase of 0.9%. For fibre (FTTH), there is even a small decrease in the number of service provides.

22. HSDPA (High-Speed Downlink Packet Access) is a packet-based mobile telephony protocol used in 3G radio networks to increase data capacity and speed up transfer rates.

More importantly, the coefficients for the 'Treated x Post-treatment' dummies are an indication of the causal effect of the aid schemes. One can observe a significantly larger increase in the number of firms for municipalities that received aid for all technologies. To put it differently, the study authors find a positive and significant average treatment effect of the aid schemes. This effect is economically large: on average, treated municipalities have 0.21 more ISPs than control municipalities: an increase of 12% over the common trend.

The effect of the aid schemes is the strongest for DSL and mobile markets. Technically, both DSL and LTE can deliver basic broadband services and were therefore covered by the aid schemes. On average, treated markets had 0.29 more DSL ISPs and 0.19 more mobile ISPs over the period 2010-2015 compared to the control group. Given the data at hand, it is unfortunately not possible to determine whether these effects are driven solely by the fact that the aid beneficiaries entered the market, or are instead due to other operators making use of open access obligations.[23]

Moreover, the aid had a significant positive effect on the application of other technologies as well. There is a statistically significant – though economically not very large – effect of 0.06 on the number of cable operators in treated municipalities (small in absolute values, but with a percentage increase of 67% compared to the common trend). For fibre markets, the effect is also positive and significant: one can observe 0.02 more operators in treated markets compared to the control group, which was however not enough to compensate for the common drop of 0.09 in the number of fibre operators between 2010 and 2015.

These results show that the aid did not displace the ISPs offering other (potentially competing) technologies. On the contrary, it enhanced their presence in the market. While precise information on whether fibre and cable technologies received aid are not available, they were not expected to be beneficiaries (*see* Footnote 13). Fibre is not suitable for the provision of basic broadband services, as it requires the installation of a new network, while cable operators tend to be unwilling to provide open access to their network. Therefore, these effects can be considered to be true spillovers of the aid schemes to alternative technologies.

Overall, these results suggest that the State aid not only helped in reducing the digital divide but also that it had positive direct effects on the number of ISPs in fixed-line broadband markets and even positive effects on the number of ISPs in other technologies, such as cable and mobile.

23. Indeed, the 2013 Broadband Guidelines of the European Commission foresee that potential entrants should be granted some form of open access to the incumbents' infrastructure when a network is realised with taxpayers' money. Unfortunately, there is no specific information on how exactly open access has been implemented in each municipality. Thus, the observed additional number of ISPs cannot be attributed to new entrants winning the aid tender, or to new entrants entering through open access imposed on the incumbents.

§9.08 ROBUSTNESS CHECKS

[A] Heterogeneous Treatment Effects

[1] Heterogeneity Between the States of Bavaria and Lower Saxony

The results presented until now discuss the average effect of the treatment across the two German states for which there is information on the municipalities that benefitted from the aid schemes: Bavaria and Lower Saxony. The first dimension of heterogeneity to look at is therefore to analyse whether the average effects holds true when the two states are taken separately.

When focusing on Bavaria only, the results show much larger effects (*see* Table 9.8) than under the main specification. The additional coverage in municipalities benefitting from the aid schemes amounts to 18.5% (2 Mbps), 27.8% (6 Mbps) and 24.8% (≥ 16 Mbps), respectively, if compared to the control group. The effects on the number of ISPs are almost identical to those reported in the previous section.

Table 9.8 Average Treatment Effect – Treated Municipalities in Bavaria Versus Other West German Municipalities

	Coverage			*Number of ISPs in Different Technologies*				
	2 Mbps	*6 Mbps*	*≥ 16 Mbps*	*Total ISPs*	*DSL ISPs*	*Cable ISPs*	*Mobile ISPs*	*FTTH ISPs*
Treated x Post-treatment	18.50*** (1.43)	27.72*** (1.63)	24.76*** (1.62)	0.29*** (0.07)	0.30*** (0.05)	0.08*** (0.02)	0.17*** (0.05)	0.06*** (0.02)
Post-treatment	31.53*** (3.59)	42.32*** (4.12)	49.87*** (4.01)	1.87*** (0.15)	1.08*** (0.12)	0.05 (0.05)	2.67*** (0.10)	-0.14*** (0.04)
R-Squared	0.509	0.602	0.664	0.843	0.748	0.208	0.913	0.110
Observations	4,233	4,233	4,233	4,228	4,228	4,228	4,228	4,228

Source: Lear, DIW Berlin and Analysys Mason (2017).
Notes: There is a control for total population, college degree, population between 24 and 65 years old, unemployment rate, public expenditure over total revenue at the municipal level, industry shares at the 1-digit, as well as municipality fixed-effects. Robust standard errors clustered at the municipality level are reported in parentheses.
The symbols ***, **, * represent significance at the 1%, 5% and 10% levels respectively.

The results for Lower Saxony (*see* Table 9.9) are quite similar in terms of sign (direction) and significance, but they are substantially smaller in terms of size with reference to coverage. Due to the aid schemes, coverage increases by 5.75% (2 Mbps), 10.4% (6 Mbps) and 13.31% (≥ 16 Mbps), respectively. Results on the numbers of ISPs are very similar to the ones obtained from the main specification. Only for fibre, no any significant treatment effect is found.

Table 9.9 Average Treatment Effect – Treated Municipalities in Lower Saxony Versus Other West German Municipalities

	Coverage			*Number of ISPs in Different Technologies*				
	2 Mbps	*6 Mbps*	*≥ 16 Mbps*	*Total ISPs*	*DSL ISPs*	*Cable ISPs*	*Mobile ISPs*	*FTTH ISPs*
Treated x Post-treatment	5.75*** (1.61)	10.35*** (1.98)	13.31*** (2.04)	0.20*** (0.07)	0.33*** (0.06)	0.14*** (0.03)	0.22*** (0.06)	-0.02 (0.02)
Post-treatment	28.65*** (4.92)	48.75*** (6.16)	50.71*** (6.53)	1.62*** (0.23)	0.81*** (0.18)	0.14* (0.09)	2.62*** (0.19)	0.04 (0.08)
R-Squared	0.485	0.576	0.650	0.859	0.764	0.280	0.925	0.255
Observations	2,021	2,021	2,021	2,021	2,021	2,021	2,021	2,021

Source: Lear, DIW Berlin and Analysys Mason (2017).
Notes: Total population, college degree, population between 24 and 65 years old, unemployment rate, industry shares at the 1-digit level, as well as municipality fixed-effects, are controlled for. Robust standard errors clustered at the municipality level are reported in parentheses.
The symbols ***, **, * represent significance at the 1%, 5% and 10% levels respectively.

There are good economic and statistical explanations for these results. First, the coverage at low speeds (1 and 2 Mbps) in Lower Saxony was higher than the average coverage in Germany – and much higher than in Bavaria – for both the treated and the control municipalities. This means that even the treated municipalities in Lower Saxony were more advanced in terms of broadband infrastructure than the average German municipality. It would therefore seem reasonable to expect that the effect of the aid schemes, if at all present, is smaller especially for low-speed broadband, where Lower Saxony was already quite advanced. Second, the differences in observable characteristics discussed above also had implications for the matching procedure. Indeed, it was more difficult to find good control municipalities for Lower Saxony than for Bavaria.

[2] Heterogeneity Depending on Observable Characteristics of the Municipalities

The next dimensions of heterogeneity considered are based on observable characteristics, including DSL internet coverage in the pre-treatment period, the degree of industrialisation and the reach of the pre-existing telecommunications infrastructure. Table 9.10 summarises the results of regressions run on the different sub-samples, leaving the set of control variables unchanged. For the sake of space, this table only reports the coefficient estimate for the average treatment effect within that particular sample.

Table 9.10 Heterogeneous Treatment Effects – Treated Municipalities in Bavaria and Lower Saxony Versus Other Municipalities in Western Germany

	Coverage			*Number of ISPs in Different Technologies*					
	2 Mbps	*6 Mbps*	*≥ 16 Mbps*	*Total ISPs*	*DSL ISPs*	*Cable ISPs*	*Mobile ISPs*	*FTTH ISPS*	*N*
Treat x Post (Low coverage)	15.34*** (1.53)	22.74*** (1.70)	22.76*** (1.65)	0.22*** (0.06)	0.22*** (0.05)	0.03 (0.02)	0.17*** (0.05)	-0.00 (0.02)	3,130
Treat x Post (High coverage)	8.15*** (1.52)	17.08*** (1.81)	19.38*** (1.78)	0.19*** (0.07)	0.35*** (0.05)	0.09*** (0.02)	0.21*** (0.05)	0.05*** (0.02)	3,131
Treat x Post (Low Industry)	10.95*** (1.45)	18.45*** (1.67)	20.19*** (1.63)	0.34*** (0.06)	0.31*** (0.05)	0.09*** (0.02)	0.28*** (0.05)	0.08*** (0.02)	3,118
Treat x Post (High Industry)	13.86*** (1.73)	23.85*** (2.01)	23.35*** (1.98)	0.04 (0.07)	0.22*** (0.06)	0.01 (0.03)	0.07 (0.05)	-0.04* (0.02)	3,143
Treat x Post (Low Distance)	7.04*** (0.79)	13.20*** (1.25)	16.52*** (1.40)	0.22*** (0.06)	0.44*** (0.05)	0.09*** (0.02)	0.22*** (0.05)	0.06*** (0.02)	3,133
Treat x Post (High Distance)	15.36*** (1.85)	25.93*** (2.08)	24.93*** (2.05)	0.21*** (0.06)	0.15*** (0.05)	0.02 (0.02)	0.15*** (0.05)	-0.02 (0.02)	3,128

Source: Lear, DIW Berlin and Analysys Mason (2017).
Notes: Each cell represents one regression. The different dependent variables are represented in the columns. A control is made for the year 2015, total population, college degree, population between 24 and 65 years old, unemployment rate, industry shares (1-digit level), as well as municipality fixed-effects. Robust standard errors clustered at the municipality level are reported in parentheses. The symbols ***, **, * represent significance at the 1%, 5%, and 10% levels respectively.

While all results are in line with the average effects – the aid was effective and increased competition in almost all subsamples – they also show some degree of heterogeneity. For instance, the effect of the aid on coverage is larger in municipalities with a below-median DSL penetration in 2010, with an above-median industrialisation structure, and farther from the MDF. This is true for all speeds. These results are rather encouraging, as they are consistent with the idea that the aid was most effective where it was most needed (i.e., in municipalities with low DSL coverage pre-aid and a high distance from the MDF). However, the aid schemes appeared to be more effective in raising broadband coverage in industrialised municipalities, probably because investments in such municipalities are likely to be more profitable.

The effects on the number of ISPs are also heterogeneous. On aggregate, the effects are significantly larger in municipalities with a below-median level of industrialisation, and in municipalities located not too far from the MDF, particularly for DSL. This would suggest that the costs of entering the DSL markets are related to distance to the MDF.

The finding that there is no additional increase in the number of ISPs in the more industrialised municipalities might be interpreted as signifying windfall gains, as the ISPs would have entered in these municipalities even without the aid. However, they would not have covered as many of the white areas within the municipalities as they did thanks to the aid.

[3] Heterogeneity Depending on the Size of the Aid

The final step of the analysis is to study whether the effect of aid is proportional to the amount spent. Such an analysis could contribute to answering the question 'How much aid is enough?' According to the data, the average grant provided to a municipality was EUR 82,449 with a standard deviation of EUR 26,780. In order to exploit the variation in this data, three categories of aids are considered: small grants up to EUR 50,000, corresponding to 27% of the treated municipalities; medium-sized grants between EUR 50,000 and EUR 100,000, corresponding to 26% of treated municipalities; and large grants of EUR 100,000 or more, corresponding to the remaining 47% of the municipalities.

Table 9.11 reports the results of the estimation. For coverage, the effect increases with the size of the grant, and this effect is independent of speed. Yet, the largest marginal gains occur between the first and the second grant categories. Instead, the extra gains derived from larger grants in excess of EUR 100,000 are relatively small. For the number of ISPs, the grant size does not seem to matter that much.

Overall, the authors of the study tentatively conclude that the most effective grants are the medium-sized ones. Grants larger than EUR 100,000 mostly add additional positive effects, but these marginal effects are not large. To make a clear welfare analysis, however, one would need a different - potentially structural - model to cleanly measure the changes in consumer surplus generated by the increased coverage and number of ISPs.

Table 9.11 Heterogeneity Depending on the Size of the Aid – Treated Municipalities in Bavaria and Lower Saxony Versus Other West German Municipalities

	Coverage			*Number of ISPs in Different Technologies*				
	2 Mbps	*6 Mbps*	*≥ 16 Mbps*	*Total ISPs*	*DSL ISPs*	*Cable ISPs*	*Mobile ISPs*	*FTTH ISPs*
Grant ≤ EUR 50,000 x Year 2015	1.23 (1.64)	5.35*** (1.85)	5.99*** (1.82)	0.16** (0.06)	0.21*** (0.05)	-0.01 (0.02)	0.11** (0.05)	-0.02 (0.02)
Grant EUR 50,000-100,000 x Year 2015	14.59*** (1.71)	22.34*** (1.92)	24.01*** (1.89)	0.30*** (0.07)	0.34*** (0.05)	0.07*** (0.02)	0.18*** (0.05)	0.02 (0.02)
Grant ≥ EUR 100,000 x Year 2015	17.32*** (1.42)	28.44*** (1.60)	29.42*** (1.57)	0.20*** (0.06)	0.32*** (0.04)	0.10*** (0.02)	0.25*** (0.04)	0.05*** (0.02)
Demographics & Technology	YES	YES	YES	YES	YES	YES	YES	YES
Municipality Fixed-effects	YES	YES	YES	YES	YES	YES	YES	YES
R-Squared	0.493	0.597	0.659	0.846	0.747	0.227	0.917	0.117
Observations	6,261	6,261	6,261	6,256	6,256	6,256	6,256	6,256

Source: Lear, DIW Berlin and Analysys Mason (2017).
Notes: A control is made for the year 2015, total population, college degree, population between 24 and 65 years old, unemployment rate, industry shares (1-digit), as well as municipality fixed-effects. Robust standard errors clustered at the municipality level are reported in parentheses.
The symbols ***, **, * represent significance at the 1%, 5% and 10% levels respectively.

[B] Alternative Control Groups

In the analysis above, the control group consists of 6,200 municipalities from Western Germany that match the treated municipalities in terms of observable characteristics. Choosing the control municipalities within all other West German states can potentially lead to results biased towards zero, as some of the control municipalities might have been potentially treated as well. Therefore, the results reported above should be seen as a lower bound of the effect of the broadband aid schemes. To enhance the robustness of the findings, this section presents results based on two alternative definitions of the counterfactual.

First, treated municipalities in Bavaria –best suited for the analysis as they received most aid – are compared to other non-treated municipalities from that same state that match them in terms of observable characteristics. As it is possible to identify precisely which municipalities in Bavaria have been treated and which have not been treated, it is certain that none of the control municipalities in Bavaria received aid. This robustness check thereby avoids the potential bias from including aided municipalities in the control group. However, as almost all municipalities in Bavaria obtained State aid, it is more difficult to find a good match for treated municipalities from a much more reduced pool of municipalities. The results presented in Appendix 2[A] confirm that the aid schemes had a large positive impact on coverage and the number of ISPs.

Second, treated municipalities in Bavaria are compared to other municipalities from a similar state that made limited use of the aid schemes. Specifically, Baden Württemberg is used as a comparator for Bavaria.[24] This control group provides a different trade-off. On the one hand, municipalities in Baden Württemberg should provide a good match as it is quite similar to Bavaria. Consequently, endogeneity problems due to unobservables are likely to be relatively limited. On the other hand, the potential number of good matches per household is significantly lower than when choosing from the whole of Germany. The results presented in the Appendix 2[B] are reassuring because they confirm the previous result, independently of chosen counterfactual.

§9.09 CONCLUSION

The case study summarised in this chapter analyses the effect of German broadband State aid schemes on the development of broadband coverage in rural areas. Its novelties are twofold. First, it combines in a single framework the analysis of the effectiveness of the aid and of its impact on the conditions of competition. Second, it uses three different approaches to measure these effects: a descriptive analysis, a matching procedure to define a control group of West German municipalities as similar as possible to the aided municipalities and a Difference-in-Differences analysis.

This analysis shows that the German aid schemes aimed at giving private operators an incentive to offer affordable basic broadband services in rural areas have been effective. First, the schemes increased coverage within municipalities benefitting from the aid relative to comparable municipalities that did not receive aid. This increase in broadband coverage ranged from almost 12 % for connections at 2 Mbps to over 20 % increases for connections at speeds larger than 16 Mbps, which suggests that the aided municipalities gained two to three years in broadband development when compared to the non-aided municipalities.

Second, the broadband aid schemes did not impair competition within the municipalities concerned. On the contrary, the number of ISPs active in aided municipalities went up by 2.0 between 2010 and 2015, which represents an increase of 12 % over the trend in non-aided municipalities, where the number of ISPs grew by almost 1.8. This difference in the number of additional ISPs can be observed for all technologies.

Third, there is some degree of heterogeneity in the effects of the aid schemes on broadband coverage and the number of ISPs active in the different municipalities. The

24. The total amount of public resources spent by Baden Württemberg in the period 2008-2013 was limited to EUR 2.7 million (also including the aid allocated under the regional aid scheme N570/2007). Baden Württemberg ranked second to last in terms of aid per capita among the German states.

effects on broadband coverage were stronger in municipalities that were lagging behind before the launch of the aid schemes. More specifically, the aid schemes had a greater effect in Bavaria as compared to Lower Saxony (where broadband coverage was already relatively high), in municipalities with low DSL coverage and in municipalities that were located further away from the MDF. This seems to indicate that the aid was most effective where it was most needed. Moreover, the effectiveness of medium-sized grants (between EUR 50,000 and EUR 100,000) appeared to be larger than that of smaller and larger grants. Finally, a number of robustness checks were carried out, showing that the main results were not affected by the choice of control group.

The case study summarised here used very detailed database, which allowed drawing a number of conclusions about the causal effects of Germany's broadband aid schemes. Nevertheless, more could have been done if it had been possible to identify which technology was subsidised in each single municipality, which operator received the aid and when, and what conditions of open access were imposed on the ISPs benefitting from the aid. For future analysis, the authors of the case study consider that the European Commission should require that aid beneficiaries be much more transparent by providing more detailed information on how the State aid has been used. Finally, it would be useful to investigate the potential effects associated with geographic proximity and/or spillovers across municipalities, which have not been taken into account in the present case study.

APPENDIX 1: DATASET

A specific dataset was constructed for the purpose of the analysis presented here. The dataset is a panel of 8,000 municipalities representing virtually all municipalities in Western Germany for the period 2008-2015. A distinction is made between the sources of information for the dependent variables (broadband coverage as well as the number and identity of ISPs) and control variables (also used in the propensity score matching procedure).

[A] Dependent Variables

The data on the dependent variables were obtained from the firm TÜV Rheinland Consulting GmbH. This component of the database contains yearly observations from 2010 to 2015 on broadband coverage at different speeds (2 Mbps, 6 Mbps, ≥ 16 Mbps). Moreover, it provides the name of the operators offering broadband services in each municipality as well as the technology used (fixed line, mobile, cable, fibre). The database had been prepared for the German Federal Ministry for Transport and Digital Infrastructure within the context of the 'Future Broadband' project. Due to budget limitations and because Eastern Germany is characterised by very different technological conditions,[25] the dataset used for the present analysis covers municipalities in Western German states only: Baden-Württemberg, Bavaria (Bayern), Hesse (Hessen), Lower Saxony (Niedersachsen), North Rhine-Westphalia (Nordrhein-Westfalen), Rhineland-Palatinate (Rheinland-Pfalz) and Schleswig-Holstein.

The dataset is completed with data from Falck et al. (2014) on internet penetration (i.e., the share of the population having access to the internet) at the municipal level for the years 2005-2008. This database allows to determine the evolution of broadband coverage before the launch of the aid schemes in 2008. Information about the trend in the dependent variable before the policy intervention is required for the correct application of the Difference-in-Differences method. Falck et al. also provide information on the broadband network in operation at the time – including the location of the MDFs.[26]

[B] Control Variables

For each municipality a rich set of variables capturing demand and supply conditions affecting broadband investment is available. These data were downloaded from the

25. The fixed line (DSL) infrastructure network in Eastern Germany was installed in the 1990s following the German reunification, as opposed to the 1960s in Western Germany. Furthermore, the East German network is partly based on a special type of fibre wires as opposed to the copper wires used in Western Germany.
26. MDFs – main distribution frames – are the nodes of the telephone grid, and each house is connected to one, and only one, of these nodes. An increase in the distance to the MDF (used as control variable of the broadband network structure) adds to the infrastructure investments required and causes a non-linear loss in speed (quality) of a DSL signal. Beyond a certain distance, the technology no longer works.

'Regionaldatenbank Deutschland' database constructed by Germany's Federal Statistical Office and the statistical offices of the German states.

Specifically, information on total population, average income, education, age structure, unemployment and the percentage of surface used by firms and industry was collected. To account for the industrial structure of a given municipality, information on the number of firms in each industrial sector (both at the 1-digit and 2-digits levels) was also gathered. Based on this information, it was possible to create variables representing the share of the firms in a specific sector over the total number of firms operating in that specific municipality. Most variables are computed at the municipal level. However, for some variables, data were available only at the more aggregate district level.[27]

This data was complemented with a dataset containing geographic contour data (altitude, ruggedness) obtained from the *Bundesamt für Kartographie und Geodäsie*. Specifically, a ruggedness index is calculated. This index is a measure that expresses the amount of elevation difference between adjacent cells of a digital elevation grid and thus captures how flat or mountainous a municipality is.

Finally, data on the broadband network structure (e.g., distance from the MDF and number of MDFs in a given municipality) were taken from Falck et al. (2014).

27. The district (Kreis) is the next administrative subdivision after the municipality. There are almost 500 districts in Germany, which means that, on average, there are 16 municipalities in each district.

APPENDIX 2: ROBUSTNESS CHECKS

This Appendix reports some further robustness checks. In particular, the main regressions presented in the core of the chapter are replicated but using different samples of treated and control municipalities.

[A] Bavaria Versus Bavaria

In this section, treated municipalities in Bavaria are compared to non-treated municipalities in Bavaria. This approach has the advantage to make sure that the control municipalities have not been treated. However, it substantially reduces the sample, as it is more difficult to find a good match for treated municipalities from a much more reduced pool of municipalities. Results in Table 9.12 are again very similar to those in the main text.

Table 9.12 Average Treatment Effect – Treated Municipalities in Bavaria Versus Non-treated Municipalities in Bavaria

	Coverage			*Number of ISPs in Different Technologies*				
	2 Mbps	*6 Mbps*	*≥ 16 Mbps*	*Total ISPs*	*DSL ISPs*	*Cable ISPs*	*Mobile ISPs*	*FTTH ISPs*
Treated x Post-treatment	17.48*** (1.27)	28.00*** (1.51)	27.11*** (1.53)	0.25*** (0.07)	0.21*** (0.05)	0.07*** (0.02)	0.05 (0.05)	0.07*** (0.02)
Post-treatment	9.34** (3.78)	14.75*** (4.77)	27.49*** (4.96)	1.98*** (0.21)	1.29*** (0.18)	0.05 (0.08)	3.04*** (0.17)	-0.11* (0.06)
R-Squared	0.474	0.589	0.662	0.843	0.774	0.214	0.918	0.126
Observations	2,660	2,660	2,660	2,660	2,660	2,660	2,660	2,660

Source: Lear, DIW Berlin and Analysys Mason (2017).
Notes: There is a control for total population, college degree, population between 24 and 65 years old, unemployment rate, public expenditure over total revenue at the municipal level, industry shares at the 1-digit, as well as municipality fixed-effects. Robust standard errors clustered at the municipality level are reported in parentheses.
The symbols ***, **, * represent significance at the 1%, 5% and 10% levels respectively.

[B] Bavaria Versus Baden Württemberg

In this section, treated municipalities in Bavaria are compared to other municipalities in Baden Württemberg. Results in Table 9.13 are qualitatively the same as in the main regressions, though the size of the effects is smaller.

Table 9.13 Average Treatment Effect – Treated Municipalities in Bavaria Versus Other Municipalities in Baden Württemberg

	Coverage			*Number of ISPs in Different Technologies*				
	2 Mbps	*6 Mbps*	*≥ 16 Mbps*	*Total ISPs*	*DSL ISPs*	*Cable ISPs*	*Mobile ISPs*	*FTTH ISPs*
Treated x Post-treatment	6.53* (3.65)	17.35*** (4.48)	16.52*** (4.33)	0.97*** (0.16)	1.24*** (0.13)	0.14*** (0.05)	0.67*** (0.11)	0.17*** (0.05)
Post-treatment	10.88* (5.63)	13.92** (6.52)	20.82*** (6.32)	1.82*** (0.22)	0.83*** (0.18)	0.27*** (0.10)	3.05*** (0.17)	-0.15* (0.08)
R-Squared	0.479	0.588	0.660	0.842	0.772	0.201	0.924	0.144
Observations	1,934	1,934	1,934	1,932	1,932	1,932	1,932	1,932

Source: Lear, DIW Berlin and Analysys Mason (2017).
Notes: There is a control for total population, college degree, population between 24 and 65 years old, unemployment rate, public expenditure over total revenue at the municipal level, industry shares at the 1-digit level, as well as municipality fixed-effects. Robust standard errors clustered at the municipality level are reported in parentheses.
The symbols ***, **, * represent significance at the 1%, 5% and 10% levels respectively.

REFERENCES

Belloc F., Nicita A. and Rossi M.A. (2012), 'Whither policy design for broadband penetration? Evidence from 30 OECD countries', *Telecommunications Policy*, 36(5), pp. 382-398.

Canzian G., Poy S. and Schüller S. (2015), 'Broadband diffusion and firm performance in rural areas: Quasi-experimental evidence', IZA Discussion Paper No. 9429.

Elixmann D. and Neumann K.H. (2013), 'The broadband State aid rules explained: An eGuide for decision makers', study prepared by WIK-Consult for the European Commission, DG Communications Networks, Content & Technology.

European Commission (2013), 'EU Guidelines for the application of State aid rules in relation to the rapid deployment of broadband networks', Communication from the Commission, (2013/C 25/01).

Falck O., Gold R. and Heblich S. (2014), 'E-lections: Voting behavior and the internet', *American Economic Review*, 104(7), pp. 2238-2265.

Heckman J.J., Ichimura H. and Todd P. (1998), 'Matching as an econometric evaluation estimator', *Review of Economic Studies*, 65(2), pp. 261-294.

Hüschelrath K., Falck O., Dürr N.S. and Briglauer W. (2019), 'Does State aid for broadband deployment in rural areas close the digital and economic divide?', *Information Economics and Policy*, 46(C), pp. 68-85.

Lear, DIW Berlin and Analysys Mason (2017), 'Economic impact of competition policy enforcement on the functioning of telecoms markets in the EU', Final report prepared for the Directorate-General for Competition of the European Commission, Publications Office of the European Union.

Nardotto M., Valletti T. and Verboven F. (2015), 'Unbundling the incumbent: Evidence from UK broadband', *Journal of the European Economic Association*, 13(2), pp. 330-362.

Nascimbene B. and Di Pascale A. (2018), 'The modernisation of State aid for economic and social development', Volume 14 of *Studies in European Economic Law and Regulation*, Springer.

Regeneris Consulting (2015), 'Final evaluation of Superfast North Yorkshire'.

Wallsten S. (2005), 'Broadband penetration: An empirical analysis of state and federal policies', Working Paper 05-12, AEI-Brookings Joint Center for Regulatory Studies.

Xiao M. and Orazem P.F. (2011), 'Does the fourth entrant make any difference?: Entry and competition in the early US broadband market', *International Journal of Industrial Organization*, 29(5), pp. 547-561.

CHAPTER 10

The Impact of State Aid on the Survival and Financial Viability of Aided Firms*

Sven Heim, Kai Hüschelrath, Philipp Schmidt-Dengler & Maurizio Strazzeri

We estimate the causal impact of restructuring aid granted by the European Commission between 2000 and 2012 on the survival and financial viability of aided firms. Using a comprehensive dataset, we find that restructuring aid decreases the hazard rate of a market exit by 58-68% and increases firms' average survival time by eight to fifteen years, depending on the definition of firm survival. We also find that aid-receiving firms have a significantly higher probability to improve their financial viability than the counterfactual group in the longer run.

§10.01 INTRODUCTION

The granting of State aid or subsidies is a traditional and important tool of public policy.[1] By reallocating funds – on a selective basis – to industries or firms, governments on the one hand may aim at compensating for market failures or market imperfections thereby improving market allocations and social welfare. On the other

---

* The chapter is based on the study *Ex post evaluation of the impact of restructuring aid decisions on the viability of aided (non-financial) firms* produced within a framework contract with the European Union by a consortium consisting of WIFO (Vienna), ECORYS (Rotterdam), Idea Consult (Brussels), SPI (Coimbra), and ZEW (Mannheim). The opinions expressed are ours only and do not represent the European Commission's official position. The European Commission has the rights to the results of the study. We are grateful to the entire project team and the European Commission for helpful discussions in the course of the project. We are further indebted to Wolfgang Briglauer, Dirk Czarnitzki, Martin Hud, Ulrich Laitenberger, Eva Pichler, Christian Rammer, Michael Schröder and Douglas Thompson for helpful remarks on earlier versions of the paper. This Chapter is a reprint of a paper published in European Economic Review, 100, pp. 193-214, Elsevier, November 2017.

1. As noted by the OECD (2010), there are no substantive differences in the definitions of 'State aid' and 'subsidies'. In the remainder of this chapter, we will use the term 'State aid' (referring to the official wording of the European Commission).

hand such selective reallocations are not only generally suspected of causing incremental societal costs by distorting competition and trade but may also be guided by less altruistic alternative governmental motives – such as, for example, the preservation of powers (*see, e.g.*, Boycko et al., 1996; Hainz and Hakenes, 2012) – typically associated with negative welfare effects.[2] This ambivalence in the motivations – together with increasing political pressure to reduce government spending – has led many countries to tie such transfers to the fulfilment of strict conditions.

For the European Union and its key objective of creating common European markets for goods and services, the control of State aid has always been of key interest. However, although the 1957 Treaty of Rome already included key provisions on State aid, it took until the end of the last century before the European Commission successfully started several stages of substantial reforms of the existing rules aiming at 'less and better targeted State aid' (European Commission, 2005) and 'good aid that supports growth' (European Commission, 2012).[3] The general success of these initiatives – such as the 2005-2009 State Aid Action Plan and the 2012-2014 State Aid Modernisation Reform – is reflected not only in the development and implementation of stricter and more transparent State aid rules but also in a shrinking significance of (non-crisis related) State aid transfers from 1.1% of GDP in 1992 to 0.49% of GDP (EU-28) in 2013.

However, despite its decreasing share, State aid continues to be an important tool of government policy in the European Union reflected in overall (non-crisis related) transfers of about EUR 64.4 billion in 2013.[4] While a large fraction of European State aid is granted for so-called horizontal objectives covering areas such as environmental protection, regional development as well as research and development (including innovation), sectoral aid (excluding both agricultural and transport sectors) still accounted for about 10% of European State aid transfers in 2013. In fact, as part of its sectoral aid activities, the European Commission considers rescue and restructuring (henceforth R&R) aid as key policy tool to support firms in difficulty, aiming at avoiding their dissolution with all the expected negative (societal and economic) consequences such as loss of employment, technical know-how and expertise or disruption to important services. However, a necessary precondition for the granting of R&R aid by the European Commission in a specific case is a sufficiently high likelihood that the respective aided firm will return to viability after going through the compulsory restructuring process (thus avoiding 'wasteful' public spending).

In this context, we estimate the causal impact of fifty-six positive restructuring aid decisions – reached by the European Commission between 2000 and 2012 – on the survival probability and financial viability of aided firms. Based on the construction of

2. *See also* Dewatripont and Seabright (2006), who developed a model in which politicians fund projects that are wasteful in order to signal their diligence. For detailed overviews of the (efficiency- or equity-related) rationales for granting State aid in general and the existence of a European State aid control in particular, *see* Nitsche and Heidhues (2006) or Friederiszick et al. (2006).
3. *See* Kassim and Lyons (2013) for a detailed overview of the history of European State aid policy.
4. Sources: 1992 data stem from Tunali and Fidrmuc (2015) while 2013 data were retrieved from the European Commission's State Aid Scoreboard.

a non-aid-receiving counterfactual group through a matching procedure, our application of survival models shows that restructuring aid increases a firm's average survival time by eight to fifteen years and decreases the hazard rate by 58-68%, depending on the definition of firm survival. Subsequently, estimating ordered response models, we find strong support that, in the longer run, aid-receiving firms have a significantly higher probability to improve their financial viability than the counterfactual group of non-aided firms. While we find that the granted aid measures were effective in increasing firm survival and long-term financial viability, we do not evaluate the efficiency of these measures. Though this would be a highly relevant extension of our research question it appears hardly feasible due to the substantial heterogeneity of the restructuring plans and the applied aid tools ranging from direct grants, different types of loans or guarantees to debt write-off and tax deferment etc. (*see* Table 10.14). This heterogeneity makes it hard to express the costs of aid in monetary units. Furthermore, it should be noted that the estimation of overall welfare effects is also beyond the scope of the chapter for the same reasons.

The remainder of this chapter is structured as follows. In section 10.02, we provide an overview of the institutional background of R&R aid transfers in the European Union and briefly review the existing literature that has estimated the impact of R&R aid on firm survival and financial viability. Section 10.03 continues with the presentation of our econometric identification strategy. Section 10.04 gives a detailed description of our data set, and section 10.05 explains our matching procedure. In section 10.06 we present our empirical results of, first, treatment effects at the end of our sample period (subsection 10.06[A]), second, survival models (subsection 10.06[B]) and, third, ordered response models (subsection 10.06[C]). The presentation of our estimation results is followed by a robustness section (section 10.07) and a discussion of selected policy implications of our empirical results (section 10.08). Section 10.09 concludes the chapter with a review of its main insights and an identification of avenues for future research.

§10.02 INSTITUTIONAL BACKGROUND AND LITERATURE REVIEW

In this section, we first provide a description of State aid in the European Union in general and the concept of rescue and restructuring (R&R) aid in particular. Subsequently, we review the rather small existing literature, which studies the impact of R&R aid on the survival and financial viability of aided firms.

[A] State Aid and Rescue and Restructuring Aid in the European Union

According to Article 107 of the Treaty on the Functioning of the European Union (TFEU), State aid is defined as 'any aid granted by a Member State or through State resources in any form whatsoever which distorts or threatens to distort competition by favouring certain undertakings or the production of certain goods'. Granting State aid is generally prohibited unless it is justified by reasons of general economic development. To ensure that this prohibition is respected and exemptions are applied equally across the European Union, the European Commission is in charge of ensuring that State aid complies with EU rules. These rules can broadly be differentiated between general rules and procedures applied to all types of State aid cases and more specific guidelines referring to different types of State aid.

With respect to the general rules and procedures, EU State aid control requires prior notification of all new aid measures to the EC by the respective EU Member State (which is not allowed to implement any measures before receiving a positive or conditional EC decision).[5] Each State aid notification is followed by a preliminary investigation by the EC as part of which it may request additional information on the case from the respective Member State. Once the information collection process is finalised, the EC has two months to decide whether the aid is compatible with EU rules or whether an in-depth investigation is necessary to closer investigate – in cooperation with the respective EU Member State – serious doubts that remained after the preliminary investigation. At the end of its formal investigation – i.e., after a preliminary or an in-depth investigation – the EC adopts either a positive decision, a conditional decision or a negative decision.

Due to the broad and general character of the State aid rules and procedures in the EU just described, reaching the aim of a transparent and strict application procedure requires several regulations and different guidelines for different types of aid. For example, the European Commission's State Aid Modernisation (SAM) reform – launched in 2012 and completed in 2014 – aimed at providing 'more efficient decision making and procedures for granting growth-supporting aid' through the reform (or creation, respectively) of both key regulations (such as the Procedural Regulation or the General Block Exemption Regulation) and several more specific guidelines (such as Broadband, Regional Aid, Research and Development and Innovation (R&D&I) or R&R Guidelines).[6]

These different types of State aid are also reflected in the European State aid statistics, which first subdivide State aid expenditures into non-crisis aid and crisis aid. Limiting our further discussions to the former category, a further sub-division into horizontal objectives aid and sectoral aid is undertaken. Horizontal aid includes transfers for regional development, environmental aid, research and development (including innovation) and aid for small and medium-sized enterprises (SMEs). Sectoral aid, however, includes government transfers to agriculture and fisheries, transport, coal, steel and shipbuilding as well as R&R aid. Figure 10.1 below provides an overview of the development of the relative significance of the two main categories over time as well as the absolute amount of government spending for R&R aid as part of sectoral aid.[7]

As shown in the left-hand chart in Figure 10.1, the total sum of EU State aid peaked in the year 2009 with a value of EUR 82.8 billion; however, experienced a

5. Our characterisation of the general rules and procedures follows European Commission (2013), 'Competition: State Aid Procedures'.
6. *See* European Commission (2015, pp. 4) for further information.
7. For illustrative purposes, agricultural aid and transport aid are reported separately (although technically part of sectoral aid).

substantial downward trend in the following years reaching the smallest value of EUR 64.4 billion in 2013. Interestingly, the share of horizontal objectives aid increased from 64% in 2008 to 74% in 2013 leading to corresponding reductions in both agricultural aid (from 15% to 13%) and transport aid excluding railways (from 4% to 2%). Sectoral aid in the narrower sense – of which R&R aid is a significant fraction – is also found to have followed a decreasing trend from a share of 16% in 2008 to 10% in 2013.

Turning to the right-hand chart in Figure 10.1, it is on the one hand revealed that the share of R&R aid out of the (narrow-defined) sectoral aid category fluctuates between 5% in 2008 and 9% in 2009. In terms of the absolute amount of R&R aid granted by the European Commission, the average amount of EUR 693 million for the entire time period from 2008 to 2013 is characterised further by a maximum value of EUR 1,079 million in 2009 and a minimum value of EUR 504 million in 2013.

Figure 10.1 EU State Aid and Rescue and Restructuring Aid (2008-2013)

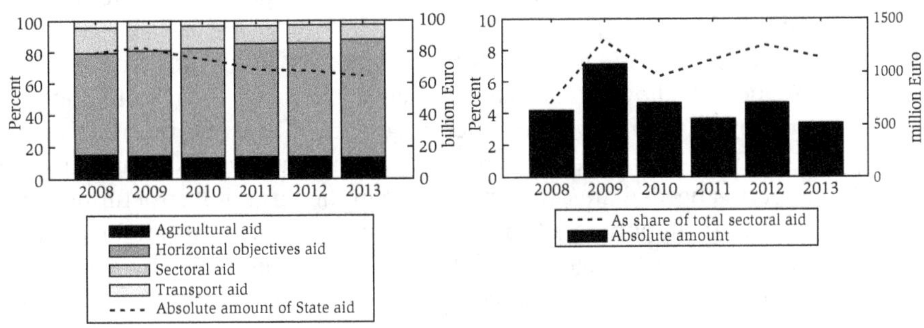

(a) EU State aid by main categories (b) EU R&R aid

Data source: EC State Aid Scoreboard

Although rather small in relative volume, R&R aid is an important policy tool for the European Commission. By definition, R&R aid can only be granted to firms in difficulty. According to the 2004 Rescue and Restructuring Guidelines[8] (hereafter referred as 2004 Guidelines), a firm in difficulty means a firm that 'is unable, whether through its own resources or with the funds it is able to obtain from its owner/shareholders or creditors, to stem losses which, without outside intervention by the public authorities, will almost certainly condemn it to going out of business in the short or medium term' (p. 3, paragraph 9, European Commission, 2004). In particular, a firm is regarded as being in difficulty in the following circumstances:

8. *See* European Commission (2004). The guidelines were adopted in 1994 and amended in 1999 and 2004. The current version of the guidelines became effective in 2014 (European Commission, 2014a).

- in the case of a limited liability company, where more than half of its registered capital has disappeared and more than one quarter of that capital has been lost over the preceding twelve months;
- in the case of a company where at least some members have unlimited liability for the debt of the company, where more than half of its capital as shown in the company accounts has disappeared and more than one quarter of that capital has been lost over the preceding twelve months;
- whatever the type of company concerned, where it fulfils the criteria under its domestic law for being the subject of collective insolvency proceedings' (p. 3, paragraph 10, European Commission, 2004).

Also according to the 2004 Guidelines, R&R aid may only be regarded as legitimate subject to certain conditions. It may be justified namely by social or regional policy considerations, by the need to take into account the beneficial role played by SMEs in the economy or, exceptionally, by the desirability of maintaining a competitive market structure when the demise of firms could lead to a monopoly or to a tight oligopolistic situation.

The 2004 Guidelines distinguish between rescue aid and restructuring aid. Rescue aid is designed to allow firms that are facing imminent collapse to stay in business for long enough to prepare a restructuring plan. It must be in the form of liquidity support (loans or guarantees) and has a maximum duration of six months. If further public support is needed after that, it must be in the form of restructuring aid. Restructuring aid aims at supporting a firm's restructuring and its return to long-term viability. It can be granted for a longer period, but must be accompanied by a detailed restructuring plan that meets a number of conditions (p. 12, paragraph 82, European Commission, 2004).

The overall objective of EU policy for restructuring aid to the non-financial sector is to contribute to successful restructuring of firms where this can be considered legitimate in the light of the justifications explained above. These justifications can only be met by firms that are viable. Moreover, the risks for distortive effects need to be minimised which implies that the amount of aid given is kept to the minimum necessary to implement the plan and appropriate measures are taken to minimise the adverse impact on competition.

In particular, the 2004 Guidelines therefore require the EC to verify the compatibility of restructuring aid according to three principles (p. 2, paragraph 7, European Commission, 2004). First, return to viability, i.e., a restructuring plan must be submitted showing that after completing its restructuring, the firm will be able to cover all its costs and to compete in the market on its own merits. Second, an own contribution, i.e., the aid recipient must make a significant contribution to the costs of the restructuring (up to 50% in the case of large companies) from its own resources. Third, compensatory measures, i.e., the adverse effects of the aid on trading conditions are minimised by divestments of assets, reductions in capacity or market presence and reduction of entry barriers to the markets concerned.

[B] Literature Review

The ex post evaluation of different types of State aid schemes has long been of interest in empirical economic research, most frequently probably with respect to the impact of R&D public policies on several outcomes such as investment and employment (*see, e.g.*, Bronzini and Piselli, 2016; Takalo et al., 2013; Czarnitzki and Lopes-Bento, 2013). More generally, in a recent meta-regression analysis Dimos and Pugh (2016) examine whether the empirical literature suggests that R&D subsidies cause a crowding out of private investments and conclude that this is not the case.

Other empirical papers have evaluated the impact of State aid on consumption growth for rural areas and income of the targeted areas. For example, in a seminal paper, Jalan and Ravallion (1998) evaluate the dynamic welfare gains from a poor-area development programme. Estimating a consumption-growth model using farm-household panel data for southern China, they find that targeted poor areas have significantly higher rates of consumption growth. Ravallion and Chen (2005) and Chen et al. (2009) find similar results.

However, the scope of applications on different types of aid measures is even wider. For instance, Grigolon et al. (2016) study the effects of scrapping schemes in the European car market, which present a subsidy for the purchase of new cars as a reaction to the financial crisis in Europe. They find that scrapping schemes helped to stabilise total car sales during the crisis and moreover also generated environmental benefits due to substitution of non-eligible to eligible (more fuel efficient) cars.

With regard to the impact of R&R aid the empirical literature is rather scarce and to our knowledge only Głowicka (2006), Chindooroy et al. (2007) and most recently Nulsch (2014) study the impact of aid on firm survival. All three papers use data on R&R aid cases decided by the European Commission. While Głowicka (2006) and Chindooroy et al. (2007) both investigate whether firms that receive both rescue and restructuring aid are more likely to survive than firms that only receive rescue aid, Nulsch (2014) also uses a control group of non-aid-receiving firms. However, as the control group is represented by the negative aid decisions by the European Commission endogeneity concerns arise and the results do not enable causal interpretation.

In this chapter we aim: (a) to identify the causal impact of receiving restructuring aid on the probability of firm survival using matching techniques; (b) based on the sample of matched non-aid-receiving firms and aided firms, to predict the difference in survival length for aided firms and the counterfactual group of non-aid-receiving firms; and (c) to estimate the impact of restructuring aid on the likelihood of a firm to recover in terms of financial viability in an ordered logit model framework.

§10.03 IDENTIFICATION OF THE EFFECT OF RESCUE AND RESTRUCTURING AID

We analyse the effect of R&R aid on the survival and financial viability of firms using the potential outcomes framework for causal inference popularised by Rubin (1974). We consider a sample of firms in which each firm i has a pair of potential outcomes, Y_{i0}

and Y_{i1}, where the former represents the outcome under control and the latter under active treatment. The two treatments under analysis here are given by the decision of the EU to grant State aid. We denote the treatment status of a firm with Z_i, where $Z_i = 1$ if the firm receives R&R aid and $Z_i = 0$ otherwise. For each firm, we observe a vector of pre-treatment variables $X_{i,pre}$ and the potential outcome of the treatment status it received.

For each firm, we define the treatment effect to be $Y_{i1} - Y_{i0}$, which is the difference in the two potential outcomes. The statistic of interest in our analysis is the average treatment effect on the treated (ATT), $E[Y_{i1} - Y_{i0} \mid Z = 1]$, which gives us the effect of R&R aid on those firms which received treatment. To calculate this statistic, both potential outcomes are required; however, we only observe one for each firm. This identification problem can be solved when treatment assignment is unconfounded (Rubin, 1978; Rosenbaum and Rubin, 1983). This assumption requires that treatment assignment is independent of the potential outcomes conditional on observable pre-treatment characteristics: $Z_i \perp Y_{i0}, Y_{i1} \mid X_{i,pre}$. In this case, we can write the ATT conditional on the observed covariates as

$$E[Y_{i1} \mid Z_i = 1, X_{i,pre} = x] - E[Y_{i0} \mid Z_i = 0, X_{i,pre} = x]$$

which is based on observable variables only (*see, e.g.*, Hirano et al., 2003). Finally, averaging the conditional ATT over the distribution of $X_{i,pre}$ yields to the population ATT.[9]

Since we consider several pre-treatment variables, many of which are continuous, it is not possible to compare firms of both groups with exactly the same pre-treatment characteristics. Rosenbaum and Rubin (1983) provide a solution to this problem using propensity scores which measure the probability of receiving treatment conditional on pre-treatment variables, $Pr(Z_i \mid X_{i,pre})$.

They show that if treatment assignment is independent of potential outcomes conditional on observable covariates, it is also independent of potential outcomes conditional on the propensity score $Pr(Z_i \mid X_{i,pre})$. This implies that adjusting for the propensity score is sufficient to correct for biases due to heterogeneity in $X_{i,pre}$.

We calculate the ATT using propensity scores with a matching algorithm. The idea is to find for each treated firm one or more control firms with a similar propensity score. After forming the matched sample, the ATT is estimated by comparing the observed outcomes between treated and control firms. Different matching algorithms have been used in the literature. We decided to use a greedy nearest neighbour matching in which a treated firm is matched with a control firm whose propensity score is closest. As we explain in more detail below, this procedure allows us to easily combine elements of direct matching (i.e., matching on a specific value of an observed covariate) and propensity score matching, which is especially useful in our analysis.

9. The unconfounding assumption stated above is necessary to derive the average treatment effect. In case of estimating the ATT, as it is the goal of this chapter, the assumption can be weakened to $Z_i \perp Y_{io} \mid Y_{ipre}$. However, to be consistent with a large part of the literature, we maintain the full unconfoundedness assumption.

So far, we have not specified the outcome variable of interest. We focus on firm survival and financial viability. With respect to firm survival, we would like to know the effect of R&R aid on, e.g., the time elapsing until a firm exits the market. As we cannot simply use the time until market exit as outcome variable (as firms live beyond the end of our sample period), we address this right censoring, by applying two complementary strategies. We first use the operating status of firms at the end of the sample period, the year 2014, as the outcome variable. In this case, the ATT provides us with the effect of R&R aid on the probability of survival of firms until 2014. While this easily implementable approach provides us with a general assessment about the effectiveness of State aid, it does not, however, quantify the impact relative to the time of treatment assignment. Consequently, our second approach makes use of survival analysis techniques, taking right censoring explicitly into account. The estimated treatment effect is the mean difference in expected survival time due to R&R. Finally, we consider an ordinal measure of financial viability (described in detail below). The treatment effect then corresponds to the effect on the probability of reaching a specific degree of financial viability.

§10.04 DATA

Our main data source, the commercial database Amadeus by Bureau van Dijk, provides an excellent opportunity to analyse the impact of State aid on the financial viability and survival of firms in the EU. Amadeus is a comprehensive database, including information of standard financial items (e.g., balance sheet items, profit and loss accounts, ratios) of around fourteen million companies across Europe. While other datasets are restricted to publicly listed firms for which information about financial items is easily accessible due to extended reporting requirements across Europe, a key element of Amadeus is that it provides financial items of private firms as well by utilising various country-specific information resources (e.g., chambers of commerce, registration offices). The detailed database of Amadeus with internationally comparable financial information for public and private firms is especially valuable in our analysis as R&R aid is given to both private and public firms.

Referring to our categorisation of State aid in the European Union introduced above, we concentrate on restructuring aid decisions by the European Commission between 2000 and 2012. Using the European Commission's online database, we first accessed the entire set of restructuring aid decisions. Out of this group of cases, we identified all positive restructuring decisions for individual firms (not aid schemes such as those that exist for SMEs). We exclude decisions in the financial sector as these are subject to specific R&R rules. Since the 2004 Guidelines are not valid for firms in the coal and steel sector either, we exclude these firms from the analysis as well. Furthermore, the agricultural sector and the fishery industry – as defined in section 5 of the 2004 Guidelines – as well as cases in which aid was granted to firms in the former German Democratic Republic in connection with the reunification of Germany were also excluded due to their status as special types of restructuring aid. In total, our case selection procedure eventually identified sixty-seven firms that received restructuring aid and fit to our criteria.

We are able to identify sixty-three out of these sixty-seven restructuring aid-receiving firms in Amadeus and obtain a large array of financial information for the years between 2000 and 2013. In addition, we construct a pool of possible matching partners which includes firms that (a) have its company headquarters within the EU28 and (b) operate in a similar industry (measured by the first two digits of the NACE Code) as the aid-receiving firms. The two restrictions capture the eligibility criteria in terms of location and industry described above to guarantee that the firms in our pool of possible matching partners are in general eligible to apply for R&R aid.

We had to cope with certain challenges in terms of data availability as Amadeus does not consistently report all financial information throughout our time period of interest. Due to the large number of possible matching partners, we are less concerned about data availability of non-aid-receiving firms. However, we aim at avoiding missing values with respect to variables of aid-receiving firms in order to keep as many of those firms as possible in our analysis. In particular, the values of variables for the years before State aid was granted are of relevance for the identification of appropriate matching partners. As a consequence, we imputed a small number of data points for some firms to avoid severe reductions in the sub-sample of aid-receiving firms. Still, due to severe gaps in the data we had to exclude six aid-receiving firms, leaving us with a sample of fifty-seven treated firms. A full documentation of the imputed data points can be found in Table 10.12 in the Appendix.

Additional country-level data is drawn from Eurostat. In particular, we obtain the following three variables: average unemployment rate of the last three years, ratio of subsidies to governmental expenditures and the percentage change in GDP per capita. These variables are measures, which might affect the propensity of a national government to provide aid to firms, and are also included in our matching procedure.

[A] Definition of Firm Survival

We use information provided in the Amadeus database to determine a firm's operating status. Based on this information we construct four different definitions of firm survival. They are summarised in Table 10.1.

Table 10.1 Definitions of Firm Survival

	Def. 1 *AM*	*Def. 2* *AMI*	*Def.3* *A*	*Def.4* *AI*
Active (A)	x	x	x	x
Insolvency procedure (I) **(In Liquidation/Bankruptcy/Default of Payment/Dormant)**	-	x	-	x
Merger or Takeover (M)	x	x	-	-
Dissolved (D)	-	-	-	-

Note: Crosses indicate that the respective status is included in the survival definition.

In survival definition one (AM), we define a firm as still being active if Amadeus reports *Active (A)* or *Merger or Takeover (M)* as the firm's operating status. However, in applying this definition, firms that are in *insolvency proceedings (I)* and firms that were *irrevocably dissolved (D)* are treated equally. This may be a too narrow definition of a firm being active since firms can possibly recover after going through insolvency proceedings. Hence, in the second definition (AMI) we utilise a less conservative definition with respect to a firm's market exit and also define firms that are in insolvency proceedings as being active since firms involved in insolvency proceedings can possibly recover.

Another concern relates to firms that were the target of a successful takeover bid. As in our definition above, we consider such firms as still being active. At times, acquired firms do not change their production capacity and how they operate in the market, in which case this definition is justified. However, many acquisitions take place in order to exploit synergies, and are followed by cost-saving measures, which may result in a significant reduction in the production capacity of the acquired firm. Here it would be more appropriate to define an acquisition as a market exit.

Since our data does not allow us to track the part of the newly formed cooperation that constitutes the acquired firm, we are not able to distinguish between a takeover which left the acquired firm unchanged and a takeover which is followed by a considerable reduction in the production capacity. Therefore, we also apply a third (A) and a fourth definition of firm survival (AI), which are equivalent to survival definition 1 (AM) and 2 (AMI) with the only difference that mergers and takeover are now considered as market exits.

The Amadeus database provides only information about a firm's operating status at a specific time. In our case, this is the year 2014, the end of our period of investigation. However, to analyse the effect of State aid on the time span in which a firm is active in the market, we need to know the year of market exit. A reasonable approach to determine the year of market exit is to use the year after the last annual financial report that is available in the Amadeus database. While this procedure might not be flawless, we are confident that it will not bias our result, as it is conducted for all firms in our sample equally.

[B] Definition of Firm's Financial Viability

In order to assess a firm's financial viability we apply the Z-score concept of Altman (1968, 2002). Altman (1968) proposes a multivariate procedure to predict a firm's probability of going bankrupt within two years. This probability can be separated into three categories: low, mid-level and high. We consider firms with a high probability of going bankrupt as firms with insufficient financial viability, firms with a mid-level probability of going bankrupt as firms with normal financial viability, and firms with a low probability of going bankrupt as firms with high financial viability.

According to Altman (1968), the probability of going bankrupt can be determined by Z-scores. These Z-scores are a linear combination of five financial ratios, weighted by different coefficients depending on the legal form of the company. The financial ratios included are: (i) working capital to total assets, (ii) retained earnings to total assets, (iii) EBIT to total assets, (iv) total revenue to total assets, and (v) market value of equity to total liabilities for public firms and book value of equity to total liabilities for private firms.[10] We use the coefficients and boundaries originally proposed by Altman (1968) to calculate Z-scores and separate firms financial viability into the three categories mentioned above.[11]

The Amadeus database includes information about almost all financial ratios needed to calculate Z-scores. The only information not provided are retained earnings and the market value of equity. Since retained earnings are part of the balance sheet item 'other equity', we use this balance sheet item as a proxy for retained earnings. With respect to the market value of equity, we use the book value of equity for both groups of firms, publicly listed and private.

[C] Descriptive Patterns

Table 10.2 shows mean values of the variables used in our matching procedure. The information provided for the treated group refers to the year before aid was granted to avoid confounding with treatment effects. As expected, firms that will receive State aid are, on average, in worse financial shape than other firms. This can be seen in lower profits, revenues per employee, liquidity ratios (current assets excluding inventories to current debt), and solvency ratios (shareholder funds to total assets). This also applies to the Altman Z-scores discussed above, which are significantly lower for treated firms.

In addition, State aid-receiving firms are older and larger. They have a higher employment level, keep more liabilities in absolute terms in their balance sheets, and are more often publicly listed in a stock market. Differences can also be seen with respect to the economic condition of the country in which the firms have their headquarters. State aid-receiving firms are, on average, from countries with better economic conditions in terms of unemployment and growth in GDP per capita. Surprisingly, countries in which treated firms are located have governments that tend to spend less on subsidies than in our control group.

There is no significant difference between the operating status in the year 2014 between both groups. Of course, this does not imply that State aid was ineffective. As shown in Table 10.2, State aid-receiving firms systematically differ with respect to many characteristics from those of our control group before aid was granted. These characteristics are likely to have an impact on our outcome variable. Firms that are in a better financial situation may prolong the time they can operate in the market as they

10. For a critical discussion of the use of Altman Z-scores, *see* Grice and Ingram (2001). Recent research suggests that the predictive power of the Altman Z-score is still high, with bankruptcy filings and financial distress being accurately predicted in over 90% of the cases (*see* Hayes et al., 2010).
11. For public (private) firms, the coefficients are 1.2 (0.717), 1.4 (0.847), 3.3 (3.107), 0.999 (0.998), and 0.6 (0.42) (the coefficients are listed in the same order as the ratios in the text). Public (private) firms are categorised as firms with: (i) insufficient financial viability if the Z-score is smaller than 1.81 (1.23); (ii) normal financial viability if the Z-score is between 1.81 and 2.99 (1.23 and 2.9); and (iii) high financial viability if the Z-score is larger than 2.99 (2.9).

can draw from larger financial resources. Hence, restricting our group of control firms to firms that are in a similar financial shape as aid-receiving firms may reduce the share of active control firms in 2014, and reveal a positive treatment effect.

Table 10.2 Mean Difference Tests Before Matching

	Control Group		*Treated Group*		
	Mean	*SD*	*Mean*	*SD*	*Significance*
Financial variables					
Profit (log)	2.082	4.305	-3.810	7.269	***
Fixed liabilities (log)	5.029	2.648	7.658	4.107	***
Current liabilities (log)	6.866	1.992	9.990	2.710	***
Revenue per employee	532.513	21,760.775	155.079	216.968	***
Altman Z-score category	2.092	0.745	1.351	0.582	***
Public firm	0.285	0.451	0.667	0.476	***
Liquidity ratio	1.543	3.252	0.671	0.647	***
Solvency ratio	33.358	25.062	7.950	37.992	***
Firm characteristics					
Employment (log)	2.682	1.560	6.107	1.764	***
Age (log)	2.672	0.785	3.055	1.137	**
Medium firm	0.397	0.489	0.298	0.462	-
Large firm	0.164	0.370	0.281	0.453	*
Very large firm	0.043	0.203	0.351	0.481	***
Macro level info					
Unemployment level (3 year avg.)	10.774	4.329	9.584	4.229	**
Share subsidies of gov. expend.	66.784	9.750	62.221	11.620	***
Pct. change in GDP per capita	0.454	2.440	2.177	2.483	***
Status in 2014					
AM	0.830	0.375	0.825	0.384	-
AMI	0.855	0.352	0.877	0.331	-
A	0.814	0.389	0.807	0.398	-
AI	0.839	0.367	0.860	0.350	-
Observations	1,132,360		57		
Number of firms	152,820		57		

Note: Significance levels: * p < 0.1, ** p < 0.05, *** p < 0.01.

See Table 10.1 for firm status definitions.

However, other differences in characteristics may work in the opposite direction. Larger firms, or firms located in countries with better economic conditions – as those in our sample of treated firms – may also stay in the market longer relative to SMEs, and firms that operate in an economically distressed environment. Adjusting our set of control firms to these characteristics may therefore increase the share of active firms in this group. Both confounding factors make it impossible to assess the impact of State aid on firm survival at this early stage of our analysis. Our matching procedure discussed in the following section aims at reducing this heterogeneity between treatment and control group, providing a clearer view of the consequences of R&R aid in the EU.

§10.05 MATCHING PROCEDURE

We estimate propensity scores, $Pr(Z_i|X_{i,pre})$, using a probit model. As covariates, we include the financial variables, firm characteristics, and macro-level information listed in Table 10.2 as well as industry dummies based on 1-digit NACE industry codes and dummies for the countries where the firms are located. The probit model is estimated with all firm-year observations of our pool of possible matching partners; with respect to treated firms, we only include the observation of the year before aid was granted.

As discussed in section 10.03, our identification strategy rests on the assumptions of unconfounded treatment assignment, which requires that treatment assignment is independent of potential outcomes conditional on observable pre-treatment characteristics. This means that our analysis can be confounded, e.g., when aided firms have systematically better political connections for which we cannot control. Unobserved heterogeneity caused by political favouritism is a potential concern in the analysis of the effectiveness of State aid. If unobserved political favouritism – such as ties to the government – increases the likelihood of receiving aid and prolongs firm survival, it is positively correlated with both treatment assignment and our outcome variable. Hence, the omission of unobserved political favouritism in the analysis would overestimate the impact of State aid. As we cannot definitely ensure that political favouritism does not play a role in at least some cases – despite the European Commission's efforts to prevent it – we will also run a robustness check using a heteroskedasticity based instrumental variable approach proposed by Lewbel (2012) to overcome this potential omitted variable bias. The results remain very stable as shown in the robustness section below (section 10.07). Additionally, we conduct a sensitivity analysis based on Ichino et al. (2008) to assess the impact of a possible overestimation. The results of this approach are also discussed in our robustness section.

The estimation results of our probit model are shown in first column of Table 10.13 in the Appendix. Our probit regression produced a reasonably good model fit (McFadden Pseudo R-Squared ≈ 0.39), indicating a high explanatory power of the included covariates. We use this model to predict propensity scores for each observation in our sample.

Matching based on propensity scores requires common support for the identification of the ATT, which implies that the distribution of pre-treatment covariates of treated and control firms overlap. We enforce this requirement based on the minimum and maximum of the estimated propensity scores in the treatment and control group. We delete observations whose propensity score is smaller than the minimum and larger than the maximum of the other group (*see* Caliendo and Kopeinig, 2008). This basic criterion avoids incomparable matches and discards one treated firm from our sample.[12]

We then proceed with our matching algorithm.[13] To select plausible control firms from our pool of potential matching partners, we conduct a greedy nearest neighbour matching with replacement based on the estimated propensity scores, in combination with elements of exact matching. We match a treated firm with a control firm whose propensity score is closest *conditional* on having the exact values on variables we consider especially important to define a valid counterfactual firm. These variables are: 2-digit NACE code, firm size, public firm, year of observation. Another potential variable for which exact matching seems appropriate is the country where the firm is located. While additionally including this variable would help control for regional policy differences, it considerably decreases the pool of potential matching firms. Especially large international firms, like airlines, have only few or no national counterparts that operate in a similar industry. Hence, we decided not to include the country where a firm is located to our set of exact matching variables, but rather control for regional policy differences by adding country dummies and other macro level information (*see* Table 10.2) as covariates in the propensity scores.

In order to examine whether our results discussed below are robust towards different specifications of neighbours, we report estimates with two different counterfactual groups. The first counterfactual group includes only the next nearest neighbour (NB1), while the second includes the three closest neighbours (NB3). Including multiple neighbours improves precision in our estimates, but it comes at the cost of increased bias.

Assessing match quality

After a successful propensity score matching procedure, we expect the distribution of the covariates to be balanced between treatment and matched control group. To check whether this is the case, we run the same probit model as before on our matched sample. Since the covariates should not significantly differ between aid-receiving and control firms after our matching procedure, the explanatory power of the model should be very low and the covariates should lack significance (Sianesi, 2004; Caliendo and Kopeinig, 2008). Indeed, comparing the Pseudo R-Squared before matching in the first column of Table 10.13 (Pseudo R-Squared $\approx$ 0.39) with the respective value of the probit regression after matching in the second and third columns of Table 10.13 (Pseudo R-Squared $\approx$ 0.17 for NB1 and Pseudo R-Squared $\approx$ 0.16 for NB3) confirms this expectation. Similarly, using a likelihood ratio test, the hypothesis that all covariates are jointly insignificant is rejected before ($p = 0.00$) but not after matching ($p = 0.83$ for NB1 and $p = 0.28$ for NB3).

12. Information on all remaining fifty-six restructuring aid cases are reported in Table 10.14 in the Appendix.
13. A matching protocol that briefly summarises the following description of our matching procedure can be found in Table 10.15 in the Appendix.

Table 10.3 Mean Difference Tests After Matching

	Treated		*NB1*		*NB3*		*Significance*	
	Mean	*SD*	*Mean*	*SD*	*Mean*	*SD*	*NB1*	*NB3*
Financial variables								
Profit (log)	-3.69	7.27	-2.50	8.11	-3.20	7.26	-	-
Fixed liabilities (log)	7.60	4.12	7.24	4.89	7.61	4.22	-	-
Current liabilities (log)	9.95	2.71	10.12	2.82	9.90	2.46	-	-
Revenue per employee	153.89	218.74	184.85	187.04	211.72	275.24	-	-
Altman Z-score category	1.36	0.59	1.39	0.65	1.49	0.71	-	-
Public firm	0.66	0.48	0.66	0.48	0.66	0.47	-	-
Liquidity ratio	0.68	0.65	0.62	0.41	0.90	2.57	-	-
Solvency ratio	9.53	36.39	15.19	30.41	14.26	28.24	-	-
Firm characteristics								
Employment (log)	6.09	1.77	5.92	2.32	5.75	2.00	-	-
Age (log)	3.05	1.14	2.67	0.91	2.88	0.93	*	-
Medium firm	0.30	0.46	0.30	0.46	0.30	0.46	-	-
Large firm	0.29	0.46	0.29	0.46	0.29	0.45	-	-
Very large firm	0.34	0.48	0.34	0.48	0.34	0.47	-	-
Macro level info								
Unemployment level (3 year avg.)	9.64	4.25	9.78	4.02	9.40	3.34	-	-
Share subsidies of gov. expenditure	62.67	11.22	63.97	8.29	64.48	8.65	-	-
Pct. change in GDP per capita	2.16	2.50	2.01	2.37	1.64	2.59	-	-
Observations	56		56		168			

Note: Significance levels: * $p < 0.1$, ** $p < 0.05$, *** $p < 0.01$. NB1 refers to the control group that includes only the nearest neighbours of treated firms; NB3 refers to the three closest neighbours. As nearest neighbour matching procedure is performed with replacement, we conduct a variance approximation as proposed by Lechner (2001).

Table 10.3 compares mean values of the covariates after the matching procedure. In comparison to the mean values before matching reported in Table 10.2, firms in our matched control group show now similar characteristics to aid-receiving firms. As shown in Table 10.3, we find only a significant difference between the selected control group (NB1) and aid-receiving firms with respect to firm age. Therefore, and in line with the above tests, the results suggests that the matching procedure was successful in identifying valid counterfactuals for the group of R&R aid-receiving firms.

As a last step we check whether both groups, aid-receiving and control firms, followed a similar trend in terms of their financial viability prior to the year in which the aid-receiving firms received the aid. This is relevant in order to ensure that post-treatment developments are not caused by different pre-treatment developments. Figure 10.2 confirms that this is indeed the case as both, the Altman Z-Score curve and the Altman Z-Score Categories curve, respectively, for aid-receiving firms and control group move parallel prior to the year of receiving aid with control firms even performing slightly better.

Figure 10.2 Assessing the Common Trend Before Treatment

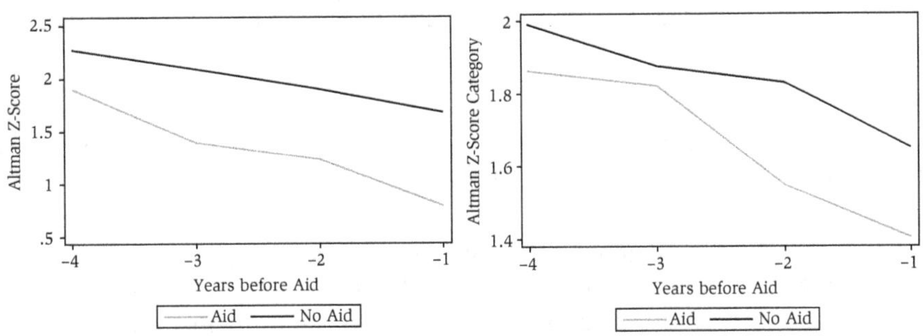

Note: Average financial viability before aid was granted by treatment status of firms. The left (right) chart measures financial viability with the continuous (categorical) Altman Z-scores explained in section 10.04.

§10.06 RESULTS

[A] Firm Survival until 2014

We first start with our analysis of the ATT using the operating status in 2014 as outcome variable. As explained in section 10.03, we can derive the ATT by comparing the observed mean average outcomes of aid-receiving and matched control firms. These values are reported in Table 10.4.

Table 10.4 Mean Difference Tests of Outcome Variable After Matching

Status	*Treated*	*Control group*		*Significance*	
		NB1	*NB3*	*NB1*	*NB3*
AM	0.82 (0.39)	0.68 (0.47)	0.67 (0.47)	*	**
AMI	0.88 (0.33)	0.73 (0.45)	0.73 (0.44)	*	**
A	0.80 (0.40)	0.63 (0.49)	0.62 (0.49)	**	***
AI	0.86 (0.35)	0.68 (0.47)	0.68 (0.47)	**	***
Observations	56	56	168		

Note: Significance levels: * $p < 0.1$, ** $p < 0.05$, *** $p < 0.01$. NB1 refers to the control group, which includes only the nearest neighbours of treated firms; NB3 refers to the three closest neighbours. As nearest neighbour matching procedure is performed with replacement, we conduct a variance approximation as proposed by Lechner (2001). Standard deviations are in parentheses. *See* Table 10.1 for firm status definitions.

Table 10.4 reveals that treatment in terms of receiving State aid exerted a significantly positive impact, which is robust to the choice of definition of the outcome variable suggesting that restructuring aid measures significantly increase the survival probability and reduce the probability of a firm's market exit, respectively.

For instance, the absolute difference in the probability of a firm to survive until at least 2014 is $0.82 - 0.67 = 0.15$ if we compare the outcome according to AM of the treated firms with the counterfactual group with one nearest neighbour. This means that whilst 82% of aided firms were active in the year 2014, only 67% of the matched non-aided firm were active, implying a difference of 15 percentage points with respect to firms operating status. As noted above, the difference of 15%, however, is the absolute difference meaning that from 100 firms 15 firms survive due to restructuring aid which otherwise had exited the market. In relative terms, the interpretation is that the average survival probability increases by 22% when a firm receives restructuring aid (0.15/0.67).

An alternative interpretation looks at the probability of a failure that is 1 minus the survival probability. Thus, aid recipients will exit the market with a probability of 18% and non-aid-receiving firms with 33% probability, respectively. In other words, receiving restructuring aid decreases the average risk of a failure by 45% (1-0.18/0.33) or, alternatively expressed, a non-aid-receiving firm from the counterfactual group has 83% (0.15/0.18) higher relative risk of failure than an aid recipient.

Table 10.5 Differences in Survival Probability and Failure Risk (NB3)

Status	*a* Absolute Difference	*b* Survival Pr. Control Group	*c = a/b* Pct. Increase of Survival Probability	*d = 1-b* Failure Risk Control Group	*e = a/d* Aid Reduces Risk
AM	15%	67%	22%	33%	45%
AMI	15%	73%	21%	27%	55%
A	18%	62%	29%	38%	47%
AI	18%	68%	26%	32%	56%

Note: *See* Table 10.1 for firm status definitions.

The differences in average outcome variables of the treated firms is statistically significant according to two-sided t-tests throughout all definitions and for both, the counterfactual groups with one and with three nearest neighbours, while there was no significant difference before in the full sample (*see* Table 10.2). Comparing the results for the different outcome definitions, we find the largest value for Definition AI, the outcome definition that considers acquisitions as market exits. In other words, aid-receiving firms are less frequently acquired compared to non-aid-receiving firms. Table 10.5 exemplary provides the respective calculations for the nearest neighbour (NB3).[14]

Limiting our discussion of the results to the very right of Table 10.5, it is shown that restructuring aid reduces the failure risk by between 45% and 56%. Also, the different definitions of survival reveal that the probability of being taken over is lower for aid recipients as is the probability to be in liquidation or under bankruptcy protection.

[B] Firm Survival Relative to Treatment

In this section, we continue investigating the impact of State aid on firm survival by using survival analysis. Survival analysis – also referred to as 'time to event' analysis or more generally duration analysis – provides an alternative perspective on our subject of study. These methods represent a common tool to analyse the time until the occurrence of an event and are frequently applied not only in economics but also in a variety of other research disciplines such as pharmaceutical statistics (e.g., to assess the efficacy of a new therapy in a clinical trial) or engineering (e.g., to study the lifetime of machine components).

In our application, the event is the market exit of firms. There are two main concepts in the field of survival analysis. The first is the survivor function which is used to determine the probability of an individual to survive beyond a certain point in time

14. The results for NB1 are very similar as can be seen in Table 10.4. In the course of the chapter we will present the estimation results for the NB3 case. All results are very similar for the NB1 case and are available from the authors upon request.

(i.e., a firm is still active after a specific time period). The second concept is the hazard rate or hazard function, which is the probability that an individual will experience the event while that individual is at risk for having an event (i.e., the probability that a firm will exit the market in t and it was operating in t-1).

Survival analysis enables us to effectively consider right censoring. Right censoring means that some individuals do not experience the event until the end of the observation period (*see* Allison, 2010, pp. 413). In our case, firms are said to be right-censored if they do not exit the market until the last year of our observation period (i.e., 2014), but potentially will do so afterwards. To adequately consider right censoring the dependent variable in survival analysis has two components: (1) the time to event and (2) the event status, which records if the event of interest occurred during the observed time period or not.

The aim of our survival analysis is to estimate and compare survival functions and hazard rates, respectively, of treated and matched control firms in our data set. Using survival analysis in this section, we aim at answering the question how the granting of restructuring aid affects the overall survival time of firms. Survival analysis can be conducted non-parametrically, parametrically or semi-parametrically with all approaches having their specific advantages and drawbacks. In the following, we limit the discussion of our estimation results to the parametric (subsection 10.06[B][1]) and semi-parametric (subsection 10.06[B][2]) duration methods (since we are also interested in studying the impact of covariates on survival).[15]

[1] Parametric Analysis

Generally, parametric survival models enable us to control co-factors with potential impact on survival probability. More importantly, they also allow to estimate the baseline hazard from which we can predict the average survival time of a firm with certain characteristics. Having chosen the appropriate model, parametric survival models deliver the highest efficiency compared to either non-parametric or semi-parametric methods. As a drawback, the accuracy of parametric survival models depends on the distributional assumptions with regard to the survival time (most common are exponential, Weibull, Gompertz, loglogistic and log-normal distributions). Parametric survival methods are implemented in a regression framework and estimated by maximum likelihood. Regression analysis steps involve (i) the identification of the distribution that best fits the underlying data and (ii) the identification of relevant covariates.

15. The results of an application of non-parametric survival methods, i.e., Kaplan-Meier and Nelson-Aalen estimates, are available from the authors upon request.

Table 10.6 Results of Parametric Survival Estimation

	AM	*AMI*	*A*	*AI*
Excluding covariates				
Aid	1.72** (0.38)	2.10** (0.67)	1.743*** (0.37)	2.119** (0.77)
Including covariates				
Aid	1.68*** (0.33)	2.07** (0.74)	1.70*** (0.33)	2.08*** (0.53)
Observations	1,438	1,464	1,406	1,432

Note: Bootstrapped standard errors in parentheses (1,000 repetitions). Significance levels: * $p < 0.1$, ** $p < 0.05$, *** $p < 0.01$. Coefficients are reported in time ratios. Covariates included are: age, public firm, firm size, share of subsidies of government expenditures, percentage change of GDP per capita, and average unemployment rate during the last three years. *See* Table 10.1 for firm status definitions.

With respect to the first step – finding the optimal distribution – we ran parametric regressions with several distributions and computed the corresponding information criteria. The model with the lowest information criteria provides the best model fit. In our case, the Akaike Information Criterion and the Bayesian Information Criterion are lowest for the log-normal model while the exponential model fits the data worst. This finding is independent of the definition of outcome and the inclusion of covariates. Thus, in the second step, the parametric regressions are conducted using a log-normal model of the form:

$$\ln(T_i) = \beta_0 + x_i' \beta_x + u_i \quad (1)$$

where T_i represents the survival time of firm i, x_i is a vector of firm specific characteristics and u_i is an error term, which follows a normal distribution with mean 0 and a standard deviation of σ. This specification implies the survivor function:

$$S(t) = 1 - \Phi\left(\frac{\ln(T_i) - (\beta_0 + x_i' \beta_x)}{\sigma}\right)$$

where Φ is the cumulative distribution function of the standard normal distribution.

Besides the treatment variable 'aid', we also include control variables such as macro-level information as well as firm age and dummies for public firm and firm size (dummies for Medium Firm, Large Firm and Very Large Firm with Small Firms being the reference category). We find that the results are also robust if control variables are included. The corresponding estimation results are reported in Table 10.6. It is important to note that parametric survival models with a log-normal distribution are parametrised in accelerated failure time (AFT) metric, i.e., the coefficients measure to what extent the treatment accelerates or decelerates a firms survival time – with the underlying assumption being that a firms survival time is generally limited. In

Table 10.6, we report the exponentiated coefficients from our estimates to make them interpretable as time ratios. This means they represent the factor by which the (expected) survival time is multiplied after a one-unit increase of the explanatory variable. Thus, a time ratio of 1.68 for 'aid' as estimated for survival definition AM can be interpreted as follows: restructuring aid prolongs the survival time by 68% (1.68-1 = 0.68) in comparison to the control group and approximately doubles the survival time if we consider survival definition A (107% lifetime expansion), respectively.

Table 10.7 Average Survival Time in Years

	AM	*AMI*	*A*	*AI*
Aid = 0	11.59	14.12	11.09	13.43
Aid = 1	19.53	29.20	18.86	27.96
Difference	7.93**	15.09**	7.78**	14.53**

Note: Significance levels: * $p < 0.1$, ** $p < 0.05$, *** $p < 0.01$. *See* Table 10.1 for firm status definitions.

As mentioned above, parametric survival models have the advantage that the intercept term is also explicitly estimated and defines the baseline survival time, which enables the prediction of a firm's survival time conditional on covariates in general, and the reception of aid in particular. Table 10.7 shows the respective results for all four definitions of a firm's survival.

Table 10.7 reveals that the average time-to-failure (or survival time) is roughly between 11 and 14 years for the non-aid counterfactual. For the aid recipients, it is approximately twice as high with average times-to-failure between 20 and 29 years, depending on the specification of our survival variable.

[2] Semi-parametric Analysis

In this section, we complete our estimations of duration models with an application of Cox proportional hazard models. Cox models (*see* Cox, 1972) are semi-parametric as they leave the baseline hazard function $h_0(t)$ unspecified meaning that they do not impose restrictions on the shape of the baseline hazard and therefore allow the baseline hazard to be as flexible as possible (however, at the cost of not explicitly estimating the baseline hazard). Thus, this class of models does not allow making any predictions on survival time. The covariates, however, enter the model parametrically:

$$\log(h_t) = \log(h_0(t)) + \beta_1 x_{i1} + \ldots + \beta_k x_{ik} \quad (2)$$

or equivalently:

$$h_i(t) = h_0(t) \exp(\beta_1 x_{i1} + \ldots + \beta_k x_{ik}) \quad (3)$$

There is no constant term in the linear predictor $\eta_i = \beta_1 x_{i1} + ... + \beta_k x_{ik}$ as the constant is absorbed in the baseline hazard $h_0(t)$ which gives the hazard (or the occurrence) of an event in t if all other predictors are equal to zero. Thus, Cox models enable us to produce covariate-adjusted hazard ratios without imposing any assumption on the baseline hazard, which yields generally more robust estimates compared to parametric analysis. In terms of interpretation, it is important to note that in contrast to the AFT metric from the log-normal parametric survival model, we report the coefficients in the Cox model as Hazard Ratios (HR), i.e., the ratio of a hazard rate with a one-unit increase of an explanatory variable and a hazard rate without such an increase. Hence, the HR represents the factor by which the hazard rate is multiplied as a result of a one-unit increase of an explanatory variable. With respect to our evaluation question, the HR is the ratio of the probability of an event (in our case market exit) in the treatment group (i.e., aid recipients) to the control group (i.e., matched non-aid-receiving firms) at any duration. Thus, the hazard ratio does not depend on the time survived in the proportional hazard model, i.e., the hazard ratio is constant over time. If this condition holds, the parameters can be estimated without consideration of the baseline hazard function. In our case, the proportional hazard assumption cannot be rejected as indicated by the test statistics based on the scaled Schoenefeld residuals from the Cox models.[16] Table 10.8 also reports the results for a Cox model with covariates, applied to the dataset with three neighbour matching and all four definitions of survival. We include a dummy for public firm, dummies for firm size (medium to very large), a firm's age as well as the macro-level variables unemployment level in the last three years, share of subsidies from government expenditures (%) and GDP per capita.

We report hazard ratios (exponentiated coefficients) rather than the actual coefficients in Table 10.8 since their interpretation is more straightforward. As revealed by Table 10.8, we find that restructuring aid significantly reduces the hazard regardless of the outcome definition. The hazard rate for those firms who received aid is only between 32% and 42% of the hazard rate for those firms that had not received the aid, or alternatively expressed, restructuring aid reduces the hazard rate between 58% and 68% - other things equal - which is measurably higher than our initial findings from the matching where we found restructuring aid to reduce the risk of a failure by 44% to 56%.

16. If the test would reject the null hypothesis of proportional hazards, one would interact the covariates with time or alternatively divide the data into strata. Since our dataset is discrete in time (calendar years), we apply the Efron method to handle tied failures.

Table 10.8 Results of Cox Regression

	AM	*AMI*	*A*	*AI*
Excluding covariates				
Aid	0.411** (0.155)	0.313** (0.143)	0.389** (0.148)	0.300*** (0.137)
Including covariates				
Aid	0.416** (0.160)	0.326** (0.155)	0.398*** (0.153)	0.315*** (0.150)
Observations	1,436	1,462	1,404	1,430

Note: Bootstrapped standard errors in parentheses (1,000 repetitions). Significance levels: * $p < 0.1$, ** $p < 0.05$, *** $p < 0.01$. Covariates included are: age, public firm, firm size, share of subsidies of government expenditures, percentage change of GDP per capita, and average unemployment rate during the last three years. Coefficients are reported in hazard ratios. *See* Table 10.1 for firm status definitions.

[C] Effect of Rescue and Restructuring Aid on Financial Viability

Although the analysis of survival rates certainly provides useful insights on the impact of restructuring aid on the aided firms, it is a relatively general measure in the sense that a firm on the verge to bankruptcy – but still alive – is treated equally to a firm that prospered again. In this section, we therefore introduce a financial performance indicator in the form of the Altman Z-score, i.e., we now estimate the development of aid-receiving and non-aid-receiving firms' financial situation over time. Hence, while we have used binary outcomes in the previous sections, we now employ a multinomial categorisation of the dependent variable based on categories of the Altman Z-score as described in the data section.

From the previous estimations, we know that non-aid-receiving firms have a statistically significant lower survival probability. Because firms with low financial viability are apparently more likely to exit the market, putting the focus only on the Altman Z-score categories per year without explicit consideration of market exits would cause a bias in favour of the non-aid-receiving firms.

This can be shown by the following example. Let us assume we have two aided firms, one with a good financial viability, one with a bad financial viability and also two non-aided firms, one with good and one with bad financial viability at time t. Assume further that the aided firm with bad viability survives until $t+3$ but still has not fully recovered while the non-aided firm with bad viability dies prior to $t+3$. Z-scores of the firms with good financial viability are unchanged in $t+3$. The Altman Z-score would incorrectly indicate that aid-receiving firms are more likely to be worse off than non-aided firms in $t+3$ as market exits are not considered.

With regard to this bias, we reclassify the outcome variable and construct a separate category for firms that have exited the market. Furthermore, we group Altman

Z-score categories 2 and 3 ('normal financial viability' and 'high financial viability') to one single category called 'safe zone' in order to avoid a lack of observations the longer the period under review. This categorisation enables us not only to analyse whether the probability of exiting the market differs between aid-receiving and non-aid-receiving firms but also whether full recovery is more likely for aid-receiving firms or not. To summarise, the Z-score categories determining the outcome variable are as follows:

- *Category 1*: The firm has exited the market (survival definitions AM, AMI, A and AI, respectively).
- *Category 2*: The firm is in the 'red zone' which is the Altman Z-score category 'insufficient financial viability'.
- *Category 3*: The firm is in the 'safe zone' which encompasses the Altman Z-score categories 'normal financial viability' and 'high financial viability'.

We now estimate ordered logit models with the Z-score categories as the left-hand side variable. Since there was no significant difference in Altman Z-score categories between treatment group and control group (before treatment) after the matching procedure, this ordered logit approach may be interpreted as a conditional difference-in-difference approach. Thus, the estimates from the ordered logit models allow for an attractive way to work around the problem of interaction terms in discrete-choice models by deriving marginal effects from the estimations. Marginal effects refer to the effect of a unit increase in the explanatory variable on the probability of selecting the respective outcome category expressed in percentage terms. With a dichotomous explanatory variable (received restructuring State aid or not), the marginal effect of receiving aid is the difference in the adjusted predictions for the two groups of firms, i.e., for treated and non-treated firms.

In order to examine the dynamics of firm survival, we estimate the ordered logit model for different time intervals of our period of analysis. In other words, for each of our three Altman Z-score categories – dead, red zone and safe zone – and for each time interval, we estimate the probability for both groups to be in the respective Altman Z-score category and subsequently calculate whether the difference in the probability of being in the same category differs statistically significant between aid recipients and the counterfactual group.

Table 10.9 below reports the ordered logit estimates for the alternative definitions of firm survival, i.e., survival definitions AM, AMI, A and AI, respectively. The row 'Marginal effect' reflects the difference in the adjusted predictions of both groups of firms while 'Av. Pr.' is the average probability for an aid-receiving and a non-aid-receiving firm, respectively, to be in the respective category.

Table 10.9 Results of Ordinal Logit Regression

Year	0		1-3			4-6			> 6		
Category	**2**	**3**	**1**	**2**	**3**	**1**	**2**	**3**	**1**	**2**	**3**
Status: *AM*											
Av. Pr. No Aid	0.63 (0.04)	0.37 (0.04)	0.14 (0.03)	0.50 (0.04)	0.35 (0.03)	0.25 (0.04)	0.42 (0.04)	0.32 (0.04)	0.46 (0.06)	0.25 (0.05)	0.29 (0.06)
Av. Pr. Aid	0.70 (0.06)	0.30 (0.07)	0.13 (0.03)	0.48 (0.04)	0.39 (0.05)	0.18 (0.04)	0.40 (0.04)	0.42 (0.05)	0.30 (0.07)	0.25 (0.05)	0.45 (0.09)
Marginal effect	0.07 (0.07)	-0.07 (0.08)	-0.02 (0.03)	-0.02 (0.03)	0.04 (0.06)	-0.07 (0.05)	-0.03 (0.02)	0.10* (0.06)	-0.16* (0.09)	0.00 (0.01)	0.16* (0.10)
Observations	224	224	221	221	221	163	163	163	92	92	92
Status: *AMI*											
Av. Pr. No Aid	0.63 (0.04)	0.37 (0.04)	0.16 (0.03)	0.50 (0.04)	0.34 (0.04)	0.29 (0.04)	0.42 (0.04)	0.30 (0.04)	0.52 (0.06)	0.22 (0.04)	0.26 (0.05)
Av. Pr. Aid	0.70 (0.06)	0.30 (0.07)	0.13 (0.03)	0.48 (0.04)	0.39 (0.05)	0.18 (0.04)	0.39 (0.04)	0.43 (0.06)	0.31 (0.07)	0.23 (0.05)	0.46 (0.08)
Marginal effect	0.07 (0.07)	-0.07 (0.07)	-0.03 (0.03)	-0.02 (0.03)	0.05 (0.06)	-0.10** (0.05)	-0.03 (0.02)	0.13* (0.07)	-0.21* (0.09)	0.01 (0.02)	0.19 (0.09)
Observations	224	224	221	221	221	166	166	166	98	98	98
Status: *A*											
Av. Pr. No Aid	0.63 (0.04)	0.37 (0.03)	0.12 (0.03)	0.53 (0.03)	0.35 (0.04)	0.23 (0.04)	0.44 (0.05)	0.33 (0.04)	0.40 (0.07)	0.29 (0.05)	0.31 (0.06)
Av. Pr. Aid	0.70 (0.07)	0.30 (0.07)	0.10 (0.02)	0.50 (0.04)	0.40 (0.06)	0.15 (0.03)	0.40 (0.05)	0.45 (0.06)	0.26 (0.07)	0.28 (0.05)	0.46 (0.10)
Marginal effect	0.07 (0.07)	-0.07 (0.07)	-0.02 (0.03)	-0.03 (0.04)	0.05 (0.06)	-0.08* (0.04)	-0.04 (0.03)	0.12* (0.07)	-0.14* (0.08)	-0.01 (0.02)	0.15* (0.08)
Observations	224	224	221	221	221	158	158	158	88	88	88
Status: *AI*											
Av. Pr. No Aid	0.63 (0.04)	0.37 (0.04)	0.13 (0.03)	0.53 (0.03)	0.34 (0.03)	0.27 (0.04)	0.43 (0.04)	0.30 (0.04)	0.47 (0.67)	0.26 (0.05)	0.28 (0.06)
Av. Pr. Aid	0.70 (0.06)	0.30 (0.07)	0.11 (0.02)	0.50 (0.05)	0.40 (0.05)	0.16 (0.04)	0.39 (0.05)	0.45 (0.07)	0.28 (0.07)	0.26 (0.05)	0.47 (0.07)
Marginal effect	0.07 (0.07)	-0.07 (0.08)	-0.03 (0.03)	-0.03 (0.03)	0.06 (0.07)	-0.11** (0.05)	-0.05* (0.03)	0.15** (0.07)	-0.19** (0.10)	0.00 (0.02)	0.19** (0.09)
Observations	224	224	221	221	221	161	161	161	94	94	94

Note: Bootstrapped standard errors in parentheses (1,000 repetitions). Significance levels: * $p < 0.1$, ** $p < 0.05$, *** $p < 0.01$. Year indicates year after aid was granted. Category refers to: 1 = market exit or merger; 2 = insufficient financial viability; 3 = normal or high financial viability. Av. Pr. No Aid (Av. Pr. Aid) shows the average probabilities of control firms (aid-receiving firms) to be in the corresponding category. *See* Table 10.1 for firm status definitions.

When looking at the Altman Z-score category 1 in Table 10.9 ('firm has exited the market'), one infers that the probability of market exit becomes significantly lower three years after the start of restructuring measures for firms that received restructuring aid. For instance, receiving restructuring aid decreases the probability of market exit by 21% in absolute terms (survival definition AMI) six years after restructuring while the difference is only 10% in absolute terms in the period from three to six years after restructuring. There is no significant difference observed in the first three years after the start of a restructuring measure. Accordingly, there is evidence of a positive treatment effect in terms of reducing the likelihood of market exit, which starts after four years, and then increases with the years elapsed since restructuring aid was granted.

This result therefore suggests that restructuring aid measures have a long-term rather than a short-term impact on survival (conditional on a firm's survival in the first years). Furthermore, the probability of a firm's full recovery from financial distress – measured in categories of the Altman Z-score – is also significantly higher for restructuring aid recipients in the long-term. Again referring to the estimates for survival definition AMI in Table 10.9, we find a 19% higher probability for aid recipients to fully recover and reach the safe zone six years after the restructuring aid was granted compared to the counterfactual, however, only a 13% difference for four to six years after the start year and no significant impact in the first three years.

The estimates are also robust to the inclusion of covariates such as age of the firm, dummy for public firms, GDP per capita, share of subsidies from government expenditures and three-year unemployment rate.[17] However, financial covariates are always excluded in these robustness checks as they are logically related to the dependent variable (as the Altman Z-score is defined on the basis of a linear combination of financial covariates). Due to missing observations, we also refrained from including the number of employees and, due to perfect prediction in some years, also firm size. As our focus is on firm survival and financial viability – and the matching shows no mean difference for these variables – these omissions do not bias our results.

In search for explanations for the observed long-term effect, the probably most straightforward one would be that the respective firm restructurings have turned out successful and the respective firms in difficulty started to prosper again. However, an alternative explanation for the identification of such a long-term effect of restructuring aid would be that politicians became active aiming at avoiding the failure of an aided firm (in order to demonstrate that they are capable of picking firms that are strong performers). Although politicians' behaviour towards aided firms is likely to be monitored closely (by the EC or the public) in the immediate aftermath of a R&R event, in the longer run, monitoring likely weakens and politicians may find channels to influence the aided firm's performance. Ceteris paribus, such an effect is more likely to exist in regulated industries (in which established ties between the State and the respective firms already exist).[18]

17. The respective regression tables are available from the authors upon request.
18. We are grateful to an anonymous reviewer for suggesting this explanation.

§10.07 ROBUSTNESS

[A] Heteroskedasticity Based IV Approach

As argued above, the quality of matching relies on the observables and the estimates may be biased if relevant unobservable factors are neglected. A potential unobservable factor influencing the probability of receiving aid is political favouritism – despite the fact that the EC is very keen on preventing such influences as part of its evaluation procedures. Aiming at investigating whether our findings are driven by such factors, we examine the robustness of our estimates using the entire set of observations (more than one million) from Amadeus (not only treated and neighbours) in an instrumental variables approach. Due to the lack of an obvious instrument for receiving State aid, we apply an estimator proposed by Lewbel (2012).

Consider the linear relationship $Y_i = X_i'\beta + Z_i\gamma + \varepsilon_{i1}$ between the outcome variable γ_i (survival, financial variability), a vector of covariates X_i, and an indicator for receiving State aid Z_i. We are interested in estimating the parameter γ. The equation determining treatment is given by $Z_i = X_i'\alpha + \varepsilon_{i2}$, hence there is no instrument to be excluded as in our setting. We require the standard exogeneity conditions $E(X_i\varepsilon_{i1}) = 0$, $E(X_i\varepsilon_{i2}) = 0$ and that $E(X_i\ X_i')$ is non-singular. For identification without external instruments, we need additional assumptions, namely that $Cov(Z_i,\varepsilon_{i1}\varepsilon_{i2}) = 0$ and that there is some heteroskedasticity in the error determining treatment, i.e., $Cov(Z_i, \varepsilon^2_{i2}) \neq 0$.

Lewbel (2017) recently provides plausible error structures that imply this heteroskedasticity for the case of a binary endogenous variable as in our case. We test the heteroskedasticity requirement based on the residuals of the first stage regression. The results of these heteroskedasticity tests are reported along with the first stage regression in Table 10.16 in the Appendix. The tests lead us to reject the null hypotheses of constant variance and homoskedasticity, respectively. Lewbel (2012) shows that given these requirements γ (and β) can be consistently estimated by using $(Z_i - \hat{Z}_i)\ \hat{\varepsilon}_{i2}$ as an instrument for Z_i in the outcome equation. The results obtained by using all control variables in X_i for Z_i are presented in Table 10.10. The standard errors are corrected for using generated instruments. We find slightly smaller point estimates, however, still very close to those from the matching for all definitions of firm survival: 0.11 to 0.15 in the Lewbel IV models versus 0.14 to 0.18 in the case of NB1 and 0.15 to 0.18 for NB3, respectively, in the matching estimates (*see* Table 10.10 below).

Table 10.10 Lewbel (2012) IV Estimation with Heteroskedasticity Based Instruments

	AM	AMI	A	AI
Including covariates				
Received aid	0.1189** (0.0452)	0.1079** (0.0429)	0.1483*** (0.0462)	0.1372*** (0.0442)
First stage F test	7,817,615	7,817,615	7,817,615	7,817,615
Observations	1,132,882	1,132,882	1,132,882	1,132,882

Note: Standard errors in parentheses. Instrumented for Aid using heteroskedasticity based IV method proposed by Lewbel (2012). Covariates are the financial items, firm characteristics, and macro-level information listed in Table 10.2 in section 10.04 as well as industry dummies based on 1-digit NACE industry codes, country and year dummies. Significance levels: * $p < 0.1$, ** $p < 0.05$, *** $p < 0.01$. *See* Table 10.1 for firm status definitions.

[B] Sensitivity to Deviations from Conditional Independence

In this section we examine the robustness of our estimates with respect to failures of the assumption of unconfounded treatment assignment with a method proposed by Ichino et al. (2008). More specifically, we analyse the impact of an unobserved binary variable U_i that is associated with both treatment assignment and outcome, implying that the unconfoundedness assumption stated in section 10.03 is violated. Instead, treatment assignment is now independent of the potential outcomes conditional on pre-treatment characteristics and the newly introduced binary variable, i.e., $Z_i \perp Y_{i0}, Y_{i1} | X_{i,pre}, U_i$.

We assume that the distribution of U_i given Z_i, Y_{i0} and Y_{i1} does not change with pre-treatment covariates $X_{i,pre}$. It follows that the distribution of U_i can be described by the probability of $U_i = 1$ in each of the four groups determined by the treatment status and the value of the outcome variable:

$$\Pr(U_i = 1 \mid Z_i = j, Y_{ij} = k, X_{i,pre}) = \Pr(U_i = 1 \mid Z_i = j, Y_{ij} = k) \equiv p_{jk} \quad (4)$$

with $j, k \in \{0,1\}$

We begin our sensitivity analysis by choosing values for the parameters p_{jk}. These values are set based on observable binary variables from our pool of pre-treatment variables. Using the four probabilities, we simulate U_i for each firm i in our sample. In a next step, we conduct our matching procedure and calculate the ATT as outlined in section 10.05 above, treating the simulated variable U_i as an additional matching variable. We simulate U_i and repeat the matching estimation 1,000 times for each set of parameters p_{jk}, and calculate the ATT for the specific failure of the unconfoundedness assumption by taking the average of the ATTs over all simulated U_i.

To measure how the unobserved binary variable influences treatment assignment and outcome, we estimate two logit models of $\Pr(Y_{ij} = 1 \mid Z_i,U_i,X_{i,pre})$ and

$Pr(Z_i = 1|U_i, X_{i,pre})$ in every iteration. The odds ratio of U in the logit regression $Pr(Y = 1 \mid Z = 0, U, X_{i,pre})$ measures the effect of U on the relative probability of having a positive outcome (outcome effect Γ), and the odds ratio of U in the logit regression $Pr(Z = 1 \mid U, X_{i,pre})$ measures the effect of U on the relative probability of receiving treatment (selection effect Λ).

Table 10.11 shows the results of our sensitivity analysis. For brevity reasons, we focus our discussion on the outcome variable that measures firm survival after the investigation period based on our definition of firm survival, which includes active and merged firms (AM). To simplify comparisons between our estimated and simulated result, the first line in Table 10.11 reports the ATT that we obtained in subsection 10.06[A].[19] The second row reports the simulated ATT if a neutral confounder is included in the analysis, which already slightly reduces the ATT.[20] The last three rows show how our estimates of the ATT is affected if we include a binary variable which mimics our observable variables *public firm*, *very large firm*, and *middle or high financial viability*.

In case U follows the distribution of public firms, the unobserved variable has a positive effect on the relative probability of being active beyond our period of investigation in case of no treatment ($\Gamma = 1.08 > 1$) and an even larger effect on the relative probability of receiving State aid ($\Lambda = 5.60 > 1$). The impact of such an unobserved variable would reduce the ATT by 4 percentage points, but does not affect its significance. An unobservable variable which mimics the distribution of very large firms in our sample would introduce an even larger outcome ($\Gamma = 2.57 > 1$) and selection effect ($\Lambda = 13.41 > 1$), and reduces our estimate of the ATT by around 30 %. Yet, as before, the coefficient remains significant.

The last row of Table 10.11 shows the ATT if the unobservable variable is distributed as the firms with high or middle financial viability. Unsurprisingly, our estimate of the ATT is less affected in this case as both, outcome and selection effect, are quite low. Overall, the results of our sensitivity analysis indicate that our estimates of the ATT are robust to failures of the assumption of unconfounded treatment assignment.

19. In Table 10.4 in subsection 10.06[A], we first round the mean of the outcome variables for each group (treated and control) to two decimal places and derive the ATT based on these numbers. In Table 10.11, we first take the difference between the mean of the outcome variables for each group and round the decimal values of the ATT to a two-digit number in a second step. The second approach leads to an ATT of 0.14 instead of 0.15.
20. Standard errors are calculated using Rubin's rule. *See also* note of Table 10.11.

Table 10.11 Results of Sensitivity Analysis

	p_{00}	p_{01}	p_{10}	p_{11}	Γ	Λ	$\overline{ATT}$	SE
No confounder	0.00	0.00	0.00	0.00	-	-	0.14	0.01
Neutral confounder	0.50	0.50	0.50	0.50	1.00	1.04	0.12	0.01
Confounder similar to								
Public firm	0.27	0.29	0.57	0.68	1.08	5.60	0.10	0.03
Very large firm	0.02	0.05	0.29	0.36	2.57	13.41	0.09	0.04
Financial viability middle or high	0.77	0.70	0.43	0.28	1.46	0.12	0.12	0.01

Note: The parameters p_{jk} give the fraction of U = 1 by treatment status and outcome as outlined in Equation (4). Based on these variables, a value for U is simulated for each firm in our sample and the ATT is obtained by the procedure described in section 10.05. This process is executed 1,000 times. The ATT shown in the table is the average over all simulated ATTs. Standard errors (SE) are calculated based on Rubin's rule:

$$SE=\frac{1}{m}\sum_{k=1}^{m} se_k^2+\frac{m+1}{m(m-1)}\sum_{k=1}^{m}(ATT_k-\overline{ATT})^2,$$

where m is the total number of iterations (1,000). The first row reports the estimation obtained by our baseline procedure of section 10.05.

§10.08 POLICY IMPLICATIONS

Our empirical results suggests that State aid granted by the European Commission to firms in difficulty is effective in significantly increasing both the probability that these aided firms survive and that they return to a status of financial viability. Even though our results cannot easily be applied to State aid cases in general – due to the specific guidelines to assess R&R aid requests – they do show that granting aid can be an effective policy tool for the European Commission. Furthermore, in the light of the European Commission's aim to only grant State aid in the case of a firm 'which, without outside intervention by the public authorities would almost certainly condemn it to go out of business in the short- or medium term' (European Commission, 2004, section 2.1, paragraph 9), it can therefore be concluded that we find evidence consistent with the European Commission reaching this aim.

Two further policy-relevant implications can be drawn from our empirical analysis. First, our application of the matching procedure in combination with the four different definitions of survival reveals that aid-receiving firms are less frequently acquired compared to non-aid-receiving firms. This finding suggests that State aid is not consistently abused as windfall profit by firms who were planning to acquire the respective firm in difficulty anyway. Second, our empirical assessment of the financial viability of aided firms find that restructuring aid have a long-term rather than a short-term impact on survival – conditional on a firm's survival in the first years – implying that the granting of restructuring aid often reaches the desired long-term survival of firms in difficulty.

Thus, we can conclude that while we find evidence supporting the hypothesis that the European Commission only grants restructuring aid conditional on 'a feasible and coherent and far-reaching plan to restore a firms long-term viability' (European Commission, 2004, section 2.2, paragraph 17), we have to leave the question whether this aim was achieved by limiting 'the amount and intensity of the aid [...] to the strict minimum of the restructuring costs necessary to enable restructuring to be undertaken' (European Commission, 2004, section 3.2, paragraph 43) for future research.

§10.09 CONCLUSION

In May 2012, the European Commission announced its SAM reform aiming at fostering growth in the internal market through streamlined rules and faster decisions. 'State aid control should more effectively target sustainable growth-enhancing policies while encouraging budgetary consolidation, limiting distortions of competition and keeping the single market open' (European Commission, 2012, p. 4). Interestingly, in working towards these goals, the Commission's strategy does not only envisage the identification of common principles for assessing the compatibility of aid with the internal market – in combination with the creation or revision of guidelines and frameworks – but it explicitly includes an ex post evaluation program as key tool to ensure an effective EU State aid policy (*see* European Commission, 2014b).

From an academic perspective, the ex post evaluation of State aid policies in general and R&R aid in particular can be subdivided further into two main research questions. First, from an effectiveness perspective, the question whether the granting of State aid had the desired direct effect suggests itself; i.e., in the case of R&R aid, did the granting of financial aid to firms in difficulty have a positive impact on their survival and financial viability? Second, from a social welfare perspective, the broader question is posed whether the respective State aid scheme or policy as such is socially desirable. In the case of R&R aid, such a broader assessment of social costs and benefits would have to go beyond the direct effects of the aid on the beneficiaries themselves (as well as their industries and sectors) and would additionally have to take various (positive or negative) indirect effects of the granting of aid on, e.g., competition, trade, employment, investment or economic growth into account.

In this chapter, we concentrate on answers to the first research question by investigating whether fifty-six positive restructuring aid decisions – reached by the European Commission between 2003 and 2012 – had a measurable impact on the survival and financial viability of the aided firms. Confronted with the challenge of a causal identification of the treatment effect of aided firms, we follow an empirical approach based on matching techniques. We first employ the matching on the whole population of firms in the Amadeus database of European companies in order to identify non-aided – but otherwise comparable – firms which act as control group. Subsequently, we apply both survival models and ordered response models on the sample of aid-receiving firms and the constructed counterfactual group to empirically investigate the impact of restructuring aid on firm survival and financial viability. Our estimates suggest that restructuring aid increases a firms average survival time by approximately eight to fifteen years or, putting it differently, decreases the exit rate by 58-68%. With respect to financial viability – measured by categories of the Altman Z-scores – we find evidence that aid recipients not only have higher survival probabilities in the long-term but that they are also more likely to improve their financial viability compared to non-aid-receiving firms.

From a policy perspective, our empirical results directly support the conclusion that the European Commission's R&R aid policy is effective in significantly increasing both the probability that firms in difficulty will survive as well as the probability that they return to a status of financial viability (in the long term). Based on these findings on the effectiveness of R&R aid, the consequential next step – left for future research – is an ex post evaluation of the overall welfare effects of R&R aid. Although both data availability and methodological issues are expected to be substantial, a thorough and complete evaluation of State aid polices and schemes will have to provide the best possible answers to the ultimate question – namely whether such government policies are likely to generate positive or negative net total effects on social welfare.

APPENDIX

Table 10.12 Documentation of Imputed Data Points in the Group of Treated Firms

Name of the Firm	*Changes Made*
Cyprus Airlines	Employment, liquidity ratio, solvency ratio from 2004 to 2005
Götzke Natursteinwerke	Revenue, profit, EBIT from 2004 to 2007 and employment from 2007 to 2008
Air Aland	Employment from 2008 to 2010
British Energy	All variables of interest from 2003 to 2004
Macedonian	Publishing All variables of interest from 2008 to 2010
Fluorite	All variables of interest from 2006 to 2007
Air Malta	All variables of interest from 2010 to 2011
Zaklad Naprawczy	Non-current assets from 2010 to 2011
Fabryka Samochobow	Employment from 2003 to 2004
Stocznia Gdansk	Employment from 2004 to 2005
Zaklady Miesne	Employment from 2010 to 2011
Fabryka Lozysk	Employment from 2005 to 2009
Konas	All variables of interest from 2004 to 2005
Bull	Solvency ratio from 2003 to 2004
Krakowskie Zaklady	Solvency ratio from 2004 to 2007

Table 10.13 Probit Estimations Before and After Matching Procedure

	Before	*After (NB1)*	*After (NB3)*
Financial variables			
Profit (log)	-0.0295*** (0.0068)	-0.0204 (0.0212)	-0.0104 (0.0165)
Fixed liabilities (log)	-0.0576** (0.0189)	0.0527 (0.0709)	-0.0476 (0.0534)
Current liabilities (log)	0.0128 (0.0516)	0.0212 (0.2220)	0.0701 (0.1420)
Revenue per employee	-0.0002 (0.0002)	-0.0004 (0.0011)	-0.0002 (0.0007)
Altman Z-score category	-0.2368** (0.0867)	0.0185 (0.3851)	-0.3004 (0.2212)
Public firm	0.2324* (0.1107)	-0.1719 (0.4552)	-0.1374 (0.3212)

	Before	*After (NB1)*	*After (NB3)*
Liquidity ratio	0.0035 (0.0314)	0.7035* (0.3394)	0.0382 (0.0643)
Solvency ratio	-0.0092*** (0.0016)	-0.0155* (0.0066)	-0.0113* (0.0045)
Firm characteristics			
Employment (log)	0.2878*** (0.0554)	0.1016 (0.2078)	0.2063 (0.1493)
Age (log)	-0.0118 (0.0502)	0.1193 (0.1738)	-0.1018 (0.1269)
Medium firm	0.0805 (0.1715)	1.0635 (1.0016)	-0.7466 (0.5631)
Large firm	-0.0706 (0.1920)	0.9087 (1.0930)	-0.6313 (0.6277)
Very large firm	-0.0632 (0.2566)	0.4756 (1.2878)	-0.7793 (0.7876)
Macro level info			
Unemployment level (3 year avg.)	-0.0503** (0.0173)	-0.0706 (0.0658)	-0.0909 (0.0498)
Share subsidies of gov. expenditure	-0.0077 (0.0120)	-0.0473 (0.1126)	-0.0728 (0.0828)
Pct. change in GDP per capita	0.0426* (0.0201)	-0.0049 (0.0880)	0.0865 (0.0634)
Observations	1,132,417	105	217
Pseudo R-Squared	0.3856	0.1681	0.1600
LR $\chi 2$	479.06	24.42	38.24
p > $\chi 2$	0.0000	0.8287	0.2830

Note: Dependent variable is a dummy variable indicating treatment assignment. All models include dummies to capture country-specific and industry-specific (determined by 1-digit NACE code) effects. The first column refers to a probit regression including all observations listed in Table 10.3 before matching. The second column includes only treated firms and their nearest neighbours; the third column includes treated firms and their three closest neighbours. Standard errors in parentheses.

Table 10.14 Information about Aid-Receiving Firms Included in the Analysis

Case Code	*Firm Name*	*Country*	*Aid*	*Instrument*	*NACE*	*Status*	*Size*
C10/2010	A NOVO COMLINK ESPANA SL	ES	2008	Guarantee, Interest subsidy, Soft loan	9522	Private	Large
SA.35205	ABBANOA S.P.A	IT	2011	Guarantee, Provision of risk capital	3600	Public	Very large
C53/2003	ABX LOGISTICS AIR & SEA WORLDWIDE	BE	2000	Debt write-off	4941	Public	Large
SA.32698	AIR ALAND AB	FI	2010	Soft loan	5110	Private	Small
C58/2003	ALSTOM S.A.	FR	2002		7112	Public	Very large
N600/2004	ARCELORMITTAL FRYDEK-MISTEK, A.S.	CZ	2003	Direct grant	2410	Public	Large
C6/2009	AUSTRIAN AIRLINES AG	AT	2007	Direct grant	7010	Public	Very large
N92/2008	BAECKER LEGAT GMBH	AT	2008	Other forms of equity intervention	4724	Private	Medium
C52/2003	BRITISH ENERGY LIMITED	GB	2003	Other, Tax deferment	7010	Private	Very large
C10/2004	BULL SA	FR	2003	Direct grant	2620	Public	Very large
N506/2007	C.HARTWIG WARSZAWA S.A. PRZEDSIEBIORSTWO SPEDYCJI MIEDZYNARODOWEJ	PL	2006		5229	Public	Medium
SA.30908	CESKE AEROLINIE, A.S.	CZ	2009	Other forms of equity intervention	5110	Public	Very large

N561/2006	CONSTRUCTIONS MECANIQUES DE NORMANDIE	FR	2005	Direct grant	3011	Public	Very large
C10/2006	CYPRUS AIRWAYS PUBLIC LTD.	CY	2004	Guarantee	5110	Public	Very large
N570/2009	DIORA – SWIDNICA SP. Z O.O.	PL	2008	Other forms of equity intervention, Soft loan	1629	Private	Medium
N632/2005	ENERGETYKA WISLOSAN SP. Z O.O.	PL	2004	Other forms of equity intervention	3513	Private	Medium
N672/2008	EXPRESS – D. KALOFOLIAS PUBLICATIONS S.A.	GR	2007	Direct grant	5813	Public	Large
SA.32024	FABRYKA LOZYSK TOCZNYCH – KRASNIK S.A.	PL	2009	Other forms of equity intervention	2815	Public	Large
C54/2006	FABRYKA PRZYRZADOW I UCHWYTOW BISON-BIAL S.A.	PL	2005	Debt write-off, Soft loan	2599	Public	Large
C3/2005	FABRYKA SAMOCHODOW OSOBOWYCH S.A.	PL	2003	Debt write-off, Guarantee	2910	Public	Very large
SA.23839	FAGORBRANDT SAS	FR	2006	Direct grant	2751	Public	Very large
N604/2009	FIEM S.R.L.	IT	2006	Guarantee	2562	Private	Medium
C60/2007	FLUORITE DI SILIUS S.P.A.	IT	2006	Direct grant	891	Public	Medium
SA.33474	FORMET S.A. FABRYKA FORM METALOWYCH W LIKWIDACJI W UPADLOSCI LIKWIDACYJNEJ	PL	2010	Other forms of equity intervention	2849	Public	Medium
N458/2008	GOETZKE NATURSTEINWERK GMBH	DE	2007	Guarantee	2370	Private	Small

Case Code	Firm Name	Country	Aid	Instrument	NACE	Status	Size
N492/2010	HYDROGEO PRZEDSIEBIORSTWO GEOLOGICZNE BUDOWNICTWA WODNEGO	PL	2009	Direct grant	7112	Private	Small
N370/2004	IMPRIMERIE NATIONALE	FR	2003	Debt write-off	1812	Public	Very large
C19/2006	JAVOR PIVKA, LESNA INDUSTRIJA, D.D.	SI	2003	Direct grant, Guarantee	1621	Public	Very large
SA.32770	KELLER ELETTROMECCANICA S.P.A.	IT	2010	Guarantee	3020	Public	Large
C42/2005	KONAS, S.R.O.	SK	2004	Tax deferment	2561	Private	Medium
N24/2009	KRAKOWSKIE ZAKLADY GARBARSKIE S.A.	PL	2007	Debt write-off, Other forms of tax advantage	1511	Public	Large
N420/2008	LONDON & CONTINENTAL RAILWAYS LIMITED	GB	2007	Direct grant	4910	Private	Very large
SA.33741	MACEDONIAN PUBLISHING PRINT S.A.	GR	2010	Direct grant	5813	Public	Large
SA.35477	MESKO – AGD SP. Z O.O. Z P H ART. GOSPODARSTWA DOMOWEGO	PL	2011	Soft loan	2751	Private	Medium
N523/2010	MOBILIFICIO FOGLIENSE S.R.L.	IT	2009	Guarantee	3100	Private	Large
C14/2007	NGP S.P.A.	IT	2005	Direct grant, Provision of risk capital, Soft loan	4675	Public	Medium
C20/2006	NOVOLES LESNA INDUSTRIJA STRAZA, D.D. – V STECAJU	SI	2003	Direct grant, Guarantee	3109	Public	Very large
C52/2006	ODLEWNIA ZELIWA ŚREM S.A.	PL	2003	Debt write-off	2451	Public	Large

C11/2007	OTTANA ENERGIA S.P.A	IT	2006	Direct grant, Soft loan	3511	Public	Large
C69/2001	PORCELANAS DEL PRINCIPADO S.L.	ES	2001	Debt write-off, Direct grant, Guarantee, and others	4644	Private	Medium
N540/2010	PRZEDSIEBIORSTWO KOMUNIKACJI SAMOCHODOWEJ W BUSKU ZDROJU S.A. W LIKWIDACJI	PL	2009	Other forms of equity intervention	4939	Public	Medium
SA.34758	PRZEDSIEBIORSTWO KOMUNIKACJI SAMOCHODOWEJ W LUBLINCU SP. Z O.O.	PL	2011	Direct grant	4939	Private	Medium
SA.33042	PRZEDSIEBIORSTWO KOMUNIKACJI SAMOCHODOWEJ W OSTROWIE WIELKOPOLSKIM SP. Z O.O.	PL	2010	Direct grant	4939	Private	Medium
SA.32612	PRZEDSIEBIORSTWO KOMUNIKACJI SAMOCHODOWEJ W PULAWACH SP. Z O.O.	PL	2010	Other forms of equity intervention	4939	Private	Medium
C49/2008	PZL DEBICA S.A. – WYTWORNIA URZADZEN CHLODNICZYCH	PL	2005		2825	Public	Medium
SA.32117	PZL SEDZISZOW S.A.	PL	2010	Debt write-off, Soft loan, Tax deferment	2932	Public	Large

Case Code	*Firm Name*	*Country*	*Aid*	*Instrument*	*NACE*	*Status*	*Size*
N726/2009	SOCIETE NATIONALE DES CHEMINS DE FER BELGES	BE	2008	Debt write-off, Direct grant, Other forms of equity intervention	4910	Public	Very large
C18/2005	STOCZNIA GDANSK S.A.	PL	2003	Debt write-off, Guarantee, Soft loan, Tax deferment	3011	Public	Very large
SA.33150	STOMIL S.A. BYDGOSKIE ZAKLADY PRZEMYSLU GUMOWEGO	PL	2010	Direct grant	2219	Public	Large
N488/2009	TARCHOMINSKIE ZAKLADY FARMACEUTYCZNE POLFA S.A.	PL	2008	Soft loan	2120	Public	Large
C6/2007	TECHMATRANS S.A. PRZEDS. PROJEKTOWANIA I DOSTAW TRANSPORTU TECHNOLOGICZNEGO I SKLADOWANIA	PL	2000	Other	7111	Public	Small
C19/2009	TV2/DANMARK A/S	DK	2008	Guarantee, Soft loan	6020	Public	Very large
N323/2007	VANYERA 3 SL.	ES	2006	Guarantee	5629	Private	Large
C8/2010	VARVARESSOS SA	GR	2008	Direct grant, Guarantee	1310	Public	Very large

SA.32965	ZAKLAD NAPRAWCZY MECHANIZACJI ROLNICTWA SP. Z O.O.	PL	2010	Direct grant	2511	Private	Medium
SA.32997	ZAKLADY MIESNE MYSLAW S.A.	PL	2010	Debt write-off, Soft loan, Tax deferment	1013	Public	Very large

Table 10.15 Matching Protocol

Step	*Description*
1	Specify and estimate the probit model to obtain the propensity scores $\hat{p}(x)$.
2	Restrict the sample to common support: delete all observations of treated firms with propensity scores larger than the maximum and smaller than the minimum of the propensity scores in the control group.
3	Choose one observation from the subsample of treated firms and delete all other observations from that subsample.
4	Restrict the subsample of control firms to firms that have the same size (small, medium, large, very large) and operate in a similar industry (measured by the 2-digit NACE code) as the chosen treated firms. In addition, delete all observations that are not in the same year as the year in which the chosen treated firm received restructuring State aid.
5	Calculate the difference of the propensity scores between the chosen treated firm and the remaining control firms.
6	For NB1: Select the observation with the minimum distance from the remaining control group. For NB3: Select the three observations with the minimum distance from the remaining control group.
7	Repeat steps 3-6 for all treated firms

Table 10.16 First Stage of Lewbel (2012) Estimation

	Coeff.	*Std. error*
Financial variables		
Profit (log)	-0.000019***	0.000002
Revenue per employee	0.000000	0.000000
Fixed liabilities (log)	-0.000012***	0.000004
Current liabilities (log)	0.000009	0.000008
Altman Z-score category	-0.000022	0.000012
Public firm	0.000043*	0.000018
Liquidity ratio	0.000005*	0.000002
Solvency ratio	-0.000002***	0.000000
Firm characteristics		
Employment (log)	0.000065***	0.000008
Age (log)	0.000015	0.000010
Medium firm	-0.000040*	0.000019
Large firm	-0.000075*	0.000033
Very large firm	0.000058	0.000054

	Coeff.	*Std. error*
Macro level info		
Unemployment level (3 year avg.)	-0.000011***	0.000003
Share subsidies of gov. expenditure	-0.000011***	0.000003
Pct. change in GDP per capita	-0.000014*	0.000007
Breusch-Pagan test for heteroskedasticity		
H_0: Constant variance		
$\chi^2(1)$	4.64×10^7	
Prob > χ^2	0.0000	
Kroenker score test for heteroskedasticity		
H_0: Disturbance is homoskedastic		
$\chi^2(1)$	4,626.28	
Prob > χ^2	0.0000	
Observations	1,151,718	

Note: Significance levels: * $p < 0.05$, ** $p < 0.01$, *** $p < 0.001$. Table presents OLS estimates from a regression of Aid on all control variables included in the matching procedure. Dummies for industries, countries, years and intercept term included but not reported.

REFERENCES

Allison P.D. (2010), 'Survival analysis', in: G.R. Hancock and R.O. Mueller (eds.), *The reviewer's guide to quantitative methods in the social sciences*, pp. 413-425, Taylor and Francis.

Altman E.I. (1968), 'Financial ratios, discriminant analysis and the prediction of corporate bankruptcy', *The Journal of Finance*, 23(4), pp. 589-609.

Altman E.I. (2002), 'Revisiting credit scoring models in a Basel 2 environment', Technical report, NYU Working Paper No. S-CDM-02-06.

Boycko M., Shleifer A. and Vishny R.W. (1996), 'A theory of privatisation', *The Economic Journal*, 106, pp. 309-319.

Bronzini R. and Piselli P. (2016), 'The impact of R&D subsidies on firm innovation', *Research Policy*, 45(2), pp. 442-457.

Caliendo M. and Kopeinig S. (2008), 'Some practical guidance for the implementation of propensity score matching', *Journal of Economic Surveys*, 22(1), pp. 31-72.

Chen S., Mu R., and Ravallion M. (2009), 'Are there lasting impacts of aid to poor areas?', *Journal of Public Economics*, 93(3), pp. 512-528.

Chindooroy R., Muller P. and Notaro G. (2007), 'Company survival following rescue and restructuring State aid', *European Journal of Law and Economics*, 24(2), pp. 165-186.

Cox D.R. (1972), 'Regression models and life-tables', *Journal of the Royal Statistical Society*, Series B (Methodological), 34(2), pp. 187-220.

Czarnitzki D. and Lopes-Bento C. (2013), 'Value for money? New microeconometric evidence on public R&D grants in Flanders', *Research Policy*, 42(1), pp. 76-89.

Dewatripont M. and Seabright P. (2006), 'Wasteful public spending and State aid control', *Journal of the European Economic Association*, 4(2-3), pp. 513-522.

Dimos C. and Pugh G. (2016), 'The effectiveness of R&D subsidies: A meta-regression analysis of the evaluation literature', *Research Policy*, 45(4), pp. 797-15.

European Commission (2004), 'Community guidelines on State aid for rescuing and restructuring firms in difficulty', *Official Journal of the European Union*, 2004/C 244/02, 10 October.

European Commission (2005), 'State aid action plan – Less and better targeted State aid: a roadmap for State aid reform 2005-2009', COM(2005) 107 final, Brussels.

European Commission (2012), 'Communication from the Commission to the European Parliament, the Council, the European Economic and Social Committee and the Committee of the Regions. EU State aid modernisation (SAM)', COM(2012) 209 final, 8 May.

European Commission (2014a), 'You can't improve what you can't measure: State aid evaluation', *Competition Policy Brief*, Issue 7, June.

European Commission (2014b), 'Guidelines on State aid for rescuing and restructuring non-financial undertakings in difficulty', *Official Journal of the European Union* (2014/C 249/01), 31 July.

European Commission (2015), 'Commission staff working document accompanying the document report from the Commission to the European Parliament, the Council, the European Economic and Social Committee and the Committee of the Regions on competition policy 2014', COM(2015) 247 final, Brussels.

Friederiszick H.W., Röller L.-H., and Verouden V. (2006), 'European State aid control: An economic framework', in: P. Buccirossi (ed.), *Handbook of antitrust economics*, pp. 625-669, Citeseer.

Głowicka E. (2006), 'Effectiveness of bailouts in the EU. Technical report', CIG Working Papers SP II 2006-05, Wissenschaftszentrum Berlin (WZB).

Grice J.S. and Ingram R.W. (2001), 'Tests of the generalizability of Altman's bankruptcy prediction model', *Journal of Business Research*, 54(1), pp. 53-61.

Grigolon L., Leheyda N., and Verboven F. (2016), 'Scrapping subsidies during the financial crisis – evidence from Europe', *International Journal of Industrial Organization*, 44, pp. 41-59.

Hainz C. and Hakenes H. (2012), 'The politician and his banker – How to efficiently grant State aid', *Journal of Public Economics*, 96(1), pp. 218-225.

Hayes S.K., Hodge K.A., and Hughes L.W. (2010). 'A study of the efficacy of Altman's Z to predict bankruptcy of specialty retail firms doing business in contemporary times', *Economics & Business Journal: Inquiries & Perspectives*, 3(1), pp. 122-134.

Hirano K., Imbens G.W., and Ridder G. (2003), 'Efficient estimation of average treatment effects using the estimated propensity score', *Econometrica*, 71(4), pp. 1161-1189.

Ichino A., Mealli F., and Nannicini T. (2008), 'From temporary help jobs to permanent employment: What can we learn from matching estimators and their sensitivity?', *Journal of Applied Econometrics*, 23(3), pp. 305-327.

Jalan J. and Ravallion M. (1998), 'Are there dynamic gains from a poor-area development program?', *Journal of Public Economics*, 67(1), pp. 65-85.

Kassim H. and Lyons B. (2013), 'The new political economy of EU State aid policy', *Journal of Industry, Competition and Trade*, 13(1), pp. 1-21.

Lechner M. (2001), 'Identification and estimation of causal effects of multiple treatments under the conditional independence assumption', in: M. Lechner and F. Pfeiffer (eds.), *Econometric Evaluation of Labour Market Policies*, pp. 43-58, Heidelberg: Physica.

Lewbel A. (2012), 'Using heteroscedasticity to identify and estimate mismeasured and endogenous regressor models', *Journal of Business & Economic Statistics*, 30(1), pp. 67-80.

Lewbel A. (2017), 'Identification and estimation using heteroscedaticity without instruments: The binary endogenous regressor case', Boston College Working Papers in Economics, Boston College Department of Economics, revised version July 2017.

Nitsche R. and Heidhues P. (2006), 'Study on methods to analyse the impact of State aid on competition', Technical report, Directorate-General Economic and Financial Affairs, European Commission.

Nulsch N. (2014), 'Is subsidizing companies in difficulties an optimal policy? An empirical study on the effectiveness of State aid in the European Union', IWH Discussion Papers 9/2014, Halle Institute for Economic Research (IWH).

OECD (2010), 'Competition, State aids and subsidies', DAF/COMP/GF(2010)5, Paris.

Ravallion M. and Chen S. (2005), 'Hidden impact? Household saving in response to a poor-area development project', *Journal of Public Economics*, 89(11), pp. 2183-2204.

Rosenbaum P.R. and Rubin D.B. (1983), 'The central role of the propensity score in observational studies for causal effects', *Biometrika*, 70(1), pp. 41-55.

Rubin D.B. (1974), 'Estimating causal effects of treatments in randomized and non-randomized studies', *Journal of Educational Psychology*, 66(5), pp. 688-701.

Rubin D.B. (1978), 'Bayesian inference for causal effects: The role of randomization', *The Annals of Statistics*, 6(1), pp. 34-58.

Sianesi B. (2004), 'An evaluation of the Swedish system of active labor market programs in the 1990s', *Review of Economics and Statistics*, 86(1), pp. 133-155.

Takalo T., Tanayama T. and Toivanen O. (2013), 'Estimating the benefits of targeted R&D subsidies', *Review of Economics and Statistics*, 95(1), pp. 255-272.

Tunali Ç.B. and Fidrmuc J. (2015), 'State aid policy in the European Union', *Journal of Common Market Studies (JCMS)*, 53(5), pp. 1143-1162.

PART IV The Broader Impact of EU Competition Policy

CHAPTER 11

How to Measure the Direct Effects of Competition Policy Interventions?*

Adriaan Dierx & Fabienne Ilzkovitz

It is more and more important for competition authorities to be able to explain in a simple way the impact of their interventions on society as a whole. The customer savings approach proposed in this chapter has been adopted by a number of competition authorities. On the basis of this approach, the European Commission calculates the direct benefits of merger and cartel decisions in terms of consumer welfare. The customer savings associated with cartel prohibitions and merger interventions by the European Commission amounted up to 0.1% of EU GDP over the period 2012-2018. A limited number of important cartel and merger decisions account for a large share of these customer savings. These decisions concern cartels in trucks as well as mergers in beer, wireless telecommunications activities and basic metals manufacturing.

§11.01 INTRODUCTION

By ensuring effective competition in product markets, competition policy encourages companies to become more efficient and increases their incentives to invest in innovation and product development. Consumers benefit from the resulting lower prices and the availability of a wider range of better quality products. Competition should therefore not be regarded as an end in itself but rather as a tool aimed at increasing consumer welfare.

It is not straightforward to convince the wider public that competition policy makes an important contribution to consumer welfare. In recent years, there has been an increased concern about the concentration of market power in a small number of large companies, especially in high-tech industries, creating risks for collusion and

* This chapter has been written under the sole responsibility of the authors and does not represent the views of the European Commission.

abuse of market power. The ability of competition policy authorities to identify and stop such anticompetitive behaviour has been put into question.

Within this context, competition authorities are making an effort to convey to the broader public what is at the heart of their mission: the promotion of competition in product markets to the benefit of consumers. The Competition and Markets Authority (CMA) in the UK even compares the estimated direct consumer benefits of its competition policy interventions with its operating costs. The benefit-cost ratio is supposed to reach a target of 10:1, in order to justify the CMA's budget for competition policy.

Other competition authorities (including those of the EU, Netherlands, Spain, the US and Japan) calculate the direct customer savings associated with their interventions primarily for advocacy and communication purposes. The results of such calculations are used in periodic reports, public speeches and the like. The kinds of interventions covered may differ between competition authorities, but usually merger interventions, cartel prohibitions and, possibly, other antitrust decisions are taken into account. The number of competition authorities that calculate the direct effects of their interventions is rather limited primarily because of the concern that such calculations provide only a partial view of the value and purpose of competition law enforcement.[1] In this chapter, it is argued that, while the results of this type of calculations should be interpreted with caution, they nevertheless provide a useful tool to monitor a competition authority's activities and their evolution over time. Moreover, they provide a rough estimate of the impact of competition policy interventions on consumer welfare.

The approach used by the European Commission to calculate direct customer savings is based on estimates of: (1) the price increase avoided due to a merger decision; and (2) the reduction in overcharges resulting from a cartel prohibition. Both lead to a reduction in prices in comparison with the counterfactual of no intervention. The estimated price reduction is multiplied by the affected turnover in the relevant market and the estimated further duration of the cartel or anticompetitive merger in the absence of an intervention by the competition authority. This approach is relatively simple, but it requires robust estimates and commonly agreed assumptions on how to measure the avoided price increase, the size of the affected market and the expected duration of the price effect in the absence of an intervention by the competition authority. These methodological aspects are discussed in detail in section 11.02 of this chapter. Sections 11.03 and 11.04 present and analyse the customer savings associated with cartel and merger decisions taken by the European Commission over the period 2012-2018. Section 11.05 describes the total customer savings from the European Commission's decisions and compares them with those calculated for other jurisdictions. The concluding section 11.06 highlights the potential benefits of customer savings calculations and suggests areas for further improvement.

1. *See* ICN (2011) and Ilzkovitz and Dierx (2015).

§11.02 METHODOLOGY

[A] Definition of Customer Savings

The rationale behind the calculation of customer savings[2] is rather straightforward. The aim of this measure is to provide an estimate of the benefits for end consumers resulting from competition policy enforcement actions. Under the presumption that less competitive markets are associated with higher prices for customers, the key element in the assessment of the impact of competition policy is the price increase avoided thanks to the competition authority's intervention. In addition, one needs to take into account the temporal dimension, i.e., the time span during which this price effect lasts, as well as the size of the markets affected by the intervention.

Thus, the customer savings from a decision equal the product of the price increase avoided, the size of the affected market and the expected duration of the price effect in the absence of an intervention by the competition authority. The customer savings associated with a specific competition policy intervention correspond to the total monetary value which customers have been able or are going to save as a result of the intervention. In aggregate, total customer savings over a certain period are nothing but the sum of the customer savings associated with each competition policy intervention made during that time horizon.

Figure 11.1 illustrates the calculation of customer savings from the detection and dismantlement of an hypothetical cartel in a market worth EUR 300 million and with a likely further duration of three years. The cartel prohibition gives rise to customer savings of EUR 90-135 million, depending on the assumption on the avoided price increase.

Figure 11.1 Calculation of Customer Savings in an Hypothetical Example

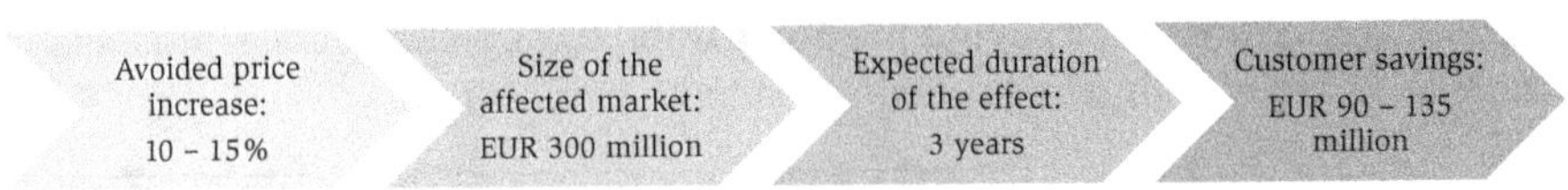

Source: Authors' own elaboration.

Like every empirical application in the field of economics, the customer savings approach has its strengths and weaknesses. On the positive side, this measure relies on a very simple calculation, namely the multiplication of three factors. As a consequence, it is easy to explain to the broader public. Moreover, both the expected duration of the effect and the size of the affected market reflect case-specific information, allowing for an estimation tailored to the decisions at hand. Finally, the assumptions regarding the

2. In this chapter, customers include both end consumers (of a final product such as beer) and users of intermediate products (such as iron and steel). We assume that the price savings of users of intermediate products are fully passed on to the end consumer (of motor vehicles, e.g.). Total consumer welfare gains are the sum of the direct savings on final products and the passed-on savings on intermediate products, which is equivalent to total customer savings.

price increase are based on the economic literature and are rather conservative. In the past, more sophisticated model simulations were used to estimate the price effects of specific merger decisions. But this approach was abandoned by the European Commission because it was very costly and not without limitations.

But this simple method has a number of weaknesses. First, it calculates only the static price effects of competition policy interventions and does not consider dynamic and non-price effects in terms of innovation, quality or choice. With the development of the digital economy, these non-price effects may even be more important than the direct price effects. Second, only the markets directly affected by the competition interventions are considered in the calculations, leaving aside deterrent effects and spillovers to other markets. As the deterrent effects of competition policy interventions are generally much larger than their direct effects (*see* Chapter 12), measures of customer savings tend to seriously underestimate the true impact of competition policy interventions. Finally, only merger and cartel decisions are covered by the European Commission's calculations, whereas positive effects arising from other antitrust decisions (e.g., cases of abuse of dominant position) or from State aid control are not considered in this framework.

[B] Main Assumptions and Data Sources

The customer savings approach relies on case-specific data and assumptions regarding the magnitude of the price effect, the size of the market directly affected and the expected duration of the price effect in the absence of an intervention by the competition authority. Fortunately, international agreement has been reached within the OECD on guiding principles for the calculation of customer savings. These common principles have been identified and published by the OECD (*see* Box 11.1) as part of a strategy aimed at promoting best practices in competition policy evaluation. Moreover, the adoption of these principles by the competition authorities making these calculations could contribute to improving the comparability of results across jurisdictions, although this type of comparison should be made with caution.

Box 11.1: OECD Guiding Principles

The OECD publication 'Guide for helping competition authorities assess the expected impact of their activities' (OECD, 2014) suggests an approach that authorities could refer to, when carrying out an assessment of their interventions. According to this Guide, the assessment should be comprehensive and include as a minimum the impact of all decisions relating to blocked mergers, mergers approved with remedies and cartels. The impact of other interventions, such as abuses of dominance, vertical agreements and market/sectoral studies may also be considered.

The Guide proposes the following general principles for calculating and reporting the benefits accruing from agencies' decisions:

- Whenever possible, use case-specific information.
- Assume that no intervention will have a negative impact.
- Estimate static consumer benefits and when possible also include dynamic ones.
- Calculate and publish the impact assessment regularly.
- Present the results both as annual figure and as an annual moving average over three years.
- Present the results by type of decisions, when possible (e.g., separate the estimated impact of cartel decisions from that of merger decisions).
- Give point estimates within a range of plausible values.

The OECD also suggests using a simple and easily applicable methodology: the static customer benefits resulting from each decision is the product of the price increase avoided, the size of the affected turnover and the expected duration of the price effect. When case-specific information is available on these three elements, this information should be used. Otherwise, the OECD suggests using the following assumption:

	Cartel Cases	*Abuse of Dominance Cases*	*Merger Cases*
Yearly price effect	Overcharge of 10%	Price increase of 5%	Price increase of 3%
Affected turnover	Ex ante turnover of the companies under investigation in the affected market(s)	Ex ante turnover of the companies under investigation in the affected market(s)	Ex ante turnover of all firms in the affected market(s)
Duration	3 years	3 years	2 years

Source: OECD (2014).

The assumptions and data sources used by the European Commission are presented in Table 11.1. The assumptions made are very similar but not identical to those proposed by the OECD. First, the European Commission considers ranges instead of single values for the yearly price effect. The lower and upper bounds of the ranges are based on recent findings of the literature. Second, as suggested by the OECD, case-specific information is used to estimate the likely duration of the price effects. More details on the information used for the calculation of customer savings from cartel decisions and merger interventions are given in the next two subsections.

Table 11.1 Assumptions and Data Sources used in the European Commission's Customer Savings Calculations

	Cartel Cases		*Merger Cases*	
	Assumption	*Source*	*Assumption*	*Source*
Yearly price effect	Overcharge of 10-15%	Empirical literature: 16-25%	Price increase of 3-5%	Empirical literature: ≥3%
Affected turnover	Turnover of the companies under investigation in the affected market(s)	Case-specific information	Turnover of all firms in the affected market(s)	Case-specific information
Duration	1/3/6-years	Case-specific information on cartel stability	2/3/5-years	Case-specific information on barriers to entry and expansion

[1] Cartels

In cartels, the affected turnover is considered to be equal to the annual value of sales by cartel members in the market directly affected by cartel. Figures on the relevant turnover come directly from the investigations carried out by the case team. It is worth noting that this definition of the affected turnover is rather narrow, in particular in comparison with the definition adopted for mergers. It is considered that the price effect generated by the cartel does not spread to the rest of the market or to the sector in which the cartel has been detected.

Cartel members are expected to charge a price higher than its competitive counterfactual, with the difference between the two being defined as the cartel overcharge. The avoided price increase due to the detection and prohibition of a cartel is considered to be equivalent to the overcharge (or increase in price) brought about by the cartel in the past. Much of the empirical work on the impact of cartel policy enforcement has attempted to estimate the order of magnitude of cartel overcharges. The recent empirical literature reports median price overcharges for cartels varying from 16% to 25%.[3] However, these estimates are based on detected cartels. As the overcharge of non-detected cartels could be larger, the estimates may suffer from selection bias (*see* Chapter 12). Based on these findings, cartel overcharges are assumed to be either 10% or 15% of the affected turnover. Compared to the literature findings, these assumptions are rather conservative.

In order to estimate what the likely duration of the cartel would have been if it had continued undetected, a two-step approach is used. First, an aggregate score of cartel stability is calculated for each cartel. Second, on the basis of this score, cartels are

3. *See inter alia* Bos et al. (2018), Boyer and Kotchoni (2015), and Connor and Lande (2008).

classified into three categories of stability, each of which is associated with a likely cartel duration.

The aggregate score of cartel stability is based on a case-by-case analysis carried out by the case team responsible. The analysis, relying on case-specific information, focuses on an assessment of a number of indicators of cartel stability, which reflect the case team's judgement. This assessment also integrates results of the empirical literature on the factors influencing cartel stability.[4] According to this literature, cartel members regularly reassess the costs and benefits of their cartel participation. If the costs of cartelisation are likely to dominate the expected benefits, they take the decision to leave the cartel. The empirical literature seems to conclude that such an exit of a cartel member substantially increases the probability of a cartel breakdown. Table 11.2 reports the thirteen indicators, along with a short description of the economic rationale behind each of them.

Table 11.2 Indicators for Cartel Stability Assessment

Indicator	*Economic Rationale*
Number of firms participating in the cartel	The larger the number of firms forming the cartel, the more likely is detection or split-up because of disagreements amongst cartel participants.
Cartel's market share	A higher market share of the cartel shields it from outside competitive pressures, thus effectively increasing cooperation incentives. This can be an estimated market share, based on a rough analysis of the likely relevant market.
Symmetry of market shares	The more symmetric the market shares of firms forming the cartel, the more sustainable is the cartel, as the partners have a higher incentive to abide by the cartel price and therefore splitting the higher profits.
Structural links (cross-shareholdings or participation in joint-ventures)	Structural links within the cartel allow for a direct monitoring and exercise of cartel discipline.
Product characteristics	Differentiation adds complexities to the pricing strategy, thus weakening the cartel.
Entry barriers	Effective entry barriers allow the cartel to enjoy enough space and time to resolve possible disagreements between the cartel partners, without competitive pressure from outside. Factors taken into account include the cost of entry, the timeframe of entry, regulatory barriers, technological barriers, reputation, experience, past episodes of attempted entry, etc.

4. *See inter alia* Hellwig and Hüschelrath (2018).

Indicator	*Economic Rationale*
Trends in demand	In a stagnating market with a stable or slowly increasing demand, the cartel will be more stable, as stagnation makes collusion more profitable. However, it is also possible that with falling demand, partners will be tempted to undercut the cartel prices in order to protect their sales volumes. Markets with rapidly increasing demand are between those two extremes.
Buyer power	Increased buyer power puts pressure on the cartel to lower prices, thus increasing the incentive of each partner to deviate from the arrangement. A simplified proxy for this option could be based on the customers' shares of the buying market. Large market shares indicate buyer power while a fragmented buying side indicates low buyer power.
Transparency (as a means to detect whether the cartel members are complying with the agreement)	The more and better means of supervision of the cartel, the more stable it is.
Ability to react timely if cheating occurs within the cartel	The ability to react timely depends on the information available to the parties (*see* under 'Transparency' above): if the information is sufficiently recent and frequent, the parties may be able to react timely, thus increasing the stability of the cartel.
Interaction in other markets	Interaction is defined as the fact that at least some of the cartel members are also present in one or more other markets where they can engage in price wars to punish deviations in the cartelised market.
Cartel deterrence in the sector concerned	Deterrence within the sector depends on the number of inspections and fining decision taken by the European Commission in the sector concerned. If there is no deterrence, the cartel is likely to be more stable.
Reach of European Commission enforcement	This indicator reflects the difficulty of enforcement by the European Commission outside the EEA territory if some or all cartel members are based outside the EEA. The difficulty of enforcement is likely to be positively correlated with the stability of the cartel.

Based on these indicators, an aggregate score of cartel stability is calculated for each cartel. On that basis, the cartels are then classified into three categories:

(1) unsustainable (corresponding to a likely duration of one year);
(2) fairly sustainable (corresponding to a likely duration of three years); and
(3) very sustainable (corresponding to a likely duration of six years).

The assumptions concerning the likely duration of the cartels are made prudently to establish a lower limit rather than to estimate the most likely values. Descriptive analyses of EU cartel cases show an average duration of detected cartels in the EU of around seven years over the period 2001 and 2015.[5] However, these analyses also conclude that there is a large variation in duration depending on the cartel characteristics. This observation pleads in favour of the case-dependent approach adopted by the European Commission.[6]

[2] Mergers

The sample of merger decisions used for the customer savings calculations consists of decisions concerning anticompetitive mergers that would have had a net negative impact on consumer welfare without the intervention of the European Commission. These 'merger interventions' consist in Phase I and Phase II merger clearance decisions,[7] that are conditional to remedies, merger prohibition decisions and merger withdrawals in Phase II provided that these withdrawals are not due to other identifiable reasons than the position taken by the Commission. Under such circumstances there appears to be a high likelihood that the Commission's intervention led to the withdrawal of an anticompetitive merger and helped to avoid a price increase.

In mergers, the affected turnover is considered to be equal to the value of total sales by the merging parties and their competitors in the relevant market. Taking the value of the entire market is justified by the observation that the price effect of a merger is unlikely to be confined to the merging parties and more likely to have repercussions on the prices in the entire relevant market.

The likely price increase avoided by merger clearance decisions subject to conditions, merger prohibitions or Phase II withdrawals is set at 3% or 5% of the affected turnover, with 3% representing a lower bound on the reported customer savings and 5% an upper bound. This 3-5% range is in line with the current literature but remains rather conservative as a measure of the expected price increase from a merger requiring the Commission's intervention. Stiebale and Szücz (2019), for example, report post-merger mark-up increases between 2% and 4% for rival firms. They attribute this rise in mark-ups to price increases, as the marginal cost reductions appear to be rather limited. They therefore conclude that horizontal mergers in the EU have, on average, led to mark-up and price increases in affected markets. A review of merger decisions in the EU by Peter Ormosi et al. (*see* Chapter 2) comes to a similar conclusion. It shows an average price increase of 5% for approved mergers and no price increase on average for the more problematic mergers approved with remedies.

5. More precisely, according to Broos et al. (2016), the average duration of detected cartels in the EU over the period 2004-2014 equals 6.9 years. Hellwig and Hüschelrath (2017) report an average duration of 7.2 years over the period 2001-2015.
6. *See* OECD (2013).
7. A Phase I merger decision is a decision which is taken within twenty-five working days following the notification of the merger. If the merger raises competition concerns and cannot be resolved in Phase I, a Phase II merger investigation is opened. Phase II is an in-depth analysis of the merger's effects on competition and requires more time (at least ninety working days from the opening of a Phase II investigation). Following the Phase II investigation, the Commission may either unconditionally clear the merger or approve the merger subject to remedies or prohibit the merger if no adequate remedies to the competition concerns have been proposed by the merging parties.

This evidence suggests that the remedies required for merger clearance reduce prices by at least 5%.

Finally, a two-step approach similar to the one followed in cartels is used to estimate the expected duration of the harm (price increase) avoided as a result of a merger intervention (such as a merger clearance subject to conditions, a prohibition, or a withdrawal in Phase II). The question is how long it would have taken for the market to self-correct and restore the conditions of competition before the merger took place. The duration of this 'restoration' process is considered to be proportionate to the barriers to entry or expansion in each market concerned. The significance of these entry barriers is assessed by the case team on the basis of twelve case-specific indicators. An aggregate score is then calculated as the sum of these single indicators. Table 11.3 lists the indicators used, together with the economic rationale for each of them.

Table 11.3 Indicators for Expected Duration of the Avoided Price Increase from a Merger Intervention

Indicator	*Economic Rationale*
Recent entry	Recent entry is evidence that the barriers to entry are probably not very high and that market entry may occur again, alleviating competition concerns.
Churn rate	The churn rate is defined as the sum of the market entry and exit rates. A high churn rate is an indication that market entry is relatively easy.
Imports from outside geographical market	This is an indicator of the likelihood of market entry from outside the geographical market.
Authorisation required to enter	If the regulatory authorities need to give their agreement to a proposed market entry, entry barriers will likely be very high.
Market regulation	A high level of market regulation is indicative of important barriers to entry.
Network effects	Network effects give rise to economies of scale, making it more difficult for smaller competitors to enter the market.
Supply chain linkages	Entry in markets with strong supply chain linkages is difficult because of the effort and resources required to establish such linkages.
Economies of scale in production	The presence of large economies of scale gives an advantage to large, incumbent producers, as potential entrants generally do not have sufficient investment resources to achieve the scale required for efficient productions and compete on an equal footing.
Fixed costs (as a share of total costs)	A high share of fixed costs requires newcomers to make substantial investments before they can start competing.
Presence of branded products	Substantial investments are required to establish a new brand on the market, creating a barrier to entry.

Indicator	*Economic Rationale*
Investments in R&D and innovation	In markets where substantial investments are required to develop new products through R&D and innovation, it is more difficult to enter.
Demand	Firms have less of an incentive to enter markets where demand is declining as profit opportunities are rarer.

On the basis of these individual indicators as well as the aggregate score, mergers are classified into three categories:

(1) markets with 'significant' entry barriers (equivalent to a duration of two years);
(2) markets with 'very significant' entry barriers (duration of three years); and
(3) markets with 'extremely significant' entry barriers (duration of five years).

The merger classification is not done in a purely mechanical fashion. Rather it is based as well on the judgement of the case team on the importance of barriers to entry and expansion in the market concerned.

The choice of the lower and the upper value of the likely duration of the price effect is based on the following considerations. First, in its Guidelines on the assessment of horizontal mergers (paragraph 74), the European Commission (2004) considers that entry is timely if it occurs within two years. If entry is not likely to take place within that period, it would not be considered as sufficiently swift and sustained to deter or defeat the exercise of market power. Therefore, the lower limit for the expected duration of the price increase due to an anticompetitive merger is fixed at two years. Second, while there does not seem to be well-developed literature that directly assesses the duration of the price effects of anticompetitive mergers, Ormosi et al. (2015) report that price changes peak at around 2-3 years following the merger. Gugler et al. (2003) estimate that the increased market power effect (and implicitly its effects on prices) of an averagely profitable merger lasts at least five years. Such observations underpin the medium and upper values chosen for the duration of the price effects.

§11.03 CUSTOMER SAVINGS FROM CARTEL DECISIONS

This section provides an overview of the customer savings associated with cartel decisions taken by the European Commission over the period 2012-2018. It also identifies the cartel decisions that have brought the largest customer benefits over that period.

[A] Overview

Table 11.4 presents the range of yearly customer savings associated with the cartel decisions taken by the European Commission over the period 2012-2018. The lower bound of the range corresponds to a 10% reduction in the price overcharge and the upper bound to a 15% reduction. During this period 4 or 5 cartel decisions were taken every year, with the exception of the year 2014, when 10 cartels were stopped. Despite the relative stability in the number of decisions taken, one can observe large fluctuations in customer savings achieved, varying between EUR 1.0-1.5 billion in 2015 and EUR 6.8-10.2 billion in 2016, which represents a ratio of 1 to 7. This illustrates that the customer savings do not only depend on the number of decisions taken but even more so on the size of the markets affected by the decisions taken and on the likely duration of the cartels if they had continued undetected. For example, in 2016, the number of decisions taken was not exceptionally high but one of these decisions concerned a trucks cartel, which affected a very large market and was considered to be very sustainable.

Finally, it is worth pointing out that the large turnover recorded for 2013 is due to the particular nature of some of the cartel cases in that year. In fact, some of the cartels concerned collusive behaviour in financial markets having an exceptionally high turnover. This can be explained by the fact that the main economic activity of financial players is not the production of goods but rather intermediation in financial assets. Consequently, the turnover proxy used for the calculation of cartel fines was considered a reasonable estimate of the turnover in the markets affected. For the customer savings calculations the effects of this high turnover were offset to a certain extent by the unsustainability of financial market cartels. In financial markets the observed duration of cartel participation tends to be relatively short for many cartelists. This can be explained by a high volatility in financial markets and the frequently updated price benchmarks, making coordination more difficult. The unsustainability of the financial market cartels explains why, despite the high turnover of the companies participating in such cartels, the value of customer savings in 2013 is lower than that in 2016.

Table 11.4 Customer Savings (in EUR billion) from Cartels Prohibitions by the European Commission (2012-2018)

Year	*Number of Decisions*	*Total Turnover in Affected Markets*	*Customer Savings*
2012	4	5.2	1.4-2.0
2013	4	13.1	1.4-2.1
2014	10	7.5	1.8-2.7
2015	4	3.3	1.0-1.5
2016	5	11.7	6.8-10.2
2017	5	3.1	1.4-2.1
2018	4	2.4	1.3-1.9

Table 11.5 classifies the cartel decisions taken over the period 2012-2018 by sector.[8] This table shows that most of the customer savings originate from a limited

8. The sector classification is based on NACE Rev.2 and is defined in Annex 1.

number of sectors. Four sectors account for 87% of the total customer savings and almost two-thirds of the cartel decisions taken, namely motor vehicles and transport equipment, electronic products and electrical equipment, financial services, and transportation and warehousing. More than half of total customer savings comes from the motor vehicles and transport equipment sector even though this sector accounts for only 25% of the number the decisions taken. Again, this points to the large size of the affected market turnover of cartel participants in this sector.

Table 11.5 Cartel Decisions by Sector (2012-2018)

Sector Codes (NACE)	*Sector Names*	*Number of Decisions*	*Share in Total Customer Savings*
C.29, C.30	Manufacture of motor vehicles and other transport equipment	9	55.6%
C.26, C.27	Manufacture of electronic products and electrical equipment	7	14.9%
K.64, K.65, K.66	Financial and insurance activities	4	9.3%
H.49, H.50, H.51, H.52	Transportation and warehousing	3	7.6%
C.28	Manufacture of machinery and equipment	1	3.9%
C.24, C.25	Manufacture of metals and metal products	2	1.6%
C.16, C.17, C.18	Manufacture of wood and paper; printing	1	1.6%
C.31, C.32, C.33	Manufacture of furniture and other products; repair and installation	1	1.4%
C.10, C.11, C.12	Manufacture of food, beverages and tobacco	2	1.4%
C.22, C.23	Manufacture of rubber, plastics and other non-metallic mineral products	3	1.3%
D.35, E.36, E.37, E.38, E.39	Electricity, gas and steam; water and waste management	2	1.0%
G.46	Wholesale trade except vehicles	1	0.3%
	Total	**36**	**100%**

Other analyses covering a longer time period confirm that a large majority of cartels in the EU occur in the manufacturing industry. A review by Hellwig and Hüschelrath (2017) of cartel decisions taken over the period 2001-2015 shows that 89 out of 113 cartel cases (about 79%) concerned the manufacturing sector, followed by eight cartels in transportation and storage and six in financial and insurance activities. Similarly, Combe and Monnier (2012) observe that over the period 1969-2009 most cartels were detected in the manufacturing industry, in particular the chemical industry and intermediate goods industry, as well as in transport and financial services.

[B] Important Cartel Prohibitions over the Period 2012-2018

Table 11.6 lists the one or two largest EU cartel prohibitions in terms of customer savings on a yearly basis. The final column of the table illustrates the important share in total customer savings of these cartel cases, exceeding 80% in every year except in 2014 when it was 49%.

Table 11.6 Most Important Cartels Prohibitions (2012-2018)

Year	*Case Number*	*Case Name*	*NACE Code*	*Sector Name*	*Share in Total Customer Savings (Year t)*
2012	AT.39437	TV and computer monitor tubes	C.26.40	Manufacture of consumer electronics	92%
	AT.39452	Mountings for windows and window-doors	C.25.72	Manufacture of locks and hinges	
2013	AT.39914	Euro interest rate derivatives	K.64.30	Trusts, funds and similar financial entities	88%
	AT.39861	Yen interest rate derivatives	K.64.30	Trusts, funds and similar financial entities	
2014	AT.39922	Bearings	C.27.32	Manufacture of other electronic and electric wires and cables	49%
	AT.39610	Power cables	C.27	Manufacture of electrical equipment	
2015	AT.39639	Optical disk drives	C.26.80	Manufacture of magnetic and optical media	83%
	AT.40055	Parking heaters	C.29.32	Manufacture of other parts and accessories for motor vehicles	
2016	AT.39824	Trucks (hybrid decision[9])	C.29.10	Manufacture of motor vehicles	97%

9. The trucks decision is part of a hybrid decision (i.e., a combination of a settlement and a prohibition decision) reflecting the fact that some participants agreed to settle in 2016 but one (i.e. Scania) declined to do so. Consequently, the Commission adopted a prohibition decision vis-à-vis Scania in 2017.

Year	*Case Number*	*Case Name*	*NACE Code*	*Sector Name*	*Share in Total Customer Savings (Year t)*
2017	AT.39824	Trucks (hybrid decision: Scania)	C.29.10	Manufacture of motor vehicles	85%
	AT.39960	Hvac – compressors – rad – fans	C.29.31	Manufacture of electrical and electronic equipment for motor vehicles	
2018	AT.40009	Maritime Car Carriers (MCC)	H.50.20	Sea and coastal freight water transport	81%

Table 11.7 ranks the five largest cartel decisions according to their share in total customer savings arising from cartel decisions taken over the period 2012-2018. Together, these five cartel decisions account for 69% of total customer savings.

Table 11.7 Top Five Cartel Prohibitions in Terms of Customer Savings (2012-2018)

Year	*Case No.*	*Case Name*	*NACE Code*	*Sector Name*	*Share of the Total Customer Savings over the Period 2012-2018*
2016	AT.39824	Trucks (hybrid decision)	C.29.10	Manufacture of motor vehicles	43.6%
2018	AT.40009	Maritime Car Carriers (MCC)	H.50.20	Sea and coastal freight water transport	6.8%
2012	AT.39437	TV and computer monitor tubes	C.26.40	Manufacture of consumer electronics	6.7%
2017	AT.39824	Trucks (hybrid decision: Scania)	C.29.10	Manufacture of motor vehicles	6.2%
2013	AT.39914	Euro interest rate derivatives	K.64.30	Trusts, funds and similar financial entities	5.3%

One cartel decision stands out regarding the benefits it provides to customers. This is a cartel involving a number of truck manufacturers, which colluded for fourteen years on truck pricing and on passing on the costs for meeting environmental standards to consumers. Together these manufacturers account for around nine out of every ten medium and heavy trucks produced in Europe. The market concerned by this cartel is very large, which explains why this cartel settlement decision alone accounts for 44%

of the total customer savings for the period 2012-2018 and 97% of the total in 2016, the year the decision was taken.

The four other cartel prohibitions listed each represent around 6% of total customer savings for the period 2012-2018. They include a cartel in the intercontinental maritime transport of vehicles; a cartel of producers of TV and computer monitor tubes which were involved in anticompetitive practices such as price fixing, market sharing, customer allocation, capacity and output coordination and exchanges of commercially sensitive information; the truck cartel prohibition decision addressed to Scania; and a cartel decision concerning the market for interest rate derivatives denominated in euros. This prohibition decision targeted four financial institutions which had tried to distort the normal course of price setting for these derivatives.

While it is interesting to gain an overview of the cartel prohibition decisions that offer the largest customer benefits, one should not forget a major limitation of the approach adopted here, in that it only considers the direct customer benefits in terms of price reduction. Other cartel decisions affecting smaller market may have an even bigger impact if they have strong deterrent effects. For example, in 2016, the European Commission imposed a fine on Riberebro, a Spanish canned and fresh vegetable company, which had participated in a cartel to coordinate prices and allocate customers of canned mushrooms in Europe for more than a year. While the direct benefits of this cartel decision account only for 0.01% of the total customer savings recorded over the period 2012-2018, this decision may have a larger impact on end consumers if it deters other companies in the food industry from forming cartels, as access to food at competitive and affordable prices is essential for European consumers.

§11.04 CUSTOMER SAVINGS FROM MERGER INTERVENTIONS

Turning to merger cases, this section presents an overview of the relevant decisions taken over the same period (2012-2018), both from a general and a sectoral perspective. It will also aim to identify the most important merger interventions made in that period.

[A] Overview

Table 11.8 describes the range of yearly customer savings associated with the important merger decisions by the European Commission over the period 2012-2018. The lower bound of the range corresponds to a 3% avoided price increase and the upper bound to an avoided price increase of 5%.

Table 11.8 Customer Savings (in EUR billion) from Merger Interventions by the European Commission (2012-2018)

Year	*Number of Decisions*	*Total Turnover in Affected Markets*	*Customer Savings*
2012	17	40.5	5.5-9.1
2013	14	4.9	0.4-0.6
2014	17	33.7	2.1-3.6
2015	22	19.9	1.7-2.9
2016	27	127.9	18.3-30.4
2017	24	22.6	2.4-4.1
2018	25	121.4	15.0-25.0

This table shows that the number of merger interventions in the period 2012-2018 varies between 14 (in 2013) and 27 (in 2016), with an average of 20 interventions per year. As is the case with cartels, we observe quite a remarkable variance over time both in terms of the size of the affected markets and in the resulting customer savings: annual customer savings range from between EUR 0.4-0.6 billion in 2013 to EUR 18.3-30.4 billion in 2016, which represents a ratio of 1 to 50. The years 2016 and 2018 were exceptional characterised both by a high number of decisions and the large size of the markets affected.

Table 11.9 applies the same sector classification as the one used for cartels to provide a description of sectors that contributed the most to the total customer savings from merger decisions over the period 2012-2018. As is the case for cartels, a large share of total customer savings is concentrated in four sectors, namely, telecommunications, food, beverages and tobacco, metals and metal products, and chemicals and pharmaceutical products. These four sectors account for 78% of total customer savings and 40% of the total number of merger decisions taken. In comparison with the cartel prohibitions, the merger interventions are somewhat more diversified across sectors.

Table 11.9 Merger Interventions by Sector (2012-2018)

Sector Codes (NACE)	*Sector Names*	*Number of Mergers*	*Share in Total Customer Savings*
J.61	Telecommunications	14	30.3%
C.10, C.11, C.12	Manufacture of food, beverages and tobacco	10	21.5%
C.24, C.25	Manufacture of metals and metal products	8	15.7%
C.20, C.21	Manufacture of chemicals and pharmaceutical products	27	10.8%
J.58, J.59, J.60	Publishing; video, television, and sound recording; broadcasting	7	5.6%
H.49, H.50, H.51, H.52	Transportation and warehousing	13	3.2%
C.16, C.17, C.18	Manufacture of wood and paper; printing	6	2.9%
C.29, C.30	Manufacture of motor vehicles and other transport equipment	11	1.8%
C.26, C.27	Manufacture of electronic products and electrical equipment	9	1.5%
B.05, B.06, B.07, B.08, B.09	Mining and quarrying	2	1,5%
C.28	Manufacture of machinery and equipment	4	1.4%
C.22, C.23	Manufacture of rubber, plastic and non-metallic mineral products	6	1.1%
M.69-M.75, N.77-N.82	Professional, scientific and technical activities; administrative and support service activities	3	0.9%
K.64, K.65, K66	Financial and insurance activities	4	0.7%
C.31, C.32, C.33	Manufacture of furniture and other products; repair and installation	8	0.4%
G.47	Retail trade except vehicles	3	0.3%
G.46	Wholesale trade except vehicles	3	0.2%
A.01, A.02, A.03	Agriculture	2	0.1%
J.62, J.63	Computer programming; information service activities	3	0.1%
H.53	Postal activities	2	0.1%
D.35, E.36, E.37, E.38, E.39	Electricity, gas and steam; water and waste management	1	0.1%
	Total	**146**	**100%**

In terms of number of decisions, one sector stands out with more than twenty-five merger decisions taken over the period 2012-2018, namely chemicals and pharmaceuticals. In the pharmaceuticals, a large number of decisions with remedies were taken to ensure that treatments remain available and prices competitive. In the case investigations on the pharma mergers proposed, the European Commission had to make a prospective analysis including the possible impact of these mergers on the development of new products and on innovation. In chemicals, some merger decisions focused on the price effects of the increased concentration, such as the 2018 decision concerning the merger between Praxair and Linde, which are two of the four largest companies active worldwide across the whole supply chains of industrial gases, medical gases, specialty gases and helium. Other decisions have looked more into the effects of the increased market concentration on innovation. A recent case in chemicals sector is the Dow/Dupont merger, affecting potential competition in the market for herbicides and insecticides used for crop protection. The Commission's remedy was designed to address concerns on both product and innovation competition. The positive effects on innovation of the European Commission's merger interventions in the chemicals and pharmaceutical sectors are not taken into account when calculating the customer savings, which is, as already discussed, a limitation of the approach used.

The telecommunication sector, on its own, is responsible for 30% of total customer savings from merger decisions taken over the period 2012-2018. This high figure should be viewed within the context of the wave of market consolidation in telecoms during this period. Consequently, the European Commission had to review several mergers between mobile-only operators and between fixed-mobile operators in Austria, Belgium, Germany, Denmark, Ireland, Italy, the Netherlands, Portugal, Spain and the United Kingdom. In all these cases, the Commission concluded that absent remedies, the mergers would have led to a lessening of effective competition and as a result to higher prices for mobile telecommunication services for consumers. In most of the cases, the parties proposed remedies addressing the Commission concerns and the mergers were cleared. In one case (the joint venture combining the Danish operations of TeliaSonera and Telenor), the parties failed to provide a remedy that would have solved the serious competition problem identified by the Commission and eventually abandoned the transaction. In another case (the proposed acquisition of Telefonica's British subsidiary operating under the brand O2 by the market challenger Hutchison), Hutchison failed to offer suitable remedies and the transaction was eventually prohibited by the Commission in May 2016.[10]

[B] Important Merger Interventions over the Period 2012-2018

Table 11.10 presents for each year the two or three merger interventions which contributed the most to the customer savings of that year. As is the case for cartels, a large share of each year's customer benefits arising from merger decisions is the result

10. *See* Manigrassi et al. (2016).

of a limited number of decisions. This share ranges between 40% (2015) and 84% (2016) of total customer savings.

Table 11.10 Most Important Merger Interventions (2012-2018)

Year	*Case Number*	*Case Name*	*Sector*	*Share in Total Customer Savings (year t)*
2012	M.6541	Glencore / Xstrata	C.24.43 – Lead, zinc and tin production	78%
2012	M.6471	Outokumpu / Inoxum	C.24.10 – Manufacture of basic iron and steel and of ferro alloys	78%
2013	M.6663	Ryanair / Aer Lingus III	H.51.10 – Passenger air transport	68%
2013	M.6944	Thermo Fisher / Life Technologies	C.26.51 – Manufacture of instruments and appliances for measuring, testing and navigation	68%
2013	M.6924	Refresco / Pride Foods	C.11.07 – Manufacture of soft drinks; production of mineral waters and other bottled waters	68%
2014	M.7018	Telefonica Deutschland / E-plus	J.61.20 – Wireless telecommunication activities	71%
2014	M.7252	Holcim / Lafarge	C.23.51 – Manufacture of cement	71%
2015	M.7278	Ge / Alstom	C.28.11 – Manufacture of engines and turbines, except aircraft, vehicle and cycle engines	40%
2015	M.7421	Orange / Jazztel	J.61.20 – Wireless telecommunication activities	40%
2016	M.7881	Ab Inbev / Sabmiller	C.11.05 – Manufacture of beer	84%
2016	M.7758	Hutchison 3G Italy / Wind / JV	J.61.20 – Wireless telecommunication activities	84%
2016	M.7612	Hutchison 3G UK/ Telefonica UK	J.61.20 – Wireless telecommunication activities	84%
2017	M.7932	Dow / Dupont	C.20.20 – Manufacture of pesticides and other agrochemical products	62%
2017	M.8633	Lufthansa / Certain Air Berlin assets	H51.10 – Passenger air transport	62%
2017	M. 8287	Nordic Capital / Intrum Justicia	K.82.91 – Other activities auxiliary to financial services, except insurance and pension funding	62%
2018	M.9041	Hutchison / Wind Tre	J.61.20 – Wireless telecommunication activities	55%
2018	M.8480	Praxair / Linde	C.20.11 – Manufacture of industrial gases	55%

Table 11.11 presents the five merger decisions accounting for the largest share in the total customer savings from merger decisions taken over the period 2012-2018. Together, these five merger decisions account for more than half of total customer savings over that period.

Table 11.11 Top Five Merger Interventions in Terms of Customer Savings (2012-2018)

Year	*Case No.*	*Case Name*	*NACE Code*	*Sector Name*	*Share of the Total Customer Savings over the Period 2012-2018*
2016	M.7881	AB Inbev / SABMiller	C.11.05	Manufacture of beer	20.2%
2018	M.9041	Hutchison / Wind Tre	J.61.20	Wireless telecommunication activities	10.9%
2018	M.8480	Praxair / Linde	C.20.11	Manufacture of industrial gases	7.2%
2016	M.7758	Hutchison 3G Italy / Wind / JV	J.61.20	Wireless telecommunication activities	6.8%
2012	M.6541	Glencore / Xstrata	C.24.43	Lead, zinc and tin production	6.6%

The top four merger interventions were taken in 2016 and in 2018, while the fifth largest merger intervention dates from 2012. This is not surprising as the value of customer savings from merger decisions is the highest during these years. In 2016, the two merger decisions which stand out are: the AB InBev/SABMiller decision which affected beer markets in nine EU Member States and the Hutchison 3G Italy/Wind/JV decision which affected retail mobile telecoms markets in Italy. Together, these two merger decisions are responsible for 66% of the customer savings from merger decisions taken in 2016 and for 27% of the total customer savings from merger decisions taken over the period 2012-2018. In the beer market, the European Commission found that the AB InBev/SABMiller transaction would have led to higher prices in EU countries and would have likely facilitated tacit price coordination among brewers in the European Economic Area. As Europeans buy around EUR 125 billion of beer every year, even a small price increase could cause considerable harm. In this case, the Commission accepted to clear the merger conditional on AB InBev selling practically the entire SABMiller beer business in Europe. The Italian telecommunications case is related to the proposed creation of a joint venture combining the Italian operations of Vimpelcom and the market challenger Hutchison. The transaction was cleared by the Commission in September 2016, subject to remedies consisting of a divestment allowing the creation of a new fourth mobile network operator in Italy.

In 2018, the top two merger decisions were Hutchison's acquisition of sole control of Wind Tre, which offers mobile telecommunication services on the Italian market, and the Praxair/Linde merger in the industrial, medical and specialty gas markets. Together, these two mergers account for 55% of the customer savings from merger decisions taken in 2018 and for 18% of the total customer savings from merger decisions taken over the period 2012-2018. Two other merger decisions taken in 2018 are also worth mentioning, i.e., the ArcelorMittal's acquisition of Ilva, an Italian steel producer, and the acquisition by The Walt Disney Company of parts of Twenty First

Century Fox. These latter two merger cases are responsible for 15% each of total annual customer savings from merger decisions taken in 2018.

The important merger decision of 2012 concerns the market for basic metals. The acquisition of Xstrata by Glencore brought together two major global players in key commodities and could have led to a significant increase in the price of zinc metal, which is an essential input for European industries such as steel galvanisers and car makers. The European Commission cleared the merger subject to conditions that preserved the ability and incentive of the largest European zinc metal producer to compete effectively with Glencore in the European Economic Area. This case illustrates that merger decisions may impact on intermediate products which are essential inputs for many European industries and affect final consumers only indirectly.

§11.05 TOTAL CUSTOMER SAVINGS OVER THE PERIOD 2012-2018

Table 11.12 summarises the development over time in the number of important merger and cartel decisions taken by the European Commission over the period 2012-2018. It also describes the annual customer savings associated with these decisions. The final two columns describe the total customer savings, both in absolute value (in billion euros) and as a percentage of the EU GDP (at current prices).

This table shows that 20 to 30 important merger and cartel decisions are taken every year, with the number of merger decisions (14-27) being larger than that of cartels (4-10). Total annual customer savings range between EUR 1.8 and EUR 25.1 billion (when applying the lower bound of the avoided price increase) and EUR 2.8 and EUR 40.6 billion (for the upper bound of the avoided price increase). This corresponds to ranges of 0.01-0.17% and 0.02-0.27% of EU GDP, respectively. The total customer savings show a significant variation over time, which may be explained not only by the fluctuation in the number of decisions taken but also by the size of the markets affected. As already mentioned, 2016 was an exceptional year, with a large number of merger and cartel decisions affecting particularly large markets.

Figure 11.2 describes the size of the markets directly affected by the merger and cartel decisions considered over the period 2012-2018. As we can see, the total affected market size varies between EUR 18 and EUR 140 billion annually. In 2016, the very large size of the affected markets is mainly driven by mergers. With the exception of 2013,[11] mergers represent a larger share (between 82 and 98%) of markets affected than cartels. This may be explained in part by the larger number of merger decisions taken. However, when calculating the customer savings, this effect is partially offset by the larger avoided price increase for cartels in comparison with mergers: on an annual basis, customer savings associated with merger decisions represent between 54% and 93% of the total customer savings (except in 2013, when they represented less than aquarter of total customer savings).

11. In 2013, two important cartel decisions affecting interest rate derivatives markets were taken.

Table 11.12 Customer Savings from Merger and Cartel Decisions

Year	*Number of Merger Decisions*	*Customer Savings from Merger Decisions (EUR billion)*	*Number of Cartel Decisions*	*Customer Savings from Cartel Decisions (EUR billion)*	*Total Customer Savings (EUR billion)*	*Total Customer Savings as a % of EU GDP*
2012	17	5.5-9.1	4	1.4-2.0	6.9-11.1	0.05-0.08
2013	14	0.4-0.6	4	1.4-2.1	1.8-2.8	0.01-0.02
2014	17	2.1-3.6	10	1.8-2.7	4.0-6.3	0.03-0.04
2015	22	1.7-2.9	4	1.0-1.5	2.7-4.4	0.02-0.03
2016	27	18.3-30.4	5	6.8-10.2	25.1-40.6	0.17-0.27
2017	24	2.4-4.1	5	1.4-2.1	3.9-6.2	0.03-0.04
2018	25	15.0-25.0	4	1.3-1.9	16.2-26.8	0.10-0.17
Annual average	21	6.5-10.8	5	2.2-3.2	8.7-14.0	0.06-0.09

Figure 11.2 Size of Markets Affected by Merger and Cartel Decisions

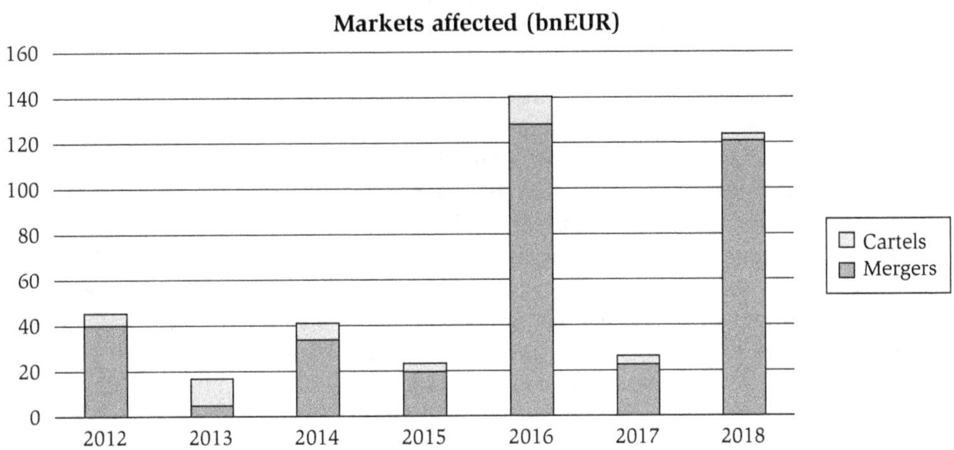

Source: Authors' own elaboration.

§11.06 COMPARISON WITH OTHER JURISDICTIONS

Table 11.13 presents data on the reported total customer savings (expressed as a percentage of GDP) from six jurisdictions, namely the EU (European Commission), the US (Department of Justice and Federal Trade Commission), Japan (Japan Fair Trade

Commission), the UK (Competition and Markets Authority), the Netherlands (Authority for Consumers and Markets) and Spain (National Commission on Markets and Competition).

Table 11.13 Total Customer Savings in Different Jurisdictions (Expressed as % of GDP)[12]

Year	*EC*	*US DOJ*	*US FTC*	*JFTC*	*CMA*	*ACM*	*CNMC*
2012	0.05-0.08	0.06	0.01	0.03	0.01	0.03	0.01
2013	0.01-0.02	0.01	0.01	0.03	0.01	0.10	0.02
2014	0.03-0.04	0.02	0.01	0.02	0.01	0.04	0.01
2015	0.02-0.03	0.02	0.02	0.01	0.01	0.02	0.21
2016	0.17-0.27	0.01	0.02	0.17	0.02	0.03	0.01
2017	0.03-0.04	0.01	0.02	0.05	0.01	0.14	0.01
Annual average	**0.06-0.09**	**0.02**	**0.01**	**0.05**	**0.01**	**0.06**	**0.05**

Clearly, the EU figure for 2016 is an outlier, not only in comparison with the EU customer savings in previous years (as noted above) but also in comparison with customer savings levels of other jurisdictions over the period 2012-2017. However, the European Commission is not the only authority experiencing a large variance over time in terms of total customer savings. On the contrary, large fluctuations over time appear to be a common feature across different jurisdictions.

While the above table allows getting an impression of the order of magnitude of customer savings from competition policy interventions in the different jurisdictions, it cannot be used to evaluate or compare the performance of the different authorities. In fact, part of the difference in customer savings levels is due to slightly dissimilar assumptions and methodologies, for example, with respect to the price effect, its duration or the size of the market affected. Differences in customer savings can also be due to the fact that the scope and number of cases as well as the type of interventions covered[13] can vary significantly across jurisdictions (and even from one year to another). Also, while, in general, higher customer savings levels are associated with more interventions in larger markets implying a more effective competition enforcement, this is not always necessarily the case: one could argue that the most efficient authority is the one that does not even need to intervene directly in the markets, given

12. Sources: EC, own calculations presented in the current chapter; US DOJ, Antitrust Division – Congressional Submission FY 2014 and 2018 Performance Budget; US FTC, Fiscal Year 2016 Performance Report and Annual Performance Plan for Fiscal Years 2017 and 2018; JFTC, calculation results made available via exchange of emails; CMA, OFT Positive Impact Report for years 2008-2014 and CMA Impact Assessment 2014/2015, 2015/2016, 2016/2017; ACM, ACM Annual Reports for the period 2013-2016 and NMa Working Paper – Outcome van NMa-optreden for 2012; CNMC, Estimating the impact of competition enforcement by the Spanish Competition Authority for 2012-2016.
13. For some jurisdictions (i.e., the US, the UK and Japan), total customer savings include antitrust cases other than cartels, whereas for the other jurisdictions (i.e., the EU and Spain) total customer savings include only mergers and cartels.

its ability to enforce competition simply through the credibility of its potential interventions.

While cross-jurisdictional comparisons are surely problematic, this may be less so when making comparisons within a given jurisdiction. Table 11.14 presents the customer savings from important merger decisions as a share of total customer savings. This figure may be indicative of the relative importance of merger control within a given jurisdiction. As observed in the previous table, the time variance is quite high. Nevertheless, the discrepancy between jurisdictions with high merger shares (such as the US Department of Justice) and low merger shares (such as competition authorities in Spain and the UK) is quite striking.

Table 11.14 Customer Savings from Mergers as a % of Total Consumer Savings

Year	*EC*	*US DOJ*	*US FTC*	*JFTC*	*CMA*	*CNMC*
2012	80-82	95	53	3	15	n/a
2013	21-22	80	56	18	13	4
2014	54-58	92	70	0	27	10
2015	63-66	97	71	10	17	2
2016	73-75	98	72	92	51	3
Weighted average	69-72	94	68	63	29	3

§11.07 CONCLUSIONS

It is more and more important for competition authorities to be able to explain in a simple way the impact of their interventions on society as a whole. The customer savings approach used by some competition authorities has the advantage of being an easy to understand method which can contribute to this objective. It allows calculating the direct benefits for consumers of important merger and cartel decisions. The customer savings associated with a specific competition policy intervention represent the total amount of monetary benefits accruing to customers as a result of the intervention.

The customer savings approach relies on assumptions regarding the avoided price increase and on case-specific information concerning the size of the market affected by the intervention and the likely duration of the price effect in the absence of an intervention by the competition authority. The customer savings stemming from a competition enforcement decision are estimated simply by multiplying these three factors. The assumptions made on the avoided price increase are based on recent findings of the literature and are rather cautious in order to avoid being criticised for inflating the calculated benefits associated with competition policy interventions.

The customer savings associated with cartel prohibitions and merger interventions by the European Commission represented on average 0.06% or 0.09% of EU GDP over the period 2012-2018 (depending on the assumptions made about the avoided price increases). These figures show a very high variability from one year to another, in line with the number of the decisions taken and more importantly with the size of the affected markets: the annual customer savings from merger and cartel decisions varied from 0.01-0.02% of GDP in 2013 to 0.17-0.27% of GDP in 2016.

A limited number of important cartel and merger decisions account for a large share of these customer savings. The top two cartel decisions (over of a total of 36 cartel decisions taken over the period 2012-2018) and the top five merger decisions (over a total of 146 merger decisions) each represent more than half of the total customer savings associated respectively with cartel and merger decisions. These decisions concern cartels in the truck and maritime car carrier markets as well as mergers in the beer and telecommunications markets and in the production of industrial gases and basic metals. While it is interesting to get an idea about the cartel and merger decisions that are most beneficial to consumers, a major limitation of the customer savings approach is that it only considers the direct benefits for consumers in terms of a reduction in price levels. Decisions affecting smaller markets may have a big impact if they have strong deterrent or non-price effects.

Therefore, future work could consider including the deterrent effects of merger and cartel decisions in the assessment of their impact. So far, competition authorities have refrained from doing this because of the uncertainties regarding the magnitude of these effects. However, as explained in Chapter 12, there is a consensus that these deterrent effects are significant and an effort is being made to improve estimates of the size of such effects. Similarly, taking account of the non-price effects (on innovation and on the variety and quality of products offered to consumers, e.g.) might lead to an increase in the magnitude of the estimated effects of competition policy interventions. While non-price effects are important, they are difficult to measure and case specific. As a first step, one could envisage including these effects when they represent an important element of the decision taken, as this was the case in recent mergers in the pharmaceutical and chemical industry. However, some caution is required, as an overestimation of the total effects of merger and cartel decisions might lead to a loss in credibility of the estimates presented. Also, one needs to be vigilant not to overcomplicate the calculation method because its simplicity is its greatest strength.

Another area for further development is to broaden the scope of the analysis by taking other activities of competition authorities into account. As suggested by the OECD, one could consider calculating the benefits for consumers of activities of competition authorities in other areas than cartel and merger control such as abuse of dominance, vertical agreements, State aid control and market studies/sector inquiries. The reasons why this has not yet been done are different for antitrust and for State aid control. In the first case, the different possible theories of harm make it more difficult to define general assumptions regarding the nature of such effects and to transform them into a price effect. In the second case, the impact of the interventions is of a different nature than the one of cartel and merger decisions. Therefore, one would need to reflect on a different method to calculate the benefits for consumers. For example, State aid control contributes to the correction of market failures and helps improve the use of public funds. This could be treated as a tax reduction benefitting consumers.

Notwithstanding these limitations, estimating the customer savings arising from cartel and merger decisions is a useful exercise which is very informative about the broad impact of competition authorities' interventions and their evolution over time. The customer savings approach has been adopted by a number of competition authorities. Moreover, international organisations, such as the OECD, are pushing for increased transparency on the underlying assumptions and a convergence of calculation methods used. Such convergence could contribute to improve the comparability of results across jurisdictions. However, great caution is required with this type of comparison: customer savings estimates cannot be used to compare the performance of the different authorities. In general, higher customer savings levels are associated with more interventions in larger markets implying a more effective competition enforcement. However, this is not necessarily the case as one could argue that the most efficient authority is the one that does not even need to intervene directly in the markets, given its ability to enforce competition simply through its credibility.

APPENDIX: SECTOR CLASSIFICATION

In order to perform the sectoral analysis, the NACE Rev.2 classification of the business economy has been aggregated into twenty-eight categories (*see* Table 11.15 below). Sectors are assigned to the same group according to their proximity in terms of products or industrial activities. Although arbitrary in some aspects, the present aggregation is necessary to implement a sectoral analysis at an acceptable level of granularity and to be consistent with the sectors covered by the QUEST macroeconomic model employed for performing simulation analyses in Chapter 13.

Table 11.15 Sector Classification

Group	*NACE Code*		*NACE Name*
1	A	01, 02, 03	Agriculture
2	B	05, 06, 07, 08, 09	Mining and quarrying
3	C	10, 11, 12	Manufacture of food, beverages, and tobacco
4	C	13, 14, 15	Manufacture of textiles, wearing, and leather
5	C	16, 17, 18	Manufacture of wood and paper; printing
6	C	19	Manufacture of coke and petroleum products
7	C	20, 21	Manufacture of chemicals and pharmaceutical products
8	C	22, 23	Manufacture of rubber, plastics, and non-metallic mineral products
9	C	24, 25	Manufacture of metals and metal products
10	C	26, 27	Manufacture of machinery and equipment
11	C	28	Manufacture of machinery and equipment
12	C	29, 30	Manufacture of motor vehicles and other transport equipment
13	C	31, 32, 33	Manufacture of furniture and other products; repair and installation
14	D-E	35, 36, 37, 38, 39	Electricity, gas and steam; water and waste management
15	F	41, 42, 43	Construction
16	G	45	Wholesale and retail trade of vehicles
17	G	46	Wholesale trade except vehicles
18	G	47	Retail trade except vehicles
19	H	49, 50, 51, 52	Transport and warehousing
20	H	53	Postal activities
21	I	55, 56	Accommodation and food services

Group	*NACE Code*		*NACE Name*
22	J	58, 59, 60	Publishing; video, television, and sound recording; broadcasting
23	J	61	Telecommunications
24	J	62, 63	Computer programming; information service activities
25	K	64, 65, 66	Financial and insurance activities
26	M-N	69, 70, 71, 72, 73, 74, 75, 77, 78, 79, 80, 81, 82	Professional, scientific and technical activities; administrative and support service activities
27	R	90, 91, 92, 93	Arts, entertainment, and recreation
28	S	94, 95, 96	Other service activities

REFERENCES

Bos I., Davies S., Harrington J.E. and Ormosi P.L. (2018), 'Does enforcement deter cartels? A tale of two tails', *International Journal of Industrial Organization*, 59(July), pp. 372-405.

Boyer M. and Kotchoni R. (2015), 'How much do cartel overcharge?', *Review of Industrial Organization*, 47(2), pp. 119-153.

Broos S., Gautier A., Marcos Ramos J. and Petit N. (2016), 'Analyse statistique des affaires d'ententes dans l'UE (2004-2014)', *Revue économique*, 67 (Hors-série), pp. 79-94.

Connor J.M. and Lande R.H. (2008), 'Cartel overcharges and optimal cartel fines', in: S.W. Waller (ed.), *Issues in Competition Law and Policy*, 3, ABA Section of Antitrust Law, Chapter 88, pp. 2203-2218.

Combe E. and Monnier C. (2012), 'Les cartels en Europe: une analyse empirique', *Revue française d'économie*, XXVII(2), pp. 187-226.

European Commission (2004), 'Guidelines on the assessment of horizontal mergers under the Council Regulation on the control of concentrations between undertakings', *Official Journal of the European Union*, 2004/C 31/03.

Gugler K.P., Mueller D.C., Yurtoglu B.B. and Zulehner C. (2003), 'The effects of mergers: An international comparison', *International Journal of Industrial Organization*, 21(5), pp. 625-653.

Hellwig M. and Hüschelrath K. (2017), 'Cartel cases and the cartel enforcement process in the European Union 2001-2015: A quantitative assessment', *The Antitrust Bulletin*, 62(2), pp. 400-438.

Hellwig M. and Hüschelrath K. (2018), 'When do firms leave cartels? Determinants and the impact on cartel survival', *International Review of Law and Economics*, 54 (June), pp. 68-84.

ICN (2011), 'Competition enforcement and consumer welfare - Setting the agenda', ICN 10th Annual Conference, The Hague, 17-20 May.

Ilzkovitz F. and Dierx A. (2015), 'Ex-post economic evaluation of competition policy enforcement: A review of the literature', DG Competition staff paper, Publications Office of the European Union, June.

Manigrassi L., Ocello E. and Staykova V. (2016), 'Recent developments in telecoms mergers', *Competition Merger Brief*, n°3, DG Competition, European Commission.

OECD (2013), 'Assessment of the impact of competition authorities' activities - Note by Prof. Stephen Davies', DAF/COMP/WP2(2013)1.

OECD (2014), 'Guide for helping competition authorities assess the expected impact of their activities', April.

Ormosi P., Mariuzzo F., Havell R. with Fletcher A. and Lyons B. (2015), 'A review of merger decisions in the EU: What can we learn from ex-post evaluations?', Report prepared for the Directorate-General for Competition of the European Commission, Publications Office of the European Union, July.

Stiebale J. and Szücz F. (2019), 'Mergers and market power: Evidence from rivals' responses in European markets', Discussion Paper No. 323, Düsseldorf Institute for Competition Economics.

CHAPTER 12

The Deterrent Effects of Competition Policy*

Adriaan Dierx, Fabienne Ilzkovitz, Yannis Katsoulacos & David Ulph

A correct measurement of deterrent effects is of crucial importance for determining the overall impact of competition policy enforcement, as such indirect effects largely outweigh the direct effects of competition policy interventions. Better information about the total (i.e., direct plus deterrent) effects of competition policy interventions is useful both for priority setting and competition advocacy. The measurement of deterrent effects requires information on the change in behaviour of market players as a result of the competition authorities' actions. While the actual behaviour may indeed be observed, the true challenge is to identify the counterfactual: how would market players have behaved if there had been no competition policy? The present chapter reviews alternative approaches proposed in the literature to assess the deterrent effects of cartel and merger enforcement policies in particular. On that basis, it proposes possible ways forward to address this challenge.

§12.01 INTRODUCTION

Better information about the total (direct plus deterrent) effects of competition policy is useful both for competition advocacy and for priority setting. The measurement of deterrent effects in particular is of crucial importance for determining the overall impact of competition policy enforcement, as such indirect effects largely outweigh the direct effects of competition policy interventions.

Nevertheless, when reporting on the outcomes of their market interventions in their annual reports, competition authorities tend to focus on the direct effects only. Competition authorities in the EU, Japan, Netherlands, Spain, UK and US, for example, report the sum of customer savings associated with important merger and cartel

* This chapter has been written under the sole responsibility of the authors and does not represent the views of the European Commission.

decisions in any given year. The customer savings associated with a given decision are obtained by multiplying the estimated reduction in prices resulting from the decision by the size of the market concerned and the expected duration of the price reduction. Any further effects on the future behaviour of market players remain unreported because they cannot be observed and require making inference about infringements that do not take place. Moreover, as discussed in this chapter, the relationship between the direct and deterrent effects of competition authorities' work is not obvious. However, there appears to be a consensus amongst policy makers and independent observers that such indirect, deterrent effects are of crucial importance to the effectiveness of competition policy enforcement (Davies and Majumdar, 2002).

The present chapter provides a review of the literature on the deterrent effects of cartel and merger control with a view to providing rough estimates of these effects. The deterrent effects of other competition policy instruments have hardly been researched. Sections 12.02 and 12.03 define the concept of deterrence, making a distinction between the deterrent effects on the parties directly affected by the decision and the effects on the behaviour of third parties. Section 12.04 introduces the main measurement issues. Sections 12.05, 12.06, 12.07 and 12.08 provide further detail on the deterrent effects of cartel enforcement, while sections 12.09 and 12.10 focus on the deterrent effects of merger control. Section 12.11 considers the interdependence between cartels and mergers. Section 12.12 proposes an alternative approach to tracking the sector diffusion of deterrent effects, and section 12.13 concludes by offering some suggestions for further research.

§12.02 THE IMPORTANCE OF DETERRENCE FOR COMPETITION POLICY

This section introduces the concept of deterrence and explains why an effective competition policy is based on the strong deterrent effects of the enforcement decisions taken. A distinction is made between deterring anticompetitive behaviour by firms directly concerned by the measures taken and the deterrence of third parties.

[A] The Concept of Deterrence

The intervention of a competition authority in cartel or merger cases raising competition concerns should produce two effects: (1) the removal of the cause for concern and its anticompetitive effects (direct effect); and (2) the prevention or reduction in severity of the anticompetitive behaviour and the consequent harm inflicted both by the parties directly involved and by others (deterrent effect).

The direct effect captures the immediate benefits of a competition policy intervention for customers. While making a quantitative assessment of the direct (price) effects of a merger or cartel decision is feasible (using structural model simulations or applying the Difference-in-Differences (DiD) technique), the measurement of the deterrent effects of such decisions is more problematic since it involves making an assessment of changes in future behaviour by market players as a result of the interventions by the competition authority. By definition these outcomes are not directly observable, and require the construction of a counterfactual behaviour. Therefore, evaluations of the impact of a specific competition policy intervention normally consider the direct effects only.

Assuming that market players behave rationally, the presumption would be that the decision whether or not to engage in anticompetitive behaviour would be based on an assessment of its costs and benefits. For example, a company's decision whether or not to join an illegal cartel will be determined by a trade-off involving on the one hand, the probability the cartel will be detected and its members be ultimately punished by a competition authority, and on the other hand the extra profits resulting from cartel participation. All mergers of a certain size cannot be hidden and need to be notified to the competition authorities. Nevertheless, companies may have the incentive to proceed with the merger notification even though they know full well that the merger may be harmful to consumers, the reason being the possibility that the competition authority mistakenly gives the go-ahead.

On this basis, one would expect that the deterrent effects of competition policy enforcement are affected by three main factors: (1) the perceived probability of detection of the anticompetitive behaviour; (2) the expected punishment following detection; and (3) the 'reputation' of the competition authority responsible. The deterrent effects of the European Commission's cartel enforcement, for example, would depend on the impact of such enforcement on the perceived likelihood of getting caught, on fining levels and on the Commission's reputation in detecting cartel cases and pursuing them in court. In the area of merger control, the deterrent effects would be defined as the extent to which companies decide to abandon or modify their merger plans in order to lessen the competitive concerns of the competition authority responsible.

These examples illustrate the differential deterrent effects of cartel policy enforcement and merger control. For cartel policy enforcement increasing the rate of cartel detection is the main challenge and competition authorities tend not to worry about possible over-enforcement. Successful cartel detection stops detected cartels from operating at least in the short term and should discourage cartel formation in the future. Moreover, it may also affect the behaviour of undetected cartels, leading to a reduction in average cartel duration or cartel overcharges. For merger control, detection is not a significant challenge if the merging parties have an obligation to notify the merger to the competition authorities, which is the case in most European jurisdictions. Rather, the competition authority's main concern is not to make an error in assessing the possible anticompetitive nature of the merger. Both over-enforcement (i.e., intervention in procompetitive mergers) and under-enforcement (clearance of anticompetitive mergers) may affect the number (frequency-based deterrence) and the nature (composition deterrence) of the mergers being notified.

[B] Why Is Deterrence Important for Competition Policy?

Effective competition is one of the main pillars of a strong and prosperous economy and the effective enforcement of competition policy by competition authorities is essential for ensuring effective competition in a modern economy. In turn, the extent to which enforcement deters anticompetitive conduct is the main determinant of the effectiveness of competition policy enforcement. Thus, the primary objective of competition authorities is to dissuade market participants from engaging in anticompetitive behaviour.

Though competition policy interventions that stop and punish such behaviour are beneficial as such, competition authorities do not have the resources to tackle all or even most of the anticompetitive actions that could potentially be taken. By undertaking interventions and so demonstrating that firms that engage in anticompetitive behaviour can and will be detected, prosecuted and penalised they hope to deter/discourage other misbehaviour from occurring in the first place. Moreover, if firms see that the competition authorities' interventions are not one-off, they may refrain from engaging in anticompetitive behaviour for a longer period of time. These deterrent effects of competition policy interventions are so important because they give a greater leverage to competition policy interventions.

However, competition authorities should not take the deterrent effects of their interventions for granted. A better measurement of these effects would help competition authorities to better target the use of their limited resources at cases having the largest total (i.e., direct plus deterrent) effects. The identification of cases having substantial deterrent effects is important for priority setting. In the same vein, better measurement would allow getting a clearer picture of the total effects of the competition authorities' activities. Such information would allow them to better illustrate the benefits of competition policy and support arguments that the work done by competition authorities is a good value for money.

§12.03 TYPES OF DETERRENCE

With a single intervention, the competition authority stops not only the competition policy infringements of the firms directly concerned, it also discourages future anticompetitive behaviour by these same firms (recidivism) and by other firms active in the same or related markets (within-sector diffusion of deterrent effects) or even in unrelated markets. Recidivism[1] is primarily an issue for cartel (or antitrust) policy enforcement. It is less relevant for merger control. Consequently, in the discussion of cartel policy enforcement we distinguish between the deterrence of repeat offenders ('recidivist deterrence') and the 'deterrent effects on other market players' ('third-party

1. The definition of the concept of recidivism is not a trivial issue. In its 2006 Fining guidelines, the European Commission defines repeated infringement (or 'recidivism') as the situation 'where an undertaking continues or repeats the same or a similar infringement after the Commission or a national competition authority has made a finding that the undertaking infringed Article [101 or 102 TFEU]'. This definition is very much in line with the definition in Werden et al. (2011) according to which a firm initiates a new cartel after having been fined for another cartel. Connor (2010) uses a wider definition and considers firms to be recidivists if they have been fined for collusion more than once, even if the different cartels existed contemporaneously. Connor (2016) explores the differences in the definition of and attitude towards recidivism between the US Department of Justice and the European Commission. Levenstein et al. (2015) provides a review of this still ongoing debate.

deterrence'). A second distinction can be made between the deterrent effects of competition policy enforcement on the number and the characteristics (e.g., level of cartel overcharges, cartel duration, horizontal versus vertical nature of the nature of the merger) of the anticompetitive activities concerned.

If companies that have been subject to an intervention consider that the intervention by the competition authority is not one-off and expect that it might monitor their future behaviour more closely and, in the case of cartels, levy increased penalties on repeat offences, they may refrain from re-engaging in anticompetitive behaviour (recidivism) for a longer period of time - possibly but not necessarily forever. The capacity to achieve more long-term deterrent effects on the parties directly affected by the competition authority's intervention depend on the level of penalties imposed and on the ex post monitoring of those having been convicted.

Interventions by competition authorities may also discourage other firms in the same or related markets from engaging in anticompetitive behaviour. There is evidence in the literature that such within-sector diffusion is indeed an important element of deterrence. In section 12.11 we further explore the sector diffusion of deterrent effects.

Finally recidivist and third-party deterrence are related because, in deciding whether or not to take an anticompetitive action in the first place, firms will in principle have in mind the extent to which they may be able to re-engage in that action following an intervention by a competition authority.

§12.04 HOW TO MEASURE DETERRENT EFFECTS?

Deterrent effects can be described as the harm that might have arisen in the absence of interventions by a competition authority but that does not arise because firms have decided to change their behaviour: they either decide to refrain from taking anticompetitive actions or agree to modify and reduce the severity of the likely impact of such actions. Deterred harm (H^{DR}) can therefore be considered as the product of two terms: (1) the number of additional cartels/mergers (N^{DR}) that would have occurred in the absence of interventions by a competition authority; and (2) the average harm (h) that would have been caused by those cartels/mergers had they occurred.

Different methods have been applied to estimate the deterrent effects of competition policy interventions. Relative measures of deterrence such as (1) the number of deterred cartels/mergers per detected cartel/merger (N^{DR} / N^{D}), or (2) the ratio of deterred cartel/merger harm over detected cartel/merger harm (H^{DR} / H^{D}) are often calculated.

The most commonly used estimation approach relies on surveys which directly ask companies and legal advisors to estimate the *number* of cartels/mergers deterred for every cartel/merger detected. One needs to take into account, however, that legal advisors may underestimate the deterrence effects because they may not have been consulted on all plans under consideration by company management. The results of these surveys are summarised in Table 12.1. They show that between 4 and 8 mergers are deterred per intervention by the competition authorities in a merger case and that between 5 and 28 cartels are deterred for every cartel detected. These surveys have some major limitations: (1) there is no certainty about the reliability of the information provided by the respondents; (2) the surveys may be biased because the sample interviewed is not randomly selected; and (3) for mergers, the ratios reported in the surveys encompass both the deterrent effects in terms of the number and the characteristics of anticompetitive actions, making it impossible to disentangle these two types of deterrent effects. For these reasons, it can be misleading to use the ratio of the number of deterred mergers/cartels over the number of detected mergers/cartels (N^{DR} / N^{D}) as a proxy of the corresponding ratio of deterred harm over detected harm (H^{DR} / H^{D}). However, until recently, such surveys were the only way to collect direct and easily obtainable information on the deterrent effects of competition policy decisions.

Table 12.1 Summary of the Results of Surveys on Deterrent Effects

Source	*Respondent and Period*	*Number of Mergers Abandoned or Modified for Every Merger Blocked or Remedied*	*Number of Cartels Deterred for Every Cartel Detected*
Twynstra Gudde (2005)	Competition lawyers and companies 2000-2003	7.5	-
Gordon and Squires (2008) based on Deloitte (2007)	Competition lawyers 2004-2006	5.3	5
	Large firms 2004-2006	-	16
London Economics* (2011)	Large and small firms 2003-2011	1.8	28
Baarsma et al. (2012) based on SEO (2011)	Companies 2005 to mid-2010	3.1-7.3	5

Source: Authors' own calculations based on Baarsma et al. (2012) and CMA (2017b).

* While the estimates by London Economics of cartel deterrence are based on a large sample of over 800 businesses surveyed, the estimates of merger deterrence are based on a sample of just thirty-three mergers and are therefore not reliable (*see also* subsection 12.09[B]).

An alternative method for assessing the importance of deterrent effects is based on comparisons over time and across countries between different competition policy regimes. Baker (2003) analyses the behaviour of US firms during historical episodes in which US antitrust enforcement was absent or lax. He shows that absent antitrust enforcement, companies in many industries use their market power to the detriment of consumers. Similarly, Hyytinen et al. (2010) find that at the end of the period during which cartels in Finland were legal (1951-1990), almost all manufacturing industries had become cartelised. Clarke and Evenett (2003) use inter-temporal and cross-sectional data to study the effects of the presence of a competition authority on overcharges and the duration of cartels in the international vitamins market. They find that, after the formation of the cartel, prices of vitamins rose more in countries without an active anti-cartel enforcement.

A third method that has been applied to assess changes over time in the deterrent effects of interventions by competition authorities is the event study. The idea underlying such studies is that cartels and anticompetitive mergers positively affect the future income streams of both the companies involved and their competitors. Stronger deterrence, on the other hand, will be reflected in a reduction of cartel overcharges and a lower frequency of anticompetitive mergers, which in turn should contribute to a reduction in future income streams and consequently lead to a decline in stock prices, all else equal (*see, for example,* Eckbo, 1992 and Duso et al., 2013).

Recently, three further methodologies aimed at measuring the deterrent effects of cartel policy in particular have been developed: the first one uses the toolbox of statistical inference; the second one employs laboratory experiments to test how market participants are affected by a change in the policy regime; and the third one is more theory based. These methods also differ in terms of the scope of the deterrent effects covered, i.e., whether they cover the deterrence of repeat offenders (in addition to third-party deterrence) and the extent to which they consider the deterrent effects on the characteristics of undetected cartels, such as the level of overcharges, cartel stability and duration (in addition to the number of cartels deterred).

The 'statistical' method attempts to reconstruct the total population of cartels (including cartels that were deterred by cartel policy enforcement) based on available observations concerning detected cartels. The main advantage of this method is that it allows taking into account the non-random nature of the sample of cases detected.

The 'experimental' method applies different market games in a laboratory setting. Each game represents a different cartel enforcement strategy. By comparing player's strategies and market outcomes a better understanding of the deterrent effects of the different enforcement strategies can be obtained. Bigoni et al. (2015), for example, apply this method to compare the deterrence effects of large penalties and high detection probabilities under different leniency policy regimes.

The 'theoretical' method uses an integrated theoretical framework describing cartel behaviour in the presence of cartel policy enforcement and attempts to explain to what extent such enforcement affects cartel formation. The principal benefit of the theoretical method is that a single analytical framework is used to explore the sensitivity of deterred and detected harm to the different competition policy enforcement parameters. Studies that apply other methods can only analyse the sensitivity to a single parameter at a time, making comparison more difficult.

§12.05 DETERRENT EFFECTS OF CARTEL POLICY ENFORCEMENT: STATISTICAL APPROACH

Cartels are illegal per se in most jurisdictions and heavy fines are imposed on companies involved. Since cartels are illegal, they are generally highly secretive and hard to find. Detected cartels on average last seven years, have six members and overcharge their customers by around 25% (Bos et al., 2017). However, since undetected and deterred cartels are not observable, one cannot exclude that their characteristics differ from the detected ones. Competition authorities use a variety of tools (including ex officio investigations and leniency programmes, *see* subsection 12.08[A]) to detect and break-up cartels.

According to Connor (2015), the average number of private international cartels detected annually worldwide has increased significantly, from less than ten in 1990-1995 to more than seventy in 2010-2015. This upward trend may be explained by improved investigation methods and the adoption of tougher cartel control policies by competition authorities worldwide, which have contributed to increased detection rates. Alternatively, it may be attributed to an increase in the number of undeterred cartels (Ormosi, 2014). The increase in the number of undeterred cartels can in turn be explained by either an increase in the total population of cartels or by a decline in the deterrent effects of anti-cartel enforcement, or both. This illustrates that one needs to have a better knowledge of the deterrent effects in order to adequately gauge the impact of cartel policy enforcement.

This section describes the newly developed statistical methods for quantifying the deterrent effects of cartel policy enforcement and presents the results obtained.

[A] Analytical Framework

The statistical approach focuses purely on third-party deterrence and on the number of cartels deterred. It draws on available information on cartels having been investigated (including their duration and estimated overcharges) to make inferences about the total population of cartels and the potential harm caused by these cartels. This is no easy task as the total population of cartels includes deterred cartels, which have not been established and so are not directly observable.

A model based on a simple analytical framework (*see* Table 12.2) proposed by Davies and Ormosi (2012) constitutes a useful starting point for thinking about how to measure the deterrent effects of cartel enforcement.

Table 12.2 Classification of Potential Cartels[2]

Total Population of Potential Cartels N		
Undeterred cartels (1-ω) *N*		Deterred cartels ω *N*
Detected cartels β (1 − ω) N	Undetected cartels (1 − β) (1 − ω) N	

2. Desirable outcomes are highlighted in grey.

If N represents the total population of all potential cartels, ω the probability that a cartel is deterred,[3] and β the probability that a non-deterred cartel is detected,[4] then the expected number of detected cartels, N^D, can be defined as:

$$N^D = \beta (1\text{-}\omega) N \qquad (1)$$

and the expected number of deterred cartels as:

$$N^{DR} = \omega N = \omega N^D / (\beta (1\text{-}\omega)) \qquad (2)$$

If moreover the average harm observed (on the basis of the detected cartels) would be representative of the average harm in the total population of undetected and deterred cartels – in other words if the average harm per cartel, h, was the same in all these different categories – then the total potential harm, H, and the deterred harm, H^{DR}, would be simple multiples of the harm associated with the detected cartels, H^D:

$$H = h N = h (N^D / (\beta (1\text{-}\omega))) = H^D / (\beta (1\text{-}\omega)) \qquad (3)$$

and

$$H^{DR} = h N^{DR} = h \omega N^D / (\beta (1\text{-}\omega)) = \omega H^D / (\beta (1\text{-}\omega)) \qquad (4)$$

On this basis, the deterrent effects can be defined as:

$$H^{DR} / H^D = N^{DR} / N^D = \omega / (\beta (1\text{-}\omega)) \qquad (5)$$

However, this seemingly simple model is based on four simplifying assumptions reflecting a more complicated reality.

First, in practice the parameters ω and β are positively correlated even though this linkage has not been explicitly modelled: an effective cartel enforcement reflected in a high detection rate β will lead to a greater rate of deterrence ω[5] with an uncertain impact on deterrent effects as measured by the ratio ω / ((1 – ω) β) (*see* Equation 5). Moreover, the impact of a more effective cartel enforcement on the share of potential cartels detected (N^D / N) and the share of potential harm avoided through detection (H^D / H) is not necessarily positive, as the effects of the increase in β may be offset by a decrease in (1 – ω) (*see* Equations 1 and 3). In other words, a more effective enforcement may reduce the share of non-deterred cartels, leaving fewer (harmful) cartels to be detected.

---

3. The probability that a cartel is deterred (ω) corresponds to the population deterrence rate, while the probability that a non-deterred cartel is detected (β) corresponds to the detection rate in the population of non-deterred cartels. Note that the share of potential cartels deterred (N^{DR} /N) is equivalent to the deterrence rate, but that the share of potential cartels detected (N^D /N) equals (β (1-ω)), which differs from the detection rate β.
4. In fact, the probability β is the product of the probability of detection and the probability of successful prosecution if detected. In the case of hard core cartels the latter probability can reasonably be taken to be 1, so in this case this crucial probability is effectively just the probability of detection.
5. One would expect there to be diminishing returns to investments in detection (as measured by the parameter β) in terms of increased deterrence (as measured by the parameter). In other words, the marginal deterrent effect of detection will decrease with the level of detection.

These mechanisms are illustrated in Figure 12.1, which presents a simulation of the simple model developed above using a given specification of the relationship between the parameters ω and β.[6] The figure shows that a more effective cartel policy enforcement (as modelled by an increase in the detection rate β) raises both the share of potential cartel cases detected (on the x-axis) and the share of cases deterred (on the y-axis). Initially, an increase in β brings about an increase in both the share of potential cartel cases detected $(N^D / N) = (1 - \omega)\beta$ and deterred $(N^{DR} / N) = \omega$. However, the increase in the share of potential cases detected levels off more rapidly than the increase in the share of potential cases deterred (a sign of diminishing returns to cartel detection). At some point a further increase in the detection rate will lead to a reduction in the share of potential cartel cases detected (N^D / N), the reason being that the associated increase in the rate of deterrence ω causes a reduction in the share of potential cartels that remain undeterred $((N - N^D)/N) = (1 - \omega)$. In other words, high detection and deterrence rates dampen the formation of illegal cartels and leave few cartels still to be detected.

Figure 12.1 Share of Potential Cartels Deterred

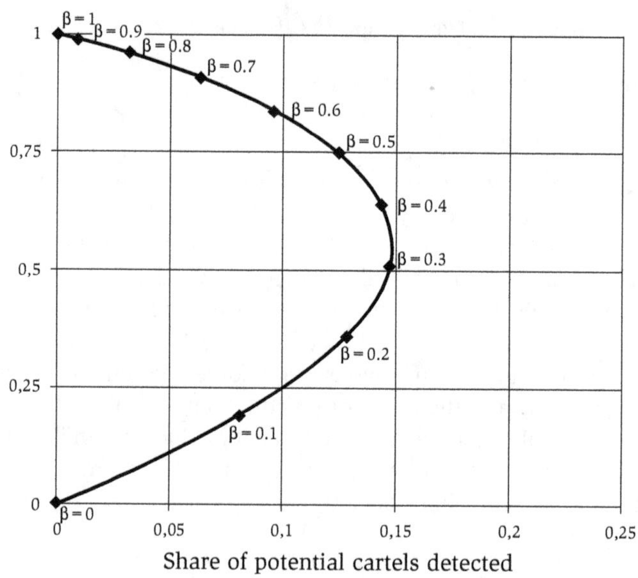

Source: Authors' own calculations.

6. The particular simulation depicted in Figure 12.1 is based on a simple quadratic function: $\omega = f(\beta) = -\beta^2 + 2\beta$. The function f(β) fulfils the following conditions guiding the relationship between ω and β: (1) f(0) = 0, i.e., if the detection rate equals zero, the deterrence rate equals zero as well; (2) f' > 0, i.e., the deterrence rate is a positive function of the probability of detection; (3) f'' ≤ 0, i.e., there are diminishing returns to investments in detection in terms of increased deterrence (*see* previous footnote); (4) f(1) = 1, i.e., if all non-deterred cases are detected, than the deterrence rate equals one because the net benefits of cartel participation are negative.

A second complication of the above modelling exercise is that the observed sample of detected cartels is not necessarily representative of the total population of (deterred) cartels due to sample selection bias. On the one hand, deterred cartels may well be less harmful than detected ones because cartels that are harmless are unlikely to be profitable and therefore more easily deterred. On the other hand, the most harmful cartels have a greater incentive to avoid drawing the attention of competition authorities. Existing estimates of cartel harm, however, are mostly related to the observed population of detected cartels and provide only limited insights about the potential harm caused by deterred cartels. Therefore, any estimates of the deterrent effects of cartel enforcement need to be corrected for sample selection bias.

A third complication is that this static modelling approach implicitly assumes that any harm that is detected (and hence prosecuted and penalised) is removed forever. More precisely it assumes that the mere act of detecting, prosecuting and penalising a cartel deters any future re-emergence irrespective of the subsequent market monitoring by the competition authority. Katsoulacos et al. (2017) relax this assumption by allowing for the possibility that, following the successful prosecution and punishment of the cartel, collusive activity might re-emerge in the same market. The probability that a cartel reappears may be influenced by: (1) the nature of post-prosecution monitoring which, given limited resources of competition authorities, may vary over time; and (2) the nature of the penalty regime for repeat offences.

A fourth and final complication is that this simple modelling framework assumes that the only deterrent effect of interventions by competition authorities is that on the decision to form a cartel. It disregards the possibility that interventions could have other effects such as on the price charged by those cartels that do form. In this case one would have to allow the possibility that the average harm per cartel, h, is affected by interventions. Katsoulacos et.al. (2017) summarise the theoretical reasons for believing that such price effects exist.[7] However, given that in this chapter we focus on the deterrence of cartels from forming, we are not reporting on findings about the size of these price effects. Therefore, this issue will not be further pursued in the present chapter.

Due to these complications, deterred harm (H^{DR}) is not a simple multiple of the direct harm avoided by competition policy interventions (H^{D}) and the calculation of the deterrent effects is more complex. It requires not only estimates of detection and deterrence rates but also methods to determine the bias in the observed sample. Moreover, due to its static nature the simple model set out above only captures third-party deterrence and does not cover recidivist deterrence. Finally, it does not consider the possible change in behaviour of (potential) cartelists.

7. In their model, such effects can be either positive or negative, depending on the penalty regime. The reason is that, when cartel participants set the cartel price, they do so anticipating the possibility of being successfully prosecuted and penalised by a competition authority. Therefore the choice of the cartel overcharge can be influenced by the associated risk of being detected and by the expected penalty they would face in case of detection. If, for example, the penalty is based on revenue and if the penalty rate is fixed, reducing the expected penalty is equivalent to reducing revenues. The least damaging way of doing so is for the cartelist to raise prices and thereby reduce output levels. Under such circumstances, the cartel price will be higher than would be the case if there were no intervention by the competition authority.

[B] Statistical Estimates

In spite of these limitations, the statistical approach allows gaining initial insights into the true extent of the deterrent effects of cartel enforcement. The validity of this approach depends on the robustness of the link between detected cartels and the total population of cartels. As explained above, the level of deterrent effects is a function of the deterrence rate ω and the detection rate β (*see* Equation 5). Let us first discuss methods used to get estimates of the detection rate β, which is defined as the probability that a non-deterred cartel is detected. The most common approach is to use observed variables (such as the duration of detected cartels) to estimate the parameters of a simple cartel formation-breakdown model. The intuition underlying this approach is that – under the assumption that all cartels are eventually detected – the probability of getting caught is inversely proportional to the average duration of existing cartels (Bryant and Eckard, 1991). A survey by Connor and Lande (2012) of US studies using such approach finds that cartel detection rates ranged between 13% and 17% prior to the introduction of cartel leniency programmes. Estimates for the post-leniency period range between 21% and 27%. Combe et al. (2008) estimate the probability of an EU cartel being discovered within a given year at around 13%. Connor (2011) concludes that there appears to be a consensus that detection rates are within the range of 10% to 33%.

A more recent study by Ormosi (2014) proposes the use of the so-called Capture-Recapture method to obtain estimates of detection rates of cartelising firms. This method is frequently used in ecology to make inferences about the characteristics of wildlife populations.[8] It has the advantage that it does not require a theoretical model based on assumptions concerning cartel formation and break-down. Moreover, it allows tracking changes in the detection rate over time. An application of this method to the EU indicates that over the period 1985-2009 less than 20% of cartels were detected. The 1991 EU/US Competition Cooperation Agreements and the introduction of 1996 EU leniency programme appear to have contributed to an increase in detection rates.

These various methods provide useful estimates of cartel detection rates but leave open the question of how to measure the deterrence rate ω. The literature provides little guidance in this respect. Conservative survey estimates by Deloitte and SEO (*see* Table 12.1) suggest that five cartels are deterred for every cartel detected, i.e., $N^{DR} / N^{D} = 5$. In combination with the assumption that the detection rate β equals 0.2 (in line with the estimates presented in the previous two paragraphs), Equation 5 implies that the deterrence rate ω equals 0.5, i.e., 50% of potential cartels are deterred.

Davies et al. (2018) use these estimates as a starting point for their Monte Carlo simulations[9] of the deterrent effects of cartel policy. The detection rate is assumed to

8. As explained by Ormosi (2014), in the simplest form of Capture-Recapture analysis, the population size of a species is estimated by taking two successive samples from the same population. The first sample is marked and placed back into the population. Under certain assumptions (no change in the population between the two sampling exercises, all individuals equally likely to be captured), the proportion of marked subjects in the second sample should be an unbiased estimate of all marked individuals to population size.
9. The Monte Carlo method runs a large number of simulations (in this case, 10,000) to obtain a probability distribution of an unobserved phenomenon.

have a uniform distribution with a range of [0.1; 0.33] while the deterrence rate is assumed to have a beta distribution[10] with a mean of 0.5 and a range of [0; 1]. Each simulation result is the outcome of randomly selected values of the deterrence (ω) and detection (β). The end result is the mean value of the deterrent effects estimated for each of the 10,000 simulations.

Box 12.1: Distribution of harm in cartel cases

Cartel induced harm can be approximated by the amount of cartel overcharges as reported in the literature. Davies et al. (2018) use the distribution of overcharges in legal cartels as a proxy for the distribution of harm in the total population of cartels. By comparing this distribution with the distribution of harm in detected cartels (as proxied by the distribution of overcharges in illegal cartels), they are able to assess the need for adjustments in their Monte Carlo simulations. The assumption underlying this type of analysis is that the distribution of overcharges of legal cartels corresponds to a situation without cartel enforcement.

Table 12.3 shows that the distribution of overcharges for illegal cartels has less mass in the lower and in the upper tail than the distribution of overcharges for legal cartels, which is an indication that cartel control is more effective in deterring very low or very high overcharge cartels. One explanation could be that cartels with low overcharges are more easily deterred by fines while cartels with high overcharges moderate their overcharge to lessen the likelihood of detection.

Table 12.3 Overcharges in Legal and Illegal Cartels

	Legal Overcharge	*Illegal Overcharge*
Cartels (number)	107	395
Cartel episodes (number)	390	1107
Median episodic overcharge (%)	27	22
Overcharge 5% or less (%)	21.7	10.7
Overcharge 5-50% (%)	50.6	74.2
Overcharge more than 50% (%)	27.7	15.1

Source: Bos et al. (2017) based on the Connor (2014) database.

10. The beta distribution is a set of continuous probability distributions defined on the interval [0, 1]. The shape of each probability distribution within the set depends on the values of two so-called shape parameters. The Lorenz curve, which is commonly used to illustrate a country's income distribution or the degree of concentration in a market, can be derived from an underlying beta distribution.

One additional challenge is to take account of the observations that: (1) the sample of detected cartels is not representative of the total population of cartels, in particular in terms of the amount of harm caused (*see* Box 12.1); (2) the probability of cartel detection is non-decreasing with cartel harm; and (3) the probability of deterrence may well be stronger for relatively harmless or relatively harmful cartels. To address the resulting selection biases, Davies et al. (2018) make adjustments to the Monte Carlo simulation selection procedure (e.g., by assigning a higher deterrence rate to simulations resulting in higher harm).

Table 12.4 presents the outcome of the Monte Carlo simulations taking into account these adjustments to the basic analytical framework developed in subsection 12.05[A]. One can interpret the 'mean' results as those of an 'average' competition authority, with a confidence interval bounded by a 'poorly performing' and 'good' competition authority. For an average competition authority, the deterrent effect as measured by the ratio of deterred harm over detected harm reach a value of 9.5.[11] The deterrent effect of cartel interventions by a good competition authority reaches a value of 17.1, while that of a poorly performing competition authority is only 7.6.

Due to the strong deterrent effects of its interventions the good competition authority is able to eliminate no less than 89% of the total potential harm, as opposed to 76% for an average competition authority and only 60% for the poorly performing competition authority. Moreover, the good competition authority detects a share of 5% of total potential harm, as opposed to a share of 7% for the poorly performing competition authority. The reason for this seeming contradiction is that the less effective competition authority is less able to deter cartels, which leaves more cartels to be detected. It can therefore be misleading to measure the performance of a competition authority simply on the basis of detected and therefore avoided harm.

Table 12.4 Total, Deterred and Undetected Harm in the Area of Cartels

Harm in Comparison with Detected Harm	*Mean 'Average' CA*		*5th Percentile 'Poorly' performing CA*		*95th Percentile 'Good' CA*	
	Multiplier	*Share*	*Multiplier*	*Share*	*Multiplier*	*Share*
Detected harm	1	0.07	1	0.07	1	0.05
Deterred harm	9.5	0.69	7.6	0.53	17.1	0.84
Total harm removed	10.5	0.76	8.6	0.60	18.1	0.89
Total potential harm	14.3	1.00	13.5	1.00	20.3	1.00

Source: Davies et al. (2018), Table 3.

11. A simple calculation based on Equation 5 using the mean values of the deterrence (ω = 0.55) and detection (β = 0.2) parameters (*see* Table 1 in Davies et al., 2018), results in a value of 6.1 for the deterrent effects (as opposed to 9.5), illustrating the importance of the adjustments made in light of possible sample selection biases.

§12.06 DETERRENT EFFECTS OF CARTEL POLICY ENFORCEMENT: THEORETICAL MODELLING

This section describes theoretical models of cartel formation and breakdown and illustrates how such models may be used to quantify the deterrent effects of cartel policy enforcement. Below, we make a distinction between models covering only third-party deterrence and models considering total deterrence, including third-party deterrence as well as recidivist deterrence.

[A] Third Party Deterrence

A number of theoretical papers, including Harrington (2004), Harrington and Chang (2009), Houba et al. (2010), Jensen et al. (2013) and Bos et al. (2017), shed light on the process of cartel formation and breakdown taking into account possible interventions by a competition authority but assuming the complete absence of recidivism.

Harrington and Chang (2009) argue that the number of cartels detected is not necessarily a good measure of competition authorities' performance and suggest that the average duration of the cartels detected might be a better measure. More effective cartel policy enforcement should lead to detected cartels having a longer duration in the short term (as the less stable cartels disappear from the market) and a shorter duration in the long term (due to the increased deterrent effects). Zhou (2013) provides supporting evidence for these theory-based hypotheses using a time series of cartel decisions by the European Commission covering the period 1985 and 2012.

[B] Total Deterrence

Other theoretical papers, including Motta and Polo (2003), Chen and Rey (2013), Marvão (2016) and Katsoulacos et al. (2017), specifically consider the possibility that cartels may re-emerge, even if they have been detected, successfully prosecuted and penalised. In this section we focus on the Katsoulacos et al. model (2017). The first subsection describes the analytical framework of the model that allows making a distinction between three sources of cartel deterrence: recidivist deterrence, third-party deterrence and changes in pricing behaviour. The second subsection illustrates the importance of such deterrence effects for a set of 'reasonable' model parameter values.

[1] Analytical Framework

Katsoulacos et al. (2017) develop a model of birth and death of cartels in the presence of interventions by a competition authority. As before, there is a certain probability β that an undeterred cartel is detected within a given period. However, detection does not necessarily imply the end of the cartel. It is possible (with a certain probability $1\text{-}\sigma$) that it continues its activities in spite of having been detected. Moreover, there is a probability $1\text{-}\lambda$ that the cartel re-emerges in the long term after having been stopped initially (*see* Table 12.5). Consequently, the intervention activities of a competition authority can be represented through three parameters: β, which is the probability that an anticompetitive action is detected; σ, the probability that cartel is forced to discontinue its operations following its detection and that the cartel participants revert to their competitive behaviour, at least in the short term; and λ, the probability that the stopped cartels remain inactive also in the long term. Note that this allows for the possibility that the short run response of the cartel participants to the cartel being detected, σ, is different from the long-run response, λ. If $\sigma = \lambda = 1$, detection implies the permanent cessation of the cartel infringement. By varying the parameters σ and λ, it is possible to examine the sensitivity of the deterrent effects to the assumption that cartel detection puts a definite end to the illicit behaviour in the market concerned.

Table 12.5 Classification of Potential Cartels[12]

<table>
<tr><td colspan="5">Total Population of Potential Cartels
N</td></tr>
<tr><td colspan="4">Undeterred cartels
(1-ω) N</td><td rowspan="4">Deterred third-party cartels
ω N</td></tr>
<tr><td colspan="3">Detected cartels
β (1 – ω) N</td><td rowspan="3">Undetected cartels
(1 – β) (1 – ω) N</td></tr>
<tr><td colspan="2">Detected cartels stopped in the short term
σ β (1 – ω) N</td><td rowspan="2">Detected but non-stopped cartels in the short term
(1 – σ) β (1 – ω)N</td></tr>
<tr><td>Permanently stopped cartels
λ σ β (1 – ω) N</td><td>Cartels re-emerging in the long term
(1 – λ) σ β (1 – ω) N</td></tr>
</table>

The deterrent effects of cartel interventions can be decomposed into: (1) avoided harm due to ex post monitoring taking into account the possibilities that the cartel will continue to be operational following detection or re-emerge in the longer term (i.e., recidivist deterrence); (2) a deterrent effect on other market players (i.e., third-party deterrence); and (3) the effects on the (pricing) behaviour of cartels that remain active (*see* Figure 12.2). The total effect of cartel interventions consists of these deterrent effects plus the direct effects from stopping cartels upon detection.

12. The objective of this table is to define the different concepts underlying the theoretical modelling approach and to compare them with the concepts underlying the statistical approach (as presented in Table 12.2). While the basic concepts underlying these two modelling approaches appear rather similar, the analytical frameworks – statistical inference versus theoretical modelling – used to exploit the information available are very different. Desirable outcomes are highlighted in grey.

Figure 12.2 Sources of Deterred Harm from Cartel Policy Enforcement

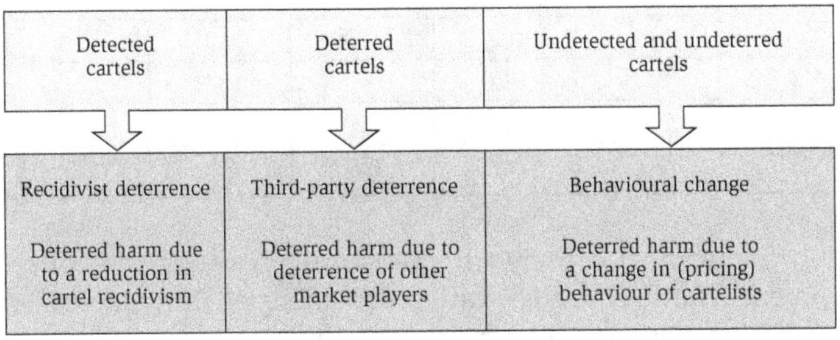

Finally, in this theoretical model the level of deterrence depends not only on the capacity of the competition authority to detect, stop and prevent the re-emergence of cartels in the long term but also on the penalty regime. The model allows exploring the effects of the penalty base and the penalty rate on deterrence, and investigating whether an improvement in the effectiveness of cartel interventions by a competition authority might be achieved more cheaply by toughening penalties rather than by putting more resources into cartel detection.

[2] Theoretical Estimates

For any given set of intervention parameters (β, σ, λ)[13] and any given penalty regime the model determines the deterrent effects of the interventions of the competition authorities or in other words the ratio of the deterred harm over the detected harm. The deterred harm includes the recidivist deterrence from a better follow-up of cartels detected, third-party deterrence from increased detection and a stricter penalty regime and indirect price deterrence. Table 12.6 illustrates the importance of such deterrent effects for a set of 'reasonable' parameter values.[14] Under the assumption that cartel interventions prevent all cartels from reappearing (i.e., $\sigma = \lambda = 1$), the ratio of deterred harm over detected harm falls within the range from 11.5 to 13.3. The magnitude of such deterrent effects is substantially smaller if competition authorities are less effective in preventing the re-emergence of collusive activity (assuming lower values of λ), illustrating the importance of market monitoring to make sure that the prohibited cartels do not reappear in one form or another.

13. Note that ω is not an intervention parameter, but rather a measure of third-party deterrence, which is the outcome of the interventions by the competition authority.
14. β, the probability of detection, is assumed to take on values of 0.1, 0.2 and 0.3, corresponding to the range of values considered by Connor (2011). As competition authorities tend to be quite effective in stopping collusion in the short run, only two alternative values for ς are used (ς = 1 and ς = 0.8). For recidivism three possible values are considered: λ = 1, which is the benchmark case where successful prosecution removes harm forever; and λ equals 0.98 or 0.9, reflecting a certain degree of uncertainty about the extent of recidivism.

Table 12.6 Deterrent Effects in the Area of Cartels

λ	*σ*	*1.0*			*0.8*		
	ß	*0.1*	*0.2*	*0.3*	*0.1*	*0.2*	*0.3*
1.0		13.3	12.0	11.5	13.8	12.6	12.0
0.98		11.4	10.4	9.9	11.9	10.9	10.4
0.9		7.4	6.7	6.4	7.6	7.1	6.8

Table 12.7 shows that a competition authority can remove between 49% and 93% of total potential harm created by cartels depending on the parameter values used. This large degree of variation illustrates that this performance measure is quite sensitive to the parameters identified. Some of this variation arises because of different values of β – the probability of detection. The degree of variation with respect to this parameter is broadly in line with that reported by Davies et al. (2018) using a statistical approach (*see* Table 12.4).

Table 12.7 Share of Total Potential Harm Removed by Competition Authorities in the Area of Cartels

λ	*σ*	*1.0*			*0.8*		
	ß	*0.1*	*0.2*	*0.3*	*0.1*	*0.2*	*0.3*
1.0		0.73	0.88	0.93	0.67	0.84	0.91
0.98		0.69	0.85	0.92	0.63	0.81	0.89
0.9		0.55	0.75	0.84	0.49	0.69	0.80

In addition to understanding the variation in the deterrent effects with respect to each intervention parameter individually – i.e., β, λ and σ – it is also very important for competition authorities to be able to compare the marginal effects on deterrence of a change in the levels of these intervention activities, since this can guide their decisions on how best to deploy their resources. However, a closer inspection of Table 12.7 shows that the marginal effects of changes in the detection and recidivism rates depend on the point of departure.[15] It is therefore difficult to draw more general conclusions on whether competition authorities should devote more resources into preventing the long-term re-emergence of cartels or into new investigations.

15. For example, if we start with a detection rate of 0.1 (i.e., β = 0.1) and a recidivism rate of 0.1 (i.e., λ = 0.9), a doubling of the detection rate increases the harm avoided by 20 pp. (from 0.55 to 0.75). Similarly, the division of the recidivism rate by five increases the harm avoided by 14 pp. (from 0.55 to 0.69), which would imply that a division of the recidivism rate by two would increase the harm avoided by around 6 pp. only. This would go to show that when taking this particular point of departure, a doubling of the detection rate would be more effective than a similar sized reduction in the recidivism rate.

§12.07 COMPARISON OF STATISTICAL AND THEORETICAL ESTIMATES OF CARTEL DETERRENCE

It is interesting to compare in more detail the ratios of total and avoided harm over detected harm in the statistical model developed by Davies et al. (2018) as summarised in Table 12.4 above with the theoretical model of Katsoulacos et al. (2017) as summarised in Tables 12.6 and 12.7 above (*see* Table 12.8 for the comparison). The Davies et al. point estimates are those of an 'average' competition authority, while the Katsoulacos et al. estimates are based on the parameter values of $\beta = 0.2$, $\sigma = 1.0$ and $\lambda = 0.98$. The corresponding ranges reflect poorly and well performing competition authorities as defined by Davies et al., and lower and upper bounds for the parameter values of β, σ and λ presented in Tables 12.6 and 12.7 above (as defined by Katsoulacos et al. (2017)).

Table 12.8 Total and Avoided Cartel Harm in Comparison of Detected Harm

	Davies et al.	*Katsoulacos et al.*	*Surveys (Number)*
Detected harm	1	1	1
Deterred harm	9.5 [7.6-17.1]	10.4 [6.4-13.8]	[5-28]
Total harm removed	10.5 [8.6-18.1]	11.4 [7.4-14.8]	[6-29]
Total potential harm	14.3 [13.5-20.3]	13.3 [8.8-22.1]	n.a.
Share of total potential harm removed	0.76 [0.60-0.89]	0.85 [0.49-0.93]	n.a.

Table 12.8 shows that the ratios of deterred harm, total harm removed and total potential harm over detected harm obtained by Katsoulacos et al. are rather similar to those of Davies et al., despite the differences in these studies. The ranges of ratios reported in the two papers show a large degree of overlap. Moreover, the ranges of the ratio of deterred harm over detected harm reported by Davies et al. (2018) and Katsoulacos et al. (2017) overlap with the range of the ratio of the number of deterred cartels over the number of detected cartels as reported by competition lawyers and other company representatives (*see also* Table 12.1). Further research aimed at narrowing the range of estimates and increasing the degree of overlap between the different simulation results would help improve current assessments of the deterrent effects of cartel enforcement.

§12.08 DETERMINANTS OF CARTEL DETERRENCE

In deciding whether a cartel would be profitable, a firm compares, on the one hand, the probability of being caught, the expected penalties and the risk of loss of reputation and, on the other, the overcharges, the gains in market share and the duration of the beneficial effects of the cartel. Therefore, as already mentioned in subsection 12.02[A], three main factors could play a role in preventing firms from engaging in illegal actions:

the probability of being detected, the expected punishment and the reputation of the competition authority. Buccirossi et al. (2013) attempt to measure the deterrent properties of competition policy regimes by taking these three determinants into account (*see* Box 12.2).

The probability of being detected depends on the capacity of the competition authority to detect cases ex officio and the effectiveness of the leniency programmes that most authorities have now implemented. Some competition authorities have also introduced 'whistle-blower' tools that allow individuals to anonymously submit information on secret agreements. Others have applied market screening tools to detect odd price movements indicative of anticompetitive behaviour. The expected punishment is related to the fining policy of the competition authority; and the reputation of the competition authority is gradually built up based on the competition authorities' willingness and capacity to pursue cartel infringements. A competition authority with a long history of ex officio investigations and a successful track record in court discourages companies from engaging in anticompetitive behaviours (Armoogum et al., 2017).

Box 12.2: Measurement of the deterrence properties of competition policy regimes

Buccirossi et al. (2013) develop composite indicators with a view to measuring the deterrence properties of competition policy regimes in thirteen OECD countries over the period 1995-2005. They make a distinction between three key determinants of deterrence: (1) the expected probability of detection and conviction; (2) the size of sanctions; and (3) the expected probability of errors in the investigation. These three determinants are in turn affected by fifty-three policy variables reflecting: the resources of the competition authority; the characteristics of competition laws and institutions (de jure and de facto); and the level of activity of the competition authority. Each competition policy variable receives a score on a scale of 0 to 1 against a benchmark of generally agreed-upon best practice.

The weighted sum of these scores represents a composite indicator of the level of deterrence of the competition policy regime in a given country. The country ranking shows Sweden and the United States on top and France, Spain and Japan at the bottom. However, this ranking needs to be considered with caution as the approach used to arrive at the ranking has a number of shortcomings: (1) the weights used to construct the composite indicator were determined subjectively (but subjected to a sensitivity analysis); (2) the additive nature of the composite indicator does not allow taking into account that the features of an optimal institutional design may be interdependent; (3) the limited variation of the composite indicator across countries and over time makes it difficult to interpret the results.

Most of the discussion in the academic literature on the determinants of effectiveness of cartel enforcement has been on the effects of leniency programmes and on the optimal level of fines to be imposed. We discuss these effects in terms of cartel detection, cartel formation, cartel stability and duration, and the level of price overcharges.

[A] Leniency Programmes

Leniency programmes were introduced in the US in 1993 and in the EU in 1996. Since then they have been introduced in many jurisdictions across the world. Leniency programmes are aimed at increasing the probability of cartel detection by encouraging companies to provide inside evidence of collusive behaviour. According to the rules underpinning the EU and US leniency programmes, the first company in a cartel to furnish inside evidence will not be fined, subject to certain conditions. Subsequent providers of such evidence may benefit from fine reductions. The increased probability of cartel detection resulting from leniency programmes should in principle lead to increased cartel deterrence, as reflected in: (1) a reduction in cartel formation; (2) a reduction in price overcharges; and (3) a reduction in cartel stability.

Since its introduction in 1996, the EU leniency programme has been heavily used in cartel enforcement. A review by Broos et al. (2016) of the fifty-two cartel decisions adopted by the European Commission between May 2004 and May 2014 found that in 94% of these cases, at least one company had applied for leniency. Moreover, 56% of the 333 companies involved had applied for leniency and 46% were granted leniency. On average the fines of the 186 companies that applied for leniency were reduced by 37.8%.

The effects of leniency programmes and their pros and cons have been extensively discussed in the literature. The theoretical model of Harrington and Chang (2009) illustrates how the introduction of a corporate leniency programme can raise cartel detection and reduce cartel formation. Miller (2009) conducts an empirical investigation of the effects of the US leniency programme on the number of cartels detected. He observes an increase in the number of cartels detected around the time of the introduction of the leniency programme followed by a decline to below pre-leniency levels around three years later. He argues (on p. 751) that such a 'pattern is consistent with enhanced cartel detection and deterrence capabilities', because in the first instance leniency programmes foster detection and only in the second instance reduce cartel formation due to a strengthening of deterrent effects. These results appear to be broadly confirmed by EU data showing that the average annual number of cartel decisions by the European Commission tripled in the aftermath of the introduction of its leniency programme in 1996 (Wils, 2016).

In terms of cartel formation, the existence of a leniency programme may on the one hand make firms more reluctant to participate in a cartel because of the higher likelihood of cartel detection. On the other hand, the reduction or even the elimination of fines to be paid by the cartel participant(s) applying for leniency may reduce ex ante disincentives to join a cartel. On balance, laboratory experiments conducted by

Apesteguia et al. (2007) indicate that leniency programmes tend to reduce cartel formation, confirming the hypotheses derived from the Harrington and Chang (2009) theoretical model. Price levels are reduced as well on average, because fewer cartels are established and overcharges are reduced (*see also* Hinloopen and Soetevent, 2008).

From a game-theoretical perspective the impact of leniency on cartel stability is ambiguous. On the one hand, leniency programmes increase the difficulty of maintaining cartels by increasing the payoff for cheaters, suggesting that leniency is bad for cartel stability. On the other hand, a stock of relatively stable cartels remains once the less stable cartels have been terminated or deterred. Brenner (2009) fails to detect a net impact of the EU leniency programme on cartel stability. Zhou (2013) on the other hand – using more sophisticated analytical tools – finds that the leniency programme has had a negative impact on cartel duration.

From the perspective of the competition authority, leniency programmes may reduce the difficulty, time and administrative costs of finding evidence of cartel infringements. At the same time, however, the follow-up by the competition authority of leniency applications requires resources that can no longer be used for ex officio investigations. This may be problematic because the disincentives to join a cartel might be diminished once potential cartel participants become aware that the competition authority no longer ventures out on its own to look for possible cartels. Another potential problem is that leniency programmes institutionalise the unequal treatment of different cartel members, which may raise moral issues. Finally, the competition authority needs to consider the possibility that leniency programmes lead to over-enforcement (i.e., Type I errors). However, in the daily practice of competition policy enforcement this does not appear to be a major issue.

[B] Sanctions and Private Damages

As part of its enforcement activities, the competition authority will sanction cartel participants by imposing a fine in the form of a monetary penalty on the corporation involved and, depending on the jurisdiction, by implementing a number of other sanctions (e.g., imprisonment of the responsible managers, monetary penalties on managers, debarment of managers[16]). In addition, in most countries there are private enforcement procedures that allow harmed parties to claim damages (often a multiple of the estimated damages) for the anticompetitive behaviour. Within the EU, the 2014 Directive on Antitrust Damages Actions has removed the main obstacles to an effective compensation of citizens and businesses for damages incurred.

Davies et al. (2015) argue that fines have strong deterrent effects on marginal cartels only since such cartels are less profitable and fines therefore weigh more heavily on their finances. More generally, Mariniello (2013) considers the level of fines applied by the European Commission to be insufficient to reach optimal deterrence. He also stresses the need to reduce the time required to complete the investigation and impose fines. It is indeed often the case that by the time that the firm is required to pay the fine,

16. For a recent review, *see* Katsoulacos and Metsiou (2017).

the managers responsible for the collusive behaviour have long changed jobs. Consequently, deterrence effects are minimal. However, with the application of the 2006 Commission Guidelines there has been a change in the fining policy which is now more directed towards the establishment of a link between the potential benefits for cartel participants and the level of fines imposed.

One way to test the adequacy of fine levels imposed is to calculate the expected profitability of price fixing: the idea is that if the expected benefits from collusion outweigh the expected sanctions and private damages, the level of deterrence will be low. Given the observation (Connor and Lande, 2012) that there is a large heterogeneity across industries in terms of the profitability of cartels, the fine levels required for deterrence will fluctuate accordingly. If uniform fining levels are applied, there is a risk that the most harmful cartels remain non-deterred (Jensen and Sørgard, 2016).

Personal fines imposed on the managers responsible for the collusive behaviour may have preventive effects as well (even for larger, profitable cartels),[17] but the European Commission has decided not to go down this road. One important reason for not doing so is that the burden of proof for the imposition of personal fines is higher, which is likely to reduce the speed of the investigative process.

Cartels are a cause of concrete harm (in terms of higher prices, e.g.) to customers. The EU Court of Justice has established that any citizen or business has a right to full compensation for the harm caused to them by an infringement of the EU antitrust rules (including rules pertaining to cartels). This right is governed by national legislation. An EU Directive adopted in 2014 has made it less costly and difficult to bring antitrust damages actions in national courts. Moreover, EU Member States were invited to introduce by 2015 collective redress mechanisms, including actions for damages. It is still too early to evaluate the deterrence effects of these new rules. However, the US has a much longer experience with private antitrust enforcement. Ginsburg (2005) considers that this experience has had mixed results. In the US, companies are often deterred from introducing innovative business practices with a legitimate procompetitive purpose for fear of being sued in court and having to pay substantial damages. On the other hand, it cannot be denied that private enforcement strengthens the deterrent effects of antitrust interventions by competition authorities. Davis and Lande (2013) provide evidence that the deterrent effects of private enforcement are as, if not more, important than those of the US DOJ.

[C] Actions to Prevent Re-emergence of Cartels

Actions preventing the re-emergence of cartels can be thought of as falling into two potential categories: (1) Actions that increase the probability of detection through the

17. Based on an online survey of Dutch firms Van der Noll and Baarsma (2017) report that both personal fines and company-level fines have statistically significant deterrent effects and raise compliance with cartel rules. Jensen and Sørgard (2016) moreover argue that the introduction of criminal sanctions (and private damages) only deters cartels from forming. However, it increases the stability of existing cartels, because with criminal sanctions the temptation to deviate becomes less attractive for cartel members.

close monitoring by the competition authority of the members of cartels that have been prosecuted, periodic dawn-raiding following prosecution and periodic screening of markets in which previously prosecuted cartelists operate; and (2) actions that reduce the ability and/or incentives of cartels to re-emerge following prosecution. These include mainly increased fines for repeat offenders and expanding the array of sanctions that the authority can potentially impose beyond monetary penalties on corporations. These sanctions would include imprisonment of managers engaged in collusion and or their debarment – something that will constrain the ability of firms to re-cartelise (especially in the short and medium term). While each action by itself may not be adequate to prevent the re-emergence of cartels, a set of actions including the different elements described above should go a long way towards tackling this challenge.

§12.09 DETERRENT EFFECTS OF MERGER CONTROL: DEFINITION AND MEASUREMENT

This section focuses on the deterrent effects of merger control. After defining more precisely what is meant by deterrence within the context of merger control, the section presents alternative approaches for measuring the deterrent effects of merger interventions by a competition authority.

[A] Definition

There is less literature on the deterrent effects of merger control as compared to cartel enforcement. One possible explanation is that the potential damage caused by an undeterred merger proposal is often less than that of an undeterred cartel. In a system of compulsory merger notification like that of the European Union, undeterred anticompetitive mergers need to be notified in any event and the merger can be remedied or prohibited following notification (*see* Table 12.9). Therefore, weak deterrence in merger cases mainly results in an increase in the number of notifications of anticompetitive mergers and in the workload of the competition authority. If the competition authority subsequently prohibits the anticompetitive merger or accepts appropriate remedies to address its competition concerns, then in principle customer harm will have been avoided.

Nevertheless, weak deterrence carries the risk that more anticompetitive mergers are notified and subsequently cleared (i.e., there is a greater risk that the competition authority commits a Type II error). Having too lenient a merger assessment would allow too many mergers to go through that in the longer run create or enhance anticompetitive conditions in markets through increased concentration.

Table 12.9 Classification of Potential Mergers[18]

<table>
<tr><td colspan="10">Total Population of Potential Mergers</td></tr>
<tr><td colspan="5">Anticompetitive mergers</td><td colspan="5">Procompetitive mergers</td></tr>
<tr><td colspan="3">Undeterred mergers</td><td colspan="2">Deterred mergers</td><td colspan="3">Undeterred mergers</td><td colspan="2">Deterred mergers</td></tr>
<tr><td>Cleared</td><td>Cleared with remedies</td><td>Prohibited</td><td>Dropped</td><td>Modified</td><td rowspan="2">Cleared</td><td>Cleared with remedies</td><td>Prohibited</td><td>Dropped</td><td>Modified</td></tr>
<tr><td>Type II error</td><td colspan="2">Direct effects</td><td colspan="2">Deterrent effects (+)</td><td colspan="2">Type I error</td><td colspan="2">Business chilling effects (-)</td></tr>
</table>

There are two possible sources of consumer harm associated with merger decisions. As already mentioned in the previous paragraph the first and most important source of consumer harm concerns the failure by the competition authority to intervene when an anticompetitive merger is proposed. A review of merger decisions in the EU (Ormosi et al., *see* Chapter 2) seems to indicate that Type II errors may well occur: in more than half of the analysed sample, prices increase after the intervention by the competition authority. However, contrary to the finding of Kwoka (2013) for the US, the merger remedies imposed by European competition authorities largely mitigate the anticompetitive price effects of the mergers proposed. Moreover, the observed price effects may be explained by other reasons than an erroneous analysis or faulty evidence: non-price effects may have played an important role in the decisions marking process or the price change may simply reflect random variation. Admittedly, the sample of merger decisions subjected to ex post evaluation is likely to be biased towards the more problematic (and anticompetitive) merger cases. Nevertheless, the evidence presented in Chapter 2 is an indication that a number of anticompetitive mergers remain undeterred leading to increased market concentration if approved by the competition authorities.

In the US, there has recently been an increased concern about merger control not being as strict as it should be (making a lot of Type II errors). Based on his review of US merger decisions, Kwoka (2013) concludes that the US competition authorities rightly intervened in the remedied cases, but that the remedies imposed were insufficient to eliminate competition concerns. The argument is being made that this could be one of the causes of the rise in concentration observed, which in turn may have negative effects on prices and investment (and hence on growth and inequality).[19]

A second possible source of consumer harm comes from an excessive degree of caution from the side of the competition authority. An overcautious authority may impose remedies or even prohibit a procompetitive merger that would have led to lower prices and/or improved quality (and thereby commit a Type I error). The awareness amongst the merging parties of the need to convince an overcautious authority of the merits of the merger might even result in the abandonment or modification by the merging parties of a procompetitive merger. However, according to

18. Desirable outcomes are highlighted in grey.
19. For evidence on the negative effects of rising concentration, *see* US Council of Economic Advisors (2016), Azar et al. (2018) and Gutierrez and Philippon (2017).

a survey (Baarsma et al., 2012) less than one in ten Dutch business respondents consider that such 'business chilling' effects are common. Similarly, a survey by Deloitte (2007) provides evidence that merger policy interventions in the UK only rarely prevent procompetitive mergers from taking place.

Sørgard (2009) models the optimal level of merger control enforcement taking into consideration both the deterrent effect of decisions taken and the likelihood that a Type I or Type II error is committed. He shows that it is optimal for a competition authority to accept the risks of mistakes in decision making because taking on more borderline cases raises the level of deterrence.

[B] Measurement

Any measurement of the effectiveness of merger control should take as its starting point its ability to deter anticompetitive mergers, since looking only at the direct effects of merger control might be misleading.[20]

A distinction can be made between frequency-based deterrence, reflecting the negative effect of merger control on the total number of anticompetitive mergers executed, and composition-based deterrence, reflecting the change in the character of mergers undertaken in light of a possible investigation or intervention by the competition authority (Aaronson, 1992).

Only a few studies have investigated composition-based deterrence. Stigler (1966) finds that a reinforcement of merger control reduces the ratio of horizontal mergers over non-horizontal mergers. A more recent paper by Clougherty and Seldeslachts (2013) confirms this result: merger interventions by US competition authorities – which focus almost exclusively on horizontal mergers – have a negative effect not only on the ratio of horizontal mergers over non-horizontal mergers but also on the absolute number of horizontal mergers executed. However a full analysis of such compositional effects would require a recognition and understanding of the different levels of harm associated with different types of merger and remains an important area for further research.

The simple model developed in subsection 12.05[A] for cartels may be a useful point of departure for a quantitative analysis of merger deterrence. Let us ignore the rather remote possibility that the competition authority intervenes in a procompetitive merger. Within a system of compulsory merger notification, the main concern of the competition authority is not to detect potentially anticompetitive mergers but rather to stop them or eliminate their anticompetitive effects.

Therefore, N^D does not correspond to the number of detected mergers but rather to the number of anticompetitive mergers detected, and consequently prohibited or modified. The detection parameter β is then defined as the probability that the

20. This would certainly be true under a very effective regime of merger control where most anticompetitive mergers are successfully deterred and the direct effects (as measured by the customer savings from merger interventions, e.g.) of the limited number of merger interventions that remain necessary underestimate the actual benefits from merger control. Instead the focus should be on the measurement of the indirect, deterrent effects of merger control.

competition authority detects the anticompetitive nature of a *notified* merger and intervenes either by prohibiting the merger or by imposing remedies:

$$\beta = N^D / N^N \qquad (6)$$

with N^N being defined as the number of notified mergers.

N^{DR} is the number of mergers deterred, i.e., the number of *planned*[21] mergers N that were abandoned or modified before notification for fear of intervention by the competition authority. The deterrence parameter ω can be defined as the probability that a planned merger is anticompetitive and deterred:

$$\omega = N^{DR} / N \qquad (7)$$

The deterrent effects of merger control can be defined as (*see* Equation 5 for a comparison with cartel deterrence):

$$H^{DR} / H^D = N^{DR} / N^D = (\omega / \beta) \times (N / N^N) \qquad (8)$$

where H^{DR} / H^D is the ratio of deterred merger harm over detected merger harm and N^{DR} / N^D is the number of deterred anticompetitive mergers per anticompetitive merger detected and stopped. In spite of the apparent simplicity of this equation, the measurement of the deterrent effects of merger control is challenging for a number of reasons.

First, as the only direct information on the number of planned mergers comes from business surveys, one option is to measure the deterrent effects of merger control purely on the basis of survey-based estimates of the detection parameter β, the deterrence parameter ω and the number of planned mergers (N) and to plug those estimates in Equation 8. The outcome of these calculations is presented in Table 12.10. As the sample size of the London Economics study is very small and the implicit intervention rate seems rather unrealistic, the results on the size of the deterrent effects should be discounted. This leaves a range for the deterrence parameter ω of 16-46% of planned mergers. Estimated deterrent effects vary from 3.7 to 7.5 times the number of anticompetitive mergers detected by the competition authority. These figures should be considered a lower bound on the size of the deterrent effects, as most of the survey results reported here are based on responses received from competition lawyers and advisers on competition law. It may well be that merger plans may have been abandoned or modified for competition policy reasons, even before the consultation of competition law experts.

21. Some planned mergers are abandoned for other reasons than the fear of being blocked by competition authorities. In this chapter, planned mergers are defined as ultimately notified mergers as well as mergers that were abandoned for competition policy reasons. Mergers abandoned for other reasons are not included in the list of planned mergers.

Table 12.10 Deterrent Effects of Merger Control

	Twynstra Gudde (2005)	*Deloitte (2007); Gordon and Squires (2008)*	*London Economics (2011)*	*SEO (2011); Baarsma et al. (2012)*
β	0.073	N.A.	0.250	0.025 – 0.06[22]
ω	0.462	N.A.	0.367	0.162
NDR / ND	7.5	5.3	1.8	3.1 – 7.3
Number of merger notifications	165	1840	24	131

Source: Authors' own calculations based on the different studies quoted.

Second, some of the deterred mergers may actually be procompetitive (as illustrated in Table 12.9). Therefore, it is not sufficient to simply determine the number of deterred mergers. Rather, the challenge is to identify the number of deterred mergers that would have had anticompetitive effects. Any deterrence of procompetitive mergers should be interpreted as a sign of over-enforcement by the competition authority and have 'business chilling' effects (similar to the Type I error discussed above). However, as discussed above, these effects are rather limited.

Third, the observed samples of notified mergers are not necessarily representative of the total population of (deterred) mergers. For example, mergers with very weak or very strong anticompetitive effects are more easily deterred. Mergers with weak anticompetitive effects may be deterred by the fact that the (administrative) costs outweigh the relatively meagre benefits from the mergers, while the high likelihood of being blocked by the competition authority deters mergers with strong anticompetitive effects from being notified (Davies and Ormosi, 2013). Mergers with very weak or very strong anticompetitive effects will therefore be overrepresented in the set of deterred mergers. However, the effect of this overrepresentation on the ratio of the harm caused by deterred mergers over the harm caused by detected mergers is uncertain: $H^{DR} / H^{D} \approx N^{DR} / N^{D}$.

In practice though, the deterrent effects of merger control are often captured by changes over time in the frequency of mergers notifications (*see* Clougherty et al., 2016, e.g.). A reduction in the number of notifications (after having controlled for business cycle and industry effects) can then be interpreted as the result of increased deterrence.

22. The SEO survey did not furnish information on the detection rate β, which in the area of merger control corresponds to the intervention rate of a competition authority. Available information on intervention rates by competition authorities has been used instead to define a range of probable values for β. More specifically, the reviews by Allen & Overy (2018, 2019) of global trends in merger enforcement in twenty-six jurisdictions over the past couple of years report that between 2% and 3% of merger notifications are either prohibited or cleared with remedies. The intervention rate of the European Commission over the period 2004-2019 averaged at around 6%.

However, such simple measures of deterrence rely on rather strong assumptions, including: (1) the observed change in the number of merger notifications reflects a corresponding change in the number of anticompetitive merger proposals; and (2) only anticompetitive merger proposals are deterred (or merger control has a much greater deterrent effect on anticompetitive mergers than on procompetitive mergers).

Eckbo (1992) and Duso et al. (2013) adopt a somewhat different approach. They track how merger interventions affect the stock prices of rival firms. If such interventions indeed have strong deterrent effects on anticompetitive mergers, newly proposed mergers should be more procompetitive and have detrimental effects on the stock prices of non-merging rival firms, for which the discounted value of future profits will decline as a result of price reductions associated with increased competition. Based on a cross-country comparison between the US with its vigorous control on horizontal mergers and Canada with its virtually unrestricted competitive environment in the pre-1985 period, Eckbo (1992) finds no evidence of such detrimental effects and therefore rejects the hypothesis that merger control has significant deterrent effects. Duso et al. (2013), on the other hand, find that following the merger reform of 2004 past prohibitions have had detrimental effects on the stock prices of rival firms, which had not been the case pre-reform. From this they conclude that the merger reform has led to a more effective deterrence of anticompetitive mergers.

§12.10 DETERMINANTS OF THE MERGER CONTROL DETERRENCE

Various authors have attempted to identify the main determinants of the deterrent effects of merger control with a view to assess and improve the performance of competition authorities. Buccirossi et al. (2013, 2014) distinguish two main determinants of deterrence: (1) the legislative regime; and (2) the enforcement of the regime by the competition authority as perceived by the merging parties.

With respect to the legislative merger regime, there has been a significant substantive convergence across jurisdictions. Today most jurisdictions apply the same standard of review despite differences in legal wording and enforce merger rules using comparable tools and principles (OECD, 2014). This leaves enforcement as the main determinant of deterrence. A young competition authority having a relatively weak record of enforcement offers merging parties an incentive to notify even an anticompetitive merger as they perceive that there is a higher probability of clearance (and commitment of Type II error by the competition authority). This is true in particular for mergers with relatively weak anticompetitive effects (Davies and Ormosi, 2013). However, as the competition authority gains experience and the outcomes of its merger investigations become easier to predict, merging parties will be less inclined to notify marginal anticompetitive mergers implying a greater degree of deterrence. The frequency of Type II errors will likely decline as well.

The deterrent effects of merger control are likely to differ according to the type of decision taken by the competition authority. Using data for twenty-eight OECD countries Seldeslachts, Clougherty and Barros (2009) find that contrary to merger remedies, outright prohibitions tend to be followed by a decrease in the number of mergers proposed in the following year. Sørgard (2015) provides more anecdotal evidence of the strong deterrent effects of merger prohibitions: two prohibitions involving the State owned electricity company Statkraft in 2002-2003 put an end to any merger activity in the Norwegian electricity market over the period 2003-2015.

With respect to the deterrent effects of remedies, Cosnita-Langlais and Sørgard (2014) go one step further in arguing that the increased use by the European Commission of merger remedies following the 2004 EU merger reform may have induced companies to more frequently propose anticompetitive mergers secure in the knowledge that they can use remedies as a fall-back position. Following this line of argument, the move in the post-reform period to a more remedy-based competition policy regime would have reduced deterrence.

Clougherty et al. (2016) extend the work of Duso et al. (2013) by updating and expanding the sample of merger decisions investigated. They observe that prior to the 2004 EU merger reform, prohibitions were the most common means of preventing anticompetitive mergers from happening. Merger remedies and withdrawals took over this role in the post-reform period. Phase I remedies in particular led to fewer merger notifications in subsequent years, indicating their strong deterrent effects. This does not appear to be the case though for Phase II remedies and prohibitions, which Clougherty and his co-authors explain by a reduced bargaining power of the European Commission in Phase II as threats by the Commission to prohibit a merger are perceived as non-credible. However, they also note that the limited sample of merger prohibitions may have made it more difficult for them to detect significant deterrent effects associated with such prohibitions and they suggest that the re-establishment of prohibitions as a viable option since 2010 may have helped to once again enhance the European Commission's bargaining power in Phase II.

Clougherty et al. (2016) also investigate whether deterrence is greater in high-concentration industries, the logic being that it would be particularly beneficial to discourage further merger activities in such industries. Using industry sector panel data describing European Commission merger decisions over the period 1990-2009, they confirm that the deterrent effects of Phase I remedy decisions are larger in high-concentration industries than in low-concentration industries.

Within the literature there is not yet a consensus on the type of decision that has the strongest deterrent effects, which is another illustration of the difficulties associated with measuring such effects. Nevertheless, most competition economists would agree with the statement that a lack of clarity in the competition authority's decision-making rules and practices encourages companies to propose anticompetitive mergers, possibly resulting in increased consumer harm. It is therefore imperative to stress the value of the competition authority being transparent on its course of action, both ex ante in the form of the publication of merger guidelines and ex post in terms of making its decisions public.

§12.11 INTERDEPENDENCE BETWEEN CARTELS AND MERGERS

In the previous sections we have looked at the deterrent effects of cartel prohibitions on cartels and the deterrent effects of merger interventions on mergers. However, we have ignored the fact that merger interventions may affect cartelisation and that cartel prohibitions may affect merger behaviour. We now look at these two possibilities in turn.

One the one hand, one could argue that a merger intervention maintains competition in the market as compared to a counterfactual situation in which the level of competition had been reduced. With this possibility for making monopoly profits having been closed off, firms will seek alternative ways to increase their profitability including through collusive behaviour. On the other hand, a more permissive merger control will help reduce the number of players in the market, making it easier to establish and sustain cartels. Cosnita-Langlais and Tropeano (2013) take the example of the air cargo market to illustrate the line of argument that a lax merger control leads to increased cartel formation. However, as there are arguments both ways, the question needs to be resolved empirically.

Establishing an impact of cartel enforcement on merger behaviour might be a bit more straightforward, the argument being that with the option of collusive profits no longer being an option, a merger might be a second best alternative. Hüschelrath and Smuda (2013) and Davies et al. (2015) indeed find that horizontal mergers in particular are more frequent after cartel breakdown, especially in markets that are less concentrated. On the basis of a more disaggregated analysis of individual mergers, they conclude that the tacit-collusion motive is likely to have been at work in a large minority of mergers investigated, especially given the observation that merger activity is most intense in the early period following cartel breakdown.

§12.12 SECTOR DIFFUSION OF DETERRENT EFFECTS

With some exceptions,[23] analyses of the deterrent effects of a competition authority's merger and cartel decisions are conducted at the aggregate national level. One would expect though that the deterrent effects of cartel and merger control are primarily felt in the markets and sectors that are directly affected by the competition authorities' interventions, because such interventions increase companies' awareness that the authorities are monitoring their behaviour. This hypothesis tends to be confirmed by business surveys showing that cartels and mergers are more likely to be abandoned in sectors where the authorities have conducted cartel investigations, where they have recently prohibited or imposed severe remedies on a merger, or where they have conducted a sector inquiry or market study (CMA, 2017a and 2017b). The survey by London Economics (2011), for example, finds companies in sectors with merger

23. *See, for example,* Clougherty et al. (2016), which includes an analysis of merger deterrence at the industry level.

investigations to be more knowledgeable about the responsibilities of the competition authority, the implication being that they will be more easily deterred.

This general observation raises the question how to relate the importance of the deterrent effects to the characteristics of market and sectors affected by the competition policy intervention. If the size of the affected market is large relative to the size of the sector concerned, the deterrent effects of a given decision within that sector are likely to be large as well. Moreover, if the sector is defined rather narrowly, there might be a diffusion of these effects to neighbouring sectors. On the other hand, if the affected market is relatively small, deterrence will be less important. However, even the relatively smaller competition policy interventions will have deterrent effects as an indication of the competition authority's objective to combat anticompetitive behaviour in all markets, no matter how small. Moreover, small decisions can serve as a precedent indicating that the competition authority intends to pursue similar cases in the future. This is true in particular in the area of antitrust, where the alleged abuse or coordinated action can take different forms, depending on the market and/or sector characteristics. Nevertheless, even in such a situation the importance of the deterrent effects will increase with the size of the affected market relative to that of the sector to which it belongs.

In Chapter 13 this line of argument will be further developed in order to model the macroeconomic effects of the European Commission's cartel prohibitions and merger interventions taken over the past eight years. Information on the direct effects of such enforcement actions will be combined with an analysis of deterrent effects at the sector level, using the estimates of the ratios of deterred harm over detected harm presented in this chapter to calibrate these effects, to arrive at a comprehensive assessment of the macroeconomic effects of EU competition policy.

§12.13 CONCLUSIONS AND AREAS FOR FURTHER RESEARCH

Better information about the total (direct plus deterrent) effects of competition policy is useful both for priority setting and competition advocacy by a competition authority. However, the measurement of the deterrent effects of competition policy interventions is quite a challenge. For example, it would be misleading to measure the performance of a competition authority in deterring anticompetitive behaviour by a simple multiple of detected and therefore avoided harm because the observed population of cases is not representative of the total population.

There is a consensus in the literature that the deterrent effects are very significant. This is corroborated by the results of surveys. They show that between 3 and 8 mergers are deterred per intervention by the competition authorities in a merger case and that between 5 and 28 cartels are deterred for every cartel detected. These survey results have a number of limitations. Therefore, new statistical and theoretical modelling tools have been developed to better measure the deterrent effects of cartel policy enforcement and merger control.

Most progress has been made with the measurement of cartel deterrence: the most recent models indicate that the amount of deterred harm is between 6 and 17 times that of detected harm. Moreover, effective cartel policy enforcement eliminates a substantial share of potential harm (up to 90%), as it deters cartels from forming in the first place. The deterrent effects of such enforcement appear to be stronger for both marginal cartels that simply cease operating and larger cartels that reduce overcharges to avoid attracting the attention of competition authorities. Also, competition authorities need to be conscious of the possibility that a cartel re-emerges in the longer term after having been stopped initially. Weak deterrence in merger control carries that risk that more anticompetitive mergers are notified and subsequently cleared (commitment of Type II error). A second possible source of consumer harm comes from the imposition of unnecessary remedies on procompetitive mergers (commitment of Type I error). However, such Type I errors appear to be much less common that Type II errors.

Measures can be taken to increase the deterrent effects of cartel policy and merger control. In the area of cartels, these measures aim at increasing the probability of detection, such as leniency programmes, at augmenting the expected punishment, via fines and private damages actions, and at reducing the risk of recidivism. In the area of mergers, there is less consensus on the type of competition policy intervention – prohibition or clearance with remedies – having the strongest deterrence effects.

The challenge for the future is to narrow the range of estimates of deterrent effects of cartel enforcement measures and merger control. Moreover, there is a need to improve our understanding of the impact on deterrence of the different components of cartel and merger control. For cartels, the question is whether to focus on raising detection rates, for example by developing new signalling instruments, or on avoiding recidivism by increasing penalty rates for repeat offenders. For mergers, the challenge is to better understand the deterrent effects of different types of decisions (prohibitions versus approval with remedies) and the impact of (Type I and Type II) errors made. Finally, one would expect that the deterrent effects of cartel and merger control are primarily felt in the markets and sectors that are directly affected by the competition authorities' interventions. Such sector diffusion effects need to be further explored. A first attempt in that direction is made in Chapter 13 of this book analysing the macroeconomic effects of competition policy.

REFERENCES

Aaronson R. (1992), 'Do companies take any notice of competition policy?', *Consumer Policy Review*, 2(3), pp. 140-145.

Allen & Overy (2018, 2019), 'Global trends in merger control enforcement', February.

Apesteguia J., Dufwenberg M. and Selten R. (2007), 'Blowing the whistle', *Economic Theory*, 31(1), pp. 143-166.

Armoogum, K.P., Davies S.W. and Mariuzzo F. (2017), 'Cartel enforcement and deterrence over the life of a Competition Authority'.

Azar J., Schmalz M.C. and Tecu I. (2018), 'Anti competitive effects of common ownership', *Journal of Finance*, 73(4).

Baarsma B., Kemp R., van der Noll R. and Seldeslachts J. (2012), 'Let's not stick together: anticipation of cartel and merger control in the Netherlands', *De Economist*, 160(4), pp. 357-376.

Baker J.B. (2003), 'The case for antitrust enforcement', *Journal of Economic Perspectives*, 17(4), pp. 27-50.

Bigoni M., Fridolfsson S.-O., Le Coq Ch. and Spagnolo G. (2015), 'Trust, leniency and deterrence', *Journal of Law, Economics and Organization*, 31(4), pp. 663-689.

Bos I., Davies S.W., Harrington J.E. and Ormosi P.L. (2017), 'Does enforcement deter cartels? A tale of two tails'.

Brenner S. (2009), 'An empirical study of the European corporate leniency program', *International Journal of Industrial Organization*, 27(6), pp. 639-645.

Broos S., Gauthier A., Marcos Ramos J. and Petit N. (2016), 'Analyse statistique des affaires d'ententes dans l'UE (2004-2014)', *Revue économique*, 67 (hors-série), février, pp. 79-94.

Bryant P.G. and Eckard E.W. (1991), 'Price fixing: The probability of getting caught', *The Review of Economics and Statistics*, 73(3), pp. 531-536.

Buccirossi P., Ciari L., Duso T., Spagnolo G. and Vitale C. (2013), 'Competition policy and productivity growth: An empirical assessment', *Review of Economics and Statistics*, 95(4), pp. 1324-1336.

Buccirossi P., Ciari L., Duso T., Spagnolo G. and Vitale C. (2014), 'Deterrence in competition law', in: M. Peitz and Y. Spiegel (eds.), *The Analysis of Competition Policy and Sectoral Regulation*, pp. 423-454, World Scientific.

Chen Z. and Rey P. (2013), 'On the design of leniency programs', *Journal of Law and Economics*, 56(4), pp. 917-957.

Clarke J.L. and Evenett S.J. (2003), 'Deterrent effects of national anti-cartel laws: Evidence from international vitamins cartels', *Antitrust Bulletin*, 48, fall, pp. 689-726.

Clougherty J.A. and Seldeslachts J. (2013), 'The deterrence effects of US merger policy instruments', *Journal of Law, Economics and Organization*, 29(5), pp. 1114-1144.

Clougherty J.A., Duso T., Lee M. and Seldeslachts J. (2016), 'Effective European antitrust: Does EC merger policy generate deterrence?', *Economic Inquiry*, 54(4), pp. 1884-1903.

CMA (2017a), 'The deterrent effect of competition authorities' work: a brief summary', note summarising the findings of a longer literature review, 'The deterrent effect of competition authorities' work'.

CMA (2017b), 'The deterrent effect of competition authorities' work: Literature review', Working Paper, 7 September.

Combe E., Monnier C. and Legal R. (2008), 'Cartels: The probability of getting caught in the European Union', Cahiers de Recherche PRISM-Sorbonne / CR-07-01-03, March.

Connor J.M. (2010), 'Recidivism Revealed: Private International Cartels 1990-2009', *CPI Journal* 6(2), pp. 101-127.

Connor J.M. (2011), 'Cartel detection and duration worldwide', *CPI Antitrust Chronicle*, September 2011(2).

Connor J.M. (2014), 'Price-fixing overcharges: Revised 3rd edition'.

Connor J.M. (2015), 'EU cartel penalties: Severity and recovery (with international comparisons)', presentation at workshop 'Looking beyond the direct effects of the work of competition authorities: Deterrence and macroeconomic Impact', Brussels, 17-18 September.

Connor J.M. (2016), 'Oceanic disparities in cartel-recidivism: Attitudes and penalties', *ABA Review*, Spring, pp. 8-14.

Connor J.M. and Lande R.H. (2012), 'Cartels as rational business strategy: Crime pays', *Cardoso Law Review*, 34, pp. 427-489.

Cosnita-Langlais A. and Tropeano J.-P. (2013), 'Fight cartels or control mergers? On the optimal allocation of enforcement efforts within competition policy', *International Review of Law and Economics*, 34(1), pp. 34-40.

Cosnita-Langlais A. and Sørgard L. (2014), 'Enforcement vs. deterrence in merger control: Can remedies lead to lower welfare?', Discussion Paper SAM 7 2014, Institutt for Samfunnsøkonomi, Norges Handelshøyskole.

Davies S.W. and Majumdar A. (2002), 'The development of targets for consumer savings arising from competition policy', Economic Discussion Paper 4, Office of Fair Trading, UK.

Davies S.W. and Ormosi P.L. (2012), 'A comparative assessment of methodologies used to evaluate competition policy', *Journal of Competition Law & Economics*, 8(4), pp. 769-803.

Davies S.W. and Ormosi P.L. (2013), 'The impact of competition policy: What are the known unknowns?', CCP Working Paper, 13-7.

Davies S.W., Ormosi P.L. and Graffenberger M. (2015), 'Mergers after cartels: How markets react to cartel breakdown', *The Journal of Law and Economics*, 58(3), pp. 561-583.

Davies S.W., Mariuzzo F. and Ormosi P.L. (2018), 'Quantifying the deterrent effect of anticartel enforcement', *Economic Inquiry*, 56(4), pp. 1933-1949.

Davis J.P. and Lande R.H. (2013), 'Defying conventional wisdom: The case for private antitrust enforcement', *Georgia Law Review*, 48(1), pp. 1-81.

Deloitte (2007), 'The deterrent effect of competition enforcement by the OFT', OFT962, Report prepared for the Office of Fair Trading, London.

Duso T., Gugler K. and Szücs F. (2013), 'An empirical assessment of the 2004 EU merger policy reform', *The Economic Journal*, 123(572), pp. F596-619.

Eckbo B.E. (1992), 'Mergers and the value of antitrust deterrence', *Journal of Finance*, 47(3), pp. 1005-29.

Ginsburg D.H. (2005), 'Comparing antitrust enforcement in the United States and Europe', *Journal of Competition Law & Economics*, 1(3), pp. 427-439.

Gordon F. and Squires D. (2008), 'The deterrent effect of UK competition enforcement', *De Economist*, 156(4), pp. 411-432.

Gutierrez G. and Philippon Th. (2017) 'Declining competition and investment in the US', NBER Working Paper No. 23583.

Harrington J. (2004), 'Post cartel pricing during litigation', *Journal of Industrial Economics*, 52, pp. 517-533.

Harrington J. and Chang M.-H. (2009), 'Modelling the birth and death of cartels with an application to evaluating competition policy', *Journal of the European Economic Association*, 7(6), pp. 1400-1435.

Hinloopen J. and Soetevent A.R. (2008), 'Laboratory evidence on the effectiveness of corporate leniency programs', *Rand Journal of Economics*, 39(2), pp. 607-616.

Houba H., Motchenkova E. and Wen Q. (2010), 'Antitrust enforcement with price-dependent fines and detection probabilities', *Economics Bulletin*, 30(3), pp. 2017-2027.

Hüschelrath K. and Smuda F. (2013), 'Do cartel breakdowns induce mergers? Evidence from EC Cartel Cases', *European Competition Journal*, 9(2), pp. 407-429.

Hyytinen A., Steen F. and Toivanen O. (2010), 'Cartels uncovered', CEPR Discussion Papers, No. 7761.

Jensen S., Kvaløy O., Olsen T.E. and Sørgard L. (2013), 'Crime and punishment: When tougher antitrust enforcement leads to higher overcharge', Discussion Paper Series in Economics 4/2013, Norwegian School of Economics, Department of Economics.

Jensen S. and Sørgard L. (2016), 'Fine schedule with heterogenous cartels: Are the wrong cartels deterred?', *Journal of Competition Law & Economics*, 12(2), pp. 263-277.

Katsoulacos Y. and Metsiou E. (2017), 'The economics of antitrust sanctioning: A brief review', in: B. Tembinkosi, E. Fox and L. Macnube (eds.), *Competition Policy for the New Era: Insights from BRICS and Developing Countries*, Oxford University Press.

Katsoulacos Y., Motchenkova E. and Ulph D. (2017), 'Measuring the effectiveness of anti-cartel interventions: A conceptual framework', TILEC Discussion Paper, No. 2016-001.

Kwoka J.E. Jr. (2013), 'Does merger control work? A retrospective on EU enforcement actions and merger outcomes', *Antitrust Law Journal*, 78(3), pp. 619-650.

Levenstein M.C., Marvão C. and Suslow V.Y. (2015), 'Serial collusion in context: Repeat offences by firm or by industry?', OECD DAF/COMP/GF (2015)12.

London Economics (2011), 'The impact of competition interventions on compliance and deterrence', OFT Report No. 1391, December.

Mariniello M. (2013), 'Do European fines deter price fixing?', VOX column.

Marvão C. (2016), 'The EU leniency program and recidivism', *Review of Industrial Organisation*, 48(1).

Miller N.H. (2009), 'Strategic leniency and cartel enforcement?', *American Economic Review*, 99(3), pp. 750-768.

Motta M. and Polo M. (2003), 'Leniency programs and cartel prosecution', *International Journal of Industrial Organization*, 21, pp. 347-379.

OECD (2014), 'Challenges of international co-operation in competition law enforcement', May.

Ormosi P.L. (2014), 'A tip of the iceberg? The probability of catching cartels', *Journal of Applied Econometrics*, 29(4), pp. 549-566.

Seldeslachts J., Clougherty J.A. and Pita Barros P. (2009), 'Settle for now but block for tomorrow: the deterrence effects of merger policy tools', *Journal of Law and Economics*, University of Chicago Press, 52(3), pp. 607-634.

Sørgard L. (2009), 'Optimal merger policy: enforcement vs. deterrence', *Journal of Industrial Economics*, 57(3), pp. 438-456.

Sørgard L. (2015), 'Merger control (and more): Direct and indirect effects', Presentation at workshop 'Looking beyond the direct effects of the work of the competition authorities: Deterrence and macroeconomic impact', Brussels, 17-18 September.

Stigler G.J. (1966), 'The economic effects of the antitrust laws', *Journal of Law and Economics*, 9(1), pp. 225-258.

Twynstra Gudde (2005), 'Research into the anticipation of merger control', Report prepared for the NMa (Netherlands Competition Authority), October.

US Council of Economic Advisors Issue Brief (2016), 'Benefits of competition and indicators of market power'.

SEO (2011), 'Anticipating cartel and merger control', Report prepared for the NMa (Netherlands Competition Authority), January.

Van der Noll R. and Baarsma B. (2017), 'Compliance with cartel laws and the determinants of deterrence – an empirical investigation', *European Competition Journal*, 13(2-3), pp. 336-355.

Werden G.J., Hammond S.D. and Barnett B.A. (2011), 'Recidivism eliminated: Cartel enforcement in the United States since 1999', *CPI Antitrust Chronicle*, October.

Wils W.P.J. (2016), 'The use of leniency in EU cartel enforcement: An assessment after twenty years', *World Competition*, 39(3), pp. 327-388.

Zhou J. (2013), 'Evaluating leniency with missing information on undetected cartels: Exploring time-varying policy impacts on cartel duration', TILEC Discussion Paper No. 2011-042.

CHAPTER 13

The Macroeconomic and Sectoral Impact of EU Competition Policy*

Fabienne Ilzkovitz, Mattia Cai, Roberta Cardani, Adriaan Dierx & Filippo Pericoli

This chapter provides an assessment of the macroeconomic and sectoral impact of merger interventions and cartel prohibitions by the European Commission over the period 2012-2018. The macroeconomic simulations consider both the direct effects of competition policy interventions and two types of deterrent effects. Intertemporal deterrence effects arise from companies' expectations that the European Commission will continue its competition policy interventions at the same pace into the foreseeable future. Sectoral deterrence effects come from the transmission of the direct effects of competition policy interventions in a given market to the remainder of the sector to which this market belongs. The sectoral diffusion of these direct effects is modelled by way of a logistic function, which has been used in the literature to model the diffusion of innovation, information, or the use of new technologies. Model simulations show that European Commission's competition policy interventions (including deterrent effects) may lead to a 0.3% GDP increase in the medium term. An input-output model is used to exploit available information on the distribution of merger interventions and cartel prohibitions across industries and to explore how the avoided price increase resulting from a competition policy intervention in a given industry is transmitted to the price levels in other industries. The total price reduction associated with competition policy interventions over the period 2012-2018 is significant (-0.2%). Price reductions occur in industries that are important for the purchasing power of consumers (motor vehicles, financial services) and the competitiveness of the European economy (telecommunications, electronics). The industry spillover price effects of competition policy interventions may be as important as their within-industry price effects. Industry spillovers were particularly high in 2013, when two important cartels in financial markets were prohibited. Spillovers tend to be higher in industries having strong interlinkages with the rest of the economy, such as network industries or intermediate goods industries.

* This chapter has been written under the sole responsibility of the authors and does not represent the views of the European Commission.

§13.01 INTRODUCTION

This book would not be complete if it did not include an assessment of the macroeconomic impact of EU competition policy. Over the recent years, both competition authorities and academics have become interested in this type of analysis (for a survey, *see, for example,* Ilzkovitz and Dierx, 2015). Some academics even questioned the capacity and willingness of competition authorities to tackle the increase in market power associated with technological change and globalisation. Weak competition policy enforcement could bring about a loss of economic efficiency and a slower diffusion of new technologies, leading to a degradation of macroeconomic performance. In this context, an assessment of the broader impact of competition policy is essential to show that the tools of EU competition policy, such as merger and cartel control, improve the functioning of markets and deliver clear benefits to consumers, businesses and society as a whole.

While the academic literature on the macroeconomic impact of competition is quite extensive, little empirical analysis has been done on the macroeconomic impact of competition policy, at least in comparison with that of other policies affecting the conditions of competition, such as trade liberalisation or deregulation policies. This lack of empirical analysis may be explained by the difficulties associated with this type of work (*see* Dierx et al., 2017 for a more detailed description of the challenges associated with such an analysis). In particular, it is not easy to find indicators of the strength of competition policy. In the literature, very simple indicators, such as binary variables indicating the existence of competition laws or authorities, are often used. Other indicators measure the inputs necessary for an effective enforcement of competition policy such as the human and budgetary resources of competition authorities or the competition laws that determine their investigative powers and the scope of their activities.

In the current chapter, the output of European Commission in its role of EU competition authority is used as a proxy for the strength of competition policy within the European Union. It is measured by the number and market impact of merger interventions and cartel prohibitions by the European Commission over the period 2012-2018. This information is used to calibrate aggregate mark-up shocks, which are then applied to a Dynamic Stochastic General Equilibrium (DSGE) model, i.e., the QUEST III model (*see* Ratto et al., 2009). A unique database containing information on the characteristics of the markets affected by the European Commission's interventions and the customer benefits of such interventions allows making a macroeconomic assessment of the impact of EU competition policy, which is based on a micro-founded general equilibrium model.

The model simulations take into account not only the direct effects of EU competition policy interventions but also their deterrent effects. These deterrent effects consist in discouraging market participants from engaging in future anticompetitive behaviour. The approach developed in this chapter considers two types of deterrent effects: a sectoral deterrence and an intertemporal deterrence. On the one hand, it is assumed that each merger intervention and cartel prohibition by the European Commission will not only have an impact on the relevant market directly affected by the Commission's intervention (direct effect) but also on the whole NACE four-digit sector concerned by this intervention (sectoral deterrence effects). A logistic function is used to model the sector diffusion of the direct effect of the intervention. This function assumes that sectoral deterrence effects are positively related to the size of the market affected by an intervention relative to the size of the four-digit sector concerned. On the other hand, intertemporal deterrence effects arise from companies' expectations that the European Commission will continue to enforce EU competition policy at the same pace into the foreseeable future. The mark-up shocks applied to the QUEST III model thus become permanent shocks, which can be used to simulate the impact of EU competition policy on macroeconomic variables such as employment and GDP growth.

However, as the QUEST III model is not disaggregated by sector,[1] it is unsuited to exploit the available information on the sector distribution of the European Commission's cartel prohibitions and merger interventions. When the European Commission breaks up a cartel or blocks a merger, the price reduction in the two-digit industry directly affected by the intervention will also benefit industries that lie downstream in the supply chain because of a reduction in the costs of intermediate inputs. To analyse these effects in more detail, the QUEST III model is complemented by an input-output model, which allows tracking the interlinkages between two-digit industries and analysing the differential effects of competition policy interventions affecting different industries of the economy.[2]

The chapter is organised as follows. Section 13.02 presents the conceptual framework used to transform the microeconomic market interventions by the European Commission into macroeconomic outcomes and to exploit the available information on the industry distribution of such interventions. Section 13.03 describes the sample of merger and cartel decisions taken over the period 2012-2018, which is used to assess the impact of competition policy in the model simulations. Section 13.04 explains how these competition policy interventions are transformed into mark-up and price shocks applied to the QUEST III and input-output model, respectively. Section 13.05 briefly presents the information used and the main assumptions made to calculate these shocks. Section 13.06 describes the method employed to estimate the sectoral deterrence effects of competition policy interventions. Section 13.07 presents the results of the QUEST III macro-model simulations and discusses the robustness of the macroeconomic results obtained, while section 13.08 describes the differential price effects of competition policy interventions affecting different industries on the

1. Nevertheless, the QUEST III model is calibrated to implicitly take into account sector spillovers. The use of a sectorally disaggregated model is necessary if one is interested in the sector specific impulse responses to sector mark-up shocks, but it is not required for analysing the aggregate macroeconomic effects of such shocks. This is the reason why the macroeconomic and input-output modelling exercises presented in this chapter are kept separate.
2. Two types of sector classifications are considered in this modelling exercise. They are both based on an aggregation of the NACE two-digit level classification. First, to calculate the aggregate mark-up shock applied to the QUEST III model, we use data on mark-ups for twenty-four sectors. Second, the input-output model employs a 64-industry aggregation of the NACE two-digit level classification. In this chapter, we refer to sectors for the first type of classification and to industries for the latter.

basis of the input-output model. The final section 13.09 concludes and offers some ideas for further research.

§13.02 CONCEPTUAL FRAMEWORK

[A] Macro-modelling Approach

The macro-modelling framework proposed here exploits the microeconomic data commonly used by competition authorities to calculate the customer savings associated with their competition policy interventions (*see* Chapter 11 for a description of the method used to calculate the customer savings). This framework is described in Figure 13.1.

Figure 13.1 An Integrated Framework to Assess the Impact of Competition Policy

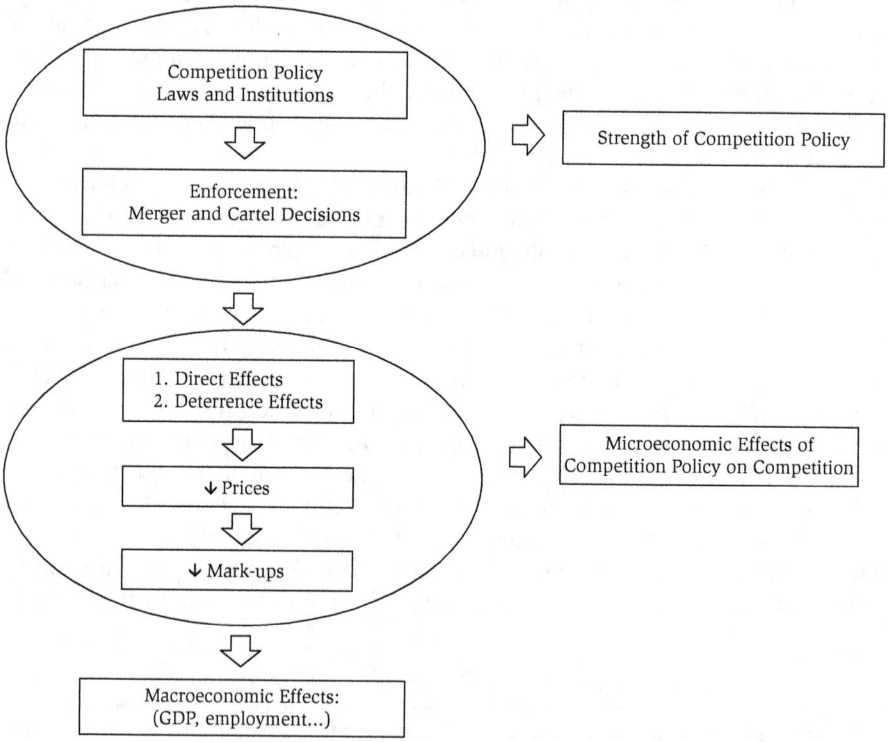

Source: Dierx et al. (2017).

The analytical framework distinguishes three main steps. First, it measures the strength of competition policy. Second, it analyses the impact of competition policy on the degree of competition and third, it assesses the impact of increased competition on macroeconomic performance.

First, competition policy is defined here as the enforcement of competition policy legislation covering the prohibition of cartels and the control of mergers. The strength of the European Commission's competition policy is measured by the number and importance of its interventions in these areas. Due to data limitations, other aspects of competition policy such as the prohibition of abuse of dominant position or State aid control are not covered here.

Second, competition policy interventions increase the level of competition, which is measured by the mark-up of prices over marginal costs, an indicator often used in empirical work. Information on the price increases avoided due to merger interventions and cartel prohibitions by the European Commission, the duration of such price effects and the size of the markets affected are used to calculate a negative mark-up shock that reflects the aggregate impact in any given year of competition policy interventions made. The deterrent effects of these interventions are taken into account as well.

Third, the QUEST III model is used to simulate the macroeconomic effects of the mark-up shocks (*see* Box 13.1). The economic logic of the QUEST III simulations can shortly be explained as follows. The reduction in mark-ups contributes to lower prices, which in turn stimulate consumer demand. In order to satisfy this greater demand, firms invest in production capacity and better technology (leading to an increase in labour productivity) and hire more workers (leading to an increase in employment). Investment and employment are increasing because the negative direct effect of reduced profitability is dominated by the positive effect of increasing demand due to lower prices. All these changes are then reflected in an increase in GDP. In the future, other transmission channels of an increase in competition should be investigated, for example, by looking at the effects of competition on business dynamism and innovation.

Box 13.1: Short Description of QUEST III

The macroeconomic assessment presented in this chapter is based on an extended version of the European Commission's QUEST III model (*see* Ratto et al., 2009 and Dierx et al., 2017 for a more detailed description). This model is a DSGE model. The model version used here is a two-region open-economy setup calibrated for the European Union and the rest of the world. For each region, the model economy is populated by households and final goods producing firms. The model includes a monetary and a fiscal authority, both following rule-based stabilisation policies. Both domestic and foreign firms produce a continuum of differentiated goods. The number of firms is fixed and firms are homogeneous in terms of their production technology. The goods produced in the home country are imperfect substitutes for goods produced abroad. The level of competition among firms is captured by the inverse elasticity of substitution between the goods varieties, which can be directly linked to the mark-up that firms charge over the marginal cost of production. Competition policy acts as an instrument to increase competition among the firms and thereby contributes to a decrease in the level of mark-ups.

From the consumers' side, we distinguish between households which are liquidity constrained and consume all their disposable income and non-liquidity constrained (so-called Ricardian) households who have full access to financial markets. The latter group of households make decisions on financial and real capital investments. The model is a fully forward-looking dynamic model in which all investment decisions are based on the expected future stream of income. Households also differ in terms of their skills and wages. Additionally, we identify the liquidity-constrained households as low skilled and the non-liquidity constrained households as high skilled. We calibrate the model by selecting behavioural and technological parameters so that the model can replicate important empirical ratios such as labour productivity, investment, consumption to GDP ratios, the wage share, the employment rate, given a set of structural indicators describing market frictions in goods and labour markets, tax wedges and skill endowments.

[B] Input-Output Analysis

While aggregate mark-up shocks are applied to the QUEST III model, a standard input-output framework (Miller and Blair, 2009) is used to exploit the available information on the distribution of merger interventions and cartel prohibitions by industry. The input-output model used distinguishes sixty-four industries defined at the NACE two-digit level and describes the economic flows in the EU28 for the year 2014. This model is applied to examine how the price effects of competition policy interventions affecting different industries are transmitted to the rest of the economy. For example, a competition policy intervention leading to a price decrease in financial services, which are used as inputs in many other industries, should have stronger spillover effects than an intervention in a consumer goods industry, which has smaller interlinkages with the rest of the economy.

To measure such spillover effects, two types of analyses are done. First, a standardised price shock is applied to different industries[3] to compare the intensity of the spillover price effects in the different industries of the economy (*see* Box 13.3 in section 13.08 for a definition of these effects). This standardised shock aims at

3. A standardised price shock needs to be defined to eliminate the impact of size differences between industries. In the analytical framework used, the change in the output value in a given industry is equal to the change in price as the physical quantity produced is assumed to remain constant. Therefore, a 10% price reduction is equivalent to 10 in an industry X having a production value of 100 and to 1 in an industry Y having a production value of 10. Everything else equal, this would lead to higher industry spillovers of a 10% price reduction in industry X than in industry Y just because of the different sizes of the two industries. To eliminate this effect, a standardised price shock is defined as a 15% price decrease in an affected market whose size is arbitrarily set at EUR 10 billion.

identifying the industries that produce the largest spillover price effects, if affected by a merger intervention or cartel prohibition. Second, the data on the industry distribution of merger interventions and cartel prohibitions over the period 2012-2018 are used to calibrate price shocks applied to the input-output model. This model calculates the total price effects of these competition policy interventions. The spillover price effects of the cartel prohibitions and merger interventions over the period 2012-2018 are then compared by industry with the within-industry price effects of these competition policy interventions.

§13.03 DESCRIPTION OF THE SAMPLE OF MERGER INTERVENTIONS AND CARTEL PROHIBITIONS

The sample of competition policy interventions used for the model simulations are merger interventions and cartel prohibitions by the European Commission over the period 2012-2018. The merger interventions included in the sample are Phase I and Phase II merger approvals subject to remedies, Phase II merger prohibitions and merger withdrawals in Phase II if these withdrawals are not due to other identifiable reasons than the position taken by the Commission.[4]

Table 13.1 describes the number of interventions in the sample and the size of the markets directly affected. The European Commission has been collecting these data since 2012 as an input into its customer savings calculations. The sample includes 146 merger interventions and 36 cartel prohibitions: around 20 to 30 important merger interventions and cartel prohibitions are made every year, the number of merger interventions (14-27) being larger than that of cartels prohibitions (4-10). The size of the markets affected by these competition policy interventions varies between EUR 18 and EUR 140 billion annually, with 2016 and 2018 being two exceptional years in terms of the number and importance of the merger interventions made. In general, mergers represent a larger share of the number of competition policy interventions and consequently, a larger share of the markets affected (more than 80%), except in 2013 when two important cartels in the interest rate derivatives markets were prohibited.

4. A Phase I merger decision is a decision, which is taken within twenty-five working days following the notification of the merger. If the merger raises competition concerns that cannot be resolved in Phase I, a Phase II merger investigation is opened. Phase II is an in-depth analysis of the merger's effects on competition and requires more time (at least ninety working days from the opening of a Phase II investigation). Following its investigation, the European Commission may unconditionally clear the merger, approve the merger subject to remedies or prohibit the merger if the merging parties were either unable or unwilling to propose adequate remedies to the competition concerns raised by the Commission.

Table 13.1 Merger Interventions and Cartel Prohibitions (2012-2018)

Year	Mergers			Cartels			All	
	Number	Affected Markets		Number	Affected Markets		Number	Affected Markets
		In EUR billion	In % of total		In EUR billion	In % of total		In EUR billion
2012	17	40.5	*88.6*	4	5.2	*11.4*	21	45.7
2013	14	4.9	*27.2*	4	13.1	*72.8*	18	18.0
2014	17	33.7	*81.8*	10	7.5	*18.2*	27	41.2
2015	22	19.9	*85.8*	4	3.3	*14.2*	26	23.2
2016	27	127.9	*91.6*	5	11.7	*8.4*	32	139.6
2017	24	22.6	*87.9*	5	3.1	*12.1*	29	25.7
2018	25	121.4	*98.1*	4	2.4	*1.9*	29	123.8
Total	**146**	**370.9**	***88.9***	**36**	**46.3**	***11.1***	**182**	**417.2**

Table 13.2 Cartel Prohibitions by Sector (2012-2018)*

Sector Codes (NACE)	Sector Names	Number of Decisions	Share in the Total Market Value
C29-C30	Motor vehicles and other transport equipment	9	33.2
K	Financial and insurance activities	4	30.3
C26-C27	Computer, electronic and electrical equipment	7	17.3
H	Transportation and storage	3	6.0
C28	Machinery and equipment n.e.c	1	4.2
C24-C25	Basic metals and fabricated metals	2	1.9
C16-C18	Wood, paper and printing	1	1.8
C10-C12	Food, beverages and tobacco	2	1.5
C31-C33	Furniture and other manufacturing	1	1.5
C22-C23	Rubber, plastic and other non-metallic products	3	1.4
D-E	Electricity, gas, water	2	0.6
G	Wholesale and retail trade	1	0.3

*The sectors are defined on the basis of the 24-sector classification used for the calculation of the aggregated mark-up shock.

Tables 13.2 and 13.3 present the sectoral distribution of the number and market value of merger interventions and cartel prohibitions over the period 2012-2018, respectively. For cartels, three sectors, i.e., motor vehicles, financial services, and electronic and electrical equipment, account for more than 50% of the thirty-six cartel prohibitions over the period 2012-2018. Prohibitions in these sectors tend to affect large markets as they represent more than 80% of the total market value of the cartel cases. Notable prohibitions concern a cartel of producers of TV and computer monitor tubes in 2012, a cartel in the market for euro interest rate derivatives in 2013 and a cartel involving truck manufacturers in 2016 and 2017 (*see* Chapter 11).

Table 13.3 Merger Interventions by Sector (2012-2018)*

Sectors Codes (NACE)	*Sector Names*	*Number of Decisions*	*Share in the Total Market Value*
J61	Telecommunications	14	29.2
C10-C12	Food, beverages and tobacco	10	18.2
C24-C25	Basic metals and fabricated metals	8	13.4
C20-C21	Chemicals and Pharmaceuticals	27	10.1
J58-J60	Publishing, broadcasting activities	7	7.8
C16-C18	Wood, paper and printing	6	4.7
H	Transportation and storage	15	4.2
C29-C30	Motor vehicles and other transport equipment	11	2.2
C26-C27	Computer, electronic and electrical equipment	9	2.1
C22-C23	Rubber, plastic and other non-metallic products	6	2.0
M-N	Professional, scientific and support service activities	3	1.3
B	Mining and quarrying	2	1.2
C28	Machinery and equipment n.e.c	4	1.2
K	Financial and insurance activities	4	1.0
G	Wholesale and retail trade	6	0.7
C31-C33	Furniture and other manufacturing	8	0.5
A	Agriculture, forestry and fishing	2	0.2
D-E	Electricity, gas, water	1	0.1
J62-J63	Computer and information service activities	3	0.1

*The sectors are defined on the basis of the 24-sector classification used for the calculation of the aggregated mark-up shock.

The sector distribution of the number and market value of merger interventions is less concentrated than that of cartels. Moreover, for mergers, a high number of interventions in a sector does not necessarily imply that these interventions add up to a large share in the total market value of merger interventions. The eleven merger interventions in motor vehicles sector, for example, account for only 2.2% of the total market value over the period 2012-2018. Four sectors stand out both in terms of the number of interventions and in terms of their share in total market value: telecommunications, food, beverages and tobacco, basic and fabricated metals, and chemicals and pharmaceuticals. Together, these four sectors account for 40% of the total number of merger interventions and for 70% of total market value. Important interventions in these sectors concern the 2012 acquisition of Xstrata, the world's fifth largest metals and mining group, by Glencore, the world's leading metals and thermal coal trader, the 2016 AB InBev/SABMiller merger affecting a number of national beer markets, and the 2018 Hutchison/Wind Tre merger in the Italian retail mobile telecoms market.

§13.04 DERIVATION OF THE SHOCKS

In this section, we describe how the shocks applied to the models are derived. A distinction is made between the mark-up shocks used for the QUEST III macro-model simulations and the price shocks applied to the input-output model.

[A] Mark-Up Shocks in QUEST III

In QUEST III, the aggregate change in mark-up (ΔMUP_N) due to a set N of competition policy interventions can be defined as follows:[5]

$$\Delta\,MUP_N = \sum_{k\in\{K_N\}} \left[\frac{\Delta\,P_k}{P_k}(1 + MUP_k)\right]\frac{GO_{2k}}{GO} \tag{1}$$

where K_N is the set of sectors k in which these interventions lead to a change in customer prices, $\Delta P_k/P_k$.

Mark-ups levels are calibrated for the available sectors based on the method proposed by Thum-Thysen and Canton (2015), which extends Roeger's (1995) mark-up calculation method by including the effects of product market reforms. Mark-ups have been estimated for the period 1995-2015 and are available for twenty-four sectors of the EU agriculture and business economy.[6] Equation (1) illustrates that the aggregate mark-up shock moves in line with price shocks in the sectors affected by the European Commission's competition policy interventions. However, they are

5. In QUEST III, it is assumed that firms charge a mark-up over the marginal cost of production: $P_k = (1 + MUP_k)\, MC_k$ (*see* Dierx et al., 2017, Equation 4). From that equation, we can derive the percentage price change in sector k as $\Delta P_k/P_k = \Delta(1+MUP_k)/(1+MUP_k) + \Delta MC_k/MC_k$. Assuming that $\Delta MC_k/MC_k = 0$ and $\Delta(1+ MUP_k) \approx \Delta MUP_k$, we obtain that $\Delta MUP_k = \Delta P_k/P_k (1+MUP_k)$. Equation (1) aggregates the relevant mark-up changes using the corresponding gross output shares in the EU agriculture and business economy as weights.

6. The agriculture and business economy is defined here as a grouping of the following activities: agriculture, forestry and fishing (Section A of the NACE sector classification), industry (Sections B-E), construction (Section F), services (Sections G-N, excluding real estate activities, as well as Sections R and S). It does not include public sector and non-market activities (Sections O-Q as well as Sections T and U). This is because mark-up data are available only at this level of sector aggregation.

weighted by the relative gross mark-up in the sector concerned $(1 + MUP_k)$ and by the share of gross output of sector k in the EU agriculture and business economy, GO_{2k}/GO. In the macroeconomic simulations, the sectors k relate to the twenty-four sectors defined at the NACE two-digit level.

To calculate the aggregate mark-up shock, information is needed on the price change in each two-digit sector k affected by competition policy interventions. This price change in sector k is computed as a weighted average of the price changes in the set of n markets affected by European Commission merger interventions and cartel prohibitions:

$$\frac{\Delta P_k}{P_k} = \sum_{n \in N_k} \frac{\Delta P_n}{P_n} MS_{nk} \tag{2}$$

where N_k are the sets of merger interventions and cartel prohibitions affecting sector k and $\Delta P_n/P_n$ is the avoided price increase, which is fixed at 3 % for merger interventions and at 15 % for cartel prohibitions under the baseline scenario.

For each merger intervention and cartel prohibition, the European Commission defines a relevant market directly concerned by the competition policy intervention. In the macroeconomic simulations, the weights MS_{nk} used to calculate the price change at the sector level are defined as the share of the affected turnover in the relevant market of competition policy intervention n in sector k (mkt_{nk}) over gross output in the sector defined at the NACE two-digit level (GO_{2k}):

$$MS_{nk} = (mkt_{nk}/GO_{2k}) \tag{3}$$

To calculate the mark-up shocks associated with the direct effect of merger interventions and cartel prohibitions, we thus make use of information on the affected turnover in the relevant market of each competition policy intervention and the price increase avoided. Moreover, we also have to take into account the duration of the direct effect. As the effects of merger interventions and cartel prohibitions may last more than one year, the mark-up change in a given year t is the sum of the effects of competition policy interventions in year t and of the interventions from previous years which continue to have an effect in year t (*see also* section 13.07[A]). The information used and assumptions made are briefly described in section 13.05.

Calculations of the direct effects of competition policy interventions ignore the sectoral deterrence effects of such interventions, which are likely to be more important than their direct effects (*see* Chapter 12). To take the sectoral deterrence effects into account, the weights MS_{nk} in Equation (3) are redefined as:

$$MS^T_{nk} = \frac{mkt^T_{nk}}{GO_{2k}} \tag{4}$$

with mkt^T_{nk} being the total market affected by competition policy intervention n in sector k. The total market affected includes both the markets directly affected by intervention n (mkt_{nk}) and the markets affected indirectly through sectoral deterrence (mkt^D_{nk}):

$$mkt^{T}_{nk} = mkt_{nk} + mkt^{D}_{nk} \quad (5)$$

The method used to determine the size of the so-called deterrence-adjusted market (mkt^{D}_{nk}) is described in section 13.06.

[B] Price Shocks in the Input-Output Price Model

The main aim of the input-output exercise presented below is to assess how a reduction (or avoided increase) in prices brought about by a set of competition policy interventions reverberates throughout the European economy. In our modelling framework, the European Commission's competition policy interventions initially give rise to price reductions in the markets directly concerned. As a result, in a generic industry k, the output price changes in relative terms by $\Delta p_k/p_k$. The term $\Delta p_k/p_k$, which we refer to as the 'within-industry' price effect, is computed according to Equation (2) and corresponds to a weighted average of the price effects of all competition policy interventions affecting industry k, with different weights for the direct and deterrent effects.

The within-industry effects are then introduced in the input-output price model as an exogenous shock. In this way, we are able to calculate how the within-industry price effects are transmitted to the rest of economy. The result is a 'spillover' price effect $\Delta ps_k/p_k$, resulting from interventions in industry k. The overall price change in any given industry is the sum of the within-industry price effect and of the spillover price effects benefitting the industry.

For a more detailed discussion of our modelling approach, the reader is referred to Box 13.3 in section 13.08. At this stage, however, it is important to note that in principle the exogenous shocks applied to the input-output model are consistent with those applied to the macro-model, as they are both based on Equation (2). The main difference is that this change in price at the industry level is directly applied to the input-output model while it is transformed into a global mark-up shock in the macro-modelling simulations.[7]

§13.05 INFORMATION USED TO CALIBRATE THE SHOCKS ASSOCIATED WITH THE DIRECT EFFECTS OF COMPETITION POLICY INTERVENTIONS

As explained in the previous section, we need information on the market directly affected by merger interventions and cartel prohibitions by the European Commission, the avoided price increase and the duration of price effect to calculate the mark-up and price shocks applied to the models. To that end, we exploit the data and assumptions

7. There are two other differences between the method used to calculate the mark-up and price shocks. First, in the input-output model, the gross output values (GO_k) used for the calculation of the weights ($MS_{nk} = mkt_{nk}/GO_k$) are defined for sixty-four industries (roughly corresponding to the NACE two-digit level classification), while in the macro-model simulations, a distinction is made between twenty-four sectors only. Second, the input-output model ignores the expected

used by the European Commission to calculate the customer savings from its merger interventions and cartel prohibitions. Chapter 11 describes the source of this information in detail. In this section, we will briefly present the information used to calibrate the shocks associated with the direct effects of competition policy interventions (*see* Table 13.4). The next section focuses on the method used to calculate the sectoral deterrence effects of these competition policy interventions.

Table 13.4 Overview of Data and Assumptions Used for the Macroeconomic Model Simulations

Competition Policy Intervention	*Cartel Prohibition*		*Merger Decision*	
	Assumption	*Source*	*Assumption*	*Source*
Affected turnover	Turnover of cartel members	Case-specific information	Total turnover in the relevant market	Case-specific information
Avoided price increase*	10-**15**-20%	Empirical literature: Median price overcharge for cartels = 16-30%	1-**3**-5%	Empirical literature: Mean price change due to remedied mergers ≥ 3%
Expected duration of the harm avoided	1/3/6	Case-specific information: Summary indicator of the stability of the cartel	2/3/5	Case specific information: Assessment of barriers to entry and expansion

*The figures in bold are used in the baseline scenario of the macro-model simulations.

Source: European Commission.

The turnover in the markets affected by a competition policy intervention can be found in the confidential versions of the merger and cartel decisions taken by the European Commission. The duration of the cartel price effect reflects the European Commission's judgment of the future sustainability of the cartel, while the duration of the merger price effect depends on the time necessary for the market to self-correct and restore the conditions of competition before the merger transaction. A specific duration is assigned to each case based on its characteristics: for cartels, the duration can be 1, 3 or 6 years and for mergers, 2, 3 or 5 years. Finally, three assumptions are made on the avoided price increase due to a cartel prohibition (10, 15 and 20%) or a merger intervention (1, 3 and 5%). These assumptions are based on the literature and are rather conservative.

duration of the avoided price increase and assumes that the effect of a competition policy intervention is felt only during the year of the decision.

§13.06 METHOD USED TO ESTIMATE THE SECTORAL DETERRENCE EFFECTS OF COMPETITION POLICY INTERVENTIONS

A primary goal of competition policy enforcement is to deter anticompetitive behaviour by enterprises, thereby maintaining a level playing field in product markets to the benefit of the end consumers. There is a consensus amongst policy makers that such deterrent effects are of crucial importance to the effectiveness of competition policy (*see* Chapter 12).

This chapter uses a novel approach to estimate the deterrent effects associated with cartel prohibitions and merger interventions by the European Commission. First, it makes the assumption that, for each merger intervention and cartel prohibition, the avoided price increase covers not only the relevant market directly affected by the competition policy intervention (direct effects) but also extends to the remainder of the sector concerned (defined at the NACE four-digit level[8]), which is referred to as the 'deterrence-adjusted market'. The competition policy interventions are assumed to discourage companies in this sector from entering into a cartel or an anticompetitive merger. For example, an important airline merger intervention addressing competition concerns about specific routes is supposed to have deterrent effects on the whole air passenger transport sector, meaning that other airline companies will be induced to abandon their planned anticompetitive mergers. This assumption rests on the idea that the deterrent effects of competition policy interventions are more likely to be diffused to other companies belonging to the same sector. The assumption has some empirical support. A survey by Deloitte suggests that mergers in the UK are more likely to be abandoned or modified if there has been a recent inquiry by the UK competition authority in the sector (Deloitte, 2007 and Gordon and Squires, 2008). Moreover, there is some evidence that cartel detection in a market decreases the rate of cartel formation in related markets (Harrington, 2008).

Second, it is assumed that the diffusion of the direct effects at the sector level follows an S-shape trajectory described by a logistic function. According to this function, the diffusion of the direct effects of a specific competition policy intervention at the sector level becomes stronger as the size of the market directly affected by the intervention (as measured by the market turnover) becomes larger relative to the size of the sector (as measured by its gross output defined at the NACE four-digit level). This implies that an intervention directly affecting large markets (and thus big companies) in a given sector will have a bigger impact on the behaviour of other companies belonging to the same sector than an intervention affecting small markets. For example, the 2016 prohibition of the cartel involving truck producers like MAN, Volvo/Renault, Daimler, Iveco and DAF and leading to a record fine of EUR 2.93 billion to these companies is assumed to have stronger deterrent effects in the car manufacturing industry than the 2017 prohibition of the cartel involving three car lighting system producers. However, if the size of the market directly affected by the competition policy intervention is very large in comparison with the size of the sector, the

8. Sectors are defined at the more disaggregated NACE four-digit level to avoid implausible deterrent effects.

diffusion effects become smaller because there are fewer companies remaining that can be deterred. The maximum size of the deterrence-adjusted markets equals the size of the sector minus the size of the market directly affected by the intervention. The use of a logistic function thus allows capturing the deterrent effects of case decisions affecting markets of different sizes.

Coming back to the definition of the shocks given in section 13.04, it is assumed that the avoided price increase by a given competition policy intervention not only affects the markets in which the intervention takes place (mkt_{nk}) but is also diffused to contiguous markets within the same sector at the NACE four-digit level. Let us denote the turnover in this 'deterrence-adjusted market' by mkt^D_{nk}. The deterrence-adjusted market should be smaller or equal to the size of the sector at the NACE four-digit level (GO_{4k}) minus the size of the market directly affected by the competition policy intervention ($mkt^D_{nk} \leq GO_{4k} - mkt_{nk}$). The 'total market affected' by an intervention n in sector k, mkt^T_{nk} is the sum of the market directly affected by this intervention and the deterrence-adjusted market:

$$mkt^T_{nk} = mkt_{nk} + mkt^D_{nk} \qquad (6)$$

We assume that the ratio of the deterrence-adjusted market (mkt^D_{nk}) over the part of the four-digit sector not directly affected by the competition policy intervention ($GO_{4k} - mkt_{nk}$) is a logistic function of (mkt_{nk}/GO_{4k}). This implies that:

$$\frac{mkt^D_{nk}}{GO_{4k} - mkt_{nk}} = f\left(\frac{mkt_{nk}}{GO_{4k}}\right) \qquad (7)$$

with the function f(.) being a transformation of a logistic function h (*see* Box 13.2 for the definition of this function). The function f(.) has a minimum equal to zero (deterrent effects are inexistent) and a maximum equal to 1 (the deterrent effects spread to the remainder of the NACE four-digit sector concerned).

Using some algebra (*see* Appendix 1), one can derive:

$$\frac{mkt^T_{nk}}{GO_{4k}} = \frac{mkt_{nk}}{GO_{4k}} + f(mkt_{nk}/GO_{4k}) \left[1 - \frac{mkt_{nk}}{GO_{4k}}\right] \qquad (8)$$

The share in gross output[9] of the total market affected by a competition policy intervention can therefore be defined as the sum of the share in gross output of the market(s) directly affected by the intervention and the transformed logistic function f(.) times the share in gross output of the markets not directly affected by the intervention. The transformed logistic function allows modelling the diffusion of the direct effects to markets within the relevant four-digit sector not directly affected by the intervention.

The total affected market weights MS^T_{nk} defined in Equation (4) can be reformulated as follows:

9. Here gross output is defined at the four-digit level. As no data are available for gross output at this level of disaggregation, GO_{4k} is estimated by ($PROD_{4k}/PROD_{2k}$) GO_{2k} with $PROD_{4k}$ and $PROD_{2k}$ representing the production values in sector k at the four- and two-digit level, respectively.

$$MS_{nk}^{T} = \frac{mkt_{nk}^{T}}{GO_{2k}} = \frac{GO_{4k}}{GO_{2k}} \frac{mkt_{nk}^{T}}{GO_{4k}} \tag{9}$$

with GO_{4k} and GO_{2k} representing gross output in sector k at the four- and two-digit level respectively, and mkt_{nk}^{T} / GO_{4k} being calculated on the basis of Equation (8).

The weights MS_{nk}^{T} can then be used to calculate a weighted average of the price changes in the set of the markets affected by the European Commission decisions, defined as the sum of the directly affected markets and the deterrence-adjusted markets. Equation (2) can therefore be rewritten as:

$$\frac{\Delta PT_k}{P_k} = \sum_{n \in N_k} \frac{\Delta P_n}{P_n} MS_{nk}^{T} \tag{10}$$

and Equation (1) becomes:

$$\Delta MUP_N^T = \sum_{k \in \{K_N\}} \left[\frac{\Delta PT_k}{P_k}(1 + MUP_k)\right] \frac{GO_{2k}}{GO} \tag{11}$$

Similarly, in the input-output model, the price change including the deterrent effects are calculated by replacing $\Delta p_k/p_k$ by $\Delta pt_k/p_k$.

Box 13.2: Definition and justification of the use of the logistic function to model the deterrent effects

Logistic functions or S-shaped curves have often been used to model the diffusion of knowledge and innovation across time and space (*see* Baptista, 1999, and Geroski, 2000, for a survey of the literature). An S-shaped curve implies that the diffusion of an innovation starts at a slow rate because of the lack of information on the new technology. However, the more firms adopt the innovation, the more likely others will also adopt it and, as the information is disseminated, the diffusion accelerates. As the innovation matures, the growth of diffusion starts to slow down, which corresponds to the inflection point F of the S-shaped curve, and progressively it reaches a saturation point. In the limit, the growth of diffusion declines to zero.

We use a (transformed) logistic function h(x) to model the sectoral diffusion of the direct effects of a competition policy intervention. We assume that the sectoral deterrence effects of a given intervention are a positive function of the size of the market directly affected by the intervention relative to the size of the four-digit sector concerned. The transformed logistic curve implies that an increase in the size of the directly affected market relative to the corresponding four-digit sector causes an exponential increase of the rate of diffusion up to the inflection point of the curve, after which the diffusion slows down and tends to zero.

The logistic function considered here is the following:

$$h(x) = \frac{1}{[1 + e^{-\chi(x-F)}]^{\frac{1}{v}}} \quad x \in [0,1]$$

with x being the relative size of the directly affected market ($x = (mkt_{nk}/GO_{4k})$). The possible values of x are restricted between 0 and 1, which implies that the size of the affected market cannot not exceed that of the four-digit sector concerned. The relative size of the deterrence-adjusted market ($y = mkt^{D}_{nk} / (GO_{4k} - mkt_{nk})$) is a functional transformation f(x) of the logistic function h(x): $y = f(x) = (h(x) - h(0)) / (h(1) - h(0))$ which ensures that the possible values of y are restricted between 0 and 1 as well. By definition, y is a strictly increasing function of x, starting from the origin and with y asymptotically reaching 1 as x approaches 1. The lower bound of the domain corresponds to the case where there is no diffusion as the direct effects of the decision are very limited, while the upper bound of the domain is reached when the sum of direct and deterrence effects covers the whole of the four-digit sector.

The parameter F represents the inflection point of the S-shaped curve where the growth rate of the sectoral deterrence effects starts to decline. The parameter χ is the steepness parameter, which reflects the speed of diffusion at the inflection point. A high value of χ implies that the majority of interventions with relatively small direct effects have less of an impact in terms of deterrence effects as well. On the contrary, the lower this parameter, the smoother is the diffusion process and the less is the differentiation across interventions in terms of the size of their deterrence effects. The parameter $v > 0$ reflects the degree of asymmetry of the S-shaped curve with respect to the inflection point, with $v = 1$ corresponding to a perfectly symmetric curve. The higher this parameter, the larger is the relative size of the directly affected market for which the maximum deterrence effect is achieved.

Table 13.5 Calibrated Parameters of the Logistic Function

	Mergers	*Cartels*
χ	100	100
F	0.0254	0.0154
v	1.0	1.0

The parameters of the logistic function (*see* Table 13.5) have been calibrated to fit the size distribution of the sample of European Commission merger interventions and cartel prohibitions over the period 2012-2018 (*see* Figure 13.2) and on the basis of reasonable assumptions regarding the shape of the logistic function.

Figure 13.2 Histogram of Merger Interventions and Cartel Prohibitions

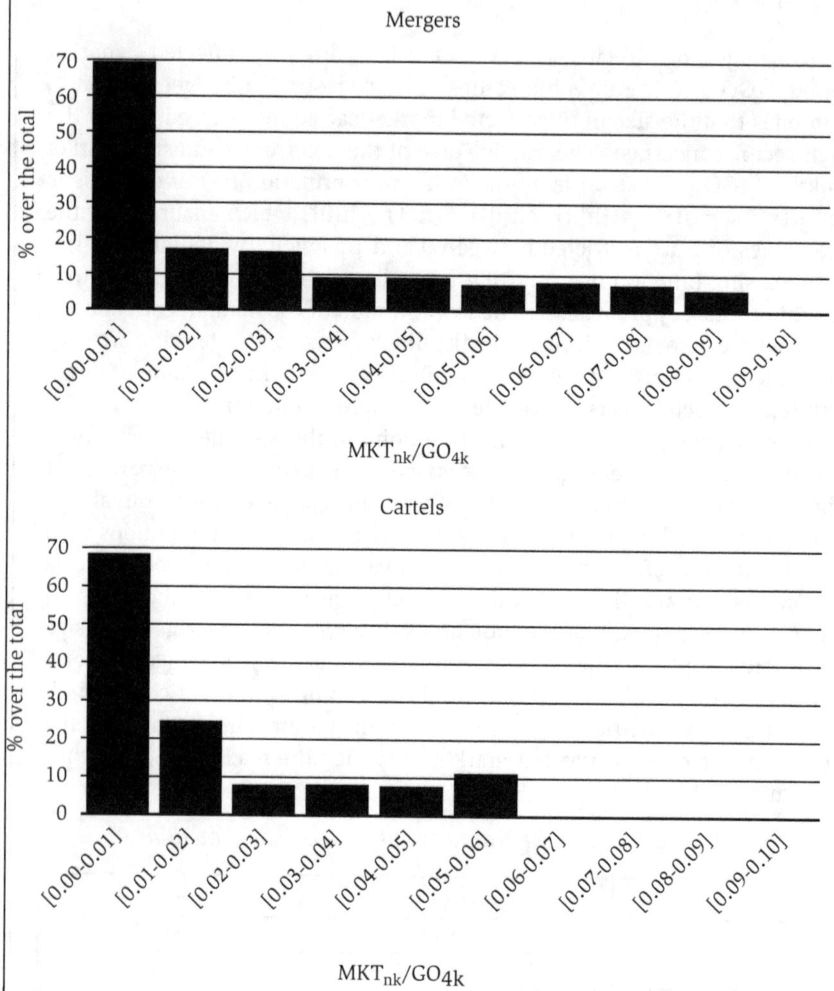

Source: Authors' own calculations.

Figure 13.2 shows that for most merger interventions and cartel prohibitions the size of the directly affected market is rather small relative to the size of the corresponding sector at the four-digit level. Consequently, the deterrence effects of such competition policy interventions are well below average. For those 'small' cases, the marginal rate of diffusion should improve with an increase in the size of the direct effects, which implies that these interventions should be located to the left of the inflection point F in the S-shaped curve. Taking this into account, the parameters of the logistic function are set as follows:

- The value of F has been calibrated in such a way that the average ratio between the deterrence-adjusted market and the size of the market directly affected by the competition policy interventions equals 10 for mergers and 20 for cartels. These two average multipliers reflect estimates found in the literature.[10] However, as available measures of deterrence are not very precise, a robustness test has been carried out to assess the sensitivity of the macroeconomic simulation results to the assumptions made with respect to these multipliers. For all values of F considered, the majority of interventions is located to the left of the inflection point in the S-shaped curve.
- The value of χ has been set at 100 to avoid unrealistically high deterrence multipliers for individual merger interventions and cartel prohibitions.
- The value of ν has been set at 1.0 to ensure that the logistic curve is symmetric.

Figure 13.3 describes the shape of the logistic functions used in the model simulations. Each dot in the graph corresponds to a merger intervention or a cartel prohibition. We can see that most of the competition policy interventions are relatively small in size in comparison to the gross output of the corresponding four-digit sector. These cases are located in the area of the curve where the speed of the diffusion of the direct effects increases with size.

10. Survey and theory based evidence (*see* Chapter 12) shows that the ratio between the deterred harm and the direct benefits associated with cartel control ranges between 5 and 28, which would imply that the size of deterrence-adjusted markets is between 5 and 28 times the size of directly affected markets. For mergers, this ratio ranges between 3 and 8. As the cartels detected and mergers notified are not necessarily representative of the population of cartels and mergers, selection bias may affect the survey based estimates of the deterrent effects of cartel and merger control. Nevertheless, the figures quoted here provide ranges indicating the importance of deterrent effects from merger interventions and cartel prohibitions, respectively. One would expect that the deterrent effects of interventions by a strong competition authority, such as the European Commission, are closer to the upper bounds of the ranges referred to in this footnote.

Figure 13.3 The Logistic Diffusion of the Direct Effects of Competition Policy Interventions

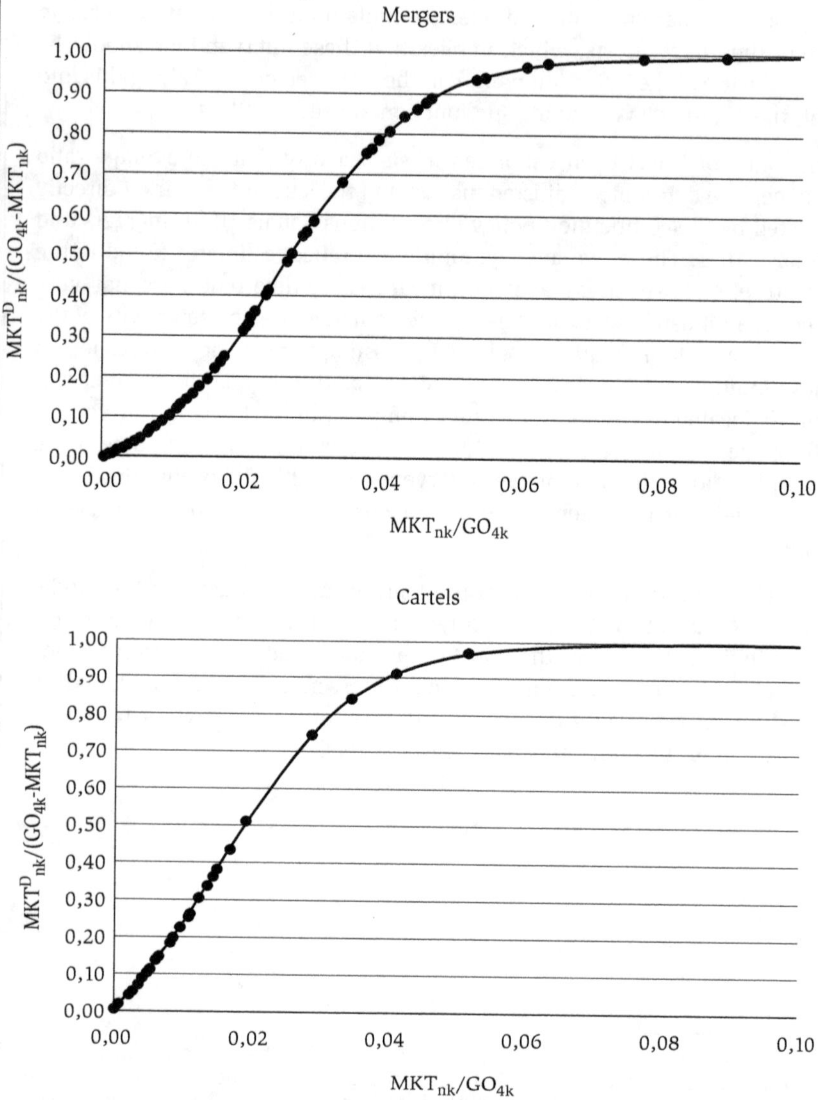

Source: Authors' own calculations.

§13.07 MODEL SIMULATIONS OF THE MACROECONOMIC IMPACT

This section starts with a presentation of the magnitude of the mark-up shocks applied to the QUEST III model. Then, it describes the macroeconomic impact of these shocks, reflecting the impact of competition policy interventions during the period 2012-2018. Finally, it illustrates the sensitivity of the macro-modelling results to different assumptions made with respect to the size of the price increase avoided and the importance of the deterrent effects.

[A] Magnitude of Mark-Up Shocks

As shown in the section 13.04[A], the impact of the European Commission's competition interventions can be assessed by summing the changes in mark-ups resulting from individual merger interventions and cartel prohibitions. In the current exercise, we look at competition policy interventions over the period 2012-2018 as described in section 13.03.

Since the price effects of competition policy interventions may last for more than a year, customers will benefit not only from the intervention in the year itself, but also from interventions with longer lasting effects made in previous years. We apply mark-up shocks to the QUEST III model from 2014 on. The mark-up shock for the year 2014 is computed by taking into account all the interventions having an impact in 2014, i.e., all interventions made in 2014 itself as well as interventions made in previous years still having an impact in 2014.[11] The same approach is used for the period 2015-2023, combining the information on observed interventions during the period 2012-2018 with estimates of missing information for the subsequent years.[12]

From 2024 onwards, a permanent mark-up shock is estimated on the basis of the full sample of competition policy interventions.[13] This permanent shock reflects the assumption that the European Commission will continue its competition policy interventions at the same pace into the foreseeable future. Such a 'permanent' mark-up shock can then be applied to a baseline scenario under which the European Commission would take no merger or cartel decision. The introduction of a permanent shock reflects the idea that a single competition policy intervention by the European

11. For example, as indicated in Table 13.4, some merger decisions can have an impact of up to five years and some cartel decisions of up to six years. In many cases though, the expected duration of the harm avoided is three years. This means that the 2014 mark-up shock applied to the QUEST III model is calculated on the basis of 2012 decisions having an impact during three years, 2013 decisions having an impact during two or three years and all 2014 decisions. No data are available for the pre-2012 period.
12. From 2019 on, historical data are used to estimate the missing information. For example, we compute the mark-up shock in 2019 by estimating the average contemporaneous shock from historical data as we do not yet have information on the 2019 decisions. As the maximum possible duration of the impact of a decision is six years, the latest year for which we have historical data is the year 2023 (we have information on the impact of cartel decisions having been taken in 2018 and lasting six years).
13. This permanent shock is calculated by summing the annual averages (over the period 2012-2018) of mark-ups shocks from decisions having an impact lasting n years, with n = 1, 2, 3, 4, 5 and 6.

Commission will have little or no enduring effects on company behaviour. The intertemporal deterrence effects of competition policy interventions come from companies' awareness of the existence of a competition authority and the expectation that the authority will continue to intervene in the market if infringements of competition law occur.

The decrease in mark-up corresponding to this permanent shock is computed using Equations (8), (9), (10) and (11): the permanent mark-up reduction ($-\Delta MUP_N^T$) equals 0.6 percentage points, which corresponds to a 4.6% reduction in the mark-up level (MUP_N^T). The magnitude of the shock and the associated simulation results largely come from deterrent effects of competition policy interventions, and reflect their direct effects only to a very limited extent.[14] As motivated above, Table 13.6 presents the 'permanent' effects of European Commission's competition policy interventions, both in absolute and relative terms.

Table 13.6 Magnitude of the Mark-Up Shock

ΔMUP_N^T *(pp)*	MUP_N^T *(%)*	ΔMUP_N^T / MUP_N^T *(%)*
-0.6	13	-4.6

The magnitude of the permanent mark-up shock appears to be reasonable in comparison with the mark-up shocks reported by studies that aim to assess the impact of a wider set of competition friendly structural reforms. For instance, in Varga and in 't Veld (2014, 2018) structural reforms aimed at narrowing the gap vis-à-vis the average of the three best EU performers in terms of market functioning correspond to an average mark-up decline across the EU of around 1.5 percentage point. Another point of comparison is the 7.8% increase in mark-up over the period 2000-2015 observed for advanced economies by the IMF (2019). As EU competition policy is estimated to reduce mark-ups by around 4.6%, one can roughly consider that the increase in mark-up in the European Union would have been equal to 12.4%.

[B] Simulations of Macroeconomic Effects

The mark-up shocks previously defined are applied to the QUEST III model. The magnitude of these shocks reflects both the direct and deterrent effects of the European Commission's merger interventions and cartel prohibition. Under the baseline scenario, the avoided price increase is assumed to be equal to 3% for merger interventions and for 15% for cartel prohibitions. Sectoral deterrence has been modelled by a logistic function whose parameters have been fixed in such a way that the ratio of deterrent over direct effects equals 10 for merger interventions and 20 for cartel prohibitions.

Table 13.7 reports the percentage change in GDP and selected macroeconomic variables of interest resulting from the above mark-up shocks. The figures reported are

14. Out of the 0.60 percentage point reduction in the mark-up level, 0.06 percentage point is due to direct effects of competition policy, while the rest comes from deterrent effects.

the percentage differences from the unshocked values. Columns report different number of years after the initial shock in 2014.

Table 13.7 Macroeconomic Effects of the Mark-Up Shock (in %)

	1	*5*	*10*	*50*
GDP	0.097	0.276	0.362	0.533
GDP deflator	-0.002	-0.074	-0.185	-0.380
Employment	0.078	0.193	0.229	0.244
Consumption	0.103	0.251	0.333	0.498
Investment	0.199	0.553	0.630	0.839
Labour productivity	0.020	0.083	0.133	0.288

Table 13.7 illustrates that competition policy interventions increase output and raise demand for the factors of productions (capital, labour). The combination of the price decline and the higher wages associated with increased labour demand and higher labour productivity yields an increase in consumption. Investment is also increasing because the negative direct effect of mark-ups on future profitability is more than offset by the positive effect of the increasing demand due to the lower prices. In terms of GDP, we can observe an increase of 0.28% after five years. In the long term, the effect on GDP doubles, increasing to 0.53%. This effect is of the same order of magnitude as the economic impact of the implementation of the Services Directive across the EU Member States (*see* Monteagudo et al., 2012 and Pelkmans, 2019) and a reduction of product market regulation more generally (*see* Égert and Gal, 2016). However, the effect is somewhat smaller than that of the European Fund for Strategic Investments (EFSI). The increase in 2019 GDP resulting from EFSI investments, which were at the core of the 2015 Juncker Plan, has been estimated at 0.9% (*see* Christensen et al., 2019).

These results can also be compared with recent IMF estimates of the impact of the observed increase in mark-ups over the period 2000-2015. The IMF (2019) estimates that 'output would be about 1 percent higher in the average economy if mark-ups had not increased since 2000'. If we had applied the observed 7.8% increase in mark-up over the period 2000-2015 to the QUEST III model, we would have obtained a negative impact on GDP by 0.8% after fifteen years (as opposed to the IMF estimate of 1.0%). This illustrates that QUEST III model simulations presented here are rather conservative.

Concerning labour market effects, our results indicate that employment goes up by around 0.2% in the mid- to long-term[15] (*see* Table 13.7), which corresponds to a job creation of around 430,000. This increase is due to positive reinforcing effects from both the labour demand and the labour supply side. From the labour demand perspective, firms require more labour (and capital) in order to ensure that production keeps up with the increased demand for lower priced products. However, the higher

15. The version of the QUEST III model used leads to positive employment effects already in the short term, because it does not model the labour market frictions associated with job search and matching, which might generate frictional unemployment in the short term.

production costs associated with increased wage levels mitigate to some extent this positive employment effect. In the longer term, increasing employment and wage income further stimulate consumption, which in turn reinforces the demand channel. From the labour supply side, households are willing to offer more labour services as declining prices lead to higher real wages.

[C] Robustness of the Macroeconomic Effects

Alternative simulations have been carried out to test the robustness of the macroeconomic results presented above. Table 13.8 illustrates the sensitivity of the results to different assumptions regarding the magnitude of the overcharges and of the deterrent effects. The first row presents the five-year GDP effect of a mark-up shock under the baseline scenario. The second and third rows of Table 13.8 describe the outcome of a lower bound and an upper bound overcharge scenario, respectively. The price increase avoided due to merger control is fixed at 1% in the former and 5% in the latter, while the price overcharge of cartels varies between 10% and 20% under the lower and upper bound scenario, respectively. These alternative scenarios are based on assumptions from the literature on the price effects of mergers and cartels (*see* Table 13.4 in section 13.05).

Table 13.8 GDP Effect after Five Years under Different Scenarios

Scenario	*Merger Overcharge*	*Cartel Overcharge*	*Merger Deterrence Multiplier*	*Cartel Deterrence Multiplier*	*Weakening of the Deterrent Effects over Time*	*GDP Effect after Five Years*
Baseline	3%	15%	10x	20x	No	+0.28%
Lower bound avoided price increase	1%	10%	10x	20x	No	+0.15%
Upper bound avoided price increase	5%	20%	10x	20x	No	+0.40%
Lower bound deterrence ratio	3%	15%	5x	10x	No	+0.18%
Upper bound deterrence ratio	3%	15%	15x	30x	No	+0.35%
Myopic agents	3%	15%	10x	20X	yes	+0.24%

A comparison of simulation results for the lower and upper bound avoided price increase scenarios is that competition authorities can multiply the positive effects of their interventions on GDP growth by more than two if they intervene in markets with more significant anticompetitive effects. The table shows that the GDP effect after five years almost triples (i.e., from 0.15% to 0.40%) if we move from the lower bound to the upper bound avoided price increase scenario. This would plead in favour of

competition interventions in markets where the anticompetitive behaviour of companies has the biggest impact in terms of avoided price increases (e.g., in highly concentrated markets).

Three scenarios reflecting various assumptions concerning the sectoral deterrence effects are defined in the last three rows of Table 13.8. In the lower bound deterrence ratio scenario, the logistic function used to model the sector diffusion of the direct effects is calibrated in such a way that the average ratio between the deterred harm and the direct benefits equals 5 for mergers and 10 for cartels. In the upper bound scenario, these ratios are fixed at 15 and 30. A shift from the lower to the upper bound scenario almost doubles the GDP effect after five years (i.e., from 0.18% to 0.35%).

The 'myopic agents' scenario assumes that the deterrent effects of competition policy interventions decrease over the duration of the interventions' effects. Under this scenario, the disciplining effect of such interventions on companies active in the same four-digit sector weakens over time as companies have short memory. Consequently, the total effect of a competition policy intervention (and the corresponding mark-up shock) diminishes over time. For the scenario presented here, the annual rate of depreciation of deterrence has been fixed at 10%. Due to such a depreciation, the simulated GDP impact of the interventions decreases from 0.28% to 0.24% after five years.

§13.08 MODEL SIMULATIONS OF THE PRICE EFFECTS BY INDUSTRY

As mentioned in section 13.02, an input-output model is used to examine how the price effects of competition policy interventions in different industries are transmitted to the rest of the European economy. A distinction is made between: (i) the within-industry price effects or price effects associated with competition policy interventions in the industry itself; and (ii) the industry spillover price effects, which are the price effects transmitted from other industries to the industry of interest. Box 13.3 provides a precise definition of these two categories of price effects and explains how they are calculated on the basis of the input-output model. The input-output model is used to: (i) compare the intensity of the industry spillover price effects in the different industries of the economy; and (ii) assess the inter-industry propagation of the price effects resulting from the merger interventions and cartel prohibitions over the period 2012-2018. It also allows calculating the total price reductions (including within-industry and industry spillovers) by industry, which are due to these competition policy interventions.

Box 13.3: Short description of the spillover price effects calculated with the input-output model

The input-output model used to calculate the cross-industry implications of the decrease (or avoided increase) in prices resulting from European Commission's competition policy interventions distinguishes sixty-four industries at the NACE two-digit level and describes inter-industry flows in the EU28 for the year 2014. This input-output table provides the basis for calculating the input-output coefficients describing the value of input necessary per unit value of output. These coefficients allow exploring how an exogenous shock to the price of a certain product is transmitted to the prices of other products. A difficulty emerges because of the coarse industry aggregation of the input-output table and because the market affected by a merger or a cartel typically represents only a small portion of the input-output industry to which it is attributed. To overcome this difficulty, a fixed proportionality assumption is introduced. The nature of the assumption is best illustrated by an example.

When the European Commission imposes remedies on a merger between two mobile telecommunication operators, this results in an avoided price increase in the mobile telecommunication services market. However, the provision of mobile telecommunication services does not appear as a distinct industry in the input-output table. Suppose, for the sake of simplicity, that the telecommunication industry is comprised of only two subsectors, namely, mobile and fixed telecommunication services and that no competition policy interventions were made concerning the market for fixed telecommunication services. Our analytical framework assumes that each industry of the economy uses mobile and fixed telecom services in the same proportion. Thus, if the mobile market represents 10% of the output of the telecommunication industry, our calculations assume that each industry (including the telecommunication industry itself) uses a combination of telecommunication services that includes 10% of mobile services and 90% of fixed services, with the value of telecommunication services used by unit value of output defined by the input-output coefficient. For example, if the banking services use EUR 0.2 of telecommunication services per unit value of output, it is assumed that this industry uses EUR 0.02 of mobile telecommunication services and EUR 0.18 of fixed telecommunication services per unit value of output.

The reduction in prices of mobile telecommunication services associated with the merger intervention will be transmitted to the fixed telecommunication industry and to the other industries of the economy that use mobile telecommunication services as inputs. These are what we refer to as the spillover effects associated with this competition policy intervention. Under the above-mentioned proportionality assumption, these spillovers can be calculated using an input-output approach as exemplified in Appendix 2. In any given industry, adding together the within-industry price effects (i.e., the price changes experienced by goods and services produced by that industry and directly targeted by

a merger or a cartel case) and the spillover price effects transmitted from other industries yields the total price effect in that industry.

Finally, the input-output model allows making a distinction between the origin and the destination of the price spillovers created. The former refers to the industry that transmits the price spillover effects and the latter to the industry on the receiving end of the spillovers. For example, regarding the former, we can calculate the total price spillovers created by competition policy interventions in the telecommunication services industry. These spillovers depend on: (i) the intensity of the initial price shocks affecting this industry, which in turn depends on the price impact of competition policy interventions within the industry; and (ii) the importance of the interlinkages between the telecommunication services industry and the other industries.

[A] Intensity of the Industry Spillover Effects by Industry

The input-output model can be used to compare the intensity of industry spillover price effects generated by industry ($\Delta ps_k/p_k$). To eliminate the impact of the size of the industry (*see* footnote 3), we have applied a standardised price shock in different industries. The objective is to see whether a competition policy intervention in an industry having significant interconnections with the rest of the economy, such as the network industries or the financial services, will generate much larger industry spillover price effects than an intervention in an industry having limited interconnections. This would allow gaining a better understanding of the extent of spillovers associated with competition policy interventions over the period 2012-2018 (*see* subsection 13.08[B]). The size of such spillovers can be explained either by the fact that the interventions concerned industries generating high spillovers by nature or by the fact that the initial price shocks were large.

The application of the standardised shock to the industries of the input-output table[16] allows classifying these industries into two categories according to the size of the industry price spillovers generated. The first category contains industries for which the ratio of industry spillovers to within-industry effects is less than or equal to 1; the second category consists of industries with a ratio exceeding 1 (*see* Table 13.9). For example, a competition policy intervention reducing prices in the energy industry (NACE code D35) by 1% will lead to a decrease in price levels in other industries that use energy as an input by 1.55%, contributing to an overall price level decrease by 2.55%.

16. As in the macroeconomic section, this analysis only considers the industries belonging to the agriculture and the business economy (*see* footnote 7 above). Therefore, the analysis covers only fifty-seven industries out of sixty-four in the input-output table.

Table 13.9 Intensity of the Industry Price Spillovers by Industry

Industries with Low Spillovers		*Industries with High Spillovers*	
*Industry**	$(\Delta ps/ps)/(\Delta p/p)$	*Industry**	$(\Delta ps/ps)/(\Delta p/p)$
R&D (M72)	0.22	**Telecom (J61)**	1.04
Entertainment (R90-R92)	0.29	**Wholesale trade (G46)**	1.05
Hotels and restaurants (I)	0.32	**IT services (J62-J63)**	1.11
Other personal services (S96)	0.34	**Refining (C19)**	1.12
Retail trade (G47)	0.43	**Agriculture (A01)**	1.20
Recreation (R93)	0.49	**Tour operators (N79)**	1.21
Furniture and other (C31-C32)	0.50	**Repair and installation (C33)**	1.27
Membership organisations (S94)	0.51	**Finance (K64)**	1.35
Pharmaceuticals (C21)	0.52	**Land transport (H49)**	1.36
Other transport equipment (C30)	0.52	**Architects/engineers (M71)**	1.37
Construction (F)	0.58	**Metal products (C25)**	1.39
Motor vehicles (C29)	0.59	**Plastics (C22)**	1.44
Textiles (C13-C15)	0.64	**Wood products (C16)**	1.44
Machinery (C28)	0.65	**Chemicals (C20)**	1.45
Food and beverage (C10-C12)	0.69	**Non-metallic minerals (C23)**	1.46
Insurance (K65)	0.70	**Rental (N77)**	1.48
Electronics (C26)	0.74	**Waste (E37-E39)**	1.51
Air transport (H51)	0.79	**Other professional (M74-M75)**	1.52
Water transport (H50)	0.80	**Energy (D35)**	1.55
Fishing (A03)	0.80	**Forestry (A02)**	1.61
Trade in vehicles (G45)	0.84	**Paper products (C17)**	1.63
Repair (S95)	0.85	**Other services (N80-N82)**	1.67
Water (E36)	0.90	**Postal services (H53)**	1.70
Electrical equipment (C27)	0.93	**Printing (C18)**	1.71
Films, music, broadcasting (J59-J60)	0.99	**Other transport services (H52)**	1.72
Publishing (J58)	1.00	**Basic metals (C24)**	1.72
		Advertising (M73)	1.82
		Legal, accounting, etc. (M69-M70)	1.82
		Auxiliary to finance/insurance (K66)	1.87
		Human resource provision (N78)	1.92
		Mining and quarrying (B)	2.02

* The figures between brackets are the NACE two-digit level codes.

Table 13.9 shows that the ratio of industry spillovers over the within-industry effects range from 0.2-0.3 (for the R&D industry and for consumer services such as hotels, restaurants and entertainment) to 1.8-2.0 (for mining and quarrying, and for enterprise services such as human resource provision, legal and accounting services as well as auxiliary financial services). All else equal, a competition policy intervention in an industry having significant interconnections with other industries - such as intermediate goods industries (metal products, plastic, chemicals), network industries (telecommunication, energy, land transport, postal services), financial services or wholesale trade - has larger industry spillover price effects than a intervention affecting industries with less significant interconnections - such as consumer goods industries (pharmaceuticals, motor vehicles, food and beverages) or consumer services (retail trade, hotels and restaurants, etc.).

Let us consider an example to illustrate this concept. The two most important cartel prohibitions in terms of customer savings are: (1) the 2016 prohibition of the truck cartel (NACE code C29); and (2) the 2013 prohibition concerning the market for interest rate derivatives (NACE code K64) denominated in euros. According to Table 13.9, the intensity of industry spillovers that are generated by the first prohibition decision (0.59) is less than half that associated with the second decision (1.35). However, the size of the industry spillovers depends not only on the intensity of such spillovers but also on the magnitude of the initial price shock (or within-industry price effects) associated with these two prohibition decisions.

The price spillovers generated by an industry may be spread out over the rest of the economy or, on the contrary, very concentrated and transmitted to a limited number of other industries. Appendix 3 shows that for the great majority of industries creating larger spillovers, these spillovers tend to be transmitted to a wide range of other industries, implying that competition policy interventions in these industries have widespread benefits.

[B] Decomposition of the Economy-Wide Price Effects Generated by Competition Policy Interventions over the Period 2012-2018

The input-output model can also be used to calculate the price effects associated with competition policy interventions over the period 2012-2018. To that end, the initial price effects of cartel prohibitions and merger interventions over that period are aggregated on the basis of Equation (2). A different price shock is calculated every year on the basis of the interventions taken in that year. In the input-output model analysis, the duration of the impact of the competition policy interventions is not taken into account. The price changes for the whole EU28 economy are obtained by calculating a weighted average of the industry-specific price changes, using the industry gross output as weights. The price shocks applied to the input-output model correspond to the within-industry price changes presented in the second column of Table 13.10.

Table 13.10 illustrates that competition policy interventions over the period 2012-2018 led to within-industry price reductions varying from 0.05% (in 2015) to 0.25% (in 2016). These price reductions reflect both the direct and deterrent effects of competition policy interventions in the industries concerned but ignore the industry spillover price effects. Under the baseline scenario, the direct price effect associated with a cartel prohibition (15%) is five times larger than the direct price effect of a merger intervention (3%). Consequently, the price shocks tend to be higher in years when important cartel prohibitions were made. In 2013, for example, two important cartels in financial services were prohibited. In other years, the price effect is largely determined by the number and size of the markets affected by merger interventions. Both in 2016 and in 2018, the total size of markets affected by merger interventions exceeded 120 billion euro (*see* Table 13.1 in section 13.03). By contrast, price reductions were less important in 2015 and 2017. During these two years, the number of interventions was similar to that of other years but the importance of the markets directly affected by these interventions was relatively small. This explains why the within-industry price effects are relatively minor.

Table 13.10 Economy-Wide Price Changes due to Competition Policy Interventions by the European Commission over the Period 2012-2018 (in %)

Year	*Within-Industry Price Effects (Δp/p)*	*Industry Spillover Price Effects (Δps/p))*	*Total Price Effects (Δp/p) + (Δps/p)*
2012	-0.080	-0.083	-0.163
2013	-0.145	-0.175	-0.320
2014	-0.120	-0.112	-0.232
2015	-0.050	-0.042	-0.092
2016	-0.249	-0.131	-0.381
2017	-0.067	-0.054	-0.122
2018	-0.106	-0.098	-0.204
Average	-0.117	-0.099	-0.216

The last column of Table 13.10 shows the total price effects associated with merger interventions and cartel prohibitions over the period 2012-2018. As explained in Box 13.3, the total price effects are the sum of the within-industry price effects and the industry spillover price effects. According to the input-output analysis, competition policy enforcement has contributed to reductions in the overall price level varying from 0.09% in 2015 to 0.38% in 2016. The annual average price reduction in the EU over the period 2012-2018 equalled 0.22%. To put this effect into perspective, one can compare this figure with the 2018 GDP price deflator, which shows a price level increase of 1.6% in 2018.

The total price reductions are particularly large in 2013 (0.32%) and 2016 (0.38%). This is not surprising for 2016, which was an exceptional year in terms of the number and importance of merger interventions and – to a lesser extent – cartel prohibitions. The price reduction of 2013, in particular, can be associated with the size of industry spillover price effects: the two main cartel prohibitions of that year were in the financial services industry, which can be characterised by significant price spill-overs. In contrast, total price changes are relatively low in 2015 and 2017, as the sizes of the markets affected by competition policy interventions were relatively small.

Table 13.11 Relative Importance of Industry Spillover Price Changes

Year	*(Δps/p)/(Δp/p)*	*(Δps/p)/(Δp/p + Δps/p)*
2012	1.05	0.51
2013	1.21	0.55
2014	0.93	0.48
2015	0.84	0.46
2016	0.53	0.34
2017	0.81	0.45
2018	0.92	0.48
Average	0.90	0.47

Table 13.11 shows that the relative importance of industry spillover price changes also varied from year to year, accounting for 34% to 55% of the total price effects. Over the period 2012-2018, the spillover effects represent on average about half of the total price effects. The ratio of spillover price effects over within-industry price effects varies between 0.53 and 1.21. This ratio is larger than or equal to one in 2012 and 2013, above the average in 2014 and 2018 and relatively low (0.53) in 2016. Table 13.12 allows exploring the reasons for these results.

Table 13.12 Number and Market Value of the Interventions in High Spillover Industries

Year	*Cartels*			*Mergers*		
	Number	*Number as a Share of Total*	*Market Value as a Share of Total Affected Markets*	*Number*	*Number as a Share of Total*	*Market Value as a Share of Total Affected Markets*
2012	2	0.50	0.17	8	0.47	0.84
2013	3	0.75	0.97	7	0.50	0.30
2014	5	0.50	0.34	12	0.71	0.96
2015	2	0.50	0.17	8	0.37	0.40
2016	0	0.00	0.00	10	0.37	0.42
2017	1	0.20	0.08	12	0.50	0.59
2018	0	0.00	0.00	13	0.52	0.72

The relatively important spillover price effects in 2013 can be explained by cartel prohibitions affecting large markets in the financial services industry. Similarly, in 2012, 2014 and 2018 the European Commission intervened in a significant number of mergers affecting large markets in industries with substantial spillover effects (such as basic metals, paper products, chemicals and telecoms). The importance of industry spillover price effects is a further indication that the customer savings calculations presented in Chapter 11 may underestimate the consumer benefits of interventions by competition authorities.

[C] Total Price Effects Observed by Industry over the Period 2012-2018

Table 13.10 above shows that competition policy interventions taken over the period 2012-2018 led to an annual average reduction in prices by 0.22% over that period, with a bit less than half of this effect coming from spillover effects. The total price reduction by industry ranges between 0.05% (employment agencies services) and 1.47% (motor vehicles). Table 13.13 describes the price effects associated with competition policy interventions taken over the period 2012-2018 in the ten industries where the total price reduction is larger than twice the average.

Table 13.13 Price Effects by Industry (2012-2018 Average)

Industry	*Within-Industry Price Effects (in %)*	*Industry Spillover Price Effects in % (Share in Total)*	*Total Price Effects (in %)*
Motor vehicles (C29)	-1.12	-0.35 *(0.24)*	-1.47
Water transport (H50)	-0.99	-0.14 *(0.12)*	-1.13
Telecommunications (J61)	-0.87	-0.12 *(0.12)*	-0.98
Air transport (H51)	-0.71	-0.09 *(0.11)*	-0.80
Finance (K64)	-0.65	-0.12 *(0.15)*	-0.77
Electronics (C26)	-0.52	-0.12 *(0.19)*	-0.65
Basic metals (C24)	-0.41	-0.16 *(0.28)*	-0.57
Electrical equipment (C27)	-0.33	-0.19 *(0.36)*	-0.52
Paper products (C17)	-0.32	-0.16 *(0.34)*	-0.48
Broadcasting (J59-J60)	-0.35	-0.10 *(0.22)*	-0.45
Average 2012-2018	-0.12	-0.10 *(0.47)*	-0.22

The ten industries reported in Table 13.13 have been affected by important competition policy interventions, which explains why the within-industry price effects are greater (3 to 10 times) than the average. The industry spillovers price effects are also above average, showing that these industries have benefitted as well from the spillovers of price reductions in other industries. However, the share of the industry spillovers over the total price effects ranges between 11% and 12% (air transport, telecommunications and water transport) and 35% (paper products and electrical equipment) indicating that the within-industry price effects are dominant in all industries recording a relatively large reduction in prices.

Some of the industries that have been mostly affected by competition policy interventions are particularly important for consumer welfare (motor vehicles, air transport, finance) or for the competitiveness of the EU economy (telecommunications, electronics). The large total price effect for motor vehicles, corresponding to a price reduction of approximately 1.5% over the period 2012-2018 and mostly related to cartel prohibitions, should be interpreted in light of an average annual increase in producer prices in this industry of 0.45% over the same period. Similarly, the 0.9% price reduction in telecommunications mostly associated with merger interventions may have been an element in the average annual decrease in producer prices of 2.35% in telecommunication services over the period 2012-2016.[17]

[D] Origin and Destination of the Industry Spillover Price Effects Created over the Period 2012-2018

Table 13.14 describes the five industries that are at the origin of the largest spillovers created over the period 2012-2018. Not surprisingly, these are also industries, for which we observe larger within-industry price changes. The higher the within-industry price effect in an industry, the larger the spillovers created by this industry.[18] These large within-industry price effects result from the relatively high number of significant cartel prohibitions (motor vehicles, finance, electronics) and merger interventions (telecommunications, basic metals) in these five industries.

Table 13.14 Origin of the Industry Spillovers Price Effects (2012-2018 Average)

Industry Transmitting the Largest Spillovers	*Share of the Within-Industry Price Effects due to Industry k (in %)*	*Share of the Industry Spillover Price Effects due to Industry k (in %)*	*Share of the Total Price Effects due to Industry k (in %)*
Motor vehicles (C29)	28.0	14.4	21.8
Finance (K64)	18.2	27.1	22.3
Telecommunications (J61)	10.9	11.0	11.0
Basic metals (C24)	5.5	8.8	7.0
Electronics (C26)	5.1	4.1	4.6
Sum	67.8	65.4	66.8

Together, these five industries account for two-thirds of the price reductions associated with competition policy interventions over the period 2012-2018. Two of these industries (motor vehicles and electronics) generate large spillovers mainly

17. Data on producer prices for telecommunications for the years 2017 and 2018 are not yet available.
18. The correlation between the share of within-industry price effects created by industry and the share of industry spillover price effects created by industry is 0.77.

because of the size of the initial price shock associated with interventions in these industries themselves. The three other industries (finance, telecommunications and basic metals) create large spillovers not only because they have been affected by large competition policy interventions but also because they produce intermediate goods and services that are used as inputs in many other industries of the economy.

Table 13.15 Destination of the Industry Spillover Price Effects in Non-shocked Industries (2012-2018 Average)

Industry Benefiting the Most of Spillovers	*Industry Spillover Price Effects (in %)*
Printing (C18)	-0.15
Insurance (K65)	-0.15
Trade in vehicles (G45)	-0.15
Tour operators	-0.14
Repair and installation (C33)	-0.14
Construction (F)	-0.11
Wood products (C16)	-0.10
Publishing (J58)	-0.10
Average 2012-2018	-0.11

In non-shocked industries, i.e., industries not affected by a competition policy intervention, the reduction in prices over the period 2012-2018 only results from spillover price effects of competition policy interventions in other industries. There are twenty-two non-shocked industries (out of a total of fifty-seven). The eight non-shocked industries benefitting from above average spillovers are presented in Table 13.15. A large share of their inputs comes from industries having benefitted from price reductions due to competition policy interventions. The printing industry, for example, is heavily dependent on paper products, an industry that has been subjected to a number of important merger interventions by the European Commission over the past years. Likewise, the insurance industry employs financial services, which were the subject of large cartel investigations in 2013 and 2014. Similarly, the wholesale and retail trade in vehicles sector uses motor vehicles as an important input, and the motor vehicles industry has seen a number of cartel prohibitions as well.

Table 13.16 reports results for 'shocked' industries having been directly affected by competition policy interventions. It describes not only the industry spillover price effects but also the total price effects including the within-industry price effects. It includes the twenty-one industries (out of the thirty-four having been subjected to interventions by the European Commission) benefitting from above average spillovers.[19] Moreover, it shows that the three industries having benefitted most from

19. One reason why there are more industries with above average spillover price effects in Table 13.16 (in comparison with Table 13.15) is that some of the most important spillover effects occur within the industry subjected to the competition policy intervention.

the spillover price effects are motor vehicles (with price spillovers equal to 0.35%), machinery (-0.19%) and electrical equipment (-0.19%). However, the shares of these spillovers represent more than 50% of the total price effects only in the machinery industry. In this industry, the large spillovers are due to its strong interlinkages with the basic metals and metal products industries. In the motor vehicles and electrical equipment industries, the spillover price effects, although significant, are lower than the within-industry price effects.

Table 13.16 Destination of the Industry Spillover Price Effects in Shocked Industries (2012-2018 Average)

Shocked Industries	*Industry Spillover Price Effects (in %)*	*Total Price Effects(in %)*	*Spillover Price Effects as a Share of Total Price Effects*
Motor vehicles (C29)	-0.35	-1.47	0.24
Machinery (C28)	-0.19	-0.37	0.51
Electrical equipment (C27)	-0.19	-0.52	0.36
Metal products (C25)	-0.17	-0.27	0.62
Paper products (C17)	-0.16	-0.48	0.34
Basic metals (C24)	-0.16	-0.57	0.28
Other transport equipment (C30)	-0.15	-0.21	0.72
Water transport (H50)	-0.14	-1.13	0.12
Advertising (M73)	-0.13	-0.14	0.94
Plastics (C22)	-0.13	-0.22	0.59
Chemicals (C20)	-0.12	-0.23	0.54
Electronics (C26)	-0.12	-0.65	0.19
Auxiliary to finance/insurance (K66)	-0.12	-0.25	0.48
Telecommunications (J61)	-0.12	-0.99	0.12
Finance (K64)	-0.11	-0.77	0.15
Furniture (C31-C32)	-0.11	-0.34	0.33
Food and beverage (C10-C12)	-0.11	-0.21	0.54
Non-metallic metals (C23)	-0.11	-0.22	0.50
Waste (E37-E39)	-0.10	-0.15	0.69
Broadcasting (J59)	-0.10	-0.45	0.22
Average 2012-2018	-0.10	-0.22	0.47

§13.09 CONCLUSIONS

This chapter analyses the macroeconomic impact of competition policy interventions by the European Commission over the period 2012-2018. It extends the work by Dierx et al. (2017) in a number of directions. First, whereas previously the mark-up shock applied to the macro-model was based on merger interventions and cartel prohibitions by the European Commission over the period 2012-2014, in the current chapter information on Commission decisions taken in the years 2015-2018 is taken into account as well.

Second, the chapter models the sector diffusion of the direct effects of competition policy interventions by way of a logistic function. In Dierx et al. (2017) limits on the size of such deterrent effects were modelled rather crudely by applying fixed multipliers to the direct effects of merger interventions and cartel prohibitions. The values of these multipliers were based on the results of business surveys. In the economic literature, the logistic function has been used to model the diffusion of innovation, information and the use of new technologies over space and time. We argue that the logistic function is well suited as well to model the sector diffusion of the direct effects of competition policy interventions. Modelling deterrence as a gradual process of sector diffusion permits imposing limits on the overall importance of deterrence in line with the business surveys, while at the same time allowing for a non-linear relationship between direct and deterrent effects. The use of a logistic function offers the additional advantage that the function's parameters can be calibrated on the basis of the characteristics of the sample of competition policy interventions. In this way, we are able to better capture the deterrent effects of both relatively small and larger case decisions. Moreover, the flexibility offered in choosing parameter values allows carrying out a sensitivity analysis, which is all the more important in light of the uncertainty concerning the size of deterrent effects associated with individual competition policy interventions.

Third, the current chapter exploits the available information on the sector distribution of the European Commission's merger interventions and cartel prohibitions over the recent period. The version of the QUEST III macro-model used is a single-sector model unsuited to explore the industry spillover effects of competition policy interventions. This is the reason why the macro-model simulations have been complemented by an input-output model analysis, which allows tracking the interlinkages between industries and identifying the differential effects of competition policy interventions affecting different industries of the economy.

The macroeconomic simulations using a logistic function to model the deterrent effects of competition policy interventions confirm that such interventions have a positive effect on growth and employment, as already reported in Dierx et al. (2017). In particular, the total effects (including the deterrent effects) of competition policy interventions on GDP are sizeable, but slightly lower than the estimated impact of the implementation of the EU Services Directive. Under the baseline scenario, GDP increases by 0.29% after five years and by 0.56% in the long term because of the European Commission's competition policy interventions. The effects on employment rise from 0.20% after five years to 0.26% in the long term. The employment effects are smaller than the GDP effects due to the increase in labour productivity associated with the increased competitive pressures.

The baseline model simulations presented here are reliant on a number of assumptions, including the level of overcharges, their duration and scope, the importance of the deterrent effects, and the specification and calibration of the general equilibrium model. Robustness tests have been carried out to assess the sensitivity of the results to the different assumptions made. However, the positive impact of competition policy interventions on growth and jobs is robust to variations in these different assumptions.

The input-output model is used to compare the size of industry spillover price effects across industries. To that end, a standardised price shock has been applied to the different industries. The comparison across industries shows that industry spillover effects are relatively large in intermediate goods industries, network industries, financial services and wholesale trade. The intensity of industry spillover price effects in an industry such as financial services can be ten times as large as that in another industry such as entertainment or hotels and restaurants. Moreover, looking at actual competition policy interventions during the period 2012-2018, we observe that five industries (motor vehicles, finance, telecommunications, basic metals and electronics) are at the origin of two-thirds of the total amount of spillovers created.

The input-output model also allows measuring the magnitude of the total price effects due to competition policy interventions over the period 2012-2018. Depending on the year, competition policy enforcement has contributed to reducing the overall price level by 0.09-0.38%. The share of this price reduction that can be associated with the propagation of the within-industry price effects to other industries ranges from 34% to 55%. Total price reductions were particularly high in 2013 and 2016. This is not surprising for 2016, which is an exceptional year in terms of number and importance of competition policy interventions. The high figure for 2013 can largely be explained by the size of the industry spillover effects of two cartel prohibition in the financial services industry. The total price effects are significant in industries important for the purchasing power of consumers (motor vehicles, financial services) and for the competitiveness of the European economy (telecommunication, electronics).

This chapter provides a more comprehensive analysis of the gains from competition policy enforcement than the customer savings approach presented in Chapter 11. It has refined the analysis of the macroeconomic impact of competition policy in a number of directions, allowing to better track sectoral deterrence effects and industry spillover effects. In spite of such progress, the chapter still provides an incomplete picture of the macroeconomic impact of competition policy interventions. In particular, it does not include an assessment of the macroeconomic effects of competition policy interventions in the areas of abuse of dominance and State aid control. Moreover, it models the impact of competition policy interventions as a decrease in mark-ups or price levels, while there are other transmission channels through which the impact of competition policy may be felt, such as increased business dynamism or improved incentives for innovation. These issues could be areas for further research.

APPENDIX 1: CALCULATION OF THE TOTAL MARKET AFFECTED BY COMPETITION POLICY INTERVENTIONS

The overall effect of a competition policy intervention (mkt^T) is given by the sum of the direct effect (mkt) and the deterrence effect (mkt^D), that is:

$$mkt^T = mkt + mkt^D \tag{12}$$

To obtain the shape of mkt^T/GO as a function of mkt/GO, from Equation (7), we have:

$$mkt^D/(GO - mkt) = f(mkt/GO) \tag{13}$$

Multiplying both sides of (13) by $\left[\frac{(GO - mkt)}{mkt^D}\frac{mkt^T}{GO}\right]$ we get:

$$\frac{mkt^D}{GO - mkt}\left[\frac{(GO - mkt)}{mkt^D}\frac{mkt^T}{GO}\right] = f\left(\frac{mkt}{GO}\right)\left[\frac{(GO - mkt)}{mkt^D}\frac{mkt^T}{GO}\right] \text{ or}$$

$$\frac{mkt^T}{GO} = f\left(\frac{mkt}{GO}\right)\left[\frac{(GO - mkt)}{mkt^D}\frac{mkt^T}{GO}\right] \tag{14}$$

From Equation (12):

$$mkt^D = mkt^T - mkt \tag{15}$$

Substituting (15) into (14):

$$\frac{mkt^T}{GO} = f\left(\frac{mkt}{GO}\right)\left[\frac{(GO - mkt)}{GO}\frac{mkt^T}{(mkt^T - mkt)}\right] \text{ or}$$

$$\frac{mkt^T}{GO} = f\left(\frac{mkt}{GO}\right)\left[\frac{(GO - mkt)}{GO}\right]\left[\frac{mkt^T + mkt - mkt}{mkt^T - mkt}\right] \text{ or}$$

$$\frac{mkt^T}{GO} = f\left(\frac{mkt}{GO}\right)\left[\frac{(GO - mkt)}{GO}\right]\left[1 + \frac{mkt}{mkt^D}\right] \tag{16}$$

Therefore, from Equation (13) we obtain:

$$mkt^D = f\left(\frac{mkt}{GO}\right)(GO - mkt) \tag{17}$$

Substituting Equation (17) into Equation (16), we obtain:

$$\frac{mkt^T}{GO} = f\left(\frac{mkt}{GO}\right)\left[\frac{(GO - mkt)}{GO}\right]\left[1 + \frac{mkt}{f\left(\frac{mkt}{GO}\right)(GO - mkt)}\right] \text{ or}$$

$$\frac{mkt^T}{GO} = \frac{mkt}{GO} + f(mkt/GO)\left[1 - \frac{mkt}{GO}\right] \tag{18}$$

Therefore, we can conclude that the total impact on the market including deterrence is a simple function both of the relative size of the affected market $x = mkt/GO$ and of the functional form $f(x)$ chosen to model deterrence:

$$mkt^T/GO = x + f(x)(1-x) \tag{19}$$

APPENDIX 2: CALCULATING CROSS-INDUSTRY PRICE SPILLOVERS: A NUMERICAL EXAMPLE

This appendix uses a numerical example to illustrate the logic underlying our price spillover calculations. To analyse how EU prices are affected by the European Commission's competition policy enforcement activity, we rely primarily on two sources of information. First, the interrelationships among the various parts of the economy are modelled using data contained in the EU's input-output table (section 13.02[B]). To keep things straightforward, it is assumed here that the economy consists of only two industries (named agriculture and manufacturing, respectively) interacting as described in the following simplified input-output table (Table 13.17).

Table 13.17 A Simplified Input-Output Table

	Agriculture	***Manufacturing***	*Final Use*	*Output*
Agriculture	6	20	14	40
Manufacturing	8	4	68	80
Value added	26	56		
Output	40	80		

All the entries of Table 13.17 are measured in currency units – say, euros (EUR). By row, the table reports how products of the various industries are employed. For instance, the first row says that the use of agricultural products by agricultural and manufacturing activities respectively amounts to EUR 6 and 20. A further EUR 14 worth of agricultural products is absorbed by final demand, so that the total agricultural output amounts to EUR 40. Conversely, the columns of the input-output table describe the cost structure of the economy. Thus, the agricultural industry buys EUR 6 worth of products from agriculture and EUR 8 from manufacturing. The residual part of the industry's output, amounting to EUR 26, is accounted for by payments to capital and labour, which are lumped together under the heading value added.

The input-output table implies that, for example, producing EUR 1 worth of agricultural products requires on average EUR 8/40 = EUR 0.20 worth of manufacturing products. Applying the same logic to all industry pairs yields the input coefficient matrix in Table 13.18. In the same spirit, one can compute a set of value added coefficients, namely, 26/40 = 0.65 for agriculture and 56/80 = 0.7 for manufacturing. The basic premise of input-output analysis is that all these coefficients represent fixed requirements of the economy's production processes (Miller and Blair, 2009).

Table 13.18 The Input Coefficient Matrix

	Agriculture	*Manufacturing*
Agriculture	0.15	0.25
Manufacturing	0.20	0.05

The second key source of input data used in our modelling exercise is a dataset of European Commission decisions in cartel and merger cases (section 13.03). Suppose that during the time span relevant for the analysis only one such case took place. Specifically, let the case in question target the market for trucks. It is assumed that the size of this market is EUR 8 and that the price of trucks decreases by 15% as a result of the European Commission's decision. For the sake of simplicity, any deterrent effects associated with the decision (section 13.06) are ignored in this example. Given that the market for trucks can be assigned unambiguously to the manufacturing industry and that no competition enforcement activity targets agriculture, the case-level information can be linked with the input-output table as described in Table 13.19.

Table 13.19 Competition Policy Enforcement by Industry

Industry	*Industry Output*	*Size of the Affected Markets*	*Affected Markets as a Share of Industry Output*	*Price Change in the Affected Markets*
Agriculture	40	0	0	0%
Manufacturing	80	8	10%	-15%

For the purpose of our analysis, the input coefficients of Table 13.18 are not detailed enough. For example, we would like to separately observe agriculture's requirements in terms of trucks on one hand, and of the remaining manufactured products on the other. Instead, the degree of aggregation in the input-output table is such that we only have information on the overall manufactured product requirements. To overcome this limitation of the data, an assumption is introduced. We know from Table 13.19 that the truck market accounts for 10% of all manufacturing. Accordingly, we assume that trucks represent 10% of the manufacturing products bought by agriculture, with the remaining 90% being made up of other manufactured goods. Thus, the coefficients describing agriculture's requirements of trucks and other manufactured products are $0.1 \times 0.2 = 0.02$ and $0.9 \times 0.2 = 0.18$, respectively. This is an instance of the fixed proportionality assumption mentioned in Box 13.3. Applying the same logic to the requirements of the manufacturing industry yields the disaggregated input coefficients of Table 13.20. It should be noted that the value added coefficients remain unaffected.

Table 13.20 The Disaggregated Input Coefficient Matrix

	Agriculture	*Manufacturing*
Agriculture	0.150	0.250
Trucks	0.020	0.005
Other manufacturing	0.180	0.045

In a nutshell, our modelling approach uses the coefficients of Table 13.20 along with the exogenously given information that the European Commission's decision causes the price of trucks to drop by 15% to model the repercussions on the prices of agricultural and other manufactured products.

As a matter of accounting consistency, the prices of trucks (p_T) agricultural (p_A) and other manufactured products (p_M) must satisfy the following equations:

$$p_A = 0.15\, p_A + 0.18\, p_M + 0.02\, p_T + v_A \qquad \text{(A1)}$$
$$p_M = 0.25\, p_A + 0.045\, p_M + 0.005\, p_T + v_M \qquad \text{(A2)}$$

where v_A and v_M respectively denote the value added coefficients of agriculture and manufacturing. Rather than actual price levels, p_A, p_M and p_T are price indices that are initially normalized to one.[20] It is indeed immediate to verify that, with the value added coefficient set at the values computed from the input-output table (i.e., $v_A = 0.65$ and $v_M = 0.7$), both equations are verified for $p_A = p_M = p_T = 1$. Effectively, what this says is merely that the sale price of a product can be decomposed into the cost of various intermediate goods used in its production and payments to the providers of labour and capital.

Using the system A1-A2, we evaluate the price spillovers associated with the European Commission's intervention in the truck market as follows. Recall that, as an immediate consequence of the European Commission's decision, the price of trucks is assumed to drop by 15% (Table 13.19). Accordingly, we exogenously reduce p_T from 1 to 0.85. At the same time, we keep v_A and v_M fixed at their initial values (0.65 and 0.7, respectively). In an input-output world with fixed input requirements, leaving the value added coefficients untouched amounts to assuming that the prices of labour and capital are not affected. Then, the system A1-A2 becomes:

20. Consider, for example, a generic economic transaction involving trucks. In an ideal world, one would be able to observe a certain number of trucks being sold at a certain price. Analyses like ours, however, typically have to be carried out in a context in which data on quantities and prices are not available separately. Instead, what can be observed is merely the overall value (i.e., price times quantity) of the trucks being exchanged. An easy way around this difficulty is by redefining the unit in which physical flows of trucks are measured. Let the new unit of measurement be the number of trucks that one euro can buy. With physical quantities measured in this unit, the price of trucks becomes one and the physical quantity of trucks is equal to the observed monetary value of the transaction. Thanks to this normalisation, data on actual prices and quantities are no longer necessary and the analysis can proceed with information being expressed in monetary values only. Clearly, the same reasoning applies to any good. The use of such price normalisations is standard in input-output price models and many other types of economic analysis.

$$p_A = 0.15\, p_A + 0.18\, p_M + 0.667 \quad \text{(A3)}$$
$$P_M = 0.25\, p_A + 0.45\, p_M + 0.704 \quad \text{(A4)}$$

which yields $p_A = 0.996$ and $p_M = 0.998$. In other words, the price of agricultural products decreases by 0.4% and that of non-truck manufactured products by 0.2%.

For ease of interpretation, it will be useful to report these results using the original – i.e., aggregated – classification adopted by the input-output table. In essence, this involves re-aggregating together trucks with other manufacturing. This operation is illustrated in the bottom row of Table 13.21. Because the truck market accounts for 10% of the manufacturing industry, a 15% drop in the price of trucks can be thought of as a 1.5% decrease in the price of manufacturing output. This is what we refer to as the 'within-industry' effect. Analogously, a 0.2% decrease in the price of other manufactured products, which are responsible for 90% of total manufacturing output, amount to a 0.18% decline in manufacturing prices. This is what we term the spillover effect of the decision to the manufacturing industry. As a result of the truck market case, the price of manufactured products is reduced by 1.5% + 0.18% = 1.68%, which we call the 'total effect' of the decision in the manufacturing industry.

Table 13.21 Within-Industry, Spillover and Total Price Effects

Industry	*Price Change in the Affected Markets*	*Price Spillover to Markets Not Affected*	*Affected Markets as a Share of Industry Output*	*Within Industry Effect*	*Spillover Effect*	*Total Effect*
Agriculture	0%	-0.4%	0%	0%	-0.4%	-0.4%
Manufacturing	-15%	-0.2%	10%	-1.5%	-0.18%	-1.68%

Finally, we aggregate the results of Table 13.21 to produce a single economy-wide indicator of the impact of competition policy enforcement on the overall price level. To this end, we simply average the estimated price changes over industries giving each industry a weight proportional to its output. The calculations are presented in Table 13.22. Thus, the intervention in the truck market is found to reduce the economy's price level by about 1.25%. A significant share of this effect is directly due the reduction in the price of trucks, which by itself is equivalent to a 1% decrease in the overall price level. The remaining 0.25% is due to spillover effects. It is perhaps worth pointing out that this economy-wide spillover effect is comprised of two distinct types of cross-market effects. The within-industry spillover (-0.12%) represents the spillover from a portion of the manufacturing industry – the truck market – to the remaining part of the same industry; the cross-industry spillover (-0.13%) relates to the repercussions of the lower truck prices on the output prices of other industries (i.e., agriculture). In the analysis presented in the core of the text, we do not make a distinction between these two categories of spillovers. Our analysis also reports the economy-wide ratio of spillovers to within-industry effects (approximately 0.25, in this example) and to total effects (about 0.2).

Table 13.22 Aggregation of the Industry Price Effects

Industry	*Aggregation Weight*	*Industry-Level Effect*			*Contribution to the Economy-Wide Effect*		
		Within	*Spillover*	*Total*	*Within*	*Spillover*	*Total*
Agriculture	40/120 = 33%	0%	-0.4%	-0.4%	0%	-0.13%	-0.13%
Manufacturing	80/120 = 67%	-1.5%	-0.18%	-1.68%	-1%	-0.12%	-1.12%
Total	**100%**				**-1%**	**-0.25%**	**-1.25%**

APPENDIX 3: CHARACTERISTICS OF THE SPILLOVERS

Table 13.23 looks at the distribution of spillovers for those industries creating above-average spillovers, as defined in Table 13.9. It allows making a distinction between industries whose spillovers are spread out over the rest of the economy and industries with spillovers being more concentrated in a limited number of other industries. For example, it is expected that spillovers from an intervention in an industry such as wholesale trade will be more widespread than spillovers originating in the wood product industry. Table 13.23 illustrates that for industries with above-average spillovers, such spillovers tend to spread widely to the rest of the economy.

Table 13.23 Characteristics of the Spillovers

Industry	*Concentration Index**	*Largest Share of Spillovers to a Single Industry (in %)*
Industries with diffuse spillovers		
Other professional (M74-M75)	0.17	6.5
Human resource provision (N78)	0.19	7.9
Other services (N80-N82)	0.19	6.4
Printing (C18)	0.21	9.0
Rental (N77)	0.25	11.0
Postal services (H53)	0.25	8.0
Advertising (M73)	0.27	9.5
Repair and installation (C33)	0.29	9.3
Legal, accounting, etc. (M69-M70)	0.30	10.9
IT services (J62-J63)	0.30	12.1
Wholesale trade (G46)	0.32	9.5
Land transport (H49)	0.40	11.0
Telecom (J61)	0.41	15.1
Architects/engineers (M71)	0.42	13.5
Refining (C19)	0.43	10.7
Finance (K64)	0.43	12.3
Waste (E37-E39)	0.55	13.5
Paper products (C17)	0.59	17.1
Other transport services (H52)	0.62	13.7
Plastics (C22)	0.62	14.4
Tour operators (N79)	0.72	21.0
Chemicals (C20)	0.86	22.0
Metal products (C25)	0.89	15.2

Industry	*Concentration Index**	*Largest Share of Spillovers to a Single Industry (in %)*
Energy (D35)	0.98	25.6
Mining and quarrying (B)	0.99	18.0
Industries with concentrated spillovers		
Basic metals (C24)	1.14	19.7
Wood products (C16)	1.32	26.1
Auxiliary to finance/insurance (K66)	1.32	23.9
Forestry (A02)	1.52	28.5
Non-metallic minerals (C23)	2.29	39.5
Agriculture (A01)	4.95	57.2

* The concentration index is the ratio of the Herfindahl-like index of the sectoral distribution of the spillovers created by an industry over the average Herfindahl-like index for the total economy.

Amongst industries with above-average spillovers, there is only a limited number for which these spillovers are very concentrated. These industries are listed in the bottom rows of Table 13.23. Three of these six industries produce intermediate inputs (such as basic metals, wood products and non-metallic metals), two are primary products industries (agriculture and forestry) and one concerns activities auxiliary to financial services and insurance activities (such as fund management activities), which by definition are closely related to financial and insurance services. Table 13.23 also indicates the largest share of spillovers transmitted to a single industry: this share ranges between 20% (basic metals) and 57% (agriculture) of the total spillovers created. This single industry often is the industry itself as there is a lot of intra-industry trading.

REFERENCES

Baptista R. (1999), 'The diffusion of process innovations: A selective review', *International Journal of the Economics of Business*, 6(1), pp. 107-129.

Christensen M., Weiers G., Conte A., Wolski M. and Salotti S. (2019), 'The European Fund for Strategic Investments: The RHOMOLO-EIB 2019 update', JRC - EIB Territorial Development Insights Series, JRC118260, European Commission.

Deloitte (2007), 'The deterrent effect of competition enforcement by the OFT', OFT962, Report prepared for the Office of Fair Trading, London.

Dierx A., Ilzkovitz F., Pataracchia B., Ratto M., Thum-Thysen A. and Varga J. (2017), 'Does competition policy support inclusive growth?', *Journal of Competition Law & Economics*, 13(2), pp. 225-260.

Égert B. and Gal P.N. (2016), 'The quantification of structural reforms in OECD countries: A new framework', OECD Economics Department Working Paper, No. 1354.

Geroski P. (2000), 'Models of technology diffusion', *Research Policy*, 29(4-5), pp. 603-625.

Gordon F. and Squires D. (2008), 'The deterrent effect of UK competition enforcement', *De Economist*, 156(4), pp. 411-432.

Harrington J.E. (2008), 'Detecting cartels', in: P. Buccirossi (ed.), *Handbook of Antitrust Economics*, MIT Press.

Ilzkovitz F. and Dierx A. (2015), 'Ex-post economic evaluation of competition policy enforcement: A review of the literature', DG Competition staff paper, Publications Office of the European Union, June.

International Monetary Fund (2019), 'The rise of corporate market power and its macroeconomic effects', in *World Economic Outlook: Growth Slowdown, Precarious Recovery*, Washington, pp. 55-74.

in 't Veld J., Varga J. and Roeger W. (2018), 'The impact of structural reforms in the EU', in: J. de Haan and J. Parlevliet (eds), *Structural Reforms: Moving the Economy Forward*, Springer International Publishing.

Miller R.E. and Blair P.D. (2009), *Input-output analysis: Foundations and extensions*, Cambridge University Press.

Monteagudo J., Rutkowski A. and Lorenzani D. (2012), 'The economic impact of the Services Directive: A first assessment following implementation', Economic Papers 456, European Economy.

Pelkmans (2019), 'Contribution to growth: The single market for services', Study for the Committee for the Internal Market and Consumer Protection of the European Parliament, February.

Ratto M., Roeger W. and in 't Veld J. (2009), 'QUEST III: An estimated DSGE model of the euro area with fiscal and monetary policy', *Economic Modelling*, 26(1), pp. 222-233.

Roeger W. (1995), 'Can imperfect competition explain the difference between primal and dual productivity measures? Estimates for U.S. manufacturing', *Journal of Political Economy*, 103(2), pp. 316-330.

Thum-Thysen A. and Canton E. (2015), 'Estimation of service sector mark-ups determined by structural reform indicators', Economic Papers 547, European Economy.

Varga J. and in 't Veld J. (2014), 'The potential growth impact of structural reforms in the EU. A benchmarking exercise', Economic Papers 541, European Economy.

Index

B

C

D

G

H

I

J

L

M

S

T

U

V

W

www.ingramcontent.com/pod-product-compliance
Lightning Source LLC
LaVergne TN
LVHW020003031026
849161LV00023B/863